Artifacts of the Spanish Colonies of Florida and the Caribbean

1500–1800

Artifacts of the Spanish Colonies of Florida and the Caribbean

1500–1800

Volume 2: Portable Personal Possessions

Kathleen Deagan

Smithsonian Books, Washington

© 2002 by the Smithsonian Institution
All rights reserved

Copy editor: Robert Burchfield
Production editor: E. Anne Bolen
Designer: Janice Wheeler

Library of Congress Cataloging-in-Publication Data
Deagan, Kathleen A.
  Artifacts of the Spanish colonies of Florida and the
Caribbean, 1500–1800.
  Bibliography: v. 1, p.
  Includes index.
Contents: v. 1. Ceramics, glassware, and beads.
  1. Caribbean Area—Antiquities.   2. Florida—
Antiquities.   3. Spaniards—Caribbean Area—
Antiquities.   4. Spaniards—Florida—Antiquities.
I. Title.
1. F2172.D43   1987   972.9   86-24772
ISBN 0-87474-392-3 (v. 1)
ISBN 0-87474-392-1 (pbk. : v. 1)
ISBN 1-58834-035x (v. 2)

British Library Cataloguing-in-Publication Data is
available

Manufactured in the United States of America
08 07 06 05 04 03 02   5 4 3 2 1

⊗ The paper used in this publication meets the
minimum requirements of the American National
Standard for Information Sciences—Permanence
of Paper for Printed Library Materials
ANSI Z39.48-1984.

Publication of this book was made possible in part by
a grant from the Program for Cultural Cooperation
Between Spain's Ministry of Culture and United
States' Universities.

For permission to reproduce illustrations appearing
in this book, please correspond directly with the
owners of the works, as listed in the individual
captions. Smithsonian Books does not retain
reproduction rights for these illustrations individually,
or maintain a file of addresses for photo sources.

Contents

List of Figures   ix

List of Tables   xxi

Acknowledgments   xxiii

Part 1. *Contexts*

Chapter 1. *Scale, Context, and Meaning in Material Culture Studies*   3

Chapter 2. *Sites and Samples*   7

    Terrestrial Sites   7
    Multicomponent Sites   19
    Marine Sites   20

Chapter 3. *Politics, Economy, and the Flow of Material Culture in the Spanish Colonies*   24

    European Goods in the Spanish Americas   24
    Transatlantic Commerce and the *Carrera de Indias*   24
    Origins of *Carrera* Merchandise   27
    The *Asiento*   27
    Problems with the *Carrera*   28
    Rescate: Contraband Foreign Trade in the Caribbean   28
    The Seventeenth-Century Depression   29
    The Eighteenth Century: Politics, Conflict, and Economic Reform   30
    Spanish American Commodity Production   31
    Intercolonial Trade   33
    Spanish-American Social Patterns and Their Material Correlates   34

Part 2. *Religion, Ritual, and Adornment*

Chapter 4. *Religious Items*   37

    Religious Material Culture   38
    Devotional Medals   41

Devotional Medals in Spanish Colonial Sites   46
Personal Crosses and Crucifixes   54
Rosaries   65
Veneras and Religious Pendants   72
Reliquaries   78
Seals and Stamps   81
Rings   83
Columns   84
Copper-Alloy Stars   84

Chapter 5. *Amulets and Magical Items*   87

Amulet Use in Spain   89
Materials with Amuletic Properties   93
Forms of Amulets   95
Summary   105

Chapter 6. *Popular Jewelry*   106

Jewelry in Colonial-Era Spain   107
Popular Jewelry in the Spanish Colonies   109
Finger Rings   122
Earrings   126
Pendants and Necklaces   130
Bracelets   134
Hair Ornaments   136

Chapter 7. *Bells*   138

Bells in the Spanish Colonies   139
Bells as Amulets   140
Rumbler Bells: Varieties and Characteristics   142
Open Bells   149
Summary   154

Part 3. *Clothing*

Chapter 8. *Clothing Fasteners and Ornaments*   157

Buttons   157
Other Clothing Fasteners   174
Clothing Ornamentation   176

Chapter 9. *Buckles, Strap Ends, and Belt Hooks*   180

Clothing Buckles   180
Armor Buckles   185
Spur Buckles   187

Harness and Baldric Buckles   189
Strap Tips   191
Belt Hooks   192

Chapter 10. *Sewing Equipment*   193

Pins   193
Needles and Needle Cases   195
Thimbles and Thimble Rings   197
Scissors and Shears   206
Lace-making Equipment   209

Part 4. *Personal Items and Accessories*

Chapter 11. *Items of Comfort and Grooming*   215

Fans   215
Umbrellas and Parasols   220
Eyeglasses   222
Combs   224
Wigs and Wig Curlers   228
Hairbrushes   228
Toothpicks and Toothbrushes   230
Razors   234

Chapter 12. *Coins and Weights*   236

Denominations, Sizes, and Values of Spanish Colonial Coins   236
Coin Production and Technology   239
The Spanish American Mints   239
Archaeologically Recovered Coins from Old World Mints   243
Summary   256
Jetons   257
Weights   259
Scales   264

Chapter 13. *Personal Firearms*   268

Firearms during the Age of Exploration   268
Matchlocks   270
Wheel Locks   273
Snaphaunce Locks, Doglocks, and Flintlocks   275
Miquelet Locks   276
Ripoll Miquelet Pistols   279
Flintlocks   280
The French, or *"a la Francesa,"* Lock   281
Firearm Accessories   284

Chapter 14. *Pastimes* 291

        Games and Gambling 291
        Children's Games and Toys 298
        Noisemakers and Music 301
        Reading and Writing 304
        Tobacco Use 310

        Glossary 313

        References 319

        Index 364

Figures

2.1.	Locations of sites used in the study	9
2.2.	The Columbus house remains, La Isabela	10
2.3.	The *fortaleza* ruins at Concepción de la Vega	10
2.4.	A shelf in the site museum of Concepción de la Vega	11
2.5.	Field laboratory, Puerto Real	12
2.6.	Cathedral ruins at Panamá Viejo	13
2.7.	Barrel well, ca. 1566, Fountain of Youth Park site, St. Augustine	13
2.8.	John Goggin at the Fig Springs site, 1952	16
2.9.	Reconstructed Spanish home of the eighteenth century, St. Augustine	17
2.10.	Excavations at Santa Rosa Pensacola, 1964	18
2.11.	Museo de las Casas Reales, Santo Domingo	20
2.12.	The Cathedral of Havana	20
4.1.	The Virgin Mary with the Christ Child	38
4.2.	*Plaquette* bearing an image of the Virgin Mary with the Christ Child	42
4.3.	Devotional medals used on a rosary	43
4.4.	Seventeenth-century religious medals from Santa Catalina de Guale (Georgia)	48
4.5.	*The Immaculate Conception* by Velásquez, ca. 1618	49
4.6.	Franciscan iconography that influenced motifs on religious medallions	49
4.7.	Immaculate Conception medal	50
4.8.	Seventeenth-century devotional medals from St. Augustine, ca. 1650–1700	51
4.9.	Eighteenth-century devotional medals from St. Augustine, ca. 1750–1800	52
4.10.	Devotional medals from the 1733 Florida plate fleet wrecks	53
4.11.	The 1832 Miraculous Medal of the Virgin Mary	54

Figures

4.12. Seventeenth-century jeweled crosses and religious pendants 55
4.13. Some forms of crosses used in the Catholic Church 56
4.14. Crucifix from La Isabela 57
4.15. Crosses from the Padre Island shipwrecks, 1554 57
4.16. Brass skeleton crucifixes 57
4.17. Seventeenth-century crosses from Santa Catalina de Guale (Georgia) 58
4.18. Carved crystal cross from San Luis de Talimali, ca. 1650–1700 59
4.19. Glass cross and pendant, 1724 59
4.20. Seventeenth-century crosses 60
4.21. Cross from *El Matanceros*, 1741 61
4.22. Crosses from the 1715 plate fleet wrecks 62
4.23. Seventeenth-century Caravaca cross 62
4.24. Coral and gold rosary, 1622 63
4.25. Maltese cross crucifix from Santa Elena 64
4.26. Decade rosary 66
4.27. Seventeenth-century jet rosary 68
4.28. Rosary beads, probably used as joining elements 69
4.29. Jet rosary beads 70
4.30. Eighteenth-century jet rosary beads with metal joining links 70
4.31. Seventeenth-century glass bead rosary elements 71
4.32. Probable glass rosary beads, seventeenth century 72
4.33. Brass mesh joining section from a rosary 72
4.34. Sixteenth-century jet *veneras* or amulets from Santa Elena, South Carolina, 1566–87 73
4.35. Jet devotional *venera* of St. Catherine of Alexandria 74
4.36. Sacred Heart *veneras* 74
4.37. Holy name *venera* 74
4.38. Nuestra Señora de Guadalupe 75
4.39. Reliquary *venera*-pendant with an image of Mary 76
4.40. Late-sixteenth-century *veneras* to the Virgin Mary 76
4.41. *Veneras* to the Virgin Mary: Santa Catalina de Guale (Georgia), ca. 1600–50 77
4.42. Nuestra Señora del Pilar *venera* 78
4.43. Sixteenth-century rock crystal reliquary pendant 79
4.44. Rock crystal reliquary used as a pendant 79

Figures xi

4.45. Glass reliquary cover, seventeenth century *80*
4.46. Reliquary pendant containing an image of the Christ Child *80*
4.47. Eighteenth-century pendant reliquary *81*
4.48. Mid-eighteenth-century reliquary pendant *81*
4.49. Seal impressions with religious motifs *82*
4.50. Fifteenth-century rings with Maltese cross motif on the bezel *83*
4.51. Seventeenth-century silver finger ring *83*
4.52. Columns bearing religious motifs, 1622 *84*
4.53. Copper-alloy star *85*
4.54. Flagellant's star-tipped lash *85*
5.1. Sixteenth-century Spanish children's amulets *88*
5.2. Eighteenth-century child's amulets and *chupeta* *91*
5.3. Varieties of characteristic Spanish amulet forms *92*
5.4. Spanish colonial amulets and ornaments recovered archaeologically *93*
5.5. Jet amulets *94*
5.6. Jet amulet of Eros *94*
5.7. Bone *higa*, ca. 1566 *96*
5.8. Complex double jet *higa* from Santa Elena, 1567–87 *96*
5.9. Jet reliquary *higa* from Santa Fe la Viega, Argentina *96*
5.10. Seventeenth-century jet *higas* from San Luis de Talimali, ca. 1650–1700 *97*
5.11. Woman's bead amulet *100*
5.12. Bead types used as amulets *100*
5.13. Glass heart *101*
5.14. Eighteenth-century shell pendant amulets *101*
5.15. Possible horn amulet *102*
5.16. Metal amulets from St. Augustine *103*
5.17. St. Christopher medallion or amulet *104*
5.18. Mermaid *(Sirena) Sonajero* form *104*
6.1. Gold and pearl unicorn pendant *108*
6.2. Bead jewelry worn in colonial New Spain *120*
6.3. Paste jewels recovered from the 1742 *Matanceros* shipwreck *122*
6.4. Finger rings from La Isabela, 1493–98 *123*
6.5. Rings from Sabana Yegua, Dominican Republic *123*
6.6. Sixteenth-century signet ring *124*

6.7.	Rings from San Luis de Talimali, ca. 1650–1700	124
6.8.	Seventeenth-century finger rings	125
6.9.	Eighteenth-century French-style finger rings	125
6.10.	Ring band designs from the 1715 Florida plate fleet wrecks	126
6.11.	Twisted copper wire rings	127
6.12.	Glass earring fragment, ca. 1580	127
6.13.	*Zarcillo* earrings	127
6.14.	Punta Rassa and San Luis pendants	128
6.15.	Gold pendant earring fragments	128
6.16.	Pendant earrings from the 1715 Florida plate fleet wrecks	129
6.17.	Copper-alloy "tinkler-cone" earring, ca. 1750	129
6.18.	Faceted glass pendant element	129
6.19.	Paste jewelry elements probably used in earrings	130
6.20.	Jewelry elements from La Isabela, 1493–98	130
6.21.	Necklace of trade beads from San Pedro Quitatoni, Oaxaca	131
6.22.	Eighteenth-century glass necklace rod fragment	132
6.23.	Gilded copper-alloy unicorn pendant	132
6.24.	Sixteenth-century pendants	133
6.25.	Spanish colonial chain elements	133
6.26.	Eighteenth-century fabric choker with bow-shaped ornament	134
6.27.	Eighteenth-century emerald *aderezo*	135
6.28.	Glass bracelet fragments from La Isabela, 1493–98	135
6.29.	Eighteenth-century bead bracelet pairs	136
6.30.	Bracelet forms recovered from shipwrecks, 1715	136
6.31.	Sixteenth-century hairpin	137
6.32.	Eighteenth-century hairpin	137
7.1.	Method of attachment for hawk bells	139
7.2.	*Der Schellenmaker* (the bell maker), 1568	140
7.3.	Bells suspended from the hem of a priest's robe	140
7.4.	Rumbler bells on a *sonajero*	141
7.5.	Rumbler and open bells used as a child's amulets	141
7.6.	Open bell used as an amulet	142
7.7.	Rumbler bells used on horse harness	142
7.8.	Rumbler bells from Sabana Yegua, pre-1550	145

7.9.	Clarksdale bells from Puerto Real, 1503–78	*145*
7.10.	Clarksdale bells from Florida sites	*146*
7.11.	Flushloop bells from American Indian mounds in Florida	*147*
7.12.	Mid-eighteenth-century Flushloop-style bells	*147*
7.13.	Rumbler bells from Concepción de la Vega, 1498–1562	*148*
7.14.	Petaloid bells and Clarksdale bells from Concepción de la Vega, 1498–1562	*149*
7.15.	Seventeenth-century bells from San Luis de Talimali, ca. 1650–1700	*149*
7.16.	Open bell components	*150*
7.17.	Sixteenth-century copper-alloy open bells	*150*
7.18.	Mission bells in Mexico	*150*
7.19.	Open bells on collars worn by captives of the Moors	*151*
7.20.	Copper-alloy handbell fragment, ca. 1580–1600	*151*
7.21.	Gold-plated silver handbell, 1733	*152*
7.22.	Bronze Florida mission bell, ca. 1650–1700	*153*
7.23.	Bronze chime bell	*153*
8.1.	Constituent parts and terminology for buttons	*161*
8.2.	Silver button from Puerto Real, ca. 1550–75	*162*
8.3.	Sixteenth-century ball-shaped buttons	*162*
8.4.	Sixteenth-century cast dome-shaped button varieties	*163*
8.5.	Sixteenth-century cast dome-shaped buttons	*163*
8.6.	Sixteenth-century glass button	*164*
8.7.	Seventeenth-century buttons from San Luis de Talimali, ca. 1650–1700	*164*
8.8.	Bone button back attachment methods on two-piece buttons	*166*
8.9.	Backings on two-piece buttons from St. Augustine	*166*
8.10.	Bone button backs and bone blanks	*166*
8.11.	Eighteenth-century carved bone buttons, St. Augustine	*166*
8.12.	Eighteenth-century single-piece brass buttons, St. Augustine	*167*
8.13.	Eighteenth-century buttons, probably used on uniforms	*168*
8.14.	Spanish colonial military button forms	*168*
8.15.	Eighteenth-century buttons, probably used on uniforms, ca. 1700–50	*169*
8.16.	Insignia on Florida's Spanish colonial military buttons	*169*
8.17.	Regimental buttons of Cuban militia in Florida	*170*

8.18.	Two-piece eighteenth-century buttons and button crowns	*171*
8.19.	Paste jewels and paste jewel buttons from the *Matanceros* wreck, 1741	*172*
8.20.	Eighteenth-century paste jewel buttons from St. Augustine	*173*
8.21.	Eighteenth-century shell buttons from St. Augustine	*173*
8.22.	Sleeve links	*174*
8.23.	Aglets	*175*
8.24.	Aglet use in sixteenth-century clothing	*175*
8.25.	Clothing fasteners from La Isabela, 1493–98	*176*
8.26.	Sixteenth-century metallic *guarnición*	*177*
8.27.	Sixteenth-century copper-alloy "stars"	*178*
8.28.	Silver sequins from San Luis de Talimali, ca. 1650–1700	*179*
9.1.	Buckle components and terminology	*181*
9.2.	Copper-alloy buckles, ca. 1500–50	*182*
9.3.	Copper-alloy buckles, ca. 1520–70	*183*
9.4.	Sixteenth-century double-frame subround ("figure-eight") buckles	*183*
9.5.	Silver harness/clothing buckle	*184*
9.6.	Clothing and shoe buckles from the 1715 Florida plate fleet wrecks	*185*
9.7.	Copper-alloy buckles from Santa Rosa Pensacola, ca. 1720–50	*186*
9.8.	Copper-alloy clothing and shoe buckles from St. Augustine, ca. 1750–90	*187*
9.9.	Buckles used on armor	*188*
9.10.	Copper-alloy armor buckles from La Isabela, 1493–98	*188*
9.11.	Iron strap lead or armor buckles, Puerto Real, 1503–78	*189*
9.12.	Manner of spur buckle attachment	*189*
9.13.	Spur buckles	*189*
9.14.	Sixteenth-century harness buckles	*190*
9.15.	Gilded and enameled harness buckle	*190*
9.16.	Late-seventeenth-century brass baldric buckle	*191*
9.17.	Fifteenth-century strap ends	*191*
9.18.	Sixteenth-century belt hook fastener	*191*
9.19.	Sixteenth-century belt hooks and fasteners, Puerto Real	*192*
9.20.	Use of belt hooks and fasteners	*192*
10.1.	The pin maker (*Der Hesstelmacher*), 1568	*194*

Figures

10.2.	Late-fifteenth-century straight pins from La Isabela (1493–98)	*194*
10.3.	Late-sixteenth-century straight pins	*195*
10.4.	Copper-alloy pin sheath	*195*
10.5.	Silver needle case (*etuí*)	*196*
10.6.	Sixteenth-century needle cases (*etuís*)	*197*
10.7.	Wood and ivory needle or pin cases	*197*
10.8.	Eighteenth-century bone needle cases	*198*
10.9.	The thimble maker (*Der Fingerhuter*), 1568	*200*
10.10.	Thimble knurling wheel	*200*
10.11.	Hand-punched and machine-knurled thimbles	*200*
10.12.	Hispano-Moresque thimbles	*201*
10.13.	Emblem of the Nuremberg Tailors Guild, 1600	*202*
10.14.	Nuremberg thimbles	*202*
10.15.	Maker's mark on a Nuremberg thimble	*203*
10.16.	Silver thimble	*203*
10.17.	Seventeenth-century Dutch-style thimble	*204*
10.18.	Dutch thimbles	*204*
10.19.	Eighteenth-century machine-knurled thimbles from St. Augustine	*205*
10.20.	Deep-drawn machine-made thimbles	*205*
10.21.	Children's thimbles	*205*
10.22.	Diagram of shears and scissors parts	*206*
10.23.	Sixteenth-century embroidery scissors	*207*
10.24.	Sixteenth-century industrial scissors	*207*
10.25.	Sixteenth-century tailor's scissors	*207*
10.26.	Utility scissors	*208*
10.27.	Sixteenth-century scissor blades	*208*
10.28.	Scissors recovered archaeologically	*209*
10.29.	Brass embroidery scissors	*209*
10.30.	Bobbin lace technology	*210*
10.31.	Lace bobbins	*210*
10.32.	Bone bobbins recovered archaeologically	*211*
11.1.	Component parts of the fan	*215*
11.2.	Spanish woman with a fixed fan, 1529	*216*
11.3.	Woman of Havana with a fixed feather fan, 1695	*217*
11.4.	The production of pleated fans	*217*
11.5.	Sixteenth-century Spanish pleated leather fan	*218*

11.6.	Eighteenth-century pleated fan in Mexico	*219*
11.7.	Articulated ivory fan sticks, 1724	*220*
11.8.	Painted ivory fan sticks, 1733	*220*
11.9.	Eighteenth-century bone fan sticks from St. Augustine	*221*
11.10.	Brass umbrella or parasol ribs, ca. 1750	*221*
11.11.	Articulated brass umbrella or parasol ribs, 1724	*222*
11.12.	Umbrella rod center ring, ca. 1820	*222*
11.13.	The spectacles maker (*Der Brillenmacher*), 1568	*223*
11.14.	Sixteenth- and seventeenth-century eyeglasses	*224*
11.15.	Spanish eyeglasses with ear attachments, 1596	*225*
11.16.	Spanish eyeglasses broadsheet, 1763	*225*
11.17.	Eyeglass lens and metal frames, pre-1750	*226*
11.18.	*"Purgat et Ornat,"* 1669	*226*
11.19.	Double-sided bone combs	*226*
11.20.	Varieties of bone combs and their production	*227*
11.21.	The brush maker (*Der Burstenbinder*), 1568	*229*
11.22.	Wire method for attaching bristles to a brush stock	*229*
11.23.	Bone hairbrush with wire grooves, ca. 1790	*230*
11.24.	French bone and ivory hairbrush stocks, 1782	*230*
11.25.	Spanish toothpicks, 1715	*231*
11.26.	Ivory toothbrush, 1733	*232*
11.27.	Bone toothbrush heads	*232*
11.28.	Bone handle for toothbrush or other personal maintenance item	*233*
11.29.	Blade merchant	*234*
11.30.	Sixteenth-century straight razor blade	*234*
11.31.	Bone straight razor, ca. 1618	*235*
12.1.	Hand hammering coin dies	*239*
12.2.	The coin stamper (*Der Munkmeister*), 1568	*240*
12.3.	Blancas and ceitils from La Isabela, 1493–98	*244*
12.4.	Sixteenth-century maravedís	*244*
12.5.	Ferdinand and Isabella reales minted in Seville for America	*245*
12.6.	Maravedís	*246*
12.7.	Four maravedís minted in Santo Domingo	*246*
12.8.	Design motifs on Spanish and Spanish American silver coinage	*248*
12.9.	Spanish American cob coins	*249*

Figures   xvii

12.10. Obverse (shield) motifs on Mexico City silver coins   250
12.11. Mexico City Phillip V pillar dollar, 1733   252
12.12. Mexico City Charles IV *bustos*   252
12.13. Counting tokens used in calculation   258
12.14. Nuremberg counting jeton   258
12.15. Eighteenth-century commemorative peace jeton   259
12.16. Coin scale and weight set   259
12.17. Sixteenth-century coin weight box   260
12.18. Fifteenth-century Spanish weights   260
12.19. Sixteenth-century copper-alloy weights from Concepción de la Vega, 1496–1502   261
12.20. Spanish coin or pharmaceutical weights   261
12.21. Weights from 1715 Florida shipwrecks   262
12.22. Eighteenth-century nested cup weights   263
12.23. Sixteenth-century cup weights   264
12.24. Examples of mastersigns on Nuremberg and other weights   265
12.25. English scale weight used in Spanish Florida   266
12.26. Colonial-era scale types   267
12.27. Arm terminals on small scale beams   267
13.1.   Fifteenth-century *hacabuche* barrel fragment   269
13.2.   Firearm nomenclature   270
13.3.   Matchlock diagrams   271
13.4.   Matchlock trigger   271
13.5.   Seventeenth-century musketeer with matchlock   272
13.6.   St. Augustine matchlock   273
13.7.   Matchlock elements from Santa Elena   273
13.8.   Wheel lock diagram   274
13.9.   Wheel lock   274
13.10. Wheel lock pans   275
13.11. Wheel lock spanners   275
13.12. Snaphaunce and doglock exteriors   276
13.13. Miquelet *a la patilla* and *a la moda* locks   277
13.14. Miquelet gunlock exterior   278
13.15. Miquelet locks   278
13.16. Ripoll miquelet pistols   279
13.17. Spanish military-issue firearms, 1752   280
13.18. Lock components of the 1752 *a la francesa* lock   281

13.19.	Hardware on 1752 issue Spanish firearms	*282*
13.20.	Spanish gun hardware, eighteenth century	*283*
13.21.	Northern European flintlock	*283*
13.22.	French flintlock, ca. 1750	*284*
13.23.	French flintlock components, ca. 1750	*285*
13.24.	Flintlock pistol elements, 1733	*286*
13.25.	English pistols, 1710	*286*
13.26.	Lead shot and ball	*287*
13.27.	Stone shot mold, La Isabela, 1493–98	*287*
13.28.	Sixteenth-century shot mold for single lead balls	*287*
13.29.	Lead sprue from multiple shot molds	*288*
13.30.	Multiple shot mold	*288*
13.31.	Colander method for making lead shot	*289*
13.32.	Sixteenth-century powder flasks	*289*
13.33.	Powder container lids	*290*
14.1.	*Astralagalas* (Knucklebones)	*292*
14.2.	Gambling with dice in thirteenth-century Spain	*293*
14.3.	Dice games in eighteenth-century Mexico	*293*
14.4.	Variants of dice layout arrangements	*294*
14.5.	Spanish colonial dice	*294*
14.6.	Board game players, ca. 1560	*295*
14.7.	Ceramic gaming pieces	*296*
14.8.	Bone gaming pieces	*296*
14.9.	Gaming pieces	*297*
14.10.	Possible gaming piece elements	*297*
14.11.	Wooden pin and ball fragment, possibly used in eighteenth-century *boliche*	*298*
14.12.	Child with hobbyhorse	*299*
14.13.	Wire bug	*300*
14.14.	Ceramic figurines	*300*
14.15.	Marbles	*301*
14.16.	Wooden spinning top with iron pin	*301*
14.17.	Whizzers	*302*
14.18.	A Jew's harp being played	*302*
14.19.	Steel Jew's harps	*303*
14.20.	Music-related artifacts	*304*
14.21.	Seventeenth-century writing equipment	*306*
14.22.	Eighteenth-century writing equipment	*306*

Figures

14.23. Majolica inkwell *306*
14.24. Eighteenth-century desk accessory pieces *307*
14.25. Sixteenth-century books *308*
14.26. Book hardware, Concepción de la Vega *309*
14.27. Book clasps and hardware, Puerto Real *309*
14.28. Book clasp type associated with Florida missions *309*
14.29. Red clay pipe bowl fragments from the Dominican Republic *311*
14.30. Gold snuffbox *312*

Tables

2.1.	Sites and Their Approximate Date Ranges	8
3.1.	Political Events Affecting the Distribution of Goods in the Spanish Caribbean and Florida	25
3.2.	Crafts and Guilds Established in the Indies and Mexico	32
4.1.	Religious Items Shipped to the Spanish Colonies, 1511–1613	39
4.2.	Images and Attributes Appearing Frequently on Spanish American Religious Medals	44
4.3.	Rosaries Listed with Prices in Shipping Records to the Caribbean, 1526–1618	67
5.1.	Common Spanish Amulets and Their Attributed Benefits	90
5.2.	Amulets and Amuletic Substances Shipped to the Spanish Colonies, 1583–1613	98
6.1.	Personal Adornment Items Shipped to the Spanish Colonies, 1511–1613	110
6.2.	Quantities and Prices of Imported Jewelry, 1592	121
7.1.	Bell Varieties from Spanish Colonial Sites	143
7.2.	Colonial-Era Chime Bells from Marine Sites	152
8.1.	Clothing Items Shipped to the Spanish Colonies, 1511–1613	159
8.2.	Bone Button Measurements from St. Augustine, 1700–1820	165
8.3.	Diameters of Round, Simple-Construction, Brass-Alloy Buttons from St. Augustine	167
10.1.	Thimble Characteristics	199
12.1.	Divisions and Weights of the Spanish Mark	237
12.2.	Average Weight, Size, and Value of Common Spanish Coin Denominations	238
12.3.	Dates and Coin Inscriptions of Reigning Spanish Monarchs of the Colonial Period	241

12.4.	Spanish Colonial Mints and Their Marks during the Colonial Period	*242*
12.5.	Size and Denomination Marks on Reales	*247*
12.6.	Pharmaceutical Weight Measures Used in New Spain	*266*
13.1.	Bore Diameters of Spanish Military Long Arms	*269*
14.1.	Writing Equipment Imported to the Spanish Colonies, 1523–1613	*305*

Acknowledgments

The original impetus for this book came in 1982 with a grant from the National Endowment for the Humanities, which provided prepublication support (Grant RS 20293–82) for what we thought would be a single-volume study. As it turned out, the research undertaken through that project generated the foundation for both Volume 1 and Volume 2 of *Artifacts of the Spanish Colonies*, as well as a projected Volume 3. Support has also been provided since that time by the Florida Museum of Natural History and the University of Florida Office of Research, Technology and Graduate Education (formerly the Division of Sponsored Research).

During the fifteen years since the beginning of this effort, I have had the good fortune to work with a remarkable range of agencies and individuals who have provided me with more intellectual, financial, and logistical support than I can appropriately acknowledge here. At the heart of the data upon which I have drawn are the pioneering studies undertaken by the first generation of Spanish colonial archaeologists who worked in the Americas—the late John Goggin, Charles Fairbanks, John W. Griffin, Hale G. Smith, Albert Manucy, and José Cruxent. Much of the information included in the following pages is essentially a synthesis of their original insights.

Financial support for subsequent projects with which I have been associated, and which generated major collections that significantly informed the research for this volume, was provided by the following agencies:

The National Endowment for the Humanities supported excavations in the sixteenth-century sites of St. Augustine (RO 32537); excavation, analysis, and interpretation of collections from La Isabela, Dominican Republic (RO 21831–89 and RK 20135-94); and excavations at Puerto Real, Haiti (RO 20935-85).

The National Science Foundation provided support for the curation and cataloging of the St. Augustine collections (RO 9208707), which made it possible to use a large segment of those important collections systematically for the first time.

The National Geographic Society supported excavations at La Isabela, Dominican Republic, and at the site of Florida's first Spanish fort in St. Augustine (8-SJ-34).

The Florida Bureau of Historic Preservation Grants in Aid Program supported research, analysis, and curation of the remains of the first sites of Spanish settlement in St. Augustine, as well as funds to organize and put all of the archaeological collections from St. Augustine in a computerized database.

The U.S. Agency for International Development provided funds for the study and curation of the collections from Concepción de la Vega.

The success of any effort of this kind depends on the quality of its illustrations, and much of the credit for the illustrations found in this book must go to the fine eye and tireless commitment of James Quine. His inventive creativity and sense of humor led him to produce splendid photographs under makeshift and often bizarre conditions in artifact repositories and field sites throughout the Caribbean and Florida.

I would also like to thank the University of Florida Office of Instructional Resources Photography and Graphics section, particularly Pat O'Brien and John Haupt, for their fine photographs of objects from the University of Florida collections. Their skill, professionalism, and uncomplaining compliance with unreasonable deadlines have enhanced this book immeasurably.

Merald Clark of the Florida Museum of Natural History created many of the excellent drawings found in the following pages, not only at the University of Florida but also at field sites in the Dominican Republic. Pauline Kulstad also contributed several fine pieces of artwork to this volume.

Although I have drawn upon more than 100 site and museum collections for this work (which are acknowledged throughout), special mention must be made of several particularly important collections that have shaped my understanding of Spanish colonial material culture, along with the individuals who helped me use them. The largest of these collections is comprised by the materials in the Historical Archaeology Laboratory of the Florida Museum of Natural History. This collection includes the scientifically excavated remains from more than 40 Spanish colonial sites throughout Florida, the Caribbean, and Mexico and, thanks to the support of the National Science Foundation, is cataloged and accessible in an electronic format. Maurice Williams, staff historical archaeologist and collections manager since 1999, and his successor, Alfred Woods, have been inextricably involved in the preparation of this book since its inception, providing hours of assistance in locating, documenting, and discussing items from the collections. Elise LeCompte, the department registrar, has also been an invaluable colleague in this effort, not only in the use of the collections but also for the research on the collections' metal objects she has carried out and shared with me over the years.

I also gratefully acknowledge the invaluable and ongoing help given to me by Jerry Milanich of the Florida Museum of Natural History and his students in locating and identifying important items from the mission sites of Florida. Jeffrey Mitchem, Brent Weisman, Rebecca Saunders, Ken Johnson, and Donna Ruhl have all brought important artifacts to my attention and have been most generous in sharing information from their projects. Fred Gaske of the Florida Division of Historical Resources has directed me to many important objects over the past ten years as well as to some very obscure publications.

Equally important to this undertaking have been the collections resulting from more than thirty years of excavation in the Spanish colonial sites of St. Augustine, Florida. That collection is the only systematic archaeological assemblage that I am aware of that spans the sixteenth through the nineteenth centuries, with documentable, discrete closed contexts. Much of the credit for this circumstance goes to the more than 300 archaeology field school students who have worked yearly in St. Augustine over the past quarter of a century. They have generated, analyzed, and reported much of the data from the town with a unique combination of enthusiasm, idealism, and irreverence, and the resulting original contributions are cited throughout the volume. Archaeologists Stanley Bond, Bruce Piatek, and Robert Steinbach, all formerly with the Historic St. Augustine Preservation Board, and Carl Halbirt, St. Augustine's city archaeologist, have provided me unstintingly with information, reports, photographs, specimens, and critiques over a twenty-year period, for which I am deeply grateful.

The Florida Bureau of Archaeological Research, Tallahassee, has been another invaluable source of information, images, and assistance, thanks largely to the help and cooperation of its chief, Jim Miller. Conservator James Levy has served as my very knowledgeable guide to the bureau's magnificent collection of shipwreck materials from Florida waters and has been extremely generous in making them available to me. He has also offered invaluable advice on the dating and identification of many of the objects, which I have gratefully accepted and used.

The San Luis Archaeological and Historical Site, also under the Florida Bureau of Archaeological Research, is one of the most comprehensive and best-controlled collections available anywhere for the study of seventeenth-century Spanish material culture. Bonnie G. McEwan, the project's director, has been tremendously helpful since the beginning of this effort, providing data, photographs, and access to collections, as well as critical review of and advice about this manuscript.

Stanley South and Chester DePratter of the South Carolina Institute of Archaeology and Anthropology have been unfailingly collegial in sharing information and images from the site of Santa Elena. South has excavated Santa Elena over the past 20 years, and this project has generated one of the most tightly dated late-sixteenth-century assemblages in the Americas. I am grateful to Stan for his comments on my use of the Santa Elena materials.

Dave Thomas and Lori Pendleton-Thomas of the American Museum of Natural History gave me help and hospitality on St. Catherine's Island and at the American Museum while learning about the assemblage from their excavations at the mission of Santa Catalina. Their generosity in providing data and images substantially influenced the sections on Spanish colonial religious items.

Several collections from sites in the Caribbean have been especially important for my understanding of sixteenth-century material culture. At La Isabela, the only fifteenth-century Spanish site in the hemisphere, the Dirección de Parques Nacionales kindly gave permission to work at the site and collaborate in its excavation and analysis. I want particularly to thank the site's principal excavator, José Cruxent of the Universidad National Francisco de Miranda of Venezuela, for his stimulating assistance, companionship, and instruction throughout our ten years of collaboration at La Isabela.

One of the most important collections of artifacts from Spanish colonial shipwrecks in the hemisphere was generated by the activities of the Comisión de Rescate Arqueológico Submarino of the Dominican Republic. These artifacts are part of the Museo de la Atarazana collections in Santo Domingo, and I would like especially to thank archaeologist Pedro Borrell and conservator Francis Soto for access to and information about those materials.

José Gonzáles, Frank Torres Petitón, and Seraphin Vásquez served as hospitable guides to the spectacular collections and remains from Concepción de la Vega in the Dominican Republic. I would like to thank both them and the Dirección Nacional de Parques for the opportunity to collaborate there.

I have also been for many years the fortunate (and appreciative) recipient of invaluable advice, assistance, and information about sites and collections in the Dominican Republic provided to me by Manuel Garcia Arévalo, Fernando Luna Calderón, Maria Nieves Sicart, Elpidio Ortega, Eugenio Pérez Montás, Marcio Veloz Maggiolo, and Bernardo Vega.

The artifact collection from the site of Puerto Real in Haiti is one of the largest and most comprehensive for the sixteenth-century Spanish colonial occupation of the Caribbean. I want particularly to acknowledge the role of the late William Hodges of the Musée de Guahabá and the Hopital le Bon Samaritain in Limbé, Haiti, not only for bringing this site to the attention of other scholars and archaeologists but also for his and his family's hospitality and assistance in our efforts to learn about Puerto Real and its material world. Thanks are also due to Albert Mangones of the Institut de Sauvegarde de

Patrimoine National D'Haiti and to the Bureau National d'Ethnologie D'Haiti for permitting us to work at the site.

Archaeologist Lourdes Domínguez of Havana was a gracious and very knowledgeable host in Havana, guiding me through collections of the Académia de Ciéncias de la Habana and the Museo de la Ciudad de la Habana. She not only led me to important Cuban artifact collections but during the ensuing years has also continued to lead me to important publications and ideas in Cuban historical archaeology.

Rick Sammon, president of CEDAM International, directed me to that organization's Pablo Bush Romero Museum in Mexico, where the extensive collections from the *Matanceros* shipwreck are curated. Rick has also generously provided me with much helpful information about CEDAM's underwater activities throughout the region.

Museum and library collections have figured prominently in the preparation of this book, as sources for contextualizing and documenting the use and meaning of artifacts in the Spanish colonies. Prominent among these is the University of Florida Latin American Collection, which has astounded me for decades with its depth and breadth of holdings and its ability to secure the most erudite and obscure of foreign publications. Because of the Latin American Collection, in combination with the Florida Museum collections, this book could not have been written anywhere but in Gainesville without an enormous travel budget.

I am also grateful for many hours of help from the staff of the St. Augustine Historical Society Library, which contains one of the most comprehensive archival collections pertinent to Spanish colonial archaeology in the United States. The holdings of the Castillo de San Marcos, revealed to me by Luís Arana, were essential to the sections of this volume dealing with military items.

Museum collections in Spain have been essential to this undertaking, and I wish to thank Begoña Torres and Maria Braña of the Museo del Pueblo Español for their assistance in learning about the important collections of that museum and for their help in identifying many of the objects from Spanish sites in the Americas. Ángela Franco of the Museo Arqueológico Nacional in Madrid was also most helpful in my efforts to locate sources and materials in their collections.

In London, the library and photographic archives of the Victoria and Albert Museum were invaluable in preparing this volume, and I would like to thank R. W. Lightbown for his helpful responses to my inquiries. Timothy Wilson and David Gaimster of the British Museum very kindly assisted me with the Medieval and Later Antiquities collections in the British Museum, and Sarah Posey of the Museum of Mankind was also most helpful in my learning about their American holdings.

Several sections of this manuscript have been reviewed by colleagues, whose comments and suggestions have resulted in substantial revision. I thank Patricia Muller of the Hispanic Society of America for her review of the chapter on jewelry; Alan Stahl of the American Numismatic Society for his assessment of the chapter on coins; and James Lavin of the College of William and Mary, James Levy of the Florida Division of Archaeological Research, and Jack "F. E." Williams of St. Augustine for their help with the chapter on firearms. Bonnie McEwan of the San Luis Archaeological and Historical Site, Deborah Peters of the American Museum of Natural History, Michael V. Gannon of the University of Florida, and Richard Ahlborn of the National Museum of American History all read various versions of the chapter on religious items. Richard Ahlborn's comprehensive review in particular resulted in important revisions to that section.

A number of colleagues and graduate students at the Florida Museum of Natural History have been pressed into service in the review, editing, and preparation of this manuscript, and I'd like to thank Jamie Anderson, Korinn Bradin, Jeremy Cohen, Matthew Curtis, Mary Herron, Kate Hoffman, Pauline Kulstad, Bonnie McEwan, Gifford Waters, Alfred Woods, and Alison Yoh for their cheerful (at least in my presence) compliance.

I owe a special thanks to Daniel Goodwin, formerly of the Smithsonian Institution Press, who showed superhuman patience and abiding trust during his ten-year wait for this manuscript. Scott Mahler and Anne Bolen of the Press took on the very belated manuscript with patience and good cheer, and my copy editor Robert Burchfield's talents have made this a much better book than it would otherwise have been.

Part 1
Contexts

Chapter 1
Scale, Context, and Meaning in Material Culture Studies

Most American archaeologists would probably agree that artifacts, in and of themselves, are not the primary focus of our work. They are, rather, tools that we use together with context, features, strata, ecological data, and other sources of archaeological evidence to reconstruct site structure and understand past cultures.
—Artifacts of the Spanish Colonies of Florida and the Caribbean, 1500–1800, Volume 1

When I began writing this volume more than ten years ago, I had a different book in mind. I intended to develop a counterpart to Volume 1 of *Artifacts of the Spanish Colonies* (1987), which was a synthesis of existing archaeological information on the classification, dating, origins, functions, and distribution of ceramic and glass artifacts in Spanish colonial sites. Volume 2 was to be an attempt to do the same for nonceramic or glass artifacts. It became apparent very quickly, however, that an approach based on physical composition would not work and that the systematic taxonomy we use for ceramic artifacts was simply not useful for many other kinds of items that evoke behavioral aspects of past society.

The ceramic and glass taxonomy approach that I used in Volume 1 was at least partly an artifact of the time when it was written (the 1980s). The heady first days of the "new" processual archaeology were past, and many historical archaeologists had come to share the concern that in our enthusiasm to address the larger processual questions of cultural organization and change we had skipped a critical step in the research process. That is, we had failed to develop a middle-range theory through which we could connect our observable material culture database to unobservable past cultural expressions. This realization was particularly disheartening for the Spanish colonial archaeologists of the early 1980s since, unlike our colleagues working in Anglo-American sites, we had yet even to develop a basic understanding of the chronology, origins, functions, distributional patterns, and economic implications of the objects we excavated, let alone their connections to past cultural expressions.

We nevertheless tended to move ahead to studying such larger issues as acculturation, foodways adaptations, ethnicity, and social status and ideology through the archaeological record with sometimes disappointing results (for a few of the many critiques of these efforts see Cusick 1997; Orser 1996; Schuyler 1988). Volume 1, for me, was an effort to step back and try to build a firmer foundation on which to develop cultural-processual models.

Obviously a great deal has changed in historical archaeology since 1987 (see, for example, Anders 1997; Orser 1996; Little 1994). For one thing, Spanish colonial archaeologists in 2002 have a much more comprehensive understanding of the past behaviors associated with several basic categories of material culture (that is, ceramics and architecture) than we did in the 1980s. This is at least in large part owing to the extraordinary surge of historical and archaeological research on Spanish colonial sites throughout the Americas generated by the occasion of the Columbian quincentenary (see Axtell 1992; Cusick 1997; Deagan and Cruxent 2002a, 2002b; Gannon 1992; Thomas 1989, 1990, 1991).

The quincentenary years also corresponded with a shift in focus among many historical and prehistoric archaeologists away from a broad-scale analysis of cultural process at a systemic level toward smaller scale analyses of social behavior at the level of individuals or single groups. The volume of new information resulting from quincentennial-related research has given rise to new questions about colonization, colonialism, and the creation of a new, multiracial social order in America. This shift has provoked many archaeologists to try to understand and incorporate the role of human agency and individual meaning into our models of past cultural activity and change, leading many of us to consider gender, race, ethnicity, and households as primary foci of our archaeological activities.

This is an entirely different—but certainly not mutually exclusive—scale of analysis from the emphasis on generalized cultural expression or process that absorbed most archaeologists in 1985. This important newer direction, however, has rarely been convincingly operationalized and realized using the archaeological record, largely because our archaeological tools and methods have been developed almost exclusively to further the goals of (largely prehistoric) processual archaeology or cultural history and tend to inform structural and chronological questions at a system-wide scale. Our methods for systematic classification, chronology, and pattern recognition were both useful and appropriate in this endeavor, and the kinds of classificatory and contextual information that Volume 1 of *Artifacts of the Spanish Colonies* contains were oriented toward that scale of analysis.

In contrast, as most archaeologists interested in such social factors as gender, race, or cultural identity have unhappily learned, there are extremely few successful methods (other than the questionable one of an archaeologist's personal intuition) designed to elicit either human agency or human meaning in the archaeological record of pre- or postcontact sites. This is especially lamentable in historical archaeology, which has the unique potential of using both parallel and convergent evidence from well-documented archaeological, documentary, iconographic, literary, and oral contexts. Although this potential is widely recognized and acknowledged, it has only rarely been applied rigorously to archaeological material culture. And material culture is, after all, not only the most basic category of our archaeological database but also the one category that separates archaeologists from social historians, geographers, philosophers, and poets.

I came to this position gradually as I worked on Volume 2, trying unsuccessfully to establish a typology for personal possessions—jewelry, amulets, religious items, clothing, items of hygiene, and so forth. Although these items can often provide important information about chronology, exchange networks, markets, and status, they are also imbued with a great deal more information about gender, beliefs, value systems, social opportunities, and social identity. As my own interest in these topics increased, it became evident that this information usually does not reside in the form or composition of the objects and cannot be elicited through traditional methods of classification and typology based only on physical attributes. It requires the integration of physical attributes with temporal, spatial, and cultural contexts together with the nonmaterial attributes provided by written and visual accounts of past production, use, and meaning.

I began this effort with the archaeocentric assumption shared by many historical archaeologists who have tried to identify the unique contributions of our discipline, that everyday and humble material culture was documented primarily, if not exclusively, in archaeological contexts. I soon learned, however (with the help of many colleagues in other fields), that the written and visual accounts of past production and use of most Spanish objects are abundant, rich, and available. Writing Volume 2 became an effort to integrate these contextual attributes with the physical and archaeological attributes of the artifacts we find in colonial sites and led to the abandonment of organization by material categories. This study instead attempts to provide a nonexhaustive synthesis of the formal, temporal, functional, distributional, and social associations for personal, portable possessions—those personal items that people chose, used, and displayed as individuals.

I concentrate on personal items not only because they are among the most frequently encountered artifacts on colonial sites but also because they are among the best material sources in the archaeological record for hypothesizing the nature of individual agency, identity, and ideology. Most of them were owned by individuals, and most were displayed or at least were visible on the person, sometimes functioning simultaneously in the technomic, sociotechnic, and idiotechnic spheres proposed more than forty years ago by Lewis Binford (1962). A pervading theme in most aspects of Spanish colonial life, for example, was the pronounced influence of Catholicism and magical belief, and this is vividly reflected in the material world of personal possessions. The chapters on religious items, jewelry, and amulets, in fact, represent a somewhat artificial distinction, since most of these items had both ornamental and symbolic significance.

The personal possessions treated in this study differ significantly in another way from the ceramics and glassware of Volume 1. A wide variety of sources—including shipping records, contemporary inventories, travelers' accounts, sumptuary regulations, paintings, literary sources, and guild records—identify personal, nonceramic items in vernacular terms and in their context of use. Therefore, to characterize these materials reliably in emic terms is often possible using these as established categories against which to identify and interpret archaeological samples.

This differs somewhat from the essentially etic systems traditionally used to identify and classify Spanish colonial ceramics and beads, using archaeological analyses as the starting point (see Volume 1 as an example and Potter 1982 for an early critique of such systems in the Anglo-colonial arena). So-called types, when they existed, were established largely through traditional attribute analysis, with dates assigned through stratigraphic and seriation studies of short-term, single-component sites (for example, Goggin's 1968 study of Spanish majolica and M. Smith's 1983 study of beads). When possible, the former emic approach has been taken in this volume.

Because this book is intended for use by archaeologists, its primary organizing criterion has been the archaeological assemblages of the Spanish colonial sites in the circum-Caribbean region. Excavation of Spanish colonial sites has increased tremendously since 1987, and it continues to be sustained beyond the Columbian quincentenary. The most important sites and collections drawn from for these chapters are discussed in Chapter 2. The major social, economic, and political vagaries that shaped the very international nature of the Spanish American material world are well documented in the explicit regulations that governed the origins and distribution of goods in the colonies, which are discussed in Chapter 3.

The material assemblage of the Spanish colonies in the New World is distinct in a number of ways from assemblages of other European American colonies. One of these is in its longevity; Spanish colonial remains date to the period between 1492 and 1898. They include items imported from numerous centers in Europe and Asia as well as a wide range of products manufactured in the Spanish colonies. The production of Spanish American material goods (for example, pottery, coinage, glassware, and jewelry) began early in the sixteenth century and still persists in the Americas.

Another characteristic of Spanish colonial material culture is the enduring influence of distinctive Iberian social processes that encouraged social and material syncretism—most notably the Moorish-Spanish syncretism of the fifteenth and sixteenth centuries (see Lister and Lister 1987:65–120) and the Spanish-American-African syncretism of the colonial period. The economic organization and trade networks in the Spanish Americas also differed considerably from those of other European colonies, in the mercantilist system attempted by Spain, in the diversity of regional Spanish American markets, and in the exchange networks that directly connected Asia, Europe, and Africa to the Americas as early as the sixteenth century. These markets, networks, and regulations changed through the centuries, providing a basis for suggesting periodicity in assemblages. These variables are addressed in Chapter 3.

Chapters 4, 5, and 6 cover religious items, amulets, and jewelry, respectively. As noted, these were often interchangeable categories, and the placement of items in one or another chapter is somewhat arbitrary. Chapter 7 deals with bells, a commonly found artifact on Spanish colonial sites and one that also served a variety of functions. Chapters 8 through 10 address artifacts related to clothing and clothing preparation (clothing fasteners, buckles, and sewing equipment, respectively), and Chapter 11 deals with items of personal comfort, cosmetics, and hygiene.

Chapter 12 considers coins and weights. While coins do not have the personal associations of some of the other categories discussed in this volume, they are one of the most frequently recovered personal possessions on archaeological sites and one of the best for establishing chronology. This can also be argued for personal firearms (Chapter 13), which, while associated with organized military activity as well as with personal use, were a nearly ubiquitous possession of Spanish men. The final chapter addresses the material aspects of individual pastimes and leisure activities in the Spanish colonies.

I should note that not only has the integration of past social context added significantly to the quantity of research and writing involved in this undertaking, but the dramatic increase in Spanish colonial archaeology during the past twelve years has expanded the sheer volume of collections in an equally dramatic way. I offer these observations not so much as an excuse for the twelve-year hiatus between volumes but rather to explain why Volume 2 has been limited to this category of portable personal possessions. A future volume is intended to address artifacts associated with military items and weaponry, architectural items, household and domestic activities, horse equipment, commercial technology, craft production, cottage industries, and tools.

I fully expect that much of this study will be revised and refined through the research that is ongoing at Spanish colonial sites throughout the Americas. For the present, however, the information here can be used as one step toward a more precise understanding of an important segment of the archaeological database, how it arrived in its archaeological context, and what it can tell us about the behavior of people in the past.

Chapter 2
Sites and Samples

As noted in Chapter 1, the starting point for this study of portable personal possessions has been artifact assemblages from the archaeological sites of the Spanish colonies themselves. Although documentary sources, museum collections, literature, and paintings have been used to establish the social contexts and meanings of these items (as well as the terminology used to describe them), the archaeological specimens provide the most unequivocal evidence for the characteristics of items used by Spanish colonists in the circum-Caribbean area.

The sites used as a database in this study represent a wide and diverse range of archaeological contexts and recovery methods, including terrestrial sites, marine sites, surface collections, systematically excavated and recorded collections, and nonsystematically recorded collections. In all cases, however, only those artifacts with reliable and archaeologically established chronological associations have been used to define and date the categories of material culture used in the Spanish colonies. Such associations have been derived through the analysis of single-component, undisturbed sites of short duration and archaeologically defined, undisturbed, closed contexts at multicomponent or long-term occupation sites.

Thirty-five assemblages from archaeological sites in Florida and the Caribbean, including both terrestrial and marine sites, provide the basis for this effort. The sites are listed in Table 2.1, and their locations are shown Figure 2.1. I have also drawn on published reports from several sites outside of the defined region because of these sites' archaeological integrity, Iberian affiliation, and well-defined date ranges. Reports from these sites, including the Padre Island shipwrecks (Arnold and Weddle 1978), Qsar es-Seghir in Morocco (Redman and Boone 1979), the Armada wrecks off the English coast (Martin 1975, 1978; Martin and Parker 1988; Stenuit 1972), and Fort Jesus, Mombasa (Kirkman 1974), have been used to help define the temporal and formal ranges of the artifacts discussed in the following chapters. Other sites, such as sites of Spanish exploration and settlement in the southwestern United States (for example, Simmons 1987; Simmons and Turley 1980), Manila galleon shipwrecks (Mathers 1990), and a number of shipwrecks in the Bahamas and Bermuda (Marx and Marx 1993; Peterson 1975), are referred to occasionally throughout the text and are cited and identified in the relevant discussions.

In order to better assess and interpret the conclusions found in the following chapters, each site used in the study is briefly discussed, with emphasis on the history and nature of colonial occupation, the archaeological excavations, and the recovery and study of the sites' material remains.

Terrestrial Sites

La Isabela, Dominican Republic (1493–98)

La Isabela was founded in December 1493 by Christopher Columbus and was the first in-

Table 2.1. Sites and Their Approximate Date Ranges

Terrestrial Sites	Date
La Isabela, Dominican Republic	ca. 1493–98
Concepción de la Vega, Dominican Republic	1496–1562
Caparra, Puerto Rico	ca. 1500–50
Sevilla Nueva, Jamaica	ca. 1502–75
Puerto Real, Haiti	ca. 1503–78
Nueva Cádiz, Cubagua, Venezuela	1515–41
Panamá Viejo	1519–1671
Fountain of Youth Park site, St. Augustine	1565–66
Sixteenth-century St. Augustine, Florida	ca. 1572–1600
Santa Elena, South Carolina	1566–87
Bayahá, Haiti	1578–1605
San Juan del Puerto, Florida	1598–1702
Baptizing Springs, Florida	ca. 1610–56
Santa Catalina de Guale, Georgia (second occupation)	1606–80
Fig Springs, Florida	ca. 1608–56
Fox Pond, Florida	ca. 1606–56
Seventeenth-century St. Augustine, Florida	ca. 1600–1702
San Luis de Talimali, Florida	1633–1704
Eighteenth-century St. Augustine, Florida	1702–63
Higgs site, Florida	ca. 1715
Santa Rosa Pensacola, Florida	1723–53
Casa Rosa scarp wall, San Juan, Puerto Rico	ca. 1784–1800
Second Spanish Period, St. Augustine, Florida	1784–1821

Multicomponent Sites	Date
Santo Domingo sites, Dominican Republic	1502–present
Havana, Cuba	1514–present
El Morro, San Juan, Puerto Rico	1591–1777

Marine Sites	Date
Padre Island wrecks, Texas	1554
Emmanuel Point wreck, Florida	1559?
Armada wrecks, Britain	1588
Atocha wreck, Florida	1622
Concepción wreck, Dominican Republic	1641
Florida plate fleet wrecks	1715
Tolosá and *Guadalupe*, Quicksilver, wrecks, Dominican Republic	1724
Florida plate fleet wrecks	1733
Nuestra Señora de los Milagros (*El Mantanceros* wreck), Yucatán	1741
El Nuevo Constante wreck, Luisiana	1766

tentional European colonial settlement in the New World. Conflict with the indigenous peoples, poor locations of the settlement, and disease, among other factors, caused La Isabela to be abandoned by about 1498 (Cruxent 1990; Deagan 1992a, 1992b; Deagan and Cruxent 1997, 2002a, 2002b; Taviani 1983; Varela 1987). The site is located on the north coast of the Dominican Republic, near present-day Puerto Plata. A portion of the settlement has been eroded by tidal action and has washed into the river and bay; however, stone foundations and the cemetery from La Isabela's occupation are still visible (Fig. 2.2). The site was badly disturbed during the twentieth century by road-building and -grading activities, but excavations have established that no post–fifteenth-century occupation existed there until the twentieth century. Artifacts can therefore be assigned a late-fifteenth-century date on the basis of morphology, since the twentieth-century material remains are easily distinguishable from them. The artifact assemblage from La Isabela was derived from excavations at the site carried out by José Cruxent between 1987 and 1995 and by the University of Florida from 1989 to 1992. It consists of more than half a million artifacts, which are presently stored at the Parque Nacional de la Isabela in El Castillo, Dominican Republic.

Sites and Samples

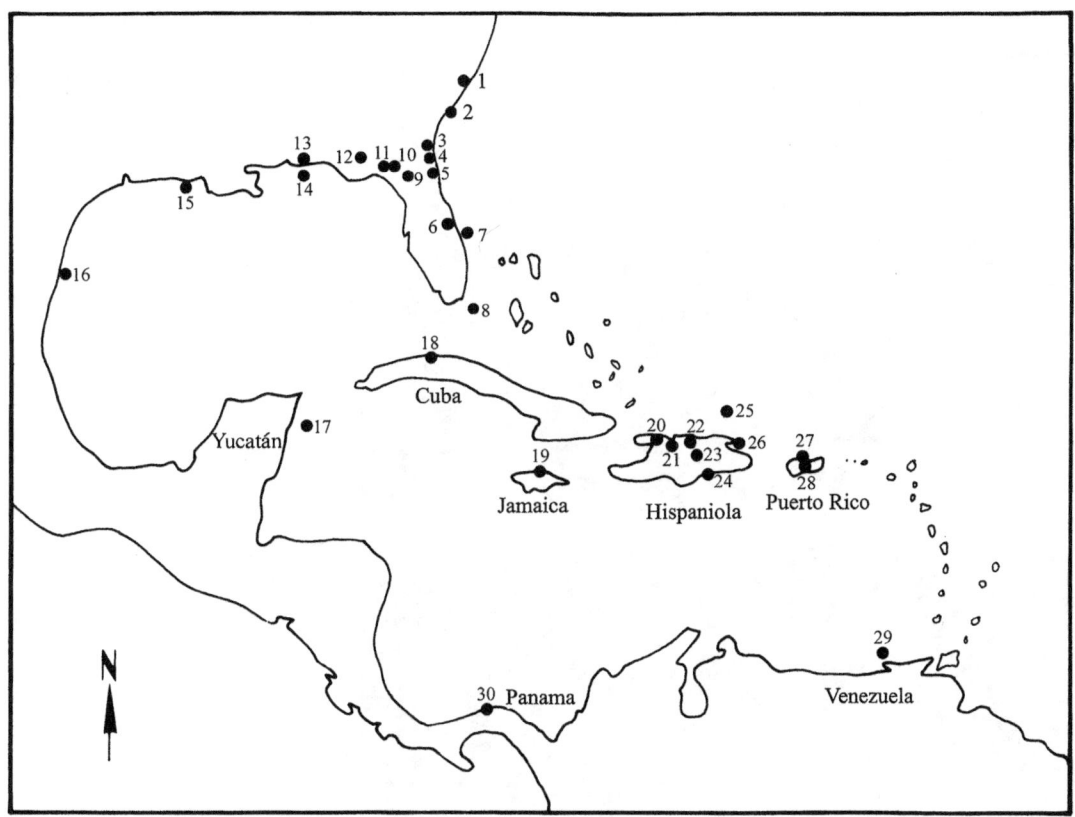

Figure 2.1. Locations of sites used in the study.

1. Santa Elena, South Carolina
2. Santa Catalina de Guale, Georgia
3. Santa Catalina de Guale, Florida
4. San Juan del Puerto, Florida
5. St. Augustine sites, Florida
6. Higgs site, Florida
7. 1715 and 1733 Spanish fleet shipwrecks
8. *Nuestra Señora de Atocha* shipwreck
9. Fox Pond, Florida
10. Fig Springs, Florida
11. Baptizing Springs, Florida
12. San Luis de Talimali, Florida
13. Santa Rosa Pensacola, Florida
14. Emmanuel Point shipwreck
15. *El Nuevo Constante* shipwreck
16. Padre Island shipwrecks
17. *Nuestra Señora de los Milagros* (*El Matanceros*) shipwreck
18. Havana, Cuba
19. Sevilla Nueva, Jamaica
20. Puerto Real, Haiti
21. Bayahá, Haiti
22. La Isabela, Dominican Republic
23. Concepción de la Vega, Dominican Republic
24. Santo Domingo, Dominican Republic
25. *Nuestra Señora de la Concepción* shipwreck
26. Quicksilver shipwrecks (*Nuestra Señora de Guadalupe* and *El Conde de Tolosá*)
27. San Juan sites, Puerto Rico
28. Caparra, Puerto Rico
29. Nueva Cádiz, Venezuela
30. Panamá Viejo, Panama

Concepción de la Vega, Dominican Republic (1496–1562)

Concepción de la Vega, also known as La Vega Vieja, is located in the central part of the Dominican Republic. It was founded around 1495 and by the early sixteenth century had become the most important town after Santo Domingo in Hispaniola. Concepción de la Vega was a gold-mining and ranching center until it was destroyed by an earthquake and abandoned in 1562 (Cohen 1997; Goggin 1968:24; Palm 1952; Torres Petitón 1988; Po-

Figure 2.2. The Columbus house remains, La Isabela.

Figure 2.3. The *fortaleza* ruins at Concepción de la Vega.

ladura 1980; Woods 1999). Portions of the town's cathedral, *convento*, and fortress are still extant at the site (Fig. 2.3).

Excavations in the central portion of the site took place between 1976 and 1994 under the auspices of the Dirección Nacional de Parques of the Dominican Republic and the Comisión para la Puesta en Valór del Sitio Histórico La Vega Vieja (González 1980; Ortega and Fondeur 1978b). From 1996 through 1999, the University of Florida carried out survey and mapping activities to identify the boundaries of the town and also undertook the inventory and curation of the more than 250,000 artifacts excavated there before 1994 (Deagan 1999). The materials from the excavations—including a remarkable collection of syncretic Hispanic-Indian pottery and one of the richest assemblages of sixteenth-century material remains in the Americas—are housed at the Museo Casas Reales in Santo Domingo and at the site itself (Fig. 2.4). Both collections were used for this study.

Figure 2.4. A shelf in the site museum of Concepción de la Vega, 1982.

Caparra, Puerto Rico (ca. 1510–50)
The site of Caparra is located in a suburb by the same name in San Juan, Puerto Rico. It is believed to have been the residence of Juan Ponce de León, governor of Puerto Rico (1509–11) and first explorer of Florida (Hostos 1938; Pantel et al. 1988). Materials in the collection from the site, which was excavated by Adolfo de Hostos, date exclusively to the first half of the sixteenth century. John Goggin (1968) used the materials in his study of New World majolicas. Most of the collections from Caparra are located at a small museum at the site, and a few examples are in the collections of the Instituto Nacional de Cultura Puertorriqueña in San Juan.

Sevilla Nueva, Jamaica (1502–75)
Sevilla Nueva was founded in 1502 by Christopher Columbus at St. Anne's Bay on the north coast of Jamaica. The town did not thrive and was largely abandoned by 1535 (Morales Padrón 1952:47–49). An earthquake destroyed the settlement in 1575, and it was thereafter completely abandoned.

Sevilla Nueva was first investigated by C. S. Cotter of Jamaica in the 1940s (Cotter 1970). The resulting materials that make up the Cotter collection are in various locations in Jamaica, with the majority in the Archeological Laboratory at Port Royal (Smith et al. 1982). The ceramic and faunal materials from that collection have been studied and reported (Woodward 1988).

Lorenzo López of the Universidad Complutense in Madrid, Spain, carried out excavations at Sevilla Nueva between 1982 and 1989 under the auspices of the Jamaica National Trust (Tony Aarons, personal communication, 1981, 1982; López y Sebastián 1986). Materials from those excavations were not available for study at the time of this writing.

Puerto Real, Haiti (1503–78)
Puerto Real is located near present-day Cap Haitien on the north coast of Haiti. It was founded by Hispaniola governor Nicolás de Ovando in 1503 as one of thirteen planned perimeter settlements established to control Hispaniola (Deagan 1995). Puerto Real developed into a cattle-raising and hide-producing center; however, it was forcibly abandoned by order of the Spanish government in 1578 in an attempt to eliminate the illegal and thriving trade between foreign traders and residents of the town (see Chapter 3). The population was resettled at Bayahá, Haiti, near what is today Fort Liberté, Haiti (discussed later).

Puerto Real was extensively excavated between 1979 and 1986 by archaeologists from the University of Florida, working in conjunction with William Hodges of the Hopital le Bon Samaritain in Limbé, Haiti, who originally located the site. Public structures, domestic sites, and commercial areas have been studied. The many project reports and publications resulting from that work are summarized and synthesized in Deagan (1995) and Ewen (1991) (Fig. 2.5).

Figure 2.5. Field laboratory, Puerto Real.

Two large collections were generated by excavations at Puerto Real. The pre-1979 assemblage excavated by Hodges is housed at the Musée de Guahabá in Limbé, Haiti, and the post-1979 materials are presently curated at the Florida Museum of Natural History but will eventually reside with the government of Haiti. Both collections were used for this study.

Nueva Cádiz, Venezuela (1515–41)

Nueva Cádiz is located on the Venezuelan offshore island of Cubagua. It was founded in 1515 as a pearl-fishing station and was a prosperous community until an earthquake destroyed it in 1541 (Willis 1976; Cruxent and Rouse 1958:136; Boulton 1952; Goggin 1968:24). The site was first investigated by José Cruxent and Alfredo Boulton in 1952 (Boulton 1952) and later by Cruxent and John Goggin in 1954. The results of the latter excavation were reported by Raymond Willis (1976), and the majolicas from that excavation were incorporated into Goggin's 1968 study. The materials used in this work are those from the Cruxent-Goggin excavations, which are housed at the Florida Museum of Natural History.

Panamá Viejo, Panamá (1519–1671)

Panamá Viejo was founded in 1519 on the Pacific coast of Panamá. It was a very rich city and a major center for New World commerce until 1671, when it was destroyed by the pirate Sir Henry Morgan. A number of impressive ruins are still extant at the site, which is located on the outskirts of modern Panama City (Fig. 2.6). Hale Smith of Florida State University made surface collections and tests at the site in 1952, and José Cruxent carried out excavations in 1953 and 1954. John Goggin used those projects in his 1968 majolica study (see Goggin 1968:48–49).

In 1962, a University of Florida expedition conducted additional stratigraphic tests at the site, which are reported by Baker (1968) and Long (1964, 1967). The collections from those excavations were used for this study; they are curated at the Florida Museum of Natural History.

The Fountain of Youth Park (8-SJ-31) and Nombre de Dios (8-SJ-31) Sites, St. Augustine, Florida (1565–66)

St. Augustine was founded in 1565 near present-day Jacksonville, Florida, primarily as a military outpost protecting Spanish shipping in the Caribbean (see Chatelaine 1941; Lyon 1976, 1997; Manucy 1997). The first fort and town site were abandoned less than a year after their establishment, and the settlement was moved across St. Augustine Bay to a location thought to be better protected from the hostile Indians of the area. In 1571–72, the fort and town were again moved back across the bay to the settlement's present location (Lyon 1997; Manucy 1997:28–31).

The site of the original 1565–66 settlement was identified about 3 km from the present town center on the grounds of the Fountain of Youth Park tourist attraction and was excavated by the University of Florida between

Figure 2.6. Cathedral ruins at Panamá Viejo.

1985 and 2001 (Fig. 2.7) (Chaney and Deagan 1989; Gordon and Deagan 1992; Stuhlman 1995).

In 1993, the remains of a sixteenth-century wood fort were discovered about 100 m from the settlement site on the grounds of the Mission of Nombre de Dios. This is thought to be the fort established in 1565 and abandoned in 1566, and excavations have been under way since 1993 (Cusick 1993; Morris 1995; Waters 1998). The collections from these sites are curated at the Florida Museum of Natural History.

Santa Elena, South Carolina (38-BU162) (1566–87)

Santa Elena was a military outpost defending the northern limits of La Florida and is located today on the marine base golf course on present-day Parris Island, South Carolina. The town was established by Pedro Menéndez de Áviles in 1566, following the founding of St. Augustine in 1565. Santa Elena served as Pedro Menéndez de Áviles's capital and was home to a somewhat more well-to-do and socially elite group of settlers than was St. Augustine (Paar 1999; South, Skowronek, and Johnson 1988; Lyon 1992). The town was briefly abandoned between 1570 and 1571 but was then reoccupied until 1587,

Figure 2.7. Barrel well, ca. 1566, Fountain of Youth Park site, St. Augustine. *Photo: James Quine.*

when it was permanently abandoned (South 1988).

Stanley South and his colleagues at the South Carolina Institute of Archeology and Anthropology, Columbia, have studied the town and its associated forts archaeologically since 1979, and excavations are ongoing at the time of this writing (South 1979, 1980, 1982, 1983, 1985; South and De Pratter 1996). The resulting collection of domestic and military materials from the period 1566 to 1587 has been synthesized and illustrated in South, Skowronek, and Johnson (1988) and is curated at the South Carolina Institute of Archeology and Anthropology.

Sixteenth-Century St. Augustine, Florida (ca. 1572–ca. 1600)

The present site of St. Augustine's downtown area was settled in 1572 (see earlier discussion). Although the town has been occupied continuously since that time, archaeological investigations ongoing in St. Augustine have been successful in locating the original settlement and in isolating the sixteenth-century component (Bond, Bell, and Parker 1994; Deagan 1981, 1985; Halbirt 1996; Singleton 1977). The sample used for this study consists of more than 2,000 artifacts from closed contexts in seven domestic home sites dating between 1571 and ca. 1600. The collection is curated at the Florida Museum of Natural History at the University of Florida.

Bayahá, Haiti (1578–1605)

Bayahá, located near present-day Fort Liberté, Haiti, was established in 1578 as a new home for settlers forcibly removed from other Spanish towns in northern Hispaniola in that year. Its establishment was part of the Spanish attempt to control and inhibit the illegal trade between colonists and non-Spanish mercenaries (Hodges and Lyon 1995; Hamilton and Hodges 1995). Bayahá incorporated the populations of Puerto Real (discussed previously) and Monte Cristi.

The efforts to eliminate illicit trade were unsuccessful, and Bayahá was forcibly abandoned and burned by the Spaniards in 1605. The site was rediscovered by William Hodges of Limbé, Haiti, who, with the assistance of Jennifer Hamilton of the University of Florida, conducted test excavations at the site in 1981 (Hamilton and Hodges 1982, 1995). The excavations resulted in a collection of materials primarily from a single domestic structure and dating between 1578 and 1605. The artifacts are housed at the Musée de Guahabá, Limbé.

San Juan del Puerto, Florida (8-DU-53) (1598–1702)

The seventeenth-century mission site of San Juan del Puerto is located on Fort George Island near present-day Jacksonville, Florida. It was established in 1598 as a Franciscan mission and endured as a major Timucua Indian mission center until 1702, when it was destroyed by English colonists from South Carolina (MacMurray 1973). In 1955, John W. Griffin (1960), under the auspices of the Jacksonville Historical Society, was the first to test the site. William Jones of Jacksonville continued excavations in 1961 (Jones 1967), and Judith MacMurray (1973) of the University of Florida synthesized and reported these earlier excavations. A large collection of Indian and Spanish materials resulting from the excavations is housed at the Florida Museum of Natural History.

Baptizing Springs, Florida (8-SU-65) (ca. 1610–56)

Baptizing Springs, located in north-central Florida, is believed to have been a small mission *visita* (an Indian town without a church but visited at regular intervals by a friar) serving the Western Timucua Indians during the first half of the seventeenth century (Loucks 1993). It may be associated with the mission of San Juan de Guacara. The date of the founding of the site is not documented, but it was established by 1612; it is nearly certain that the *visita* was abandoned after 1656, when a major Timucua Indian rebellion took place in that area (Hann 1996:180; Worth 1992:59). The site includes an aboriginal component with an associated European structure, which was probably the church (Loucks 1993).

The University of Florida carried out excavations of Baptizing Springs in 1977–78, which L. Jill Loucks analyzed and reported as part of a doctoral dissertation (1979). The resulting collection is curated at the Florida Museum of Natural History.

Santa Catalina de Guale, Georgia (1606–80)

In 1567, Pedro Menéndez de Áviles and a group of Jesuit friars visited the island of Santa Catalina (which is today St. Catherine's Island) off the coast of Savannah, Georgia (Jones 1978; Thomas 1988). They established a small presidio there, and the island became the headquarters for the Jesuit mission effort among the Guale Indians of that region until rebellion forced its abandonment in 1597.

The mission of Santa Catalina de Guale was reestablished by the Franciscans in 1606 and was occupied until 1680, when it was permanently abandoned. The site included a substantial mission complex and a sizable Indian town during the latter period of occupation (Thomas 1993). David H. Thomas of the American Museum of Natural History carried out excavations of Santa Catalina between 1980 and 1994 (Thomas 1988, 1990, 1993). The excavations have concentrated upon the mission complex structures (the *convento* and the church and its interior burials), which appear to be largely from the second period of occupation. The ongoing project has resulted in a large collection of seventeenth-century Spanish colonial materials, which is particularly notable for its remarkable assemblage of religious objects and glass beads. The collection is currently housed at the Department of Anthropology laboratory of the American Museum of Natural History and at the archaeological field laboratory on St. Catherine's Island.

Fig Springs, Florida (8-CO-1) (ca. 1608–56)

Fig Springs, located on the Ichtucknee River in north-central Florida, is believed to have been associated with the Franciscan mission of San Martín de Ayacuto, which was established in 1608 and abandoned after the 1656 Timucua rebellion (Hann 1996; Worth 1992; Weisman 1992). The site itself includes both a terrestrial component and a spring in the river, which apparently was used as a dump by the mission inhabitants. John Goggin and his associates salvaged the spring between 1949 and 1952, collecting more than 5,000 artifacts (Fig. 2.8) (Goggin 1968:74–75; Deagan 1972). The Florida Bureau of Archaeological Research excavated the terrestrial portion of the site from 1987 to 1988, revealing the church, the *convento*, and a section of the associated Indian residential area (Weisman 1992). The collection Goggin assembled is housed at the Florida Museum of Natural History, and the collection excavated by Weisman (more than 5,400 artifacts) is curated at the Florida Bureau of Archaeological Research in Tallahassee. Both collections were used for this study.

Fox Pond, Florida (8-A-272) (ca. 1606–56)

The Fox Pond site, also located in north-central Florida, is believed to have been the site of a Spanish mission settlement (possibly San Francisco de Potano) of the early seventeenth century (Symes and Stephens 1965; Goggin 1968:23). San Francisco was established in 1606 and abandoned after the Timucua rebellion of 1656 (Hann 1996:165; Worth 1992). Fox Pond was first located and surface collected in 1956 by the University of Florida under the direction of John Goggin. Charles Fairbanks reexcavated it in 1964 (Symes and Stephens 1965). The collections from both investigations are housed at the Florida Museum of Natural History.

Figure 2.8. John Goggin at the Fig Springs site, 1952.

Seventeenth-Century St. Augustine, Florida (ca. 1600–1702)

In the course of the past twenty-five years of excavation at St. Augustine, a number of occupation components dating to the seventeenth century have been located. These include closed, undisturbed contexts datable to the periods 1600 to 1650 and 1650 to 1702. Dating is based upon historical documentation, stratigraphic placement, and the *terminus post quems* for seventeenth-century artifact types. The seventeenth-century occupation of St. Augustine has been addressed most recently by Hoffman (1994), who has synthesized the data from seventeenth-century contexts, expanding the initial work of King (1981). These materials are curated at the Florida Museum of Natural History.

San Luis de Talimali, Florida (8-LE-1) (ca. 1633–1704)

San Luis was established in 1633 as a mission center and military garrison near present-day Tallahassee, Florida. A Spanish village was also established at San Luis, where several powerful Florida families maintained residences and engaged in ranching and shipping (Hann 1988; Hann and McEwan 1998; McEwan 1991b, 1993a, 1993b). It was the headquarters for the Franciscan mission effort among the Apalachee Indians until 1704, when it was destroyed by English colonists and Indians from South Carolina (Boyd, Smith, and Griffin 1951).

John W. Griffin partially excavated part of the mission complex at the site in 1948, and the results of these excavations are reported in Boyd, Smith, and Griffin (1951). In 1983, the state of Florida initiated a long-term program of historical and archaeological investigation as well as public interpretation at San Luis under the direction of the late Gary Shapiro. That program has continued under the direction of Bonnie McEwan, generating one of the largest and most diverse collections of seventeenth-century materials in the region (McEwan 1991a, 1992, 1993a, 1993b; Hann and McEwan 1998; Shapiro and McEwan 1992; Shapiro and Vernon 1992). Collections from the excavations are housed at the on-site laboratory and museum at San Luis.

Eighteenth-Century St. Augustine, Florida (ca. 1702–63)

The largest systematically collected assemblage of materials from eighteenth-century Spanish

Figure 2.9. Reconstructed Spanish home of the eighteenth century, St. Augustine. *Photo: James Quine.*

contexts comes from St. Augustine. Most of these contexts are undisturbed deposits in multicomponent sites that have been determined through stratigraphy, contents, and *terminus post quems* of associated artifacts to have been deposited between about 1702 (when St. Augustine was burned by James Moore) and 1763 (when Florida was ceded to England and evacuated by the Spaniards). The assemblage used in this study includes more than 60,000 items from eleven sites excavated between 1972 and 1997 through field schools of Florida State University and the University of Florida, by the city of St. Augustine archaeological programs under Carl Halbirt, and by archaeologists with the Historic St. Augustine Preservation Board. These include the de la Cruz (SA-16-23), de Hita (SA-7-4), Avero (SA-7-5), and Palm Row (SA-36-4) sites, which are reported in Deagan (1983). Other sites include the Nuestra Señora de la Soledad site (SA-36-7; Koch 1980), the Ximenez-Fatio house (SA-34-2; Ewen 1985), the de Mesa site (SA-7-6), the Trinity Episcopal site (SA-34-l; Deagan 1981), the Castillo de San Marcos (Williams 1982), the de León site (SA-26-1), and the Puente site (SA-24; Bond, Bell, and Parker 1994).

All of these except the Castillo de San Marcos (a fort) and the Soledad site (a church and cemetery) represent domestic occupations (Fig. 2.9). With the exceptions of the collection from the Castillo de San Marcos, which is housed at the Southeast Archeological Center of the National Park Service, Tallahassee, and that from the Soledad site, which is housed at the Sisters of St. Joseph's convent in St. Augustine, all of the materials used for this study are curated at the Florida Museum of Natural History in conjunction with the city of St. Augustine.

Higgs Site, Florida (8-Bri-1) (ca. 1715)
The Higgs site is located on Florida's east coast in what is today Brevard County. The site is believed to have been the location of eighteenth-century salvaging activities carried out to recover materials from the 1715 plate fleet shipwrecks (Smith 1949:23–24). Hale Smith and Charles Higgs tested the site in 1946. Their excavations resulted in a large collection of Indian artifacts and Spanish

Figure 2.10. Excavations at Santa Rosa Pensacola, 1964. *Courtesy of the National Park Service Southeastern Archaeological Center.*

shipwreck materials, which are housed at the Florida Museum of Natural History.

Santa Rosa Pensacola, Florida (8-ES-22) (1723–52)

The town of Santa Rosa, which was established as a settlement in 1698, was relocated in 1723 to the Santa Rosa Sound of Pensacola Bay, an area that offered a more protected location than its original site (Smith 1965). The town was essentially a military outpost occupied by Spanish soldiers and Indian inhabitants, who were forced by lack of supplies and isolation into commercial exchange with the French colony in Mobile, Alabama (Smith 1965:3). The settlement in its relocated position was destroyed by a hurricane in 1752, after which the community relocated again, to the present site of Pensacola.

Hale Smith of Florida State University excavated this single-component site in 1964 (Smith 1965). The excavations (see Fig. 2.10) yielded a collection of some 26,000 artifacts dating between 1723 and 1752. These are housed at the Southeast Archeological Center of the National Park Service and the Department of Anthropology at Florida State University, both in Tallahassee.

Casa Rosa Scarp Wall, San Juan, Puerto Rico (ca. 1784–ca. 1800)

The Casa Rosa scarp wall site is adjacent to a section of the old city wall in the La Perla section of San Juan. It was apparently a trash dump for residents of the city during the last decades of the eighteenth century. The site was initially tested by the Instituto Nacionál de Cultura Puertorriqueña, San Juan, during a restoration project for the wall. The work was continued by the University of Alabama Office of Archeological Research (Solís 1988). Both collections were used for this study and are housed at the Instituto Nacionál de Cultura Puertorriqueña, San Juan.

Second Spanish Period, St. Augustine, Florida (1784–1821)

Florida was ceded to England by the Spaniards in 1763 as a condition of the Treaty of Paris. Some twenty years later, in 1784, the colony was returned to Spain and remained under Spanish rule until 1821. The Second Spanish Period occupation (1784–1821) is well represented in the archaeological record of St. Augustine, and all of the sites so far excavated have contained a Second Spanish Period component. The components have been identified by stratigraphic position, by *terminus post quems* provided by the presence of pearlwares, and by the absence of post-1820 artifacts.

Several of the Second Spanish Period occupation components have been the subject of synthetic reports: the de León site (SA-26-1) in Zierden (1981) and the Ximenez-Fatio site (SA-34-2) in Ewen (1985). The Second Spanish Period data from these and several other sites have more recently been synthesized and reported by Cusick (1993). Materials from Second Spanish Period contexts at all of the other sites have also been used for this study and are housed at the Florida Museum of Natural History.

Multicomponent Sites

Several important collections resulting from excavation of multicomponent urban sites, often under salvage conditions, were used in the course of this research. In many cases it was not possible to date the items from these collections with confidence by reference to their archaeological associations, as was possible for all other artifacts used in this study. Many morphologically and typologically interesting specimens do occur in these collections, however, and can often be dated typologically or by cross-reference with other dated sites. Such items have occasionally been included in the following chapters as useful illustrations of certain artifact types or attributes and as examples of variation within a type group.

St. Augustine Restoration Commission Collection (1600–1800)

A large collection of archaeological materials resulted from renovation activities carried out in the town of St. Augustine from the 1930s through the 1950s, before John W. Griffin and Hale Smith began archaeological studies in the 1960s. The materials include primarily eighteenth- and nineteenth-century artifacts from properties along St. George Street. Little or no information on their provenience is available, but they are curated for purposes of comparative study and type collection at the Florida Museum of Natural History.

Santo Domingo (1502–present)

Santo Domingo is the oldest European capital and the longest continuously occupied European city in the Americas. Established in its present location on the west bank of the Ozama River in 1502, it was the center of Spanish dominion in the New World during the sixteenth century. Although it gradually lost its influence to New Spain after the mid-sixteenth century, it remained an important religious and administrative center for the Spanish Caribbean during the colonial period.

In addition to nearly 500 years of intensive urban occupation, Santo Domingo has also undergone considerable restoration and renovation during much of the twentieth century (see Lopéz Penha 1992; Pérez Montás 1984). The result has been a rich but often disturbed archaeological record in the city, reflecting components dating from ca. 1500 through the nineteenth century.

Much of the material from Santo Domingo has been recovered through restoration activities and has been reported by Elpidio Ortega and his colleagues (Ortega 1971, 1980, 1982; Ortega and Cruxent 1976). Many of these materials are housed at the Museo Casas Reales in Santo Domingo (Fig. 2.11).

Before its establishment in its present location, the site of Santo Domingo was located between 1496 and 1498 on the east bank of the Ozama, opposite the present city. That site was discovered and tested by Marcio Veloz and Elpidio Ortega in 1988, who documented not only the presence of the site but also the badly disturbed nature of its deposits (Veloz Maggiolo and Ortega 1992).

Havana, Cuba (1514–present)

The Museo de la Ciudad de la Habana and the Académia de Ciéncias de Cuba have con-

Figure 2.11. Museo de las Casas Reales, Santo Domingo.

Figure 2.12. The Cathedral of Havana.

ducted extensive projects to renovate, restore, and salvage Habana la Vieja, or Old Havana (Fig. 2.12), over the past decade. Havana was established in 1514 and for most of the colonial era served as the major commercial and administrative entrepôt for the circum-Caribbean area. It was there that the treasure fleets regrouped and provisioned for their return journey to Spain (see Chapter 3).

Like Santo Domingo, centuries of intensive occupation of Havana and the building and rebuilding at most of the sites have resulted in a rich but disturbed archaeological record in the city (Domínguez 1981, 1984; Romero 1981). The range of materials in the assemblage, however, is remarkable and adds to our understanding of variability in form and decoration for many categories of colonial artifacts. Collections at both the Museo de la Ciudad de la Habana and the Académia de Ciéncias de Cuba were studied in the course of research for this project.

El Morro, Puerto Rico (1591–1777)

The fortress of El Morro was constructed and expanded between 1591 and 1777, and it still visually dominates the waterfront of Old San Juan (Manucy and Torres-Reyes 1973). It served as a military installation until 1949 and is now maintained and interpreted by the U.S. National Park Service.

Hale Smith carried out excavations at El Morro in 1961, recovering a large assemblage of materials from predominantly mixed deposits (see Smith 1962). The collection is currently curated by the National Park Service's Southeast Archeological Center in Tallahassee, Florida. Small type collections from the site are also maintained at El Morro and at the Department of Anthropology at Florida State University.

Marine Sites

Shipwrecks constitute one of the most important categories of sites for dating the material culture of the Spanish colonies. Although recovery procedures and philosophies have varied widely in the investigation of Spanish colonial shipwrecks, their remains are well preserved and the sites can be confidently dated, factors that make such assemblages especially critical to understanding the temporal aspects of Spanish colonial material culture. For this reason, Spanish shipwrecks that are appropriately dated but located outside of Florida or the Caribbean have also been included in this study.

The following discussion of Spanish colonial marine sites by no means encompasses all of the sites that have been identified or investigated. Only those sites for which collections are available for research or which have detailed reports on the artifact assemblage were used.

Padre Island Wrecks (1554)

Three of the ships in the 1554 treasure fleet *flota* en route from Veracruz to Spain were wrecked off the coast of what is today Padre Island, Texas. The ships were carrying cargoes of gold, silver, cochineal, and other New World products.

Excavation of the wrecks took place from 1972 to 1975 under the auspices of the Texas Antiquities Commission, and the results of that work are reported in Arnold and Weddle (1978) and in Olds (1976). The extensive collections recovered from the three wrecks were conserved at the Texas Archeological Research Laboratory of the University of Texas at Austin and are curated at the Texas Maritime Museum in Corpus Christi.

Emmanuel Point Wreck (1559?)

The earliest Spanish shipwreck identified thus far in Florida was discovered in October 1992 by a team led by State Underwater Archaeologist Roger Smith. The wreck was located in Pensacola Bay and is thought to have been one of the ships in the fleet of Tristan de Luna during his unsuccessful colonization attempt in 1559. Three years of excavation at the site recovered a variety of organic, ceramic, and metal artifacts dating to the mid-sixteenth century or earlier. These are illustrated and reported in Smith et al. (1995), and the collections are curated at the Florida Bureau of Archaeological Research in Tallahassee.

Armada Wrecks (1588)

The defeat of the Spanish Armada by the English navy in 1588 resulted in the sinking of a number of Spanish vessels off the coasts of Ireland, Scotland, and England. Five of these wrecks have been located and at least partially salvaged. Two of the best-known salvage efforts are of the *Trinidad Valencera* (Martin 1975, 1978) and the *Girona* (Stenuit 1972). The wrecks have yielded a considerable number of personal and domestic items of Spanish and Portuguese origin, as the Armada was at least partially provisioned in Lisbon (Martin:1978:296). Publications on the project, rather than the collections themselves, were referred to in this study.

Nuestra Señora de Atocha (1622)

The *Nuestra Señora de Atocha* (hereafter *Atocha*) sank off the Florida Keys in 1622 en route to Spain from Cartagena, Colombia, and Portobello, Panama (Lyon 1979; Matthewson 1986). Its cargo was principally gold, silver, and New World products.

The site, which was salvaged by Treasure Salvors, Inc., of Key West, Florida, contained a large assemblage of materials dating to an inadequately known period of Spanish colonial material culture. The collection was the focus of a long-term litigation battle between Treasure Salvors and the state of Florida (Cockrell 1980), which the state lost. As of this writing, the remaining materials are in the possession of Treasure Salvors.

This study has made use of the drawings and photographs of the *Atocha* collection prepared by the Florida Division of Archives, History and Records Management, Tallahassee (today the Florida Bureau of Archaeological Research, Division of Historical Resources), before their transfer, as well as on the illustrations in Matthewson (1986).

Nuestra Señora de la Pura y Limpia Concepción (1641)

The *Nuestra Señora de la Pura y Limpia Concepción* (hereafter *Concepción*) sank off the north coast of the Dominican Republic in 1641 en route to Spain from Mexico. The ship was part of the 1641 fleet, carrying cargoes of New World silver and other products. Burt Webber and Pedro Borrell salvaged the widely reported wreck (Borrell 1983b; Peterson 1979b). They recovered a rich and varied collection of material, much of which is included in the permanent collections of the Museo de la Atarazana in Santo Domingo. Those collections, as well as reports and publications, were used in the course of this work.

Plate Fleet Wrecks (1715)

A hurricane in 1715 caused the destruction of the annual treasure fleet en route to Spain from Mexico off the east coast of Florida. Eleven ships and 700 people were lost. Several of the ships were located and excavated under the auspices of the Florida Division of Archives, History and Records Management, Tallahassee (Clausen 1965; Burgess and Clausen 1982; Wagner and Taylor 1972). A large and well-preserved collection of artifacts resulting from the excavation, housed at the Florida Bureau of Archaeological Research, was used in this study.

Plate Fleet Wrecks (1733)

A disaster comparable to the fleet destruction of 1715 occurred in 1733, again off the Florida coast, when the *flota* was ravaged by storms en route to Spain. At least four of the sunken vessels have been salvaged under the auspices of the Florida Bureau of Archaeological Research (Logan 1977; Skowronek 1982). Collections from the wrecks, curated at the Florida Bureau of Archaeological Research, Division of Historical Resources, and the Museum of Florida History, Tallahassee, were used in this study.

Quicksilver Wrecks (1724)

The *Conde de Tolosá* (hereafter *Tolosá*) and the *Nuestra Señora de Guadalupe* (hereafter *Guadalupe*) are also known as the "Quicksilver wrecks" after the quantities of mercury they carried as cargo. They sank in a storm off the northeastern coast of the Dominican Republic in 1724, en route from Spain to the New World (Apestegui, León, and Borrell 1996; Borrell 1983a; Santiago 1980; Peterson 1979a). Although the principal cargo was quicksilver, the ships are also exceptional for the quantities of small personal and religious items, glassware, and household goods they carried.

The Museo Casas Reales, the Dirección Nacional de Parques, and the Centro de Inventario de Bienes Culturales of the Dominican Republic salvaged the wrecks between 1977 and 1979. A major part of the site collections, on exhibit at the Museo de la Atarazana in Santo Domingo, was used in this study.

El Matanceros (1741)

The ship *Nuestra Señora de los Milagros,* also known as *El Matanceros,* was a Spanish merchant vessel that sank off the coast of Yucatán in 1740 or 1741. The wreck was excavated in 1957–58 by Robert Marx and Clay Blair, working with CEDAM International (Blair 1960; Marx and Marx 1993:91–95). More than 50,000 items were recovered from the wreck, most of which were small personal and religious items (much, apparently, as contraband) destined for New Spain. A large part of the collection is on display at the CEDAM Pablo Bush Romero Museum, Puerta Aventuras, Quintana Roo, Mexico, and those materials as well as the reports on the site were used in this study.

El Nuevo Constante (1766)

El Nuevo Constante was wrecked in the Gulf of Mexico off the Louisiana coast in 1766. The ship was en route from Veracruz to Spain with a cargo of precious metals and New World products. The Louisiana Department of Culture, Recreation and Tourism excavated the wreck in 1980–81 (Pearson 1981; Pearson and Hoffman 1995). The collections from the site are also curated at that agency in Baton Rouge, and the reports on the project were consulted for this study.

Chapter 3
Politics, Economy, and the Flow of Material Culture in the Spanish Colonies

Perhaps more than in any other part of colonial America, the material assemblage of the circum-Caribbean Spanish colonies reflects the rich cultural diversity of the global post-Columbian New World. Spanish colonists in the region incorporated an international melange of goods into their daily lives, not only from various indigenous and creole American traditions but also from virtually all European colonial powers active in the hemisphere.

The disparate economic, political, and social factors that converged to shape the unique character of the colonists' material world included Spain's mercantilist commercial policies governing colonial trade (and the failures of that policy); the inability (or disinclination) of Spain to industrialize the production of consumer goods; patterns of shifting political alliances in Europe; the early development of craft and production traditions in the Spanish Americas; and the patterns of intercultural exchange and intermarriage that were established very early in the region. The following discussion is intended to consider these factors in a very general way, with particular attention to those that shaped both the distribution of material goods and periodicity as recognized in the archaeological record (Table 3.1).

European Goods in the Spanish Americas

From the establishment of Isabela in 1493 until the late sixteenth century, the majority of European-style manufactured goods in the New World came from Europe rather than from local production sources. Shipping manifests suggest that before about 1550, imports were predominantly food, cloth, tools, and other subsistence-related items (see Avery 1997:7; Parry 1990:123). The archaeological record of the earliest Spanish colonies, however, reveals that such luxury goods as ornate book hardware, jewelry, Venetian glassware, and Italian ceramics were in fact present in quantity before 1550. These items probably arrived in the Americas as personal possessions. By the middle of the sixteenth century, the Age of Discovery was over, and the establishment of colonial society led to a demand for the commercial import of luxury goods (Elliott 1963:185; Hoffman 1994; Parry 1990:123; Pike 1966:56; Torre Revello 1943; Vicens Vives 1969:317). European goods from a variety of legal and illegal sources circulated in the region, entering through official Spanish trade, smuggling, intercolonial commerce, and a limited amount of foreign trade sanctioned by the Spanish crown. These routes for entry are considered later.

Transatlantic Commerce and the *Carrera de Indias*

Spanish trade with the American colonies operated under a mercantilist policy, that is, the colonies were permitted to import from and export to Spain alone. To implement the policy and control trade, a system of annual trade fleets known as the *Carrera de Indias* (hereafter *Carrera*) was implemented in 1503

Table 3.1. Political Events Affecting the Distribution of Goods in the Spanish Caribbean and Florida

1492	Reconquest of Spain complete, expulsion of Jews and Muslims
1492	First European trade goods introduced in America on Columbus's first voyage
1493	Columbus settles La Isabela
1499	Columbus dynasty ends and imperial Spanish rule begins in America
1503	Casa de la Contratación established in Seville
1503	Gov. Nicholas de Ovando mandates establishment of 13 Spanish towns in Hispaniola
1511	Spanish conquest of Puerto Rico and Cuba
1516	Death of Ferdinand
1517	Hapsburg Charles I arrives in Spain
1519	Formal establishment of the Council of the Indies, centralizing control of the colonies
1519	Charles I becomes Holy Roman Emperor Charles V
1519–22	Cortés invades and takes Mexico
1521–29	Spain at war with France, reduced shipping to Caribbean
1533	Inca empire falls to Pizarro (Lima established—1535)
1550–59	Spain (and Holy Roman Empire) at war; reduced shipping to the Indies allowed greatly increased French privateering
1555	Charles V abdicates to Philip I
1571	Spanish victory over Turks at Lepanto
1588	Spanish Armada defeated by English navy
1598	Philip II dies, Philip III ascends the throne of Spain
1609	Expulsion of Moriscos from Spain
1621	Philip IV ascends the throne of Spain
1640	Portugal secedes from Spain, loses *asiento* to provide slaves to colonies
1648	Treaty of Munster—Holland /Spain—Holland granted freedom of trade with the Spanish colonies
1665	Charles II ascends the throne of Spain
1667	Treaty of Breda—Dutch exchanged New York for English-held Surinam
1668	Treaty of Aix la-Chapelle—France/Spain—ended warfare in Europe
1670	Treaty of Madrid—Spain/England—agreed to suppress and forbid pillage of one another in Caribbean; Spain recognized legitimacy of English colonies in Caribbean; Charleston, S.C., established by England
1684	Treaty of Ratisbon—Spain/France—agreed to peace in Europe and in colonies
1697	Treaty of Ryswyck—Spain, France—Ceded St. Domingue to France after French buccaneers capture Cartagena
1700	Death of Charles II of Spain (childless)—Bourbon prince Philip V ascends throne
1702–16	France (French Guinea Company) given Spanish *asiento* to provide slaves (and one ship of trade goods annually) to Spanish colonies in Caribbean
1702–16	War of the Spanish Succession—England/Spain
1716	Peace of Utrecht—England/Spain—ended War of Spanish Succession, England got Spanish *asiento* privilege for 30 years
1717	*Casa de la Contratación* moved to Cádiz
1739–41	War of Jenkins's Ear (Spain/England)—ended English *asiento*, increased English privateering in the Caribbean
1740	Havana company formed
1740–48	War of the Austrian Succession—France and Spain fight England
1756–63	Seven Years' War—England/France (after 1762 England/France and Spain)
1755	Barcelona Company formed
1762	Havana and Manila lost to English
1763	Treaty of Paris ended Seven Years' War—Florida ceded to English in exchange for Havana

Continued on next page

Table 3.1 continued

1765	End of Cádiz monopoly, direct trade with colonies opened to nine Spanish ports
1774	Trade permitted between South American (Río de la Plata and Peruvian) colonies and the rest of the Indies
1778–90	Volume of trade between Spain and America quadrupled
1779–83	Spain and England at war
1783	Florida restored to Spain
1789	Free trade permitted to New Spain and Venezuela
1790	Casa de Contratación closed

(for detailed discussions of the *Carrera* and its impacts, see Avery 1997; Haring 1947; Morales Padrón 1992; Parry 1990; Phillips 1990).

The *Carrera* was controlled by an institution known as the *Casa de la Contratación de las Indias* (hereafter *Casa*), which was located in Seville. Through the *Casa,* Seville came to establish a monopoly on the control of Spanish American shipping, and throughout most of the colonial period the mechanisms for the distribution of goods were designed to work to the advantage of the powerful Sevillian merchants. This situation proved to be neither efficient nor advantageous for the colonies (Haring 1947:55–56).

All goods bound for America before 1717 were shipped from Seville, and all cargoes had to be registered with the *Casa,* which levied various taxes and duties (for discussion of the tax and duty structure during the colonial period, see Haring 1947:256–263). After 1526, all shipping to the New World from Spain was done by convoys for protection against foreign corsairs, and after 1542 it was forbidden to leave for the Indies in groups of fewer than ten ships (Phillips 1986:10). The convoys were accompanied by other vessels to protect the fleet from pirates, but the protection was paid for by a tax (*avería*) levied on the merchants, which raised the cost of shipped goods for the colonists. Single trading vessels, known as *sueltos,* were occasionally permitted under special circumstances to sail to the Indies without a convoy.

From 1503 until 1510, the Sevillian trade monopoly was absolute. Between 1510 and 1575 under Charles V, the policy generally relaxed, and authority gradually dispersed to Cádiz (Vicens Vives 1969:328). In 1529, in fact, Charles not only permitted German merchants to participate in the New World trade but also opened ten other Castilian ports to such trade, although ships still had to put in for registry at Seville (Elliott 1963:182).

From 1543 until 1554, a single convoy sailed each year to the Caribbean, where it would split into three groups. One went to New Spain (Mexico), one to Panamá, and the other to Tierra Firme (northern South America) (Phillips 1986:10–11). By 1564, the American demand for imported goods had increased to the point that two annual fleets were needed, one bound for New Spain (the *flota*) and another bound for Tierra Firme (the *galeones*). These would leave from Seville at different times of the year, winter in the Indies, and, if possible, meet in Havana and return together in early summer before the start of the hurricane season (Parry 1990:134–135; Phillips 1986:130). This organization was actually based on Spain's earlier medieval shipping system of sending two annual fleets to transport large quantities of wheat, oil, and wine to northern Europe (Reitzer 1960:218).

Most of the commerce related to the American fleets was done at trade fairs throughout the region, where the merchandise brought by the *Carrera* was exchanged for American products and precious metals. The most important of these was on the Caribbean coast of Panamá, first at Nombre de Diós (1555–97) and thereafter at Portobello, the primary nexus between Peru and Europe (see Ward 1993).

Origins of Carrera Merchandise

Although foreign merchants and foreign ships were excluded from the *Carrera*, at no point during the colonial era were the European goods sent to the Spanish American colonies exclusively of Spanish origin. Although the Spanish industries of ceramics, glass, textiles, and metallurgy were well established internally, the developing postmedieval Spanish industrial sector was unable to meet the steadily increasing demands of the New World colonists for manufactured goods (for more extended discussions of this phenomenon, see Avery 1997:20–23; Elliott 1963:188–190; Haring 1964:113; Kamen 1978, 1991; Parry 1969:181). To satisfy the demands of the colonial market and continue their trade monopoly, it was necessary for merchants to import foreign goods to Seville for re-export to the New World. The consequent richness and international flavor of Seville during the American colonial era were captured in 1613 by Spanish playwright Lope de Vega in the opening lines of his *Arenal de Sevilla* (Lope de Vega 1989):

> we will see all of the great treasure that leaves for the Indies . . . and what is more reason to boast is to see leaving from these ships so many diverse nations . . . for knives, merchandise and rouan cloth, the French, they carry oil; the German brings linen, coarse cloth and llantés; they load wine of Alanís. The Vizcaino carries iron, shot, wood planks and pine; those of the Indies, ambergris, pearls, gold, silver, Campeche wood, and skins; all of this is money. . . . it is a port of the Indies, to which comes so many millions; a port of many nations, an open door for everyone. All of Spain, Italy and France live for this Arenal; for it is the principal place for all business and profit.

Genoa was an important source of non-Spanish goods, channeled through the merchants in the thriving Genoese colony who had been present in Seville since the fifteenth century (Pike 1966; Vicens Vives 1969:336). Sevillian merchants also had close ties with German traders, particularly after 1528, when the Hapsburg Charles V gave the Germans a place in the *Casa* and permitted them to trade directly with the Americas (Haring 1964:98–99). Northern European items were also routed to the New World colonies via the Genoese merchants of Seville, who themselves had close ties to trade in The Netherlands (Pike 1966:17–18).

It has been estimated that under the Hapsburg rule in Spain, up to 83 percent of the cargo leaving Seville was of foreign origin (Haring 1964:113). As early as 1504, the governor of Hispaniola commented that most of the merchandise available there belonged to the Genoese or other foreigners, and a sixteenth-century visitor to Seville noted goods in the city from Flanders, Greece, Genoa, England, Germany, Brittany, and Italy (Pike 1966:55, 30). Ship registries of the sixteenth century provide additional details about these non-Spanish export goods, listing cloth from France, Holland, Portugal, England, Italy, and Germany; combs from Paris and Italy; and beads and jewelry from Paris and Italy (Torre Revello 1943).

The Asiento

Non-Spanish goods also legally entered the American colonies through the *asiento*, which was an exclusive monopoly on the right to supply African slaves to the Spanish colonies granted by Spain to foreign merchants. The *asiento* also generally included the right to trade a certain amount of merchandise each year in the Americas (see Parry 1969:240, 268–305). Before 1595, enslaved Africans had to be brought to and registered in Seville before traveling to the Americas, an inefficient practice that could not keep up with the growing demand for slaves in the colonies. The first *asiento* was granted to Portuguese merchants in 1595 and was in place until 1640, when Portugal rebelled and separated from Spain. During the second half of the seventeenth century, the trade was carried out largely as contraband, although contracts were made variously with Dutch, French, and English merchants (McAlister 1984:333).

With the beginning of the Bourbon dynasty in Spain, the *asiento* was awarded to the French Guinea Company in 1702. The *asiento* also permitted one boatload of goods to be sold each year at the Portobello (Panamá) trade fair and offered abundant opportunities to smuggle trade goods into the Spanish Americas.

The English victory in the War of the Spanish Succession (1701–14) resulted in the Peace of Utrecht, which conceded the *asiento* to the Jamaica-based English South Seas Company for thirty years. The English merchants, as had the French merchants before them, generally abused the *asiento* privilege, and soon many more than the single permitted ship entered Portobello, Veracruz, and Cartagena (Harman 1969:6–7; Parry 1969:291–297; Williams 1970:92–93). English goods entered the Spanish colonies in greatly increased numbers between 1713 and 1739, when the outbreak of war between Spain and England ended the English *asiento* (Parry 1990:300).

Problems with the Carrera

The *Carrera* system proved to be inefficient and in many ways unable to meet the needs of the Spanish American colonists. Irregularity in scheduling the convoys, pirate attacks, hurricanes, shipwrecks, and a multitude of taxes and duties on shipped goods all contributed to the inadequacy of the Sevillian system as the exclusive mechanism for colonial trade. These problems provoked widespread dissatisfaction in the colonies and contributed to the colonists' willingness to engage in illicit, non-Spanish sources of trade (Wright 1939:341–343; Haring 1964:115–122).

The colonies of the Caribbean region were the earliest to be affected by the inefficiencies of the *Carrera* system. The first half of the sixteenth century was the only time during which Spanish trade was focused primarily in the Antilles, since by 1550 attention had turned to New Spain and South America in response to the greater output of gold and silver from those regions. Major shipping often bypassed the colonies of the Caribbean after the mid-sixteenth century, and colonists frequently asked for *sueltos* to call at their ports to supply badly needed commodities. Their requests, however, were consistently denied by the Sevillian merchants who controlled transatlantic trade and for whom *sueltos* were not profitable.

The effects of the Sevillian monopoly were exacerbated by artificially higher prices of Spanish goods in the Americas. Throughout most of the sixteenth century, Seville was permitted to sell goods in the New World at whatever price the market would sustain, which was generally inflationary owing to the large supply of money and short supply of goods. Prices were additionally increased by taxes and duties levied on Spanish-shipped goods and by delays, inefficiencies, and losses in shipping (Parry 1969:182; Gibson 1966:162). These circumstances led inevitably to the chronic contraband trade that was to distinguish the Caribbean through much of its colonial history (see Andrews 1978:70).

Rescate: *Contraband Foreign Trade in the Caribbean*

The Treaty of Tordesillas in 1494 had established the New World as a closed Iberian area. It divided the Americas into two spheres of jurisdiction, Spanish and Portuguese, by a line extending north-south at about the mouth of the Amazon River. Although it was confirmed by a papal bull, other European nations began almost immediately to disregard not only the Church-sanctioned arrangement but also Spain's policy of exclusive mercantilist relations with its colonies. Because the merchandise offered by the foreign traders was more abundant, often of better quality, and cheaper than the legal Spanish goods, the islands' inhabitants eagerly engaged in regular illegal commerce (for discussions of *rescate* in Cuba, see Wright 1939 and Hoffman 1980; in Florida, see Bushnell 1982:89–90; in Hispaniola, see Hernández Tápia 1970:283–294 and Hodges and Lyon 1995). The efforts of England, France, Portugal, and The Netherlands to countermand Spanish exclusionary economic policy came to be the major influencing factor in the distribution of goods in the circum-Caribbean area after 1550 (see Haring 1964:122).

By the 1520s, Portuguese, French, and English corsairs were active in the Caribbean, preying upon and trading with Cuba, Hispaniola, Jamaica, and Puerto Rico (Parry 1969:180; Haring 1964:69). The French dominated this activity until the 1560s, when English corsairs eclipsed them, largely as a consequence of France's military losses to England (Parry 1969:180–185; Gibson 1966:162; Haring 1964:113). The English continued to dominate the illicit market in the Caribbean until the early decades of the seventeenth century, when their control gave way to the Dutch.

The Dutch West India Company was chartered in 1621, with the considerable force of the Dutch navy behind it. The company's ships and agents began an aggressive strategy designed to disrupt Spanish shipping and defense in the Caribbean (Parry 1969:187–188; Gavin 1999:47–49). In 1628, Piet Heyn struck a disastrous blow to the Spaniards by capturing the entire Spanish fleet and its cargo of 15 million guilders in gold, and the Dutch captured Bahia and the control of Brazil's north coast the following year. These events dealt a permanent blow both to Spain's credit in Europe and to Spain's shipping and defense systems in the Caribbean (Parry 1969:188). The weakening of Spain's position ultimately allowed France and England to expand and settle in the Lesser Antilles, rupturing Spain's hegemony in the Caribbean and opening a new economic era in the region.

The Seventeenth-Century Depression

Spain's economic condition—still suffering from the blows dealt by the Dutch in the Caribbean—worsened with the nation's loss of the Thirty Years War in 1648, an event that also underscored Spanish military and economic weakness during the seventeenth century. Much has been written about the seventeenth century as a period of serious economic decline for Spain, as it also was for much of Europe (for example, Avery 1997:18–24; Elliot 1961; Gibson 1966:160–166; Hamilton 1938; Kamen 1978, 1991; Phillips 1987; Vicens Vives 1969:410–412). Among the many factors implicated by these authors in this decline were the inevitable dwindling of precious metal and labor supplies in the colonies; the devaluation of silver and the dispersal of Spanish colonial treasure throughout Europe in exchange for manufactured goods; the costs of sixteenth-century imperial expansion in Europe (the wars against the Protestants in the Netherlands and the Turks in the Mediterranean); the costs of seventeenth-century wars, including the Thirty Years War with Flanders and England (1618–48) and the partially concurrent wars with France (1635–59); revolts in the Spanish territories of Portugal, Catalonia, and Italy; poor agricultural output; severe population loss through epidemics; and increasing threats and intrusions to the New World colonies by other European powers (Avery 1997:18–24; Elliot 1961; Gibson 1966:160–166; Hamilton 1938; Kamen 1978, 1991; Phillips 1987; Vicens Vives 1969:410–412).

This depression impacted the Spanish colonies in the Caribbean both politically and economically, and the *Carrera* shipping convoys declined steadily during the second half of the seventeenth century (Parry 1990:260–261). Much of the shipping between Spain and America during the late seventeenth century was carried out in *sueltos*, which made commerce more flexible in meeting the needs of the colonies but at the same time lowered the quantities of materials imported. Avery (1997:165) suggests that from 1684 to 1754, 87 percent of all shipping between Spain and the Americas was carried out in *sueltos*. By the end of the seventeenth century, Jamaica and Haiti had been taken by the English and the French, respectively; the Lesser Antilles and the southeastern United States were colonized by the English, French, and Dutch; and Spain was near bankruptcy.

The Eighteenth Century: Politics, Conflict, and Economic Reform

The death of Charles II without an heir in 1700 and the ascendancy of the Bourbon prince Philip to the Spanish throne as Philip V initiated the "Bourbon Century" of French-influenced Spanish imperial administration. The Bourbon monarchs—Philip V (r. 1700–46), Ferdinand VI (r. 1746–59), and Charles III (r. 1759–88)—imposed a series of administrative and economic reforms during the eighteenth century that markedly affected the distribution, exchange, and character of material culture in the Spanish American colonies (see Gibson 1966:165–174). These reforms were carried out, however, in a larger context of international conflict and Spain's attempts to resolve its consequences.

The War of the Spanish Succession in which France and Spain were allied against England was at least partly provoked by Spain. Part of the provocation was the awarding of the lucrative *asiento* to the French Guinea Company in 1702. The Peace of Utrecht (1714) marking the English victory in that war conceded the *asiento* to the Jamaica-based English South Seas Company for thirty years, which provided greatly enhanced opportunities for the entry of English goods into the Spanish Americas. Although the French merchants lost the *asiento*, they still maintained a strong commercial connection with the Indies through their influence over the *Casa* and the goods leaving Spain (Parry 1990:300).

In addition to the increase in legal trade permitted by the *asiento*, English privateers and traders continued to violate the trade restrictions placed by Spain on its Caribbean colonies. Spanish reprisals for these violations and English objections to such reprisals culminated in 1739 in the War of Jenkins's Ear (part of the War of the Austrian Succession in Europe), which did a great deal between 1739 and 1743 to encourage even more privateering and illicit trading in the circum-Caribbean Spanish colonies (see Blair 1960; Harman 1969:12–22; Lietch-Wright 1978:138–141). It also brought the official English *asiento* to an end in 1739.

At the same time, the origins of goods shipped legally to the Americas through the *Casa* became even less Spanish, and in 1704 it was reported that only one-sixth of the commercial activity of the *Casa* was controlled by Spanish merchants (Sánchez-Barba 1992:193). The *Casa* was moved to Cádiz in 1717 under Philip V, and several monopolistic joint-stock trading companies were established under its control to manage all trade between specific colonies and Spain. The Havana Company, for example, was created in 1740 and was intended to control Spanish-Cuban trade, and the Catalonia (also called Santo Domingo) Company, established in 1755, controlled trade between Spain (primarily Barcelona) and Hispaniola and Puerto Rico (Haring 1964:168).

Important economic reforms were made under Charles III, including opening trade in the Caribbean to nine other Spanish ports in 1765. Duty exemptions and tax reductions were introduced, and intercolonial trade restrictions were relaxed after 1770 (Haring 1964:169). These reforms were highly effective in encouraging commerce with the Americas, and between 1778 and 1790 the volume of trade between Spain and America more than quadrupled (Parry 1969:317–318). Much of this trade was with Barcelona and Madrid, both of which had energetically taken advantage of the liberalization of American trade policies. They exported Spanish-manufactured products, such as Catalonian and Talaveran pottery, silks, laces, and other fabrics (Parry 1969:317–318).

In 1790, the *Casa* was closed and disbanded, and in 1793 trade between foreign merchants and the Spanish colonies was openly permitted as long as the commerce was carried out using Spanish ships (Gibson 1966:169; Parry 1990:316). From that time until the twentieth century, American and English manufactured goods dominated the archaeological assemblages of the colonies.

Spanish American Commodity Production

Craft guilds (*gremios*) were established in New Spain during the first half of the sixteenth century to regulate the commercial production of a wide variety of commodities (Table 3.2). A number of these products, particularly ceramic and glass tablewares, have been recovered archaeologically in contexts dating to after about 1580 in the circum-Caribbean colonies (Deagan 1987).

The earliest European ceramic production in the Americas began in 1493 at La Isabela, Columbus's first settlement in what is today the Dominican Republic (Deagan and Cruxent 2002a). On the basis of the archaeological evidence, this production appears to have been abandoned along with La Isabela in about 1497 and not resumed in Spanish America until the second or third decade of the sixteenth century. A European-style ceramic industry producing glazed wares was established in Mexico by the middle of the sixteenth century (Lister and Lister 1987), and it is likely that unglazed and lead-glazed utilitarian production began shortly after conquest. Panamanian production of majolica and utilitarian wares also took place from the 1570s onward (Long 1967), and in Guatemala a ceramic industry had developed after 1580 (Luján Muñoz 1975). A strictly utilitarian European pottery industry is also believed to have been present during colonial times in the Dominican Republic (Ortega 1980). The products of those kilns—most frequently those of Mexico—are found in the sites of the circum-Caribbean region, with the majolica dating to after about 1580 and the utilitarian earthenwares to after the middle of the sixteenth century (Deagan 1987:Chapter 4).

Glassmaking began in Puebla, Mexico, during the 1530s and has continued to the present (Frothingham 1941:121). Puebla remained the glass-producing center for the Spanish New World throughout the colonial period, exporting glasswares to Central and South America as well as to the Caribbean and Florida (Frothingham 1941:121).

Blacksmiths were present in virtually all of the Spanish settlements from the earliest days of colonization. Working with imported raw iron, they produced weaponry, horse equipage, construction hardware, and the other miscellaneous iron objects indispensable to domestic life (hooks, chains, tacks, trivets, and the like) (see, for example, Simmons and Turley 1980). At least a portion of the forged iron objects in use in the colonies was probably locally made at most of the sites of the circum-Caribbean area.

The first royal mint in the Spanish New World was established in Mexico in 1535 (Nesmith 1955), followed by mints in Santo Domingo (1537), Lima (1568), Potosí (1574), and Bogotá (1627) and in Guatemala, Popayán, Chile, Guanajuato, and Guadalajara during the eighteenth century (Haring 1947:287–291; Burzio 1956–58).

Gold- and silversmithing, as well as copper

Table 3.2. Crafts and Guilds Established in the Indies and Mexico

Earliest Documented Date of Guild Activity	Guild
1514	Artisans active in Santo Domingo* (Various blacksmiths, carpenters, metal founders, lime makers, masons, tailors, locksmiths)
1524	*Herreros* (Blacksmiths)
1526	*Arte mayor de la seda* (Workers in silk)
1528	*Plateros* (Silversmiths) and *lapideros* (Gemstone cutters) active in Mexico**
1537	*Alfareros* (Potters) active in Mexico***
1542	Glassmakers active in Mexico****
1546	*Bordadores* (Embroiderers)
1549	*Silleros* (Chair makers)
1549	*Guarnicioneros de sillas y aderezos de caballos* (Decorators of chairs and horse regalia)
1550	*Cordoneros* (Cord and braid makers)
1556	*Espaderos* (Sword makers)
1556	*Escultores* (Sculptors)
1557	*Doradores y pintores* (Gilders and painters)
1560	*Zapateros* (Cobblers)
1561	*Curtidores* (Tanners)
1568	*Herreros* (Blacksmiths)
1568	*Carpinteros, entalladores, violeros* (Carpenters, wood carvers, instrument makers)
1570	*Hiladores de seda* (Silk spinners)
1571	*Sombrereros* (Brimmed hat makers)
1572	*Sayalos y sayaleros* (Coarse cloth makers)
1574	*Cereros y candeleros* (Candle makers)
1575	*Zurradores* (Tanners)
1575	*Gorreros y boneteros* (Cap and hat makers)
1576	*Cardas y carderos* (Wool carders)
1581	*Perros* (Dog handlers)
1583	*Tintoreros* (Dyers)
1587	*Regatoneros* (Makers of walking sticks and ferrule tips)
1589	*Pasamaneros y orilleros* (Fringe, crochet, edging makers)
1590	*Calceteros y sastres* (Stocking makers and tailors)
1593	*Agujeteros y clavadores de cintas* (Makers of laces, ribbons, and studs for belts)
1595	*Guanteros y agujeteros* (Makers of gloves and lacings)
1596	*Chapineros* (Wooden shoe makers)
1598–99	*Batihojas y batihojas de oro* (Metal and gold leaf workers)
1599	*Albañiles* (Stone masons)
1616	*Agujeros* (Needle makers)
1659	*Alfareros* (Pottery makers)
1720	*Caldereros* (Copper pan makers)
1746	*Plateros* (Silverworkers)
1757	*Algodoneros* (Cotton weavers)

Source: Barrio Lorenzot 1920 (unless otherwise noted)
* Arranz Márquez 1991:535–539
** Torre Revello 1932:12
*** Lister and Lister 1987:221
**** Toussaint 1967:121–123

working and brass working, were also carried out in sixteenth-century Santo Domingo, Mexico, and Peru, continuing the rich pre-Columbian traditions of work in precious metals in these areas (see Cruz Valdevinos and Escalera Ureña 1993:36–38; Davis and Pack 1963; Gallo 1967; Toussaint 1967:63–66). Jewelry, tablewares, and religious objects were made throughout Mexico and Peru and distributed to Spain and probably to the other Spanish New World colonies. Specific information relevant to these commodities is considered in the chapters that follow.

Intercolonial Trade

Until the middle of the sixteenth century, most of the European material items in the Spanish American colonies were of Old World origin. Once the colonies began to manufacture various kinds of commodities, however, they could potentially supply an increasing portion of the material goods used by Spanish colonists in the circum-Caribbean region, and in some aspects such as foodstuffs, leather, iron and wood items, and ceramics, they did (see Deagan 1987).

A full realization of this potential, however, was inhibited by Spanish mercantilist commercial policy until the second half of the eighteenth century. The Spanish government was "chronically suspicious of the commercial activities of its colonial subjects. If they traded with one another they could not easily be prevented from trading with foreigners" (Parry 1990:317). Direct shipping did take place irregularly between Veracruz and Havana, Hispaniola, Puerto Rico, Florida, and Jamaica during the sixteenth and early seventeenth centuries and also between Panamá and the colonies of Cuba, Puerto Rico, Hispaniola, and Jamaica (Chaunu and Chaunu 1957:108–110, 112–113). But by the early decades of the seventeenth century, Spain had prohibited (although apparently could not prevent) all intercolonial trade in those commodities that were important Spanish exports, including wine, raisins, olives, almonds, silk, metals, and china. These prohibitions remained in effect until the final quarter of the eighteenth century, when the reforms instigated by Charles III permitted New Spain, New Granada, Guatemala, Peru, and the Río de la Plata to engage in reciprocal commerce (Parry 1990:317).

Many of the Caribbean colonies, however, either purposefully or inadvertently circumvented these restrictions. Because the islands of the Indies were for the most part bypassed by the convoys after 1600 in favor of the major trade fairs (see earlier discussion in this chapter and Andrews 1978:70), those colonies were generally ill supplied and depended greatly upon American goods brought in on the homeward-bound fleets from New Spain and Tierra Firme. From initial colonization until about 1550, Santo Domingo was the major trade entrepôt in the Caribbean (Andrews 1978:58), but this distinction passed to Havana after midcentury as the ships of the *galeon* and *flota* convoys met there to combine forces and reprovision for the trip across the Atlantic (see Wright 1939 for a more detailed discussion of the market in Havana). During the reconnoiter in Havana, a wide variety of items from New Spain and South America were available to Cuban shops and merchants, and through them informally to the other Spanish colonies in the Caribbean and Florida.

The economic roles of many Spanish Caribbean colonies such as Puerto Rico and Florida tended also to place them outside of both intercolonial and foreign trade restrictions. Although these colonies were economically unproductive, their role in the defense system of the Spanish Caribbean was critical, and they were subsidized by the crown to ensure their existence (see Hoffman 1980). The presidios of Havana, Florida, and Puerto Rico were financed by a subsidy (*situado*) from the treasury of New Spain (Haring 1947:206), with the majority of the goods on the *situado* coming from New Spain. (For discussions of the specific mechanisms in one example—the Florida *situado*—see Bushnell 1982:63–74; Deagan 1983:34–37; Harman 1969; Sluiter 1985).

The treasuries of Spain and New Spain were sometimes unable to meet the needs of the dependant *situados* by usual means and turned to foreign trade. In 1683, for example, the Spanish crown was unable to supply the colony in Florida adequately and was forced to grant the governor permission to obtain needed supplies from English merchants in the hated British colonies to the north (Bushnell 1982:89).

In the sites of Cuba, Puerto Rico, the Dominican Republic, and Florida, therefore, the circumstances of distribution and exchange resulted in an archaeological assemblage consisting of locally produced items and contraband European items throughout their occupation; legal items from Spain and its European trading partners (most commonly from 1500 to 1600 and again from 1770 to 1790); and New World products, most notably from Mexico, after about 1580.

Spanish-American Social Patterns and Their Material Correlates

While it is obvious that all material culture is generated by complex and dynamic arrays of culture and behavior, certain patterns of social interaction in the circum-Caribbean region had specific consequences for shaping the Spanish colonial material world in ways that set it apart from other Euro-American colonial societies. The most influential of these interactions were the nearly universal patterns of multicultural and multiracial exchange that created a syncretic Euro-African-American society, both socially and materially. This was achieved largely through intermarriage among Spaniards, Indians, and Africans within Spanish-established towns. Through these unions, non-European and syncretic European American traits were incorporated into Spanish households on a regular basis (Deagan 1996; Deagan and Cruxent 2002b). More than a quarter of a century of excavation at post-1500 Spanish colonial sites has shown that such elements were consistently incorporated in female domestic activities—most often those of the kitchen—and that syncretic forms also emerged most often in female domestic activities. Items associated with male activities or those that were perceived to function as socially visible symbols (clothing, ornamentation, tablewares, and architecture, for example) were primarily European, with very little American influence. Although the material details differ among regions, this pattern can be documented throughout the Spanish Americas (see Deagan 1996).

The incorporation of non-European material traditions in Spanish colonial life is reflected most visibly in categories that are not treated directly in this volume (for example, ceramics, foodways, and domestic organization). It is likely, however, that the past contexts of use and meaning for many of the items that are discussed in the following chapters were altered from their original (and better-documented) European meanings by the unique social dynamics of the Americas.

Part 2

Religion, Ritual, and Adornment

Chapter 4
Religious Items

The profound influence of the Catholic Church in shaping both daily life and public policy in the Spanish colonies cannot be overemphasized. Church, state, and people were inextricably interconnected through the *Patronato Real,* by which the pope granted the kings of Spain papal authority in the administration of Church and ecclesiastical affairs in Spain. This power included the rights to establish churches and monasteries and to receive and administer such ecclesiastical benefices as tithes and endowments. At the request of Ferdinand and Isabella, the *Patronato Real* was extended to the Spanish Americas in papal decrees being between 1493 and 1508. This recast the agreement between the crown and the pope that ecclesiastical control of the Americas would remain in the hands of the crown as long as the monarchs fulfilled their obligation to convert the American natives and ensure that Church precepts were properly administered. In 1524, this responsibility was delegated to the Council of the Indies, which also governed secular affairs in the colonies (Haring 1947:103, 180; Kapitske 1999:29–32). Through these arrangements, the very organization and purposes of the colonization effort were to a large extent religiously motivated.

Rules of social conduct for both Indians and Spaniards were largely set forth and enforced by the Church (backed by the state); social activities were scheduled and organized by the annual round of religious feasts and observations; and the policies that structured Spanish-Indian relations were largely governed by the Church (see Gannon 1965; Gonzáles 1969; Hanke 1949; Kapitske 1999; McAlister 1984:133–183). Catholicism has furthermore maintained stability as the dominant social and religious institution throughout Spanish America since 1492.

One of the consequences of the Church's pervasive influence in Spanish colonial life was the ubiquitous presence of religious motifs in the fine arts, decorative arts, and jewelry of the colonial era. Recognizing this, the category of "religious items" as used in this chapter is admittedly somewhat arbitrary, since it is often impossible to separate "religious" items and symbols from those that served decorative, magical, or social identification purposes. It would be difficult and probably misleading to attempt a rigid classification of exclusively "religious" objects, as opposed to objects with aesthetic, magical, or social functions. The difficulty of such a challenge would probably have been as perplexing to a seventeenth-century Spaniard as it is to a twenty-first-century archaeologist.

Items with religious significance nevertheless constitute a particularly fascinating category of Spanish colonial material culture, largely owing to the very detailed written documentation about much of their ritual and religious meanings. Only rarely are archaeologists provided with such a glimpse into the ideological realm of a culture through material objects; therefore, this chapter is intended to be used by archaeologists, and its organization is not necessarily a reflection of functional classification in the past. With this caveat, the following discussion will consider those personal objects recovered archaeologically with a primary use and documented identification as religious items. Other items used in a religious context, such as holy water, oil cruets, or book clasps that could have been used on missals or on Bibles, are discussed in Chapter 13 (see also Deagan 1987:139).

Religious Material Culture

The daily lives of Catholics contain many material religious elements. Various kinds of devotional symbols and images—saints, medals, rosaries, stations of the cross, sculptures, reliquaries—are typically part of Catholic life. When used in a Catholic context, they are not considered to be charms, amulets, or idols but rather are tangible reminders to Catholics of their faith, religious duties, and rewards (Mulhern 1967:547). The most popular of these objects also award Church indulgences to those who use them properly. Indulgences generally provide a reduction in the amount of time one will have to spend after death in purgatory to expiate pardoned sins (see Lea 1968).

Throughout Spain and Spanish America, however, the material distinctions between religion and magic apparently remained quite fluid during most of the colonial era. Crosses, religious medallions, and other devotional items were often worn and used in combination with secular amulets and were sometimes used as amulets rather than religious items (discussed further in Chapter 5; see also Alarcón Román 1987). This flexibility is illustrated in Figure 4.1, which shows a seventeenth-century Peruvian painting of the Virgin Mary and the Christ Child wearing a variety of religious items (medals, crosses, and reliquaries) in combination with secular amulets (clenched-fist *higas*, beads, and bells).

Shipping records and the materials recov-

Figure 4.1. The Virgin Mary with the Christ Child. Religious elements are combined with amulets such as *higas* and bells. School of Leonardo Flores in Peru. Late seventeenth century. *Reproduced courtesy of the Mt. Cavalry Retreat House collection, Order of the Holy Cross, Santa Barbara, California.*

ered from shipwrecks show that religious items were regularly shipped from Spain to the Spanish American colonies throughout the colonial era. Table 4.1 presents the items shipped between 1511 and 1613. Many of these were the component parts of rosaries (beads, crosses, and medals), which were apparently made into complete rosaries in the Americas.

Artifacts reflecting religious life are found consistently on Spanish colonial sites but are usually numerically infrequent. Sacred objects were undoubtedly curated more carefully than utilitarian objects and apparently did not enter the archaeological record in the same relative proportions as other, more

Table 4.1. Religious Items Shipped to the Spanish Colonies, 1511–1613

	1511–26	1583	1590	1592	1603	1613	Total
Rosaries							
ROSARIOS (Rosaries)		3	60	714	762	780	2,319
ROSARIOS DE EBANO GUARNECIDOS (of gilded ebony)			394				394
ROSARIOS LEONADOS (tawny colored)			384				384
ROSARIOS COMUNES (common)						340	340
ROSARIOS DE TAVOR (of wood from Mt. Tabor)				96		240	336
ROSARIOS CORRIENTES (ordinary)					300		300
ROSARIOS DE EBANO (of ebony)			55	118	48		221
ROSARIOS TOSCOS (crude)				192			192
ROSARIOS PEQUENOS (small)					108		108
ROSARIOS DE AZABACHE (of jet)			96				96
ROSARIOS GUARNECIDOS (gilded or decorated)					84		84
ROSARIOS DE TABOR PEQUENOS (small, of wood from Mt. Tabor)			78				78
ROSARIOS DE VIDRIO (of glass)			37	1	36	2	76
ROSARIOS DE OTRA CLASE (of another kind)					72		72
ROSARIOS ENTEROS DE EBANO (complete, of ebony)				66			66
ROSARIOS DE PORTUGAL (of Portugal)				36			36
ROSARIOS GRANDES (large)					24		24
ROSARIOS DE HUESOS BLANCOS (of white bone)		24					24
ROSARIOS DE GRANADILLO (of red glass or stones)				12			12
ROSARIOS DE PALO DE BRASIL (of Brazilwood)			12				12
ROSARIOS COLORADOS GUARNECIDAS (of colors, gilded or decorated)			12				12
ROSARIO DE PASTILLA CUGASADOR (tablet or bar-shaped beads)			11				11
ROSARIOS DE AZABACHE (of jet)				10			10
ROSARIOS DE PASTA (of paste)			9				9
ROSARIOS DE CUENTAS DE VIDRIO DORADO (of gilded glass beads)				6			6

Continued on next page

Table 4.1. continued

	1511–26	1583	1590	1592	1603	1613	Total
ROSARIOS DE CORALES FALSOS (of imitation coral)			6				6
ROSARIOS DE CORAL (of coral)				5			5
ROSARIOS DE CUENTAS (of beads)		2					2
ROSARIO AZABACHE GORDO (of fat jet beads)				1			1
ROSARIO CORAL CON EXTREMOR FALSO (of coral with an imitation terminal piece)			1				1
ROSARIO CRISTAL CON EXTREMOR DE ORO (of crystal with gold terminal piece)		1					1
ROSARIO DE AMBAR (of amber)	1						1
ROSARIO DE CORAL CON CRUZ (of coral with a cross)		1					1
ROSARIO DE CORAL PARA GUARNECER (of coral to decorate)			1				1
ROSARIO DE OLOR (scented)					1		1
ROSARIO DE VIDRIO AZUL Y NEGRO (of blue and black glass)						1	1
ROSARIO LEONADO CON PASOS DE LA PASION (tawny-colored, with medals representing the passions of Christ)					1		1
ROSARIOS AZUL (blue)						1	1
ROSARIOS VERDE DE VIDRIO (of green glass)						1	1
Total Rosaries	1	31	1,156	1,257	1,436	1,365	5,246
TERCIOS DE ROSARIOS (packs of rosaries)				60			60
TERCIOS DE ROSARIOS GUARNECIDOS (packs of decorated rosaries)					24		24
TERCIOS DE ROSARIOS NEGROS (packs of black rosaries)						12	12
Total Tercios of Rosaries				60	24	12	96
Crosses and Images							
CRUCES DE VIDRIO (glass crosses)			12				12
VENERAS DE AZABACHE (jet veneras)					6,040		6,040

Table 4.1. continued

	1511–26	1583	1590	1592	1603	1613	Total
GUARNICIONES PARA ROSARIOS (decorations for rosaries)				72			72
IMAGENES PARA ROSARIO (images for rosaries)				75			75
MEDALLAS DE ROMA ROSARIO (medals from Rome for rosaries)					1,872		1,872
MEDALLAS DE ROSARIOS					3,600		3,600
Total Crosses and Images			12	147	11,512		11,671
Other Items							
CENCERROS Y CAMPANILLAS (cowbells and open bells)						276	276
ROLLETITOS DE CERA PEQUENOS (small rolls of wax)					576		576

Sources: *Registros de la Casa de Contratación,* Archivo Generál de las Indias, Seville (microfilm copy in the P. K. Yonge Library of Florida History, University of Florida, Gainesville)
1511—*Contratación* #1451
1523—*Contratación* #1079
1583—*Contratación* #1080
1590—*Contratación* #s1089, 1092
1592-93—*Contratación* #1099
1603—*Contratación* #1143
1613—*Contratación* #s 1159, 1160

pedestrian categories of the material world. This is underscored archaeologically by the distribution of religious articles, which, when they do occur, are found most frequently in cemeteries and shipwrecks. In these situations, purposeful placement or disaster caused their deposition rather than the discard, abandonment, or loss more common on living sites.

Religious items recovered archaeologically in the region include devotional medals, crosses, rosaries, *veneras* (symbols of devotion and identity in a confraternity), seals, rings, reliquaries (containers for holy relics or objects), certain bells, and badges. Religious and devotional themes also dominated the fine jewelry of the fifteenth through seventeenth centuries in Spain (Muller 1972; Evans 1970:73–80; see also Chapter 6), and many of the humbler religious medals and rosaries followed these in style if not in materials. The production of religious and devotional objects in a fine jewelry tradition continued throughout the colonial era to the present.

Devotional Medals

Devotional medals are usually coin-shaped metal objects bearing a religious symbol or image and often an inscription. They represent devotion to a saint, event, or symbol in the Church. Although devotional medals have been used by Catholics in one form or another since the third or fourth century, religious medals as they are known today did not become common until the sixteenth century, when Pope Pius V inaugurated the custom of papal blessing of popular medals (Mulhern 1967:547). The first mention of *medallas* and *imágenes* (images) in the *Contratación* (shipping contract) records is in 1592 (Table 4.1), and they do not appear in New World sites until the closing decades of the sixteenth century.

The well-known and respected medalists of the late medieval and early Renaissance periods tended to concentrate on important civil figures and political events rather than on religious themes (see Salton 1969; Catholic Church 1883), and it was not until after the first third of the sixteenth century that popular devotional medals became accessible to the average citizen (Mulhern 1967:547; Thurston 1913:114). These were typically of brass, bronze, pewter, or lead and were nearly always struck rather than cast (Salton 1969:58–59).

The religious medals of the modern (post-1500) era evolved from the pilgrims' tokens and hat badges that were common among medieval and early Renaissance Catholic pilgrims (Evans 1970:78–79; Thurston 1913:112). These were lead or pewter tokens of saints or miraculous events produced at religious sites and worn suspended around the neck or as hat badges. They were extremely popular and widely used during the later Middle Ages. One monastery in Switzerland, for example, sold 130,000 badges in a single fortnight of 1466 (Spencer 1990:10). *Jetons*, or flat token disks inscribed with religious themes, were also common during this period but were generally carried rather than worn (Spencer 1990:10). The use of *plaquettes*, or small badges with holy images stamped on them, continued at least into the middle of the seventeenth century (Fig. 4.2).

Several scholars have suggested that the earliest use of religious medals in the modern sense occurred in 1566 with the revolt of Gueux in Flanders. Pope Pius V blessed a Spanish medal with the head of Christ on one side and Our Lady of Hal on the other

Figure 4.2. *Plaquette* bearing an image of the Virgin Mary with the Christ Child. Copper alloy, 1680–1702. Height 3.8 cm. Santa Catalina de Guale (Florida). (8NA41) FLMNH Collections. *Photo: University of Florida Office of Instructional Resources.*

and granted an indulgence to those Spanish soldiers who wore it on their hats (Thurston 1913:114). From this time onward, the practice of blessing medals and attaching indulgences to them was established, and by the seventeenth century nearly every Catholic capital in Europe was producing devotional medals (although regulated by Churchwide edicts). Large numbers of medals were struck, blessed with special indulgences, and distributed on the occasion of canonizing a new saint (Lea 1968:518). The distribution of these medals served to introduce and popularize the new saint very quickly after canonization.

There appears to have been no documented regular production of religious medals in the American colonies, and this lack of production is supported by the immense numbers of medals shipped from Spain to the Americas during the seventeenth and eighteenth centuries, both listed in shipping records and recovered from shipwrecks. *Medallas,* both *"de Roma"* and *"para rosarios,"* appear in the *Contaduría* shipping account records after 1592 and were recorded and priced by the gross. They were quite inexpensive compared to glass and jet images and *veneras,* with the latter costing between three and four reales a dozen and the *medallas* costing from five to six reales a gross. By the eighteenth century, these European-produced medals also included American images, such as Our Lady of Guadalupe and Saint Rose of Lima (Medina 1924:275–281).

Medals found on colonial American sites could have been produced in any of a number of centers in Europe, although Spain and Rome are probably the primary places of origin. Those made in Rome sometimes had "ROMA" inscribed at the base of the medal, a practice also used by earlier sixteenth-century medalists depicting nonreligious themes (Norris and Weber 1976:24, Plate 48). The medals generally represent the saints, cults, and events that figured most prominently in either the place of origin or the religious order distributing them.

Local clergy are responsible for maintaining Church standards and regulations dictated by the Vatican to govern medals (see Lea 1968). The medals must be blessed by a priest who has been granted the necessary faculties to perform the blessing; they must be made of a solid, nonperishable substance; and the person or event portrayed on the medal must be certified by the Church (Mulhern 1967:547). The medals are blessed with a prayer intended to obtain a favor from God through the intercession of the person represented on the medal. Certain saints and events are associated with particular kinds of

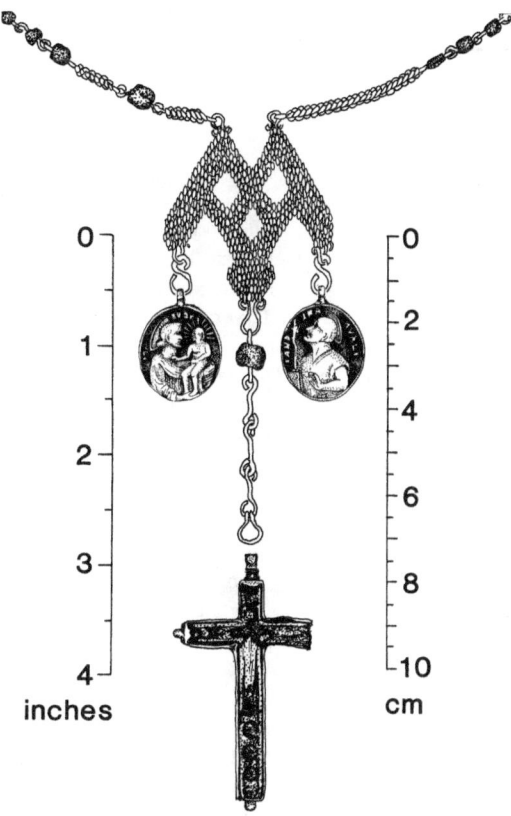

Figure 4.3. Devotional medals used on a rosary. Chaplet of silver-plated, copper-alloy links and 63 black wooden (probably ebony) beads. Cross and medals are suspended from the chaplet. The cross is wood sheathed in silver. St. Peter/Toulouse Street cemetery, New Orleans (1725–88). *From Owsley et al. 1985:Fig. 6; reproduced with permission. Courtesy of the Louisiana Division of Archaeology, Baton Rouge, and Charles Orser.*

favors, such as assistance in locating lost objects, protection from sudden death, or prevention of plague (Table 4.2). Other medals carry Churchwide indulgences, such as those representing the Christ Child, Our Lady of Guadalupe, St. Bernard, and St. Benedict (Mulhern 1967:549).

Devotional medals were worn suspended around the neck, attached to clothing, as

Table 4.2. Images and Attributes Appearing Frequently on Spanish American Religious Medals

Image	Attributes	Intercession/Associations	Dates of Most Frequent Archaeological Occurrences
Anne	Shown with Mary	Mother of Mary	1700–50
Anthony of Padua	Christ Child on book; book and lily	Franciscan devotion; finder of lost articles	1630–70
Barbara	Tower; sword, chalice	Patroness of miners, gunners; protection from lightning	1750–1800
Benedict/Benedictine cross	Monastic cowl on head, holding up a rule or rod, book in hand	Patron of Benedictine order	1720–80
Bernard of Siena	Tablet with IHS surrounded by rays	Franciscan devotion	1650–70
Carlos Borromeo	Rope around neck; one hand raised in benediction, other holding book	Benedictine devotion (ca. 1610)	1700–1800
Catherine-Alexandria	Spike wheel; palm leaf and sword	Protectress of the dying; patroness of young girls, students, and artisans	1600–1750
Catherine of Siena	Lily	Dominican devotion	1650–1700
Christ Corcovado	Christ with back bent, carrying cross		1730–80
Christopher	Crossing water with Christ Child on his shoulder	Patron of travelers, protector against danger in water and sudden death	1730–1800
Crucifixion	Christ on cross		1720–50
Dominic	Rosary, lily	Dominican devotion	1700–50
Holy Eucharist	Chalice with kneeling angels		1650–1750
Felipe Neri	Globe of fire; heart on exterior of body	Founder of the Italian Oratorians	1740–1800(?)
Frances Xavier	Jesuit robe; JAVIER or XAVIER inscription	Jesuit devotion; patron of foreign missions (ca. 1622)	1680–1780
Francis Assisi	Vision of Christ Child in rays; receiving stigmata	Founder of Franciscans	1680–1750
Francisco de Paula		Franciscan devotion; patron of seafarers	1740–1800(?)
George (Giorgio, Jorge)	Dragon; depicted on horseback	Patron of soldiers and armorers; invoked against plague, syphilis, and leprosy	1700–50
Head of Mary/Head of Christ	Name inscriptions		1650–1700
Holy Name	"IHS" with three arrows below and a cross above	Symbol of Bernardino de Siena, a Franciscan in 1700s, a Jesuit symbol	1630–70
Ignatius Loyola		Jesuit devotion	1750–1800(?)

Table 4.2. continued

Image	Attributes	Intercession/Associations	Dates of Most Frequent Archaeological Occurrences
James (Santiago)	Scallop shell, armor	Patron of Spain; protector of soldiers in battle	1630–70
Jerome	Hermit with lion, skull, loincloth	Patron of Hieronymites	1580–1600
John Evangelist	Lamb lying on a book, hermit with long cross in hand, dressed in skins; cup with serpent	Patron of booksellers, protector against poison	1600–25; 1720–50
Joseph	Accompanied by Mary and/or Jesus	Patron of fathers, artisans, and carpenters	1720–50
John of the Cross (Juan de la Cruz)	Crucifix and lilies, barefoot	Carmelite devotion, founder of Reformed Carmelites (ca. 1726)	1740–1800(?)
John Capistrano	Crucifix, banner and cross	Franciscan devotion (ca. 1724)	1700–1780
Nicolas Tolentino	Basket of bread	Intercedes for the sick and women in labor	1740–1800(?)
Pascual de Baylon	In adoration before a host	Protector of the Eucharist (canonized in 1690)	1700–1780
Paul	Sword and a book	Patron of missionaries, basket makers, and rope makers	1750–1800
Peter	Keys, sometimes a fish, boat, inverted cross	Patron of Catholic Church, gatekeeper to heaven	1630–1730
Peter Alcantara	Star over head, walking with lay brother	Franciscan devotion (ca. 1669)	1740–1800(?)
Rosa de Lima	Roses, crown of thorns, Christ Child on rose	First American saint; patroness of South America (ca. 1671)	1740–80
Stanislaus Kostka	On couch with angel by his side	Jesuit devotion (ca. 1726)	1750–1800
Teresa de Avila	Nun with fiery arrow in breast or dove above her head, inscription of name	Carmelite devotion; founder of reformed Carmelites (ca. 1622)	1725–50
Holy Family	Jesus, Mary, and Joseph	Protectors of families	1720–50
Thomas Aquinas (Tomás Aquino)	Sun on breast, book shedding rays	Dominican devotion	1740–1800(?)
Vincent Ferrer	Has wings, crucifix	Dominican devotion (ca. 1455)	1720–50
Virgin (del Rosario)	Virgin holding rosary, monks kneeling at her feet; winged angels, roses	Dominican devotion	1740–1780

Continued on next page

Table 4.2. continued

Image	Attributes	Intercession/ Associations	Dates of Most Frequent Archaeological Occurrences
Virgin (Carmel)	Virgin with Carmelite habit, Christ Child on one arm, scapular, souls at feet	Intercedes for souls in purgatory; Carmelite devotion	1650
Virgin (Guadalupe)	Virgin on crescent surrounded by rays	Protectress of Mexico	1680–1750
Virgin (Immaculate Conception)	Virgin on crescent moon with halo of stars	Franciscan devotion	1580–1650
Virgin (Misericordia, "Mother of all")	Virgin with outstretched arms, sheltering people with cloak	Protector of all but especially of sailors	1700–1750
Virgin (Pilar)	Virgin standing on pillar	Associated with Santiago, patron of Spain	1730–80

Sources: De Bles (1925); Duchet-Suchaux and Pastoureau (1996); Ferguson (1961); Trens (1946); New Catholic Encyclopedia (1967)

Note: Only images recovered from more than a single archaeological site are included; dates are derived from archaeological contexts only.

part of rosaries, or on necklace chains that included multiple medals (Figs. 4.1, 4.3). Necklace medallions were sometimes set into frames.

A few attempts have been made to classify and organize religious medals (Thurston 1913; Kuncze 1885); however, the immense number of images and the complexity of design variations have made these efforts relatively unsuccessful. Kuncze (1885), for example, identified more than 700 different depictions of the Virgin Mary alone, and there are undoubtedly many more. Because the designs on many medals were inspired by contemporary religious art, paintings are often useful for identifying specific images and devotions (useful sources with this orientation include DeBles 1925; Duchet-Suchaux and Pastoureau 1996; Trens 1946; Ferguson 1961).

Devotional Medals in Spanish Colonial Sites

Medals found on Spanish colonial sites dating between 1575 and 1800 fortunately are somewhat more limited in their variety, particularly before the eighteenth century. They were apparently produced most often in Spain or in Rome and were introduced by a restricted number of New World religious missionary orders. Competition among the Spanish missionary orders for jurisdiction over mission fields was fierce, and this may have affected both the distribution and production of medals (Ahlborn 1991). The eagerness of individual orders to promote their patron saints and particular devotions in some cases apparently led to the unauthorized production of devotional medals. The medal of Lourdes, for example, was first struck before the canonization of Bernadette (Ahlborn 1991).

In the Spanish colonial sites of La Florida, the Franciscans were the only order active in the missions after the regular use of devotional medals began (see Gannon 1965; Hann 1988, 1996). In the Caribbean and Mexico, a number of different orders including the Franciscans, Dominicans, Augustinians, Hieronymites, Jesuits, and Mercedarians carried out missionary and other Church activities (see González 1969; New Catholic Encyclopedia 1967). Both the singularly Franciscan presence in Florida and the diversity of orders in the Caribbean and Mexico are reflected in the archaeological records of these regions, most dramatically in the materials recovered from wrecked ships that were bound for New Spain.

Medals can often be roughly dated by their size and shape as well as by their motifs. Motifs are especially useful when medals bear inscriptions of saints whose canonization dates can be used as a *terminus post quem*. Useful sources for the identification of saints and symbols on devotional medals include Ahlborn (1991); Muller (1972); Ferguson (1961); Roig (1950); Malé (1932); and De-Bles (1925). Table 4.2 lists some of the most frequently occurring saints and symbols on devotional medals, along with their symbolic attributes.

Sixteenth- and Seventeenth-Century Devotional Medals

All reported Spanish colonial archaeological religious medallions dating to before about 1650 have been found in either underwater or frontier mission contexts. No devotional medals, for example, have been reported from such extensively excavated Spanish sites as sixteenth-century St. Augustine (1565–1600); Santa Elena, South Carolina (1566–86); Puerto Real, Haiti (1503–78); Nueva Cádiz, Venezuela (1503–45); or Concepción de la Vega, Dominican Republic (1498–1562).

Some of the earliest reported archaeological examples of devotional medals appear to be those from the 1588 Spanish Armada wrecks off the coast of Ireland. At least eight medals made of brass, pewter, or lead have come from the wrecks, representing the Virgin Mary, the Immaculate Conception, the head of Christ, and the Holy Family (Martin 1978:42, 1975:192; Stenuit 1972:176, 203).

The earliest Spanish devotional medal reported from the New World was recovered at the site of San Gabriel del Yunque in New Mexico (Ellis 1987:32; Boyd 1961), the site of the first capital of New Mexico, administered under Juan de Oñate from about 1601 to 1609. This oval brass medallion depicted the Holy Family and St. Jerome, patron of the Heironymite fathers.

The most extensive sample of pre-eighteenth-century medallions comes from the Florida mission sites, particularly that of Santa Catalina de Guale on St. Catherine's Island, Georgia (Thomas 1988, 1993; Ahlborn 1991). Like the medals from the Armada wrecks and San Gabriel de Yunque, those from the missions are without exception oval in shape and less than 3 cm in maximum diameter. All pre-eighteenth-century medals reported archaeologically range from 2.8 to 4.4 cm in height. In addition to a top loop for suspension, 43 percent of these medals had one or more additional flanges projecting from the sides of the medal (see Fig. 4.4), sometimes serving as points of attachment to a frame or other linking element. This feature was not noted on any medals dating to after 1650 except for gold medals set into frames and used as jewelry (see Skowronek 1982:143).

The standard iconography of seventeenth-century religious medals follows that found in contemporary Spanish and Italian paintings. Much of the art in Europe during the Counter-Reformation served to reinforce Catholic belief and to challenge Protestantism (see Malé 1931, 1932). The Council of Trent, in response to Protestant threats to the Church, issued a series of edicts in 1563 governing the representation of religious subjects

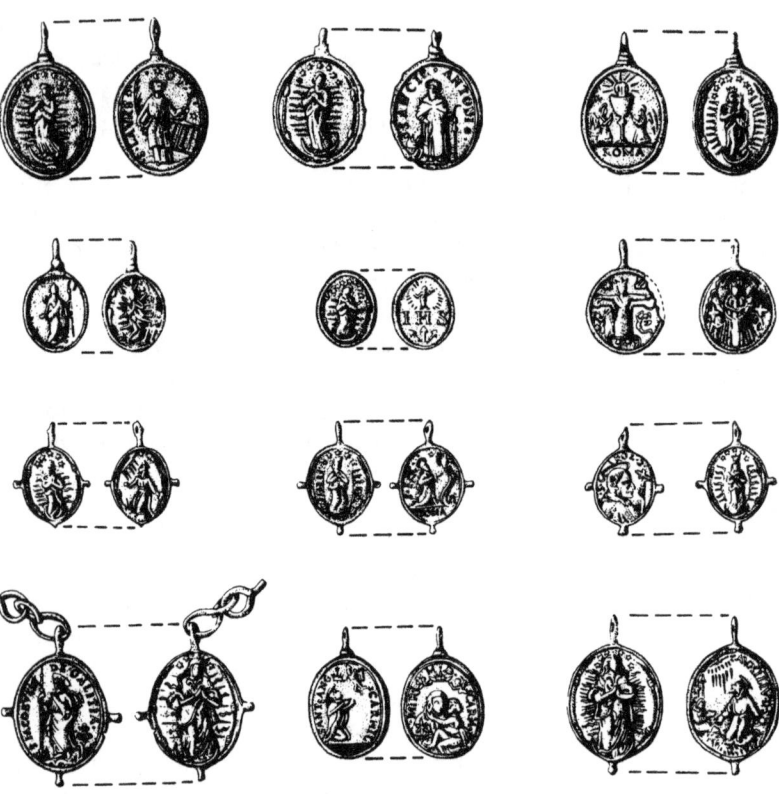

Figure 4.4. Seventeenth-century religious medals from Santa Catalina de Guale (Georgia). Height of top left medal, including loop, 2.1 cm. *Courtesy of the American Museum of Natural History, the Edward John Noble Foundation, and David H. Thomas.*

in art, which in turn affected Catholic iconography of the subsequent era (Malé 1932:1–3, 15–16).

Spanish artists of the early seventeenth century were particularly devoted to these goals and were often commissioned by Catholic orders to create works of art for their churches. Much of the greatest art of seventeenth-century Spain was religious in theme, and these themes were also used in the minor arts, including medal production (see Figs. 4.5, 4.6). Because so many of the images seen on religious medallions were based on the paintings of such Sevillian artists as Bartolomé Murillo (1618–82) and Francisco de Zurburán (1598–1664), it is possible that many of the Spanish-produced medals came from Andalucia.

This point of origin is especially suggested by the many seventeenth-century medals bearing the image of the Virgin of the Immaculate Conception (Figs. 4.4, 4.5, 4.7, 4.8). The Immaculate Conception is the Catholic precept that Mary, unlike all other human beings, was conceived and born without original sin. This dogma was not always accepted by all orders in the Church, and from the fourteenth through the seventeenth centuries it was a point of heated contention between the Franciscans, who fervently believed in the Immaculate Conception, and the Dominicans, who did not but believed instead that Mary was sanctified after she was conceived (Holweck 1910:678–680). In 1497–98, universities in Seville, Salamanca, Toledo, and Valencia decreed that nobody could enter as a member of the university unless they swore to defend the Immaculate Conception of Mary (Holweck 1910:680). The Council of Trent in 1563 failed to make a

Figure 4.5. *The Immaculate Conception* by Velásquez, ca. 1618. This early depiction of Mary is an example of Spanish religious iconography that influenced motifs on devotional medals. National Gallery Picture Library #NG6424. *Courtesy of the National Gallery, London.*

Figure 4.6. Franciscan iconography that influenced motifs on religious medallions. *Top:* Murillo's *The Stigmatization of St. Francis* (1665). *Bottom:* Murillo's *The Vision of St. Anthony of Padua* (1665). *Courtesy of the Museo de Bellas Artes de Cádiz, Cádiz .*

decision in this debate, which inspired a surge of artistic effort (particularly in Spain) to represent the Immaculate Conception.

The devotion to *La Immaculada* came to the Americas with the first Spaniards. The second Spanish settlement in the Americas (Concepción de la Vega) was named in honor of the Immaculate Conception, and it is thought that the first formal lay confraternity devoted to Mary in America was organized in Santo Domingo in 1502 (see Cipriano de Utrera 1947:20).

The concept of the Immaculate Conception—as well as the image—was attacked by Martin Luther and passionately defended by sixteenth- and seventeenth-century Catholics. The cult was particularly fervent in Spain and reached its peak during the first third of the seventeenth century as devotees of Mary insisted that the Church accept her Immaculate Conception as dogma (Malé 1932:41–43; O'Connor 1967:381). Between 1617 and 1622, Popes Gregory V and Paul V gave official papal sanction to the teaching and forbade the Dominicans to teach that Mary was conceived in original sin (Holweck 1910:680). In 1621, the Virgin of the Immaculate Conception became the Patron of the Franciscans (or Friars Minor), who were thereafter bound by oath to teach it publicly.

It was during the middle years of the seventeenth century that the familiar image of the

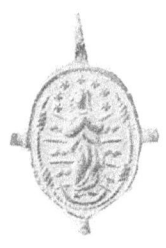

Figure 4.7. Immaculate Conception medal. Copper alloy, pre-1650. Height 1.45 cm. Baptizing Springs site (8SU65), FLMNH Collections. *Photo: James Quine.*

Immaculate Conception (seen in Fig. 4.5) became fixed in Catholic iconography and established on medals (although the Immaculate Conception did not become official Church dogma until 1854). The Franciscan orders were particularly devoted to the Immaculate Conception, and several of Murillo's classic paintings of the subject were originally commissioned for Franciscan churches and hospitals in Seville (Malé 1932:41, 491).

One of the earliest medals depicting the Immaculate Conception was recovered from the 1588 Armada wrecks (Martin 1978:42). The image of the Immaculate Conception is by far the most common motif found on Spanish colonial medals prior to 1700, and most of these come from Franciscan mission sites in Florida (for example, that shown in Fig. 4.7). These medals show the Virgin Mary on a crescent moon, crowned by stars and surrounded by an aureole of rays. The words, or variations on the words, "SIN PECADO" (without sin) or "CONCEBIDA SIN PECADO" (conceived without sin) also frequently appear. The classical image of the Immaculate Conception—featuring Mary with her hair on her shoulders, hands clasped in prayer, stars, and a crescent moon—appears in representations as early as the late fifteenth century, such as Albrecht Dürer's *The Virgin on the Crescent* (1498) (Strauss 1973:56) and the first years of the sixteenth century (Malé 1932: 212). A medal made by Rizzaridi around 1500 shows Mary standing and praying with winged cherubs below her feet and a crescent below the cherubs. Winged cherubs and aureole rays surround the figure (Victoria and Albert Museum collections, #A.10-1957). An even earlier image used as the stamp and icon of the fifteenth-century London brewers guild shows the same praying figure of Mary standing over winged cherubs, surrounded by rays (Museum of London collections). The Immaculate Conception, however, was the most widespread Catholic imagery during the early seventeenth century.

No medals bearing this particular iconography of the Immaculate Conception have been reported from any sites occupied exclusively after 1650. Although devotion to the Immaculate Conception was considerably less fervent after 1650, medals of the eighteenth century do sometimes commemorate that Mystery.

Other saints were also regularly depicted on seventeenth-century religious medallions; for the most part, these are saints associated with Franciscan devotions. However, the archaeological sample of seventeenth-century medals from Spanish American sites comes nearly exclusively from the Florida mission sites, which were dominated by the Franciscans. The few medals recovered from reliably dated seventeenth-century contexts in St. Augustine, for example, do not necessarily depict saints and subjects associated with Franciscans (such as that shown in Fig. 4.8). Medals from sites of the same period affiliated with Jesuits or Dominicans should display a different array of saints and symbols, such as those at the Lasanen site (Cleland 1971:29–34) or those from eighteenth-century shipwreck sites in the Caribbean.

Important Franciscan saints and images appearing on seventeenth-century medallions

Religious Items 51

Figure 4.8. Seventeenth-century devotional medals from St. Augustine, ca. 1650–1700. *Left:* The Virgin Mary/St. Anthony (SA-30-3-63). *Center:* Holy Sacrament/Immaculate Conception (SA-24-469). *Right:* Immaculate Conception/Annunciation (SA-24-371). Height of Immaculate Conception medal 2.3 cm. FLMNH/CSA Collections. *Photo: James Quine.*

include St. Anthony of Padua, St. Peter, John the Evangelist, the Holy Family, St. James (Santiago), and symbols of the Eucharistic host. The IHS monogram occurs both on both Franciscan medals, where it may represent St. Paul's sign *"In Hoc Signum,"* and on Jesuit medals, where it represents the first three letters of Christ's name in Greek (Ahlborn 1991). St. Francis of Assisi, the founder of the Franciscan order, curiously appears only rarely on medals until the eighteenth century.

Eighteenth-Century Devotional Medals
After about 1700, devotional medals became considerably more varied in motif, size, and shape. Archaeological sample bias must again be considered as a factor in this observation, however, since the great majority of medals in the eighteenth-century sample came from the wrecks of ships carrying goods for distribution throughout Mexico, Central America, Florida, and the Caribbean. The medals on these ships were undoubtedly intended for a wide variety of religious orders and constituencies, depending upon who ordered them or chose the selection for shipping.

This increased variety probably also reflects the increased number and maturity of local medal-producing centers outside of Rome that had developed by this time (Thurston 1913:114). The inscription "ROMA," which appears on medals made in Rome, occurs on 14 percent of the seventeenth-century examples, dropping to 7 percent of the eighteenth-century medals. Another characteristic of eighteenth-century medals is the absence of small flanges on the sides or bottom of the medals. Richard Ahlborn points out that both of these changes might be attribu-

Figure 4.9. Eighteenth-century devotional medals from St. Augustine, ca. 1750–1800. *Top, obverse; Bottom, reverse. Top rows, left to right:* Mary Magdalen dei Pazzi/Peter of Alcantara (ca. 1669), height 2.0 cm (HTC); St. Francis Xavier/ROMA, image on obverse only, height 2.7 cm (AO181); Cross fragment (AO166) height 2.4 cm; Giacomo della Marca, O.F.M., height 3.2 cm (SA-7-7-337). *Bottom rows, left to right:* St. Francis Xavier/St. Stanislaus Kostka (AO389), height 2.1 cm; Symbol of the Benedictine Order/St. Benedict of Nuria (SA-7-7-358), height 1.7 cm; St. Benedict/St. John of Capistrano (SA-7-7-265), height 1.8 cm; Enthroned Virgin/Angels with Eucharistic symbol, height 2.0 cm (SA-7-7-251). Identified by María Brana, Museo del Pueblo Español, Madrid. FLMNH/CSA Collections. *Photo: James Quine.*

table to the start of mass production and concomitant simplification of devotional medals (personal communication, 1989).

Oval, round, and octagonal medals have been recovered from eighteenth-century sites (Figs. 4.9, 4.10). Oval medals account for 42 percent of the measured sample (24) and range in diameter from 2.5 to 3.5 cm. The mean diameter for the group is 3 cm. These measurements are quite distinct from those of the oval medals from pre-eighteenth-century contexts, which ranged from 4.4 to 2.8 cm in height, with a mean height of 4.9 cm.

Octagonal medallions account for 33 percent of the measured sample from the eighteenth century and range from 2.0 to 3.8 cm in height, with a mean height of 3.3 cm. Round medals account for 25 percent of the overall reported sample and range from 3.0 to 5.0 cm in diameter. Although they have not been formally quantified, round medallions were the most commonly recovered variety from the Dominican Republic's Quicksilver wrecks (Santiago 1980:115), as well as from the *Matanceros* (*Nuestra Señora de los Milagros*) wreck (CEDAM Museum, Akumal, Yucatán). It appears that after the first quarter of the eighteenth century, round medals became the most common form and increased in size through the century.

Some of the most remarkable collections of devotional medals are those from ships wrecked while making the journey from

Religious Items

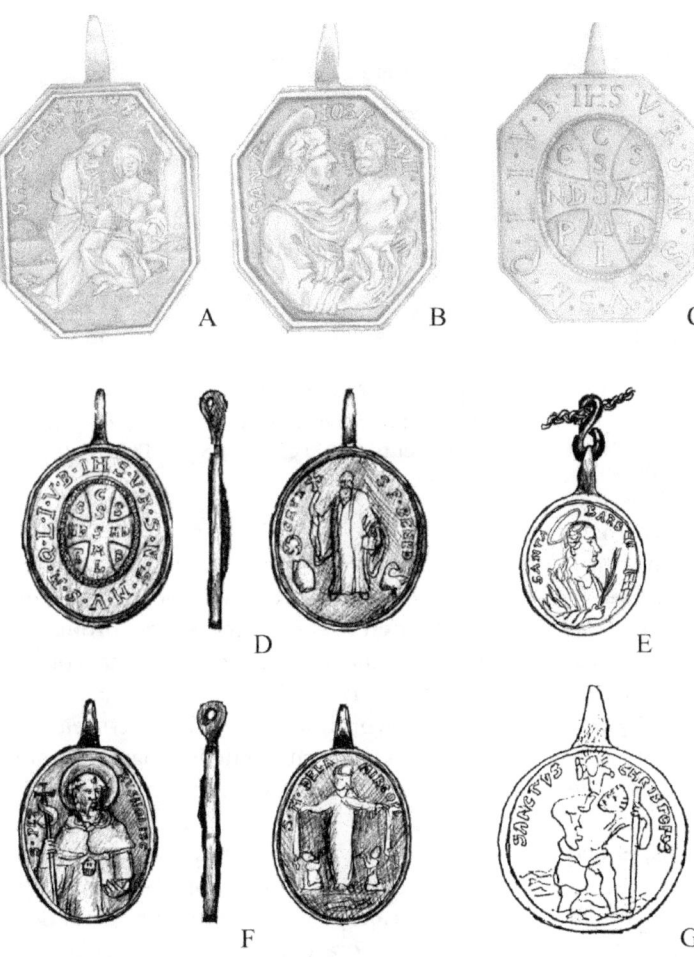

Figure 4.10. Devotional medals from the 1733 Florida plate fleet wrecks. A. St. Anne with the Virgin Mary; B. St. Joseph with the Christ Child; C. Benedictine symbol; D. St. Benedict/Benedictine symbol; E. Santa Barbara; F. Our Lady of the Rosary/St. John; G. St. Christopher. Height of A–C, with loop, 4.8 cm; Diameter of G 2.5 cm. *Courtesy of Florida Bureau of Archaeological Research. Drawings: Frank Gilson.*

Spain to the Americas, such as the Quicksilver wrecks (the *Tolosá* and *Guadalupe*), which sank off the coast of the Dominican Republic in 1724 (Borrell 1983c; Santiago 1980), and the *Matanceros* wreck, which sank off the coast of the Yucatán peninsula in 1741 (Blair 1960; Pope 1979:75–87; CEDAM Museum, Akumal, Yucatán). These ships carried thousands of religious medals and other objects, apparently intended for distribution throughout the New World Spanish colonies. Many different saints associated with a variety of indulgences appear on these medals, including several who were canonized during the seventeenth and even eighteenth centuries. Far fewer medals have been found on ships bound from the Americas to Spain (the 1733 Florida plate fleet wrecks, for example), and these were probably the personal possessions of crew members or passengers (Allender 1995; Skowronek 1982:140–144; Fig. 4.10).

Late-Eighteenth- and Nineteenth-Century Devotional Medals

Religious medallions dating to the later eighteenth century (ca. 1770–1800) are somewhat larger in size than those used earlier in the century and are most often round. They frequently have more regular and precise inscriptions, and they sometimes have images on one side only (Fig. 4.9). Examples from both St. Augustine and the southwestern

U.S. missions dating to this period are as large as 3.5 cm in diameter (Di Peso 1976:192; FLMNH collections).

Two examples from late-eighteenth-century contexts in St. Augustine are both 3.3 cm in diameter. One bears a traditional image of Francis of Assisi on the obverse, with no inscription other than the word "ROMA" on the reverse. The other medal bears images of St. John of Capistrano (canonized in 1724) on the obverse and of St. Bernard of Siena on the reverse (Fig. 4.9). Both were important Franciscan saints.

Medals of the later eighteenth and nineteenth centuries in Spain tended to become somewhat more ornate in their designs, adding filigree, openwork scrolls, wreaths, and cornucopias as frames around the religious themes (Berges 1984:41; Contreras y López de Ayala 1952:5). These later medals often had pointed oval shapes, referred to as *mandorlas,* or almond shapes. They were used most frequently with images of the Virgin Mary and the Holy Trinity (Ferguson 1961:148; DeBles 1925:29). Necklaces often had several of these medals, along with amulets, reliquaries, and crosses, suspended from them.

A revival of the popular cult of the Immaculate Conception occurred in the early nineteenth century with the issuance of the "Miraculous Medal" (Fig. 4.11). In 1830, the Virgin Mary appeared to a French nun with instructions to produce a medal that would bring many graces to whomever wore it. The medal, struck in 1832, has an obverse image of Mary with rays, holding a globe, and the inscription "O Mary conceived without sin, pray for us to have recourse to thee." The reverse bears the letter "M," surmounted by a cross, over the sacred hearts of Jesus and Mary. Jesus' heart is surrounded by a crown of thorns and shows flames, and Mary's is pierced by a sword and shows a cross. The medal's popularity was enormous, and it is claimed that by 1875 there were more than 30 million of them in circulation throughout

Figure 4.11. The 1832 Miraculous Medal of the Virgin Mary. St. Augustine (SA-7-7-396), nineteenth century, 2.0 cm by 2.8 cm. FLMNH/CSA Collections.

the world (Lea 1968:521; Moell 1967:818). The miraculous medal was used by both men and women in the United States through the 1960s (Michael V. Gannon, personal communication, April 1997).

Medals continue to be manufactured today, often using the same iconography found on colonial-period devotional medals (Anonymous 1926). These medals, however, are made in a wider variety of shapes, including the *mandorla* and scalloped-*mandorla* shapes, scalloped circles and ovals, and floral shapes. Elaborate filigreed frames are also common (Anonymous 1926). The medals are made in a variety of lightweight white base metals as well as the brass that typically comprised the colonial-period medals.

Personal Crosses and Crucifixes

Crosses and crucifixes—a representation of Christ on the cross—were present from the earliest days onward in the Spanish colonies as items of jewelry, personal and community devotional objects, parts of rosaries, church furniture, and sculptures. Design and decoration on Spanish crosses were frequently distinct from those of other European crosses (see Dusenbury 1960:16–18).

Crosses found on archaeological sites are

Religious Items

Figure 4.12. Seventeenth-century jeweled crosses and religious pendants. *Top:* Rock crystal, gold, and enamel reliquary pendant. Height 6.0 cm. V&A #347-1820. *Center left:* Gold cross set with gemstones. Height 9.0 cm. V&A #213-1864. *Center:* Gold and enamel pendant of Nuestra Señora del Pilar. Height 5.5 cm. V&A #299-1866. *Center right:* Gold and enamel cross set with gemstones. Height 7.5 cm. V&A #299-1866. *Bottom:* Gold, enamel, and gemstone Immaculate Conception *venera*. Height 7.2 cm. V&A #396-1872. V&A Picture Library. *Courtesy of the Victoria and Albert Museum, London.*

generally parts of rosaries or small personal devotional items; however, many crosses of gold and jewels that apparently served as fine jewelry for the very wealthy are found in museum collections and on shipwreck sites (see, for example, Borrell 1983b:115–118; Muller 1972:59–63; Peterson 1977:733; Oman 1967; Victoria and Albert Museum collections, #s 213-1864, 344-1870; Walters Art Gallery 1979:493; Fig. 4.12). These, however, are not typically found on terrestrial archaeological sites and are included in the category of fine jewelry.

The cross is a universal Christian symbol, representing Christ's crucifixion and the essence of Christianity. Crosses have been used as symbols in Christian iconography since the beginning of the Christian era but were rarely displayed until after the fourth century. Before that time, the cross, although probably used in private devotion, was a dangerous symbol of identification for early Christians, who were still outlawed (Benson 1976). Furthermore, early Christians saw the cross as a repugnant and barbaric Roman instrument of torture (Lesage 1960:21–22; Meinberg 1967:475). It was not until Constantine was converted to Christianity after having a vision of a cross in the heavens that the symbol became widely and openly used. Finally, when Constantine's mother, Helena, discovered the true cross, Christians everywhere adopted it as their sign and an object of devotion (Lesage 1960:22).

Widespread use of the crucifix came somewhat later. Not until the sixth century did the first representations of Christ on the cross commonly appear (Pérez-Bueno 1952:5; Meinberg 1967:475). By the fifteenth century, the familiar image of Christ without clothing and in intense physical suffering had emerged (Lesage 1960).

The two basic forms of crosses are the Greek cross, with four equal-sized bars or arms, and the Latin cross, which has a longer vertical bar than horizontal bar (Fig. 4.13). The crossbar is usually placed so that the upper arm and two horizontal arms are of the same length, with the lower vertical arm longer (Benson 1976:68; Ferguson 1961:154). Other well-known but less common forms in the Americas include the Tau, or St. Anthony's cross, which is a T-shaped cross, and the St. Andrew cross, which is in the form of an x. This latter cross is named after St. Andrew, who asked to be crucified on an x-shaped cross since he (like St. Peter

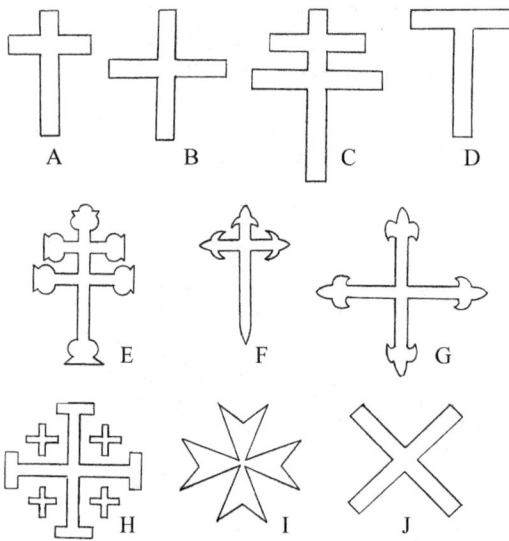

Figure 4.13. Some forms of crosses used in the Catholic Church. A. Latin cross; B. Greek cross; C. Patriarchal cross; D. Tau cross; E. Caravaca cross (Spanish ca. 1650–nineteenth century); F. Avellan cross (seventeenth century); G. St. James Cross (Knights of Santiago); H. Jerusalem cross (Order of the Holy Sepulchre); I. Maltese cross (Order of St. John Hospitallers); J. St. Andrew's cross.

before him) felt unworthy of the same form of cross on which Christ died. Many variations on these basic forms evolved, largely through the impetus and development of heraldry (Heim 1978; Meinberg 1967:475). Figure 4.13 shows some of the most common cross forms and their associations.

Certain adaptations of the Latin cross, known as Ecclesiastical crosses, are used symbolically to distinguish different ranks in the hierarchy of the church. The double cross, that is, a cross with two crossbars, signifies patriarchs and archbishops, while the triple cross, with three crossbars, exclusively symbolizes the pope (Heim 1978:74; Ferguson 1961:165). Variations of the double-barred cross were also used by some Catholic laypeople in their personal devotions (see Benson 1976:77).

Crosses and rosaries in the Spanish colonies probably came from a variety of New and Old World sources. Only 12 crosses (*cruces de vidrio*) are listed specifically in the *Contaduría* records of 1513–1613 (Table 4.1); however, a great many were imported from Spain by the eighteenth century. For example, more than 5,000 crosses were recovered from the 1741 *Matanceros* wreck (Blair 1960; Marx 1973:14–17). Crosses and probably rosaries were almost certainly produced in the New World as well. Small, simple, hollow-cast crosses and crucifixes were mass produced during the eighteenth century in Mexico (see Toussaint 1967:368), and many simple and ornate crosses were produced in Mexico, Peru, and other silver-mining areas during colonial times (Davis and Pack 1963; Oman 1968; Taillard 1941). Crosses, rosaries, and reliquaries made in Asia were also shipped to Spanish America from the Philippines on the Manila galleons (Marx 1983:14; Schurz 1939:33).

Latin Crosses and Crucifixes

Dating crosses is difficult owing to the universality and durability of the many variants of the cross form. The simple Latin cross is the most common form found during all periods on Spanish colonial sites. These can be undecorated, engraved with designs, or have a corpus attached. The earliest example from a Spanish American colonial site is a crucifix excavated at the site of La Isabela in the Dominican Republic. The cross is made of copper alloy, with a smaller overlaid cross of white metal and a copper-alloy corpus attached to that by small pins (Fig. 4.14). A scroll with an undecipherable inscription is attached to the top of the cross. The crucifix is similar in size and form to that shown by the Flemish painter Quentin Massys (1465–1530) in *Portrait of a Man*. Both crucifixes are of complex construction, showing Christ in a loincloth with bent head and surmounted by a scroll.

Although they are depicted in portraits of the late fifteenth and early sixteenth cen-

Figure 4.14. Crucifix from La Isabela. Copper alloy and white metal, ca. 1493–98. Height 4.4 cm. Excavated by José M. Cruxent. FS 1874. Parque Nacional de La Isabela, Dominican Republic. *Drawing: Patricia D. Farrior.*

Figure 4.15. Crosses from the Padre Island shipwrecks, 1554. *Left:* Gold-covered wooden cross (41KN10 No. 129-2). Sheet gold lines the edges and is secured by gold wire. Height 2.55 cm. *Right:* Gold crucifix with suspension loops for pearls or jewels and a skull at the base. (41YW3, No. 1436). Height (including loop) 2.9 cm. From Arnold and Weddle (1978: Fig. 63). *Reprinted with permission of the authors, Academic Press, and the Texas Historical Commission.*

turies (see, for example, Fig. 7.6), crosses for personal use are rare in archaeological contexts dating to before about 1570, and the archaeological record supports Pérez-Bueno's (1952:5) suggestion that simple, undecorated metal crosses in general were not used widely for personal devotions prior to the early seventeenth century. None, for example, have been recovered from Puerto Real (1503–78), Nueva Cádiz (1503–45), or Concepción de la Vega (1498–1562). The only archaeological examples reported from before about 1570 (other than the La Isabela crucifix) have come from shipwrecks. The 1554 shipwreck of the *San Esteban* off Padre Island, Texas, contained a simple Latin cross of wood covered in gold, along with a more ornate gold crucifix with a gold corpus and small pearls attached (Arnold and Weddle 1978: 291; Olds 1976:145; Fig. 4.15).

A brass crucifix was recovered from a Bermuda shipwreck thought to date to about 1560 (Peterson 1975:86). This was a distinctive cross form in that there were small skeleton figures at the terminal ends of the cross forming open Greek crosses with their legs (Fig. 4.16). A preoccupation with death was reflected in the art and jewelry of Counter-Reformation Europe during the second half of the sixteenth century and the early part of the seventeenth century, manifest by the death's head designs that were frequently incorporated into material culture (Evans 1970:142–143; Lanllier and Pini 1983: 87, 99). These crosses were most often used as

Figure 4.16. Brass skeleton crucifixes. *Left:* Brass crucifix with skeleton terminals from a shipwreck thought to have sunk ca. 1560 (Peterson 1975:86). *Reproduced with permission of the Smithsonian Institution. Right:* Terminal fragment of brass crucifix with skeleton terminal and attachment hole for a corpus. Length 3.2 cm. St. Augustine (SA-34-2). FLMNH/CSA Collections. *Photo: James Quine.*

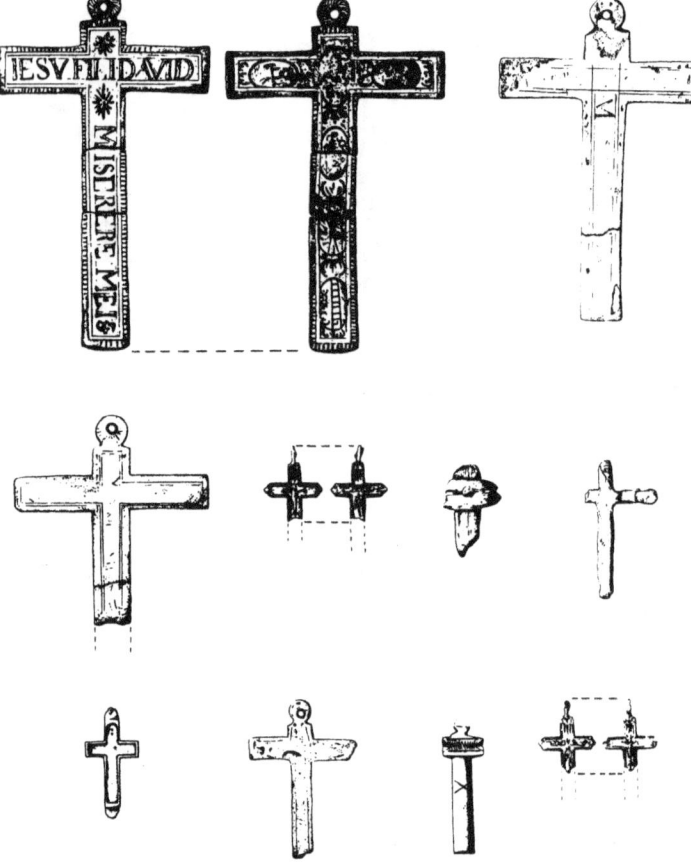

Figure 4.17. Seventeenth-century crosses from Santa Catalina de Guale (Georgia). Height of top left cross 12 cm. *Reprinted by permission of the American Museum of Natural History. Courtesy of the American Museum of Natural History, the Edward John Noble Foundation, and David H. Thomas.*

symbols of mourning (Evans 1970:142). A fragment of a cross nearly identical to that found in Bermuda was recovered from a multicomponent site in St. Augustine in a context dated to about 1780. It is possible, however, that it was originally deposited in and then disturbed from a sixteenth-century context.

Crosses and crucifixes become much more common after about 1600 and have been found at several of Florida's Spanish mission sites (Deagan 1972:38; Vernon and McEwan 1990:37). The largest sample comes from the seventeenth-century mission site of Santa Catalina de Guale in Georgia, where both plain and engraved examples have been recovered (Thomas 1988:131, 1993:14;

Fig. 4.17). Engravings on the crosses include religious motifs, such as the symbols of Christ's passion, and inscriptions, such as "Jesus, son of David, have mercy on me" (Thomas 1993:14).

One of the most beautiful crosses recovered in the Americas was found in association with Native American burials in the church at the seventeenth-century mission of San Luis de Talimali in Florida (Fig. 4.18; McEwan, Davidson, and Mitchem 1997). This quartz crystal cross was skillfully pressure flaked and carved on the surface with facets and ridges using a metal file, and the reverse is smooth. It is suspected to have been of Native American production because of the biconical drilling technique used in the

Figure 4.18. Carved crystal cross from San Luis de Talimali, ca. 1650–1700. Quartz crystal, second half of the seventeenth century, found in association with Native American burials at the church site of Mission San Luis. Height 7 cm. FS 7104 (see also Hann and McEwan 1998:121). *Courtesy of the Florida Bureau of Archaeological Research, the San Luis Historical and Archaeological Research Site, and Bonnie McEwan.*

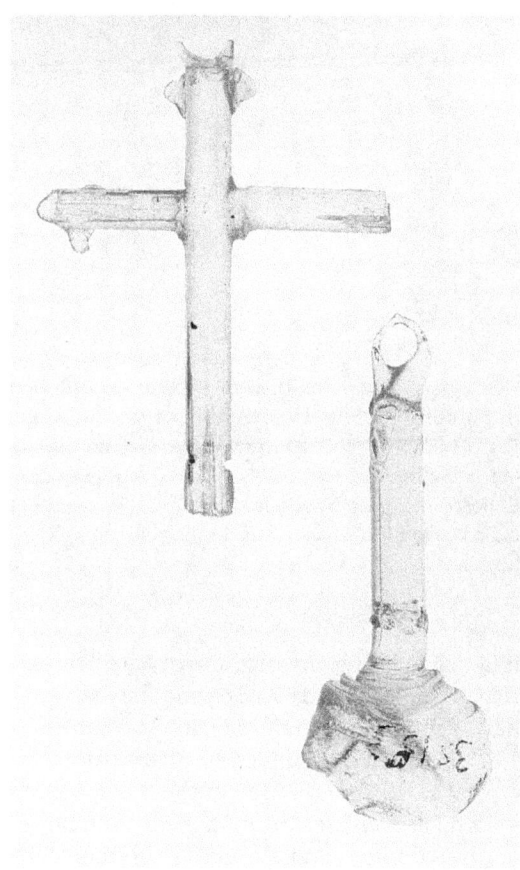

Figure 4.19. Glass cross and pendant, 1724. Quicksilver wrecks (1724). Length of intact cross 4.2 cm. *Courtesy of the Museo de la Atarazana, Santo Domingo. Photo: James Quine.*

suspension loop (McEwan, Davidson, and Mitchem 1997). The well-established tradition of an indigenous Mexican lapidary tradition and the early introduction of European faceting techniques suggest the additional possibility that this cross, like many seventeenth-century cut crystal beads (see Chapter 5), may have been made in Mexico (Allender 1995:207–208).

The simple glass cross shown in Figure 4.19, however, is undoubtedly far more typical of those used in the Spanish colonies. This example, recovered from an America-bound ship in 1724, probably represents the *cruces de vidrio* listed in various shipping manifests of items being imported to the colonies from Spain (for example, those in Table 4.1).

A small, undecorated pewter cross with a loop for suspension was recovered from the

Figure 4.20. Seventeenth-century crosses. *Left:* Copper alloy (with fabric impression), late seventeenth century. St. Augustine, Sisters of St. Joseph Convent collection (SA-36-7-54). *Center:* Copper alloy, first half of the eighteenth century. Height 3.3 cm. (SA-7-4-592). FLMNH/CSA Collections. *Right:* Silver, first third of the seventeenth century. Height 2.5 cm. Fig Springs site (8CO1). FLMNH #HTCCO1. FLMNH/CSA Collections. *Photo: James Quine.*

mid-seventeenth-century site of Fig Springs (Fig. 4.20; Deagan 1972:38) and may also have been produced in Mexico (Toussaint 1965:278). This example is probably more typical of the crosses used in the missions.

Two Latin crosses from St. Augustine have decorated finials and a central cartouche decoration (Fig. 4.20). One of these was part of a rosary associated with a late-seventeenth-century Spanish burial (Koch 1980:337). Muller (1972:59) notes that the cartouche decoration on fine jewelry crosses was characteristic of the second half of the sixteenth century, and it clearly persisted through the seventeenth and probably into the early eighteenth century in the Spanish colonies.

Thousands of small, copper-alloy Latin crosses were shipped to the Spanish colonies during the eighteenth century and have been recovered from the wrecks of nearly all ships bound from Spain to America (see Blair 1960:149, 165, 263; Borrell 1983a, 1983c; Museo de la Atarazana, Santo Domingo). A wide variety of cross forms occur archaeologically, but the most commonly occurring eighteenth-century form is that of a small, flat Latin cross with plain terminals. Used on rosaries or as pendants, these often have engraved or molded figures of Christ or the saints on one side and inscriptions on the other (Fig. 4.21).

The use of simple, wooden Latin crosses sheathed in gold or silver was a long-lived tradition in the Americas, dating from at least the sixteenth century (see, for example, Fig. 4.15). A crucifix of wood sheathed in silver and bearing a silver corpus was recovered from a 1715 shipwreck site (Fig. 4.22), and silver-sheathed wood crosses have also been reported from late-eighteenth-century Peru (Museum of Mankind, London, #AM1123.1968) and from a late-eighteenth-century burial in New Orleans (Owsley et al. 1985:83).

The Caravaca Cross

During the second half of the seventeenth century, a double-barred patriarchal cross with cyma molding at the termination of the top and horizontal arms became popular (Figs. 4.13, 4.22, 4.23). This form is known in Spain as the Caravaca cross (see Alarcón Román 1987; Pérez-Bueno 1952; Hildburgh

Religious Items

Figure 4.21. Cross from *El Matanceros*, 1741. Reproduction of a copper-alloy cross in the collection of CEDAM, Akumal, Yucatán, Mexico. Height 5 cm. Thousands of crosses of this kind were recovered from the wreck. *Front:* Figure of Christ on the cross. Inscription: INRI. *Reverse:* Figure of Virgin Mary as the *Immaculada*. Inscriptions: Top, IMMACULATA; Cross arms, VITAM PRAESTA; Foot, PVRADI. *Photo: University of Florida Office of Instructional Resources.*

1940) and in France as the Lorraine cross (Benson 1976:71).

The Caravaca cross was used widely throughout Spain during the seventeenth century, when extensive papal indulgences were attached to it (Lea 1968:565). Although the cross is patriarchal in its form, is thought to have been permitted for general use in Spain by a papal dispensation commemorating the cessation of the plague there (Benson 1976:77). The Caravaca form also has amuletic and protective properties, particularly when made of silver or bronze, and these crosses continue to be used extensively in Spain as protection against lightning and rabies and, in Andalucia, to aid in childbirth (Alarcón Román 1987:35; Hildburgh 1940).

Caravaca crosses are often engraved with corpus designs and religious inscriptions or with Christ on one side and the Immaculate Conception on the other. They also frequently served as reliquary crosses. During

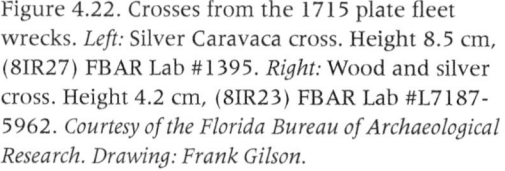

Figure 4.22. Crosses from the 1715 plate fleet wrecks. *Left:* Silver Caravaca cross. Height 8.5 cm, (8IR27) FBAR Lab #1395. *Right:* Wood and silver cross. Height 4.2 cm, (8IR23) FBAR Lab #L7187-5962. *Courtesy of the Florida Bureau of Archaeological Research. Drawing: Frank Gilson.*

Figure 4.23. Seventeenth-century Caravaca cross. Copper-alloy reliquary cross segment, ca. 1686–1702. Height 5.5 cm. Santa Catalina de Guale on Amelia Island (8NA41). 8NA41-2293. FLMNH/CSA Collections. *Photo: University of Florida Office of Instructional Resources.*

the seventeenth century, these crosses were often engraved with the symbols of the passion of Christ (see "Reliquaries").

With a single exception, Caravaca crosses recovered from circum-Caribbean sites occur in eighteenth-century contexts. The exception is a small, 5.5 cm high brass Caravaca crucifix from a seventeenth-century Florida mission site, which appears to have been part of a reliquary cross (Fig. 4.23). Except for the attached corpus, it is undecorated (Saunders 1988).

Eighteenth-century Caravaca crosses recovered archaeologically are generally engraved and are larger and more ornate than the seventeenth-century example from Santa Catalina de Guale on Amelia Island, Florida (Fig. 4.22). Reported examples include that shown in Figure 4.22 and those from the Quicksilver wrecks (1724), the 1741 *Matanceros* wreck, and eighteenth-century St. Augustine (HSAPB collections AO166).

The Avellan Cross
The Avellan cross is a Greek cross with rounded and molded arms (Fig. 4.13; Dusen-

bury 1960) and appears in Spanish contexts during the seventeenth century. The arms of this cross taper toward the ends and can be decorated with bosses, ribbing, and floral elements. Gold Avellan-type crosses are shown in paintings of the seventeenth century, for example, Velázquez's *Lady with a Fan* (1635), and have been found on shipwrecks of the 1622 fleet (Florida Bureau of Archaeological Research Conservation Lab #O94) (Fig. 4.24). The Baltimore Art Museum has a similar example that adorns a crown for a seventeenth-century religious figure, believed to have been made in Peru (Lesley 1968:170–172), and a silver Avellan cross occurs on a rosary in the collection of the Museo del Pueblo Español (2.446).

The Avellan crosses found archaeologically are ornate and made of precious metals. They seem to be associated with such costly rosaries as those made of coral beads (used traditionally by women). In paintings, they are associated with women of status or the Virgin Mary and thus may reflect feminine use.

Crosses Associated with Religious Orders, Brotherhoods, and Confraternities

Certain cross forms, such as Santiago and Maltese crosses, were associated with and used as symbols of identification by religious-military confraternities or knightly religious orders. These crosses are also considered to be *veneras* (see *"Veneras"*).

Cofradías (religious confraternities) were extremely widespread in Spain and its colonies throughout the colonial era. Many of these socioreligious organizations were originally formed with a military function during the times of the Crusades, and most have continued in a civilian capacity to the present day. They were devoted to a particu-

Figure 4.24. Coral and gold rosary, 1622. Chaplet with five decades of coral beads and five gold paters. A gold Avellan cross is suspended. Cross arms are 3.7 cm high. *Nuestra Señora de Atocha*, 1622. Florida Division of Archaeological Research (see also Matthewson 1986: C28). *Courtesy of the Florida Bureau of Archaeological Research. Drawing: Frank Gilson.*

lar religious cause, to fostering fraternity, and to promoting the interests of the Church (Meyers and Hopkins 1988). Others were prestigious secular organizations appointed by nobility, such as the Order of the Golden Fleece. Each group had a particular symbol, many of which were crosses. Others, such as those devoted to the Immaculate Conception, had other symbols as *veneras*.

The three major religious-military orders in Spain during the sixteenth through eighteenth centuries were the Knights of Alcantara, the Knights of Malta (also known as the Sovereign Military Order of the Hospital of St. John of Jerusalem), and the Knights of Santiago (St. James) (O'Callaghan 1967:215). Each had its own insignia.

The Maltese cross is associated with the Knights of Malta, who were famous for their charitable hospital on Malta and their role in repelling the Turks from the Mediterranean during the battle of Lepanto in 1571 (Heim 1978:70; Sherbowitz-Wetzor and Toumanoff 1967). Maltese crosses have been found in sixteenth-century archaeological contexts, including the Armada wrecks (Stenuit 1972:214–217) and Santa Elena (South, Skowronek, and Johnson 1988:160). The Armada cross was of embossed gold, originally enameled, and pierced in the angles of the cross by four fleur-de-lis-like objects. A similar design dating to 1641 is shown by Muller (1972:Fig. 182), and ornately jeweled gold Maltese crosses of this type were also recovered from the 1715 Spanish fleet wrecks in Florida (see, for example, Marx and Marx 1993:88).

The crucifix from Santa Elena is in the form of a Maltese cross, with a simple, stylized figure of Christ (Fig. 4.25). No later archaeological examples of nonprecious Maltese crosses have been reported, and it is likely that they were most typically used during the sixteenth and first half of the seventeenth centuries. This is supported by Muller's analysis of jewel designs in Spain, which include Maltese crosses primarily dur-

Figure 4.25. Maltese cross crucifix from Santa Elena. Brass, ca. 1566–87. Maximum width 3.04 cm, height 1.62 cm. Santa Elena #38BU162C-14B. South, Skowronek, and Johnson (1988: Fig. 95D). *Courtesy of the South Carolina Institute of Archaeology and Anthropology and Stanley South.*

ing the first half of the seventeenth century (Muller 1972).

The Santiago cross is a slender Latin cross, painted or enameled in red, with fleur-de-lis at the termination of the horizontal arms and upper tip (Fig. 4.13). It is often superimposed on a scallop shell (the symbol of St. James) or on a heart and used as a *venera*. The Knights of Santiago were very popular in Spain during the seventeenth and eighteenth centuries, and the Santiago cross appears not uncommonly in archaeological assemblages of that period. It was also depicted frequently in paintings, embroidered on the tunics of kings of Spain and such noblemen as Pedro Menéndez de Áviles of Florida. All but a single reported example from archaeological sites have been made of gold, and most are quite ornate. The 1724 Quicksilver wrecks (Borrell 1983c; Peterson 1979a:106–107) also yielded two gold examples, one mounted on a heart and one on a four-lobed plaque.

The cross of the Knights of Alcantara is a Greek cross with fleur-de-lis forming the termination of all four arms (Fig. 4.13). A gold

Alcantara cross came from the Armada wrecks (Stenuit 1973:193, fig. op. 192).

Other nonknightly confraternities and religious organizations were widespread in Spain and in the colonies and also had cross emblems. The cross of St. Dominic is a Greek cross with fleur-de-lis terminating at all four arms and is a symbol of the Dominican Order. A gold *venera* cross of St. Dominic enclosed in a four-lobed frame was recovered from the 1724 Quicksilver galleons (Borrell 1983a:80). When the Dominic cross is double-barred in black and white, it is the symbol for the Order of the Militia of Christ (also known as the Order of St. Dominic) and was used to represent the Holy Order of the Inquisition (Heim 1978:78; Muller 1972:117–118). In its simplest form, the four-arm fleur-de-lis cross appears on Spanish coinage of the New World (see Chapter 12).

Small, stylized crosses carved from jet have been recovered from sixteenth-century contexts in Spanish La Florida and are considered to be amulets because of their material and unorthodox designs. These are discussed and illustrated in Chapter 5.

Rosaries

The rosary is another uniquely Catholic object that occurs frequently in Spanish colonial archaeological assemblages. The term "rosary" refers both to a pious exercise of prayer and meditation and to the string of objects designed as a physical guide to those prayers. The full devotion, known as the Dominican Rosary, consists of fifteen sets (decades) of ten Hail Marys (*Aves*) each, preceded by a recitation of an Our Father (*Pater* or *Pater noster*) and followed by recitation of a Glory Be to the Father (*Gloria*). At the end of the rosary the Apostles' Creed is recited and followed by two *Paters,* three *Aves,* and one *Gloria.* Each decade is devoted to 1 of the 15 church Mysteries (5 sorrowful, 5 glorious, and 5 joyful) that summarize the lives of Mary and Jesus and describe the liturgical year (see Hinnebusch 1967; Casanowicz 1909).

Many papal indulgences were attached to the saying of the rosary after 1495 and again after 1571, and it was during the sixteenth century that the rosary assumed its present form (Lea 1968:484–488; Hinnebusch 1967:668). The production of rosaries was an important commercial activity from medieval times onward in the capitals of Europe, still evidenced today by streets in the older sections that bear names reflecting rosary makers, such as Paternoster row in London or Via Coronari in Rome (Evans 1970:52; Casanowicz 1909:255). The rosary has been a very popular form of devotion since the sixteenth century and was especially promoted by the Dominican Order. It assumed greater importance in the Church after 1572, when the Feast of the Rosary was established following Spanish victory over the Turks at the battle of Lepanto in 1571, an event believed to have been successful due to the intercession of the Virgin of the Rosary (Lea 1968:488–489).

Of particular interest to archaeologists are the devices used to guide the rosary prayers. These are usually strings (chaplets) of beads or small stones of varying sizes, with sets of ten small beads representing *Aves,* separated by larger beads representing the *Paters.* A crucifix or medallion accompanied by large beads or amulets is usually suspended from the chaplet and used for the concluding prayers.

There are several varieties of rosaries, and the organization of beads varied from the sixteenth to the nineteenth centuries. Studies of tombs in churches show rosary chaplets containing 80, 75, 40, and 33 beads, often with no divisions (Casanowicz 1909:359). The full, or Dominican, rosary is made up of 150 small *Ave* beads, separated by 15 large *Pater* beads. A shorter string is suspended from the chaplet with one large and three small beads for the concluding prayers, which include a *Pater* on the large bead, *Aves* on the small beads, and the Apostles' Creed at the termination. A cross, crucifix, medallion, or other devotional object terminates the smaller string.

The "lesser" rosary is more commonly used than the full rosary and has a chaplet with only five decades of *Ave* beads separated by five large *Pater* beads. This could be said five times to complete a full rosary (Casanowicz 1909:351).

The Franciscan rosary contains seven decades to celebrate the seven Mysteries of Mary, while the Crown of Our Lady rosary (*corona*), also used by the Franciscans, has 72 *Aves* and seven *Paters* commemorating the tradition of Mary's age (Casanowicz 1909:354–357). Other Spanish rosary combinations include the *trisagio*, or three decades in honor of the Holy Trinity, and the *septenario*, consisting of seven sets of seven *Ave* beads, each in honor of the Virgin of Sorrows (Contreras y López de Ayala 1951:5).

Decade rosaries were common during the fifteenth, sixteenth, and seventeenth centuries, comprised of ten large (and usually stone) beads with a cross or medallion at the end (Fig. 4.26; Evans 1970:Plate 38). It could be used repetitiously to complete a whole rosary or for only a single set of Mysteries.

Rosaries were omnipresent accompaniments of Spanish women, and it was fashionable to wear them as necklaces or bracelets, on the belt, or over the arm (Mason 1974:97; Muller 1972:170; see also Fig. 11.6). Madame Marie-Catherine D'Aulnoy, in her acerbic social commentary on seventeenth-century Spain, described the importance of the rosary to well-to-do Spanish women:

> In every house at a certain stated hour, all the women meet with the mistress of the family in the chapel, there to repeat their rosary aloud. . . . It is a strange thing to see how continually fond they are of their beads. Every woman there has a pair fastened to her girdle, and so long that they almost touch the ground. They are perpetually without ceasing using them in the streets, as they play at ombre [cards], as they discourse, nay, as they are making love, when they are telling lies, or speaking

Figure 4.26. Decade rosary. Silver with glass beads. Peru, colonial era. Museum of Mankind #AM1972 A712-14, British Museum, London. *Courtesy of the Museum of Mankind, London.*

> evil of their neighbors. They are continually muttering over their beads . . . nothing of this hinders them still to keep on at their pace. I leave you to judge what devotion there can be in this; but custom has great power in this country. (1930:198–199)

Rosaries for the very wealthy were often made of gold, pearls, ivory, cameos, coral, and precious and semiprecious stones (Muller 1972:56, 62, 129; Casanowicz 1909:354). Common rosaries were made of glass beads, stone beads, bone, wood, or seeds. Throughout the colonial period, rosary chaplets often had medallions, crosses, reliquaries, *veneras*, or other ornaments suspended from them (Fig. 4.3; see also Muller 1972:62–68 for additional examples).

Tables 4.1 and 4.3 document the kinds of rosaries shipped to the Spanish Americas during the sixteenth and early seventeenth centuries. No designation of size is given,

Table 4.3. Rosaries Listed with Prices in Shipping Records to the Caribbean, 1526–1618

Rosary Type	Number	Percent	Price Range
Wood	1,143	59.0	
Ebony			6–8 rls./dozen
Gilded Ebony			10 rls.–5 ducats/dozen
Mt. Tabor wood			1–4.5 rls./dozen
Mt. Tabor wood, small			4.5 rls. each
Brazilwood			2 rls. each
Leonados			
Tawny-colored	385	19.4	7.5 rls./dozen
With medals showing the passion of Christ			7.5 rls. each
Glass			
Plain	240	12.4	3 rls./dozen, 4.5 rls. each
Gilded			19 rls. each
Jet	107	5.5	2–6 rls. each
White bone	24	4.2	18 rls./dozen
Paste	18	0.9	3 rls. each
Pastilla cugasador			12 rls. each
Other	11	0.6	
Coral			30 rls. each
Coral to decorate			8 ducats each
Ambar			not given
Crystal			3,740 mvds. each
"de olor"	24		340 mvds. each

Note: 1 real (rl.) = 44 maravedis (mvds.); 1 ducat (esscudo) = 16 reales or 704 maravedis.

other than the mention of *tercios de rosarios*, which may refer to *trisagios*. Most of the rosaries were not identified in the records as to material composition (2,251, or 53 percent of those listed). The majority of the remaining rosaries (1,928) were made of wood, including plain and gilded ebony, "Tavor" or "Tabor" (wood from Mt. Tabor), and "Palo de Brasil" (Table 4.3). Wood was probably the most common material for rosary beads in general. Wood beads constitute the majority of beads in existing collections of rosaries, such as that of the National Museum of American History (Casanowicz 1909) and a large proportion of the Museo del Pueblo Español's eighteenth-century rosary collection (Contreras y López de Ayala 1951). Wood beads are rarely recovered archaeologically except on shipwreck sites (see, for example, Skowronek 1982:148).

Bone beads were used more frequently in rosaries than they were in jewelry. Ivory and bone rosary beads occur frequently on French colonial sites (see Stone 1974:74–75, 114–116) but are relatively uncommon in Spanish colonial sites. Only 24 bone rosaries were listed in the shipping records shown in Table 4.3. Simple, spherical bone beads, probably used in rosaries, have been reported from sixteenth-century Puerto Real, Florida (Ewen 1987:Fig. 6-14k), and from sixteenth-century St. Augustine (Deagan 1985:12).

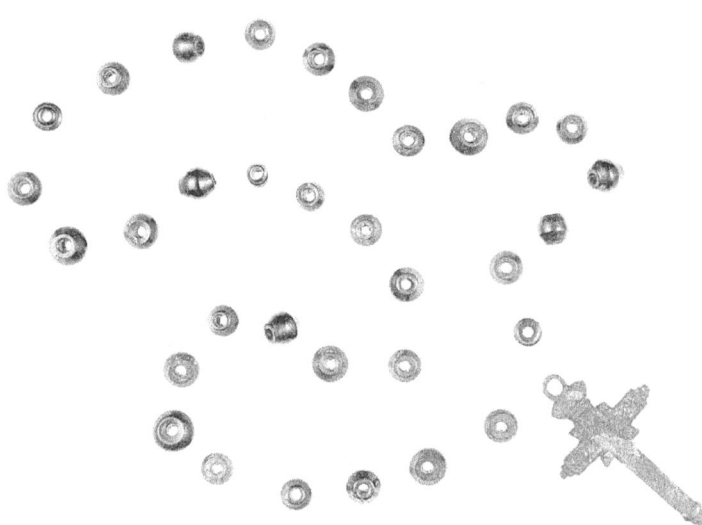

Figure 4.27. Seventeenth-century jet rosary. Silver wire with jet beads and silver cartouche cross suspended. Sixty-eight nonarticulated carved beads were recovered with a late-seventeenth-century Spanish burial (Koch 1980:159). Height of cross 3.3 cm. (SA-36-7-54). St. Augustine, Sisters of St. Joseph Convent collection. *Reproduced with permission from Deagan 1987:Fig. 7.15. Photo: James Quine.*

An unusual and probably perishable category of rosary listed in 1603 was the *rosario de olor*, costing 340 maravedís (about 7.7 reales) each. The *rosario de olor* could have been made of sandalwood or possibly of ambergris. Ambergris, a secretion of the sperm whale and an important ingredient in perfume, gradually hardens and assumes a sweet scent after exposure to the air. Pendants and other jewelry items were carved from ambergris during late Renaissance times in Europe (McConnell 1991:40).

More durable materials for rosaries include coral, jet, amber, crystal, metal, and glass, although some of these materials were very costly and would have been less likely than others to enter the archaeological record through loss or breakage. Coral rosaries, for example, are the most expensive kind of rosary listed in the shipping records, costing between 30 reales and 12 ducats each. Coral was believed in Spain to have a number of special qualities, probably stemming from its red, bloodlike color, which promotes the belief that it restores strength and protects against illness (Alarcón Román 1987:28–29; see also Chapter 5). A rosary of simple spherical coral and gold beads recovered from the 1621 wreck of the *Atocha* provides an example of the upper end of rosary production (Fig. 4.24; Matthewson 1986:C28).

Jet rosary beads are often recovered in Spanish colonial sites and, while more expensive than glass or wood rosaries, were considerably less costly than coral or crystal beads (Table 4.3). Magical and protective qualities have been attributed in Spain to jet since the Middle Ages, and it was an extremely popular material for a wide range of religious items, amulets, and ornaments (see Chapter 5).

Although jet rosaries were imported to the Spanish colonies as early as 1590 (Tables 4.1, 4.3) and were probably used in Spain somewhat earlier, jet rosary beads on colonial sites have been reported only from seventeenth-century and later contexts. These rosary beads often have distinctive forms not found on necklace beads. A rosary of 68 carved jet beads strung on thin silver wire was recovered from a mid-seventeenth-century burial in the parish cemetery of St. Augustine (Fig. 4.27; Koch 1980:159). The small beads occurred in two shapes, a spherical ellipsoid shape averaging .5 cm in diameter and a barrel shape with a sharp equatorial ridge averaging .3 cm in diameter. A silver cross with a cartouche element (shown in Fig. 4.20) was suspended from the chaplet.

Religious Items

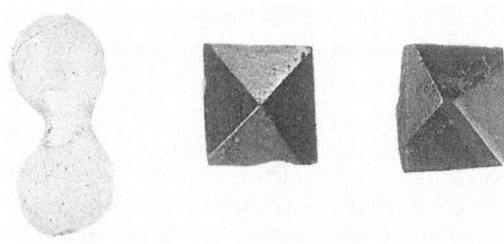

Figure 4.28. Rosary beads, probably used as joining elements. Clear glass double bead, ca. 1500–50. Length 1.55 cm. St. Marks Wildlife Refuge, Florida, Florida State University Anthropology Department, Tallahassee. Geometric jet beads, early eighteenth century. 8 mm square. St. Augustine (SA-7-4-164). FLMNH/CSA Collections.

Another distinctive type of jet rosary bead found widely throughout the North American Spanish borderlands (and therefore possibly related to the Franciscans) is a square, cubelike bead with a faceted upper surface, often with two perforations at right angles (Fig. 4.28). These beads are found in contexts dating from the second half of the seventeenth century to the late eighteenth century in St. Augustine and Santa Rosa Pensacola, as well as from the Spanish mission site of San Luis (Boyd, Smith, and Griffin 1951:146; Deagan 1987:183; Smith 1965:71, 97). They have also been reported from French-influenced Tunica sites (Brain 1979:221), the Guevavi mission in Arizona (Robinson 1976), and the Los Adaes site in Louisiana (Avery 1996; Gregory and Webb 1965).

Round, oval, and teardrop-shaped faceted jet beads have been recovered from eighteenth-century contexts (Deagan 1987:Fig. 7.16) and may also have been rosary beads. Such beads were, however, widely used for jewelry as well (see Chapter 3). They are present on the 1733 Florida plate fleet wrecks (Skowronek 1982:147), in eighteenth-century Spanish contexts in St. Augustine, and at Santa Rosa Pensacola (1723–52) (Smith 1965:101).

A large (more than 2.2 cm long) and ornately carved jet rosary bead was recovered from a late-sixteenth-century context in St. Augustine (Stanley Bond, personal communication, 1995). This bead is similar in concept to the similarly large and ornate rosary beads known to have been used in Spain during the sixteenth century (Gómez Tabanera 1977; Osma y Scull 1916). One example in the Walters Art Gallery collection is nearly 2.5 cm high, carved with the conjoined heads of Christ and St. James (Walters Art Gallery 1979:486). The bead from St. Augustine is shown with other carved jet items in Figure 5.5.

Prices for rosaries of the same material varied little between 1583 and 1613. Coral was the most expensive rosary material, costing up to 12 ducats for a decorative coral rosary (*de coral para guarnecer*), and the rosaries of Tavor were the least expensive at 1 to 4.5 reales per dozen (see Table 4.3). Gilding on any material increased the price substantially.

Given that the majority of rosary beads brought to the Americas from Spain during the late sixteenth and early seventeenth centuries were made either of perishable or valuable materials, it is probable that rosaries in general are underrepresented in the archaeological record. It is also likely, however, that many of the hundreds of thousands of glass beads (as well as the medallions) imported during the same period were used in the local production of rosaries (see Chapter 3). Only about 5,000 complete rosaries were imported during the first century of commerce, but nearly 12,000 items to be used in the production of rosaries (not including the millions of beads; see Table 6.1) arrived during the same period.

Unfortunately, it is not possible to distinguish confidently glass beads used in jewelry from those used in rosaries. There are certain categories of archaeologically recovered glass beads, however, that seem to have been used more frequently in rosaries. The easiest to identify are those that form joining elements in the rosary, either between the necklace portion and the pendant portion or between

Figure 4.29. Jet rosary beads. Faceted jet rosary beads from San Luis de Talimali, ca. 1650–1700. Diameter of bottom right bead 13 mm; diameter of bottom left bead 7 mm. *Clockwise from top center bead:* FS 7885bb; FS 7885a; FS 7885ff; FS 6886; FS 8115. *Courtesy of the Florida Bureau of Archaeological Research, the San Luis Historical and Archaeological Site, and Bonnie G. McEwan. Photo: James Quine.*

Figure 4.30. Eighteenth-century jet rosary beads with metal joining links. *El Conde de Tolosá* shipwreck (1724). Bead diameter 1.6 cm. *Courtesy of the Museo de la Atarazana, Santo Domingo. Photo: James Quine.*

the necklace portion and other pendant elements. These beads are often double lobed or jointed, or they have three or four holes (the usual longitudinal perforation as well as a vertical perforation) (Fig. 4.28). Rosary beads occasionally have fragments of the metal links that connected the rosary elements protruding from the perforations, and these often have flattened ends on the axis parallel to the perforation and irregular wear patterns resulting from handling the beads during prayer (Figs. 4.29, 4.30; see also Stone 1974:74–75).

Articulated glass rosary beads have occasionally been recovered with their metal linking elements attached. A portion of a seventeenth-century rosary was found at the site of San Luis de Talimali (Boyd, Smith, and Griffin 1951:147, Plate 5), made with 39 barrel-shaped, twisted, and grooved green beads (Fig. 4.31). Beads of this type are found infrequently on Spanish colonial sites and may be typical of rosaries.

Certain of the beads recovered from excavations at the San Luis site church, cemetery, and *convento* are probably also associated with rosaries rather than jewelry, given their association with friars and Catholic burials (Mitchem 1992, 1993). The most distinctive of these is a wire-wound, barrel-shaped gilded bead of burgundy glass, with appliquéd wavy stripes of blue or green glass (Fig. 4.32).

As noted earlier, gilding added considerably to the price of beads of any material (see Table 4.3). For example, rosaries of gilded glass beads cost 19 reales each as compared to 4.5 reales for plain glass rosaries. Gilded glass beads, including the variety known as Seven Oaks Gilded Molded (Goggin 1960), have been found associated with churches and *conventos* at several Franciscan mission sites in Florida spanning the seventeenth century, including San Luis de Talimali (Mitchem 1993:402), the Fig Springs Mission (Weisman 1992:146), San Juan del Puerto (Deagan 1987:176), Mission Patale (Marrinan 1993:273), and Santa Catalina de Guale in Georgia (Peter Francis, personal communica-

Religious Items 71

Figure 4.31. Seventeenth-century glass bead rosary elements. San Luis de Talimali, ca. 1650–1700. Copper-alloy linking elements with green glass beads. Height of cross 4 cm. *Courtesy of the Florida Bureau of Archaeological Research, the San Luis Historical and Archaeological Site, and Bonnie G. McEwan.*

tion, 1996). John Goggin also recorded a Seven Oaks Gilded Molded bead from the *convento* at Casas Grandes in Chihuahua, Mexico.

The largest sample of beads from a Spanish colonial church site is the assemblage from Santa Catalina de Guale in Georgia (Thomas 1988, 1993). This assemblage is currently under study and will undoubtedly enhance and modify our current understanding of beads in Spanish colonial religious contexts.

The Soledad cemetery site in St. Augustine (SA-36-7) was used by the Spaniards from 1598 until 1763 (Koch 1980). In both seventeenth- and eighteenth-century burials, the most frequently encountered beads were of bone known to have been associated particularly with rosaries or of brown to amber-colored glass (Koch 1980:275, 278). A large

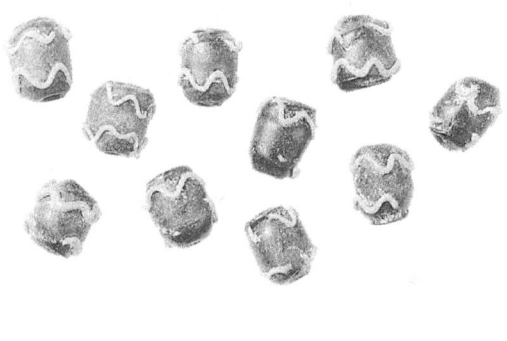

Figure 4.32. Probable glass rosary beads, seventeenth century. Wire-wound burgundy glass, gilded with applied stripes of blue and green glass. Approximately 7 mm by 8 mm. San Luis de Talimali, ca. 1650–1700. FS 3685 (from Mitchem 1993:Fig. 15.1). *Courtesy of the Florida Bureau of Archaeological Research, the San Luis Historical and Archaeological Site, and Bonnie G. McEwan. Photo: James Quine.*

Figure 4.33. Brass mesh joining section from a rosary. Copper-alloy links form a mesh that connects the rosary's chaplet to its terminal pendant elements. In use from mid-seventeenth century to ca. 1800 (see also Fig. 4.3). Approximately 3.5 cm by 4.5 cm. St. Augustine (SA-7-4-498). FLMNH/CSA Collections. *Photo: James Quine.*

number of rosaries in the *Contaduría* shipping lists (Tables 4.1, 4.3) were described as *leonados*, which indicates a deep tawny color, and at 7.5 reales per dozen, these were probably of glass. The Soledad beads may have fallen into this category. Amber- or tawny-colored glass beads are otherwise uncommon in colonial sites and may be primarily associated with rosaries.

Sections of small, connected metal links forming a mesh have been recovered from several Spanish colonial archaeological sites and served as joining elements in rosaries (Figs. 4.3, 4.33). They occur in contexts dating from about 1650 through the late eighteenth century.

Veneras *and Religious Pendants*

Veneras are symbols of cults, saints, religious orders, knighthoods, confraternities, and other religious organizations. Lay religious orders and confraternities were part of Spanish colonial social and religious life from the earliest days of colonization. They functioned to organize community life around the Christian calendar. *Cofradías* also provided welfare to the needy; organized religious fiestas, devotions, and processions; helped raise funds for the church; and attended to church maintenance. Some also cared for the sick and dying (Bushnell 1994:91–92; Kapitzke 1999; Meyers and Hopkins 1988). In St. Augustine, for example, *cofradías* were present in 1576, and by 1688 there were six *cofradías* active in the community. When the town was abandoned in 1763, there were eight active *cofradías* (Kapitzke 1999:24; Parker 1999).

Cofradías were also established at Indian missions, where symbols of the devotion were carried in processions and venerated. An Indian *cofradías* dedicated to Our Lady of the Rosary was present at San Luis de Talimali (Hann and McEwan 1998:120), and among the seventeenth-century Timucuans there were several *cofradías* of the True Cross (Hann 1996:160–161). These latter *cofradías* had twice-yearly "Processions of the Blood," during which banners of the true cross were carried and flagellation was practiced (Hann 1996:160–161). During the eighteenth century, there was a fervent devotion and *cofradías* devoted to Nuestra Señora de la Leche (Our Lady of the Milk) at the Timucuan mission of Nombre de Dios in St. Augustine (Bushnell 1994:89).

Symbols of religious organizations assume many forms, depending upon the devotions of the group to which they pertain. Many *veneras* included cross symbols, such as those of the Knights of Malta, Alcantara, and Santiago and the Orders of St. Dominic and the Inquisition, which were discussed earlier. Other groups used such symbols as the scallop shell (Knights of Santiago) or a sheep suspended by its midsection (Order of the Golden Fleece). Even more common were images of the figures or beliefs to which confraternities were devoted, such as various images of the Virgin Mary, the Christ Child, the Sacred Heart of Jesus, and the Immaculate Conception. Useful sources in English for identifying *venera* symbols include Duchet-Suchaux and Pastoureau (1996), Ferguson (1961), Heim (1978), Muller (1972), and the New Catholic Encyclopedia (1967).

A number of *veneras* have been recovered from Spanish colonial archaeological sites. Most of these *veneras* are based on the heraldic crosses of the military and religious orders; however, others (discussed later) represent saints and the Virgin Mary. Jesus as a child is also sometimes represented; for example, a small, gilded pendant figure of the Christ Child holding a scepter and globe was found at Santa Catalina de Guale in Georgia (1606–80) (Judge 1988:355). Similar pendants were used in Spain in the sixteenth and seventeenth centuries, often made in precious metals and enamels (Muller 1972:74, 128).

Jet *Veneras*

Jet, as discussed earlier and in Chapter 5, was widely held to have strong protective and

Figure 4.34. Sixteenth-century jet *veneras* or amulets from Santa Elena, South Carolina, 1566–87. *Left:* Scallop shell, Knights of Santiago *venera*, 1.25 cm by 1.06 cm. #38BU162G-225 (after South, Skowronek, and Johnson 1987:Fig. 95A). *Right:* Dominic cross form 1 cm square. #38BU162G-225 (after South, Skowronek, and Johnson 1987:Fig. 94). *Courtesy of the South Carolina Institute of Archaeology and Anthropology and Stanley South.*

magical qualities and is a common substance for amulets. The carving of religious objects in jet was a monopoly in Spain under the jurisdiction of the Church and was associated with the shrine of St. James (Santiago) at Compostela. The jet carvers at Compostela formed a guild during the fifteenth century, and their art reached a peak of development during the sixteenth century. It declined in the seventeenth century as the great pilgrimages to such shrines as Santiago's declined (Gómez Tabanera 1977:410; Proske 1938:92–93). Scallop shells, symbols, amulets, and images related to St. James are most commonly carved, as are a variety of objects with decorative and religious themes (see Osma y Scull 1916). Several small jet statues of Spanish saints are present in the collections of the Hispanic Society of America (D800, D801) (Osma y Scull 1916).

Jet *veneras* of the sixteenth century have come from the site of Santa Elena, South Carolina, where a jet scallop shell (the symbol of St. James) and a small, flat, carved piece that appears to have been a Dominic cross were excavated (South, Skowronek, and Johnson 1988:59–60; Fig. 4.34; see also Chapter 5). Similar carved jet objects have come from late-sixteenth-century contexts in St. Augustine, where a piece of a carved jet pendant

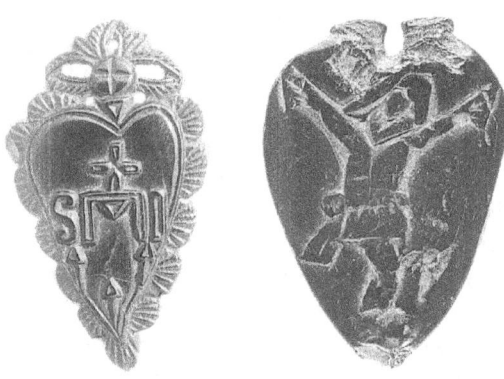

Figure 4.35. Jet devotional *venera* of St. Catherine of Alexandria. Image of St. Catherine and her wheel, ca. 1580. Height 2.7 cm. St. Augustine (SA-24-454, TU 23). FLMNH/CSA Collections. *Photo: James Quine.*

Figure 4.36. Sacred Heart *veneras*. Left: *Venera* with crucifix motif. Savataneta, Trinidad, 1689–1759. Right: *Venera* with Jesuit inscription, *El Conde de Tolosá* shipwreck (1724). Height 4.6 cm (see Borrell 1983:13). *Courtesy of the Museo de la Atarazana, Santo Domingo.* Height 3.0 cm. *Courtesy of Peter O'B. Harris. Photo: University of Florida Office of Instructional Resources.*

depicting St. Catherine of Alexandria surrounded by her wheel was recovered (Fig. 4.35) in association with a jet figure of Eros (Stanley Bond, personal communication, 1988; the latter figure is shown in Fig. 5.6).

A carved jet Sacred Heart *venera* with the inscription IHS was recovered from one of the 1724 Quicksilver wrecks (MCR Collections; Borrell 1983b:13; Fig. 4.36). This symbol is especially associated with the Jesuit Society of Jesus and did not become part of Catholic iconography until the second half of the seventeenth century (Morris 1967:820). A considerably less well carved and more worn jet Sacred Heart *venera* was found at the site of Savataneta, Trinidad, which was an Indian mission from 1689 to 1759 (Peter O'B. Harris, personal communication, 1996). Rather than the IHS symbol, the heart bears a carved image of a crucifix (shown in Fig. 4.36). Some of these jet pendants probably functioned as amulets in addition to or rather than devotional objects, given their often unusual forms and the popularity of jet for amulet pendants (see Chapter 5).

The letters "IHS," as noted, were also associated with the Jesuit order. These letters are

Figure 4.37. Holy name *venera*. Copper alloy. Quicksilver wrecks (1724). Diameter without loop 2.8 cm. *Courtesy of the Museo de la Atarazana, Santo Domingo. Photo: James Quine.*

associated with devotion to the Holy Name of Jesus and represent Jesus' initials in Greek (Fig. 4.37).

Veneras Devoted to the Virgin Mary

Some of the most remarkable and certainly the most numerous *veneras* found in the region are associated with devotions to the Virgin Mary, which reached their pinnacle with the seventeenth-century cult of the Immaculate Conception (discussed earlier). *Veneras* to Mary came to the Americas on Columbus's first voyage, as Bartolomé de las Casas recounts that Columbus obliged a member of the *Santa Maria*'s crew to wear a silver image of the Virgin Mary around his neck because the sailor had said "some mischievous and derogatory things against our Holy Faith" (Las Casas 1985:Book 1, Chapter 86:358). Many of the conquistadores were devotees of Mary and carried images of her constantly, attributing victories in the Caribbean and in Mexico to her intervention (Hodges 1991:8–9). The Marian devotion has remained fervent in Spanish America since that time (see, for example, Cipriano de Utrera 1947; Dávila Rodríguez 1989).

The most prominent cult and pilgrimage site in the Catholic Americas was that of the Virgin of Guadalupe. It was established in Mexico City in 1531, when an apparition of the Virgin appeared to an Aztec Indian named Juan Diego and imprinted her image on his cloak (Martí 1971). The hill at which she appeared, Tepeyacac, was also the home of the Aztec goddess Tonantzin, helping to forge a syncretic concept of female deity in Mexico. The image of the Our Lady of Guadalupe shows Mary standing on a crescent moon surrounded by golden rays and wearing a crown (Fig. 4.38). These elements were already in place in European iconography of the late fifteenth century and can be seen in several of Albrecht Dürer's early woodcuts (Hodges 1991:6; Strauss 1973). Many versions, although suggested to be

Figure 4.38. Nuestra Señora de Guadalupe. Image of the Virgin Mary as Our Lady of Guadalupe as she appeared on the *tilma* (garment) of Juan Diego in 1536 (www.sancta.org).

later than the original image, also include fleur-de-lis on the mantle and stars on the crown (J. Smith 1983:69–70).

Relatively few *veneras* or images of the Virgin Mary have been reported from sixteenth-century Spanish colonial contexts. One of the earliest, found near the site of Puerto Real in Haiti by William Hodges (Hodges 1991), was a reliquary pendant depicting the Virgin Mary (with iconography similar to that of the Immaculate Conception and the Our Lady of Guadalupe) on one side and a Latin cross on the other (Fig. 4.39). A small, copper-alloy

Figure 4.39. Reliquary *venera*-pendant with an image of Mary. Silver. Associated with Puerto Real (1503–80). Diameter 5.3 cm. Hodges Collection, Musée de Guahabá, Limbé, Haiti. *Drawing and photos courtesy of William Hodges.*

Figure 4.40. Late-sixteenth-century *veneras* to the Virgin Mary. *Left: Nuestra Señora de Nieva (Segovia).* Copper alloy. Height 2.9 cm. St. Augustine, Sisters of St. Joseph Convent collection (SA-35-1). Identified by Maria Brana, Museo del Pueblo Español, Madrid. *Photo: James Quine. Right:* Our Lady of Sorrows *venera*. Silver. Height 3.0 cm. Thomas Mound, Florida. South Florida Museum, #A5652. *Courtesy of Jeffrey Mitchem and the South Florida Museum, Tampa.*

venera of the Virgin of Nieva (Santa María de Nieva) was identified from a late-sixteenth- or early-seventeenth-century context in St. Augustine (María Brana, personal communication, 1985; Fig. 4.40). Santa María de Nieva had a popular cult in the region of Segovia, Spain, and her shrine is still extant there. Silver-mounted slate heart amulets bearing reference to her are present in the collection of the Museo del Pueblo Español (13.025), and another was collected during the nineteenth century by Hildburgh, who interpreted it as a women's lactation amulet (1951:438–439).

Many of the archaeologically recovered *veneras* to the Virgin Mary are made from precious metals. Part of a silver image of a sorrowful Madonna was excavated by Montague Tallant at the Thomas Mound site in southwest Florida (8HG7), which is thought to date to the sixteenth century (Fig. 4.40; Allerton, Luer, and Carr 1984). A similar image in size, construction, and composition was found at the early-seventeenth-century site of Santa Catalina de Guale in Georgia (Thomas 1988:100). This is a circular, ornately framed silver medallion with a pieta image of Mary holding Christ, just taken down from the cross (Fig. 4.41). Two side

 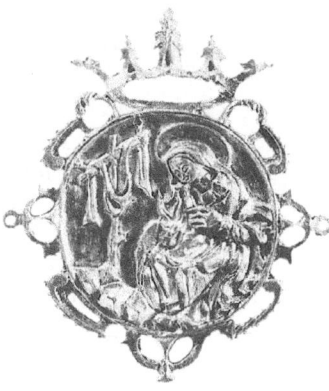

Figure 4.41. *Veneras* to the Virgin Mary: Santa Catalina de Guale (Georgia), ca. 1600–50. *Left: Sin Pecado* Immaculate Conception *venera*. Gold-plated silver with glass stones. Height 7 cm. AMNH #28.0/6509. *Right:* Silver *Pieta (Our Lady of Sorrows) venera,* AMNH #28.0/6503. *Courtesy of the American Museum of Natural History, the Edward John Noble Foundation, and David H. Thomas.*

loops are attached for suspension, indicating that it was intended to be worn against the wearer's skin or attached to clothing or on a hat rather than as a pendant (Baroja de Caro 1945:20; Walters Art Gallery 1979:485).

Immaculate Conception *veneras* are found most commonly on seventeenth-century sites for the reasons discussed previously. A small gold *venera* from the early-seventeenth-century Fig Spring mission site consists of the interlocking letters of "M" and "A" surmounted by a crown (Weisman 1992:152–153). This was a symbol of Mary, "Queen of Heaven and Immaculate" (Muller 1972:118–121). A more ornate Immaculate Conception *venera* was excavated from the mission burials at the site of Santa Catalina de Guale in Georgia (Thomas 1988:100; Fig. 4.41). This image of copper, enamel, and gold was 7 cm high, depicting the classic image of the Virgin of the Immaculate Conception surrounded by a four-lobed frame bearing the motto of the confraternity of the Virgin of the Immaculate Conception, "CONCEBIDA SIN PECADO ORIGINAL" (conceived without original sin) (see also, "Seventeenth-century Religious Medals"). A very similar Immaculate Conception *venera* made of gold and inlaid with topaz was recovered from one of the 1715 Spanish plate fleet wrecks (Cockrell 1981:i). This latter example was in an oval frame and was 7 cm high.

Immaculate Conception *veneras* were widespread in Spain, particularly during the seventeenth century, and they were often made of precious metal encrusted with gems. Muller (1972:122) illustrates several examples. The seventeenth-century examples Muller shows have the four-lobed frame shape of the Santa Catalina example rather than the oval shape from the 1715 plate fleet wreck.

An extensive collection of eighteenth-century *veneras* and religious pendants came from the wrecks of the 1724 Quicksilver galleons (Borrell 1983b; Peterson 1979a). Hundreds of small images of the Virgin of Pilar (Our Lady of the Pillar of Saragossa) were recovered from the 1724 Quicksilver wrecks in the Dominican Republic (Fig. 4.42; see also Fig. 4.12, center, for a jeweled example of this image). Similar figures documented in Spain date from the seventeenth and eighteenth centuries and are often made of precious metals, gems, and enamel (see Muller 1972:124; Oman 1967:405; Victoria and Albert Museum collections #s 468-1864, 341-1870, 342-1870). Those from the Quicksilver shipwrecks were in most cases made of brass, but gold examples were also recovered (Borrell 1983a, 1983c; MCR Collections).

The shrine of Our Lady of the Pillar (Nuestra Señora del Pilar) is in Zaragoza, Spain, on the spot where, according to tradition, she

Figure 4.42. Nuestra Señora del Pilar *venera*. El Conde de Tolosá shipwreck (1724). Copper alloy. Height 4.4 cm. *Courtesy of the Museo de la Atarazana, Santo Domingo. Photo: James Quine.*

appeared to St. James in A.D. 40 (Oman 1967:400). A major church in her honor was begun there in 1681, and the Cult of the Virgin of the Pillar was most popular after this time. Several towns in the Americas are named for her (Vargas Ugarte 1947:98), and the devotion is also reflected in the religious medallions from the 1741 wreck of *El Matanceros* that bear her image (Table 4.2; CEDAM Museum, Akumal, Yucatán).

Reliquaries

Reliquaries are containers for safeguarding or displaying the relics of saints. They have been in use since about the third century of Christendom, and their popularity spread rapidly after the discovery of the true cross by St. Helena in the second century and the discovery during the fourth century of the bodies of a number of early martyrs (see Farnik 1967). Relics and reliquaries are still widely used today by Spanish and other Catholics.

A relic is an object that was part of the person of a saint, touched or blessed by a saint, or closely associated with a saint during his or her life. Hair, wood, bone, teeth, and cloth fragments are typical relics. All relics, however, must be sanctioned by the Church in Rome, and Church doctrine holds that the relics serve to gain intercession with heaven by the saint whose relic is possessed (Farnik 1967). Relics do not, in and of themselves, have miraculous properties.

Personal reliquary containers have included great works of jewelry as well as very humble devices since the third century (for examples of precious personal Spanish reliquaries, see Dennis 1943:Figs. 21, 22; Evans 1970:74–75, Plates 12, 37; Lesley 1968:63–73; Muller 1972:63, 70–72). One of the earliest examples of what may be a reliquary from the Americas was part of a heart-shaped pendant locket of gilded copper alloy recovered at the site of La Isabela (see Fig. 6.20). A metal reliquary pendant with an image of the Virgin Mary was also found near Puerto Real,

Figure 4.43. Sixteenth-century rock crystal reliquary pendant. Puerto Real (1503–78). Length 5.5 cm. Hodges Collection, Musée de Guahabá, Limbé, Haiti. *Photo: James Quine.*

Haiti, (discussed earlier and shown in Fig. 4.39).

During the late fifteenth and early sixteenth centuries, personal reliquary pendants were frequently circular or oval. Throughout the sixteenth century, however, small reli-

Figure 4.44. Rock crystal reliquary used as a pendant. Detail from *Retrato do Doña Anna Vich* by Antonio Stella, sixteenth century. *Courtesy of the Museo Provincial de Bellas Artes, Valencia* (#496).

quaries in the form of books were popular. A book reliquary was recovered from the 1588 Armada wreck (Stenuit 1972:220). Made of gold and measuring 4 cm by 3 cm, it opened to reveal five circular compartments around a central rectangular compartment.

Another reliquary form popular in Spain during the second half of the sixteenth century was the rock crystal column, often embellished with gold, gems, and enamel work (see Rowe 1975:46; Muller 1972:70–72). A crystal column measuring 5 cm in length and enclosing a red, yellow, and blue image of a saint or monk was recovered from Puerto Real, Haiti (Fig. 4.43; Hodges Collection, Musée de Guahabá). The terminal ends of the column have been broken off, and it may originally have had a setting that permitted suspension as a pendant in the manner shown in Figure 4.44 (see also Dennis 1943:Fig. 21).

Rock crystal was also used in reliquary rings, which opened to reveal a cavity for the relic. A reliquary ring of rock crystal and gold was reported to have been recovered from the 1622 shipwreck of the *Atocha* (Schneider 1981:32).

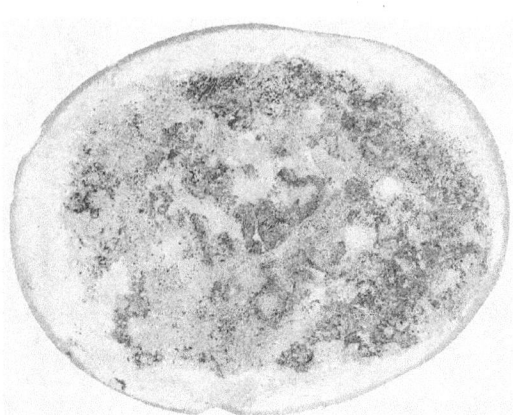

Figure 4.45. Glass reliquary cover, seventeenth century. Santa Catalina de Guale (Florida), ca. 1680–1702. Height 3.5 cm. 8NA41. FLMNH/CSA Collections.

Pendant crosses were used in Spain as personal reliquaries from medieval times until at least the middle of the eighteenth century (Muller 1972:61–62; Evans 1970:49–54). Caravaca crosses were especially used as reliquaries (see "Caravaca Crosses"). A brass reliquary Caravaca crucifix with a compartment on the back of the cross came from the 1724 Quicksilver wrecks (Peterson 1979a:869) and another came from a late-seventeenth-century Spanish mission context in Florida (Saunders 1988; Figs. 4.22, 4.23). Caravaca and other reliquary crosses were often engraved in the late sixteenth and seventeenth centuries with symbols of the Passion (representing the suffering and death of Christ), which include the crown of thorns, column and staff, monogram symbols of Mary, the IHS symbol, lances, nails, arrows, pincers, ladders, whips, dice, 20 coins, rods, and palm leaves (for other examples, see Thomas 1993:14; Victoria and Albert Museum collections #M.242-1975).

Framed reliquary pendants in a variety of materials were extremely popular during the seventeenth and eighteenth centuries (Muller 1972:124). These pendants often held an image of a saint or holy symbol rather than a physical relic (Muller 1972:124;

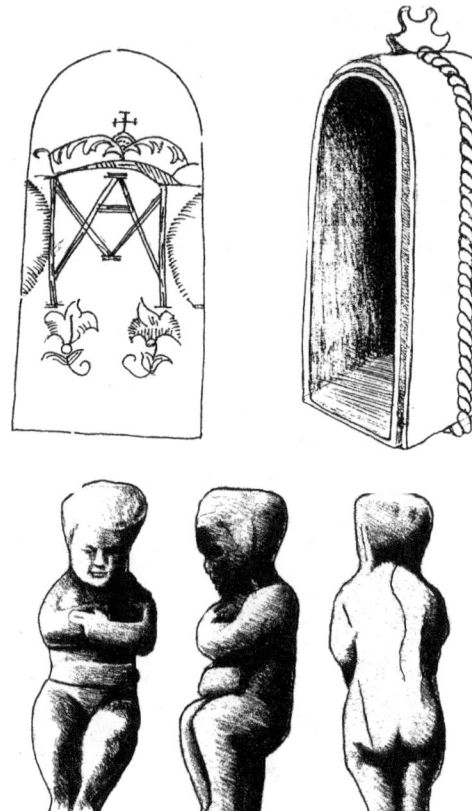

Figure 4.46. Reliquary pendant containing an image of the Christ Child. 1715 Florida plate fleet wrecks, 8SL17. Silver reliquary has anagram of the Virgin Mary on back and contained a ceramic Christ Child. Height of reliquary 4.25 cm. FBAR Lab #L5199. *Courtesy of the Florida Bureau of Archaeological Research. Drawing: Frank Gilson.*

Walters Art Gallery 1979:488). Thin, oval, or circular pieces of flat glass found at some mission sites (such as San Luis de Talimali and Santa Catalina de Guale on Amelia Island, Florida) were probably parts of reliquaries. The example shown in Figure 4.45 is gilded on one side, but the original image is lost.

A tiny, silver container (4.4 cm high) containing a ceramic figure of the Christ Child was recovered from a 1715 Florida shipwreck (Fig. 4.46). This was probably an elaborate

Religious Items

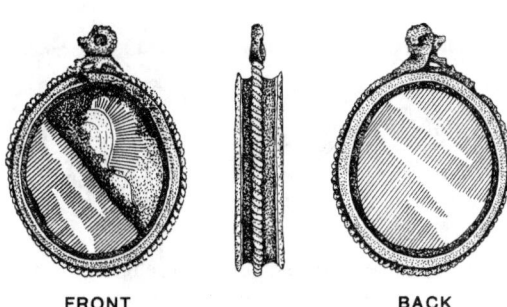

FRONT   BACK

Figure 4.47. Eighteenth-century pendant reliquary. Glass-covered copper image with frame, ca. 1725–88. St. Peter/Toulouse Street cemetery, New Orleans. Height including loop 6.1 cm. French or Spanish. Reprinted from Owsley et al. (1985). *Courtesy of the Louisiana Division of Archaeology, Baton Rouge, and Charles Orser.*

Figure 4.48. Mid-eighteenth-century reliquary pendant. Wound copper wire and mica enclosing plant or other fiber. Height 3.3 cm. St. Augustine (SA-36-4-282). FLMNH/CSA Collections. *Photo: James Quine.*

reliquary pendant that had lost its glass front. The back of the pendant was engraved with the crowned "M" and "A," symbolizing Mary, "Queen of Heaven and Immaculate."

Toward the end of the seventeenth century and into the eighteenth century, oval, round, or octagonal ornately cast frames for reliquaries were apparently mass produced in base metals and gilt (Muller 1972:127). Large numbers of these have been recovered from eighteenth-century shipwrecks (see Borrell 1983c:90). Examples of silver pendant lockets with glass faces that may have served as reliquaries were recovered from the 1733 Florida plate fleet wrecks (Skowronek 1982:135) and from the eighteenth-century parish cemetery in New Orleans (Owsley et al. 1985; Fig. 4.47).

Reliquary pendants of more humble materials have also been found on eighteenth-century Spanish colonial sites. A fragile pendant dating to the first half of that century was excavated in St. Augustine, Florida, comprised of a looped copper wire frame surrounding what appears to have been translucent layers of mica or shell that enclose a plant, fabric, or hair fiber (Fig. 4.48). Another probable reliquary pendant with a sheet of what appears to be translucent mica came from the *Matanceros* shipwreck. It has a simple circular frame of lead or pewter approximately 2.5 cm in diameter, enclosing the translucent center (CEDAM collections, Pablo Bush Romero Museum, Puerta Aventuras, Mexico).

At the risk of redundancy, it must be emphasized that these pendants with religious themes and reliquary functions probably also served as ornaments and jewelry. As noted, it is extremely difficult and probably incorrect to try and classify objects as either "religious" or "secular" in the meaning they had for their owners.

Seals and Stamps

Seals and seal impressions related to Church concerns have been occasionally recovered from Spanish colonial sites. The most famous of these are the *Agnus Dei* (Lamb of God) seals, usually impressed in wax from a papal candle sometimes embedded with dust from the relics of martyrs. They were inscribed with religious motifs, including but not limited to the flag-bearing lamb sitting on a book that symbolizes Christ. The seals are also inscribed with the name of the pope who blessed them and carry both indulgences and protection for their owners (Muller 1972:72–74).

Madame D'Aulnoy commented in 1679 that the Spanish women "carry upon their sleeves, their shoulders and all about their bodies *Agnus Deis* and little images" (1930: 203). In 1613, 576 *"rolletitas de cera pequeña"* were shipped to the Americas from Spain and may have been used for *Agnus Dei* seals (Table 4.1). Because the wax was fragile, special lockets or reliquaries were frequently used to hold and protect them (see Mason 1974:96; Muller 1972:72–74). Some of the reliquary pendants from colonial sites may, in fact, have been used to hold *Agnus Dei* seals.

Bishops and archbishops owned seals that bore their arms and were used to seal directives and official correspondence (for a discussion of ecclesiastical heraldry, see Heim 1978). The earliest seal found at a Spanish colonial site is from Concepción de La Vega in the Dominican Republic (Poladura 1980:16; Torres Petitón 1988). It is an almond-shaped bronze seal of Pedro Suárez de Deza, bishop of La Vega between 1512 and 1522. A clay impression of a seal depicting the Immaculate Conception (for which the town was named) was also found at the site (Poladura 1980:16).

Seals and seal impressions have also been recovered from seventeenth-century Spanish mission sites in Florida, including a brass bishop's seal from Santa Catalina de Guale on Amelia Island, Florida (Hardin 1986:83). The seal bears an image of the mission's namesake, St. Catherine of Alexandria (Fig. 4.49), and is thought to have been brought there from the earlier Santa Catalina de Guale mission in Georgia.

A clay tablet stamped on both sides with images of saints was recovered from the site of the Georgia Santa Catalina de Guale mission cemetery (ca. 1604–80). This may have been produced from a seal, possibly in anticipation of the missionaries' long journeys. The oval stamps depict St. Helen on one side and another saint believed to be St. Francis on the

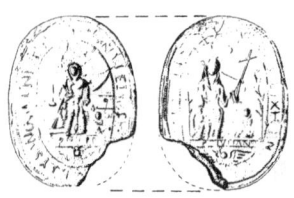

Figure 4.49. Seal impressions with religious motifs. *Left:* Seal impressions in clay. Santa Catalina de Guale, Georgia, ca. 1650. Height 7.1 cm. *Obverse:* Possibly St. Francis; *Reverse:* St. Helen. AMNH #28.1/1624. *Courtesy of the American Museum of Natural History, the Edward John Noble Foundation, and David H. Thomas. Drawing by Pauline Kulstad after Thomas (1988:100). Right:* Design on a brass seal depicting Saint Catherine of Alexandria. Height 9.4 cm. Excavated in the *convento* area of Santa Catalina de Guale mission on Amelia Island Florida (8NA41) (1683–1702) and probably brought from Santa Catalina de Guale in Georgia (1601–ca. 1683). FLMNH Collections. *Drawing by Pauline Kulstad after Hardin (1986:83).*

other (Thomas 1988:100). The inscriptions around the edge are eroded and indistinct (Fig. 4.49).

Papal seals were also used on bullae, apostolic letters containing some important religious pronouncement or decree made by the pope (such as definition of dogma concerning a Mystery). A bull is more solemn than a papal directive or brief, known as an encyclical. Lead seals were used on bullae from the sixth century until 1878. They bore the inscription of the pope who issued them on one side and the images of St. Peter and St. Paul on the other (Skeabek 1967). Bullae were often consigned to Franciscan friars embarking for America and the Philippines, and the seals themselves often carried benefits that were conferred on the owner, such as exemption from fasting (Santiago 1980:120).

Several identical examples of lead papal seals were recovered from the 1724 Quicksilver wrecks (Borrell 1983c:10; Santiago 1980:119–120; Peterson 1979a:870). Each has the name of Pope Innocent XIII (1721–

Religious Items

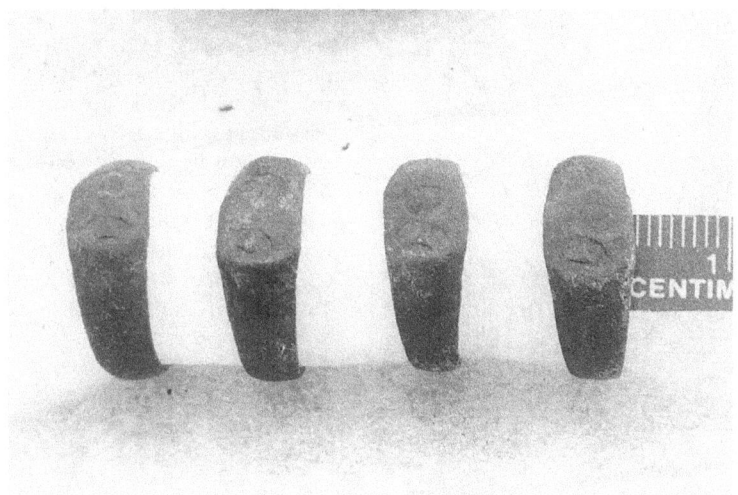

Figure 4.50. Fifteenth-century rings with Maltese cross motif on the bezel. Bezel, 9 mm by 8 mm. Copper alloy. Possibly used as trade items at La Isabela (1493–96). La Isabela, FS HP-1. Parque Nacional de La Isabela, Dominican Republic.

24) on one side and the image of St. Peter and St. Paul with a cross on the other.

Rings

Rings bearing religious motifs, which appear to have a primarily religious function apart from that of a reliquary or as jewelry, also occur on Spanish colonial sites. Some of the earliest in the New World are from the site of La Isabela, where a number of copper-alloy finger rings with flat, oval bezels bearing a raised Greek cross were recovered (Fig. 4.50). Other finger rings from La Isabela bore engraved images of the Virgin Mary (Deagan and Cruxent 2001a).

A more valuable specimen in gold came from the 1588 Armada wrecks. This was a gold band with a raised, circular bezel (4.7 cm diameter) engraved with the inscription IHS with a cross above the I (Stenuit 1972:177). This inscription is associated with the Jesuits, as well as with the Order of the Holy Sepulchre, and the ring may have belonged to a canon or priest.

More than a dozen silver finger rings were recovered from the seventeenth-century mission cemetery site at Santa Catalina de Guale in Georgia (Thomas 1988:99, 119;

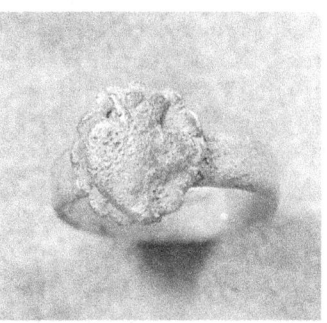

Figure 4.51. Seventeenth-century silver finger ring. Santa Catalina de Guale (Georgia). Ring with flame-crowned heart motif recovered from a mission burial. Bezel diameter 1 cm. *Courtesy of the American Museum of Natural History, the Edward John Noble Foundation, and David H. Thomas.*

Judge 1988:354). Several of these rings have a circular scalloped and fluted bezel, over which is imposed a heart shape crowned with a form that apparently represents flames (Fig. 4.51). These rings are quite distinct from the contemporary and later "Jesuit rings" found on French colonial sites (see Thomas 1988:119) and most closely resemble images of the flame-crowned Sacred Heart of Jesus. In Catholic symbolism, such hearts represent extreme religious fervor and are often an attribute of St. Augustine (Ferguson 1961:48–49; DeBles 1925:25). Other

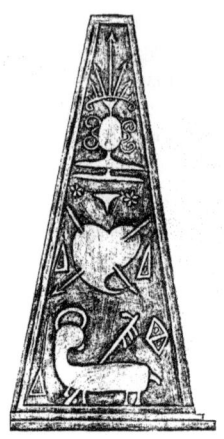 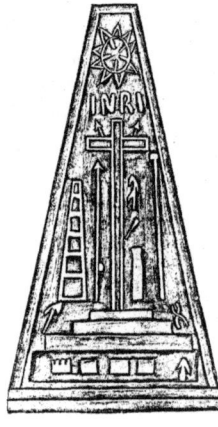 

Figure 4.52. Columns bearing religious motifs, 1622. Examples of pyramid-shaped silver columns with symbols of the Passion, possibly used as bases for religious figures or crosses or as taper holders. Columns have central vertical holes and range in height from 9.5 to 13.5 cm. Recovered from the 1622 shipwreck of *Nuestra Señora de Atocha*. Courtesy of the Florida Bureau of Archaeological Research. Drawings: Frank Gilson.

hearts are depicted as pierced by an arrow (Judge 1988:354), which is a Catholic symbol for contrition, deep repentance, and devotion under extreme trial (Ferguson 1961:49), attributes that could certainly describe the lot of the Florida missionaries. Still other rings are plain or have simple raised concentric circles as bezels and do not appear to have religious significance. Rings of the type found at the Santa Catalina mission in Georgia have not been reported from other Spanish colonial sites. Another type of devotional ring, the decade ring, was used in Europe from the fifteenth through the eighteenth centuries but is not reported from Spanish colonial sites. These rings have ten raised knobs or bumps around the band that could be used in repeating the rosary (see Bury 1984:46).

Columns

One of the most curious categories of objects from any Spanish colonial site is the group of artifacts from the 1621 *Atocha* shipwreck referred to as devotional columns (Florida Bureau of Archaeological Research collections, Tallahassee; Schneider 1981:33). More than 20 silver or silver-washed ceramic columns were recovered from the wrecks, ranging in reported height from 9.5 to 13.5 cm. The columns have small (4–6 mm in diameter) holes extending vertically through their centers. Some are four-sided and some three-sided, and all bear raised designs (Fig. 4.52).

Catholic symbols of the Passion of Christ occur on many of the columns, suggesting that the columns had a religious association. These symbols, discussed earlier under "Reliquaries," were commonly used on reliquaries during the seventeenth century and are also closely associated with the founder of the Jesuit order, Ignatius Loyola, who stressed devotion to the Passion as a means to daily perfection (Mead 1967).

The function of the columns remains unknown, but the central sockets suggest that they may have been intended as reliquaries or as bases for reliquaries. It is also possible that they were intended to serve as taper holders. No other examples have been reported from New World sites.

Copper-Alloy Stars

Small, copper-alloy star-shaped objects are found regularly on sites of the sixteenth century, including St. Augustine, Santa Elena (Radisch 1988:145–151), Puerto Real (Ewen 1991:95; Willis 1984:193), and Concepción de la Vega. They measure between 2.0 and 4.5 cm in diameter and have a central perfo-

Figure 4.53. Copper-alloy star. Possible tip for a flagellation lash, ca. 1565. Maximum diameter 13.2 mm. St. Augustine, 8SJ34, FLMNH Collections.

Figure 4.54. Flagellant's star-tipped lash. Detail from Antonio Salas's *Mary Magdalen in Meditation* (1826). *Courtesy of the Museo Filanbanco, Quito, Ecuador.*

ration and from four to ten points (Fig. 4.53). Some of these stars from Caribbean sites were cut from four-maravedí pieces minted in Santo Domingo.

In his study of copper-alloy stars from Santa Elena, William Radisch (1988) has offered several possible functions of these objects. He documents the use of similar stars in sixteenth-century Spanish imagery as clothing ornaments, as grommets for fastening studs to leather saddlery and leather jerkins, as religious symbols, and as parts of scourges used for flagellation (Radisch 1988:145–151). At least some of the stars found on Spanish colonial sites may have had religious significance, either as self-flagellation implements or as badge-symbols.

Self-flagellation was practiced as a form of penitence and piety in Spain beginning in the twelfth century (see Toke 1910). The Flagellants, or Disciplinants, were organized into lay societies throughout Spain and the Americas (Toke 1910). Although the pinnacle of the practice occurred in the thirteenth century, it was still very much alive in late-seventeenth-century Madrid, where it combined religious, social, and amorous elements. An appalled Madame D'Aulnoy supplied a secondhand description of Spanish flagellation in 1687:

> Tis an unpleasant thing to see the disciplinants . . . fancy a man coming so near you that he'll cover you all with his blood. This, it seems is one of their [Spaniards'] pastimes; there are certain rules by which to discipline themselves handsomely, and masters to teach the art, just as to dance and to fence . . . on the back of their waistcoats they have two great holes upon their shoulders. . . . They give themselves most terrible cuts and slashes upon their shoulders, from whence runs streams of blood; they present themselves before their mistress's window, and there with wonderful patience lash themselves. The lady, through the lattice of her chamber, sees this fine sight and by some sign encourages her gallant to flay himself alive, and lets him know how very kindly she takes this action of his. When they meet a handsome woman they whip themselves after such a rate as to make the blood fly upon her. This is esteemed as a particular civility, and the lady acknowledges and thanks them for it. (1930:223–224)

High-ranking individuals sometimes made processions through the streets with many attendants, and D'Aulnoy goes on to describe an encounter between two rival Knights of

Discipline who marched with their entourages into the same street. "Each of then would have the upper hand, and neither of them would yield it . . . armed only with this instrument of penance, (*they*) begin a most terrible battle. After they have used a little discipline about one another's ears, and covered the ground with the ends of their whip cords, they fall to downright fisticuffs like a porter" (1930:225).

Among the "ends" of the whipcords may have been the small stars of the type known archaeologically. The implements used for flagellation occasionally appear in paintings of the period, which usually show star-shaped tips on the leather scourges (Fig. 4.54; see also Radisch 1988).

Flagellant societies were introduced into the Americas with the Spaniards of the sixteenth century (Espinosa 1911:636; Toke 1910), often through high-ranking officials and nobles. The first royal governor of Santo Domingo, Nicholas de Ovando, was a member of the Third Order of Penitents (Ciprano de Utrera 1947:23), which was a Franciscan organization devoted to penitent flagellation (Espinosa 1911:636). It is possible that some of the star-shaped objects from sixteenth-century Spanish American sites were used in this way.

Stars are also important in Catholic symbolism, and some of these objects could have functioned as badges reflecting this. Various images of the Virgin Mary, including the Immaculate Conception and the Queen of Heaven, are depicted with twelve stars in a halo around her head, and stars were a symbol of these devotions (Ferguson 1961:44, 95–96).

Chapter 5
Amulets and Magical Items

Like religious objects, amulets and magical items provide a rare and unusually well documented material glimpse into Spanish colonial ideology and worldview. An "amulet" is an object believed to possess magical powers of protection against a variety of ills or the power to bring about a favorable outcome for its wearer. This power is attached to the object itself as one of its intrinsic qualities rather than being conferred on the object by a higher governing force (for example, the Catholic Church). Nor are amulets used as intermediaries between their owner and a higher power, as are the objects discussed in the preceding chapter as "religious" items.

Talismans also have magical powers but are intended to bring about a specific event or end (such as the use of a copper bracelet to relieve arthritic pain or a garlic clove to ward off vampires) rather than to provide the generalized protection provided by amulets. Just as it is often difficult to distinguish an individual "religious" use from an individual "magical" use in either material culture or the archaeological record, it is equally difficult to distinguish talismanic from amuletic uses of such objects. Unless an object is independently documented as a talisman, the term "amulet" will be used throughout this chapter.

Witchcraft, spells, and demons were urgent concerns in Europe during the centuries of Spanish colonization of the Americas, and these concerns were undoubtedly transferred to the Americas. Many of the beliefs and practices related to witchcraft in the sixteenth and seventeenth centuries, documented in such works as the *Compendium maleficarum* (written in Milan in 1598 by Francesco Guazzo, an Ambrosian father), reflect the close connections between religion and magic that were characteristic of medieval life. Both of these beliefs and their material expressions have persisted into modern times in many parts of Europe and the Americas, particularly in rural areas (for discussions of this phenomenon, see Caro Baroja 1973; Gómez Tabanero 1977; Hildburgh 1950–51; Maloney 1976; Meaney 1981). This is particularly pronounced in the Iberian peninsula and in Ibero-America, where many people maintain strong traditions of amulet use and where amulets with origins in the colonial era and earlier can be bought today in markets throughout the region (see Caro Baroja 1973; Limón Delgado 1981; Maloney 1976; Salgado Jerrera 1977).

Magic and the superstitious use of amulets have long vexed the Catholic Church. In 1525, for example, the Holy Roman Emperor and king of Spain Charles V issued a largely ineffective *pragmatica* forbidding the use of profane jet amulets against the evil eye (Hildburgh 1914:209). Nevertheless, as noted in the previous chapter, the material distinctions between religion and magic apparently remained quite fluid in much of Spain and Spanish America. Amulets were frequently combined on necklaces or chains with such religious objects as devotional medals and reliquaries (see Figs. 4.1, 5.1). Madame D'Aulnoy, writing in 1679 from travel accounts, described their use among Spanish

Figure 5.1. Sixteenth-century Spanish children's amulets. Detail from Pantoja de la Cruz's *La Infanta Ana* (1602). Museo del Monasterio de las Descalzas Reales, Madrid, #00612229. *Copyright © Patrimonio Nacional.*

women: "They wear girdles all of medals and relics. There are diverse churches that have not so many" (1930:202). Examples of such chains dating from the colonial era to the present can be seen in the collections of the Museo del Pueblo Español (for example, Cat. #11.587; see also Berges 1984:25,71; Contreras y López de Ayala 1951).

Father Guazzo, writing in 1598 about Church-approved methods for avoiding demons and witches, noted that protection could be gained by "pious writings or sacred amulets hung around the neck, such as the Apostles' creed . . . but for this remedy to be lawful St. Thomas says that there must be two conditions: first, that nothing superstitious is mingled with the sacred words, as that one should put faith in the shape or color of the letters . . . ; and the second is that the wearer's intention must be righteous"(Guazzo 1988:180). He also decries "[s]uperstitious folk" who use saints' images as magical items rather than intermediaries with the divine (Guazzo 1988:160–162). The profound failure of such injunctions in the Americas, at least, is reflected in the numerous clenched fist–shaped amulets known as *higas* (discussed later) that have been found archaeologically in both burials and domestic contexts at the seventeenth-century Franciscan and Dominican *conventos* in Santa Fe la Vieja, Argentina (Zapata Gollán 1988:114, 122–125; see also Fig. 4.1).

Because of the preoccupation with magic and the nature of spells, the intended functions of amulets and talismans—like those of religious objects—are often well documented in Spanish treatises dating to the colonial period and earlier (for example, Caro Baroja 1974; Castañega 1946; Guazzo 1988; Morales 1977). The persistence of many of these beliefs in parts of the modern world furthermore offers an unusual convergence of documentary, ethnographic, and material cultural evidence on which to base archaeological interpretation.

Unfortunately, however, most American historical archaeologists are largely unaware of the nature and meaning of specific amulets and materials, and most examples of amulets have not been reported as such in the archaeological literature (an important exception to this is Zapata Gollán 1988). It is also often difficult to identify fragments of amulets; for example, jet, amber, and carnelian beads were popular components not only of amulets but also of necklaces and rosaries. It is nevertheless important to be aware of the many possible functional roles of these items and substances in the lives of the colonists.

Some of the most useful sources for the identification and discussion of Spanish amulets include a series of articles by the folklorist W. L. Hildbergh (1906, 1913, 1914, 1915, 1938, 1940, 1941, 1942, 1951) and the publications of the Museo del Pueblo Español (Alarcón Román 1987; Baroja de Caro 1945). These sources should be consulted for lengthier discussions of the identification and symbolic meaning of amulets not included in this chapter.

Amulets fall in general into three functional categories: those that protect against the evil eye, those that provide protection against other ills, and those that assist in the basic life cycle events of reproduction and death. The power of an amulet is derived through both the material from which it is made and the form that it assumes. These materials and forms have specific meanings and are generally combined to suit specific needs (see Alarcón Román 1987; Zapata Gollán 1988; Table 5.1).

Amulet Use in Spain

The origins of ancient Spanish amulet forms (and probably of many of concomitant beliefs) can be traced to precedents in the classical societies of Greece and Rome and to Islamic traditions (Hildburgh 1906:459–460). The famous *higa* closed-hand symbol (discussed later) was found widely throughout Italy (where it is known as the *mano fica*) and is identical in form to documented Roman and Phoenician amulets (Gómez Tabanero 1977; Hildburgh 1906:458). The common open-hand symbol, also referred to as the "hand of Fatima," was a Muslim symbol used to ward off the evil eye (Gómez Tabanero 1977:397).

The evil eye (*mal de ojo*) was the most common evil against which amulets were intended to protect. This concept is both ancient and widespread, with a history going back thousands of years in the Mediterranean region (Maloney 1976; Elsworthy 1895; Salillas 1905). It refers to envious or malevolent glances from those who might covet another's fortune and wish one ill or from inherently evil people. Such glances and intentions are thought to cause a wide variety of illnesses and afflictions, including the dreaded *fascinación,* or enchantment. Children, being young and relatively weak, are thought to be more susceptible to the evil eye, and thus many amulets against it are designed for and worn by children.

Evil air (*mal de aire*) is a less common but nevertheless widespread source of evil against which amulets are also used. This is provoked by the emanations, intended or not, of certain people, places, or circumstances. Cats who have recently given birth, pregnant women, poisonous animals, air from a tomb, stars, and dirty places are examples of some sources of evil air. It can also be transmitted by contact with anything ugly, dirty, abnormal, mysterious, or socially impure. Specific beliefs about the causes of evil air vary regionally within Spain, but the concept is consistent (Alarcón Román 1987:15; Salillas 1905).

Amulets were (and are) worn most commonly by those who were in need of protection or were considered vulnerable. This traditionally included children, women, sick people, and animals (Alarcón Román 1987; Hildburgh 1906, 1951:430–432). Children, as noted, were considered to be particularly vulnerable to both illness and the evil eye, and all classes of society used amulets to protect children during the centuries of colonial dominion in Spanish America (Figs. 5.1, 5.2). The Spanish linguistic scholar Covarrubias, writing in 1611, cited the following items as useful in protecting children: wild boar tusks; coral, jet, and crystal fragments; amber beads; clay figures of St. Teresa; the written name (*firma*) of St. Teresa; Caravaca crosses; "eagle" stones; jet *higas* with crescent moon symbols; a Christ Child figure with outstretched arms in the form of a cross; chestnuts encased in silver; and mercury (Gómez Tabanero 1977:403; Baroja de Caro 1945:8).

The *higa,* however, seems to have been the amulet most often associated with children. Writing in 1679, Madame D'Aulnoy described an account of an undernourished baby in the Spanish countryside who "had above a hundred little hands like those of

Table 5.1. Common Spanish Amulets and Their Attributed Benefits

Substances

Amber	Aids in and protects from problems of gestation, birth, and lactation in women; aids teething in infants; protects from poisonous things; protects against witches and spells.[1, 3]
Agate	Women's amulet; helps lactation (white agate); prevents problems of the breast; stops hemorrhage (red agate); cure for snakebite and scorpion poison; in powdered form can clarify vision; taken by mouth can produce sterility in women (seventeenth century).[1]
Beryl	Water in which beryl was soaked can cure stomach problems;[2] also said to encourage love.[3]
Carnelian	Stops excessive menstrual flow; protects against dropsy and protects kidneys; cures hemorrhoids and dysentery.[1, 3]
Coral	Protects against evil, especially children; restores the strength of blood; staunches nosebleeds; aids in teething and the prevention of tooth decay; quells vomiting; protects against lightning, whirlwinds, and storms.[1, 3]
Garnet	Lightens the heart and relieves sadness; protects from and releases air corrupted by peste.[1]
Jasper	Greenish with colored veins; stops the flow of blood, brings down fevers, protects against dropsy.[2]
Jet	Strong protection against evil eye and evil in general. Causes demons to flee; can cause abortion; can detect virginity.[1, 2, 3]
Rock crystal	Protects against evil eye; when ground and eaten, causes mothers' milk to flow; relieves thirst—all depending upon form in which it is cut.[2]
Serpentine	Long, thin forms protect against lightning; heart-shaped forms are a symbol of Christ and guard against evil.[3]
Silver	Enhances and strengthens the qualities of substances that it encases;[2] finger rings of silver protect against epilepsy.[3]

Objects

Badger paws, claws	Protect against evil eye.
Beads	Used singly or in combination to acquire the benefits of the stones from which the beads are made, see "Substances."
Bells	Ward off evil spirits, see "Sonajeros."
Bezoar stone	Protects against rabies.
Caravaca cross	Protects against lightning and fire; protects against rabies; aids in birth.
Chestnut	Relieves and protects against earaches, hemorrhoids, epilepsy; protects, relieves skin ailments such as mange, impetigo, and erysipelas (acute skin infection usually affecting the face that was widespread and dreaded before advent of antibiotics).
Chupador	Child's amulet to promote dentition and protect against witches.
Fish	Enhances fertility; aids children in learning to speak.
Heart	Symbol of Christ, protects against evil; also used as a love amulet when carried over the heart; carried to gain success in enterprises and undertakings.
Higa (Figa)	Protects against evil eye.
Horns, animal	Protects against evil eye, especially children; protects against bites of poisonous animals.
Lunar crescents	Aids lactation; promotes fertility; protects against *alunamiento* (moon madness).
Pineapples	Fertility symbols.
Shells	Women's fertility symbols.
Sonajeros sirens, lizards, lions with bells	Protects women and children against the evil eye and enchantment.
Teeth, animal	Protects against evil eye; assists in children's teething; aids lactation
Trochus shell operculum	Aids in vision problems; relieves headache; promotes fertility.

Sources:

[1] Morales 1977

[2] Arfe 1678

[3] Alarcón Román 1987

Note: Sixteenth through nineteenth centuries, after sources indicated.

Figure 5.2. Eighteenth-century child's amulets and *chupeta*. Detail from a Mexican *casta* painting, ca. 1760: From *Spaniard and mestizo woman, castiza. Courtesy of the Museo de América, Madrid.*

jointed babies hanging about his neck and on all sides of him. I asked his mother what this meant. She answered me, this was good against *evil eyes* . . . (which) looking on anyone with an evil intention strike them with such languishment that they become lean like skeletons; and her child, she told me, had been struck in this manner and the common remedy is these little hands" (1930:158).

Amulets governing women's reproductive activities were also especially widely used. White-colored stones (*cuentas de leche*) were used in various combinations in amulets intended to aid in lactation (see Hildburgh 1951). This belief was so common that the Real Academia Española's *Diccionário de la lengua Español* includes *"cuenta de leche"* as "a little ball of chalcedony which lactating women customarily wear at the neck, in the belief that through it they attract milk to their breasts" (1939:380).

Agate and carnelian beads, either round or lozenge shaped, were particularly favored by women not only because of their red color representing blood and life forces but also because of their association with St. Agatha (Agata). Agatha was a martyr tortured by having her breasts severed, and she is invoked by Spanish women against diseases of the breast.

People who habitually worked in dangerous situations also used amulets, such as the seahorse amulets known among horsemen, to protect themselves from hazard (Baroja de Caro 1945:13). Table 5.1 lists some of the most common Spanish associations between amulets and protective qualities.

Amulets were frequently used in combinations that probably had special significance (see Alarcón Román 1987:16; Baroja de Caro 1945; Hildburgh 1906, 1914, 1915). Women and children generally wore them quite visibly, often in combinations and frequently in attractive settings that also served ornamental functions. Like religious items, amulets were made both in valuable forms of precious metals and gems and in humble materials. Those recovered archaeologically generally fall into the latter category (Figs. 5.3, 5.4).

Late-sixteenth- and early-seventeenth-century shipping records provide an indication of the kinds and quantities of amulets being shipped to the Spanish American colonies at that time (Table 5.2). Among them were thousands of *higas*, most commonly made of jet but also made of glass and crystal. Some were set with stones. Charms or amulets for women (*diges de mujeres*) were imported for use in necklaces, and trinkets of jet and glass may have had amuletic properties. The extremely large quantities of coral in branches, beads, and pieces that were imported to the colonies undoubtedly also served in amulets.

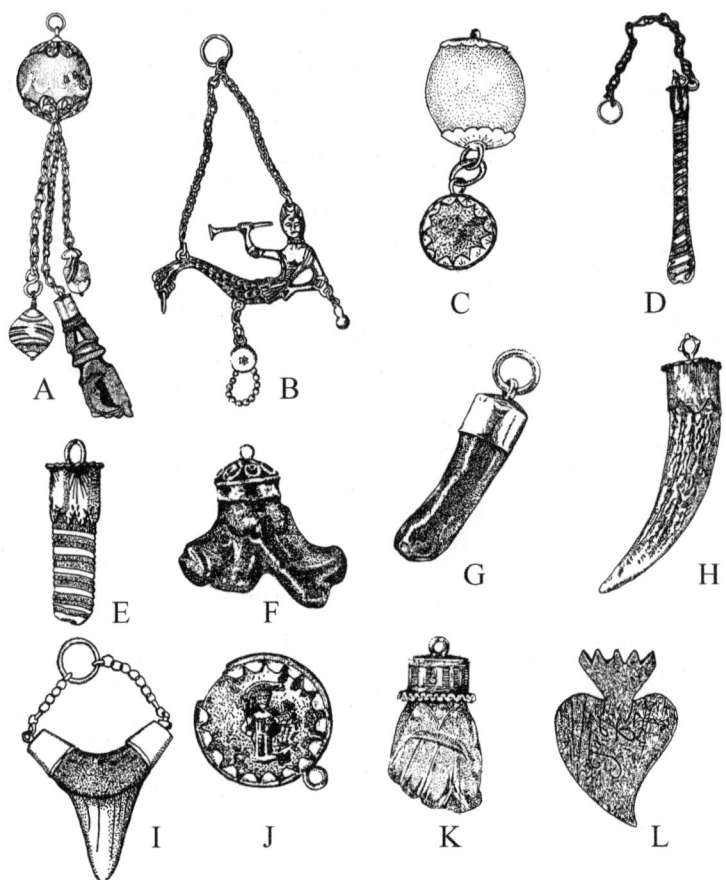

Figure 5.3. Varieties of characteristic Spanish amulet forms. A. Compound amulet. Glass bead with three pendant elements including an agate bead, a jet *higa* (left-handed with fingers engraved on one side and crescent moon with a human face on the other), and a jar-shaped agate bead. Overall length 230 mm; *higa* length 75 mm; large bead diameter 35 mm. Museo del Pueblo Español #8.855. B. Mermaid (*Sirena*) pendant, possibly used as *sonajero*. Silver, 120 mm by 55 mm. Museo del Pueblo Español #4.815. C. Bead amulet, heliotrope bead with bezoar stone mounted in silver. Length 23 mm. Museo del Pueblo Español #1.985. D. Glass *chupador* (child's teething aid and protection against the evil eye). Spiraled clear, blue, red, and white glass with silver cap and chain. Length of glass 155 mm. Museo del Pueblo Español #9.578. E. Glass *chupador*. Clear glass with red and white spirals, silver cap, and chain. Length 35 mm. Museo del Pueblo Español #10.425. F. Double coral branch in silver, 35 mm by 13 mm. Museo del Pueblo Español #7.809. G. Single coral branch in silver, 55 mm by 14 mm. Museo del Pueblo Español #1.840. H. Deer horn point with silver cap. Length 90 mm. Museo del Pueblo Español #7.810. I. Fossil shark tooth in silver mount, 30 mm by 45 mm. Museo del Pueblo Español #1.768. J. *Medalla de Santa Elena*. Byzantine bronze coin set in silver. Museo del Pueblo Español #1.534. K. Higa. Left-handed *higa* of rock crystal with silver cap, 48 mm by 20 mm. Museo del Pueblo Español #7.377. L. Bone heart with crown, 85 mm by 59 mm. Museo del Pueblo Español #4.722. *Drawings by Pauline Kulstad after examples in Alarcón Román 1987.*

Figure 5.4. Spanish colonial amulets and ornaments recovered archaeologically. *Top row, left to right:* White glass set in copper-alloy rim (no number), diameter 1.3 cm; white glass set in scalloped silver rim, ca. 1780 (SA-7-4-592), diameter 1.1 cm; trilobed jet bead or ornament fragment, ca. 1580 (SA 24-24); oval agate bead (SA-24-385); Carnelian bead (SA-24-118). *Bottom row, left to right:* Copper-alloy floral grommet, not an amulet; pierced copper-alloy fragment (SA-24-27-17-52); cap holder for stone, ca. 1750 (SA-7-4-498); copper-alloy ring with pink glass stone (SA-39a-11-27); gilded copper-alloy fish (SA-7-4-497), length 2.5 cm. St. Augustine, FLMNH/CSA Collections. *Photo: James Quine.*

Materials with Amuletic Properties

Certain materials such as jet or agate are believed to carry protective properties in and of themselves and can in that sense be considered as amulets. They are, however, often formed into distinctly religious symbols or *veneras* that carry Church sanction and are thus at the same time religious (see Chapter 4).

A wide variety of organic materials and semiprecious stones are believed to have special magical and protective properties and have been used in Spanish amulets since medieval times (Table 5.1). Colonial-era Spanish beliefs about organic and lithic gems were explicated in Gaspar de Morales's 1598 treatise, *Libro de las virtudes y propiedades de las piedras preciosas* (Morales 1977). Stones acquire their properties by virtue of their color, shape, or unusual markings and are typically associated with the colors of vital life fluids: red and white.

Jet (*azabache*), a black fossil resin, is the most common of these materials and was discussed in Chapter 4 as a popular medium for religious *veneras* and crosses. Jet has been carved in Compostela and elsewhere in Spain since early medieval times not only in religious themes but also in a variety of amulets and ornamental items (see Gómez Tabanero 1977:386–401; Figs. 5.5, 5.6). It was thought to be especially strong and efficacious in repelling the evil eye. Jet was also believed to have the ability to make demons flee, to cause pregnant women to abort, to cause menstruation to begin, and to produce virginity (Alarcón Román 1987:27; Morales 1977).

Jet carving was carried out most actively at Compostela, where scallop shell jet *veneras* of Santiago de Compostela (St. James) were made by the hundreds of thousands for dis-

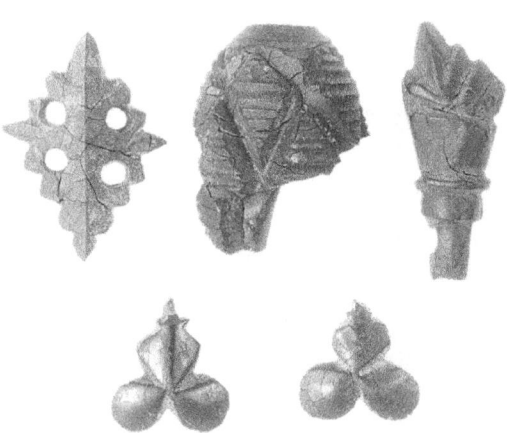

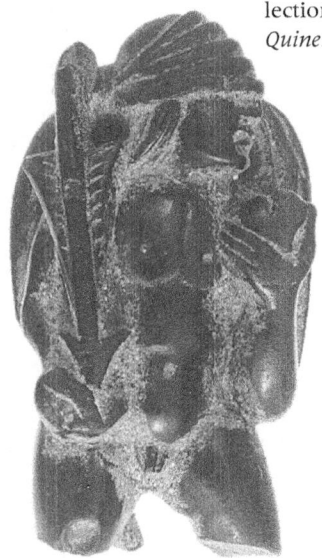

Figure 5.6. Jet amulet of Eros. Jet image of Eros, ca. 1580. Height 3.3 cm. St. Augustine (SA-24-454). FLMNH/CSA Collections. *Photo: James Quine.*

Figure 5.5. Jet amulets. *Top row, left to right:* Carved and pierced cruciform jet ornament, last quarter of the sixteenth century, height 2 cm (SA-24-TU2); large carved jet bead, last quarter of the sixteenth century (SA-24-385); left-handed jet *higa*, ca. 1720–40 (SA-16-23). *Bottom row:* Trilobed jet beads or pendant element, last quarter of the sixteenth century (SA-24-24). All St. Augustine. FLMNH/CSA Collections. *Photo: James Quine.*

tribution to pilgrims. The jet-carving guild was centered at Compostela, and many kinds of amulets were produced there along with quantities of beads and other ornamental items. Other centers (most notably in Asturias, where excellent sources of jet are located) also had jet-carving industries beginning in the late sixteenth century. These arose in response to the decline of Compostela, as pilgrimages lost popularity and fewer people made their way to the shrine (Gómez Tabanero 1977:408–410).

The most common jet amulets are *higas*; however, many kinds of beads, crosses, scallop shells, and saints' images were also made. A stylized Santiago cross carved from jet and superimposed on a central square cartouche of jet was recovered from a sixteenth-century context in St. Augustine, and a similar cross reminiscent of the Dominic cross was found at sixteenth-century Santa Elena (Fig. 4.5; see also South, Skowronek, and Johnson 1988:158–161). Amulets were occasionally made from fragments of jet mounted in metal.

Coral, another material used in both religious and magical items, is also believed to have a variety of beneficial properties. Possibly because red coral is close to the color of blood, it is believed to restore blood, strength, and health. It is also attributed with protection against lightning flashes and whirlwinds, saddle sores, and stomach problems (Morales 1977:304).

Amber beads are frequently found as parts of amulets (Alarcón Román 1987:65; Museo del Pueblo Español collections #1.987) and have apparently been used as amulets since Greek and Roman times (Meaney 1981:10–11; Alarcón Román 1987:29). Morales attributed amber with the ability to resist venom and repel venomous animals, produce milk in lactating women, make birth easier, provoke menstruation, and break spells (1977:304).

Semiprecious stones in extant or recently recorded amulet collections (such as those of the late W. L. Hildburgh and the Museo del Pueblo Español) are usually of quartz: agates, jasper, rock crystal, chalcedony, carnelian, and heliotrope. Table 5.1 shows some of their commonly attributed properties.

Animal products such as shells, mother-of-pearl, teeth, claws, horns, fish otoliths, bezoar stones (renal calcifications found in deer), badger paws, and stag beetle jaws are also known to have been used as amulets. They were usually framed or placed in a collar of metal and suspended.

Vegetable remains were also sometimes used as amulets, but these are less likely to be recovered archaeologically than amulets of more durable materials. Chestnuts (*castaña de Indias*) and unusually shaped seeds and nuts mounted in silver are recorded (see Alarcón Román 1987; Hildburgh 1906, 1914, 1915, 1942, 1951). Other common but perishable amulet materials include red cloth, figures made of bread dough, bits of wheat, garlic cloves, and invocations and saints' names written on paper. Several such items were often kept in small, embroidered bags known as *evangélios* (Alarcón Román 1987; Salillas 1905:84–87).

Although materials occurring in nature are the most common amulet substances, human-made materials are also used, often in combination with natural materials. A variety of metal and glass amulets occur in forms believed to provide protection against diverse ills (for example, lunar crescents, Caravaca crosses, hearts, beads, and *higa* hands).

Forms of Amulets

The possible combinations of forms and materials for amulets are virtually endless, and this discussion will include only those that occur most frequently in existing collections or that have been recovered archaeologically from Spanish colonial sites.

Higas

By far the best-known and most commonly recognized amulets are the small, clenched fists known as *higas* (used more commonly in Spain) or *figas* (used more commonly in Italy). These amulets (rarely exceeding 2 cm in height) are found throughout the Mediterranean and Latin America (Figs. 5.7–5.10). The term *"higa"* entered common use in Spain during the first half of the sixteenth century, and these amulets were referred to before that time as *"manos de azabeche, crystal,"* and so forth (Gómez Tabanero 1977:402). They are believed to provide powerful protection against the evil eye and, as discussed earlier, were especially used to protect very young children. Such Spanish painters as Sanchez Coello, Pantoja de la Cruz, and Velásquez, as well as the eighteenth-century *casta* paintings of Mexico, illustrate the use of *higas* among aristocratic and royal children (see García Saiz 1989; Fig. 5.2).

Higas were not, however, restricted to use by children or to protection from the evil eye. That they were considered useful for general health in the seventeenth century is attested by the prolific seventeenth-century Mexican writer Siguenza y Góngora's refrain: *"Buen orina y buen color, Y tres higas al doctor"* (Good urine and good color, and three *higas* to the doctor) (quoted in Zapata Gollán 1988:15).

Jet was (and remains) the favored material for *higas,* but coral, glass, crystal, metal, shell, amber, bone, and other materials were also used. Jet *higas* were shipped to the Spanish colonies in enormous quantities during the colonial period (Table 5.2; Blair 1960:261; Borrell 1983:261; Museo de la Atarazana collections, Santo Domingo). The costliest *higas* were those of jet garnished with stones or metal, and the least costly were small, undecorated *higas* of jet and of bone. Zapata Gollán records much more valuable *higas* from seventeenth- and eighteenth-century inventories in Argentina, including *higas* of gold and

Figure 5.7. Bone *higa*, ca. 1566. Carved bone stained with black pigment. Length 2.2 cm. Outer side of fist is carved with a representational eye symbol. 8SJ31-F74 (Fountain of Youth Park site). FLMNH Collections.

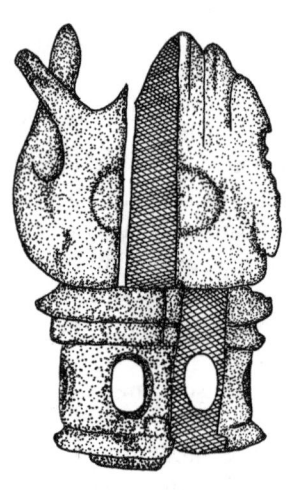

Figure 5.8. Complex double jet *higa* from Santa Elena, 1567–87. Length 1.49 cm. Santa Elena, South Carolina. #38BU162G-241A. South, Skowronek, and Johnson (1988:Fig. 94). *Courtesy of the South Carolina Institute of Archaeology and Anthropology and Stanley South.*

Figure 5.9. Jet reliquary *higa* from Santa Fe la Vieja, Argentina. Sixteenth-century *higa* found with a Spanish burial at the Convento de San Francisco in Santa Fe, Argentina. A notch in the dorsal side of the *higa* contained a quartz crystal enclosing a relic thought to be of St. James (Zapata Gollán 1988:49–50). Length 3.95 cm. Museo Etnográfico de Santa Fe, Argentina #32.365. *Drawing by Pauline Kulstad, after Zapata Gollán 1988.*

coral decorated with pearls, diamonds, and emeralds (1988:47–48).

Higas do not appear in Spanish colonial archaeological contexts or in shipping records until the second half of the sixteenth century. None have been reported at Puerto Real (1503–78), Concepción de la Vega (1496–1562), or Nueva Cádiz (1515–41), and the earliest reported example comes from the 1565–66 campsite of Pedro Menéndez de Áviles in St. Augustine, Florida (Fig. 5.8). An elaborate *higa* was also found at Santa Elena, South Carolina (1566–87; another site established by Menéndez), from a post-1574 context (South, Skowronek, and Johnson 1988:159–161; Fig. 5.7).

Several scholars have suggested that *higas* made during the sixteenth century were most frequently left hands and that those of

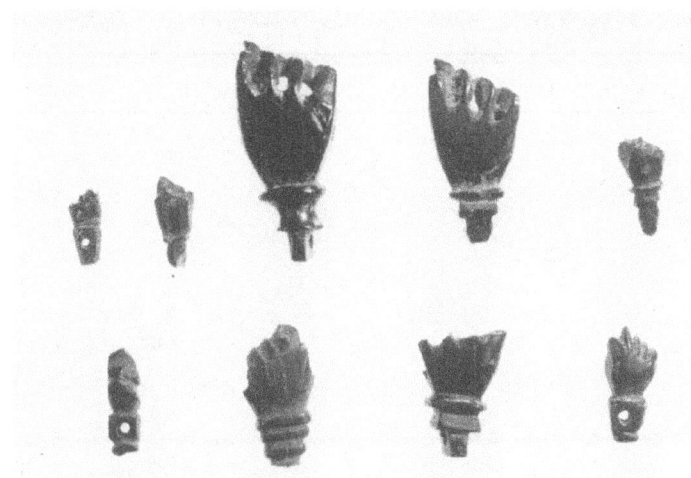

Figure 5.10. Seventeenth-century jet *higas* from San Luis de Talimali, ca. 1650–1700. Height of top center *higa* 3.1 cm. *Top row, left to right:* FS 6947, FS 6929, FS 5043, FS 7291, FS 7291. *Bottom row, left to right:* FS 7286, FS 7446, FS 6940, FS 7286. *Photo courtesy of Florida Bureau of Archaeological Research, the San Luis Historical and Archaeological Site, and Bonnie G. McEwan.*

the seventeenth century were primarily right hands (Caro Baroja 1945:16; Osma 1916:1). During the sixteenth and earliest decades of the seventeenth century, *higas* were often elaborately carved, sometimes combining the clenched fist with carved flowers, lunar crescents, hearts, and fleur-de-lis. One of these complex *higas*, probably made at Compostela, was that excavated by South at the site of Fort San Felipe in Santa Elena (Fig. 5.7). This was a triple, left-handed *higa* figurine measuring 1.5 cm in height with a suspension loop at the wrist (see South, Skowronek, and Johnson 1988:158–159). Hildburgh reports a *higa* with four small hands dating to the same period (1914:210), and an extensive collection of similarly complex *higas* can be seen in the collection of the Instituto de Don Juan de Valencia in Spain (see also Osma 1916).

A jet reliquary *higa* was excavated from a late-sixteenth- or early-seventeenth-century burial at the Convento de San Francisco in Santa Fe Viejo, Argentina. This complex carving combined the amuletic properties of jet and the *higa* with a Catholic relic in a Catholic burial (Zapata Gollán 1988:50–51; Fig. 5.9). Many of the symbols carved on *higas* had Catholic religious significance, particularly related to Christ and Mary. Some sixteenth-century *higas* had figures of saints or the Virgin carved at the wrist and were referred to at the time as *santiagos de higas* (Alarcón Román 1977:27). This combination of religious motifs with the profane *higa* hand may have been a response to the 1525 *pragmatica* forbidding the use of jet amulets against the evil eye (Hildburgh 1914:209).

Higas produced after the early seventeenth century tend to be simpler and less adorned than sixteenth-century examples. Those from the seventeenth-century mission site of San Luis de Talimali (Fig. 5.10), the 1641 *Concepción* wreck (Borrell 1983b:65), and eighteenth-century contexts in St. Augustine are very similar in their simplicity. Jet *higas* have been recovered from several eighteenth-century shipwreck sites, including the 1741 *Matanceros* and the 1724 Quicksilver wrecks (Borrell 1983c:60; Santiago 1980:121). They were most commonly of jet, although rock crystal *higas* and a number of glass *higas* mounted on stems were also recovered (Museo de la Atarazana collections, Santo Domingo). Glass *higas* are listed in the shipping records of goods bound for the colonies during the late sixteenth century, and Hildburgh (1906:459–460) has reported them in Spain. *Higas* are quite common today in the markets of most Spanish Caribbean countries and are made in a wide variety of materials

Table 5.2. Amulets and Amuletic Substances Shipped to the Spanish Colonies 1583–1613*

	1583	1590	1592	1603	1613	Total
ITEMS						
Higas						
AZABACHE DORADO CON PIEDRAS ILUMINADAS (gilded jet with sparkling stones)		2,736				2,736
AZABACHE, BASTARDAS CHICAS (jet, crude and small)			1,212			1,212
AZABACHE (jet)		324	948	3,042	1,800	6,114
AZABACHE DORADOS (gilded jet)		36				36
AZABACHE COMUNES (common, of jet)			48			48
AZABACHE MONTAN (jet, in a mounting)			72			72
AZABACHE PEQUEÑO (small jet)			78		264	342
CRISTAL	20					20
HUESO (bone)		60				60
VIDRIO (glass)				432		432
HIGUITAS DE AZABACHE (small higas of jet)	36					36
HIGUITAS DE VIDRIO			150			150
Medals, Trinkets, Charms						
BRINQUINOS DE VIDRIO (trinkets of glass)				120		120
JUGUETES DE VIDRIO (toys or trinkets of glass)			300			300
MEDALLAS DE VIDRIO Y AZABACHE (medals of jet and glass)			48			48
MEDALLAS DE ALQUIMIA (gilded medals)			240			240
MEDALLAS DE AZABACHE (jet medals)			12	216		228
PRIZAS DE ANIMALEJOS Y HIGAS DE AZABACHE (bunches of odd-looking creatures and jet higas)			100			100
VENERAS DE AZABACHE (jet veneras)	6,040					6,040
Bells						
CASCABELES (rumbler bells)					15,840	15,840
CASCABELES DANZANTES (bells of dancers)					432	432
CASCABELES DE TODOS TIPOS (rumbler bells of all kinds)					3,168	3,168
Total	6,096	3,156	3,208	3,810	21,504	37,774
SUBSTANCES						
AZABACHES Y CORAL EN UNA CAJITA (jet and coral in a little box)		2				2
CORAL			3,000	4,000		7,000
CORAL DE CEVADILLA (horn coral)			4,000			4,000
CORAL FALSO (imitation coral)		30,000	1,000	21,000		52,000

Table 5.2. continued

	1583	1590	1592	1603	1613	Total
CORAL FALSO CONTRAHECHO DE PALO (imitation counterfeit coral of wood)					30,000	30,000
CORAL MENUDO (bits of coral)			4,000			4,000
CORAL REDONDO (round coral)			1,000			1,000
CORALES FALSOS DE VIDRIO (imitation coral of glass)					3,863	3,863
EBANO GUARNECIDOS (decorated ebony)		24				24
PANECILLOS DE AZABACHE (small loaves of jet)				2,540		2,540
PIEZAS DE AZABACHE (pieces of jet)	44	12				56
Total	44	30,038	13,000	27,540	33,863	104,485

Sources: *Registros de la Casa de Contratación*, Archivó Generál de las Indias, Seville (microfilm copy in the P. K. Yonge Library of Florida History, University of Florida, Gainesville)

1511—*Contratación* #1451
1523—*Contratación* #1079
1583—*Contratación* #1080
1590—*Contratación* #s 1089, 1092
1592-93—*Contratación* #1099
1603—*Contratación* #1143
1613—*Contratación* #s 1159, 1160

*1511–26 no amulets recorded in Contaduría records

including jet, wood, amber, coral, glass, silver, copper, and semiprecious stone. The modern *higas* are also right-handed and have a more elongated and narrow wrist than do the colonial examples.

Beads as Amulets

Few types of amulets are as easy to recognize as *higas*. Many others have several components that, when separated from their constituent parts, may appear to be simply beads or ornaments. One of the most common amulet forms in the collections of the Museo del Pueblo Español is, in fact, a series of two to eight stone beads connected by short links of chain (Fig. 5.11; see also Hildburgh 1951:432). These most frequently incorporate white stones (*cuenta de leche*) such as white quartz, glass, or mother-of-pearl and such reddish stones as amber, agate, and carnelian (Alarcón Román 1987; Hildburgh 1940:432–433). These white and reddish stones are associated in Spain with women's amulets, intended to aid in lactation and other reproductive functions (see Hildburgh 1951:430–434). Agate beads of rectangular, lozenge, or conical shape in particular were thought to provide protection against breast tumors and mastitis (Alarcón Román 1987:23, 64).

Some of the beads used for amuletic purposes have small, metal caps from which they are suspended (see Fig. 5.3D for an eighteenth-century example of such a cap from St. Augustine), and others simply have a hole through which chain links are passed. Many isolated beads of amber, agate, carnelian, and jasper are found on Spanish colonial sites

Figure 5.11. Woman's bead amulet. *Cuenta de leche* (mother-of-pearl) and amber with tin links. Length 4.3 cm. Museo del Pueblo Español #1.987. *Reproduced from Alarcón Román (1987) with permission of the Museo del Pueblo Español, Madrid.*

Figure 5.12. Bead types used as amulets. *Clockwise from left:* Spherical amber bead, late sixteenth century. Diameter 2.23 cm. Florida (8PI8; 7 Oaks Mound). Faceted agate bead, ca. 1750–75 (6 facets). Length 2.6 cm. St. Augustine (SA-7-4-HTC). Faceted spherical amber bead, sixteenth century. Diameter 1.32 cm. Loring Collection #20924-HTC. Faceted spherical amber bead, sixteenth century. Diameter 0.95 cm. FLMNH #20924-HTC. Faceted red and white agate bead. Length 2.65 cm. Nueva Cádiz (1515–41) A1117-HTC; FLMNH Collections. *Photo: University of Florida Office of Instructional Resources.*

dating through the entire time range of the colonial period (Fig. 5.12; see Deagan 1987:180–182). Although it is usually not possible to determine the original function of these beads with great confidence, the possibility that they served as women's amulets should not be ignored.

Other semiprecious and nonprecious stones were also commonly used in amulets, including rock crystal, heliotrope (bloodstone), serpentine, beryl, garnet, *piedra de águila* (hematite), andalucita, and slate (see Table 5.1 for amuletic associations of some of these stones). These are most often flat and formed into geometric shapes (oval, round, square, rectangular, trapezoidal) or hearts and are frequently mounted in a silver frame with a characteristic toothed design (Fig. 5.3C).

This particular kind of serrated, denticulate frame is also a common characteristic of seventeenth-century popular jewelry (Angela Franco, personal communication, 1988). A ring made of a trochus shell encased in a serrated silver frame of this kind is included in the Victoria and Albert Museum's ring collection, attributed to the seventeenth century (#M249-1962; Bury 1982:205). The form appears to have persisted into the nineteenth century, however, and occurs on rings bought by Hildburgh at the turn of the twentieth century in Granada (1906:466–467). No examples of this amulet form have been reported from Spanish colonial sites in Florida or the Caribbean; however, stones that may have once been encased in frames have been found (FLMNH/CSA collections, SA-24-358, SA-24-388).

Hearts

Heart-shaped ornaments could have religious or amuletic significance, depending on form, material, and context. The asymmetrical Sacred Heart *venera* is especially associated with the Jesuit Society of Jesus and did not become part of Catholic iconography until the second half of the seventeenth century (Morris 1967:820; see Chapter 4). It represents the love of Christ and is extended through amuletic use to human love. Heart amulets (presumably to inspire and protect love) occur in a wide variety of materials, including silver, bone, glass, and jet (see, for example, Figs. 5.3L, 5.13). They are also worn in Spain to help achieve triumph in business or in love (Alarcón Román 1987:86, 96).

Glass heart shapes have been recovered from seventeenth- and eighteenth-century contexts in St. Augustine and may have served as parts of an amulet. Several undated examples of glass heart amulets exist in the Museo del Pueblo Español collections, one of which is formed by two flat, heart-shaped pieces between which is a fragment of cloth (Alarcón Román 1987:97).

Shells

Shells have consistently been used as amulets in Spain, and cowrie shells, olive shells, cockle shells, and various univalves are common (see Alarcón Román 1987:32–33; Hildburgh 1906:465–466). Shells are a feminine symbol, believed to provide protection from the evil eye as well as protection from many diseases (Alarcón Román 1987:33; Hildburgh 1906:466).

Shells mounted with metal rings for suspension have been recovered archaeologically from Spanish colonial sites and probably served as amulets (Fig. 5.14). In St. Augustine, they occur most often in contexts dating to after 1780. The examples from St. Augustine were shells that occur in Florida and the Caribbean and were probably fabricated into amulets in the colonies.

Other shell amulets have drilled holes rather than metal caps for suspension. Examples from St. Augustine include a small, perforated West Indian top shell (*Trochidae tegula lividomacualta*) with its outer coating removed and four drilled holes for attachment (Deagan 1976:72; see Chapter 8, Fig. 8.21) and a flat circle of clam shell perforated for suspension (Shephard 1983:93).

The operculum of the trochus shell is a common amulet in Spain (Alarcón Román 1987:33; Hildburgh 1906:466), often set in a

Figure 5.13. Glass heart. Clear glass, possibly used as an amulet and/or *lagrimario* (receptacle for wept tears). Maximum height 2.4 cm. Mid-eighteenth century, St. Augustine (SA-7-7-20). (See Deagan 1987:155.) FLMNH/CSA Collections. *Photo: University of Florida Office of Instructional Resources.*

Figure 5.14. Eighteenth-century shell pendant amulets. *Left:* Checkered nerite (*Nerita tessellata*) with loop suspension. Length 2.2 cm. St. Augustine, HSAPB-RC. *Right:* Common marginella (*Prunus apicinum*) with copper alloy loop, late eighteenth century. Length 1.6 cm. St. Augustine (SA-34-2). FLMNH/CSA Collections. *Photos: James Quine.*

serrated frame and suspended. Known there as *"haba de Sta. Lucia"* (St. Lucy's bean), it is believed to be efficacious in protecting against migraine headaches. Its eyelike appearance is also believed to provide protection from problems of vision, and St. Lucy is invoked in general for eye problems (Alarcón Román 1987:33; Amades 1951; Hildburgh 1906:465). Although no framed or mounted trochus shells have been reported from Spanish colonial contexts, trochus shell operculi have been recovered from these sites and may, in fact, have been used in amulets.

Figure 5.15. Possible horn amulet. Deer antler with ground end and polished tip to receive a cap, mid-eighteenth century. Length 7 cm. Although this could also have served as a handle for an awl, it illustrates the typical form of the horn amulet. St. Augustine (SA-7-4-165). FLMNH/CSA Collections. *Photo: University of Florida Office of Instructional Resources.*

Animal Claws, Teeth, and Horns

Animal claws and teeth—particularly those of deer and wild boar but also of crabs and wolves—were mounted for suspension and used widely as amulets (Figs. 5.3H, 5.15). These often have a shape similar to lunar crescents, which have powerful amuletic significance in Spain (see Hildburgh 1942; see also "Metal Amulets"). Alligator teeth capped with gold and metal were exported from Asia to the Spanish colonies through the Manila galleon trade (Schurz 1939:33), probably as amulets, and crocodile teeth amulets have been recorded in Spain (Hildburgh 1914:212). Teeth, claws, and horns found on archaeological sites should be examined for evidence of wear or mounting.

Horns or horn fragments of deer, goat, and other ruminants were believed to be effective protection against poisonous snakes and animals, as well as the evil eye (Caro Baroja 1950). In Spain, the deer is thought to be the mortal enemy of serpents (Alarcón Román 1987:35). The Museo del Pueblo Español collections contain a number of goat and deer horn amulets, both unmodified and carved, some mounted for suspension and others simply drilled. A deer horn tip with a modified, socketed end was recovered from an eighteenth-century context in St. Augustine (SA-7-4-165) and may have served as an amulet (Fig. 5.15). A curved bear claw—unusual in the criollo sites of St. Augustine—also came from the site.

Glass Amulets

Several kinds of glass charms and shapes with amuletic properties were imported to the Spanish colonies, including *higas,* hearts, charms, trinkets (*juguetes*), and medallions of glass (Table 5.2, Fig. 5.13).

Chupadores were slender, elongated glass drops with a circular section used as "suckers," or pacifiers, for children (Figs. 5.2, 5.3 D, E). They are believed to aid in both teething and repelling the evil eye. *Chupadores* were generally made of glass, often incorporating spiral designs in red, white, and/or blue. Most examples in the Museo del Pueblo Español and the Hildburgh collections are mounted for suspension in a metal cap and measure about 10 cm in length (Alarcón Román 1987; Hildburgh 1915:405–406). Some *chupadores* were combined with suspended bells, *higas,* and other amulets, presumably to provide stronger protection (see Hildburgh 1915; Fig. 5.3A). No *chupadores* have been reported from colonial sites; however, fragments of polychrome, unperforated glass with a circular section may be fragments of these types of amulets.

Glass was also formed into various shapes with amuletic significance and mounted in metal frames. The most common of these are glass hearts, discussed previously. Hexagonal glass shapes are also known; for example, a blue glass amulet of this sort was purported in the seventeenth century to aid in vision problems as well as in restraining carnality (Alarcón Román 1987:57).

Metal Amulets

In addition to being used to make frames and mounts, metals were used to fashion specific amulet forms. One of the commonest of these in Spain was the lunar crescent (Fig. 5.16). Lunar crescents were, and in some areas still are, believed in Spain to provide protection against the evil eye and against *alunamiento*, a certain kind of lunar influence that is similar to the evil eye (Oxea 1965; Hildburgh 1942:73). They were made in a very wide variety of both solid and openwork crescent forms, often combining anthropomorphic elements, *higas*, celestial elements, flowers, and religious motifs in elaborate designs (see Alarcón Román 1987; Hildburgh 1942). They were tied on infants' cribs and clothing, worn by women, and also used as amulets for animals (Alarcón Román 1987:38; Oxea 1965). No elaborate lunar crescents like those in the Hildburgh and the Museo del Pueblo Español collections have been reported from Spanish colonial sites, but seventeenth- and eighteenth-century metal toothpicks assumed this form and may have had amuletic significance (see Chapter 11).

A curious pendant that may have been an amulet was recovered from a stream adjacent to the eighteenth-century free black fort and town of Mose, near St. Augustine (Deagan and MacMahon 1995). This was a small, apparently hand-crafted silver disk engraved with a crude image of St. Christopher (the patron of travelers) on one side and a mariner's compass rose on the other. It may have had amuletic significance for one of the black watermen who lived at the site during the second half of the eighteenth century (Fig. 5.17).

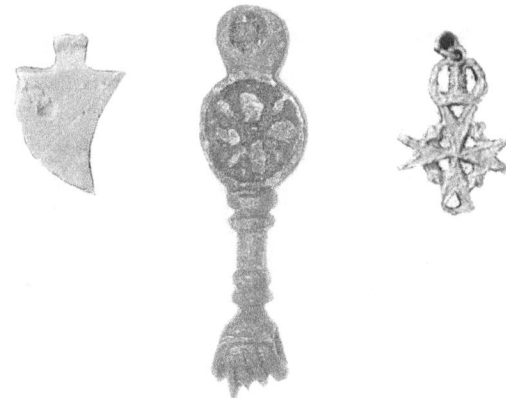

Figure 5.16. Metal amulets from St. Augustine. *Left:* Lead claw or lunar crescent pendant, ca. 1680. Length 1.8 cm (SA-30-3-369). *Center:* Copper-alloy *higa*, with fist clenched to hold an object. Length 4.5 cm. HSAPB-AO. *Right:* Copper-alloy St. Andrew cross link, ca. 1780. Length 2 cm (SA-7-7-251). FLMNH/CSA Collections. *Photos: James Quine.*

Sonajeros (rattles) were common children's amulets, comprised of a metal figure of an animal or mythological creature from which small bells were suspended (Figs. 5.3B, 5.18). One of the most common *sonajero* amulet forms was that of a *sirena* (mermaid)(see Alarcón Román 1987:35–36; Caro Baroja 1952; Fig. 5.18), which was believed to help protect people against enchantments and spells as well as the evil eye (Elsworthy 1895:356–359). A siren, according to myths known since classical times, was half woman and half animal and was able to enchant men (such as Ulysses) with her beauty and her singing.

Other *sonajero* amulet forms include lions and lizards, also with small bells attached. Lizards were believed in Spain to be poisonous and enemies of women, and lizard amulets were used to protect against and cure *mal de ponzona*, a disease characterized by inflammation and eruptions of the skin (Bouza Brey 1949).

Figure 5.17. St. Christopher medallion or amulet. Handmade silver, St. Christopher on one side; mariner's compass rose on the other. Diameter 2.1 cm. Found at Ft. Mose, 8SJ40. St. Augustine. F. E. Williams Collection. *Courtesy Jack Williams. Photos: James Quine.*

Figure 5.18. Mermaid (*Sirena*) *Sonajero* form. Silver, 28.5 cm by 9.3 cm. Similar to Museo del Pueblo Español collection #1.686 (after Hildburgh 1903:464).

Intact *sonajeros* have not been identified or reported on Spanish colonial sites; however, some of the small rumbler bells (1–3 cm in diameter) found on sites might have been for that purpose. Bells of this type were also used commonly in Spain, suspended from children's clothing as protection from evil spirits and evil sounds (*mal de oido*) (see Chapter 7). Those in the Museo del Pueblo Español collections range from 2.6 to 5.0 cm in height.

A curious Spanish metal amulet form is the *Medalla de Santa Elena*, widespread in Spain but unreported from colonial sites (Fig. 5.3J). These are actually Byzantine coins of the eleventh through thirteenth centuries, concave in form and mounted in silver (see Alarcón Román 1987:37–38). Imitations of Byzantine coins, mounted and used in the same way, are also known. According to testimony given in Inquisition trials, these amulets or talismans were used in the seventeenth century to make love spells and conserve fidelity (Alarcón Román 1987:37). They are also attached to the body against the skin to cure convulsions.

The Caravaca cross, discussed and illustrated in Chapter 4, was used as an amulet. As an amulet, it is believed to provide special protection against lightning and rabies, as well as protection during childbirth in some parts of Spain (Alarcón Román 1987; Hildburgh 1940).

Metal amulets in the shape of a fish

(Fig. 5.4) were believed to have beneficial influence in fertility and reproduction and were also attached to infants' clothes to help them begin talking (Alarcón Román 1987:36). Fish were common and popular symbols in Mexican folk jewelry and were made both in solid cast pieces and in series of flexible plates allowing the fish to wiggle (see Davis and Pack 1963:9, 99).

Summary

Many aspects of Spanish and Moorish belief systems persisted in Spain and Spanish America into postcolonial times, particularly those related to the evil eye. The material amulets that expressed these ideas and provided at least emotional protection against various threats persisted as well and are found on Spanish colonial archaeological sites. They are particularly important in documenting the presence of children (coral, *higas, chupadores,* and *sonajeros*) and women (agate and white stone beads).

A few amulets, such as *higas*, are easily recognizable by their form. Other items, such as the beads, bells, horns, shells, claws, and mineral substances that were often parts of amulets, are not. Although even careful contextual analysis is sometimes inadequate to determine the specific use of such items in past households, we should consider the possibility that archaeological examples may have been related to amulets.

Chapter 6
Popular Jewelry

Virtually all people since Paleolithic times have worn some form of jewelry or personal adornment, making use of a vast array of natural and human-made items. In the Spanish colonial Americas, precious and popular jewelry were both imported and locally produced and were available in some form to most members of colonial society. This chapter concentrates on archaeologically recovered popular jewelry rather than on fine or precious jewelry. "Popular jewelry," as used here, refers to that portable, personal, nonprecious adornment that was generally available to a person of average means. Today such ornaments would be considered costume jewelry or trinkets. Although popular jewelry is rarely preserved in museum collections, it does occur regularly on archaeological sites from the period from 1500 to 1800.

Precious jewelry, in contrast, rarely occurs on archaeological sites. When it does, it is under very specific depositional circumstances, such as disaster, burial, or caching prior to abandonment. Normal processes of loss and discard do not generally apply to precious objects such as these, and most archaeologists working on Spanish colonial terrestrial sites do not often encounter precious jewelry.

Shipwreck sites, however, frequently do contain quantities of precious metals and stones, often in the form of jewelry. Highly publicized finds of precious jewels by commercial salvors on Spanish shipwrecks have occurred in recent years; however, these finds are not included in this study unless they illustrate a morphology typical of popular jewelry. Not only do these items fall outside the scope of this chapter, but a great many of these archaeological specimens are also sold to private holders and removed from both scholarly study and public access and appreciation.

Because inexpensive adornment followed the form and decoration of the more valuable pieces (using humbler materials and poorer artisanship) and also often preserved styles that were fashionable decades earlier in fine jewelry, the study of popular jewelry in the Spanish American colonies draws by necessity on the corpus of scholarly research on fine jewelry. A great deal of information about fine jewelry is available from primary sources, including existing collections, documents, and paintings. These have been extensively treated in both scholarly and popular sources, the most important of which is Patricia Muller's *Jewels in Spain, 1500–1800* (1972), a basic reference source for Spanish fine ornament that should be referred to by any archaeologist who encounters jewelry in a Spanish colonial site. Spanish jewelry is also treated and illustrated in a number of other useful publications—although generally not with an exclusive emphasis on Spanish pieces—and these will be referred to throughout this chapter. These sources draw for the most part on important nonarchaeological Spanish jewels surviving in private, public, and church-owned European and American collections (British Museum 1976; Bury 1982; Cruz Valdovinos and Escalera Ureña 1993; Dennis 1943; Evans 1970; Lesley 1968; McConnell 1991; Oman 1967, 1968; Tait and Gere 1978; Walters Art Gallery 1979).

In contrast to the attention given to fine jewelry, very little was recorded or written specifically about popular jewelry in the past. Furthermore, popular jewelry is rarely preserved in museum collections unless it was derived from preliterate ("ethnographic") cultures. One of the few sources apart from archaeological collections for the study of Spanish folk and popular jewelry is the jewelry collection of the Museo del Pueblo Español in Madrid. Although most of the pieces are undated, they still constitute an important comparative collection of popular jewelry from the eighteenth and nineteenth centuries (Baroja de Caro 1947, 1952; Berges 1984; Contreras y López de Ayala 1951).

Other geographically peripheral but nevertheless useful comparative sources for popular jewelry in the Spanish colonies of Florida and the Caribbean can be found in the literature devoted to Mexican and South American colonial silverwork. Some of the most accessible and helpful include Anderson (1956); Davis and Pack (1963); Fernandez, Munoa, and Rabasco (1984); Oman (1968); and Taillard (1941). Much of the popular jewelry from Mexico and South America was the work of Native American artisans and combined elements and motifs of pre–Hispanic American jewelry with Spanish traits. This American-Hispanic ornamental tradition was, and still is, widely used in the Native American and mestizo cultures of South and Central America. Although the native populations of Florida and the Caribbean disappeared very early, the criollo and mestizo peoples of the region were undoubtedly influenced to some extent by the crafts and products of South and Central America and particularly by those of Mexico.

Because of the inextricably pervasive nature of religious belief in all aspects of Spanish colonial life, much of the precious and popular jewelry used in Spain and in the Spanish colonies was designed with religious symbols and motifs. As emphasized in earlier chapters, it is therefore not only inappropriate but also impossible to rigidly segregate "religious," "magical," and "ornamental" functions in many of these pieces. This is especially true of jewelry dating to the seventeenth century, when a long series of *pragmaticas* from the Church and the crown strictly limited the personal displays of extravagance and luxury that had reached a peak in the silver-and-gold-rich sixteenth century (see Muller 1972:105–106). Because of this, the chapters on religious items (Chapter 4) and amulets (Chapter 5) should also be consulted for discussions of archaeologically recovered jewelry.

Jewelry in Colonial-Era Spain

Jewelry was worn by both men and women during the sixteenth and seventeenth centuries and in its popular forms by nearly all social classes. Certain items of jewelry were associated exclusively with feminine use, such as hair ornaments, pendant earrings, and bracelets. Other pieces, such as chains, most rings, or religious motif pendants, cannot be confidently assigned a gender-specific function.

Trends in precious jewelry of the colonial era are discussed in detail by Muller (1972) and are only briefly summarized here as a general framework for interpreting stylistic development in popular jewelry. By the time Spanish colonies were established in the Americas, Renaissance style, influenced by classical antiquity and based in sculptural techniques, was clearly manifest in the jewelry traditions of Europe (see Evans 1970:81–83). At the same time, the earliest Spanish explorers in the Americas encountered flourishing and sophisticated indigenous gold- and silversmithing traditions (see, for example, Gallo 1967; Taillard 1941). The motifs and techniques of Native American jewelry traditions fascinated and ultimately influenced

Spanish jewelers of the sixteenth century, particularly in their emphasis on single, pendant elements of naturalistic forms (see Muller 1972:28–32; Santiago Cruz 1960).

Jewels, jewelry design, jewelers' pattern books, and jewelers themselves circulated throughout Europe during the sixteenth century, frequently making it difficult to identify the national origin of many pieces (see Muller 1972:40). The pattern books and goldsmiths guild records are especially useful in the identification and dating of trends, and among the most useful of these for Spanish jewelry are the guild records of Barcelona, contained in volumes known as the *Llibres de Passanties* (see Muller 1972:5, 9), and the drawings of the sixteenth-century Nuremberg jeweler Victor Solís (Evans 1970:89–90).

Early-sixteenth-century jewelry in Spain frequently retained Moorish design elements, such as filigree, scrollwork, loops, and interlocking geometric patterns. This practice does not appear to have been sustained much past the middle of the century. Elite classes during the sixteenth century wore wide, elaborate collars of enameled and jeweled sculpted links, square cut stones set in elaborate foliage-like settings, and a variety of precious religious jewels. One of the distinctive features of the second half of the century was the predominance of single-figure pendants in zoomorphic, anthropomorphic, or fantastic forms (see Muller 1972:77–83; Fig. 6.1), discussed later. Scent holders in the form of urns, fruits, caskets, and balls were common, as were small, book-shaped pendants. Pendant crosses, reliquaries, and religious images were also widely used (see Chapter 4).

Muller (1972:103) characterizes sixteenth-century Spanish jewelry as the product of wealth combined with fine artisanship and fantasy. This changed somewhat during the seventeenth century, when Church and crown regularly issued prohibitions against excesses in adornment. These *pragmaticas* stipulated precisely which jewels could be worn by whom. In a 1600 *pragmatica*, for example, women were permitted only a single strand necklace of pearls or a single kind of stone, while men were permitted only gold chains and hat ornaments (Muller 1972:105). The *pragmaticas* were generally ineffective, however, and the wealthy apparently found ways to circumvent these restrictions (Deleito y Piñuela 1946:234–253). During the first half of the seventeenth century, chains replaced the elaborate jeweled collars of the sixteenth century, pearls became even more prevalent, gems replaced enamels as additions of color to jewelry, hat ornaments had great popularity, and religious motifs dominated jewelry. Simpler, more classical designs were in general more common throughout Europe after 1600 (Evans 1970:126–127).

In the second half of the seventeenth century, the most characteristic jewelry form for women in Spain was the bow shape, or *lazo*. The popularity of this form continued through the eighteenth century in the Americas, however. Women also wore elaborate hairpins with attached ornaments, and earrings became very much larger and more

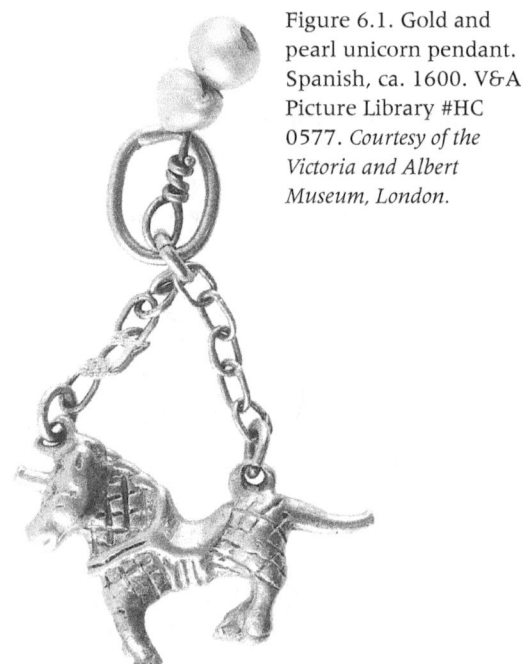

Figure 6.1. Gold and pearl unicorn pendant. Spanish, ca. 1600. V&A Picture Library #HC 0577. *Courtesy of the Victoria and Albert Museum, London.*

elaborate, with many pendant elements (see Muller 1972:137–140). Matched sets of jewelry, known as *aderezos,* were also popular in the latter part of the century. These could consist of matched design earrings, hair ornaments, necklaces, bracelets, rings, buckles, and brooches. *Aderezos* of glass beads were also imported to the Spanish colonies in the late sixteenth and early seventeenth centuries (Table 6.1).

Madame D'Aulnoy, writing in 1679 from travelers' accounts of Spain, commented on the use of jewelry by both common and elite women. Of the poor women in the country, she observed unkindly that "they have glass necklaces which hang twisted about their necks like ropes of onions, but, however, serve to cover the nastiness of their skin" (1930: 70). Her description of the jewelry of the privileged classes was hardly more flattering:

> above all, anything made of their false stones ravishes them with joy. That they have so many that are right and so excellent, yet wear a prodigious quantity of these false ones, which in reality are nothing neither than bits of glass set, and just like those our chimney sweepers sell to our provincials . . . the ladies of the greatest quality are loaded with these false stones, which they buy at a dear rate; and when I asked them why they were so fond of these counterfeit diamonds they told me it was because they could have of them as big as they desired. And indeed they have of them in their pendants as big as an egg, and all of these come to them either from France or Italy. For, as I have told you, few things are made at Madrid, idleness reigns too much there. (D'Aulnoy 1930:320)

By the end of the seventeenth century, Spanish jewelry—along with nearly all Spanish crafts—was dominated by influence from other parts of Europe. French influence was particularly strong, strengthened with the ascendancy of the Bourbon dynasty in 1700, and, as Madame D'Aulnoy suggested, much of the jewelry in Spain was of French origin. Matched sets of jewels continued in popularity and assumed a greater lightness and delicacy of form than that seen in earlier centuries (Evans 1970:149). During the second half of the eighteenth century, naturalistic motifs such as multicolored floral bouquets appeared (see Evans 1970:156–157).

Precious jewelry in New Spain appears to have retained older styles into the eighteenth century. Inventories from the first half of the century include earrings shaped like parrots, baskets, and small hats; mermaid pendants; Immaculate Conception jewels; bow-shaped pendants; very large earrings; and quantities of pearls (Toussaint 1967:261). Emeralds and gold dominate in the materials. Later eighteenth-century jewelry, as indicated in portraits of the era, suggest that pearls were the most favored and widely used stones (Toussaint 1967:367; Davis and Peck 1963:56).

Popular Jewelry in the Spanish Colonies

The production of jewelry in the Spanish colonies began soon after the first colonization efforts in the Caribbean. A Spanish master silversmith, Pablo Belvis, was already present in Hispaniola by 1495 (Torre Revello 1945:41), and silversmiths and gemstone cutters were present in Mexico before 1530 (Toussaint 1967:67; Santiago Cruz 1960:54). Both Indians and Spaniards belonged to the crafts guilds, and the theme of Ibero-American cross-fertilization pervades most scholarly works dealing with colonial-era jewelry.

Jewelry was also imported to the colonies throughout the colonial period (Cruz Valdevinos and Escalera Ureña 1993). From the 1520s until the end of the eighteenth century, popular jewelry and amulets were shipped in quantity from Europe to the Americas. Items of precious and nonprecious jewelry were also sent to New Spain from Asia via the Manila galleon trade and from there to Spain (see Schurtz 1939; Mathers 1990; Provoyeur 1996).

Table 6.1 shows the items of personal

Table 6.1. Personal Adornment Items Shipped to the Spanish Colonies, 1511–1613

	1511–26	1583	1590	1592	1603	1613	Total
Beads and Stones							
ABALORIOS (common beads)		395,000	512,000	166,000	531,000	1,130,000	2,734,000
ABALORIOS FINO (fine)			20,000				20,000
ABALORIOS VERDE/ AMARILLO (green and yellow)	102,000						102,000
ABALORIOS BLANCO (white)				70,000			70,000
ABALORIOS CRISTALINOS (crystal-like)				6,000		4,000	10,000
ABALORIOS CRISTALINOS DE COLORES (crystal-like and colored)			15,000				15,000
ABALORIOS DE COLORES (of colors)					140,000	181,600	321,600
ABALORIOS DE COLORES DE FRANCIA (French, of colors)			12,000				12,000
ABALORIOS DE FLANDES (of Holland)				30,000			30,000
ABALORIOS NEG. CANASTILLA (small black baskets)				2,000			2,000
ABALORIOS NEGROS Y COLORES (of colors and black)					6,000		6,000
ABALORIOS DE 50 MILLARES (lots of 50,000 beads)				20,000			20,000
TALEGAS DE ABALORIOS Y CANUTILLO BLANCO (sacks of beads and white tube beads)						6	6
AGUAMARINAS (aquamarines)		10,000	98,000	1,132,000	652,000	351,000	2,243,000
ARGENTERIA DE VIDRIO (glass beads inlaid or worked with gold or silver)				26,000			26,000
ARGENTERIA DE VIDRIO NEGRO (black glass beads inlaid or worked with gold or silver)				7,000			7,000
CALABACITAS DE VIDRIO (pumpkin-shaped, fluted?)				36	288	288	612

Table 6.1. continued

	1511–26	1583	1590	1592	1603	1613	Total
CANUTILLOS DE VIDRIO (glass tube beads)		3,000	12,000				15,000
CANUTILLOS DE VIDRIO NEGRO (black glass tube beads)				4,000			4,000
CANUTILLOS LARGO DE VIDRIO (large tube beads)					60,000		60,000
CRISTALINA AZUL (clear blue glass)				5,000			5,000
CRISTALINA DE COLORES (clear glass of colors)				50,000	10,000		60,000
CRISTALINA DE ITALIA (clear glass of Italy)				57,000	50,000		107,000
CRISTALINA EN 40 MACITOS (clear glass in 40 bunches)				20,000			20,000
CRISTALINA GRUESA (fat clear glass beads)				860,000			860,000
CRISTALINA NEGRA (clear black glass)		8,168		30,000			38,168
CRISTALINA NEGRA Y DE COLOR (black and colored clear glass)			330,000				330,000
CRISTALINA NEGRA/COLORES (black and colored clear glass)					100,000		100,000
CRISTALINAS (clear glass beads)		44,000	365,000	517,072	447,000	416,000	1,789,072
CRISTALINAS AZUL GRUESA (fat clear blue glass)				6,000			6,000
CRISTALINAS AZULES DE CANUTILLO (clear blue glass tube beads)						14,400	14,400
CRISTALINAS DE COLORES (clear glass of colors)						130,000	130,000
CRISTALINAS DE COLORES DE VENECIA* (clear glass of colors from Venice)			151,000				151,000
CRISTALINAS DE FRANCIA (from France)			30,000				30,000
CRISTALINAS DE ITALIA (from Italy)						75,000	75,000
CUENTACITAS DE AZABACHE (small jet beads)						44,000	44,000

Continued on next page

Table 6.1. continued

	1511–26	1583	1590	1592	1603	1613	Total
CUENTACITAS DE VIDRIO DORADO (small gilded glass beads)			1,000				1,000
CUENTAS (necklace beads)	60,000		2,000				62,000
CUENTAS DE COLOR CON CRUZ (of colors, with a cross)			2,000				2,000
CUENTAS DE AGUAMARINAS (of aquamarine)						11,000	11,000
CUENTAS DE ALQUIMIA (gilded)				9,096	3,000	5,000	17,096
CUENTAS DE BRONCE (of bronze)						2,000	2,000
CUENTAS DE CARRETILLA (wheelbarrow-shaped, possibly bunches of beads?)	17,000						17,000
CUENTAS DE CRISTAL (of crystal)		500	300		1,000		1,800
CUENTAS DE CRISTALESTRIN (clear glass?)		500					500
CUENTAS DE ESTANO (of tin)		2,000					2,000
CUENTAS DE HUESO COLORADOS (of colored bone)			9,000				9,000
CUENTAS DE VIDRIO (of glass)		326,000					326,000
CUENTAS DE VIDRIO A MODO DE OLIVA (of glass, olivelike)		4,000					4,000
CUENTAS DE VIDRIO AZUL (of blue glass)				76,000			76,000
CUENTAS DE VIDRIO AZUL/ BLANCO (of blue and white glass)		500					500
CUENTAS DE VIDRIO BLANCO (of white glass)			300,000			28,000	328,000
CUENTAS DE VIDRIO LISTADO (of striped glass)				140,000			140,000
CUENTAS DE VIDRIO VERDE (of green glass)		15,000					15,000
CUENTAS VERDE/AMARILLO (yellow and green)		48,000					48,000
MARGARITAS ("pearls")			9,000				9,000
MARGARITAS AZULES (blue "pearls")					3,000		3,000
MORILLAS (?)			31,440				31,440

Table 6.1. continued

	1511–26	1583	1590	1592	1603	1613	Total
PERLILLAS FALSAS DE VIDRIO (false glass pearls)			52,000			715,288	767,288
ROCALLAS DE VIDRIO (pebbles of glass)						58,000	58,000
CANTERIA AZUL (blue stone)						4,000	4,000
TURQUI (deep blue bead)		138,000	88,000		2,000		228,000
TURQUI CRISTALINO (clear)		28,000					28,000
TURQUI DE FRANCIA (of France)			2,000		3,000		5,000
TURQUI DE VIDRIO (of glass)				4,000			4,000
TURQUI GRUESO (fat or thick)		22,000					22,000
TURQUI NEGRO Y AZUL (black and blue)			4,000				4,000
TURQUI VERDE (green)		60,000					60,000
TURQUIS DE 1,000 CUENTAS DORADAS (of 1,000 gilded deep blue beads)			4,000				4,000
GRANADILLOS (*lit.* passion fruit, red beads?)				60			60
GRANATES (garnets, or possibly cut stones or glass)			1,750	5,000	32,000	3,000	41,750
GRANATES AZULES Y BLANCAS (blue and white)						10,000	10,000
GRANATES BLANCO DE CRISTAL (crystal)				7,000			7,000
GRANATES COLORADOS (colored)				2,000			2,000
GRANATES DE AZABACHE (of jet)			27,000	6,000		5,000	38,000
GRANATES DE COLORES DE FRANCIA (of colors, from France)						33,000	33,000
GRANATES DE VIDRIO (of glass)						576	576
GRANATES ENGARRADOS (in mounts)		5,000					5,000
GRANATES FALSOS AZULES (imitation, blue)						1,000	1,000
GRANATES FALSOS DE COLORES (imitation, of colors)		4,000	4,000			30,000	38,000
GRANATES FINOS (fine)		7,000		13,000	2,000		22,000
GRANATES FINOS MENUDOS (small, fine)			3,000				3,000

Continued on next page

Table 6.1. continued

	1511–26	1583	1590	1592	1603	1613	Total
GRANATES LEONADOS FALSOS (false, tawny-colored)			1,700				1,700
GRANATES MENUDITOS (very small)			5,800				5,800
GRANATES MORADOS FINOS (fine, purple)			12,000				12,000
GRANATES NEGROS (black)			2,000			85,000	87,000
Sartas (Strings)							
SARTAS			168		14,000	144	14,312
SARTAS DE ABALORIOS (of common beads)			54	420	4,752	2,880	8,106
SARTAS DE ABALORIOS DE UN COLOR (of common beads of a single color)					11,288		11,288
SARTAS DE DOS COLORES (of two colors)					648		648
SARTAS DE CUENTAS DE ALQUIMIA (of gilded beads)				11			11
SARTAS DE AGUAMARINA (of aquamarine)			8,000				8,000
SARTAS DE CUENTAS DE AMBAR ENGARZADAS (of strung amber beads)	1						1
SARTAS DE CUENTAS AMBAR PEQUENOS (of small amber beads)				3			3
SARTAS DE AZABACHE (of jet)			12				12
SARTAS DE GRANATES DE AZABACHE (of jet granates)					1,008		1,008
SARTAS GRANATES ENGARRADOS (of mounted or connected granates)				1			1
SARTAS CORAL CONTRAHECHO DE VIDRIO (of glass, imitation coral)						1	1
SARTAS DE CORAL QUE PESA 12 ONZAS (coral, weighing 12 ounces)				21			21
SARTAS DE CORAL DE CARRETILLA (wheelbarrow-shaped?)			127				127
SARTAS DE CORAL DE CEVADILLA (branch coral)				2			2

Table 6.1. continued

	1511–26	1583	1590	1592	1603	1613	Total
SARTAS DE CORALES FALSOS DE VIDRIO (of glass, imitation coral)			864				864
SARTAS DE CORALES REDONDAS (of round coral)			4				4
SARTAS DE CRISTALINAS (of clear glass)			948	636			1,584
SARTAS DE CUENTAS (of necklace beads)	9						9
SARTAS DE CUENTAS DE VIDRIO (of glass necklace beads)					24		24
SARTAS DE CUENTAS DE VIDRIO AZUL (of blue glass necklace beads)					1		1
SARTAS CUSARTADAS (?)		144					144
SARTAS DE MORILLAS (?)		6					6
SARTAS DE VIDRIO (of glass)		61	36		195		292
SARTILLA DE CUENTA DE OLOR DORADO (of gilded, scented beads)				1			1
SARTILLA DE CUENTAS DE PLATA (of silver necklace beads)			1				1
SARTILLA DE GRANATES MORADAS (of purple granates)			1				1
SARTILLAS DE ABALORIOS (of common beads)			168	130		3,456	3,754
SARTILLAS DE CRISTALINA (of clear glass)				540			540
Bracelets							
SARTAS DE MANILLAS DE VIDRIO (strings of glass bangle bracelets)	18						18
SARTAS DE VIDRIO PARA LOS BRAZOS (strings of glass for the arms)			12				12
PARES DE BRAZALETES (pairs of bracelets)					17		17

Continued on next page

Table 6.1. continued

	1511–26	1583	1590	1592	1603	1613	Total
Finger Rings							
ANILLOS (finger rings)				288			288
ANILLOS COMUNES DE VIDRIO (common, of glass)			6,912	4,116			11,028
ANILLOS DE ALQUIMIA (gilded)				36			36
ANILLOS DE AZABACHE (of jet)	200		3,816	432			4,448
ANILLOS DE AZABACHE TORNEADOS (of lathe-turned jet)			576				576
SARTAS DE ANILLOS DE AZABACHE (strings of jet rings)			576		2		578
ANILLOS DE BUFANO LUMINADO (shiny wood from the cuban bufano tree)				60			60
ANILLOS DE EBANO PIEDRAS (ebony and stones)				576			576
ANILLOS DE LO PROPIO OCHAVADOR (?)			288				288
ANILLOS LUMINADOS (shiny)			348				348
DIAMANTILLOS DE CRISTAL PAR ANILLOS FALSOS (small crystal artificial diamonds for fake rings)			36				36
GRANATES PARA ANILLOS (granates for rings)			216				216
SORTIJAS DE ALQUIMIA (rings with metalwork)					432		432
SORTIJAS DE AZABACHE (rings of jet)			6			2,880	2,886
SORTIJAS DE AZABACHE Y EBANO (of jet and ebony)		15					15
SORTIJAS DE BUFANO (bufano wood)						60	60
SORTIJAS DE BUFANOS CON VIDRIERAS (of bufano wood set with mirrors)			216				216
SORTIJAS DE BUNA? CON PIEDRAS AZULES (of bufano wood with blue stones)			9				9

Table 6.1. continued

	1511–26	1583	1590	1592	1603	1613	Total
SORTIJAS DE VIDRIO (rings of glass)			7,200	366			7,566
SORTIJAS DE ZERDAS CON PERLAS (horsehair rings with pearls)		24					24
SORTIJAS DOMINADAS				216			216
SORTIJAS LUMINADAS (shiny rings)			144				144
SORTIJILLAS DE BUFANO CON PIEDRAS (small rings of bufano wood with stones)			36				36
Necklaces							
COLARES DE VIDRIO (choker of glass)						288	288
COLLARETES Y GARGANTILLAS DE VIDRIO (chokers and necklaces of glass)						432	432
GARGANTILLAS (necklaces)		24					24
GARGANTILLAS AZULES (blue)				168			168
GARGANTILLAS COMUNES (common)			784	3,898	1,632	752	7,066
GARGANTILLAS DE ABALORIOS (of common beads)			461	1,818		3,168	5,447
GARGANTILLAS DE ALQUIMIA* (of gold or silver metalwork)				41			41
GARGANTILLAS DE AZABACHE (of jet)			124	600	24	480	1,228
GARGANTILLAS DE CANUTILLO (of tube beads)				360			360
GARGANTILLAS DE CRISTALINAS (of clear stones)			168				168
GARGANTILLAS DE CUENTAS DE VIDRIO (of glass beads)			7				7
GARGANTILLAS DE MEDALLA AZABECHE (of jet medallions)			60				60
GARGANTILLAS DE NACAR (of mother-of-pearl)						25	25
GARGANTILLAS DE PLATA** (of silver)				6			6
GARGANTILLAS DE VIDRIO (of glass)				684	2,034	1,272	4,099

Continued on next page

Table 6.1. continued

	1511–26	1583	1590	1592	1603	1613	Total
Necklace Pieces							
GARGANTILLAS SENCILLAS DE AZABACHE (simple jet necklaces)						240	240
MEDALLAS DE VIDRIO PARA GARGANTILLAS (glass medallions for necklaces)					1,584		1,584
PIEZAS DE AZABACHE PARA GARGANTILLAS (pieces of jet for necklaces)			7,000				7,000
PIEZAS DE GARGANTILLAS (pieces of necklaces)				576			576
PIEZAS DE VIDRIO VERDES PARA GARGANTILLAS (pieces of green glass for necklaces)					306		306
Earrings							
MEDALLAS ZARCILLOS VIDRIO (glass medallions for pendant earrings)					1,152		1,152
ZARCILLOS (dangling earrings)			18	600			618
ZARCILLOS CHIQUITOS DE CORAL (small, of coral)				6			6
ZARCILLOS DE ABALORIO (of common beads)			50			1,440	1,490
ZARCILLOS DE ALQUIMIA (of gold or silver work)					168		168
ZARCILLOS DE AZABACHE Y VIDRIO (of jet and glass)				648			648
ZARCILLOS DE CRISTAL SON DE HIGUITAS (of small crystal *higas*)				6			6
ZARCILLOS DE LANTERNILLOS (of small lantern shapes)			864				864
ZARCILLOS DE NACAR (of mother-of-pearl)						24	24
ZARCILLOS DE PERLAS DE VIDRIO (of glass pearls)			120				120
ZARCILLOS DE VIDRIO (of glass)			1,072	822	696	2,040	4,630
ZARCILLOS DE VIDRIO DE FRANCIA (of glass from France)						60	60

Table 6.1. continued

	1511–26	1583	1590	1592	1603	1613	Total
ZARCILLOS VERDES DE CORAZON (of green glass hearts)			14,400				14,400
Other Jewelry							
ADEREZOS DE ABALORIOS (sets of jewelry of common beads)					6		6
BANDA DE VIDRIO (glass band or strip)			1				1
CADENA DE VIDRIO DE ROSAS AZULES (chain of blue glass roses)						1	1
CADENILLAS DE AZABECHE (small jet chains)						24	24
CLAVITOS DE VIDRIO BLANCO Y DE COLORES (hairpin ornaments of white and colored glass)				100,000			100,000
CLAVITOS DE VIDRIO PARA TOCADOS (glass hairpins for hairdos)				100,000			100,000
SOBRETOCAS DE ABALORIO (hair ornaments of beads)			6				6
TIQUILLEOS DE ABALORIO (fancy, silly ornaments of beads)		24					24
PULSERAS Y AHOGADERAS DE VIDRIO (bracelet bands and throat bands of glass)						1,344	1,344
FLORES DE VIDRIO (glass flowers)			84				84
Total	179,336	1,120,942	2,163,043	3,491,604	2,078,970	3,358,169	12,392,064

Sources: *Registros de la Casa de Contratación,* Archivo Generál de las Indias, Seville (microfilm copy in the P. K. Yonge Library of Florida History, University of Florida, Gainesville)

1511—*Contratación* #1451

1523—*Contratación* #1079

1583—*Contratación* #1080

1590—*Contratación* #s 1089, 1092

1592-93—*Contratación* #1099

1603—*Contratación* #1143

1613—*Contratación* #s 1159, 1160

*Complete entry is "gargantillas de alquimia con piedras falsas de vidrio."

** Complete entry is "6 gargantillas de plata con piedras doradas."

adornment that were shipped between 1526 and 1613. Taken from shipping records of that period, these records provide insight into the identification and meaning of jewelry items recovered archaeologically from Spanish colonial sites of the later sixteenth, seventeenth, and eighteenth centuries (see also Torre Revello 1943:780).

The majority of these items appear to be glass beads of various kinds, ready for use in the fabrication of jewelry or rosaries. These include *abalorios* (small glass beads or seed beads), *aguamarinas* (aquamarine colored beads), *canutillos* (tubular beads), *cristalinas* (clear or crystal beads), *granates* (semiprecious stones, often garnets), *turquis* (turquoise-colored stones), as well as *cuentas* (beads) of amber, *alquimia* (damascene work), bronze, bone, glass, gilded glass and wood, crystal, and jet (see Table 6.1; for additional discussions of glass beads on Spanish colonial sites, see Deagan 1987; Fairbanks 1968; Smith 1983; Smith and Good 1982). Beads arrived in huge quantities. In 1592 alone, for example, more than 3.25 million beads of various sorts were shipped to Mexico and the Caribbean, not including an additional 65 libras (about 26 kg) of beads (Table 6.2).

Beads varied considerably in cost. The most expensive beads were of coral (30–60 reales per *libra* [about 1.25 kg]) and *granates*, cut stones that cost between 40 and 60 reales per thousand. Rings, necklaces, and earrings made mostly of glass, crystal, coral, and jet were also shipped to the colonies. Two kinds of finger rings are noted—*anillos*, which were inexpensive and most commonly made of glass (20 maravedís per gross) or jet (2–3 reales per dozen), and *sortijas* (3–5 reales per dozen). The *sortijas* were probably those with settings, and examples of both *sortijas* and *anillos* have been found archaeologically (discussed later). Inexpensive glass earrings (1 real per dozen) were also imported throughout the colonial era.

Such ornaments were probably similar to the many examples of bead jewelry shown in

Figure 6.2. Bead jewelry worn in colonial New Spain. Detail from a *casta* painting by Miguel Cabrera, From *Spaniard and Indian woman, mestiza*, 1763. Mother wears white beads with white and coral pendant beads; daughter wears white, black, and coral-colored beads. *Courtesy of the Museo de América, Madrid.*

the Mexican *casta* paintings of the eighteenth century (Fig. 6.2; García-Saíz 1989). During the eighteenth century, mass production of glass and paste jewels was perfected, and all classes of people widely used them in jewelry of the same style as that worn by the wealthy (Muller 1972:164–166; Evans 1970:151–152; Lewis 1970). The materials recovered from the 1741 shipwreck of *El Matanceros*—which include thousands of paste jewels and paste-set items—illustrate the range and quantity of popular jewels sent to the Spanish colonies (Blair 1960:260–267; Fig. 6.3). Pinchbeck, a gold-colored alloy of zinc and copper, was also developed during the early eighteenth

Table 6.2. Quantities and Prices of Imported Jewelry, 1592

	Mazos*	Gruesas**	Libras	Individual	Price
Beads					
Abalorios (Small, common beads)		244	4	50,000	5–8 reales/1,000
Aguamarinas (Aquamarine beads)		300		832,000	1–3 reales/1,000
Arginteria de vidrio (Glass with metal inlay)				31,000	2–8 reales/1,000
Canutillos (Tube-shaped beads)				4,000	10 reales/1,000
Cristalinas (Clear glass)	624		44	910,000	6–8 reales/1,000
Cuentas de Alquimia (Beads of metalwork)				9,096	10 reales/1,000
Cuentas de Ambar (Amber beads)			17		30–60 reales/libra
Cuentas de Vidrio (Glass beads)	68			148,000	6–9 reales/1,000
Granates (Garnets or cut stones)	7			26,000	40–60 reales/1,000
Margaritas azules (Blue "pearls")				3,000	not given
Jewelry					
Anillos de vidrio (Glass finger rings)		49		84	20 maravedis/gross
Anillos (other)		9		60	2–3 reales/dozen
Gargantillas de vidrios (Glass necklaces)		8.5		2,466	2 reales/dozen
Gargantillas de azabeche (Jet necklaces)		4		24	2–4 reales/dozen
Gargantillas de metal (Metal necklaces)				36	30 reales–1 ducat/dozen
Sartas y Sartillos de vidrio (Strings of glass pieces)		2		1,932	2–5 reales/dozen
Sortijas (Rings)		1.5			3–5 reales/dozen
Zarcillos de vidrio (Pendant earrings of glass)				184	1 real/dozen

Source: *Registros de la Casa de Contratación,* Archivo Generál de las Indias, Seville (microfilm copy in the P. K. Yonge Library of Florida History, University of Florida, Gainesville)

1592–93—*Contratación* #1099

*Mazos (bunches) = ±1,000; **Gruesas (gross = 144)

1 real = 44 maravedís, 1 ducat = 135 maravedís

Figure 6.3. Paste jewels recovered from the 1742 *Matanceros* shipwreck. Some of the thousands of green, blue, and clear stones recovered from the site. CEDAM Museum, Akumal, Yucatán, Mexico. *Photo: James Quine.*

century and was used widely along with gilt and silver in popular jewelry.

As with precious jewelry, it is often difficult to distinguish Spanish paste pieces from those of other European countries. It has been suggested that some distinctive qualities in Spanish paste jewelry include uniformity of stones, an absence of relief in pieces, a tendency to use white and green stones, a predominance of crosses and religious motifs, and very large, nearly hand-sized earrings (Lewis 1970:42).

Shoe buckles and clasps were also important items of personal adornment during the eighteenth century, often set with paste or real gems, gilded and engraved according to the station of the owner. During this period, jewelry conforming to prevailing ideas of taste became generally accessible to a much wider variety of people in relatively inexpensive materials. This development can be seen clearly in the archaeological record of the Spanish colonies, which includes a wide variety of jewelry items. Finger rings, earrings, necklaces and pendants, bracelets, and pins have been reported, even though it is often difficult to recognize and identify fragmentary elements of jewelry when they are disarticulated. Many beads, small pendant elements, unusually shaped copper-alloy fragments, and perforated objects could once have been part of jewelry elements, and the preceding chapters on religious items and amulets should also be considered in the identification of such objects.

Finger Rings

Apart from glass beads, finger rings are the most frequently reported jewelry items on Spanish colonial sites. Simple bands of glass, jet, or metal (*anillos*) and rings with settings (*sortijas*) are present throughout the colonial period. Precious finger rings of the sixteenth century were carefully sculpted and enameled, with high, decorated box mounts (Bury 1984:7); however, this was not the case with the early finger rings from archaeological sites, which tend to be quite humble in both design and material.

The earliest examples of Spanish rings in the Americas come from the site of La Isabela in the Dominican Republic (1493–98) (Deagan and Cruxent 2002a). Some of these are shown in Figure 6.4. The most frequently occurring variety of ring was a copper-alloy band with a flat, widened bezel bearing a raised Maltese cross emblem (discussed in chapter 4 and illustrated in Fig. 4.50). Two of these rings were recovered from within the

Popular Jewelry

Figure 6.4. Finger rings from La Isabela, 1493–98. *Left to right:* Copper-alloy band, FS 1701; copper-alloy band with incised lines, FS 1703; gilded copper alloy with setting for stone, FS 3277; copper alloy with crowned F, FS C7P1; copper-alloy ring with Maltese cross on bezel, FS 2895; copper-alloy stirrup ring with blue turquoise stone, FS 795. Bezel of center ring, 1.2 by 1 cm. Parque Nacional de La Isabela, Dominican Republic.

Figure 6.5. Rings from Sabana Yegua, Dominican Republic. Late fifteenth or early sixteenth century. Copper-alloy stirrup rings with round turquoise and dark blue stones, and stirrup-type rings with square paste stones set into bezel. Ring diameters, 2 cm. Vega Collection, Santo Domingo. *Courtesy of Bernardo Vega.*

town site, and a cache of six others was found outside the town walls in an area thought to have been occupied by Taíno Indians.

Although not identical in form, these rings are quite similar in concept to the copper-alloy rings known to have been brought by Jesuit and Franciscan missionaries to the North American missions in the seventeenth century (see, for example, Cleland 1971:30), suggesting that the practice of bringing rings with Christian symbols as gifts for newly converted souls began very early in the Americas.

Bartolomé de Las Casas recorded that Columbus also gave rings to the Taíno Indians during his earliest explorations (Las Casas 1965[I]:288). One of the rings recovered at La Isabela is identical to a group of six brass rings reported by Bernardo Vega from a late-fifteenth-century cache of Spanish and Taíno artifacts from the rock shelter site of Sabana Yegua in the Dominican Republic (Vega 1979). These rings have no applied bezel but are thickened and widened at the top and set with small, round, colored stones (Fig. 6.5). Known as "stirrup rings," they were popular throughout the Middle Ages (see Egan and Pritchard 1991:326; Hinton 1982:14, 31). A single ring of this type was recovered from La Isabela, but they have not been reported from other Spanish sites, and this form may have been used primarily for very early New World trade.

Several rings probably not intended for trade with the Taíno were also found at La Is-

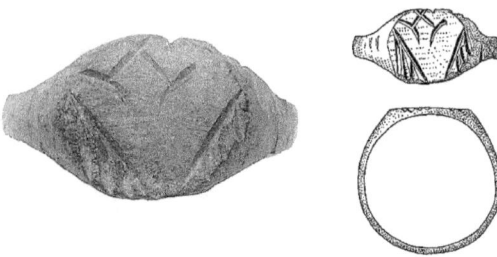

Figure 6.6. Sixteenth-century signet ring. Copper alloy, pre-1580. Design incised after production. St. Augustine, 8SJ31-1667 (Fountain of Youth Park site). Ring diameter 1.86 cm, bezel height 0.8 cm. FLMNH Collections. *Drawing: Merald Clark. Photo: University of Florida Office of Instructional Resources.*

abela and were probably worn by men, since European women are not recorded to have been at the colony until quite late (if at all) (Deagan and Cruxent 2002a, 2002b). The most ornate ring is of gilded copper alloy, cast with a setting for a stone. Plain copper-alloy bands were also recovered from La Isabela, both smoothly finished and with horizontal cast ridges (Fig. 6.4).

Signet rings are found most often on sixteenth-century sites. Two cast, copper-alloy signet rings were recovered from La Isabela, one with a crowned letter "R" and the other bearing an image of the Virgin Mary with the Christ Child (Fig.6.4; Deagan and Cruxent 2002a). A sixteenth-century signet ring was also found at the Fountain of Youth Park site in St. Augustine, which is thought to have been the initial campsite for Pedro Menéndez de Áviles in 1565–66 (Gordon and Deagan 1992). This ring appears to have been crudely engraved after its production (Fig. 6.6).

Finger rings found on other sixteenth-century Caribbean sites are rare, despite the numbers that were shipped to the colonies. The single ring recovered from the site of Puerto Real in Haiti (1503–78) is a band of carved jet, popularly believed to protect one from the evil eye (see Chapter 5). A faceted and incised jet band was also found at the seventeenth-century Florida mission site of San Luis de Talimali (ca. 1650–1700) (Fig. 6.7).

A common style of finger ring during the seventeenth century was a simple, thin, copper-alloy band with a raised square bezel, set with a colored glass or paste stone (Fig. 6.8). These rings, reported from several seventeenth-century contexts, are very similar in form to examples made from gold and pre-

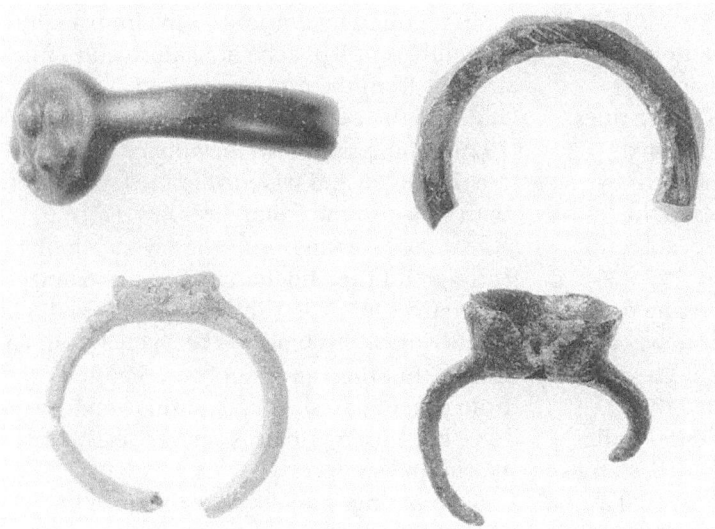

Figure 6.7. Rings from San Luis de Talimali, ca. 1650–1700. *Top left:* Black molded glass, FS 6946. *Top right:* Faceted and incised jet, FS 4280. *Bottom left:* Copper alloy with square bezel for stone, FS 4329. *Bottom right:* Copper alloy with square bezel for stone, FS 3926. Maximum exterior diameter of jet band 2.3 cm. *Courtesy of the Florida Bureau of Archaeological Research, the San Luis Historical and Archaeological Site, and Bonnie G. McEwan. Photo: James Quine.*

Popular Jewelry

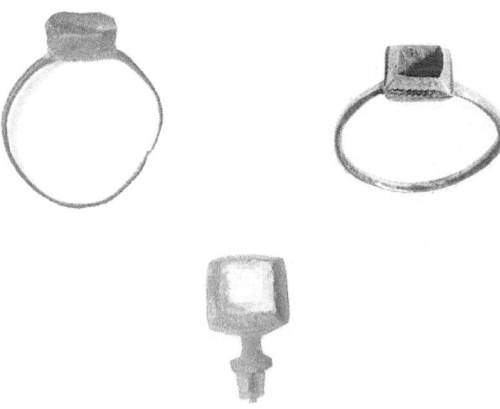

Figure 6.9. Eighteenth-century French-style finger rings. Copper alloy with glass stones, mid-eighteenth century. Probably of French origin. *Left:* Green glass stone flanked by blue stones. St. Augustine (SA-30-3-127). *Right:* Blue stone flanked by clear stones. St. Augustine (SA-36-4-13). FLMNH/CSA Collections. *Photos: James Quine.*

Figure 6.8. Seventeenth-century finger rings. *Top left:* Copper-alloy with square setting for missing stone. First half of the seventeenth century. Diameter of band, 1.75 cm. Fig Springs site (8CO1). *Center:* Fragment of copper-alloy ring with square pink table-set stone. Late seventeenth to early eighteenth century. Diameter of bezel 8 mm. St. Augustine (SA-39A-11-27). *Right:* Gilded copper alloy with green glass table-set stone, ca. 1650–1700. Band diameter 1.8 cm. St. Augustine (SA-30-3-17). FLMNH/CSA Collections. *Photo: James Quine.*

cious gems known from the sixteenth century and earlier (see, for example, those from the Armada wrecks in Stenuit 1972:274; see also those illustrated by Hinton 1982:26). Rings of this style have been found in seventeenth-century contexts at the Convento de San Francisco in Santo Domingo; from the mission site of Fig Springs, Florida (Deagan 1972:38); and at San Luis de Talimali, Florida. A slightly more ornate example of this ring style came from a seventeenth-century context in St. Augustine. This was of copper alloy, with a large, square bezel holding a pink, table-cut stone (Fig. 6.8).

A considerably wider variety of rings appear on eighteenth-century sites, a period during which popular jewelry became more generally accessible. The French Bourbon influence can also be seen in these rings, since many of them are of the same designs as examples found on contemporary French sites

(see, for example, Stone 1974:126–131). Rings set with both semiprecious stones and paste jewels fall into this category. Several eighteenth-century sites have produced silver or copper-alloy rings featuring a large central stone set into a serrated bezel, flanked by from one to three smaller stones on each side (Fig. 6.9). These have included examples of silver set with a garnet and tourmaline as well as brass set with glass.

Rings with large central stones flanked by smaller ones have been recovered in brass and glass at Santa Rosa Pensacola (1723–52), which sustained a lively trade with French Mobile during its occupation (Smith 1965:97). This ring style was also quite common at eighteenth-century French Fort Michilimackinack (Stone 1972:123–126), suggesting that these rings may have been of French origin.

Simple brass and gold bands have been recovered from a number of eighteenth-century contexts. These are sometimes engraved with inscriptions but most often are plain (see Shephard 1983:93; Skowronek 1982:130–133; Smith 1965:97). Several plain, nonprecious rings as well as decorated gold band rings came from the 1715 and 1733 Florida plate fleets wrecks (Skowronek 1982; Fig. 6.10).

Finger rings of a curious form have been recovered from eighteenth-century criollo

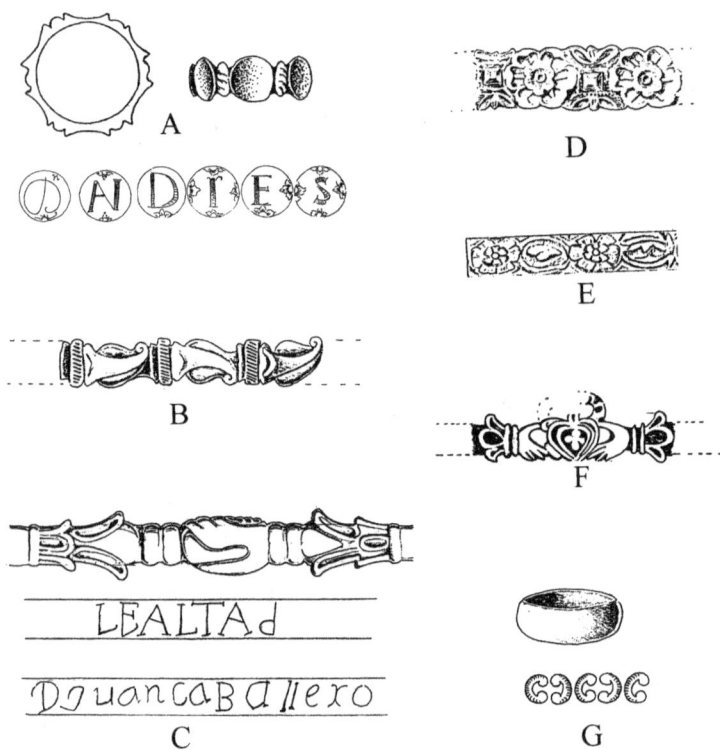

Figure 6.10. Ring band designs from the 1715 Florida plate fleet wrecks. Some of these may have been made in the Americas, since the fleet was bound to Spain. Bands are expanded to show detail. A. Gold alloy with interior inscription, band width 1.6 cm, (8SL17) FBAR Lab #L7391; B. Gold alloy, heart design, band width 0.7 cm, (8SL17) FBAR Lab #L7184; C. Gold, clasped hands, *Riomar* wreck, FBAR Lab #86-021; interior (*top*) and back (*below*) inscriptions shown; D. Gold alloy, floral design, band width 0.9 cm, (8SL17) FBAR Lab #L7183; E. Gold, alternating flowers and circles, band width 0.65 cm, (8MO101) FBAR Lab #L2633; F. Silver, Irish "Cladagh" design, band width 1.4 cm, (8SL17) FBAR Lab #L6654; G. Metal alloy, engraved with repeating design shown below band, band width 0.6 cm, (8SL17) FBAR Lab #L6655. *Courtesy of the Florida Bureau of Archaeological Research. Drawings: Frank Gilson.*

sites in St. Augustine (Shephard 1983). These were made of twisted copper wires shaped into a floral or spiral form at the bezel area. Finer copper wire was then wrapped around the bezel decoration (Fig. 6.11). Other examples are simple bands made of twisted and spiraled wires. Although twisted wire rings of this kind have not been reported from other Spanish sites, similar techniques are known to have been used in clothing decoration and in rosaries, such as the rosary "beads" of twisted copper wires recovered from Santa Rosa Pensacola (Smith 1965:71, 97).

Earrings

Earrings and earring fragments have been reported infrequently from Spanish colonial sites, although many earring elements such as beads and fasteners have probably gone unrecognized. Heart-shaped glass beads pierced vertically by copper wires with loops at both ends were excavated at sixteenth-century Santa Elena and identified as earrings by comparison to a very similar earring in a Spanish painting done in 1555 (Fig. 6.12; South, Skowronek, and Johnson 1988:159, 162; South and DePratter 1996:61).

Figure 6.11. Twisted copper wire rings. Ca. 1725–60. *Left:* Length 3.1 cm. *Right:* Band diameter 1.4 cm. St. Augustine (SA-7-4-215). FLMNH/CSA Collections. *Photo: James Quine.*

Figure 6.12. Glass earring fragment, ca. 1580. Blue glass. Maximum length 3 cm. Santa Elena, South Carolina. #38BU162H-81A. South, Skowronek, and Johnson (1988:Fig. 81). *Courtesy of the South Carolina Institute of Archaeology and Anthropology and Stanley South.*

Shipping records of the early seventeenth century (Table 6.1) identify earrings of glass, glass beads, damascene work, jet, mother-of-pearl, and glass "pearls." Some of the glass beads found on Spanish colonial sites were certainly used in earrings, and many were undoubtedly quite elaborate. In 1679, Madame D'Aulnoy described Spanish women's earrings as "longer than one's hand and so heavy that I have wondered how they could carry them without tearing out holes in their ears, to which they add whatever they think is pretty. . . . some have good large watches hanging there, others with padlocks of precious stones, and even your fine-wrought English keys, and little bells" (1930:203).

During the seventeenth century, elaborate pendant *zarcillos* that combined up to 13 pendants became quite popular (Muller 1972:138–139). Between 1590 and 1613, large numbers of *zarcillo* elements were shipped to Mexico, including *medallas zarcillos vidrios* (glass medallions for earrings), crystal *higuitas*, *lanternillas* (small lantern shapes), and green glass hearts (Table 6.1). The *casta* paintings indicate that these remained in use among most classes of women in the colonies

Figure 6.13. *Zarcillo* earrings. Detail from South American *casta* painting, ca. 1770. "China. Produce Quarteroon de Chino." *Courtesy of the Museo Nacional de Antropología, Madrid.*

Figure 6.14. Punta Rassa and San Luis pendants. San Luis de Talimali, ca. 1650–1700. *Top:* Punta Rassa pendants (aquamarine glass). All FS 3685. Length of center pendant 2.3 cm. *Bottom:* San Luis pendants. *Left to right:* Turquoise glass, FS 4271; light amber glass, FS 7224; green glass, FS 5188; turquoise glass, FS 7291a; light turquoise glass, FS 7224. Length of center pendant 1.2 cm. *Courtesy of the Florida Bureau of Archaeological Research, the San Luis Historical and Archaeological Site, and Bonnie G. McEwan. Photo: James Quine.*

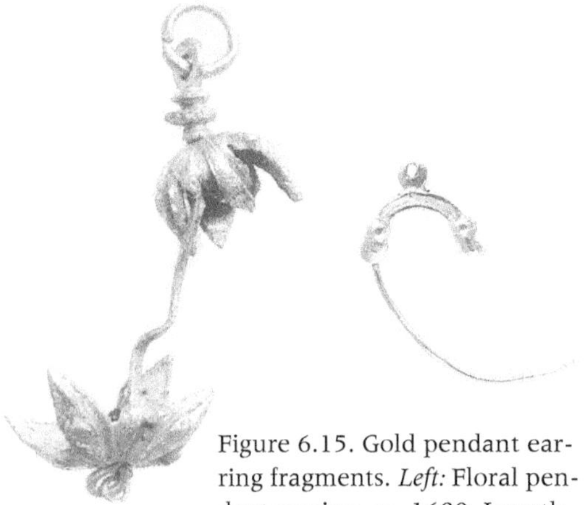

Figure 6.15. Gold pendant earring fragments. *Left:* Floral pendant earring, ca. 1680. Length 2.5 cm; diameter of floral element 1.0 cm. St. Augustine (SA-30-3-426). *Right:* Fragment, ca. 1750. Frame at top supports a ring from which other elements were probably suspended. Width of frame 1.1 cm. St. Augustine (SA-7-4). FLMNH/CSA Collections. *Photos: James Quine.*

through the eighteenth century (Fig. 6.13; see also García Saíz 1989).

Small, perforated glass pendants that may have been parts of earrings have been recovered from a number of seventeenth-century sites in Florida and the southeastern United States. These pendants are known as Punta Rassa Teardrop pendants and San Luis pendants (Mitchem 1992, 1993:407; Smith 1981; Fig. 6.14). The Punta Rassa Teardrop pendants, first defined by John Goggin (1960), are blue-green (aquamarine), pear shaped, and made in a mold with an attachment loop at the narrow end. They are between 1 and 2 cm long. The San Luis pendants, defined by Mitchem (1992), have been found in blue, amber, green, and aquamarine glass. Smaller than the Punta Rassa Teardrop pendants, they are triangular in section. They also could have been used in necklaces.

Dangling earrings are found most frequently in eighteenth-century contexts, and the earrings from this period underscore the international character of jewelry designs and styles in eighteenth-century Europe. Many of the examples from Spanish contexts overlap and are in some cases identical to earrings found on contemporary French colonial sites. Fragments of gold earrings recovered from early-eighteenth-century contexts in St. Augustine consist of the uppermost earring element, which holds the ear wire and a projecting loop from which the rest of the earring would have been suspended (Fig. 6.15). Intact pendant earrings with multiple elements were recovered on the eighteenth-century Florida plate fleet wrecks (Fig. 6.16).

Several fragments of brass, cone-shaped pendant earrings have been recovered from mid-eighteenth-century domestic contexts in St. Augustine. They consist of a simple metal cone or elongated drop-shaped pendant from a hollow sphere to which a wire is attached (Fig. 6.17). Unlike the "tinkler cones" associated with the fur trade (see Quimby 1966), the pendant cones on these earrings are carefully finished and regular in form and do not

Popular Jewelry

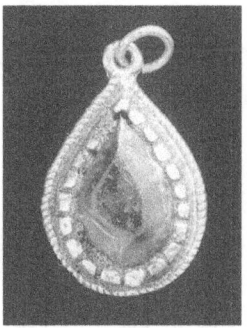

Figure 6.16. Pendant earrings from the 1715 Florida plate fleet wrecks. *Left:* Gold with mother-of-pearl drops. Length 4 cm, (8SL17) FBAR Lab #L6449. *Right:* Gold with emerald drops. Length 6 cm, (8IR19) FBAR Lab #LL7185. *Courtesy of the Florida Bureau of Archaeological Research. Drawing: Frank Gilson.*

Figure 6.18. Faceted glass pendant element. Green glass set in copper-alloy pendant, ca. 1780–1800. This could have been used in earrings or necklace. Length, 1.6 cm. St. Augustine (SA-7-4-46). FLMNH/CSA Collections. *Photo James Quine.*

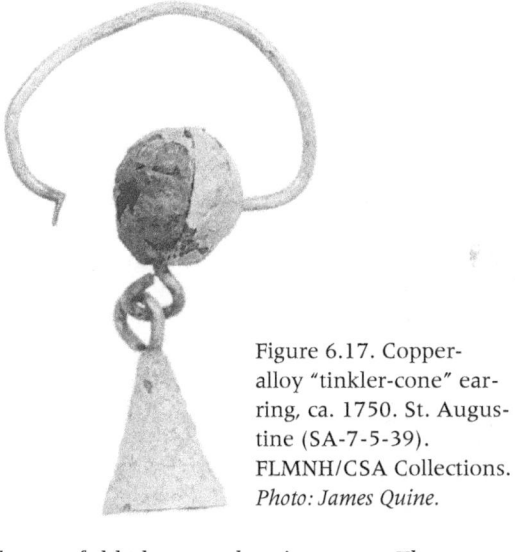

Figure 6.17. Copper-alloy "tinkler-cone" earring, ca. 1750. St. Augustine (SA-7-5-39). FLMNH/CSA Collections. *Photo: James Quine.*

have a folded or overlapping seam. The cones sometimes served as cap holders for stones or other elements, and a number of similar earrings are present in the collections of the Museo del Pueblo Español (Cat. #s 11.265, 11.689; Berges 1984).

The colonial examples are typically made of brass or copper alloy, although silver examples have been reported from later eighteenth-century contexts in Florida (Goggin 1952:147, Plate 12). Silver earrings of this style are nearly always associated with sites of American Indian trade (see Brain 1979:191). These earrings are virtually identical to the earbobs reported from eighteenth-century French colonial sites, where they appear to have been used primarily in the American Indian trade (see Maintfort 1979:394; Stone 1974:136–137; Brain 1979:191).

Paste-set pendant earrings and earring elements have also been recovered from eighteenth-century Spanish sites. These are usually in the form of small, flat, decorated pieces of copper alloy, set with paste stones and having attached loops or perforated holes (Fig. 6.18). Such pieces were recovered in large quantities from the 1741 *Matanceros* shipwreck (Figs. 6.19, 6.3), as well as from St. Augustine and Santa Rosa Pensacola (Smith 1965:111). The earrings made from paste stones set in metal usually incorporated several of these elements linked together, with additional paste stones suspended. Examples are present in the Museo del Pueblo Español collections (Berges 1984:49–51), and very similar paste-set earrings have been reported from eighteenth-century French-influenced sites (Brain 1979:191; Stone 1974:137).

130 Religion, Ritual, and Adornment

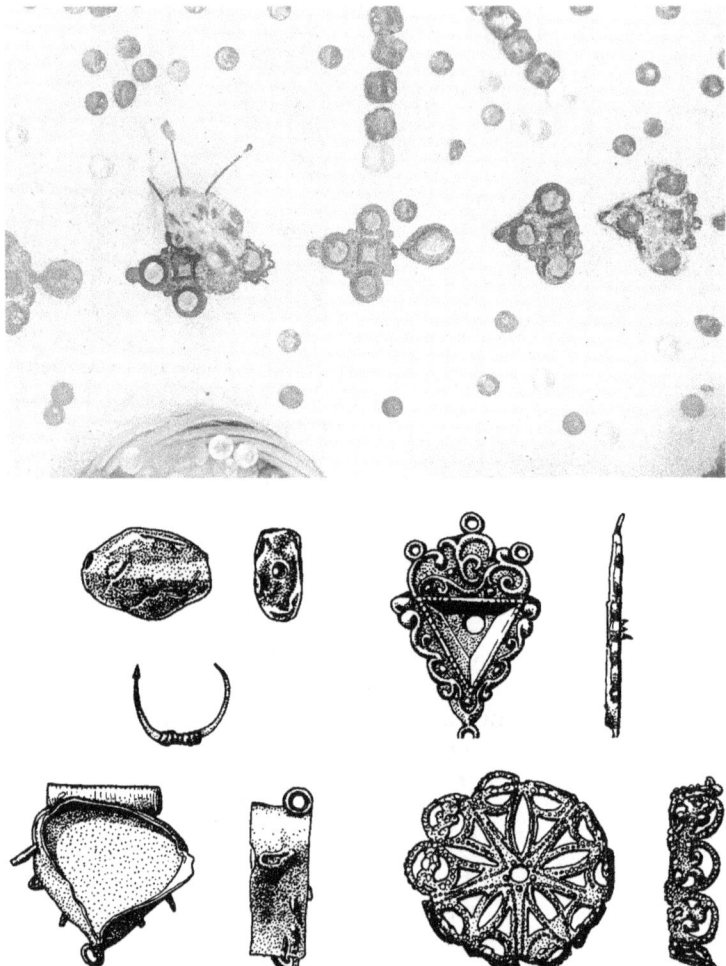

Figure 6.19. Paste jewelry elements probably used in earrings. Blue, green, and white glass stones in copper-alloy settings. Length of center pendant 3.4 cm. *El Matanceros* shipwreck (1741). CEDAM Museum, Akumal, Yucatán, Mexico. *Photo: James Quine.*

Figure 6.20. Jewelry elements from La Isabela, 1493–98. *Top left:* Agate bead, length 1.3 cm, FS 155. *Under agate bead:* Copper-alloy earring fragment, FS118. *Top right:* Gilded copper-alloy joining element, length 2.4 cm, FS 779. *Bottom left:* Copper-alloy and white metal locket or reliquary fragment, maximum width 1.7 cm, FS 212. *Bottom right:* Copper-alloy filigree cap, possibly from a cassolette. Diameter 2.0 cm, FS 56. Parque Nacional de La Isabela, Dominican Republic. *Drawing: Merald Clark.*

Many late-eighteenth- and early-nineteenth-century earrings, particularly those made in Mexico, were constructed of filigree (see Davis and Pack 1963:91–96). Hispano-Moresque filigree work was used in the production of fine jewelry in both Spain and the Indies since the first half of the sixteenth century (see Muller 1972:58–59, 98), although most examples of silver or base metal filigree work surviving in Mexican museums date to the later period (Davis and Pack 1963).

Pendants and Necklaces

Pendant and necklace fragments are among the most frequently recovered jewelry items from Spanish colonial sites. The earliest of these come from the late-fifteenth-century site of La Isabela, including a filigree-work, copper-alloy cap (Fig. 6.20) that may have been part of a *cassolet,* or a hollow, tubular necklace element such as those shown by Muller (1972:22–23). Moorish-inspired filigree work was popular and widespread in late-fifteenth-century Spain (Muller 1976:21–23) but has not been reported from sixteenth-century sites in the Americas.

Other pendants found on the site include the back half of a locket or reliquary with ornamented silver sides and a copper-alloy back. An ornately cast, gilded copper-alloy pendant in a triangular form has three loops for pendant elements and may have been a joining element on a necklace or a rosary (Fig. 6.20).

After 1500, beads are the most common necklace components recovered archaeologically, although not all beads recovered from sites were used in necklaces. Seed beads, of course, were often used in embroidery as clothing decoration, while many varieties of glass and stone beads were used in rosaries (see Chapter 4; Deagan 1987:156–181). Other beads, particularly those of semi-precious stone, coral, crystal, or jet, were used as amulets (see Chapter 5).

Colonial bead necklaces have survived in a number of places, such as Peru and Mexico. Examples from Peru include necklaces of both twisted and plain turquoise Nueva Cádiz beads separated by gold linking elements and beads; combinations of gold beads, navy and turquoise Nueva Cádiz twisted beads, and unfaceted chevron beads; and tubular blue and white striped beads in combination with red, white, and blue striped beads and gold beads (Gallo 1967:#s 258, 259, 260, 262, 263). Other necklaces included combinations of coral beads, ivory beads, and gold beads and links. All of these necklaces date to the sixteenth century and could probably be considered to have been fine jewelry given the quantities of gold used in them.

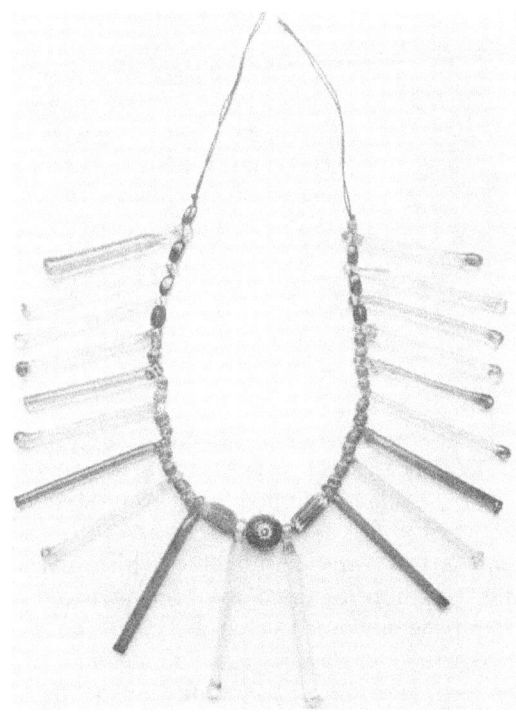

Figure 6.21. Necklace of trade beads from San Pedro Quitatoni, Oaxaca. Chevron beads with clear and green glass rods. From Davis and Pack (1982:Plate 46). *Courtesy of the University of Texas Press.*

Sixteenth-century glass beads were also used in the folk jewelry of Mexico. A peculiar necklace style characteristic of the Oaxaca area uses chevron beads alternating with long glass rods ending in a loop to permit stringing (Fig. 6.21; Davis and Pack 1963:88–89). These translucent rods are about 6 cm long. Although Davis and Pack (1963) attribute the beads in the necklace shown in Figure 6.21 to the sixteenth century, a fragment of one of these glass rods was recovered from an eighteenth-century context in St. Augustine (Fig. 6.22), and these necklaces are still in use today in the town of San Pedro Quiationi (Davis and Pack 1963:88–89).

During the sixteenth century, several kinds of *gargantillas* (necklaces) and *sartas* (strings) made of beads were imported to Mexico and

Figure 6.22. Eighteenth-century glass necklace rod fragment. Translucent turquoise colored glass, ca. 1750. Length 2.4 cm. St. Augustine (SA-36-4-222). FLMNH/CSA Collections. *Photo: University of Florida Office of Instructional Resources.*

Figure 6.23. Gilded copper-alloy unicorn pendant. Puerto Real (ca. 1550–78). Maximum length 2 cm, FS 3148. *Bureau National D'Ethnologie D'Haiti, Port au Prince. Photo: James Quine.*

the Caribbean (Table 6.1). In 1511, the only kind of necklaces shipped to the Americas were *gargantillas de vidrio,* but by 1613 the *Contaduría* records identify blue, white, black, and "common" *gargantillas* as well as *gargantillas* made of women's charms (*diges de mujeres*), *abalorios,* glass, crystal, jet, *alquimia* (gilded metal), silver, and mother-of-pearl. *Collares* were listed for the first time in 1613, as were chains of jet and blue glass roses (Table 6.1). The most costly of these necklaces were *gargantillas* of silver or *alquimia,* and the least expensive were of glass beads and *abalorios.* As noted earlier, many other kinds of beads were shipped loose (unstrung) in very large quantities, probably to be made into jewelry (including necklaces) or rosaries in the Americas (Table 6.1).

Jet was a popular material not only for rosaries and amulets but also for necklaces, particularly during the sixteenth century. Most archaeologically recovered jet necklace beads are found on sixteenth-century sites. A type of small, trilobed jet bead with a perforation for suspension (see Fig. 5.4, top center) has been recovered from Santa Elena (South, Skowronek, and Johnson 1988:158–159) and from sixteenth-century contexts in St. Augustine. They are from 1.3 to 1.5 cm high with a suspension hole at the narrowest point. Beads of this type were produced during the sixteenth century in Compostela, where they were made and sold in quantity as both ornaments and amulets. Some had smooth lobes, some had carved lobes, and some had three holes for stringing (Gómez Tabanero 1977:409). A necklace made of these trilobed beads is shown in a sixteenth-century Spanish painting identified by South, Skowronek, and Johnson (1988:159).

The sixteenth century was a time of "unparalleled wealth, fantasy and craftsmanship in the fabrication of jewels" in Spain (Muller 1972:103), which is reflected in the ornately crafted *gargantillas* made of metals, enamels, and fanciful pendants. A gilded silver unicorn pendant recovered from Puerto Real reflects this sixteenth-century Spanish style in a popular form (Ewen 1987:87; Fig. 6.23). The use of fantastic creatures such as unicorns, mermaids, and dragons was particularly popular during the second half of the sixteenth century in Spain and dates at Puerto Real to between about 1550 and 1578. A gold and ruby lizard pendant in the same tradition was recovered from the 1558 Armada wrecks (Stenuit 1972:212).

The use of enamels was also characteristic of sixteenth-century Spanish jewelry. An

Figure 6.24. Sixteenth-century pendants. *Left:* Enameled and gilded pendant element; red, white, and green enamel over gilded copper alloy. Concepción de la Vega, Dominican Republic (1496–1562). Parque Nacional de Concepción de la Vega, Dominican Republic. *Right:* Brass pendant medallion, late sixteenth century. Length 2.2 cm. St. Augustine (SA-26-1-39). FLMNH/CSA Collections. *Photo: James Quine.*

Figure 6.25. Spanish colonial chain elements. *Top:* Gold. Length 4.0 cm. 1715 (8IR19) FBAR Lab #028. *Bottom:* Gold. Length of chain 6.4 cm. 1733 (8MO101) FBAR Lab #2637. *Courtesy of the Florida Bureau of Archaeological Research. Drawings: Frank Gilson.*

enameled pendant element from Concepción de la Vega (1496–62) is shown in Figure 6.24, with green, red, and white enameled floral design on a gilded copper-alloy background.

Medallions were used in combination with chains and other pendant elements in sixteenth-century jewelry, and medallions of glass, jet, and metal were recorded in the *Contaduría* records (in addition to the *"medallas* for rosaries" and *"medallas* with images of saints") (Table 6.1). A small, oval, brass pendant from a late-sixteenth-century context in St. Augustine has a distinctly secular floral motif with a wreathlike design framing it and a loop for suspension at the top (Fig. 6.24). This may have served as a necklace element.

By the early seventeenth century, sumptuary rules restricted the role of jewelry, and although they were generally ineffective, a trend developed toward the use of necklace chains and away from the elaborate pendants, enamels, ornate metalwork, or jewels used in sixteenth-century necklaces (Muller 1972:106–110). Many examples of extraordinarily elaborate gold chains have been recovered from seventeenth- and early-eighteenth-century Spanish shipwrecks

(Borrell 1983b:107; Marx and Marx 1993:71, 89, 130; Mathers 1990:52–53; Matthewson 1986:c13–c16; Wagner 1972:80), but unfortunately few of them remain in the public domain. Many of these were apparently intended to serve as an easily transportable form of personal wealth, and many others were crafted in Asia for export to Spain via the Americas (see particularly Mathers 1990). Gold chains of this kind are unlikely to be found on colonial terrestrial sites, where occasional disarticulated copper-alloy links constitute most of the evidence for chains.

Many of the chains used to suspend medallions or connect beads during the eighteenth century are constructed in the manner shown in Figure 6.25, that is, short lengths of wire, onto which beads could be strung or medals attached, that were looped and connected to one another at each end. This type of chain is of considerable antiquity in Iberia, and examples have been recovered in late-fifteenth-century contexts at Qsar es-Seghir (Redman 1986:206).

Although the ornateness of necklaces diminished in the early seventeenth century, it was also at this time that the *Contaduría* records reflect an increase in the diversity of popular necklace types imported to the Spanish colonies (Table 6.1). In addition to *gargantillas* and *sartas,* the registers list *cadenas de vidrio de rosa azules* (glass chains of blue roses; price not listed) and *cadenillas de azabache* (small jet chains) costing 476 maravedís, or more than 10 reales each. *Collares, collaretes,* and *agohaderas* (choker-type necklaces) are also listed for the first time in the 1613 registers. *Agohaderas* apparently remained popular in the Americas into the eighteenth century, since it is the overwhelmingly most common type of necklace depicted in the Mexican *casta* paintings for women of all ages and classes (Fig. 6.2). These consisted of from one to four strands of beads, usually with pendant beads or other ornamental elements suspended from the lowest stand. Many women's chokers consisted of a fabric band from which a single, large, elaborate ornament was suspended at the throat (Fig. 6.26). These pendants were frequently in the bow- or butterfly-shaped *lazo* ornaments that became the most characteristic jewelry form during the late seventeenth and eighteenth centuries in Spain (Muller 1972:134).

Another late-seventeenth-century jewelry development that was undoubtedly reflected in the popular jewelry of that period and later was the *aderezo,* or matched set of jewelry (Muller 1972:136, 142–147). *Aderezos* could consist of a necklace, earrings, finger rings, bracelets, hair ornaments, bodice bands (*bandas*), and individual pendant jewels that could be used in combination with other pieces. Madame D'Aulnoy commented on the passion for many sets of jewels among the elite women of late-seventeenth-century Madrid: "Neither is it enough to have one set of jewels, as our ladies in France have, but these must have eight or ten; some of diamonds, others of rubies, emeralds, pearls, Turkey-stones, and in short, of all sorts" (1930:202). *Aderezos* were shipped to the colonies as early as 1603, along with most of the individual pieces comprising them. An eighteenth-century emerald *aderezo* from Mexico is shown in Figure 6.27.

Figure 6.26. Eighteenth-century fabric choker with bow-shaped ornament. Detail from a *casta* painting of the Mexican School, mid-eighteenth century. From *Coyote and morisca woman, the mocking, joke-playing albarazado.* Mexico, private collection.

Bracelets

Bracelets have been infrequently reported from Spanish colonial archaeological sites, particularly those dating to the seventeenth century or later. The earliest examples come from La Isabela, where fragments of several thin, ring-shaped glass bracelets were found (Fig. 6.28). Glass bracelets have also been recovered from the late-fifteenth-century Portuguese colony of Qsar es-Seghir in Morocco, where they were found archaeologically on the wrists of adolescent Christian female burials (Redman 1986:204; Boone 1980:148–

Popular Jewelry

Figure 6.27. Eighteenth-century emerald *aderezo*. Necklace, cross, bow pendant, *zarcillo* earrings, small earrings, and finger ring. Probably late seventeenth or early eighteenth century. Museo Nacional de Historia, Chapultapec, Mexico. Davis and Pack (1984:Plate 25). *Courtesy of the University of Texas Press and the authors.*

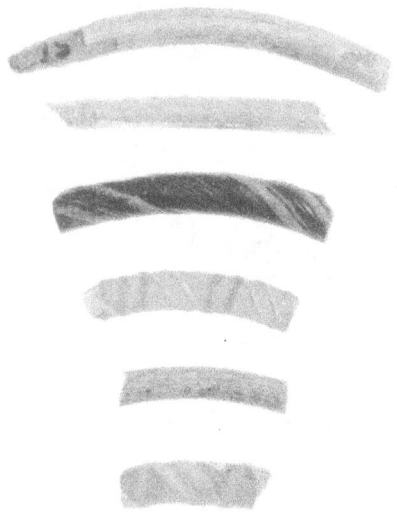

Figure 6.28. Glass bracelet fragments from La Isabela (1493–98). *Left to right:* Pale green, FS 13; clear glass tube, FS 176; black with white spiral stripes, FS 615; light green with latticinio stripes, FS 761; aqua, FS 132; green with dark green and white spiral stripes, FS 729. Length of top fragment 3.6 cm. Parque Nacional de La Isabela, Dominican Republic. *Photo: James Quine.*

149), and from seventeenth-century contexts at Fort Jesus in Kenya, where they are attributed to East Indian origin (Kirkman 1974:158, 317).

There is some indication that glass bracelets may have been associated with young or adolescent girls, since they were found in this context with the burials at Qsar es-Seghir, and bracelets (*manillas*) of glass are also known to have been ordered by Isabella of Spain for her daughter, the infanta (Muller 1972:25).

Glass bracelets have not been reported from Spanish American sites other than La Isabela and Puerto Real, and only a single example was found at the latter. Glass bracelets do, however, have a long-standing tradition of use dating from the medieval era to the present in the Islamic world and in India, where they are still made and used today (Spaer 1994).

The bracelets from La Isabela included fragments of opaque black glass with white spiral appliqué stripes, very dark green glass with white spiral appliqué stripes, and pale green glass with lattice-pattern (*latticinio*) appliqué white stripes. Other bracelets were of plain glass in light colors (pale green, clear, and aqua green), and one was constructed of twisted glass. The single example from Puerto Real is of dark blue glass. None of the American fragments are large enough to reconstruct diameter reliably, but the example from Qsar es-Seghir has a diameter of approximately 5.3 cm.

Figure 6.29. Eighteenth-century bead bracelet pairs. Detail from a *casta* painting of the Mexican School, mid-eighteenth century. From *Spaniard and mestizo woman, castizo. Courtesy of the Museo de América, Madrid.*

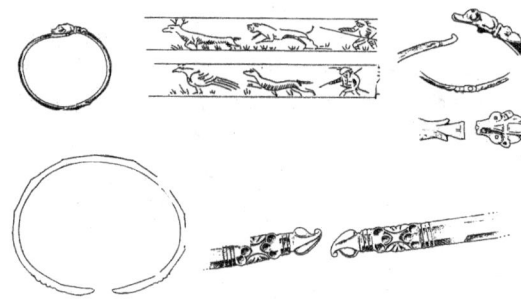

Figure 6.30. Bracelet forms recovered from shipwrecks, 1715. *Top:* Gold, with animal head terminal, and engraved with hunt design. Diameter 6.4 cm (8IR19) FBAR Lab #L-316. *Bottom:* Gold with molded finials (8SL17) FBAR Lab #L7189. *Courtesy of the Florida Bureau of Archaeological Research. Drawings: Frank Gilson.*

Ring-shaped bangle bracelets made of twisted copper wire have been reported from sites ranging from the sixteenth through the eighteenth centuries in both the Americas and Europe. Examples were found in a nineteenth-century context in association with the glass bracelets described earlier at Fort Jesus and are identified as having an Arabic origin (Kirkman 1974:316–317). A very similar example was recovered from the sixteenth-century Molasses Reef shipwreck in the Bahamas (Kieth 1987:270), and bracelets of this sort were widely used in the fur trade in late-seventeenth- and eighteenth-century North America (see Stone 1974:135; Cleland 1971:23).

Although pairs of *brazaletes* and *pulseras* were listed in the *Contaduría* shipping records for 1613, none have been recovered from seventeenth-century contexts, and, in fact, Muller (1972:141) notes that there was a notable lack of Spanish interest in bracelets during the seventeenth century (at least until the *aderezo* ensembles gained ascendancy). This trend seems to have been altered by the eighteenth century, when multistrand bracelets of pearls or beads were worn widely in Spain (Muller 1972:74) and in the Americas, where bracelets are consistently shown in the *casta* painting series (Fig. 6.29). These are shown worn in pairs, one pair on each wrist, and beads found on eighteenth-century sites may have been used in such bracelets.

The best source of direct information for other kinds of eighteenth-century bracelets has come from shipwrecks. The Florida plate fleet wrecks of 1715 and 1733 yielded examples of thin, metal, bangle bracelets of gold, which may suggest forms for bracelets of common materials in the colonies (Fig. 6.30).

Hair Ornaments

Jewelry for the hair was used by Spanish women throughout the colonial period. Muller (1972:25) notes that the hair jewels of Isabella included *pinjantes* (hairpins with pendants) and *alfiletes* (hairpins) designed *"para jugar y para tocar"* (to dance about and finish the headdress). Hair ornaments also included the *punzón* (single-pronged hairpin), *tembladeras* (bouncing ornaments to be attached to pins), and *clavillos* (ornamented hairpins). The latter were used with securing pins referred to as *agujas* (Muller 1972:136–137).

Hairpins with ornamental finials were also an important component of the *aderezos* of the seventeenth and eighteenth centuries.

Figure 6.31. Sixteenth-century hairpin. Copper alloy, Concepción de la Vega (1496–1562). Length 6.8 cm. Parque Nacional de Concepción de la Vega, Dominican Republic.

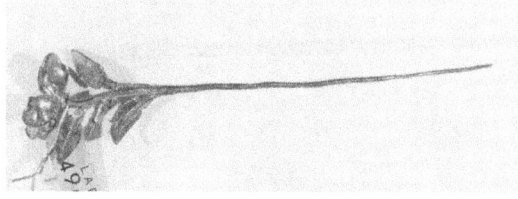

Figure 6.32. Eighteenth-century hairpin. Gold, with floral design. 1715. Length 9.8 cm. FBAR Lab #L4694. *Courtesy of the Florida Bureau of Archaeological Research.*

Madame D'Aulnoy comments of Spanish women in 1679 that "they all have their heads stuck full of bodkins, some made of diamonds in the shape of a fly, others like butterflies whose colors are distinguished by various stones" (1930:203).

Hair ornaments were undoubtedly used as well in the Spanish colonies, and the 1592 *Contaduría* records list a shipment of 100,000 *clavitos de vidrio tocado* (glass hairpins) costing 3 reales per thousand and 100,000 *clavitos de vidrio blanco y de colores* costing 4.25 reales per thousand. *Sobretocas de abalorios* (headdress ornaments of beads) were also sent to the colonies. Few hair ornaments have been archaeologically reported, however. A single, large, double-pronged hairpin was recovered at Concepción de la Vega (Fig. 6.31) and could have attached a pendant ornament. A white metal bodkin was recovered at the site of San Luis de Talimali (McEwan 1991a:308), and an ornamental hairpin with a floral design was recovered from the 1715 treasure fleet wrecks off the coast of Florida (Fig. 6.32). An example of hair ornaments worn by Spanish and mixed-blood women in eighteenth-century Mexico is shown in Figure 6.13.

Chapter 7
Bells

Bells were among the first European artifacts introduced in the Americas, and although they are not found in abundance on most archaeological sites, they can often provide useful chronological and functional information. Many kinds of bells have been recovered from sites, including those used for religious purposes, as amulets, as trade goods, for clothing ornaments, in musical instruments, and on animal harness and trappings.

Columbus brought copper-alloy bells on his first American voyage of exploration (1492–93), and they proved to be enormously popular with the Taíno Indians (see Vega 1979:41–45). One of the earliest and most infamous references to bells was the edict issued by Columbus in 1495 that every Indian over the age of 14, living near the Hispaniola mines, was to bring every three months in tribute "a bell of Flanders, that is the hole of the bell, filled with gold" (Las Casas 1985[I, CV]:417). The largest such bells known from contact period Hispaniola sites are approximately 3 cm in diameter, with a volume of approximately 14 cubic cm. This translates in gold weight to about 272 g (or 8.7 troy ounces.)

For much of the ensuing colonial period, bells continued to be important items in the trade repertoires of Spanish explorers and colonists throughout North America and the Antilles (Brain 1975). Three varieties for personal use are listed in the shipping records of the late sixteenth century, including *cascabeles* (closed, hawk bell–type bells), *campanillas* (small, open bells) and *cencerros* (open animal bells). *Cencerro* is defined by the Real Academia Española as "a small cylindrical bell, coarse and common, made with a clapper of iron. It is used for livestock and is usually fastened around the necks of cows" (1939:281).

Bells were used in many social and material contexts in the Spanish colonies, including as trade goods, as clothing adornment, on horse harness decoration, on animals and birds as locators, at gates and as doorbells, in a variety of church functions, and on amulets (particularly those for children). In many cases, the bells are physically indistinguishable from one another, and function must be inferred from archaeological context.

Two basic categories of bells are found archaeologically. The most common is the crotal, or closed, bell generally referred to in the archaeological literature as the rumbler bell. Rumbler bells are closed, are usually spherical or oval in shape, and enclose a loose clapper. They range from about 2 to 6 cm in diameter (although Spanish colonial archaeological examples are rarely larger than 3 cm in diameter). Rumbler bells are often popularly called jingle bells, sleigh bells, or hawk bells.

Open, or clapper, bells are open at one end and have a metal clapper attached to the inside of the bell. Most often cup or "bell" shaped, they occur in a much wider range of sizes than the rumbler bells, from small ornamental bells a few centimeters in height to the massive bells of Spanish churches and missions.

Bells in the Spanish Colonies

Most of the published information pertinent to the origin and history of Spanish colonial bells concerns large church bells (Carillo y Gariel 1989; Howe 1956; Walsh 1934). Such bells—whole or fragmentary—are only rarely found on archaeological sites (some exceptions are discussed later). Detailed descriptions of bell founding in the sixteenth century appear in Biringuccio's *Pirotechnia* (Smith and Gnudi 1990:260–275) and in Carillo y Gariel's discussion of Spanish colonial bell founding methods used in eighteenth-century Mexico (1989:11–13). Bell founding was an itinerant trade, and large bells were most often cast and founded near the building in which they were to be installed. Bell founding in this tradition was introduced into Spanish America before 1530, shortly after the arrival of the earliest colonists. Bells for the Mexico City Cathedral were first cast there in 1528, and Simón and Juan Buonaventura cast one of the massive tower bells in 1578 (Carillo y Gariel 1989:33; Price 1984:215). Church and other large bells were made throughout the Spanish colonies, including the southwestern borderlands of New Mexico (Howe 1956). These massive bells have been well documented; however, considerably less has been written about the smaller bells, both rumbler and open, which are found most frequently on archaeological sites.

Unlike many other aspects of Spanish colonial material culture, the long Moorish occupation of southern Spain did not influence the form of bells, since bells were forbidden in the Muslim tradition. The ringing of bells was thought to disturb the repose of souls and reflect infidelity (Coleman 1928:31). The origins of Spanish colonial small bells are probably, like those of most of western Eu-

Figure 7.1. Method of attachment for hawk bells. *Drawing: Pauline Kulstad.*

rope, found in the Roman *tintinabula*, small, musical, copper-alloy bells made in both open and rumbler varieties. Some of the earliest small bells found on Spanish American sites are quite similar to bells reported from European Roman colonial sites (see, for example, Coleman 1928:30).

During the fifteenth century, cast-metal rumbler bells—sometimes as large as 6.5 cm in diameter—frequently adorned both men's and women's clothing; however, the use of bells as dress accessories does not seem to have persisted in secular clothing much beyond the end of the fifteenth century (Payne 1965:222–223, 226–227; Egan and Pritchard 1991:336–337).

Rumbler bells were also frequently used during medieval times as hawk bells in falconry (Wood and Fyfe 1961:140–142; Fig. 7.1). The practice of falconry as a leisure activity was typically restricted (particularly after the early sixteenth century) to the elite classes and does not appear to have been practiced widely in the Americas after that time. Other than their use as hawk bells, rumbler bells were probably used most frequently in the colonies as trade items, on children's toys, as amulets, and on animal

Figure 7.2. *Der Schellenmaker* (the bell maker), 1568. Woodcut by Jost Amman in *Der Standebuch*. Originally published by Sigmund Feyerabens in Frankfurt am Main (Amman 1973:82).

Figure 7.3. Bells suspended from the hem of a priest's robe. Detail from Zurburán's *The Circumcision* (1639). *Courtesy of the Museé de Beaux Artes, Grenoble.*

gear, particularly on horse harness and trappings.

The production of small bells was not an occupation meriting a guild in the Spanish Americas, and no mention of bell making appears in the guild ordinances for New Spain (Lorenzot 1920). The bell maker, or *Schellenmacher*, was illustrated as a craftsperson, however, in the *Standebuch* (Book of trades) published in Nuremberg in 1568 (Amman and Sachs 1973; Fig. 7.2). This was a separate occupation from that of the bell founder (*Glockengeisser*), who made, in addition to large bells, guns, mortars, cauldrons, and ovens of bell metal (Amman and Sachs 1973:62).

It is likely that many, if not most, of the sheet-metal rumbler bells used in the Spanish American colonies were produced in northern Europe. Columbus, as noted earlier, specified that hawk bells of Flanders be used as a measure of Taíno gold tribute, and a 1496 English treatise on falconry comments on the excellence and low cost of "Dutche" hawk bells (Berners 1966:cv).

Bells as Amulets

The use of bells by Spaniards as part of their personal accouterments had roots in ancient Judeo-Christian traditions of attributing protective or amuletic properties to bells. One use for bells in Spain during the colonial era—that of trimming the robes of priests, for example (Fig. 7.3)—was also documented in biblical times, when golden bells trimmed the high priest's robes to impress the ears of both gods and people and to drive away evil spirits (Exodus 28:33–35; Price 1984:209).

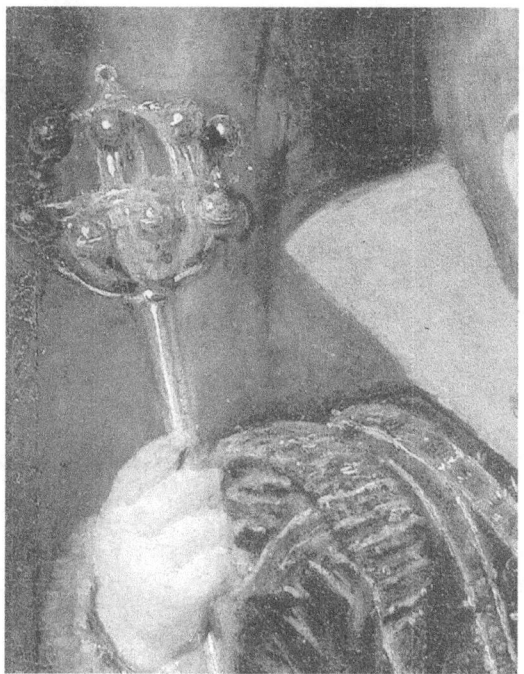

Figure 7.4. Rumbler bells on a *sonajero*. Detail, *Don Baltasar Carlos with a Dwarf* (1632). Diego Velásquez. Henry Lillie Pierce Fund #01.104. Courtesy Museum of Fine Arts, Boston. Reproduced with permission © 2000 Museum of Fine Arts, Boston. All rights reserved.

Figure 7.5. Rumbler and open bells used as a child's amulets. Detail from Velásquez's *Prince Felipe Próspero* (1659). Courtesy of the Kunsthistorisches Museum, Vienna. #GG319.

The belief that bells had protective properties against witches, spells, evil spirits, and other sources of supernatural harm was prevalent through the colonial period and persists today in some parts of Spain and Latin America. The *Compendium maleficarum*, a treatise on witchcraft published by an Ambrosian monk in 1608, describes the effects of bells as "so hostile and inimical to demons that they are prevented by it from raising up violent storms." It states further that "it is commonly confessed by witches that if, when they are carried by a demon to the Sabbat . . . the sound of bells is heard, the demons carrying them at once set down their foul burden and escape in terror" (Guazzo 1988:180, 206). Bells have been used for centuries in Spain as protective amulets to ward off storms and hearing problems (Alarcón Román 1987:129, 134), and both Church and laity acknowledged their protective properties (Thurston 1907).

This belief system is manifest archaeologically in small bells—both rumbler and open types—that were probably used as amulets. Of the 292 amulets cataloged in the Museo del Pueblo Español collections (Alarcón Román 1987), 14 (5 percent) included bells. Of these, eight were open bells of silver, and six were children's *sonajeros* incorporating small rumbler bells.

Bells as amulets appear to be associated most frequently with children. These are usually very small rumbler bells attached to rattles or small open bells suspended from cords around a child's waist (Figs. 7.4, 7.5). Adults also incorporated bells into amulets, such as those shown on the priest's robes in Figure 7.3 and that in Figure 7.6. Bells worn

Figure 7.6. Open bell used as an amulet. Detail from *The Man Holding a Pink Flower,* Dutch, ca. 1436. *Courtesy of the Staatliche Museum, Berlin-Preussischer Kulturbesitz. Gemäldegalerie. Photo: Jörg P. Adaders.*

Figure 7.7. Rumbler bells used on horse harness. Detail from Amman's *Cavalryman with Spear* (1599), *Der Kunstbuchlin* (4th ed.). *Pictorial Archive of Decorative Renaissance Woodcuts* (*Kunstbuchlin*) (Reprint, New York: Dover, 1968).

by animals could serve both as protective amulets and as decoration (Fig. 7.7). Bells used in amulets do not appear to differ physically from those used in other activities, although amulet bells are usually quite small and open bells used as amulets were usually made of silver (Alarcón Román 1987).

Rumbler Bells: Varieties and Characteristics

Several useful studies of archaeological bells have produced typologies and chronological sequences for rumbler bells in the Spanish colonies. The most detailed of these are found in Brown (1979) and Mitchem and McEwan (1988); however, several other sources provide important additional information (Brain 1975; Brown 1975; Jelks 1967; Smith 1987:42–44).

Rumbler bells can be produced either by casting or by shaping sheet metal. Each of these categories has been divided into "types" according to their method of construction and further subdivided into "varieties" according to their decorative attributes (Brown 1979:197–202). Table 7.1 is adapted from this classificatory system, based on Brown (1979:197–202).

Sheet-Metal Rumbler Bells

The most common bells on Spanish colonial sites are roughly spherical, sheet-metal rumbler bells. These bells are made in two halves, joined horizontally at the equator. Types are distinguished by the manner in which the two halves are joined, which can be lapped-edged, flanged-edged, or flush-edged (Jelks 1967:87; Brown 1979:197).

Lapped-edged Rumbler Bells

Lapped-edged bells are among the earliest in the Spanish colonies. On a lapped-edged bell, one of the hemispheres is slightly larger than the other, and its edges overlap the edges of the smaller hemisphere. These overlapped edges are crimped and/or soldered together to form a flat, squarish flange around the bell's equator. Three varieties of lapped-edged bells have been described from archaeological sites. These include Sabana Yegua, Clarksdale, and Lapcross bells.

The site of Sabana Yegua, a contact period

Table 7.1. Bell Varieties from Spanish Colonial Sites

	Dates*	Attachment Method	Holes	Joining	Size**	Decoration	Figure or Citation
CAST RUMBLER BELLS							
Petaloid	1493–1550	Cast circular loop	Open at base forming wide slit	Petaloid shape, joined at sides	Height 2.4–2.6	Thin wire wrapped around top under attachment loop	Figs. 7.13, 7.14
Key*							
La Vega	1500–1550	Cast tapering rectangle, wider at base with round punched hole	None recorded in upper halves	Flanges protruding from base of top half (possibly fitting into grooves in lower half)	3–4	Spiral lines or series of horizontal panels enclosing vertical lines	Fig. 7.13
Flower-key	1700–1800	Cast tapering rectangle, wider at base with round punched hole	2 in upper half, 4 in lower half, with 2 of these connected by narrow slit	Soldered, seam apparent but smoothed	2.4–5.5	Flowers with petals separated on larger bells by vertical ridges	Brown 1979: 198
Arch*							
Circarch	1675–1800	Cast square or rectangle with arch-shaped hole	2 in upper half, 2 in lower half connected by slit	Soldered, seam slightly projecting	2.7–6.0	Can have semicircles and vertical loops, letters "K" and "W"	Brown 1979: 199
SHEET BRASS RUMBLER BELLS							
Flush Edged*							
Bayou	1700–1730	Narrow strip of metal formed into a circle and soldered directly to top of bell	2 round holes at base joined by wide slit	Halves joined flush and soldered or brazed, no ridge or flange	2.3–2.7	None reported	Brown 1979: 203
Flushloop	1600–1850	Narrow strip of metal passed through bell top and soldered inside	2 round holes at base joined by slit	Halves joined flush and soldered or brazed; no ridge or flange	1.2–2.5	Some have 4 grooves encircling bell (2 above and 2 below equator	Fig. 7.11; Brown 1979: 201

Continued on next page

Table 7.1. continued

	Dates*	Attachment Method	Holes	Joining	Size**	Decoration	Figure or Citation
Flanged-Edged							
Saturn	1650–1850	Narrow strip of metal passed through bell top and soldered inside	2 round holes at base joined by slit	Edges of halves turned out and brazed together forming narrow flange	1.4–4.4	Occasional maker's mark on base	Brown 1979: 202
Lapped-Edged*							
Sabana Yegua	1492–1500	Narrow strip of metal passed through bell top and soldered inside	2 round holes at base joined by slit	Lapping, crimping, and brazing edges into a narrow protruding flange	1.6	None recorded	Fig. 7.8
Clarksdale	1492–1575	Wide strip of metal passed through bell top and soldered inside	2 round holes at base joined by slit	Crimped and folded join producing a squarish flange	2.0–3.2	Rare, incised designs on lower half	Figs. 7.9, 7.10 Brain 1975
CAST OPEN BELLS							
Bowl-shaped	1500–1550	Cast tapering rectangle, wider at base, with round punched hole	n/a	n/a	2.5–4.0	Cast spirals or geometric lines, occasional makers mark	Fig. 7.13
"High-waisted" copper	1500–1750	Cast loop	n/a	n/a	Height 4.0–5.0	None reported	Fig. 7.17
Small, copper alloy or silver	ca. 1500–1800	Cast loop; cast rectangle or oval with drilled hole	n/a	n/a	Height 2.0–8.0	Can have raised, molded figures or letters; incised lines	Figs. 7.5, 7.6, 7.21

* Dates are based on reported archaeological associations.
** Size is diameter in centimeters at center of bell unless otherwise indicated. Based on reported archaeological examples.
*** For descriptions of other bells in these categories not reported so far from Spanish colonial sites, see Brown (1979:197–202).

Figure 7.8. Rumbler bells from Sabana Yegua, pre-1550. *Top row:* Clarksdale bells. *Bottom row:* Sabana Yegua bells. Diameter at equator 1.6 cm. Vega Collection, Santo Domingo. *Courtesy of Bernardo Vega.*

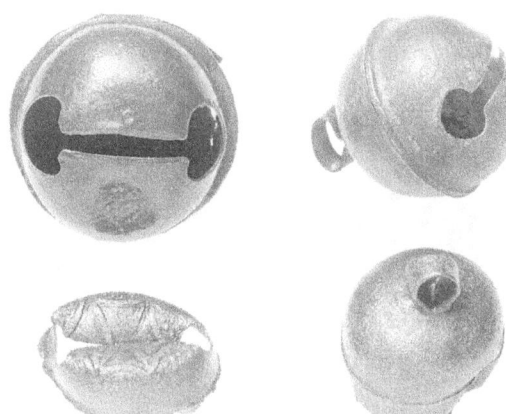

Figure 7.9. Clarksdale bells from Puerto Real, 1503–78. Maximum diameter of top left bell, 2.94 cm. Hodges Collection, Musée de Guahabá, Limbé, Haiti. *Photo: James Quine.*

Taíno Indian site in the Dominican Republic, yielded five early-sixteenth-century lapped-edged rumbler bells (Vega 1979). Two of these were large Clarksdale bells, measuring 2.7 cm in diameter (discussed later), and the other three bells were considerably smaller and distinct in their construction (Fig. 7.8). These small bells each measured 1.6 cm in diameter. They had slightly different sizes of upper and lower hemispheres, which were joined at the bell's equator by lapping, then crimping and brazing the joined edges into a narrow protruding flange, similar in form to the flange on the flange-edged Saturn bell. The suspension attachment on these early bells was a strip of metal passed through a hole in the top of the bell and crimped or soldered on the inside. The bottom of the bells has two round holes connected by a slit. These small, flanged, lapped-edged bells are referred to here simply as Sabana Yegua bells and are presumed to date to the late fifteenth and very early sixteenth century. This early date is supported by the presence at La Isabela (1493–98) of two fragments of what appear to be Sabana Yegua bells. They constitute the only evidence of bells recovered at this wholly fifteenth-century site.

The best-known lapped-edged sheet-metal rumbler bells from archaeological sites are those known as Clarksdale bells, first described by Brain (1975). The Clarksdale bell is a reliable marker for the sixteenth century, although it has been reported from a few contexts dating to the first quarter of the seventeenth century (Mitchem and McEwan 1988; Smith 1987:43). Its distinguishing characteristics include: a crimped and folded seam producing a squarish flange around the bell's equator; a squarish or slightly "squashed" shape rather than a true spherical shape; the presence of two round holes connected by a slit at the bottom of the bell; and a wide (ca. 1.5–2.5 mm) attachment loop made of a strip of metal passed through a hole in the top of the bell and soldered to the interior surface.

Most Clarksdale bells have an undecorated surface; however, Mitchem and McEwan (1988:41) note examples from Florida with grooved or incised lines encircling the lower halves of the bells. One example of what may also have been a Clarksdale bell from Puerto Real, Haiti (1503–78), bears an embossed design on its lower half (Fig. 7.9).

Clarksdale bells from sixteenth-century Native American sites in Florida range in di-

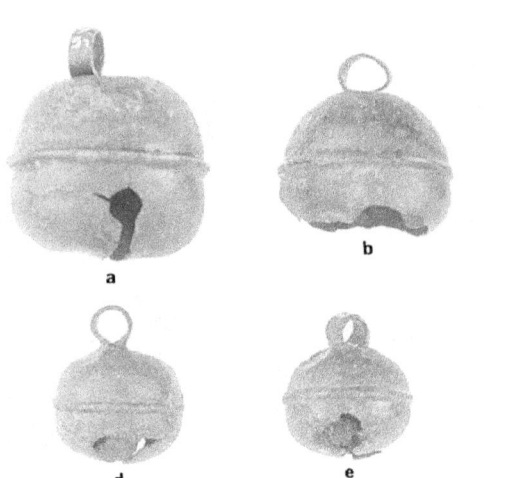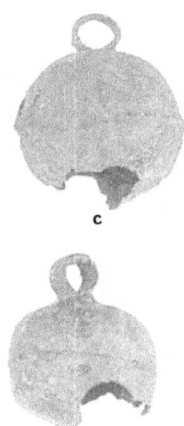

Figure 7.10. Clarksdale bells from Florida sites. A–E. St. Marks Wildlife refuge; F. Bee Branch site. A, B, D, E, F, South Florida Museum, Bradenton, #s A-1966, A-1965, A-1964, A-1963, 4-6183. C, Florida Museum of Natural History #102657. Bell A diameter 2.2 cm. Reprinted from Mitcham and McEwan (1988:Fig. 2). *By permission of Southeastern Archaeology and the authors.*

ameter from 2.0 to 2.8 cm (Mitchem and McEwan 1988:41). Examples from sixteenth-century Spanish sites in Florida and the Caribbean range from 2.0 to 3.2 cm in diameter (see, for example, Figs. 7.9 and 7.10). The larger sizes typical of these bells on Spanish sites may reflect a different use by Europeans, such as use on horse harness rather than as trade goods or clothing adornment.

Brown (1975:195) describes another variety of a lapped-edged, sheet-metal rumbler bell known as a Lapcross bell. This variety has not been reported from Spanish colonial sites and cannot be confused with the Clarksdale bell. The Lapcross bell is smaller and made of copper, it has a wire attachment loop, and the lower hemisphere has two perpendicular slits forming a cross rather than the two holes connected by a slit found in the Clarksdale bell. It also occurs primarily in nineteenth-century contexts and is thought to be of American manufacture (Brown 1979:204).

Flanged-edged Rumbler Bells
Flanged-edge bells differ from lapped-edged bells in that the two hemispheres are bowl shaped and of equal size (rather than, as in the latter, being squarish and of slightly unequal sizes), and their edges meet and are turned out. The turned-out edges are brazed together to form a narrow, protruding flange (as opposed to the flat, squarish flange on the Clarksdale bell).

Brown distinguishes two varieties of flanged-edged bells, "Flancross" and "Saturn" bells (1979:197, 202–203), neither of which has been reported from Spanish colonial contexts (South, Skowronek, and Johnson [1988:142] describe an iron Saturn bell from Santa Elena found in a post-Spanish context). The Saturn variety has two holes connected by a slit in the lower bell hemisphere, while the Flancross bell has two slits forming a cross in the lower hemisphere. The Saturn bell appears to be the more common of the two, and its distribution suggests that it is associated with French and American sites between about 1650 and 1850.

Flush-edged Rumbler Bells
In contrast to the lapped-edged and flanged-edged types, flush-edged bells do not exhibit any kind of protruding or elevated flange around the bell equator. The two bowl-shaped hemispheres are instead placed flush together and soldered or brazed into place, leaving a seam but no discernable flange (Jelks 1967:87; Brown 1979:201). Silver-colored solder is sometimes evident on the seam.

Brown (1979:203–204) distinguishes two flush-edged varieties, the "Flushloop" and

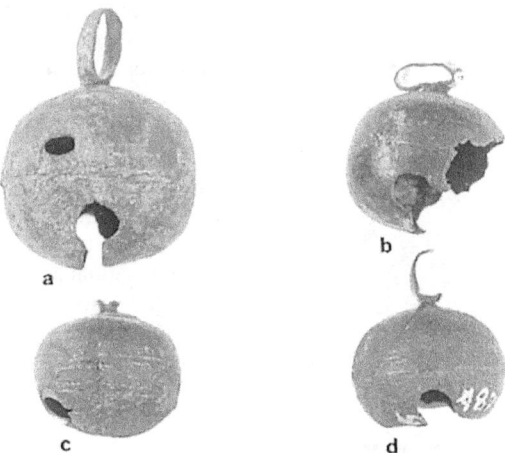

Figure 7.11. Flushloop bells from American Indian mounds in Florida. A. Thomas Mound (SFM #A5657). B–D. Rattlesnake Mound (SFM A8748, A8747, A8746). South Florida Museum, Bradenton. Diameter of bell A 1.75 cm. Reprinted from Mitchem and McEwan (1988:Fig. 3). *By permission of Southeastern Archaeology and the authors.*

Figure 7.12. Mid-eighteenth-century Flushloop-style bells. *Left:* Gilded copper alloy. Diameter 1.8 cm. St. Augustine (SA-36-4-340). *Right:* Copper alloy. Diameter 1.3 cm. St. Augustine (SA-7-4-95). FLMNH/CSA Collections. *Photos: James Quine.*

the "Bayou." Of these, the Flushloop is the most common and long-lived, spanning the period from about 1600 or earlier to about 1825. Its distinguishing characteristics (in addition to the absence of a flange) is an attachment loop made of a thin strip of metal looped and passed through a hole in the top of the bell, two holes connected by a slit in the lower hemisphere of the bell, and the frequent presence of four grooved lines encircling the bell.

The Bayou bell can be distinguished by a very smooth external surface with a barely perceptible or imperceptible seam line and an oval-shaped loop attachment soldered directly to the top of the bell. Its temporal distribution appears to have been restricted to the first third of the eighteenth century (Brown 1979:204), and it has not been reported from Spanish colonial sites.

Flushloop bells occur on colonial-era Native American sites in Florida thought to date from the second half of the sixteenth century through the seventeenth century (see Gordon and Deagan 1992; Mitchem and McEwan 1988:41–44). These range from 12 to 21 mm in diameter (Figs. 7.11, 7.12). Small (12–20 mm diameter) Flushloop-type bells are found on eighteenth-century domestic sites in St. Augustine; however, these often have a wire loop for suspension rather than a loop made from a strip of brass, as is typical of the Flushloop bells described by Brown (Fig. 7.12).

Flushloop bells from non-Florida sites range from 11 to 25 cm in diameter. They are found in seventeenth- through nineteenth-century contexts and are thought to have been of English or French manufacture (see Brown 1979:201–204; Mitchem and McEwan 1988:41–44).

Cast Rumbler Bells

The second basic category of rumbler bells reported in the Americas include bells cast of brass or copper alloy rather than shaped of sheet brass. Cast bells are easily distinguished by the attachment loop, which is cast as an integral part of the top half of the bell rather than added separately. They are thicker and heavier than sheet-brass bells and are often decorated with a molded relief design, rather than the embossed, impressed, or incised designs found occasionally on sheet-metal bells.

Brown (1979) offers a classification of cast rumbler bells based on the shape of the

148   Religion, Ritual, and Adornment

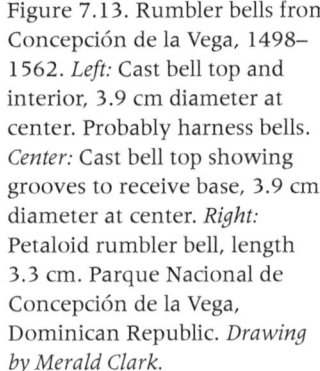

Figure 7.13. Rumbler bells from Concepción de la Vega, 1498–1562. *Left:* Cast bell top and interior, 3.9 cm diameter at center. Probably harness bells. *Center:* Cast bell top showing grooves to receive base, 3.9 cm diameter at center. *Right:* Petaloid rumbler bell, length 3.3 cm. Parque Nacional de Concepción de la Vega, Dominican Republic. *Drawing by Merald Clark.*

attachment loop. Those with an attachment shaped somewhat like an inverted block letter "v" and with the point flattened are designated as Key types; those with attachment loops shaped like a square or a rectangle are called Arch types; and those with rounded, dome-shaped attachment loops are referred to as Dome types. Each of these three categories is further divided into types based on the nature of the design cast onto the bell's surface (Table 7.1). Most of the bells Brown describes are of French or English manufacture and date to the eighteenth century. He suggests that most of the cast rumbler bells from that period are of English manufacture (Brown 1979:197–200).

Spherical cast brass rumbler bells have also been recovered from sixteenth- and seventeenth-century Spanish sites, and these may have been of German origin, given the trade patterns of that period (see Chapter 3). The upper halves of several ornately cast bells were recovered from Concepción de la Vega in the Dominican Republic (1498–1562) (Fig. 7.13). These range in size from 3.0 to 4.0 cm in diameter at the center and from 2.3 to 3.2 cm in height. The cast attachments are of the Key type described by Brown (1979:198). One of the bells has a soldered loop inside for the attachment of a clapper, while the others have no such attachment piece, suggesting that loose rumblers were used. The bells' surfaces are decorated with spiral lines or a series of horizontal panels enclosing vertical lines. Cast bells of similar size and shape to those from Concepción de la Vega have been reported from seventeenth-century contexts. These later bells, however, do not have cast decoration, and their tops are of the Arch-type rather than the Key-type. Examples occur at San Luis de Talimali (ca. 1650–1700) (McEwan 1992:45; Fig. 7.14) and the 1641 shipwreck of the *Concepción* (Borrell 1983c:106; Peterson 1979a:18).

Cast rumbler bells of a very distinctive form have been recovered in quantity at the site of Concepción de la Vega. These bells are of an elongated-pear shape ("petaloid"), joined at the sides rather than around the center. They are cast with a round loop attachment at the top and have a slot at the bottom of the bell following the curve of the lower edge (Fig. 7.15). Examples from Concepción de la Vega range from 2.4 to 2.6 cm in length, and this bell variety has not been reported from any other sites. They are similar to the petaloid bells that occurred com-

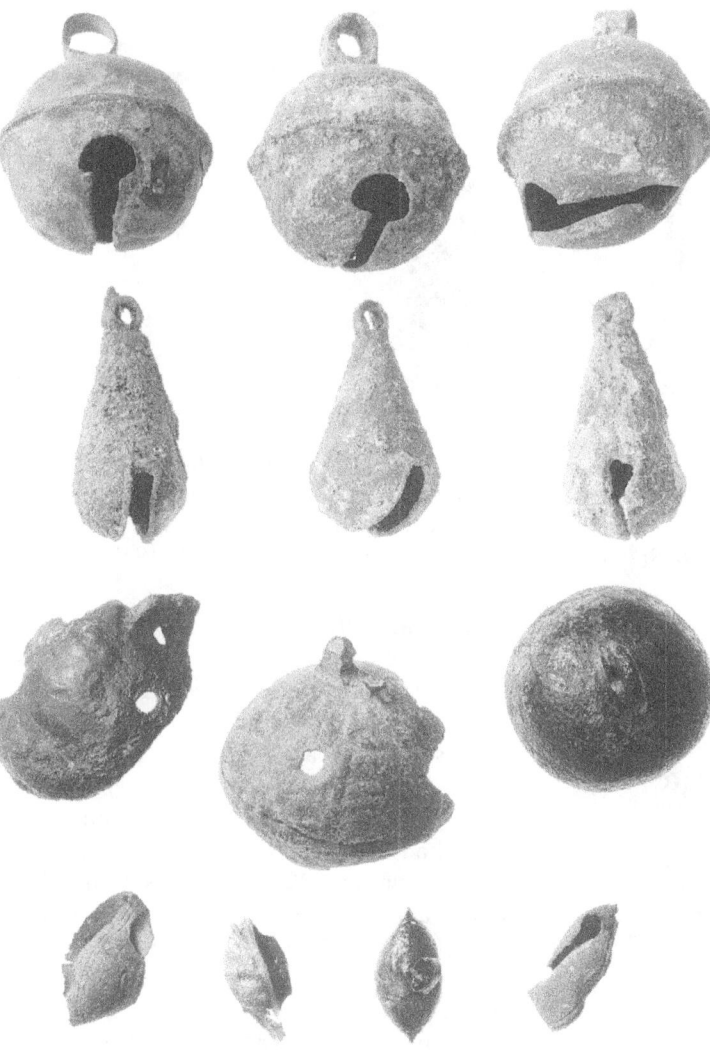

Figure 7.14. Petaloid bells and Clarksdale bells from Concepción de la Vega, 1498–1562. *Top row:* Clarksdale bells, center bell diameter 3.3 cm. *Bottom row:* Petaloid bell lengths: 3.2 cm, 3.5 cm, 3.9 cm. Parque Nacional de Concepción de la Vega, Dominican Republic. *Photo: James Quine.*

Figure 7.15. Seventeenth-century bells from San Luis de Talimali, ca. 1650–1700. *Top row:* Cast bells, left to right: FS 7360; FS 74-36-132, 169, 143; FS 6205. Diameter of top right bell: 3.9 cm. *Bottom row:* Flushloop bell fragments, left to right: FS 4329, FS 4249, FS 6327, FS 1648. *Courtesy of the Florida Bureau of Archaeological Research, the San Luis Archaeological and Historical Site, and Bonnie G. McEwan. Photo: James Quine.*

monly as clothing decoration in late medieval Europe (see Egan and Pritchard 1991:339–340).

Open Bells

Without inscribed dates, most open bells are not particularly useful as chronological indicators on Spanish colonial sites. By the middle of the sixteenth century, the modern bell shape of an inverted, skirted cup was standard and has continued without significant change to the present century (Fig. 7.16). The few sixteenth-century examples recovered archaeologically have cast and drilled suspension holes (see Fig. 7.17), while two open bells from eighteenth-century shipwrecks—the 1733 Florida plate fleet wrecks (Skowronek 1982:153) and the 1724 Quicksilver wrecks (Museo de la Atarazana, Santo Domingo)—have large, circular loop attachments and three sets of three incised lines encircling the bodies. The small size of the available sample, however, precludes suggesting that these traits serve as chronological markers.

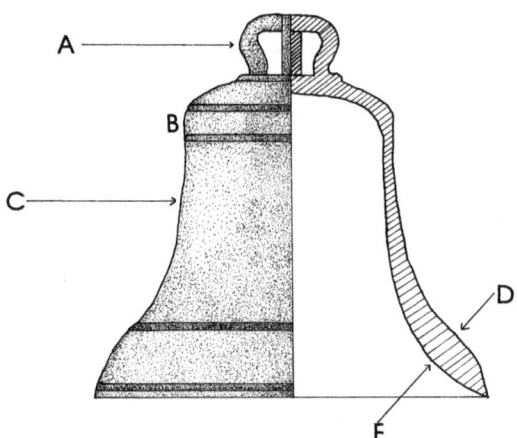

Figure 7.16. Open bell components. A. Cannons or loops; B. Incised lines (optional; inscriptions are usually placed near or within lines, iconography in the middle); C. Waist; D. Sound bow; E. Rim or lip. *Drawing: Pauline Kulstad.*

Figure 7.17. Sixteenth-century copper-alloy open bells. Concepción de la Vega (1498–1562). *Left:* Mouth diameter 4.5 cm. Height (including loop) 5.1 cm. *Right:* Small chime bell, mouth diameter 12.0 cm. Height (without loop) 12.0 cm (including loop, 16.5 cm). Parque Nacional de Concepción de la Vega, Dominican Republic. *Photos: James Quine.*

Figure 7.18. Mission bells in Mexico. Detail from *Crónica de Michoacán* by Frey Pablo Beaumont (eighteenth century). *Publicaciones del Archivos Generál de la Nacion* (Mexico), Vol. 19, 1932.

Both large and small open bells were important elements in the repertoire of Spanish missions during the seventeenth and eighteenth centuries (Fig. 7.18). John Hann's analysis of Florida mission inventories documents bells in various contexts. In 1681, for example, the 34 extant Florida Indian missions had 92 bells to toll for mass (nearly 3 per mission) and 238 "little bells, some in circles and some loose, to ring for the Sanctus" (Hann 1986:151). The former bells were probably large mission bells, recorded as having been buried in 1704 when the missions were abandoned, because the Spaniards were unable to carry everything away. Hann (1986:148–160) interpreted the 238 "little bells" to have been handbells, some of them probably welded together in rings.

Open bells were often used on animal, and sometimes human, collars to help control mobile property. The cylindrical *cencerro* (cowbell) described previously served for livestock, and smaller animals undoubtedly had smaller bells on their collars. An eighteenth-century Ecuadorian painting depicts another use for small open bells: they were suspended on the collars of manacled prisoners of the Moors (Fig. 7.19).

Figure 7.19. Open bells on collars worn by captives of the Moors. Detail from Manuel de Samaniego (1767–1824), *Virgen de Mercedes con cautivos.* Courtesy of the Museo Filanbanco, Quito, Ecuador.

Handbells

Handbells of about 12 to 18 cm in length are occasionally found on Spanish colonial sites, particularly on shipwrecks. Some examples, such as that shown in Figure 7.20, have come from domestic contexts and were probably used for summoning or for personal devotions. Others, particularly such ornate handbells as that shown in Figure 7.21, may have been used for a variety of religious purposes, both in the Mass and as part of many other Devotions of the Catholic Church (see Thurston 1907:19). Handbells were among the earliest cast bells in Europe, first made by Italian Benedictine monks at the end of the sixth century, and have been part of the Christian missionary's repertoire since that time (Price 1984:212). Handbells often appear in portraits of prelates and popes by seventeenth-century Spanish artists such as Zurburán (Fig. 14.21).

Large Open Bells

Large open bells in a vast range of sizes were used as signaling devices both in churches and on ships in the Spanish colonies. These bells are generally foundered in bronze, using proportions close to 20 parts tin or pewter and 80 parts copper (Howe 1956:149; Noel Hume 1980:58). Bells of the sixteenth cen-

Figure 7.20. Copper-alloy handbell fragment, ca. 1580–1600. Length 8.5 cm. St. Augustine (SA-24-279). FLMNH/CSA Collections. *Photo: James Quine.*

tury typically had an elongated shape, which gradually evolved by the late seventeenth century to a shape with less length and greater diameter (Toussaint 1967:267).

Churches and missions usually had bells in sets of three or more (as in Fig. 7.18), and each bell was sanctified, named, and considered a member of the spiritual community (Foster 1960:159). Most large bells were inscribed with some or all of the following information: the bell's name, its dedication, the date and place of the founding, the bell founder, the priests in residence at the time of founding, and the financial patron of the bell.

The sizes of such bells were extremely varied. The largest known bell in the world is the "Tsar Kolokol II," cast in 1735 and hanging in the Kremlin in Moscow. It weighs more than

Figure 7.21. Gold-plated silver handbell, 1733. Height 14 cm (8MO101) FBAR Lab #S12-19133. *Courtesy of the Florida Bureau of Archaeological Research. Drawing: Frank Gilson.*

210,000 kg with a lip diameter of 6.9 m (Price 1984:209). The largest bell in the Mexico City cathedral was smaller but still immense at 20,240 kg (440 *quintales*) (Carillo y Gariel 1989:34–39). Many of the church bells in the larger churches of Mexico measured more than a meter across in diameter (see Carillo y Gariel 1989). These bells are not recovered archaeologically, for they were refounded into new bells once they broke or lost tone.

Most of the signaling bells that have been recovered archaeologically—those on ships and in the Spanish frontier missions—were considerably smaller than the bells just described, and most fall into the category of "chime bells" (Table 7.2). Chime bells generally weigh less than 45.5 kg, are from 22.0 to 40.0 cm in height, are 4.5 to 6.6 cm thick, and have a lip circumference of from 66.0 to 165.0 cm (Howe 1956:148–149). They also tend to be longer in relation to their width during the sixteenth and seventeenth centuries, in comparison to the eighteenth century, when the height and mouth diameter of the bell are often equal.

Some chime bells were inscribed and dated, with inscriptions found most commonly around the sound bow. A characteristic Spanish inscription, seen on bells from Florida, Mexico, New Mexico, and Spain, is a cross made up of small squares or diamonds, sometimes with each square or diamond con-

Table 7.2. Colonial-Era Chime Bells from Marine Sites

Site	Date	Bell Height (cm)	Base Diameter (cm)	Decoration	Suspension
Tolosá	1724	50–60	50–60	Inscriptions	obscured
Tolosá	1724	18	15	Raised figures	3-lobe
Bronze bell wreck	1677	34	28	Figures, inscriptions	3-lobe
H-1, Florida	1650–1700	30	28	Cross	3-lobe

Figure 7.22. Bronze Florida mission bell, ca. 1650–1700. Height 30.2 cm, mouth diameter 28.2 cm, weight 13.64 kg. Ben Waller Collection, Ocala (Site H-1). *Drawing by Pauline Kulstad, after Denton 1991.*

taining a floral or geometric design. Another characteristic feature of Spanish colonial chime bells is the crown attachment, which is often comprised of three rings or loops arranged in a pyramid shape (Figs. 7.18, 7.22, 7.23).

The 1772 inventory of the San Antonio de Valera mission in Texas provides specific information about the kinds of large bells that might typically have occurred at Spanish frontier mission sites (Leutenneger 1977). The inventory lists seven bells; three of these were large bells weighing 15 to 18 *arrobas* (approximately 170 to 200 kg), two were small bells weighing 5 to 7 *arrobas* (62 to 175 kg), and there were two considerably smaller bells weighing from 2.25 to 3 kg and 3.5 to 4.5 kg (Leutenegger 1977:34–35). It was additionally noted that because the new church tower was not completed, the bells were hung from two poles supported by upright forked supports (Leutenegger 1977:34–35).

A few Spanish colonial bells of this type have been recovered archaeologically, and a large number of them are still in use in the churches of Spanish America and the American Southwest (for descriptions of such bells, see Howe 1956; Walsh 1934). Figure 7.22 shows a Florida mission bell of this type, and fragments of mission bells have been recovered at the seventeenth-century missions of

Figure 7.23. Bronze chime bell. Mouth diameter 50 cm. *El Conde de Tolosá* (1724). *Courtesy of the Museo de la Atarazana, Santo Domingo. Photo: James Quine.*

Santa Catalina de Guale in Georgia and San Damian de Escambe in La Florida and at Awatovi in Arizona (Thomas 1988:104).

Several large chime bells were recovered from the 1724 *Tolosá* wreck (Borrell 1983a:116). These range from 15 to 60 cm in diameter at the mouth and about 18 to 50 cm in height, excluding the three-lobed suspension piece. The largest bell (Fig. 7.23) is dated 1710, and the others have two inscribed lines encircling the skirt and relief figures of standing people on the sides.

An elaborately cast bronze bell with a date inscription of 1677 was recovered from an early-eighteenth-century shipwreck off the coast of Wales. Not only is the bell inscribed and dated, but it also has figures of the Virgin Mary, Christ, and cherubs molded in relief (Davies et al. 1981:49–50). This bell is similar in size to the somewhat simpler late-seventeenth-century bell shown in Figure 7.23, recovered from a Florida river (Denson 1991). Both of these bells were thought to have been intended for use in churches and are similar in their size, date, attachment rings, and the religious nature of their decorations.

Summary

Closed rumbler (crotal) bells and open bells are both found on Spanish colonial archaeological sites. The category of open bells can be usefully divided further into small amuletic or ornamental bells, handbells, chime bells, and the massive church bells. All of the rumbler bells reported from archaeological sites have been small (under 6 cm in diameter), and the majority have been sheet-metal Clarksdale bells (ca. 1500–1630) or Flushloop bells (ca. 1580–1700). Cast rumbler bells are only rarely reported. Small rumbler bells found on Spanish colonial domestic sites were probably used on amulets or children's toys and larger examples on horse or other animal gear.

Open bells are more varied but less useful for dating purposes. Small, "bell-shaped" copper-alloy or silver open bells span the entire colonial period. Those of the eighteenth century tend to be shorter in relation to their diameter than are open bells of the sixteenth or seventeenth centuries. Small open bells on domestic sites, particularly bells made of silver, were often used as amulets.

Church-related bells include handbells, chime bells, and large church bells, which, unless they are inscribed with dates, are not especially useful as temporal markers. Chime bells produced in the Americas occur most commonly on frontier church sites, and many are still in use in Mexico and the southwestern United States.

Part 3
Clothing

Chapter 8
Clothing Fasteners and Ornaments

This chapter addresses archaeologically recovered items associated with clothing, including fasteners and various forms of clothing adornment. Although buckles are often associated with clothing, they are considered in the following chapter because of their multiple functions as clothing, shoe, armor, harness, and spur fasteners.

Obviously, most colonial clothing was made of organic materials and was unlikely to survive archaeologically except under very unusual circumstances. Several studies of Spanish colonial clothing, however, have been based on paintings and museum specimens and provide a more complete survey of the range of clothing worn by Spaniards and Spanish colonists of the sixteenth through eighteenth centuries. Among the most useful of these for archaeological interpretation are Anderson (1979) and Berners (1962) on sixteenth-century Spanish clothing; Carillo y Gariel (1959) on colonial-period New Spain; and Duarte (1984) on colonial-era Venezuela. Although not specifically addressing clothing, the eighteenth-century Mexican and Andean *casta* paintings compiled by García Saíz (1989) provide what is probably the most comprehensive survey of nonelite clothing during that period.

Buttons

Buttons were used both as clothing fasteners and as ornaments throughout the Spanish colonial era in the Americas. Although they are not common on archaeological sites before the middle of the seventeenth century, they can be useful in dating sites and interpreting social attributes. Buttons were used by the Romans as fasteners and were used for centuries on medieval-era Asian and Moorish clothing. It is thought, however, that buttons were not widely employed in Europe until the thirteenth century (Egan and Pritchard 1991:272; Nevison 1977:38; Payne 1965:109–110). Moorish dress style, which was more closely fitted than most medieval European clothing and typically featured long rows of buttons, influenced European costume after its introduction by returning Crusaders (Anderson 1979:92–93).

By the fourteenth century, buttons were an important decorative element in European dress as well as a means of fastening clothing (Nevison 1977; Payne 1965:180). They appear in paintings as long rows of small, round buttons down the fronts of men's doublets and women's dresses, along the edges of women's sleeves, and on caps (Payne 1965:180–181, 190–193). Buttons continued to be used as fasteners, but their popularity as decorative elements apparently declined in most nonelite European clothing during the fifteenth and sixteenth centuries.

Button-makers guilds were not designated in Spain or New Spain during the colonial period (Lorenzot 1920; Santiago y Cruz 1960), nor was such a group noted for sixteenth-century Córdoba or Seville (Córdoba de la Llave 1990). Button making (particularly making buttons of bone and thread) appears to have been a cottage industry, or buttons were made by craftspeople in a variety of different guilds. Metallic and silk thread buttons, for example, were made by the silk tailors in sixteenth-century Mexico, and glove makers were mandated to make purses or pouches with buttons "trimmed in deerhide" (Lorenzot 1920:125). Metal buttons were probably made by jewelers (*plateros*) in precious metals and by other metalworkers such as brass workers (*latoneros*) in base metals.

Considerably more is known about the early button industry in England (Noel Hume 1980:88–93; White 1977), which produced and distributed many of the buttons found in the eighteenth-century Spanish colonies. Before the middle of the eighteenth century, button production in England was largely a cottage industry concentrating on cloth-covered and thread buttons. By about 1760, however, metal and gilt buttons were the most popular adornment fasteners on men's clothing, and these required specialized production processes that could not be met in a cottage industry (White 1977:68).

Button making thus became considerably more standardized in the eighteenth century, and by the time Diderot's *Encyclopédie* was published (1751–97), three separate entries were devoted to cast-metal, resin, and cloth-covered button production, respectively (Diderot 1751–65). Many of the buttons found in eighteenth-century Spanish colonial sites are of English, Dutch, or French origin, imported to the Spanish colonies either legally or through contraband (see, for example, Blair 1960).

Buttons in the Spanish Colonies
The great majority of buttons reported from Spanish colonial sites date to after the beginning of the eighteenth century, when a change to French-influenced fitted clothing styles was manifest at all levels of society. Before that time, clothing of nonelite colonists tended to be laced, tied, belted, or hooked rather than buttoned. Carillo y Gariel's document-based study of dress in New Spain treats the clothing of slaves, the nobility, religious orders, and soldiers (Carillo y Gariel 1959).

Most studies of pre-eighteenth-century Spanish costume and costume accessories (for example, Anderson 1979; Davenport 1948; Payne 1965; Reade 1951) depict rows of small buttons (often of thread or cloth) as a consistent feature of Spanish clothing from the sixteenth through the nineteenth centuries. Most of these works, however, are based on paintings and museum specimens, which usually portray elite individuals or special occasions. The archaeological record of nonelite daily life in the Spanish colonies provides a somewhat different portrayal of button use in that the great majority of buttons recovered from sites dating to before 1650 are from military contexts, and no buttons have been reported from any reliable contexts dating before about 1560.

In spite of the archaeological record, there is considerable documentary evidence for the importation and use of buttons in the sixteenth-century Spanish colonies. Torre Revello (1943:778) notes that buttons of crystal, gilded brass (*latón dorado*), and thread (*espigados de hilera*) were imported to New Spain between 1534 and 1586.

Contratación (shipping contract) records for New Spain provide additional details. Nine crystal buttons, three costing 227 maravedís each and six costing 61 maravedís each, were imported to Cartagena in 1583 (Table 8.1; A.G.I. *Contratación* 1080). These were obviously ornamental luxury items, compared to the 20 gross of glass buttons imported to New Spain in 1613, which cost 20 maravedís a gross (A.G.I. *Contratación* 1159). Other glass buttons were imported to New Spain in 1592–93, including six gross without prices listed and five dozen costing 2 reales a dozen (A.G.I. *Contratación* 1100, Folio 34). In addition to the glass buttons imported to New

Table 8.1. Clothing Items Shipped to the Spanish Colonies, 1511–1613

	1511	1583	1590	1592	1603	1613	Total
ABALORIOS PARA BORDAR (embroidery beads)					50,000		50,000
CORTES DE ABALORIOS PARA MANTOS (bead edgings for cloaks)					3		3
BOTONES DE ALQUIMIA (buttons of metalwork)				13,824			13,824
BOTONES DE CRISTAL (crystal buttons)		9					9
BOTONES DE VIDRIO (glass buttons)				924		2,880	3,804
PUNTILLAS BLANCAS (white lace tips)				1,000			1,000
PUNTILLAS DE VIDRIO (glass lace tips)			66,000	29,000			95,000
PUNTILLAS DE VIDRIO LISAS (smooth plain glass lace tips)				2,000			2,000
PUNTILLAS MORADAS DE VIDRIO (purple glass lace tips)				1,000			1,000
DEDALES DE MARFIL (ivory thimbles)				4			4
Total	0	9	66,000	47,752	50,003	2,880	166,644

Source: *Registros de la Casa de Contratación,* Archivo Genérál de las Indias, Seville (microfilm copy in the P. K. Yonge Library of Florida History, University of Florida, Gainesville)

1511—*Contratación* #1451
1523—*Contratación* #1079
1583—*Contratación* #1080
1590—*Contratación* #s 1089, 1092
1592-93—*Contratación* #1099
1603—*Contratación* #1143
1613—*Contratación* #s 1159, 1160

Spain in 1592, 96 gross of *"alquimia"* ("alchemy," probably gilded) buttons costing 3 reales per gross entered Veracruz (A.G.I. *Contratación* 1100 Folio 49).

Eugene Lyon's study of late-sixteenth-century St. Augustine material culture documents the presence of several kinds of buttons, which appear both in wills and in supply lists (Lyon 1992). Large quantities of buttons referred to as *atauxia* (enameled or damascened) and *acero* (steel) buttons were imported with the colonies' supplies. Four gross of *atauxia* buttons arrived in 1569, 40 gross and 10 dozen in 1570, and 600 dozen in 1578. These buttons cost 9.5 reales per gross. South, Skowronek, and Johnson (1988:131–132) have suggested that the term *"atauxia"* refers to gilded, ball-shaped buttons, based on the findings at the site of Santa Elena, South Carolina (1566–87), discussed later.

Contratación records for Florida also document the importation of very large quantities of *acero* buttons. In 1567, for example, 2,250 dozen *acero* buttons arrived and were to be used on 900 soldiers' jackets (*ropillas*) issued to the Florida troops. Each uniform used 30 buttons, 22 buttons on each jacket (16 on the chest and 6 on the sleeves) and 8 on the breeches (Lyon 1985; South 1985:54; South, Skowronek, and Johnson 1988:134–135). A number of unadorned, ball-shaped iron buttons have been recovered at the site of Santa Elena and are thought to represent *acero* buttons (South, Skowronek, and Johnson 1988:135).

Acero buttons either were not used commonly on civilian clothing or were not considered worthy of note in personal property inventories. Although buttons of the 1566–87 period in St. Augustine were noted and described for garments listed as part of personal property inventories, they were specified for only a relatively few pieces of clothing. A total of 142 items of potentially buttoned clothing (breeches, jackets, doublets, shirts, capes, and coats) were listed among the goods of 23 soldiers and sailors (or approximately six items per man) (Lyon 1992:22–34). Three of the clothing items (2 percent) noted buttons, including "black and gold buttons," "buttons of Moorish inlay work," and "buttons of crystal." Two sailors also had undescribed loose buttons listed among their properties.

Officials and noble colonists owned considerably more clothing, averaging 30 items per man and 23 items per woman, based on 131 items listed for five people (Lyon 1992:68–78). Buttons were specifically described for approximately 2 percent of the clothing listed among the goods of the town's elite. All of the buttons listed for men's clothing were of silk, and the single example of buttons on women's clothing was a gold-embroidered taffeta skirt with two dozen (obviously decorative) crystal buttons adorned with gold. This was apparently a form of elite clothing decoration known throughout Europe during the later sixteenth century, and a 1631 chronicle (cited in White 1977:67) recounts that

> at the beginning and before the reign of Elizabeth [1558–1603] the making or wearing of silk buttons was very little or not at all known to the common people, they having their buttons constantly made of the same stuff with their doublets, coats and jerkins. The honorable personages as well women as men did wear borders of great crystal buttons about their caps or headbands, to distinguish between the gentry and others; but in the tenth year of Elizabeth many young citizens and others began to wear crystal buttons upon their doublets, coats and jerkins . . . and within a few years afterwards, buttons of thread, of silk, of hair and of gold and silver twist became common and were chiefly worn.

The few records of seventeenth-century buttons in Spanish Florida tend to support the predominance of thread or silk (and therefore perishable) buttons. The inventory of the wealthy Captain Francisco de la Rua's personal property after his death in St. Augustine in 1649 lists eight dozen "horsehair" buttons (*botones de zerda*) from Campeche and 12 dozen buttons of white thread (Hann 1991:506–507). Later seventeenth-century wills of wealthy residents (1673 and 1680) describe clothing with large, silver, filigree buttons; silver thread buttons; and silk buttons (El Escribano 1971, 1972). "Points" (lacing ends), however, were noted much more frequently than buttons in these wills.

Very little documentary information is available about eighteenth-century button production or use in the Spanish colonies, and the best source of information is the archaeological record (discussed later). Button manufacturing is known to have taken place in the Anglo-American colonies during the eighteenth century; however, it is thought that the great majority of British colonial buttons were still imported from Europe until the nineteenth century (Noel Hume 1980:92–93). Buttons in the Spanish colonies

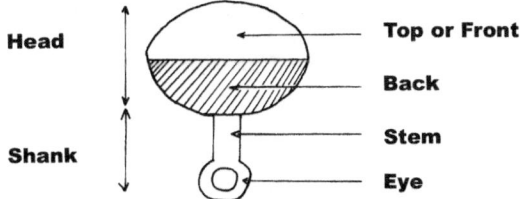

Figure 8.1. Constituent parts and terminology for buttons. Following Egan and Pritchard (1992:273).

were probably also imported both legally from Spain and illegally (through contraband trade with English merchants) during the eighteenth century (see, for example, Blair 1960).

Button Description and Classification

Typologies have been developed for archaeologically recovered eighteenth- and nineteenth-century English and French buttons (South 1964; Stone 1974:45), as well as for plain brass-alloy buttons (Olsen 1963). Although these systems do not include pre-eighteenth-century buttons, they provide useful guidelines for the consistent description and comparison of buttons. Both employ the following standard attributes in classifying buttons:

1. Construction refers to the number and method of combination of button parts (Fig. 8.1 shows the constituent parts of a button). Button bodies are usually of one- (simple) or two-piece (compound) construction. Two-piece buttons have separate crowns and backs, while on one-piece buttons the crown and back are the obverse and reverse of a single piece, respectively. Either type of button can have an integral shank or a separately added eye. The construction type of a button is usually the highest-order distinction.
2. Material composition, such as bone, wood, glass, shell, copper, brass, pewter, and so forth.
3. Manufacturing method can include casting, soldering, cutting or punching, brazing, crimping, and lathe turning.
4. Method of attachment to clothing can include holes (as in simple, flat buttons); wire eyes either soldered to the back of the button or inserted through the back of the button through a hole; and shanks, which are flat, U-shaped pieces of metal soldered to the back of the button and drilled with a hole for attachment.
5. Shape, such as spherical, flat, round, domed, concave, convex, and so forth.
6. Decorative method and motif can include the design on the crown of the button and the method by which the decoration is made, such as embossing, carving, punching, enameling, inlaying, gilding, or silvering.
7. Size or diameter.

Sixteenth- and Seventeenth-Century Buttons Found Archaeologically

The few buttons recovered archaeologically from sixteenth- and early-seventeenth-century Spanish sites are of one-piece, molded construction and are made of metal or glass. These buttons are all either spherical or dome shaped and can be gilded, inlaid, or molded in a relief design. They either have an attached wire eye or an integral shank with a drilled hole for attachment and are smaller than 1.5 cm in diameter. As noted earlier, these are most frequently recovered from military contexts, and no buttons have been reported from pre-1550 contexts in the Caribbean or Florida. The earliest nonmilitary button reported from a Spanish colonial site came from Puerto Real in a context dating to about 1550–75. This was a small, molded silver button with a soldered silver wire eye, probably used on a doublet (Fig. 8.2).

The most common sixteenth-century buttons in the Spanish colonies are one-piece, solid, cast-metal, spherical or dome-shaped

Figure 8.2. Silver button from Puerto Real, ca. 1550–75. Diameter 9.8 mm. Soldered silver eye attachment. PR L19-FS3327.

Figure 8.3. Sixteenth-century ball-shaped buttons. White metal alloy, ca. 1550–1600. Diameter 1.2 cm. St. Augustine (SA-23-341). Buttons of this type occur commonly in military contexts at both St. Augustine and Santa Elena, South Carolina. South, Skowronek, and Johnson (1988:Fig. 81). FLMNH/CSA Collections. *Photo: James Quine.*

buttons with attached wire eyes (Fig. 8.3; Powell 1994a, see also www.artifacts.org). They occur frequently at St. Augustine and at Santa Elena and appear to have been used primarily by the military men at these sites. They are especially numerous at Santa Elena, where the town's forts were excavated. Three types of these solid ball or dome buttons have been distinguished on the basis of the Santa Elena sample, which includes 31 buttons (South, Skowronek, and Johnson 1988:131–135; Polhemus 1988:414). Each of the varieties occurs in both gilded and plain forms, and they include:

1. Gray metal (lead and copper pewter alloy) with iron wire eyes (39 percent) and diameters of 9.5 to 10.9 mm. Only 1 of these 12 buttons (the smallest) was gilded;
2. Gray metal with brass wire eye (6 percent), with diameters of 10.0 to 10.3 mm. One of these two examples was gilded;
3. Brass with brass wire eye (15 percent), with diameters of 9.5 to 9.9 mm. Three of these five buttons were gilded; and
4. Gray metal with missing eyes (40 percent), with diameters of 10.3 to 11.4 mm.

Polhemus (1988:414) notes that at least two of the gray metal buttons were dome shaped. Overall, 20 percent of the buttons were gilded, and South, Skowronek, and Johnson (1988)

suggest that these may have been the *atauxia* buttons discussed earlier and that the gray metal, ungilded buttons were the *acero* buttons. The Real Academia Española (1939:134) defines *ataujia* as "work that the Moors do of silver, gold and other metals, inserted and pressed (*embutidos*) into one another, and with enamels of various colors, which serves as decoration for stirrups, bits, etc." This description is consistent with the ornately molded and gilded sixteenth-century buttons described later, which may also have once held decorative inlay in their molded surface grooves. It is possible that these more elaborate buttons may be examples of the *atauxia* buttons in the St. Augustine inventory, while the simple, metal, ball-shaped buttons may have been those listed as *acero* buttons.

South (1985:54) notes that jackets made with Spanish cloth had *atauxia* buttons, while those made of English cloth, which was a common Spanish import in the sixteenth century, had *acero* buttons. Whatever their sixteenth-century designation might have been, however, the ball-shaped buttons from Santa Elena and St. Augustine were undoubtedly standard-issue buttons used by members of the military.

Although the solid-metal ball buttons occur in sixteenth-century contexts in St. Augustine, a different kind of metal button is somewhat more common there (Figs. 8.4, 8.5). These are one-piece, dome-shaped, solid-cast buttons with an integral molded shank bearing a drilled hole for attachment. Various designs are cast into the crown surface, and the top of the button dome ends in a small, metal nipple. The most commonly noted design is a gridlike network of lines or raised dots contained in panels or flutes around the button dome. The buttons range in diameter (at the dome base) from 1.2 to 1.43 cm and in height from 1.3 to 1.4 cm. Of the six examples excavated in St. Augustine, all but one bear traces of gilding in the crevices of the design. These buttons are also candidates for the identification of the *atauxia* buttons discussed previously.

Molded, dome-shaped decorative buttons were apparently in widespread use from the mid-sixteenth century into the first few decades of the seventeenth century. They have been found in St. Augustine contexts dating to 1565–66 (Fountain of Youth Park site) and in post-1572 contexts in the town. Two examples have also been reported from the site of San Gabriel del Yunque in New Mexico, believed to be associated with Juan de Oñate's settlement of 1597–1609 (Simmons 1987).

Very similar buttons appear in Spanish paintings of the mid-sixteenth century, several of which are reproduced by Reade (1951): Antonio Mor's *Catherine of Austria, Queen of Portugal* (1552) and *Ann of Austria, Queen of Spain* (1570) and Sánchez Coello's *The Archduke Rudolph of Austria* (1567). They do not, however, appear in Anderson's (1979) exhaustive study of Spanish dress from 1480 to 1530. The buttons depicted in these paintings were worn by noble individuals and were undoubtedly of precious metals. The base-metal examples reported archaeologically were a common version for use by soldiers and people of lesser economic means.

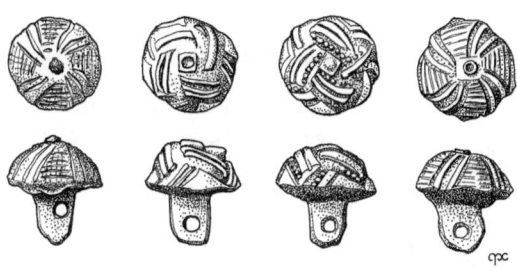

Figure 8.4. Sixteenth-century cast dome-shaped button varieties. Copper alloy with gilt, cast in one piece with a drilled shank. Diameters 1.1 to 1.25 cm. St. Augustine (*left to right:* SA-34-1-322, SA-26-1-32, SA-31-1518, SA-26-1-233). FLMNH/CSA Collections. *Drawing: Merald Clark.*

Figure 8.5. Sixteenth-century cast dome-shaped buttons. Copper alloy, cast in one piece with a drilled shank. St. Augustine (*left:* SA-30-3-247; *right:* SA-30-3-237). FLMNH/CSA Collections. *Photo: James Quine.*

Another variety of sixteenth-century button made in precious metal was recovered from the 1588 wreck of the *Girona*, one of the Spanish Armada ships (Martin and Parker 1988:48). These were two-piece, cast and soldered, hollow, ball-shaped buttons with attached wire eyes. The surfaces of these buttons were covered with molded geometric and medallion designs, and the designs surrounded a central metal nipple on the button crown. They averaged 15 mm in diameter (see also Stenuit 1973:222).

Three glass buttons have been recovered from St. Augustine contexts dating to approximately 1580 to 1600. All are spherical with wire eye attachments. One of these was a simple ball of black glass (10.0 mm in diam-

Figure 8.6. Sixteenth-century glass button. Molded white glass with enamel inlay and loop eye, ca. 1580–1600. Total length 1.2 cm, diameter of glass top 0.7 cm. St. Augustine (SA-34-1-342). FLMNH/CSA Collections. *Drawing: Merald Clark.*

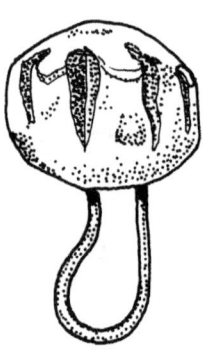

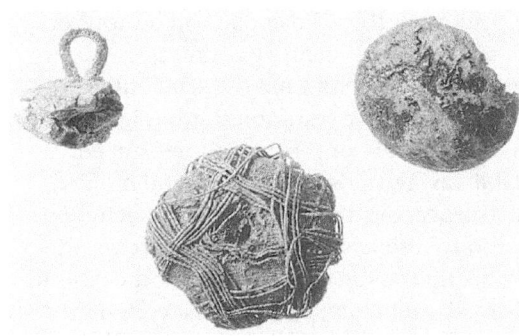

Figure 8.7. Seventeenth-century buttons from San Luis de Talimali, ca. 1650–1700. *Left:* Pewter with wire eye, diameter 9 mm, FS 6646. *Center:* Copper-alloy thread over pewter, diameter 1.6 cm, FS 7143. *Right:* Hollow pewter button fragment, diameter 2.0 cm, FS 4097. *Courtesy of the Florida Bureau of Archaeological Research, the San Luis Archaeological and Historical Site, and Bonnie G. McEwan. Photo: James Quine.*

eter), and the other was of white or clear glass (7.5 mm in diameter) and was molded, fluted, and inlaid with gilt (Fig. 8.6). The third button was made of black glass inlaid with enamel but is extremely deteriorated.

Even fewer buttons have been reported from seventeenth-century Spanish colonial contexts than from sixteenth-century contexts. Among these, the most common method of attachment is a wire eye. The earliest were found on the 1622 *Atocha* shipwreck, which yielded both base-metal and ornamental gold buttons (Florida Bureau of Archaeological Research Conservation Laboratory records). The single base-metal button reported was a one-piece, cast copper-alloy, dome-shaped button with a wire eye (8 mm in diameter). The size and general shape were consistent with dome-shaped buttons from the sixteenth century; however, the seventeenth-century example had no decoration on the surface and was attached with a wire eye rather than by a drilled shank. Dome-shaped pewter buttons with wire eye attachments were also recovered from the seventeenth-century mission site of San Luis de Talimali. Buttons made of metallic thread, however, were more commonly found at the San Luis de Talimali site (Fig. 8.7).

Two-piece, hollow-cast, round or dome-shaped metal buttons were also present in French and English sites through the seventeenth century. Usually ornamented with a cast relief design of flowers, stars, or basketry, they had wire eye attachments and often had small holes on the reverse near the eye to allow the escape of gasses during joining (see Noel Hume 1980:88–89, 1983:280–281, 314; Cleland 1971:25–27). The only examples of this kind of button construction in Spanish contexts that resemble these are the gold buttons from the Armada wrecks.

The earliest flat, disk-shaped, copper-alloy buttons from Spanish colonial contexts date to the closing decades of the seventeenth century. Eight flat, disk-shaped, copper-alloy

Table 8.2. Bone Button Measurements from St. Augustine, 1700–1820 (in millimeters)

Period	1-Hole Range	x̄	2-Hole Range	x̄	4-Hole Range	x̄	5-Hole Range	x̄
ca. 1700–40	10–19	15	12	12				
ca. 1740–65	8–23	15	21	21				
ca. 1765–85	8–15	12	19	19				
ca. 1785–1800	8–25	15	12–17	14	10–18	14		
ca. 1800–20	12–21	14	14	14	10–17	14	11–18	15
ca. 1820–45	12–21	17	4–19	16	16–19	17		

buttons with drilled shank attachments were found on a late-seventeenth-century burial in St. Augustine (Koch 1980:329, Plate 5). These were of uneven sizes—13 to 16 mm in diameter—and some were irregularly shaped.

Among the European gentry, jeweled buttons reached a peak in popularity during the seventeenth century (Lester and Oerke 1954:474–475); however, these are not likely to be found on colonial domestic sites. Cloth and thread buttons also increased in popularity during this period, but these, too, are less likely to have been preserved in buried sites.

Eighteenth-Century Buttons

By the eighteenth century, French fashion dominated Europe and the Americas, and the use of buttons by all manner of people greatly increased. Very few of the eighteenth-century buttons recovered from either Spanish shipwrecks or land sites can be identified as exclusively Spanish, since most of the varieties are also found in English or French colonial sites. The studies of buttons by Stanley South at Brunswick Town, South Carolina (1964), and by Lyle Stone at Fort Michilimackinack (1974), for example, are based on large collections of eighteenth-century English and French buttons and are useful for the dating and identification of buttons on Spanish colonial sites.

Eighteenth-century buttons were made of fabric, thread, leather, wood, bone, horn, shell, glass, ceramic, and virtually every kind of metal. Two or more of these materials were often combined in a button, particularly those of complex, two- or three-piece construction, which was a common feature of buttons in the second half of the eighteenth century.

The most useful collection for the study of eighteenth-century Spanish colonial buttons is that from St. Augustine, Florida (1565–1763, 1784–1821). A sample of 368 buttons from seven domestic sites was assessed in order to characterize the assemblage (Yoh 1993). The sites of Santa Rosa Pensacola (1722–52) (Smith 1965) and the Florida 1733 plate fleet wrecks (Skowronek 1982) provide additional useful and more tightly dated information about eighteenth-century Spanish buttons.

Bone Buttons and Button Backs

One of the most common button varieties throughout the eighteenth century was a flat bone disk with a single central hole. These range in size from 8 to 25 mm in diameter (Table 8.2) and served as backing for metal or cloth button tops. A metal eye was attached through the single hole (Figs. 8.8, 8.9).

These bone disks were both made locally and imported. The 1741 *Matanceros* shipwreck yielded hundreds of single-hole bone disks, as well as metal button tops (CEDAM collec-

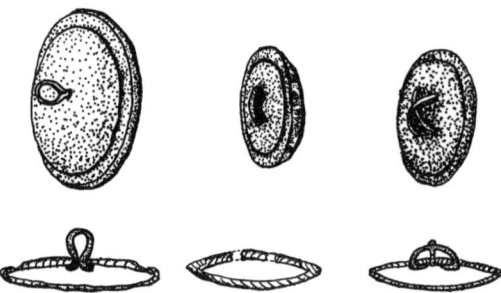

Figure 8.8. Bone button back attachment methods on two-piece buttons. *Left:* One-hole backing. *Center:* Two-hole backing. *Right:* Four-hole backing. *Drawing: Pauline Kulstad.*

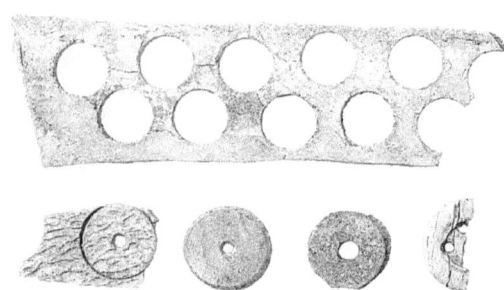

Figure 8.10. Bone button backs and bone blanks. Eighteenth century. St. Augustine. Length of blank at top 8.3 cm. Diameter of center button 1.5 cm (SA-39A-11-43). FLMNH/CSA Collections. *Photo: James Quine.*

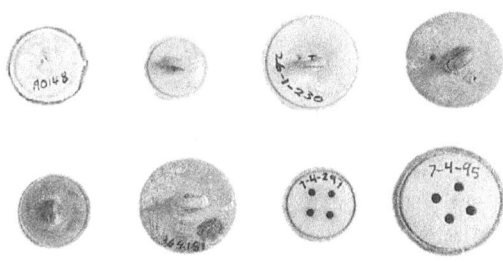

Figure 8.9. Backings on two-piece buttons from St. Augustine. *Top row,* ca. 1725–50, left to right: Single-hole shell back with gilded white metal top (AO148); bone back with copper loop (SA-36-4-342); bone back with copper eye (SA-26-1-230); copper-alloy back with soldered eye and gas holes (SA-16-23-9). *Bottom row,* ca. 1780–1800, left to right: Copper alloy with loop eye (SA-7-7-337); copper alloy with loop eye (SA-36-4-181); four-hole bone back (SA-7-4-297); four-hole bone back (SA-7-4-95). Diameter of bottom right button 2.5 cm. FLMNH/CSA Collections. *Photo: University of Florida Office of Instructional Resources.*

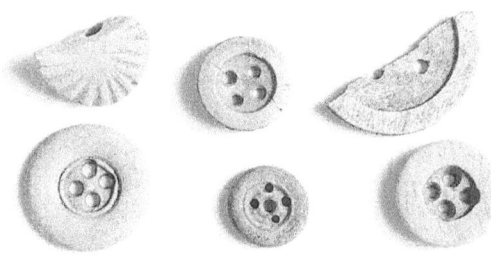

Figure 8.11. Eighteenth-century carved bone buttons, St. Augustine. *Top row,* ca. 1720–60, carved with drilled shank for attachment, left to right: SA-28-1-14, SA-7-4-205, SA-36-4-57. *Bottom row,* ca. 1780–1800, left to right: SA-16-23-44, SA-26-1-396, SA-16-23-44. Diameter of bottom right button 1.4 cm. FLMNH/CSA Collections. *Photo: James Quine.*

tions, Pablo Bush Romero Museum, Puerta Aventuras, Mexico). The backs were apparently replaced through the life of the button, and abundant evidence for their production in the colonies has been recovered archaeologically (such as that seen in Fig. 8.10).

In general, there were fewer single-hole bone button backs present during the first half of the eighteenth century (39 percent simple brass buttons and 24 percent bone backs), suggesting that two-piece buttons requiring bone backs were not used as commonly before 1750 as were flat brass buttons of simple construction. This is supported in the assemblages of the 1733 Florida plate fleet shipwrecks and of Santa Rosa Pensacola, neither of which contained bone button backs.

By the middle of the eighteenth century,

these proportions are reversed in the St. Augustine collection, with single-hole bone backs accounting for about 40 percent of all buttons and flat, simple-construction brass buttons accounting for approximately 18 percent of the later assemblages.

Carved bone buttons with four holes are present throughout the eighteenth century, although they do not exceed 5 percent of the assemblages until the nineteenth century. Those of the about 1700 to 1760 period are often carved with a raised ridge around the outer edge (Fig. 8.11; see also Skowronek 1982:114). Bone buttons with five holes do not appear until late in the eighteenth century (ca. 1780s) and are consistently present into the first decades of the nineteenth century.

Eighteenth-Century Copper-Alloy Buttons

Copper-alloy buttons (usually brass) of one-piece construction were used from the late seventeenth century to the end of the colonial period (see Olsen 1963). In Spanish collections, these are typically flat or slightly domed brass disks (Fig. 8.12). None of the

Table 8.3. Diameters of Round, Simple-Construction, Brass-Alloy Buttons from St. Augustine (in millimeters)

Dates	Range	$\bar{x}$	Frequency
1700–40	11–20	15	8
1740–65	12–34	18	11
1765–85 (British period)	13–25	18	10
1785–1800	12–34	18	35
1800–20	16–18	17.6	12

examples dating to before about 1760 are decorated; however, Second Spanish Period eighteenth-century disk buttons (ca. 1785–1800) do sometimes have a small floral element engraved in the center of the disk (Fig. 8.12).

Metal disk buttons of the first half of the eighteenth century are smaller in general than those of the second half (Table 8.3), a trend that is consistent with that noted for English buttons (Noel Hume 1980:90). Diameter decreased again during the early nineteenth century.

Figure 8.12. Eighteenth-century single-piece brass buttons, St. Augustine. *Top row,* ca. 1700–50, left to right: SA-7-4-161, SA-7-5-17, SA-7-4-118. *Second row,* ca. 1700–50, left to right: SA-7-4-161, SA-1623-128, SA-7-4-162. *Third row,* ca. 1780–1800, left to right: SA-26-2-282, SA-36-4-233. *Bottom row,* ca. 1790–1820, left to right: SA-7-5-12, SA-RC. Diameter of lower right (largest) button 3.6 cm. FLMNH/CSA Collections. *Photo: University of Florida Office of Instructional Resources.*

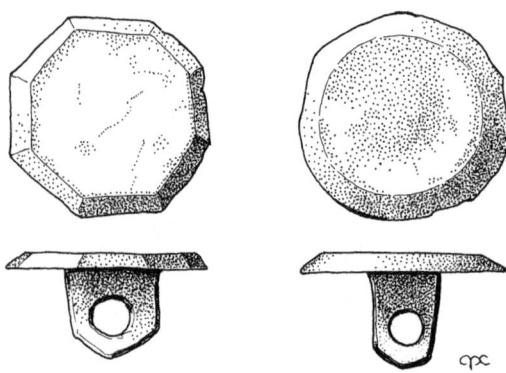

Figure 8.13. Eighteenth-century buttons, probably used on uniforms. Brass, single-piece construction with beveled edge and drilled shank, ca. 1700–50. Diameter of hexagonal button 1.8 cm; diameter of round button 1.9 cm. St. Augustine (SA-7-4-161). FLMNH/CSA Collections. *Drawing: Merald Clark.*

about 1700 to 1740 are solid-cast flat disks or octagons, with cast and drilled shanks. The outer edge of the crowns on these buttons are usually beveled, and many examples retain traces of gilding (Fig. 8.13). Buttons of this kind are not reported in the major eighteenth-century French or English collections from Fort Michilimackinack (Stone 1974) or Brunswick Town (South 1964), probably because these buttons are associated with Spanish military uniforms (Fig. 8.14; see Powell 1994a, 1994b, 1996, see also www.artifacts.org). They may be, in fact, one of the few categories of eighteenth-century buttons identifiable as Spanish.

Both the round and the octagonal forms of these buttons occur in two diameter sizes, 1.5 cm for sleeves or trousers and 2.0 cm for coats. Examples of the octagonal, beveled-edge buttons were also recovered from the 1733 Florida plate fleet excavations (Skowronek 1982:116).

Another type of brass button thought to be associated with Spanish naval uniforms (see Powell www.artifacts.org) is shown in Figure 8.15. These are one-piece, slightly domed, cast buttons with drilled shanks soldered to the back of the button. The upper surface of the crown is decorated with three concentric circles. They also occur in two sizes, 1.6 and

Another temporal trend in the simple-construction brass buttons from St. Augustine is the change from drilled integral shanks to attached wire eyes. After about 1760, drilled shanks cast as part of the button are rare, and attached brass or copper wire eyes are instead the rule.

Military Buttons

The most commonly occurring metal buttons found in St. Augustine contexts dating to

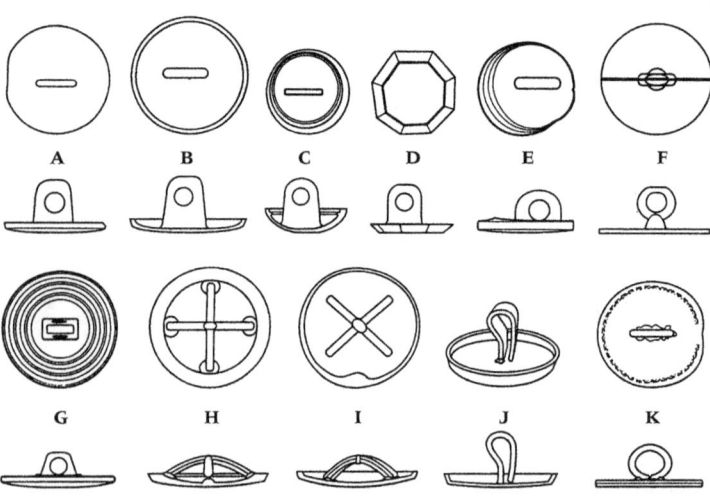

Figure 8.14. Spanish colonial military button forms. A–F. Cast brass Spanish buttons with drilled wedge shanks as worn by Spanish regular and provincial troops until marked buttons appeared after ca. 1795. Cast brass buttons continued in use, however, by the local urban militias until the end of the colonial era. G. Late eighteenth century. H–I. "Cross-wire" types contemporary with A–E; J–K. Post-ca. 1780. Reproduced from Powell (1996:16). *Courtesy of John Powell.*

Clothing Fasteners and Ornaments

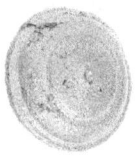  

Figure 8.15. Eighteenth-century buttons, probably used on uniforms, ca. 1700–50. Brass with drilled soldered shank, 1733 (8MO101). Large button diameter 2.0 cm; small buttons' diameters 1.6 cm. FBAR Lab #L2501. *Courtesy of the Florida Bureau of Archaeological Research. Photo: James Quine.*

2.0 cm in diameter. They have been recovered from the 1733 plate fleet wrecks (Skowronek 1982:114) and in eighteenth-century St. Augustine contexts dating to the First Spanish Period (1700–63).

Insignia appeared on military buttons between about 1770 and 1785 (Emilio 1911; Olsen 1963:552; Powell 1994a, 1994b). Figures 8.16 and 8.17 show buttons bearing the regimental insignia of Florida- and Caribbean-based troops. Representations of Spanish uniforms in the Museo del Ejército of Madrid show large, undecorated, somewhat dome-shaped round buttons on eighteenth-century uniforms, similar to those known for French uniforms of about 1730 to 1760 (Stone 1974:49, Fig. 48-I). At Fort

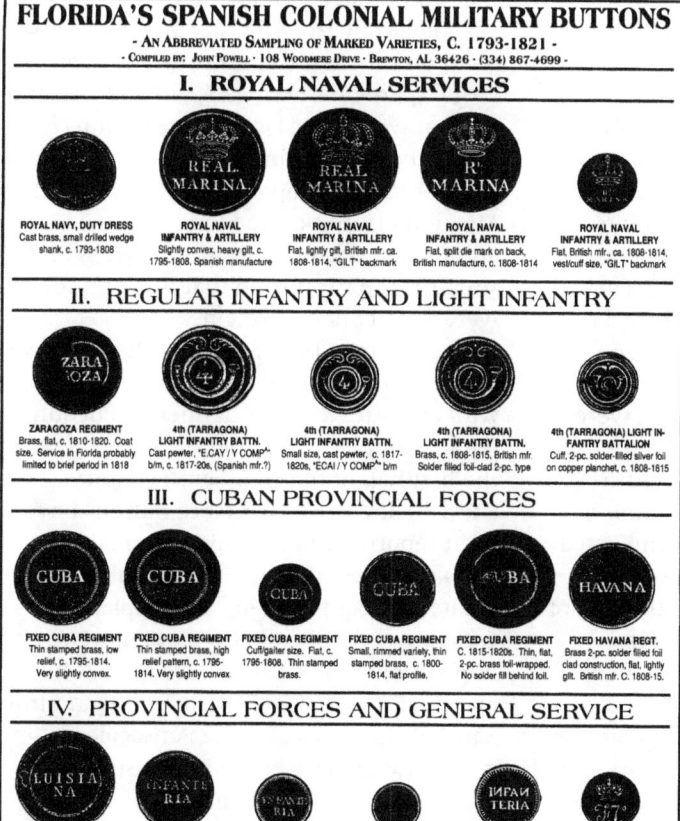

Figure 8.16. Insignia on Florida's Spanish colonial military buttons. By John Powell. *Courtesy of John Powell.*

Figure 8.17. Regimental buttons of Cuban militia in Florida. All copper alloy, from St. Augustine. *Left: Regimiento de Cuba.* Enlisted man (1789–1821). Diameter 1.8 cm. (SA-23-188). *Center: Regimiento de Cuba.* Enlisted man (1789–1821). Diameter 2.6 cm. (SA-12-26-3.018). *Right: Dragones de América de la Habana* (ca. 1788–1821), 2.4 cm. FLMNH/CSA Collections. *Photo: James Quine.*

Michilimackinack, these occur in two sizes, 1.70 to 1.95 cm and 2.35 to 2.45 cm. Such buttons have also been found in St. Augustine; however, they occur in contexts dating to the period of about 1785 to 1800.

Two-piece Metal Buttons
Convex brass-alloy button tops (used with a filler and bone or wood back to form a composite button) are not found in the St. Augustine assemblage until after the middle of the eighteenth century (Fig. 8.18), and none were reported from either Santa Rosa Pensacola (abandoned in 1752) or the Florida plate fleet wrecks (1715, 1733). They are, however, present in large quantities on the *Matanceros* shipwreck (1741) and thus were probably present in the Spanish colonies by the second third of the eighteenth century.

The earliest of these two-piece buttons are plain, disk-shaped crowns with no embossed decorations, and the single intact example from the First Spanish Period has a backing of shell rather than of bone. The early (ca. 1750) undecorated button crowns in the St. Augustine collection were also somewhat smaller than the later (ca. 1780) examples. The former measure approximately 1.6 cm in diameter, while the later examples from St. Augustine range from 2.0 to 2.5 cm in diameter and are usually decorated (Fig. 8.18).

Decorated button crowns bear an embossed design and are crimped around the edge to fasten to a backing. Examples from both the 1741 *Matanceros* and eighteenth-century St. Augustine are flat or slightly convex.

Hundreds of these button tops—both decorated and undecorated—were recovered from *El Matanceros*. They are decorated with a variety of floral, pinwheel, diamond, scroll, geometric, and curvilinear motifs, and their diameters ranged from about 20 to 25 mm. Large numbers of single-hole bone button backs and smaller numbers of metal button backs with attached wire eyes were recovered in association with these crowns.

The *Matanceros* assemblage also featured a large quantity of contraband French and English goods, including cloth seals from merchants in London and Nimes. Blair (1960) notes that much of the material recovered archaeologically from the site was not registered on the manifest and was undoubtedly illegal (particularly since Spain and England were at war in 1741). That the buttons from *El Matanceros* were in many cases identical to those from contemporary contexts at Fort Michilimackinack (see Stone 1974:62–64) and Brunswick Town (South 1964:Fig. 8.1) supports the suggestion that these buttons were not of Spanish origin.

Noel-Hume (1980:89) notes that hollow-cast, two-piece metal buttons with attached wire eyes are the most frequently encountered button type on English colonial sites of the first half of the eighteenth century. Only a few hollow-cast, two-piece buttons have been reported from Spanish colonial sites, and all of these date to the first half of the eighteenth century. Single examples have come from the site of Fort San Francisco de Pupo in Florida (8-Cl-10), occupied from about 1670 to 1730 (Goggin 1951), and from Santa Rosa Pensacola. The Pensacola button was cast with a basket-weave design on the surface of the crown (Smith 1965:72), and the Fort Pupo example is undecorated (Fig. 8.12). Both buttons, however, differ from those described for English sites in that

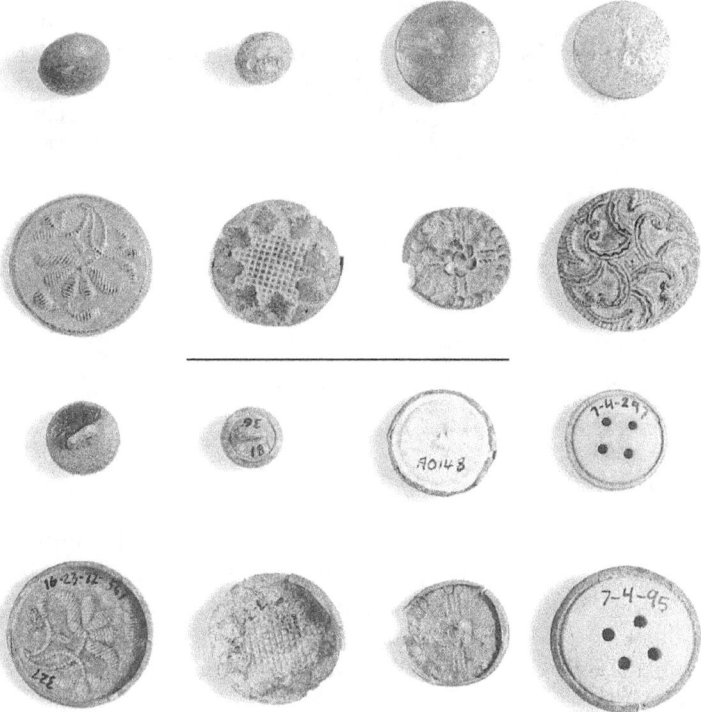

Figure 8.18. Two-piece eighteenth-century buttons and button crowns. *Top:* Button tops; *Bottom:* Button backs. *Top row, left to right:* Copper alloy with soldered shank, ca. 1670–1730, Ft. Pupo (8CL10); molded copper alloy with wire eye, ca. 1785–1800, St. Augustine (SA-36-4-187); copper alloy with gilt top, single hole shell back, ca. 1700–50, St. Augustine (AO148); white metal with four-hole bone back, ca. 1780–1800, St. Augustine (SA-7-4-297). *Bottom row, left to right:* Embossed copper-alloy top, ca. 1750, St. Augustine (SA-16-23-327); embossed copper-alloy top, ca. 1750–80, St. Augustine (SA-7-7-286); embossed copper-alloy top, ca. 1780–1800, St. Augustine (SA-36-4-35); embossed copper alloy with 4-hole bone back, ca. 1780–1800, St. Augustine (SA-7-4-95). Diameter of top left button 1.2 cm; diameter of bottom right button 2.5 cm. FLMNH/CSA Collections. *Photo: University of Florida Office of Instructional Resources.*

they have soldered shanks with a drilled hole for attachment rather than a wire eye. All of the Spanish buttons furthermore lack the two small holes for gas escape often found on either side of the eye on hollow-cast buttons (Noel Hume 1980:88; South 1964).

"Jeweled" Buttons

As noted previously, gold and silver buttons set with precious stones were in vogue during the seventeenth century among elite Spaniards, but such items are rarely found archaeologically. By the early eighteenth century, however, imitations set in base metal (usually brass or white metal) were apparently widely available through French and English merchants, and copper-alloy buttons set with paste or glass jewels were used thereafter throughout the eighteenth century in the Spanish colonies. Many of those found

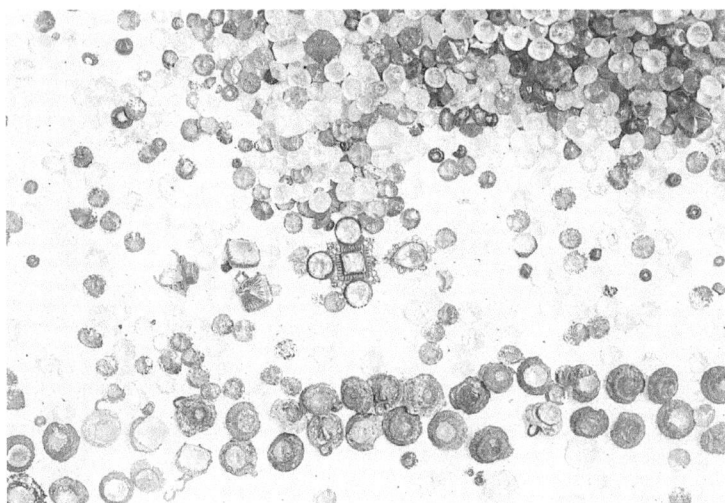

Figure 8.19. Paste jewels and paste jewel buttons from the *Matanceros* wreck, 1741. Clear, green, and blue stones. CEDAM Museum, Akumal, Yucatán, Mexico. *Photo: James Quine.*

archaeologically were in use as sleeve buttons (cufflinks, discussed later).

Paste jewel buttons occur in St. Augustine in contexts dating from about 1700 to about 1820, and certain general observations about trends through time can be suggested. Those of the 1700 to 1750 period are more varied than later examples in both shape and color. Green, blue, and clear "jewels" were used, and the settings are oval, square, and round. The great majority of "jeweled" buttons from the Second Spanish Period (1785–1821) are round, with clear or dark blue "jewels" dominating. No green stones were recorded among the St. Augustine examples dating to after about 1750, although they are quite common in the 1741 *Matanceros* assemblage (Fig. 8.19).

A small but consistent trend toward an increase in size through time is also evident. "Jeweled" buttons of the about 1700 to 1750 period range from 10 to 12 mm in diameter, with a mean diameter of 11 mm; those from the period of about 1785 to 1821 range from 10 to 13 mm in diameter, with a mean diameter of 12 mm; and those of the 1800 to 1820 period range from 12 to 15 mm in diameter, with a mean diameter of 13 mm. One of the most elaborate "jeweled" buttons, dating to the period of about 1785 to 1800, has seven square-cut clear stones set around a central stone (Fig. 8.20). "Jeweled" buttons comprise a larger proportion of the assemblage dating to the first half of the eighteenth century than they do of later periods.

Shell and Glass Buttons

Buttons carved from shell or mother-of-pearl are found in St. Augustine's Spanish contexts from about 1750 to the end of the colonial period (1821) (Fig. 8.21). Only two examples have been recovered from early- or mid-eighteenth-century contexts, and these date to about 1750 to 1765. They are the largest of the flat, round, shell buttons in the assemblage (11–12 mm), and both are undecorated, with two holes for attachment.

These disk-shaped shell buttons generally decrease in size through the colonial period. Two shell buttons from 1785 to 1800 contexts have simple designs carved into them, and one example from this period is unfinished, suggesting local production. Shell buttons of the early nineteenth century (1800–21) measure from 7 to 9 cm in diameter and most frequently have four holes for attachment.

All of the glass buttons reported from eighteenth-century contexts were set into frames in the manner of the "jeweled" buttons or sleeve links discussed previously. Examples

Clothing Fasteners and Ornaments   173

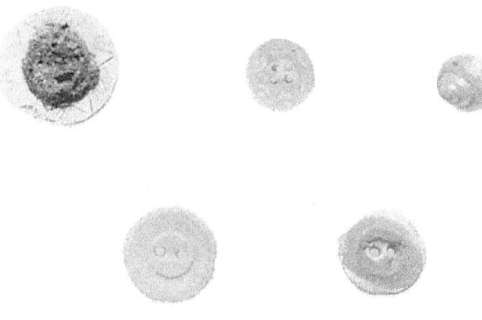

Figure 8.20. Eighteenth-century paste jewel buttons from St. Augustine. *Top row, left to right:* Copper alloy with blue stone and drilled shank, 1.0 cm square, ca. 1730–60 (SA-7-4-8); white metal with clear stone, diameter 1.0 cm, ca. 1730–60 (SA-36-4-257); copper alloy with eight clear stones, diameter 1.5 cm, ca. 1785–1800 (SA-7-4-95). *Center:* White metal with clear stones, loop attachment, diameter 1.2 cm, ca. 1785–1800 (SA-7-4-95). *Bottom row, left to right:* Copper-alloy sleeve link with clear, engraved, and gilded stone, 1.3 cm square, ca. 1785–1800 (SA-26-1-3); copper alloy with blue stone, drilled shank, length 1.2 cm, ca. 1785–1800 (SA-7-4-95); white metal with white stone and dentate frame, loop back, diameter 1.2 cm, ca. 1700–50 (SA-7-4-166). FLMNH/CSA Collections. *Photo: University of Florida Office of Instructional Resources.*

Figure 8.21. Eighteenth-century shell buttons from St. Augustine. All but the top left were recovered from the same mid-eighteenth-century feature. *Top row, left to right:* Mother-of-pearl incised with a star pattern, corroded iron loop attachment, diameter 1.7 cm, ca. 1750–80 (SA-16-23); incised mother-of-pearl, diameter 1.0 cm, ca. 1730–60 (SA-7-5-38); West Indian top shell (*Trochidae tegula lividomaculata*) with surface removed and four drilled attachment holes, diameter of shell base 8 mm, ca. 1730–60 (SA-7-5-38). *Bottom row, left and right:* 2-hole carved shell, diameter 1.3 cm, ca. 1730–60 (SA-7-5-38). FLMNH/CSA Collections.

from St. Augustine are of clear molded or engraved glass and are gilded. Simple-construction white and clear glass buttons with two or four holes are not found until the early nineteenth century, and after that time they dominate the button assemblage.

Sleeve Buttons
Although small, linked pairs of buttons were used to fasten sleeves in the English colonies during the seventeenth century (Noel-Hume 1961), none have been reported from Spanish contexts prior to the eighteenth century. They are present on Spanish sites throughout the century and are usually both smaller and more ornate than associated buttons (Fig. 8.22).

Square sleeve links set with paste jewels are encountered most frequently during the first half of the eighteenth century and have been reported from St. Augustine, Pensacola, and the 1733 Florida plate fleet wrecks. After the middle of the eighteenth century, metal sleeve links become more common. Because of the overlap in size, decoration, and construction methods between buttons and sleeve links, it is possible that some buttons may actually have been used as parts of sleeve links and vice versa.

Summary
Some general observations can be made about the periodicity of buttons on Spanish colonial sites; however, none of these are unequivocal. Although buttons are known to have been in use from the fifteenth century onward, they are not found on Spanish colo-

 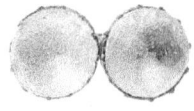 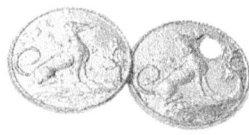

Figure 8.22. Sleeve links. *Left:* Silver scallop shells, height 1.4 cm, ca. 1760 (SA-7-5-18). *Center:* White metal set with clear stones, diameter 1.4 cm, ca. 1750 (no number). *Right:* Copper alloy with greyhound motif, diameter 1.9 cm, ca. 1780–1820, St. Augustine (SA-38-6-4). FLMNH/CSA Collections. *Photo: James Quine.*

nial sites until the second half of the sixteenth century. Buttons from about 1560 to 1600 are small, solid-cast metal, ball or dome shaped, sometimes with gilding and molded decoration. These were possibly military-issue buttons. Plain glass ball buttons and inlaid, enameled glass ball buttons with wire eyes have also been reported from sixteenth-century contexts dating to about 1575 to 1600.

Very few seventeenth-century buttons have been recovered archaeologically, and all of these are from the last quarter of the century. Small (13 mm in diameter), flat, brass-alloy disks with soldered eyes and small, single-hole bone button backs (possibly for cloth buttons) have been documented in late-seventeenth-century contexts.

Button use increased dramatically after 1700, although the majority of eighteenth-century buttons on Spanish sites appear not to be of Spanish origin. Three varieties of simple-construction brass-alloy buttons not documented on English or French sites do occur consistently in Spanish contexts, however, and are thought to represent standard-issue Spanish buttons, probably for military use. They include both octagonal and circular flat buttons with beveled edges and integral cast and drilled shanks, and round, slightly domed buttons with three inscribed concentric circles on the crown. The latter buttons have drilled shanks soldered to the crown. These varieties occur through the entire eighteenth century, differentiated temporally only by some of the attachments, which after 1785 tend to be soldered wire eyes rather than integrally cast or applied drilled shanks.

During the first half of eighteenth century, simple-construction brass and copper-alloy buttons with integral or soldered drilled shanks dominate the assemblage. Wire eye attachments are relatively uncommon, and the metal buttons of this period average 15 mm in diameter. Single-hole bone button backs are common, although no metal crowns for these backs have been reported from contexts dating to before 1740. Buttons inlaid with paste or glass stones are also proportionally most common during this period.

By the middle of the eighteenth century, composite buttons with single-hole or four-hole backings and decorated brass crowns are more frequent and may be of French or English origin. Simple-construction buttons of brass alloy are noticeably larger than those of the preceding period, averaging 18 mm in diameter. These trends continued in a general way to the closing decades of the century. After that time, glass buttons and composite brass and bone buttons dominate the assemblages.

Other Clothing Fasteners

Aglets

Laces were the most common method of fastening clothing in the Spanish colonies until the second half of the seventeenth century. Relatively few buttons are found on Spanish

Clothing Fasteners and Ornaments

Figure 8.23. Aglets. Rolled copper-alloy aglets from the burial of a Spanish man in St. Augustine, ca. 1580. *Left to right:* length 2.8 cm (SA-24-446); length 2.8 cm (SA-24-78); length 3.1 cm (SA-23-341); three right aglets, lengths 3.7 cm, 3.6 cm, 2.7 cm (SA-24-76). FLMNH/CSA Collections. *Photo: James Quine.*

colonial sites before 1700, but there are large quantities of small, rolled copper or copper-alloy tubes (lace ends), known in English as aglets, lace chapes, or tags and in Spanish as *agujetas* (Fig. 8.23). These objects served to enclose and reinforce the ends of the laces, known as *puntas* or *correas*, which fastened many elements of clothing to one another (hose to breeches, breeches to jackets, sleeves to doublets, and so forth) (Fig. 8.24). Aglets were also a form of clothing ornamentation throughout the sixteenth century on elite clothing and could be made of precious metals elaborately engraved and ornamented with enamels and precious stones (Anderson 1979:91, 223–225). Such lace ends are often mentioned in wills (Lyon 1992:84; Hann 1991).

Aglets found on archaeological sites, however, are usually simple, rolled copper-alloy tubes, measuring between 1.5 and 3.5 cm in length. A single silver aglet (2.6 cm long) was excavated at Puerto Real (Ewen 1991:82). Aglets are usually, but not always, tapered in a cone shape. At the fifteenth-century site of La Isabela, aglets occur in two lengths, 1.5

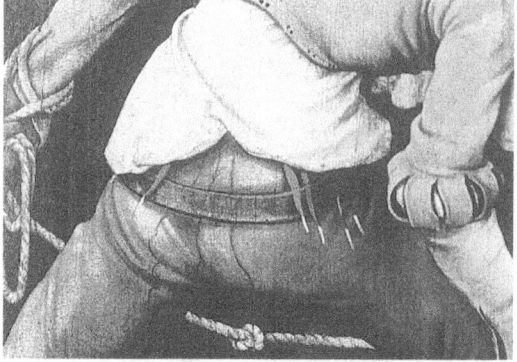

Figure 8.24. Aglet use in sixteenth-century clothing. Detail from Matthias Grunewald's *Mocking of Christ* (1503). *Courtesy of the Bayerische Staatssemäldesammlungen, Alte Pinakothek, Munich. #10352.*

and 2.0 cm. There is considerably more variation in size reported at sixteenth-century sites; for example, at Santa Elena (South, Skowronek, and Johnson 1988:418–419) and St. Augustine the aglet sizes range from 1.7 to 3.4 cm. Aglets are rare on Spanish colonial sites after about 1650 and have not been reported from eighteenth-century contexts.

Laces were drawn through holes that were

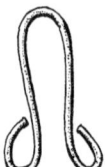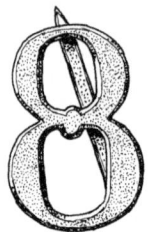

Figure 8.25. Clothing fasteners from La Isabela, 1493–98. *Left:* Copper-alloy "eye," length 1.5 cm, FS 7. *Center:* Copper-alloy grommet, diameter 1.3 cm, FS 1949. *Right:* Copper-alloy "figure-eight" pin, length 1.82 cm, FS 566. Parque Nacional de La Isabela, Dominican Republic. *Drawing: Merald Clark.*

sometimes finished with thread and occasionally with smooth or toothed metal grommets, particularly on leather garments (Egan and Pritchard 1991:227–228). Copper-alloy eyelets and toothed grommets that have the same form as modern examples have been found at sites ranging from the fifteenth to the eighteenth centuries (Fig. 8.25).

Hook-and-Eye Fasteners

Both copper-alloy and iron hooks and eyes are found on Spanish colonial sites from the fifteenth through the nineteenth centuries (Fig. 8.25) and were used to fasten doublets, jerkins, bodices, and other clothing elements. In sixteenth-century Spain, the hook element was known as the *corchete* and the eye as the *hembra* (female) (Anderson 1979:89). The fifteenth- and sixteenth-century hooks and eyes tend to be somewhat more narrow and elongated than modern examples (see Fig. 8.25). These elongated hooks and eyes were used throughout the colonial period, but by the seventeenth century copper-alloy examples with the configuration of modern hooks and eyes were also present.

Clothing Ornamentation

Clothing worn during the Spanish colonial period—especially during the sixteenth century—was often bordered or trimmed with nonperishable decoration. Elaborate crystal and metal buttons, not intended for closure, were commonly used in the sixteenth and seventeenth centuries to ornament capes and have been discussed earlier.

Equally common on elite clothing, including military officers' uniforms, was the metallic lace, braiding, or crochet work known in the English-language archaeological literature as *bordado* (see South, Skowronek, and Johnson 1988:140–142). The term *"bordado,"* however, properly refers to embroidery, while the term *"pasamanería"* refers to braided, corded, woven, or pleated trim, and *"encaje"* refers to lace (González Mena 1982:390–391). As a group, these items of clothing adornment are known as *guarnición* (Córdoba de la Llave 1990:111). The metallic decoration can include gold, silver, or alloy metal threads, as well as cloth string wrapped with metal threads.

Metallic lace for trimming clothing was known as *caierele* and was produced by a separate group of artisans known as *caireladores,* who were part of the cloth-makers guild (Anderson 1979:92; Córdoba de la Llave 1990:114). The metallic braiding, weaving, and cording of *pasamanería,* however, were thought to have been produced by members of the *guarnecioneros* guild, who made decoration to trim cloth, clothing, leather goods, and saddles (Córdoba de la Llave 1990:113).

Guarnición figured prominently in the long series of sumptuary laws and *pragmaticas* that nearly two centuries of Spanish monarchs tried unsuccessfully to implement (Deleito y

Piñuela 1946:275–296; Salmerón 1915). These attempts to curb extravagance had economic as well as sociological motives. Ferdinand and Isabella issued a *pragmatica* in 1494 that prohibited indulgence in costly cloths and trimmings because:

> our subjects and native born have forgotten all respect and exceeded all rule in their gowns (*ropa*), and suits of clothes (*traje*), and also in their trimmings (*guarnición*) and horse trappings (*jaeces*) . . . with the result that in order to satisfy their appetites and conceit, many squander their revenues, while others sell, pawn, and consume their capital and inheritances and revenues . . . in order to buy brocades, cloths of drawn gold and embroideries of gold and silver for their own wear and even to adorn their horses and mule. There is another universal damage to all our kingdoms in that commonly these brocades and cloths of gold are brought hither by foreigners, who take out of our kingdoms the gold and silver they obtain by their sales. (quoted in Anderson 1979:140)

The prohibition was largely ignored, and metallic trimmings were used extravagantly on elite Spanish clothing throughout the sixteenth century, reaching a peak in the early decades of the seventeenth century despite various other attempts at sumptuary control (Payne 1965:264–265; Reade 1951). The most stringent series of sumptuary laws were the Articles of Reformation promulgated in 1623 by Philip IV, which prohibited the high, stiff, lace–adorned ruff known as the *lechuguilla*, which was not only expensive but provoked the complaint that "young people who are both intelligent and strong are occupied in ironing and fluting these extravagant baubles and would be far better employed in doing some useful work for the state or in cultivating land" (cited in Defourneaux 1966:57; Deleito y Piñuela 1946:234–253). Philip IV's *pragmaticas* also prohibited the use of clothing embroidered with gold or silver thread and all manner of *guarnición*. These laws, too, were generally ineffective, and it has been noted with irony that the peak of

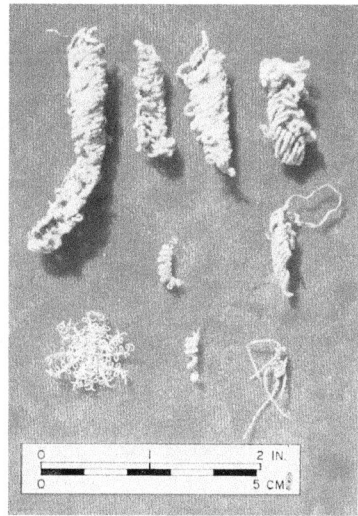

Figure 8.26. Sixteenth-century metallic *guarnición*. Santa Elena, South Carolina, ca. 1575. *Top and center right:* #38BU162D-67; *Center and bottom left:* #38BU162E-40C; *Bottom right:* #38BU162-72. South, Skowronek, and Johnson (1988:Fig. 84). *Courtesy of the South Carolina Institute of Archaeology and Anthropology and Stanley South.*

excess and ostentation in Spanish costume occurred while these rules were in effect (Deleito y Piñuela 1946:276).

Metallic clothing trim has been recovered from American sites spanning the entire Spanish colonial period and does not appear to be useful for dating. Metallic trim is, however, acknowledged by the sumptuary regulations as an index for costly clothing and was from the sixteenth through the nineteenth centuries an element of officers' clothing (Gonzáles Mena 1982:409–410). Examples of both *pasamanería* and of *cariele* have been recovered from Spanish colonial sites, although it is often very difficult to distinguish these from the few remnant threads that are typically encountered (Fig. 8.26). Braided, twisted, corded, or spiraled elements are most commonly identified, however, suggesting that *pasamanería* ornamentation was more common that true *cariele*. For additional examples of archaeologically recovered *guar-*

Figure 8.27. Sixteenth-century copper-alloy "stars." *Top row, left to right:* 18 points, diameter 1.6 cm, pre-1578, Puerto Real, Hodges Collection; 17 points, 1.7 cm by 1.6 cm, pre-1578, Puerto Real, FS 3354; 6 points, maximum diameter 1.4 cm, Puerto Real, FS 3297. *Center row, left to right:* 7 points, diameter 1.32 cm, ca. 1566, St. Augustine (8SJ31-2135); 8 points, maximum diameter 1.3 cm, pre-1578, Puerto Real, FS 3327; 7 or 8 points, maximum fragment diameter 1.4 cm, pre-1578, Puerto Real, Hodges Collection; 15 points (made from a four-maravedí piece), maximum diameter 2.2 cm, pre-1578, Puerto Real, Hodges Collection; 11 points, maximum diameter 1.1 cm, ca. 1580, St. Augustine (SA-26-1-256). *Bottom row, left to right:* 10 points, maximum diameter 1.3 cm, pre-1578, Puerto Real, FS 3354; half star, 8 points, maximum diameter 1.3 cm, pre-1578, Puerto Real, FS 3354. Hodges Collection, Musée de Guahabá, Limbé, Haiti, and FLMNH Collections. *Photos: James Quine.*

nición, see Ellis (1987:58), Smith (1965:71–73), and South, Skowronek, and Johnson (1988:140–142).

Small, metallic or glass ornaments often referred to as mounts or bosses were also commonly used to decorate clothing of the fifteenth and sixteenth centuries, particularly hats, belts, and collars (see Egan and Pritchard 1991:162–203; Anderson 1979:77, 22). Examples of some of these items have been recovered from Spanish colonial sites dating to that period. A small, copper-alloy pin in the form of a figure eight was found at the site of La Isabela, identical to those used as clothing and belt decoration in late medieval London (Egan and Pritchard 1991:204; Fig. 8.25). This particular example may have been Moorish in inspiration, since it is known that Queen Isabella ordered quantities of small pins known as *Cifras moriscas* (Moorish letters) with which to decorate collars, belts, and mantle borders (Muller 1972:21–23). These are not known to have been used after the early sixteenth century.

Small, star-shaped cutouts of thin copper-alloy sheets have been reported from several sixteenth-century sites and may have been used as clothing ornamentation (Fig. 8.27) (these are discussed in a religious context in Chapter 4). They measure between 1.5 and 2.0 cm in diameter and usually have a central perforation. Stars with from four to ten points have been reported (Ewen 1991:95;

Radisch 1988:145–151; Willis 1984:193), and at Puerto Real and Concepción de La Vega, the stars were cut from four-maravedí pieces minted in Santo Domingo.

These star-shaped objects have been variously suggested to have functioned as spur rowel replacements, clothing ornaments, saddle ornaments, self-flagellation implements, and religious symbols (Ewen 1991:95; Radisch 1988:145–151; Willis 1984:193). At least some of these stars probably functioned as clothing ornamentation, owing to their similarity to clothing mounts that have been well documented in medieval English sites (Egan and Pritchard 1991:162, 179) and that appear in sixteenth-century paintings (South, Skowronek, and Johnson 1988:147). The latest dating of such star-shaped ornaments reported archaeologically is from the Portuguese Fort Jesus, Mombasa, where they are attributed as Arab-influenced ornaments of the seventeenth century (Kirkman 1974:316–317).

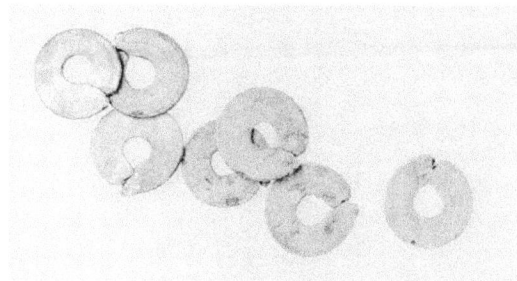

Figure 8.28. Silver sequins from San Luis de Talimali, 1650–1700. Average diameter 8 mm. FS 4257. *Courtesy of the Florida Bureau of Archaeological Research, the San Luis Archaeological and Historical Site, and Bonnie G. McEwan. Photo: James Quine.*

Clothing was also decorated with small, metallic spangles or sequins throughout the colonial period, although these are rarely recovered archaeologically. A number of silver sequins of about 8 mm in diameter were excavated at the seventeenth-century Spanish village at San Luis de Talimali (ca. 1650–1700) and are shown in Figure 8.28.

Chapter 9
Buckles, Strap Ends, and Belt Hooks

Buckles have been used as fastenings for clothing, harness, armor, and weaponry since pre-Roman times, and they are found archaeologically throughout the entire span of Spanish occupation in the Americas. They are generally more useful for suggesting function rather than chronology, although some broad chronological distinctions in buckle typology can be suggested. Figure 9.1 shows the components of a buckle and the terminology used throughout this chapter (following Egan and Pritchard 1991:50–56). Other useful sources on archaeologically recovered buckles and their classification and dating include Abbitt (1973), Noel Hume (1980:4–88), Stone (1974:25–43), and, for military buckles in particular, Powell (www.artifacts.org). Although these sources are concerned primarily with English or French buckles of the eighteenth century, they are also useful references for buckles found on eighteenth-century Spanish colonial sites as well, since French and English buckles (like buttons) were imported in quantity to the Spanish colonies after 1700.

Three broad categories of buckles are found archaeologically: clothing and shoe buckles, armor and spur buckles, and harness and tack buckles. Clothing buckles are in general the most common of these, although on sites predating 1550 they are often outnumbered by armor buckles. The clothing buckle group includes shoe, belt, hat, and knee buckles, and by the eighteenth century shoe buckles outnumber other categories on both Spanish and English American sites (see Noel Hume 1980:84–88).

Most Spanish colonial buckles recovered archaeologically are made of iron or copper alloy, although a few eighteenth-century examples have been reported in silver (discussed later). Harness and tack buckles are in general (although not exclusively) made of iron, while clothing buckles are most often made of a copper alloy.

Sixteenth-century Spanish guild ordinances indicate that brass buckles were made by the *latoneros* (brass-workers guild), but iron buckles were made most often by the *freneros* (bit and bridle–makers guild, which was a division of the blacksmiths guild) and buckles of gold or silver were made by the *joyeros* (gold-workers) and *plateros* (silver-workers) guilds, respectively. If iron or copper-alloy buckles were to be gilded or enameled, this decorative work was done by a separate artisan who was a *dorador*, or member of the metal-decorators guild (Córdoba de la Llave 1990:238, 251, 260–262).

Clothing Buckles

Buckles have been used as clothing fasteners since ancient times and can include belt, baldric (a leather shoulder belt for supporting and suspending a sword), shoe, knee, and hat buckles. The function of a particular buckle can sometimes be indicated by its size and shape, although there is considerable overlap among the groups, and there are no absolute guidelines for determining buckle function from morphology alone. The dating criteria for buckles are equally general, in that cer-

Buckles, Strap Ends, and Belt Hooks

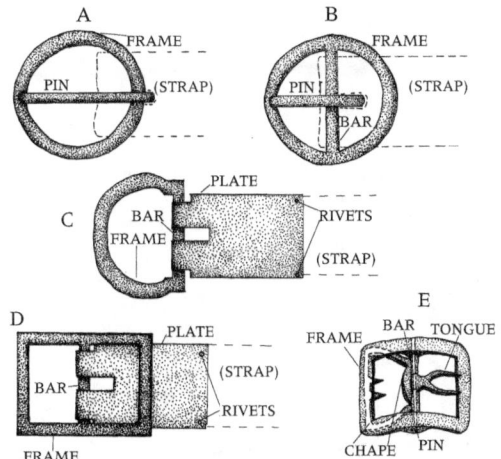

Figure 9.1. Buckle components and terminology. A. Simple, round frame, "ring and pin" buckle; B. Simple, round frame with bar; C. Simple, subround frame; D. Simple, rectangular frame with bar; E. Eighteenth-century shoe buckle with tongue and chape. *Drawing: Pauline Kulstad following Egan and Pritchard (1990:51–52) and Abbitt (1973:35).*

tain shapes and sizes tend to occur during certain periods, although this, too, cannot be attributed absolutely.

The use of clothing buckles also varied with trends in fashion, and thus an understanding of clothing evolution is important in any consideration of buckles or other durable clothing elements. The most detailed source of information about specific items of clothing is in art, though paintings tend to depict elite clothing rather than the humble apparel that is more likely to be represented in an archaeological site (see, for example, Anderson 1979; Davenport 1948; Kohler 1963; Payne 1965).

Some general functional and chronological tendencies in colonial-period buckles can be suggested. Buckles for knee britches tend to have the center bar running parallel to the length rather than the width of the buckle, as is the arrangement on other kinds of clothing buckles. Shoe buckles are most often curved in section to fit on a shoe and tend to be the largest of buckles (up to 12 cm across). Hat and breeches buckles are similar in form to shoe buckles but are generally about half the size and flat (Noel Hume 1980:86).

Shoe buckles are not reported from Spanish colonial sites dating to before 1700, nor are they common on English sites before that time (Abbitt 1973; Noel Hume 1980:86). They tend to become larger and more elaborate through the eighteenth century. Breeches buckles (small buckles used to fasten breeches at the knee) were also not introduced until about 1700 (Lester and Oerke 1940:282–283).

Fifteenth- through Seventeenth-Century Clothing Buckles

Buckles of many kinds are commonly found in sites dating to the first half of the sixteenth century. During the seventeenth century, however, clothing buckles are relatively uncommon as compared to those related to military activities. Like buttons, clothing buckles on (nonmilitary) Spanish colonial sites are not common again until the eighteenth century, when the influence of French fashion was manifest in nearly all sectors of material life.

The earliest form of clothing buckle on Spanish colonial sites (and also the most common late medieval buckle form; see Egan and Pritchard 1992:57–64) is a simple circle of copper-alloy metal, with or without a central bar. The ring and central bar (when present) were cast as a single piece. Those without a central bar often have a pin attached and are virtually identical to those known from Bronze Age sites as "ring and pin" fasteners or "annular brooches" (Egan and Pritchard 1992:65; Lester and Oerke 1940:280). These ring-shaped buckles range in size from 3.0 to 5.5 cm in diameter. Although they are usually undecorated, some examples are scalloped or molded around the ring (Fig. 9.2). They occur during the first half of the sixteenth century on Spanish sites. Circular frame buckles from late medieval

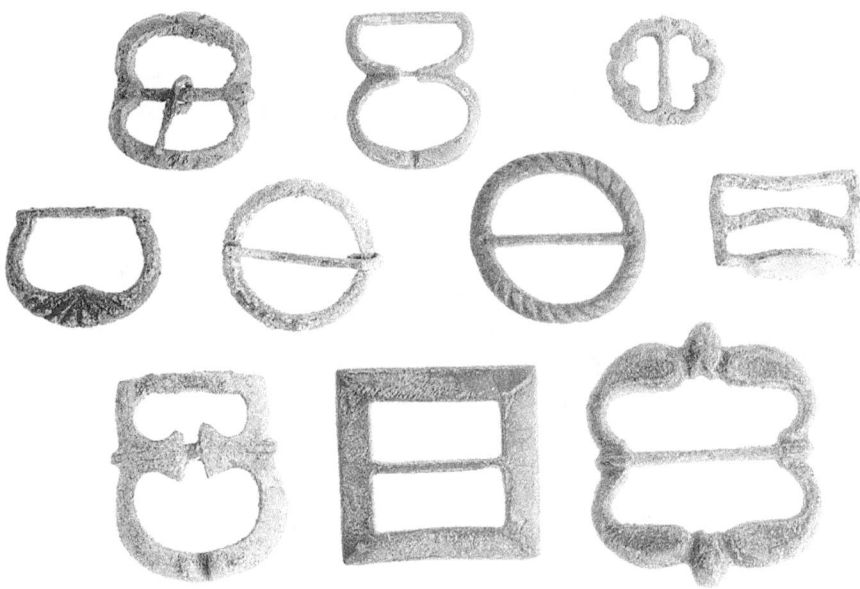

Figure 9.2. Copper-alloy buckles, ca. 1500–50. All from Concepción de la Vega. *Top row, left to right:* Subround double frame with bar and pin (length 2.8 cm); asymmetrical double-frame strap lead/buckle (length 2.8 cm); ornamental spur buckle (length 1.9 cm). *Center row, left to right:* Ornamented subround buckle (length of bar 2.5 cm); "ring and pin" buckle (diameter 2.6 cm); round molded frame with bar (diameter 3.0 cm); rectangular double-frame buckle with perpendicular oval integral plate (length 2.7 cm). *Bottom row, left to right:* Asymmetrical double-frame belt (length 3.8 cm); square buckle with bar (3.5 cm square); ornate double-frame belt buckle with bar (maximum length 5.0 cm). Parque Nacional de Concepción de la Vega, Dominican Republic. *Photo: James Quine.*

sites in Europe were used most commonly on shoes, but they also functioned as fasteners for breeches and belts (Egan and Pritchard 1991:57, 64–65).

Other belt buckles of the sixteenth century are generally double-frame buckles and include double oval and subround frames (figure eight) and rectangular, square, flared square, and flared rectangular double frames (Figs. 9.3, 9.4). These were generally cast of copper alloy in one piece and are only occasionally decorated. The most commonly occurring of these, particularly during the later sixteenth century, is the oval double-frame buckle in either iron or copper alloy (Fig. 9.4). Certain of the oval, subround, or D-shaped double-frame buckles have a hook or a loop attached at one end and were used on sword belts to attach the scabbard lead to the belt (see Fig. 9.4; see also Fig. 9.20; South, Skowronek, and Johnson 1988:124, Fig. 73).

In an analysis of sixteenth-century paintings with depictions of buckles, Cusick (1993) suggests that the subround or oval double-frame buckles in general are associated primarily with sword belts and leads of the sixteenth and early seventeenth centuries. These double-frame buckles (cast in a single piece) were apparently in use on Spanish sites into the first quarter of the seventeenth century, as indicated by the presence of a half-round, double-frame sword belt buckle of this type on the 1622 *Atocha* wreck (Florida Bureau of Historical Resources Conservation Laboratory Catalogue #2194).

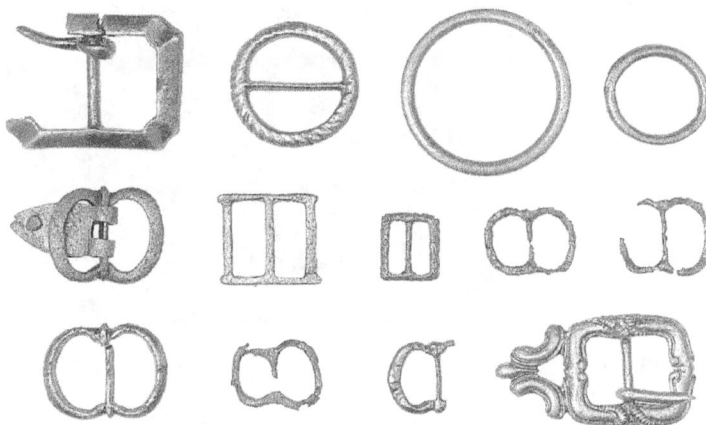

Figure 9.3. Copper-alloy buckles, ca. 1520–70. All from Puerto Real. *Top row, left to right:* Belt buckle (height 4.0 cm); ring buckle (diameter 3.5 cm); ring buckle (diameter 5.0 cm); ring buckle (diameter 3.2 cm). *Center row, left to right:* Double-frame subround armor buckle with plate (4.1 cm by 2.8 cm); square armor buckle (2.5 cm square); rectangular spur buckle (2.0 cm by 1.7 cm); double-frame subround spur or armor buckle (2.6 cm by 1.8 cm.); double-frame subround armor buckle (2.8 cm by 2.1 cm). *Bottom row, left to right:* Double-frame subround armor buckle (3.5 cm by 2.1 cm); double-frame subround spur buckle (2.0 cm by 2.4 cm); double-frame subround armor or spur buckle (height 2.1 cm); ornate clothing buckle (3.8 cm by 3.4 cm). Hodges Collection, Musée de Guahabá, Limbé, Haiti. *Photo: James Quine.*

Few clothing buckles have been reported from Spanish colonial sites of the seventeenth century, either terrestrial or marine. Only a single clothing buckle fragment, for example, has been recovered from seventeenth-century contexts in St. Augustine (Hoffman 1994). Clothing, including shoes, was most frequently fastened with laces or hooks during the seventeenth century, before the advent of French fashion in Spain.

Eighteenth-Century Clothing Buckles

French fashion influence, provoked by the Bourbon rule after 1700 in Spain and the Spanish colonies, made buckles (particularly shoe buckles) extremely popular. Clothing buckles on eighteenth-century Spanish American sites are for the most part identical to many of those recovered from contemporary Anglo-American and French American

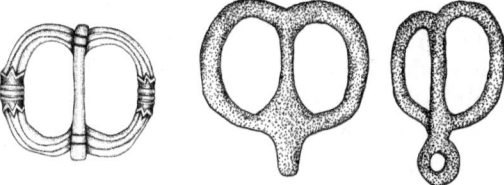

Figure 9.4. Sixteenth-century double-frame subround ("figure-eight") buckles. *Left:* Molded copper alloy, *San Esteban* shipwreck, Padre Island, Texas, 1554. 5.2 cm by 4.6 cm. Texas Historical Commission #156-5. Reproduced from Arnold and Weddle (1978:Fig. 66). *Courtesy of the Texas Historical Commission, the authors and Academic Press. Center and right:* Typical form of a "figure-eight" buckle with a sword lead. *Drawing by Pauline Kulstad following examples from Santa Elena, South Carolina, 1566–87 (South, Skowronek, and Johnson 1988:123–124), and the Spanish Armada wreck (1588) (Martin and Parker 1988:34).*

sites (see Brain 1979:190; Abbitt 1973; Stone 1974; Sullivan 1986:76; Noel Hume 1980). The 1741 *Matanceros* shipwreck, for example, carried more than 3,000 copper-alloy buckles of apparent French and English origin (Blair 1960:237).

Buckle manufacturing was well established in Birmingham, England, by the first quarter of the eighteenth century, and by 1750 the city is said to have produced 2.5 million pairs of buckles annually (Abbitt 1973:26). One characteristic that distinguishes eighteenth-century buckles in general from those of earlier periods is the separate production of the frame, chape, pin, and tongue, particularly on shoe buckles (see Fig. 9.1). Most earlier examples were cast with the central bar and frame in a single piece, with the pin and often a strap end (rather than a chape) attached to the center bar. Clothing buckles of the first third of the eighteenth century are usually small and often square or rectangular. By midcentury, oval shapes cast in rococo designs were made, and buckles were larger, with men's shoe buckles measuring 4.4 to 5.5 cm across and women's somewhat smaller (Abbitt 1973:26).

Plain brass baldric or strap buckles, presumably for use with arms, continued to be made with the center bar. These are generally double-frame, D-shaped, copper-alloy or iron buckles, differing from the earlier "figure-eight" buckles with the same functions in their more elongated D shape rather than the subround shape of earlier periods (see, for example, Fig. 9.16).

Several technological developments that affected the production of buckles occurred after 1750 and are summarized by Abbitt (1973:2). These included a shift to setting paste jewels after 1750 in openwork metal backs, in contrast to the solid-metal backings more typical before 1750. In 1742, the technique for plating copper items with silver was developed in Sheffield, England, and was soon applied to buckles. The buckle-manufacturing process (like that for thimbles)

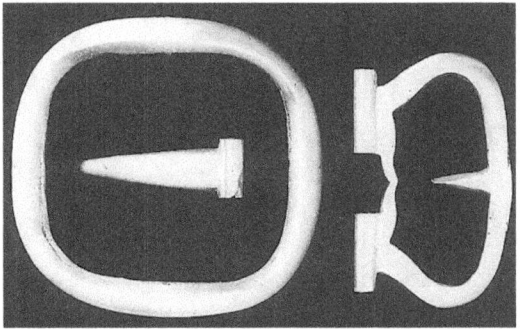

Figure 9.5. Silver harness/clothing buckle. Silver or silver gilt harness-type buckles of this type were fashionable for clothing during the later eighteenth century. Frame: 4.5 cm by 4.7 cm. St. Augustine (SA-12-26-2.013) FLMNH/CSA Collections. *Photo: James Quine.*

was revolutionized after 1769, when the metal stamping machine was developed in Birmingham and buckles could be pressed in quantity from prepared dies.

Buckle size grew larger throughout the eighteenth century, and buckles reached their largest sizes during the final quarter of the century. Large, plain harness buckles of silver or silver gilt were particularly popular on clothing of fashionable young men in London during that period (Abbitt 1973:26), and an example of one of these buckles from St. Augustine is shown in Figure 9.5.

Shoe buckles and large ornamental buckles fell out of popularity by the end of the eighteenth century, and after that time shoes were fastened with laces. The buckle industry fell into decline, and shoe buckles are quite rare on sites of the nineteenth century.

More than 50 buckles were recovered from the 1715 and 1733 Florida plate fleet wrecks (Skowronek 1982:119–127; Fig. 9.6), and 30 buckles were found at Santa Rosa Pensacola (1728–52) (Smith 1965:115). These two collections provide a useful cross section of Spanish colonial clothing buckles in use during the first half of the eighteenth century (Figs. 9.6, 9.7).

Like those of colonial Williamsburg, the

Buckles, Strap Ends, and Belt Hooks

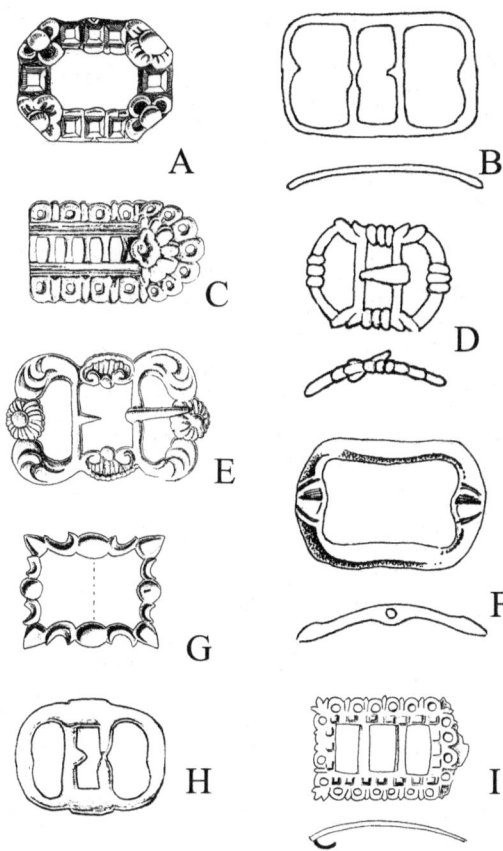

Figure 9.6. Clothing and shoe buckles from the 1715 Florida plate fleet wrecks. A. Gold, 7.0 cm by 5.7 cm (8SL17) FBAR Lab #L7394-0987; B. Copper-alloy shoe buckle, 4.5 cm by 2.7 cm (8SL17) FBAR Lab #L1147; C. Gold clasp buckle, 4.0 cm by 2.3 cm (8SL17) FBAR Lab #L7210; D. Silver shoe buckle 3.3 cm by 2.5 cm (8SL17) FBAR Lab #L1415; E. Silver, 3.1 cm by 2.0 cm (8IR23) FBAR Lab #6294/2505; F. Brass shoe buckle, 4.3 cm by 3.0 cm (8IR17) FBAR Lab #L7549; G. Gold, 3.0 cm by 2.6 cm (8IR23) FBAR Lab #L6460. H. Brass belt buckle, 3.5 cm by 2.6 cm (8SL17) FBAR Lab #L6284; I. Gold, 3.5 cm by 2.3 cm (showing detail of clasp on reverse) (8IR23) FBAR Lab #L6467. *Courtesy of the Florida Bureau of Archaeological Research. Drawings: Frank Gilson.*

clothing buckles in the early-eighteenth-century samples are square or rectangular in shape, usually with rounded corners. Only one example from the 1715 collection had a separate chape and pin (see Burgess and Clausen 1976:132), and all others had either one or two center bars. The chape-type buckle seems to have been used primarily after 1715.

Ornate cast decoration in base metal is found primarily on shoe buckles, but elaborate decoration is almost always found on gold or silver buckles, whether they are for clothing or shoes. The materials recovered from the 1715 fleet included several gold and silver buckles, which may have been products of American goldsmiths (since the ship was bound for Spain). Several of these were formed in three sections with two internal cross bars, a shape not found on French or English buckles. Only 1 of the 42 buckles from the 1733 fleet materials was in this form, and it was of silver. Some of these ornate gold buckles fastened by means of a hook at one end rather than by a pin (Fig. 9.6).

During the second half of the eighteenth century, oval and rectangular frames with molded openwork, floral, and other baroque designs appeared on Spanish sites (Fig. 9.8). Small, rectangular breeches buckles, often ornately cast, became more common. Except for these breeches buckles, clothing and shoe buckles of this period were also considerably larger in size than those of the first part of the century, and during the latter part of the eighteenth century harness-type buckles of silver or silver gilt were fashionable for clothing wear (Fig. 9.5). Such studies as Stone (1974) and Abbitt (1973) are useful for classifying and dating these later clothing buckles.

Armor Buckles

All of the major categories of armor used during the first century of Spanish colonization (that is brigandine plate armor, chain mail,

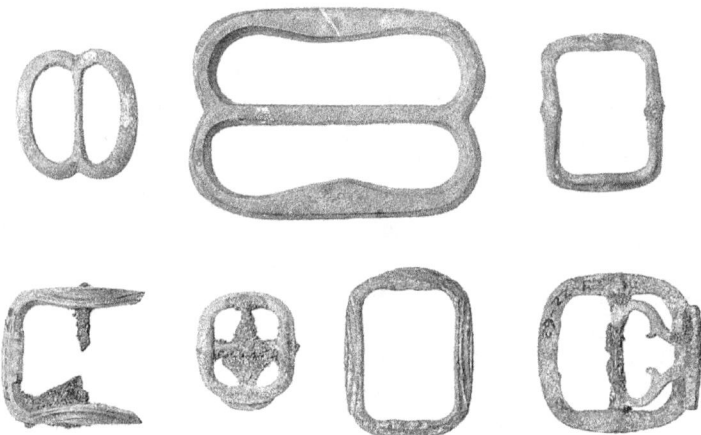

Figure 9.7. Copper-alloy buckles from Santa Rosa Pensacola, ca. 1720–50. *Top row, left to right:* Clothing buckle, center height 2.8 cm, FS 101; harness or bandolier buckle, center bar length 6.3 cm, FS 20; shoe buckle, length 3.9 cm, FS 29. *Bottom row, left to right:* Copper-alloy and iron shoe buckle, center bar height 3.5 cm, FS 69; copper-alloy and iron clothing buckle, center height 2.8 cm, FS 43; clothing buckle, length 4.2 cm, FS 43; shoe buckle with intact chape, center height 3.9 cm, FS 62. Florida State University Anthropology Department Collections. *Photo: James Quine.*

and to a much lesser extent, full body armor) used small buckles and straps to fasten sections of the armor together, employing from five to ten or more buckles per set of armor (Fig. 9.9; for a discussion and illustration of these basic categories of armor, see Calvert 1907; Ffoulkes 1988; Karcheski 1990). Armor buckles have been reported from Spanish colonial sites dating from approximately 1492 to 1600. They are generally small, flat buckles of no more than 3 cm in length and are most commonly made of copper alloy.

At the fifteenth-century site of La Isabela in the Dominican Republic (1493–98), the most frequently occurring buckles are simple, oval frames with offset, narrowed bars (Fig. 9.10). Several retain the separately added metal plate attached to the straight part of the frame to receive a strap. These buckles are flat and undecorated on the inner side, are convex on the exterior, and measure between 2.0 and 2.8 cm in length. Most of them have a small, cast notch at the center of the frame face to hold the tip of the pin, and some examples have scalloped and molded decoration on their faces. The simple, oval frame armor buckles from La Isabela are of a very ancient design, resembling those found on Roman sites (Lester and Oerke 1940:281, Fig. 356). Other fifteenth-century armor buckles from La Isabela include both D-shaped, simple-frame and square, double-frame examples.

Although they are reported from medieval English sites (Egan and Pritchard 1991:85–87), no double oval frames have been recovered from later fifteenth-century contexts in the Caribbean (these are also described as "figure-eight" buckles, for example, in Noel Hume 1980:85). By the sixteenth century, however, double oval frame buckles are the most common shape on Spanish colonial sites. Although a simple, copper-alloy oval buckle with an offset, narrowed bar (similar

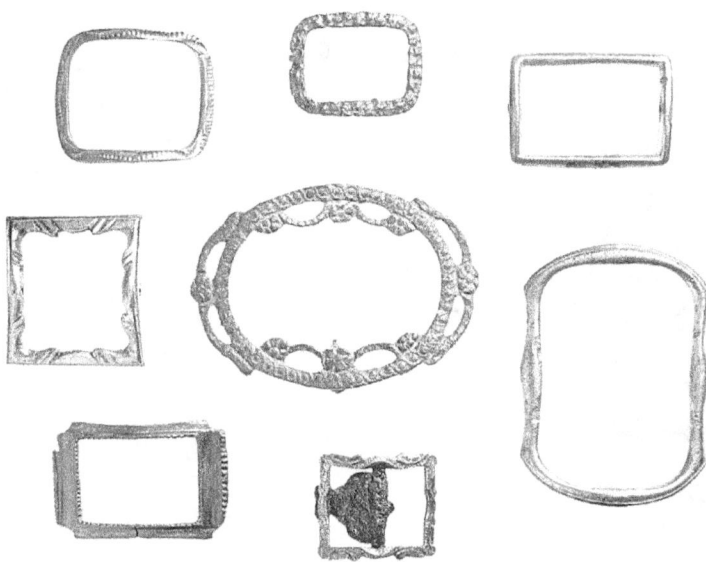

Figure 9.8. Copper-alloy clothing and shoe buckles from St. Augustine, ca. 1750–90. *Clockwise from top center:* Breeches buckle, width 3.0 cm (SA-AO061); clothing buckle, maximum width 3.6 cm (SA-AO229); shoe buckle, maximum width 5.8 cm (SA-AO229); breeches buckle with chape, maximum width 3.0 cm (SA-7-7-279); clothing buckle, maximum width 3.7 cm (SA-7-7-300); clothing or shoe buckle, maximum width 3.5 cm (SA-10-1-1); shoe buckle, maximum width 3.5 cm (SA-38-6-4). *Center:* Clothing buckle, maximum width 7.2 cm (SA-16-23-63). FLMNH/CSA Collections. *Photo: James Quine.*

to the La Isabela examples) was found attached to a fragment of body plate armor at Santa Elena, South Carolina (1566–83), double-frame examples were much more common at that site (South, Skowronek, and Johnson 1988:111, Fig. 63). Double-frame armor buckles are also the most commonly encountered type at such sixteenth-century sites as Concepción de la Vega (1498–1562); Puerto Real, Haiti (1503–78); and Caparra, Puerto Rico (1500–50), suggesting a general trend toward double-frame oval armor buckles of a slightly larger size (about 3 cm) through the sixteenth century.

Small, rectangular and trapezoidal buckles of iron and brass have been reported from both fifteenth- and sixteenth-century sites (Fig. 9.11). An example from Santa Elena was found attached to a fragment of Tasset Lame (overlapping armor plates that covered the upper thigh).

Spur Buckles

Spur buckles are used to attach the metal spur assembly to the leather spur straps that pass over and under the wearer's instep (Fig. 9.12). Small, rectangular buckles were sometimes cast as part of the metal heel plate itself (as in Fig. 9.13); however, this did not become standard until the nineteenth century (Noel Hume 1980:243). Before that time, the spur heel plate commonly terminated in a double (or "figure-eight") loop, to which a buckle was attached by means of a hook, loop, or riveted plate.

Free-standing spur buckles were usually smaller than other buckles, measuring 2 cm

Figure 9.9. Buckles used on armor. Detail from drawing of a Spanish conquistador, ca. 1500. From the Florida Museum of Natural History exhibit, *First Encounters. Courtesy of the Florida Museum of Natural History and Merald Clark. Drawing: Merald Clark.*

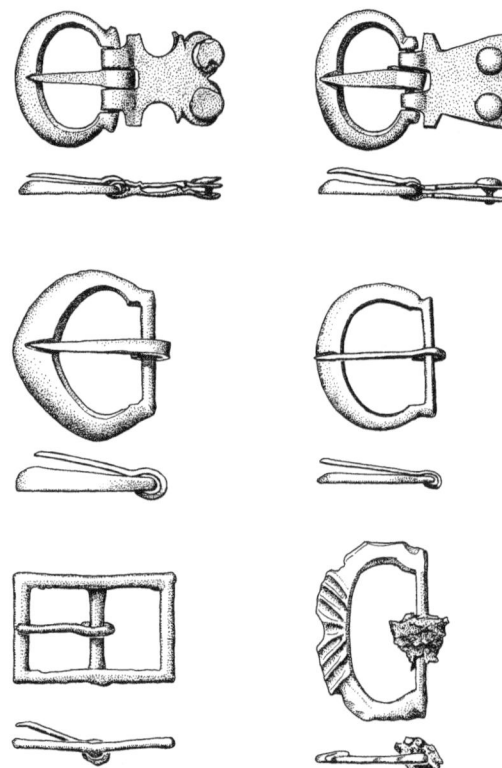

Figure 9.10. Copper-alloy armor buckles from La Isabela, 1493–98. *Top left:* Subround frame with pin and plate attached; buckle height 2.0 cm, plate length 1.75 cm, FS 5941. *Top right:* Subround frame with pin and plate attached; buckle height 2.0 cm, plate 1.5 cm by 1.7 cm, FS 5612. *Center left:* Subround frame with pin attached, 2.5 cm by 2.0 cm, FS 5856. *Center right:* Subround frame with pin attached, 2.1 cm by 1.8 cm. *Bottom left:* Rectangular double frame with pin on central bar, 2.4 cm by 1.65 cm, FS 1855. *Bottom right:* Ornate subround frame with remnant iron pin, 2.7 cm by 1.68 cm, FS 5840. Parque Nacional de La Isabela, Dominican Republic. *Drawing: Merald Clark.*

or less across (Noel Hume 1980:87). These can be difficult to distinguish from armor buckles on very early military sites, but after the mid-sixteenth century, buckles of a few centimeters in length were almost certainly used on spurs.

The forms of spur buckles generally follow those of other kinds of buckles. At the late-fifteenth-century site of La Isabela, buckles are generally of simple-frame design, although a single, brass, double-frame buckle was cast as an integral part of a heel plate (Fig. 9.13). Sixteenth-century examples are most frequently double frame in form, either the oval double frame or a simple, rectangular frame with a vertical center bar (see Figs. 9.2, 9.3).

During the second quarter of the seventeenth century, boots became extremely popular as footgear for men in Europe, and spurs, often with elaborate straps and buckles, were an essential accessory "whether or not their wearers ever went near a horse" (Payne 1965:334). Butterfly-shaped ornamental spur buckles were typical of the mid-seventeenth century, and examples have

Figure 9.11. Iron strap lead or armor buckles, Puerto Real, 1503–78. Lengths, left to right: 4.3 cm, 3.5 cm, 2.5 cm. Hodges Collection, Musée de Guahabá, Limbé, Haiti. *Photo: James Quine.*

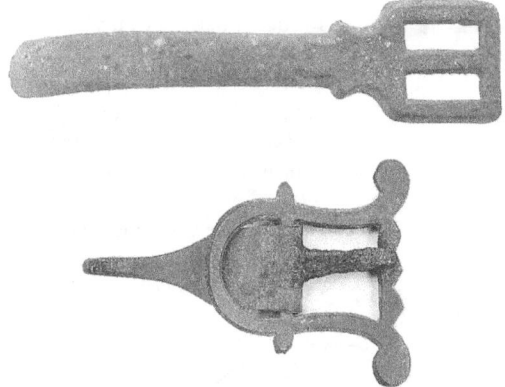

Figure 9.13. Spur buckles. *Top:* Copper-alloy spur buckle cast with heel plate (1493–98). Total length 8.5 cm; buckle 2.0 cm by 2.5 cm. La Isabela, FS 3591. Parque Nacional de La Isabela, Dominican Republic. *Bottom:* Seventeenth-century copper-alloy French-style "butterfly" spur buckle. Maximum length 5.5 cm. St. Augustine (SA-30-3). FLMNH/CSA Collections.

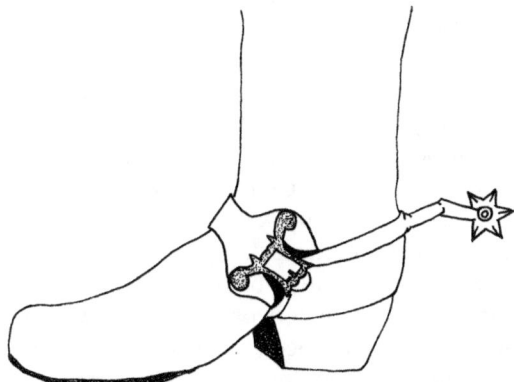

Figure 9.12. Manner of spur buckle attachment. *Drawing by Pauline Kulstad after Faulkner and Faulkner (1987:Fig. 9.3).*

been recovered from both French (Faulkner and Faulkner 1987:253) and Spanish sites (Fig. 9.13) of this period.

Noel Hume (1980:87) notes that small, often ornamental double-frame oval buckles were also characteristic of the seventeenth- and early-eighteenth-century spur buckles in the English colonies (see also Cotter and Hudson 1957:51); however, these have not been reported from seventeenth-century Spanish sites. Somewhat larger spur buckles, ranging from 2.3 to 3.8 cm in length, have been reported from eighteenth-century Spanish colonial sites in the southwestern United States. These are generally double frame and rectangular and made of iron (Simmons and Turley 1980:113). By the nineteenth century, most spurs had buckles cast as integral parts of the spur heel plate, often eliminating the need for free-standing buckles (Noel Hume 1980:237).

Harness and Baldric Buckles

Buckles used with harness and baldrics generally range from about 6 to 15 cm in length and are considerably larger than typical clothing buckles. Smaller buckles (but larger than spur or armor buckles) were also used on belts and strapping as part of military equipage. Even after the eighteenth century, these buckles tend to have center bars around which straps could be attached, rather than the chapes found typically on shoe buckles.

Figure 9.14. Sixteenth-century harness buckles. Concepción de la Vega (1496–1562). *Top:* Double-frame round buckle, copper alloy, diameter 11.8 cm. *Bottom:* Half of a double-frame subround buckle, copper alloy, 8.0 cm by 4.9 cm. Parque Nacional de Concepción de la Vega, Dominican Republic. *Drawing: Merald Clark.*

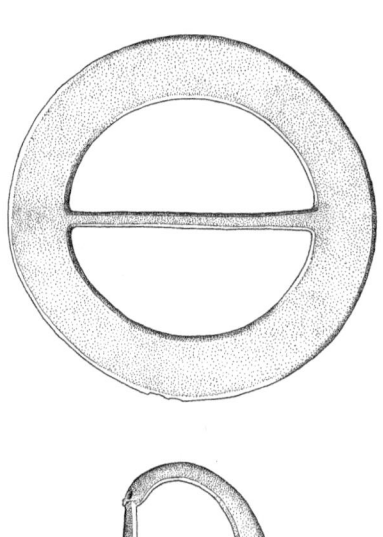

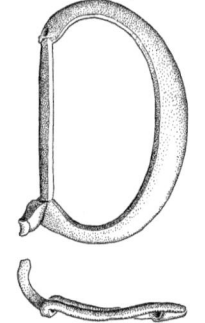

Figure 9.15. Gilded and enameled harness buckle. Concepción de la Vega (ca. 1500–62). Copper alloy, 8.0 cm by 9.0 cm (width of frame at center 2.5 cm). Parque Nacional de Concepción de la Vega, Dominican Republic. *Photo: James Quine.*

Two large, copper-alloy buckles from Concepción de la Vega—a flat, circular, brass buckle with a central bar and a D-shaped, double-frame buckle—may have been baldric or harness buckles (Fig. 9.14). Harness buckles are more likely to be made of iron than are either baldric or clothing buckles, although very ornate enameled harness buckles have been recovered at early-sixteenth-century sites (Fig. 9.15). Narrow, rectangular buckle frames thought to have been used with harness have been reported from sites ranging from the fifteenth through the eighteenth centuries, including La Isabela, Puerto Real, St. Augustine, and the 1715 and 1733 Florida plate fleet wrecks. These are between 6.0 and 8.0 cm long and about 1.5 to 2.0 cm wide. Those of the sixteenth century are of iron and have no central bar (Fig. 9.11), while a 1715 example was of copper alloy with a vertical bar in the center (Fig. 9.6).

Figure 9.16 shows a large, brass baldric buckle from St. Augustine, recovered from a context dating to the second half of the seventeenth century (Stanley Bond, personal

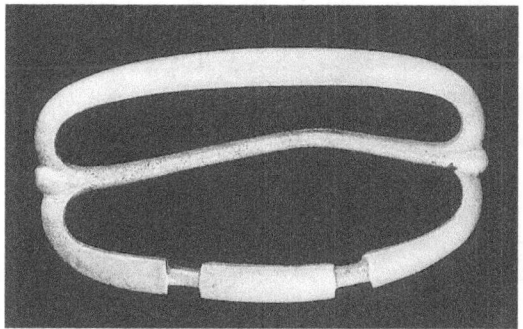

Figure 9.16. Late-seventeenth-century brass baldric buckle. Length 9.5 cm. St. Augustine (SA-30-1-285). FLMNH/CSA Collections. *Photo: James Quine.*

Figure 9.17. Fifteenth-century strap ends. La Isabela, copper alloy. *Clockwise from top left:* FS 745, FS 176, FS 745, FS 134. *Center:* FS 39. Upper left strap end, tip, 2.0 by 2.5 cm. Parque Nacional de La Isabela, Dominican Republic. *Photo: James Quine.*

Figure 9.18. Sixteenth-century belt hook fastener. Concepción de la Vega, copper alloy. Length 7.5 cm. Parque Nacional de Concepción de la Vega, Dominican Republic.

communication, 1992). It is an elongated, D-shaped, double-frame brass buckle, 12 cm in length and 4 cm wide, and this form was in use from at least the mid-seventeenth century through the end of the eighteenth century (see Noel-Hume 1980:Fig. 20-11).

Strap Tips

Metal tips intended to fit over the ends of leather straps are found alone or attached to the center bar of early buckles (in the eighteenth century, these were replaced by chapes). These strap ends have been recovered primarily at early Spanish colonial sites (dating before 1600); however, they have also been occasionally found on buckles from seventeenth-century Anglo-American sites (Noel Hume 1980:85). The earliest Spanish examples consist of a folded sheet of brass in a double-lobed form, with the closed end crimped into a tube to fit around the center bar of a buckle. The open (lobed) end was riveted to a strap (Fig. 9.17). They range in size from 1.0 to 2.0 cm in length and are either 0.7 or 1.0 cm wide where the strap was attached to the buckle bar. This is a medieval form of strap end and is a common type on medieval English sites (Egan and Pritchard 1991:124–225). Those found on late-sixteenth- or early-seventeenth-century English sites are usually a simple folded rectangle or rounded rectangle of copper alloy with a single rivet (see, for example, South, Skowronek, and Johnson 1988:11; Noel Hume 1980:85).

A number of strap or belt ends that were not intended to be attached to buckles were recovered at fifteenth-century La Isabela. These are in general more ornate than the buckle strap ends and served a decorative and a functional role (see Fig. 9.17 top right and bottom left). Strap ends of this kind have not been reported from Spanish colonial sites dating to later than 1550.

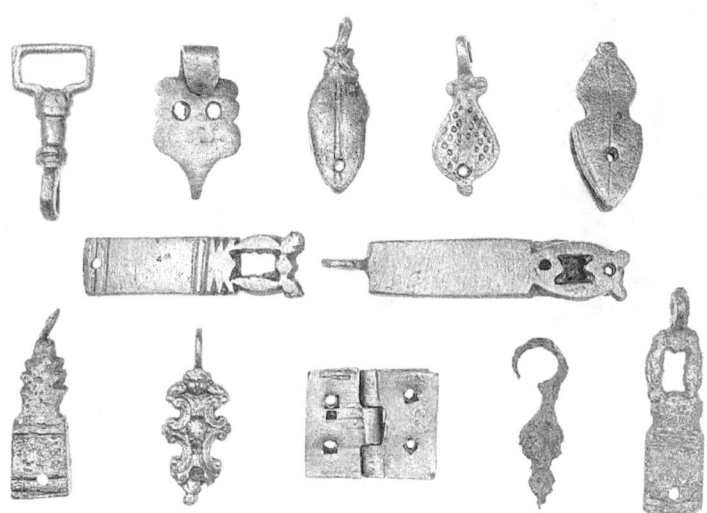

Figure 9.19. Sixteenth-century belt hooks and fasteners, Puerto Real. *Top row,* copper-alloy belt hooks, *left to right:* Length 4.4 cm, 3.8 cm, 4.4 cm, 4.2 cm, 4.3 cm. *Center:* Copper-alloy hook and loop fasteners. *Left:* Length 5.2 cm. *Right:* Length 7.5 cm. *Bottom row, left to right:* Belt hook, length 4.7 cm.; belt hook, length 4.55 cm; armor or box hinge, width 3.25 cm; iron hook, length 4.2 cm; loop fastener, length 5.7 cm. Hodges Collection, Musée de Guahabá, Limbé, Haiti. *Photo: James Quine.*

Belt Hooks

From the late fifteenth through the mid-seventeenth centuries, strap tips with hooks, buckles with hooks, and mounts with hooks were attached to belts in order to suspend objects or connect straps. These strap tips were used both for military and domestic purposes, such as attaching leads for swords, powder kegs, purses, knives, keys, or scissors and were often quite ornamental (Figs. 9.18, 9.19). Twelve less elaborate iron hook mounts with bilobed attachment plates were recovered from Santa Elena, all in domestic contexts (South, Skowronek, and Johnson 1988:127–130). Hooks were used to attach leads to sword belts or baldrics during the sixteenth and seventeenth centuries (Fig. 9.20) but occur much less frequently after the middle of the seventeenth century.

Figure 9.20. Use of belt hooks and fasteners. Detail from Cristóbal de Morales's, *Don Sebastián de Portugal* (1565). Monasterio de las Descalzas Reales, Madrid, #00612069. *Copyright © Patrimonio Nacional.*

Chapter 10
Sewing Equipment

The construction and repair of fabric and clothing were major domestic activities in all colonial households and were generally the domain of women in Spanish homes (Anderson 1979:187; Perry 1990:16; Riaño 1890:272). Depending upon a household's circumstances, needlework might be a domestic necessity, a means of economic support, or an important social and leisure activity for Spanish women (González Mena 1982; Martín 1983:37; Perry 1990:16–17). Nearly all domestic colonial sites yield material evidence of sewing and needlework, including pins, needles, thimbles, scissors, and bobbins.

Pins

Pins (*alfileres*) are the most commonly occurring needlework-related artifact in archaeological sites, particularly when sampling and recovery methods incorporate small mesh size (25 mm or smaller) in screening. Copper-alloy straight pins had been used for centuries in Europe when Columbus arrived in the Americas, not only for holding fabric together during tailoring but also to fasten clothing as it was worn. Straight pins are also an integral part of pillow or bobbin lace-making (discussed later), which was practiced in Italy by the fifteenth century and probably came to the Americas with some of the first Spanish women to emigrate in the late fifteenth century.

Pin making was one of the earliest industries organized by task specialization and mass production (Caple 1995), and up to 24,000 pins a day could be produced by a specialized colonial-era workshop (Tylecote 1972:183). The technology of pin making did not change significantly from medieval times until the second quarter of the nineteenth century (see, for example, Amman's 1583 illustrations [Amman and Sachs 1973:110; Fig. 10.1] and Diderot's 1750 illustrations [Diderot 1751–65, 1969]). In 1824, the flat-headed solid pin, stamped out in a single process, was patented (Noel Hume 1980:254). Before that time, the shanks and heads of straight pins were made separately and joined by hand.

Nearly all colonial-era pins were made of brass. Pin shanks were made of drawn wire, pulled through metal draw-plates with openings the size of the desired pin diameter. This technique was well established in Europe by the sixteenth century (see Grove 1966:53) and permitted the standardization of pin shank diameter. After drawing, the wires were cut and bundled into short lengths and sharpened to points on both ends by using a grinding wheel. The cutting and grinding process was repeated until the intended pin lengths were obtained. In a separate process, other pieces of brass wire were wound in spirals of two wrapped loops onto a mandrel of the same diameter as the pin shank. These were annealed and served as the heads, which were attached to the shanks using a small drop stamp or by hand with a hammer. The wrapped heads were sometimes hammered into shapes or flattened after applica-

Figure 10.1. The pin maker (*Der Hesstelmacher*), 1568. "The pin maker produces fine, smooth, round-headed pins out of brass wire. He also makes clasps for clothing" (Amman and Sachs 1973:110).

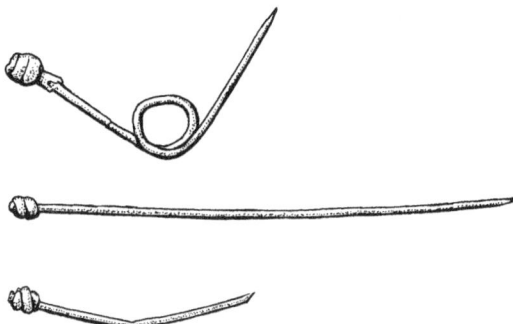

Figure 10.2. Late-fifteenth-century straight pins from La Isabela (1493–98). Copper alloy with wound heads. *Top:* (twisted) FS 914; *Center:* Length 4.4 cm, FS 5856; *Bottom:* Length 2.4 cm, FS 5856. Parque Nacional de La Isabela, Dominican Republic. *Drawing: Merald Clark.*

tion (for discussion and examples of late medieval pins made in this way, see Egan and Pritchard 1991:299–301).

Solid balls were also used as pinheads, attached to the shank by soldering. These solid ball heads could be either cast or hammered into shape and were often highly decorative. Few examples of such pins have been recovered from Spanish colonial sites, but they are quite common in English medieval sites (Egan and Pritchard 1991:300–304).

Most pins were tinned after construction to give them a silvered appearance, although the silvered surface is often lost on archaeological examples through postdepositional processes. Tinning was a simple electromagnetic process achieved by boiling the pins in a solution of potassium bitartrite containing granules of tin. After tinning, the pins were polished by rotating them in a polishing barrel (containing a mild abrasive such as bran).

Straight pins are not particularly useful for dating, since their materials and construction methods changed little from medieval to modern times, and pin sizes varied widely throughout this period according to their intended uses. Smaller pins were needed for dressmaking and tailoring, particularly with light or fine fabrics. Larger pins were used to hold headdressings, veils, clothing pleats, and folds in place.

The earliest pins on Spanish American sites are found at La Isabela (1493–98), and all of these were of brass with wrapped wire heads (Fig. 10.2). They are somewhat longer than pins from sixteenth-century Spanish sites such as Santa Elena, South Carolina (see South, Skowronek, and Johnson 1988:422–424); St. Augustine; or Puerto Real, Haiti (see, for example, McEwan 1995:221). The larger sizes of pins at La Isabela, however, probably had more to do with the use of the pins in heavier military clothing than with the early date of the site.

There was considerable variation in the sizes of pins used with clothing, as indicated by the pins from a single late-sixteenth- or

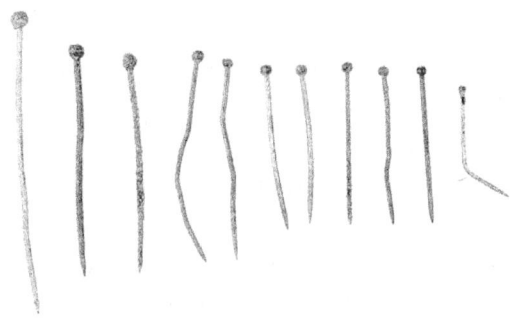

Figure 10.3. Late-sixteenth-century straight pins. Copper alloy with wound heads. St. Augustine (SA-24A-FS 272), FS 134, FS 326, FS 120. Longest pin, 5 cm; shortest pin, 2.5 cm. FLMNH/CSA Collections. *Photo: James Quine.*

Figure 10.4. Copper-alloy pin sheath. Note hole in side for attachment to cloth. Length 20 mm. St. Augustine (SA-34-1). FLMNH/CSA Collections. *Photo: University of Florida Office of Instructional Resources.*

early-seventeenth-century burial in St. Augustine (Fig. 10.3). All were of brass with wrapped wire heads and ranged from 2.8 to 4.8 cm in length.

To diminish the danger of pricking from the exposed pinpoint, pin holders or sheaths into which pin ends could fit were often attached to clothing. These sheaths were tapered, rolled metal tubes, very similar in size and appearance to aglets or lace points. Pin sheaths, however, were fastened to clothing by thread and, unlike aglets, have a small hole in one side for fastening the sheath to fabric (Fig. 10.4).

Needles and Needle Cases

Needles (*agujas*) were indispensable household items, but few of them have been recovered archaeologically. Pedro Menéndez de Avilés of Florida was sent 3,800 needles in 1567 (Lyon 1992:43), but none have been recovered from sixteenth-century contexts at St. Augustine or Santa Elena. Not only were most of the needles after 1500 made of steel, which has notoriously poor preservation qualities, but they were also considerably more costly than pins and probably curated more carefully. Like pins, needles were manufactured by hand in a series of specialized tasks. The production of steel needles, however, was more complex, time consuming, and costly than that of pins, requiring some 80 separate operations. The process included several annealings in a furnace in addition to cutting and straightening the steel wires from which they were made, stamping and punching eyes, preparing a thread groove, sharpening the points, cleaning, and polishing (for detailed descriptions of needle making, see Córdoba de la Llave 1990:241–243; Grove 1966:21–23). Needles were made in a large range of sizes according to their intended function, from fine, slender needles for sewing light fabric to large, sturdy needles used for such rugged products as sails, baskets, and carpets. The latter very large needles are often referred to as bodkins.

Steel needles were manufactured in the Islamic Near East for centuries before the arrival of Europeans to America, and they were introduced to Spain with the Moorish occupation of Iberia. During the Middle Ages, Córdoba became a world-renowned needle-making center, exporting steel needles throughout Europe (Córdoba de la Llave 1990:240–241) and, during the sixteenth century, to the Spanish-American colonies (Torre Revello 1943:80). Spanish needles remained highly prized by European seamstresses and tailors throughout the eighteenth century, despite the fact that guild ordinances and commercial regulations in both England and Mexico prohibited the importation and sale of Spanish needles after needle-making indus-

Figure 10.5. Silver needle case (*etuí*). 1733 Florida plate fleet wrecks. Height 8.2 cm (8MO101) FBAR Lab #12659. *Courtesy of the Florida Bureau of Archaeological Research. Photo: James Quine.*

tries were established in these areas during the early seventeenth century (Barrio Lorenzot 1920:135; Grove 1966:19–20). Torre Revello (1943:780) records three kinds of needles imported to America between 1534 and 1586: *agujas capoteras* (greatcoat- and bonnet-makers' needles), *agujas cordobesas* (Córdoban needles), and *agujas de coser sedano* (needles for sewing silk).

Spanish steel needles were categorized both by function and by shape during the sixteenth century and presumably through the colonial period. *Agujas de obra redonda* (round-sectioned needles) were used for sewing and other work in fabric, and the diameter of their heads (in which the eye was punched) was larger than that of the rest of the needle. *Agujas cuadradas,* used by shoemakers and leather workers, were characterized by a hand-filed edge running along the shaft (*cuadra*) of the needle to aid in cutting and penetrating the leather. These needles did not have larger heads than shafts, owing to the added difficulty of penetrating leather, and the points were filed by hand rather than being round in section. Another category of needles was known as the *aguja de tres esquinas* (needle with three corners) and was presumably triangular in section. These were used primarily by glove makers and hide tanners (Córdoba de la Llave 1990:244).

Ordinances governing the needle-workers guild (*agujeros*) were established in 1617 in Mexico, specifying the quality controls for all kinds of needles, from "the thickness of those used by the a*rrieros* (muleteers, animal pack makers) to those of the *essartar aljofar* (pearl stringers)" (Barrio Lorenzot 1920:135–137). Those used by shoemakers, workers in chamois or silk, surgeons, pack makers, and cushion makers were sold at four to the real; those used by pearl or bead stringers and scabbard makers were sold at six to the real; and the least-expensive needles were sewing needles, sold at eight to the real (Barrio Lorenzot 1920:135–137). Fines were levied if needles were made of iron rather than steel or if the needle shops or merchants sold any needles from Spain. Neither American Indians, blacks, mestizos, nor mulattos were permitted to become needle makers (Barrio Lorenzot 1920:135).

From early medieval times onward, women kept needles used for domestic sewing in small needle cases, often worn suspended from a belt (see Egan and Pritchard 1991:384–386 for medieval English examples). Needle cases could be highly ornate and made from a wide range of materials, including precious metals (see Grove 1966:Plates 5–10). An ornate silver needle case with loops both for suspension and for lifting the cap without separating it from the case was recovered from one of the 1733 Florida plate fleet wrecks (Fig. 10.5). Such cases, known as *étuis*, were made in Germany and France from the sixteenth to the eighteenth centuries (see Von Boehn 1929:212–222; Fig. 10.6). What is believed to have been the bottom part of an embossed brass needle case was found at Puerto Real (1503–78) (Fig. 10.6); however, the great majority of needle cases were made from bone, wood, or ivory. Most of those found archaeologically in the Americas are slender, carved bone or wood tubes ranging from 7 to 12 cm in length and 1 to 3 cm in diameter. These had removable, often screw-on tops and were sometimes decorated with simple carved patterns. Because of the perishable nature of these artifacts, they are found only rarely in terrestrial archaeological sites and are usually fragmentary (Fig. 10.6). Most of the examples reported from Spanish colonial sites are from eighteenth-century shipwrecks, including carved bone and carved wood cylinders from the 1724 Quicksilver wrecks (Borrell 1983c; Figs. 10.7, 10.8); the 1733 Florida plate fleet wrecks (Skowronek 1982:137); and the 1741 *Matanceros* wreck (CEDAM collections, Pablo Bush Romero Museum, Puertas Aventuras, Mexico).

Thimbles and Thimble Rings

Thimbles and thimble rings (open-topped thimbles) are among the best-studied sewing items and can be quite useful for dating and identifying production origins (Grove 1966:36–41; Hill 1995; Holmes 1985, 1987; LeCompte 1988; McConnell 1990; Von Hoelle 1988). Closed, or dome, thimbles protect the end of the sewer's finger when the needle is passed through fabric. Thimble rings (also known as sewing rings) protect the side of the finger and are usually used for stitching very heavy fabrics or leather. Thimble rings are traditionally used by tailors (Holmes 1985), and it has been suggested that they may reflect the specialized, male-attributed production of clothing on archaeological sites in contrast to the domestic, feminine needle-

Figure 10.6. Sixteenth-century needle cases (*etuís*). *Left:* Lower portion of a copper-alloy *etuí*. Height 6.2 cm. Hodges Collection, Musée de Guahabá, Limbé Haiti. *Right:* Design for etuí and thimble, ca. 1585, Nuremberg. Reproduced from Von Boehn (1929:222).

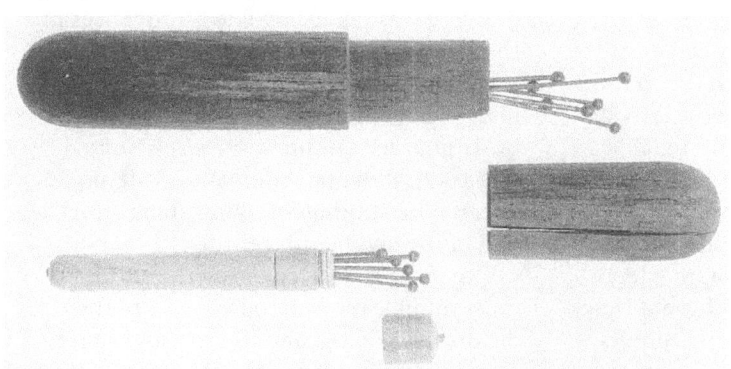

Figure 10.7. Wood (*top*) and ivory (*bottom*) needle or pin cases. Total length of wood case, 9.5 cm; ivory case, 5.5 cm. From the *Nuestra Señora de Guadalupe* shipwreck (1724). Museo de la Atarazana, Santo Domingo. *Photo: James Quine.*

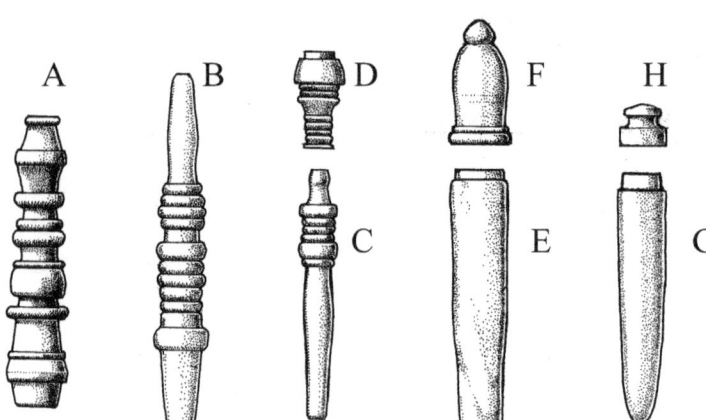

Figure 10.8. Eighteenth-century bone needle cases. From the Quicksilver wrecks (1724). A. Length 7 cm; B. Length 8.3 cm; C. Length 5.7 cm; D. Length 2.2 cm (threaded top); E. Length 6.5 cm; F. Length 2.78 cm (threaded top); G. Length 6.4 cm; H. Length 1.1 cm (*top*). Museo de la Atarazana, Santo Domingo. *Drawing: Merald Clark.*

work associated with closed thimbles (Hill 1995:90).

For extremely heavy, industrial sewing such as sail making, a "palm" was used to help push the needle through the fabric. This was a leather, canvas, or wood pad, often with a metal reinforcement at the center, that was held in the palm of the hand in order to exert pressure on a needle with the whole arm.

Metal thimbles were widespread throughout Europe by the fourteenth century and undoubtedly came to the Americas with the Columbian expeditions (although none were recovered from the site of La Isabela). They were made in silver, gold, iron, ivory, and brass; however, for reasons of curation and preservation, the overwhelming majority of archaeologically recovered thimbles are of brass. Thimbles are somewhat more useful as chronological markers than are needles or pins, since various innovations in the manufacturing of thimbles occurred between 1500 and 1800. These changes are more reliable guides to dating than is shape or size, since these attributes varied widely depending upon the intended use of the thimble. Distinctive manufacturing and decorative techniques, however, were used at different times in different thimble-manufacturing centers (Table 10.1).

Manufacturing Methods

Brass thimbles could be produced in several ways. The earliest method was by casting in a mold, and cast thimbles were produced intermittently until the end of the eighteenth century. Stamping was another early method in use by medieval times but largely discontinued by the eighteenth century. It involved annealing sheet brass and hammering it into a die or mold. The sheet brass used in this process was generally of uneven thickness, and the frequent annealing needed to permit hammering sometimes caused the brass to settle into small folds on the inside or near the base of the thimble. A third method, known as deep drawing, involved annealing disks of sheet brass and punching or press-stamping them into a series of graduated dies until the desired shape was achieved. Deep drawing was made possible by advances in the founding preparation of sheet brass and was first practiced in Nuremberg, Germany, after 1530, where the technique was jealously guarded (Holmes 1985:28–30; Fig. 10.9). It did not come into widespread use in other thimble-making areas until the end of the eighteenth century.

The indentations covering the surface of most thimbles served to help secure the needle during sewing, and the size and shape of the indentations vary according to the kind of

Table 10.1. Thimble Characteristics

Date	Origin	Construction Method	Shape	Crown Details	Surface Design	Comment
Pre-1500	Spain–Cordoba(?)	Cast	Helmet shape	Pointed top, not decorated	Hand punched, round	Leather working
Pre-1500	North Europe	Cast (frequent) or stamped (infrequent)	Short, domed	Round top, hole at apex tonsure	Hand punched, various designs	Some makers' marks; no rim at opening
1500–1620	Nuremberg	Deep drawn	Taller, narrow	Flattish or gently pointed, no tonsure	Hand punched, spiral design	Folded or hollow rim if present
1530–1620	Holland/England(?)	Stamped (sometimes with annealing folds)	Short, wide	Rounded with tonsure	Hand punched, spiral design	Solid rim if present
1620–50	Holland	Cast–2 pieces	Tall, narrow, cylindrical	Rounded with tonsure	Wheel knurled, waffle design	Usually no rim
1600–1700	England	Stamped (sometimes with annealing folds)	Tall, narrow, cylindrical	Rounded with tonsure	Hand punched, waffle design, strap work	Solid rim if present
1650–1730	Holland	Cast–1 or 2 pieces	Becomes shorter and wider through the period	Rounded, no tonsure, hand-punched crown	Wheel-knurled sides, ring-shaped punches, circular design	Solid rim if present
1700–1750	England	Cast–2 pieces	Short, wide	Rounded, no tonsure	Wheel-knurled sides, top, circular design	Solid rim if present
1750–1800	England/Holland	Cast–1 piece	Tall, narrow with wider base	Rounded with wheel knurls on crown	Wheel knurled sides and top	Solid rim if present
Post-1800	England	Deep-drawn–1 piece	Rounded beehive shape	Rounded	Wheel knurls, sides and top to base	Folded rim if present

sewing and needle for which the thimble was intended. The method of making the indentations is more useful for dating purposes than are their size and shape, since earlier indentations were made individually by punching or drilling, while most of those dating to after about 1625 bear indentations made by knurling. The knurling process required fixing the thimble on a form fitting its internal dimensions and then revolving the form

Figure 10.9. The thimble maker (*Der Fingerhuter*), 1568. "The thimble maker manufactures his products from brass which is heated, shaped and riddled with holes; they are used by cobblers, tailors, embroiderers and seamstresses" (Amman and Sachs 1973:63).

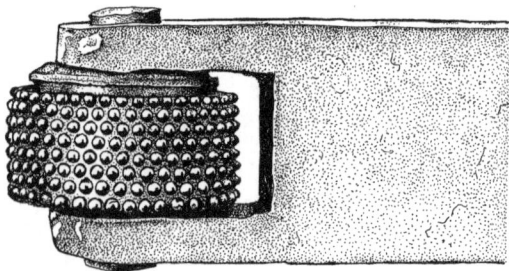

Figure 10.10. Thimble knurling wheel. *Drawing: Merald Clark.*

Figure 10.11. Hand-punched and machine-knurled thimbles. *Top:* Nuremberg thimble, ca. 1550. Height, 1.73 cm; base diameter 1.66 cm. Puerto Real, FS 3123. *Bottom:* Machine-knurled thimble, ca. 1785. Height 1.98 cm, base diameter 1.73 cm. St. Augustine (SA-34-2-5855). FLMNH Collections. *Photo: Elise LeCompte.*

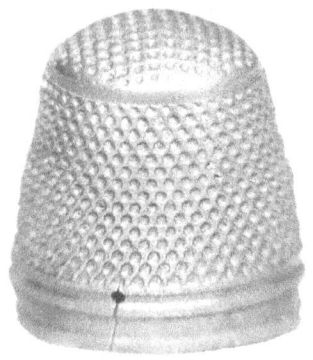

while a wheel with a raised pattern of knurls, knobs, or teeth in rows was pressed against the thimble (Fig. 10.10). Hand-punched indentations are irregular in size, depth, and spacing, while knurled examples are regular and precise in size, shape, and spacing (Fig. 10.11). It is thought that the knurling wheel was developed about 1620 in the Netherlands (Holmes 1987:3); however, examples of thimbles thought to have knurled indentations have been recovered from late-sixteenth-century English sites (see Grove 1966:36–37).

Sixteenth-Century Thimbles

Before 1530, most thimbles were made by casting or stamping. European cast and stamped thimbles tended to be squat in form with rounded, dome tops and were made in a single piece. Cast thimbles are usually thicker and heavier than the stamped varieties, and they often have a small hole in the top and notches around the open base. These notches, however, were used to secure the thimble to a lathe for finishing and can also appear on early stamped varieties (Holmes 1987). If a solid rim of metal protrudes around the base of the thimble, the thimble is cast; if a folded or rolled protuberance occurs, it is stamped or drawn. As noted, the walls of early stamped thimbles are less regular in thickness and quality than either cast or later deep-drawn examples, and the annealing and hammering processes sometimes caused the metal to settle in folds near the base (opening) of the thimble (Holmes 1985:135).

During the fifteenth-century Islamic occupation of Andalucia, Córdoba was an important metalworking center and probably produced many of the distinctive cast Hispanic-Moresque thimbles found at sites there (McConnell 1990:14). These were cast in a single piece but had a distinctive pointed top and bullet shape rather than the squat, dome-shape of cast medieval thimbles from northern Europe (Fig. 10.12). Their size and weight suggest that they were used for heavy stitching such as saddlery and leatherwork.

Little is known, however, of sixteenth-century or later production of thimbles in Spain, and those recovered from Spanish colonial sites in the Americas are almost always attributable to a German, Dutch, or English origin. During the sixteenth century, it is likely that most were imported from Nuremberg, where the leading brass thimble-production center of the time was located. There were also thimble-production centers at that time in the Netherlands and perhaps in England (Greif 1984; Grove 1966:36–38),

Figure 10.12. Hispano-Moresque thimbles. Bronze, fifteenth century. Height of left thimble 5 cm. *Reproduced with permission from McConnell (1990:14). Courtesy of Wellfleet Books, Inc.*

but Nuremberg dominated the sixteenth-century export market.

An important development in thimble manufacture took place after 1530, when the Nuremberg thimble-makers guild was established (Fig. 10.13). Before that date, the thimble makers were part of the coppersmiths guild (*caldereros* in Spain) and produced cast thimbles. Techniques for producing metallically pure zinc were developed in Nuremberg during the first half of the sixteenth century, which made the production and working of high-quality alloy sheet brass easier. After that time, the thimble makers separated from the coppersmiths and began to produce deep-drawn thimbles in large quantities (see McConnell 1990:21–22; Grief 1984:28–30; Holmes 1985:26–27). Nuremberg thimbles were characterized by thin, lightweight sheet brass of very consistent thickness and by a regular, light, bright gold color (McConnell 1990:21). They were lighter in both color and weight and more regular in form and thickness than were the cast or annealed and stamped examples. This in turn permitted more variety in shapes and decoration than before. Nuremberg thimbles tended to be taller than the medieval domelike thimbles, they were usually a bit wider at the base than at the top, and the tops were slightly curved

Figure 10.13. Emblem of the Nuremberg Tailors Guild, 1600. Source: Mummenhoff (1901:100).

or gently pointed (rather than rounded) (Fig. 10.14). Both one-piece and two-piece thimbles were made, the latter with the caps soldered or brazed onto the sides.

The indentations on Nuremberg thimbles were punched by hand in a spiral pattern, beginning at the open base and spiraling up the sides and across the cap to cover the top of the thimble. Although most Nuremberg thimbles did not have rims around the base, many bases had bands of decoration, and many also bore makers' marks near the base (Fig. 10.15).

Nuremberg thimbles are the most frequently encountered type on Spanish colonial sites of the sixteenth century, such as Puerto Real, Concepción de la Vega, Nueva Cádiz, and Santo Domingo (Hill 1995; LeCompte 1988; Von Hoelle 1989); the 1554 Padre Island shipwrecks (Olds 1976:147); and Santa Elena (South, Skowronek, and Johnson 1980:155) (see Figs. 10.11, 10.14).

The guild closely guarded the techniques for the production of Nuremberg deep-drawn thimbles. Sixteenth-century thimble makers in other areas continued to use some casting but primarily worked with annealing and stamping techniques (Holmes 1987:2; comprehensive treatment of sixteenth-century Dutch thimble production is provided in Langedijk and Boon 1999). Toward the end of the sixteenth century, mechanized methods of punching the indentations with knurling wheels were developed in the Netherlands; however, the Nuremberg thimble makers did not adopt this innovation, presumably to preserve jobs for guild members. It was not only the development of better metallurgical techniques for zinc alloys outside of Nuremberg but also the refusal of the Nuremberg guild to permit these innovations that ultimately led to the decline of the Nuremberg industry in the seventeenth century (Grief 1984:28; Holmes 1985:29–30).

Seventeenth-Century Thimbles

Few brass thimbles have been reported from firmly dated seventeenth-century contexts in the Spanish colonies, and thus direct archaeological evidence for the kinds of thimbles in

Figure 10.14. Nuremberg thimbles. All from Puerto Real (1503–78). Hodges Collection, Musée de Guahabá, Limbé, Haiti. *Photo: James Quine.*

Sewing Equipment

Figure 10.15. Maker's mark on a Nuremberg thimble. Ca. 1520–75. Key-shaped mark at lower right edge. Puerto Real, FS 3123. Thimble height 1.79 cm; base diameter 1.64 cm. FLMNH Collections. *Photo: Elise LeCompte.*

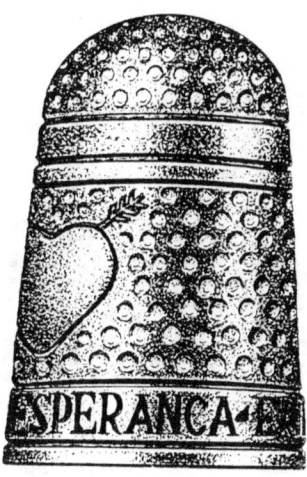

Figure 10.16. Silver thimble. Ca. 1600–50. Probably of Dutch production. Engraved with the legend: "ESPERANCA^EREI^ FORE^AE^MORE^" (Hope is the sum of all love). From the Phillips Mound, Polk County, Florida. *Redrawn by Pauline Kulstad from Hoelle (1988:7); Original drawing by Matt Regine.*

use during this period is poor. An ornamented silver thimble was found in an American Indian burial mound in Florida dating to the first half of the seventeenth century (Benson 1967:126–127). It is tall, narrow, and cylindrical, with wheeled knurls, and is thought to have been of German or Dutch production (Von Hoelle 1989:7). The thimble has a heart pierced by an arrow engraved on the side and a Latin inscription around the base, "ESPERANCA^EREI^FORE^AE^MORE^" (Hope is the sum of all love) (Fig. 10.16).

It is likely that most brass thimbles on Spanish colonial sites of this period were imported from Holland, since Dutch thimbles dominated the European markets of the seventeenth century (Holmes 1985:135–137, 1987:3). It is less likely that any of those imported to the Spanish colonies came from England or Germany, the only other (but minor) thimble-producing areas during that time. Tens of thousands of thimbles, in fact, were imported into England from the Netherlands during the seventeenth century (Holmes 1985:37–38).

Early-seventeenth-century brass thimbles made in Holland (as well as in England) were typically tall, narrow, and cylindrical, with slightly rounded heads (Fig. 10.17). They were usually made in two parts by stamping. After about 1620, Dutch thimble makers reintroduced the use of casting as a principal manufacturing method, but English thimble makers continued to use annealing and stamping as the primary production method until the end of the seventeenth century (Holmes 1987:2; Grove 1966:38).

Before about 1620, the designs on thimbles were usually hand punched. The indentations generally followed a spiral design, starting at the open end of the thimble and spiraling around it to the top. Many of those produced outside of Nuremberg, however, left a bare, undecorated area at the top of the thimble, known as a tonsure. This practice continued only until the mid-seventeenth century (Holmes 1987:3; Noel-Hume 1980:26), and thus the presence of a tonsure both dates the thimble to before about 1650

Figure 10.17. Seventeenth-century Dutch-style thimble. Height 2.5 cm; base diameter 1.9 cm. En Bas Saline, Haiti. FLMNH Collections. *Photo: University of Florida Office of Instructional Resources.*

  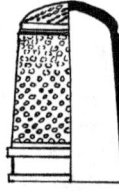

Figure 10.18. Dutch thimbles. *Left:* Dutch type I, 1620–50. Height 2.6 cm. *Center:* Dutch type III or English, 1730–1800. Height 2.2 cm. *Right:* Dutch Type II, 1650–1730, or English, 1690–1730. Height 2.5 cm. *Drawing by Pauline Kulstad after Holmes (1987:4).*

and identifies it as not being from Nuremberg.

By 1620 (and possibly earlier), the surface indentations on Dutch thimbles were produced by mechanical knurling and were thus quite regular in size and distribution (Fig. 10.18). Knurling is thought to have been Dutch monopoly until the 1690s (Holmes 1987:3). The indentations on English and Dutch thimbles of the first half of the seventeenth century were hand punched or machine knurled, respectively, with geometrically shaped punches in a wafflelike design that covered the sides of the thimble (in contrast to the earlier spiral design). The top, or crown, of the thimbles was undecorated (the tonsure) until after about 1650. English thimbles of the first half of the seventeenth century also sometimes bear strap-work decoration around the sides, that is, bands of reserved, nonindented areas usually in a geometric design (McConnell 1990:25).

Although the tops of thimbles were decorated after about 1650, this was often done by hand or by stamping rather than by machine knurling, so that in some cases the sides of a thimble were knurled and the crown hand punched. As the century progressed, the waffle design was replaced by decorative ring or donutlike circles arranged in rows or concentric rings around the thimble, and the shape of the thimbles became shorter and wider (Holmes 1987:4; McConnell 1990:25–26; Fig. 10.19).

Eighteenth-Century Thimbles

The eighteenth-century thimble industry was dominated by English production. A significant innovation in English thimble making occurred after 1696, when John Lofting, a Dutch thimble maker, obtained a patent to produce thimbles by a new process that included a superior sand-casting method in combination with machine knurling the surface indentations (Holmes 1985:137–138; Grove 1966:38). For the next hundred years, both English and Dutch thimbles were cast rather than stamped (Figs. 10.18, 10.19). Those made in Holland were cast in two pieces until about 1730 (Holmes 1987:4) and in England until about 1750 (McConnell 1990:29). The indentations were knurled by machine over the sides and crown of the thimbles, although often in different patterns in the two respective areas. Cast thimbles are generally heavier with thicker walls than stamped or drawn thimbles, and if they have a rim, it is solid (that is, not turned, rolled, or folded).

Thimble shapes changed throughout the eighteenth century, from the short, squat form favored at the end of the seventeenth

Sewing Equipment

Figure 10.19. Eighteenth-century machine-knurled thimbles from St. Augustine. *Left to right:* Round knurls in concentric circles, rolled rim; height 2.1 cm, base diameter 1.62 cm; FLMNH #91739. Round knurls in waffle shape; height 1.79 cm, base diameter 1.72 cm; FLMNH #97460. Round knurls in waffle shape, raised bands around the rim; height 2.28 cm, base diameter 1.12 cm; FLMNH #97415. Round knurls in waffle shape, raised bands around rim; height 1.98 cm, base diameter 1.73 cm; FLMNH SA-34-2-855. FLMNH Collections. *Photo: Elise LeCompte.*

century to a tall, cylindrical form with a rounded head by the middle of the eighteenth century. At the end of the eighteenth century, a shorter, "beehive" shape with rounded walls was popular (McConnell 1990:28–29).

In 1769, another thimble-making innovation was patented by John Ford in Birmingham, England. This was the deep-drawing method, similar to but more mechanized than the method of producing sixteenth-century Nuremberg thimbles. A disk of sheet brass was shaped into the desired form by a series of size and shape-graded pressing operations using a stamp-and-die machine. This led to the mass production of almost completely machine-made thimbles by the end of the eighteenth century, deep drawn in a single piece and machine knurled on top and sides. The knurling extended to the base of the thimble, which, if having a rim, was folded or rolled rather than solid (Fig. 10.20). The shape of deep-drawn thimbles was also taller and narrower than the earlier cast thimbles (Grove 1966:143), and this basic method of producing deep-drawn thimbles is still in use.

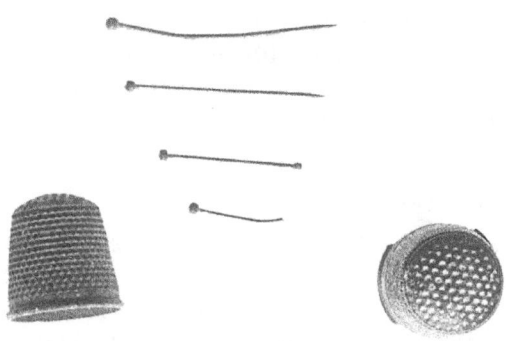

Figure 10.20. Deep-drawn machine-made thimbles, ca. 1810–21. *Bottom left:* Height 1.7 cm, base diameter 1.7 cm. Length of top pin 3.3 cm. St. Augustine (SA-16-23). FLMNH/CSA Collections.

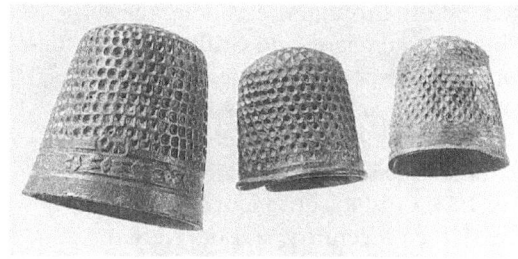

Figure 10.21. Children's thimbles. First third of the eighteenth century, St. Augustine. *Left:* Adult-sized thimble, height 1.73 cm, is shown for size comparison. *Center:* Height 1.3 cm (SA-7-4-208). *Right:* Height 1.1 cm (SA-7-4-242) FLMNH/CSA Collections. *Photo: University of Florida Office of Instructional Resources.*

Children's Thimbles

Young girls throughout Europe were expected to learn needlework at an early age, and thimbles were commonly made for them (Holmes 1985:167–169). These came as nested sets of thimbles in graduated sizes to allow for the child's growth (Grove 1966:39), and the smallest thimbles might be a centimeter or less in diameter. They were produced in the same way as adult thimbles, differing only in their smaller size. Child-sized thimbles serve as one of the few material indices to female children in the archaeological record and have been recovered from sixteenth- and eighteenth-century Spanish colonial contexts (Fig. 10.21). The absence of seventeenth-century examples is undoubtedly owing to archaeological sample limitations.

Scissors and Shears

Scissors and shears were indispensable implements not only for seamstresses and tailors but also for a wide variety of domestic and industrial tasks. "Scissors" refer to cutting implements based on riveted and pivoting blades and loop handles, while "shears" generally refer to cutting implements with unconnected blades operating on a spring action (Fig. 10.22). Both scissors and shears were in general use through the Middle Ages (see Cowgill, Neergaard, and Griffiths 1987). Tailors and seamstresses in medieval Córdoba, for example, used hinged scissors (*tijeras de eje*) in their cutting work, while fullers and barbers used shears (Amman and Sachs 1973:53; Córdoba de la Llave 1990:116). By the sixteenth century, scissors were much more common than shears and used for a wider variety of tasks. Shears remained in use into the eighteenth century for certain specialized production tasks in textile work such as trimming the pile of woolen material, cutting long lengths of cloth, and shearing sheep (Grove 1966:45). Although rare examples of seventeenth- and eighteenth-century shears are found in museum collections, they have not been reported from Spanish colonial sites in the circum-Caribbean region.

The basic elements of scissors include the blades, the arms (sometimes called the hafts), and the bows (also referred to as eyes, loops, or finger grips) (Fig. 10.22). Most utilitarian scissors and shears were made of iron or steel by *cuchilleros* (cutlers) (see Córdoba de la Llave 1990:266–267; Diderot 1959:179) or, in frontier areas, by blacksmiths (Simmons and Turley 1980:128–130). Ornate sewing scissors were also made in gold or silver by jewelers (Diderot 1959:408–409; Mandel 1990:4).

The production of scissors involved shaping

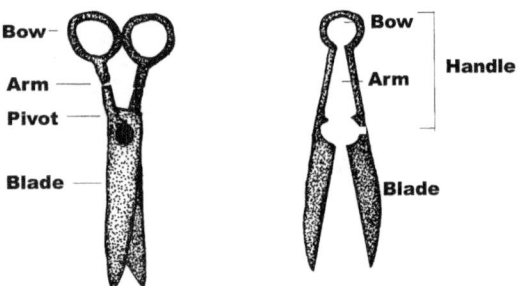

Figure 10.22. Diagram of shears and scissors parts. *Left:* Scissors. *Right:* Shears. *Drawing: Pauline Kulstad.*

of the blades by forging and hammering, then drawing the blade up to form the haft and the bows. The bows were usually looped extensions of the blade and haft on utility scissors, although some more finely wrought scissors had bows made by piercing the ends of the haft and enlarging the hole (see Simmons and Turley 1980:129). Iron blades were usually overlaid with a steel cutting edge, and the inside of the blade was beveled. Once the blade, haft, and bows were complete, the two sides were joined by a rivet through the haft.

Smaller, ornate scissors for sewing were often made in separate parts with cast copper-alloy bows and hafts attached to steel blades. These were modeled on the small, highly ornamental scissors of gold or silver produced by jewelers and were frequently accompanied by ornamental cases, or "scabbards" (which can easily be mistaken for long, narrow, dagger scabbard tips). From the sixteenth to the eighteenth centuries, fine French and Italian needlework scissors were renowned and were exported worldwide, including to the Spanish Americas (Mandel 1990:4; Torre Revello 1943:780).

The various forms of scissors have remained basically unchanged from medieval times to the present and are better indications of function than of date. For example, scissors used for fine snipping work, such as in lace making and embroidery, have very short, pointed blades with comparatively

Sewing Equipment

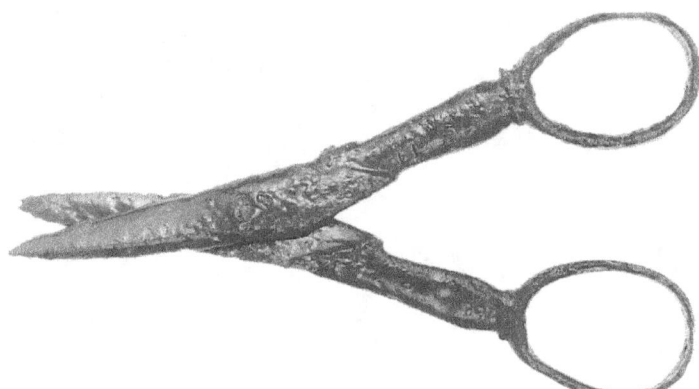

Figure 10.23. Sixteenth-century embroidery scissors. Steel, bow length 2.5 cm, blade length 4.0 cm. Puerto Real (1503–78). Hodges Collection, Musée de Guahabá, Limbé, Haiti. *Photo: James Quine.*

long hafts and large eyes (Fig. 10.23). This form permits frequent snipping action with the worker's fingers resting easily in the eyes but left free. Scissors for heavy work and industrial tasks had wide blades with very short hasps and large eyes (Figs. 10.24, 10.25), while those intended for everyday cutting and trimming have long, tapering blades; medium-length hafts; and relatively small eyes set vertically above (rather than to the side of) the haft (Fig. 10.26).

Figure 10.24. Sixteenth-century industrial scissors. Iron, length of bow 9 cm, length of blade 20 cm. Concepción de la Vega (1496–1562). Parque Nacional Concepción de La Vega, Dominican Republic. *Photo: James Quine.*

Noel-Hume (1980:267–269) has offered some observations about temporal trends in scissor forms on British-American colonial sites. He notes that "rat tail" bows, that is, those formed by drawing the ends of the haft into narrow rat tails and looping them outward and back toward the haft but not attaching them to the haft, are characteristic of the first half of the seventeenth century. Scissors of this type are also seen in images dating to the sixteenth century (for example, Amman and Sachs 1973:53) and are not common past that date. Scissors with unattached rat tail bows were also made, however, during the eighteenth century by Spanish frontier blacksmiths (see Simmons and Turley 1980:128).

Other features of scissors from Spanish colonial sites, such as blade shape and bow shape, also appear to be related more closely to function than to time period. A blade

Figure 10.25. Sixteenth-century tailor's scissors. Detail from Giovanni Battista Moroni's *The Tailor*. National Gallery Picture Library #NG697. *Courtesy of the National Gallery, London.*

Figure 10.26. Utility scissors. Iron, length 15.3 cm. Puerto Real (1503–78). Hodges Collection, Musée de Guahabá, Limbé, Haiti. *Photo: James Quine.*

shape thought to be characteristic of the eighteenth century—that is, wide and cut at an oblique angle to the point rather than tapering to a point—is frequently depicted in images of tailors from the sixteenth through the eighteenth centuries but may be related more to that activity than to time period (see Fig. 10.25; Diderot 1959:440; Noel-Hume 1980:268). Most of the tailoring scissors shown in these works have very short hafts and long blades, as is appropriate for heavy cutting.

Iron scissors have been recovered from a number of Spanish colonial sites, although the preservation is usually quite poor. Among the largest and earliest assemblages are those from Puerto Real and Concepción de la Vega, where embroidery or lace scissors, as well as a variety of general-purpose cutting scissors, were found. Cutting scissors with long hafts and small, drawn bows and large, heavy-duty scissors have been found at several sixteenth-century sites (Figs. 10.27, 10.28A–C).

Several pairs of iron scissors were recovered from the 1622 wreck of the *Atocha* (Florida Bureau of Archaeological Research Conservation Lab #s 1226, 1880). These ranged from 9 to 15 cm in length, and all had small, looped bows positioned directly above (as opposed to everted) the side of the hafts (Fig. 10.28D–F). The hafts on two of the *Atocha* scissors are curved rather than

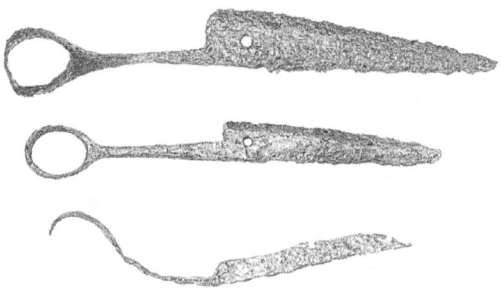

Figure 10.27. Sixteenth-century scissor blades. *Top:* Length 22.5 cm; *Center:* Length 18.0 cm; *Bottom:* Length 16.0 cm. Puerto Real (1503–78). Hodges Collection, Musée de Guahabá, Limbé, Haiti. *Photo: James Quine.*

straight, a trait that had not been documented for utilitarian scissors of the eighteenth century.

By the early eighteenth century, sewing scissors with ornamental cast brass bows and hafts and steel blades were in widespread use in the Spanish colonies (Figs. 10.28G, 10.29). In many instances, the brass bows and hafts were apparently shipped without their blades, since quantities of these handles with no evidence of rust or iron have been recovered from such shipwrecks as the 1724 Quicksilver wrecks (Borrell 1983:98), the 1733 Florida plate fleet wrecks (Skowronek 1982:118), and the 1741 *Matanceros* wreck (CEDAM collections, Pablo Bush Romero

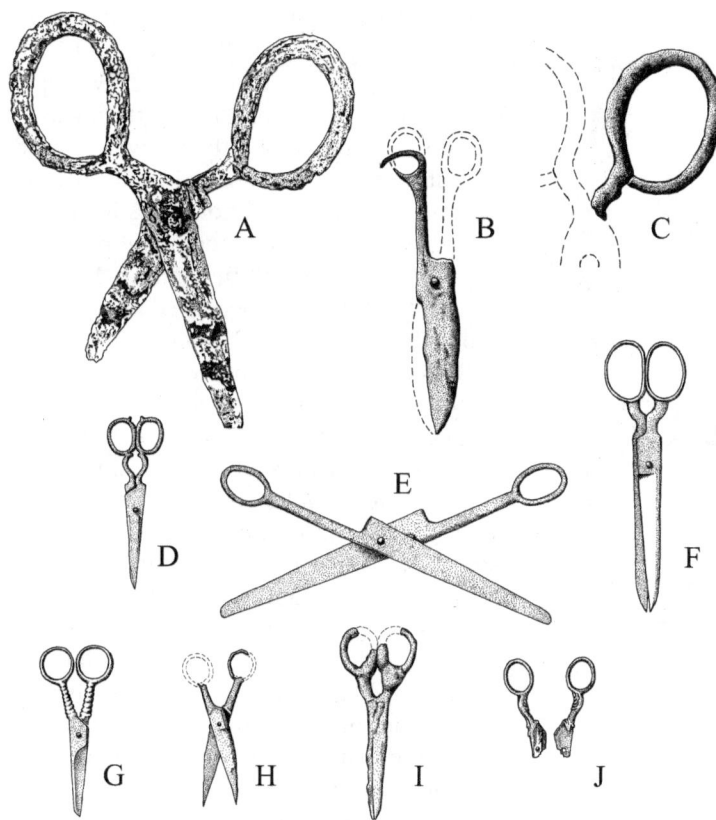

Figure 10.28. Scissors recovered archaeologically. A. Molasses Reef wreck, early sixteenth century, maximum length of A, 25.5 cm (after Keith 1987:Fig. 172); B, C. Santa Elena, South Carolina, 1566–87, maximum length of B, 17.0 cm (after South, Skowronek, and Johnson 1988:Fig. 90); D–F. *Nuestra Señora de Atocha,* 1622, FBAR Lab #s 18800, 1262, maximum length of E, 20.0 cm; G–I. Mission San Antonio, California, ca. 1770–1830, maximum length of G, 10.0 cm (after Hoover and Costello 1985:65); J. 1733 plate fleet wrecks, 8MO146. *Drawings: Merald Clark.*

Museum, Puertas Aventuras, Mexico). The blades were presumably added by cutlers in the Americas. Examples of similar scissors have also been recovered from Santa Rosa Pensacola (1722–52) (Smith 1965:98) and early-eighteenth-century contexts in St. Augustine (Fig. 10.29).

Lace-making Equipment

Lace making and embroidery are among the oldest and most admired crafts in Spain and by the sixteenth century were considered among the essential accomplishments of refined Spanish women (see D'Aulnoy 1930:198; González Mena 1982). Throughout the colonial era, lace making in Spain was often a cottage industry producing lace for export—much of it to the Spanish Ameri-

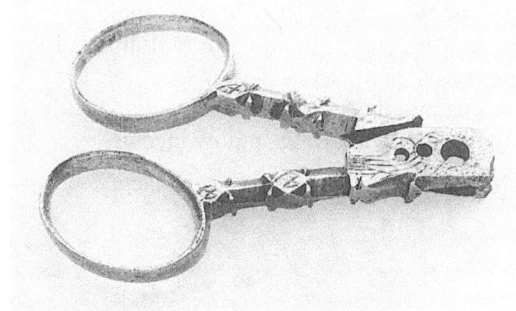

Figure 10.29. Brass embroidery scissors. First half of the eighteenth century. Length 6 cm. (Steel blades are missing.) St. Augustine (HTC). FLMNH/CSA Collections. *Photo: James Quine.*

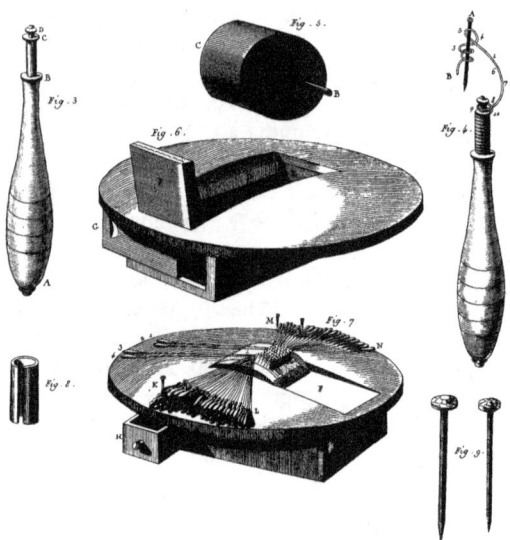

Figure 10.30. Bobbin lace technology. Detail of Plate 140, Part 1, Diderot, *L'Encyclopédie* (Diderot 1751–65). *Courtesy of the University of Florida Library, Special Collections Department.*

can colonies (González Mena 1982:411–412), although lace making was also practiced in the households of some colonists.

Most of the lace produced in domestic settings was the type known as bobbin or pillow lace, or *encaje de bolillos*. This lace-making technique is also one of the few that requires the use of distinctive needlework tools that are potentially recoverable archaeologically. Figure 10.30 illustrates pillow lace in progress. A pattern for the lace was drawn on parchment or paper, and holes were pricked along curving lines and at all points where the threads were to cross. This pattern was affixed to a firm pillow, and pins were placed at the strategic pricked points in the pattern to guide the threads and hold the stitches in position. One end of a meters-long thread was attached to each of these pins, with the other end of the thread wrapped around a bobbin. The bobbins held and manipulated the threads as well as provided tension on the threads as the lace progressed.

Working from the back of the pattern forward, the lace makers would cross and recross the threads, following the pattern by twisting and plaiting and manipulating the bobbins backward and forward with the tips of their fingers. As one segment of the pattern was completed, the pins would be lifted and replaced farther forward on the pillow. Many English lace makers used pins with special heads or pins onto which small seed beads were strung and crimped as markers for critical places in the design (Grove 1966:119), and it is quite possible that Spanish lace makers may have done the same. For a simple edging there might be 50 threads to be held in position, and up to 500 or 600 threads might be used for a wide, elaborate trounce (Grove 1966:115). Each thread would have a pin and a bobbin attached to it.

The bobbins onto which the lace threads

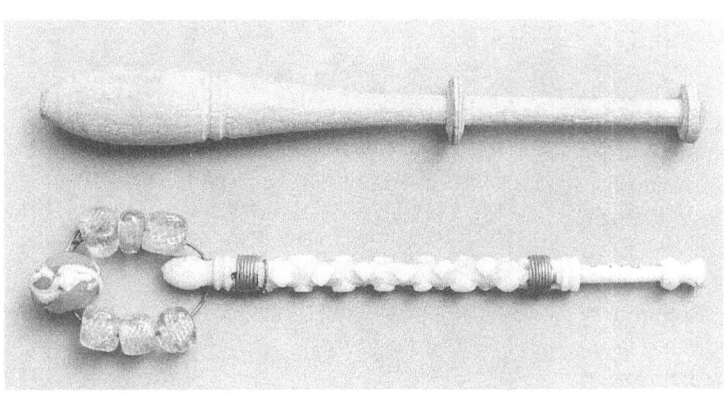

Figure 10.31. Lace bobbins. *Top:* Wood, length 7.5 cm. *Bottom:* Ivory with bead weights, length 6.2 cm. Probably nineteenth century. Lightner Museum Collection, St. Augustine. *Photo: James Quine.*

Sewing Equipment

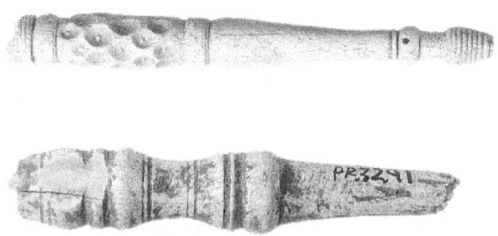

Figure 10.32. Bone bobbins recovered archaeologically. *Top:* ca. 1740–60, length 8.0 cm. St. Augustine (SA-7-4-200). *Bottom:* ca. 1550–75, length 5.2 cm. Puerto Real, FS 3291. FLMNH Collections. *Photos: James Quine.*

were wound were typically made of wood and occasionally of bone or ivory. They are round in section and consist of a long shank surmounted by a narrow neck onto which the thread is wrapped. Above the neck a carved or turned top is usually present, often with a second, smaller neck or hole for securing the thread while allowing it to be gradually unwound from the bobbin (Figs. 10.30, 10.31). Bobbins range from approximately 8 to 15 cm in length, and their general size is determined by the fineness of the threads to be woven. Because tension is an important consideration, the base of these bobbins is often heavier and larger in diameter than the shank. On English bobbins, it is common to find a loop of wire strung with glass or stone beads attached to the base (Fig. 10.31; Grove 1966:117–118), and it is possible that Spanish bobbins may have sometimes been treated in the same way (accounting for at least some of the beads on Spanish colonial sites). Because of the perishable nature of wood, relatively few bobbins survived in Spanish colonial sites, and all of these are of bone (Fig. 10.32). Many other bobbin fragments have probably gone unidentified and unreported and instead have been identified as "carved bone items" rather than bobbins owing to the relative absence of archaeological attention to and information about these items of typically female activity.

Part 4

Personal Items and Accessories

Chapter 11
Items of Comfort and Grooming

For millennia, people have made and used material items to improve their appearance, health, hygiene, and physical comfort. Although the forms of these items were designed to serve functional needs, many of them in the Spanish colonies and elsewhere assumed additional roles as social and economic indicators. Recognizing this, the following discussion attempts to consider those items of personal comfort and grooming that occur most consistently on archaeological sites. Some of them, like fans and toothpicks, could be as easily considered with dress accessories or jewelry, respectively, and these alternative functions will be addressed when appropriate.

Fans

Fans (*abanicos*) have been rarely reported as such from archaeological sites in the Americas, and they come almost exclusively from Spanish American sites. None, for example, are reported from such well-studied English American sites as Williamsburg or Jamestown or from equally well studied French American sites such as Fort Michilimackinack (Stone 1974), Pentagoet (Faulkner and Faulkner 1987), or the *Machault* shipwreck (Sullivan 1986). It is not clear whether this is a function of cultural differences in the colonial past or of archaeological recovery and recognition biases.

Fans for personal use—cooling, fly whisking, adornment, or flirtation—are generally categorized as either fixed or folding. Fixed fans consist of a fanning material (feathers, fibers, paper, or leather) attached to the end or side of a rigid handle, while folding fans are constructed of rigid sticks connected together at their bases by a pivot, allowing the fan to open and close (Fig. 11.1).

Fixed Fans

The fixed fan is an accoutrement of ancient standing in Asia and the Middle East and is depicted in Chinese and Egyptian iconography thousands of years old (Ruiz Alcón 1982:621; Von Boehn 1929:33–36). Very large fans used by one person to fan another and smaller, hand-held fans are illustrated and have remained in use in these areas to the present day. These small, fixed fans were also used by Greek and Roman women and men as cooling devices, fly whisks, and dress accessories (Alexander 1984:7–8).

It has been suggested that fixed fan as personal accessories were introduced to Europe

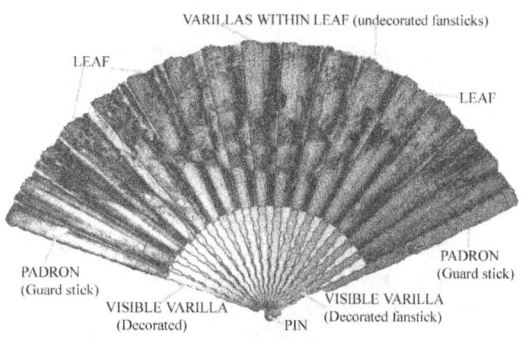

Figure 11.1. Component parts of the fan.

from the Middle East during the Crusades. They remained for centuries an elaborately made and expensive items for elite use and were often made of gilded leather or feathers on a long handle of silver, gold, or ivory (Alexander 1984:7–9; Von Boehn 1929:38–40). Even after the introduction of folded fans, fixed fans remained in use among European women through the nineteenth century.

The adoption of hand-held, fixed fans of feathers in Europe during the sixteenth century may have been in part owing to the interest stimulated by the elaborate feather fans introduced to Europe from the Americas. Columbus, in fact, presented an ornamental feather fan of Caribbean origin to Queen Isabella in 1493 on his return from the first voyage (Alexander 1984:8). Europeans were greatly impressed by the marvelous feather work of the American Indians, and Moctezuma presented Cortés with two magnificent feather fans on golden handles (Von Boehn 1929:40). Small, fixed feather fans were apparently used by Spanish women of high status throughout the sixteenth and seventeenth centuries (Allard 1966:Plates 5, 83; Weiditz 1994:Plate 57; Figs. 11.2, 11.3). Remnants of fixed fans have not been reported from Spanish colonial sites, either because they were not used frequently in the colonies, not preserved, or not recognized.

Folding Fans

The folding fan, rather than the fixed fan, is associated in art, literature, and the popular imagination with Spain. Japan is credited with originating the folding fan during the fifth century A.D. (Lester and Oerke 1954:439), and it is thought to have been introduced to Spain and Portugal during the sixteenth century via Iberian trade connections with Asia (Alexander 1984:10; Ruiz Alcón 1982:622; Von Boehn 1929:43). Spain was the first European production center for folding fans and remained the only country in Europe producing folding fans until the seventeenth century (Ruiz Alcón 1982:622).

Figure 11.2. Spanish woman with a fixed fan, 1529. *"Thus the women in Spain look."* Plate 57 in the Weiditz *Trachtenbuch* (1529). The fan is white embossed with gold, with a violet center and handle, and the edges embossed in green (Weiditz 1994).

Folding fans came into general use somewhat later in the rest of Europe. The opinionated English encyclopedist Randle Holme, for example, described folding and fixed fans in seventeenth-century England: "A gentlewoman's folding fan, half opened, garnished or adorned with a variety of fancies, stories or landscapes. . . . Some term it a circle fan, because being opened to its full extent, it is just the half of a semicircle." This is contrasted with "a feathered fan or handled fan. This is also termed a Matron's fan, being more comely and civil for old Persons than the former, which is stuft with nothing but vanity" (Holme 1972:Book 3, Chapter 1:21).

Folding fans are of two basic kinds: the

Items of Comfort and Grooming 217

Figure 11.3. Woman of Havana with a fixed feather fan, 1695. Plate 83 in Carolus Allard, *Orbis Habitabilis* (Allard 1966).

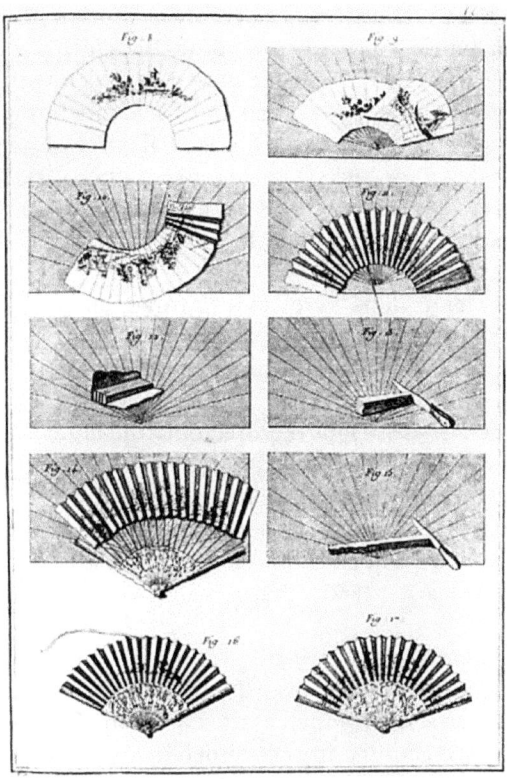

Figure 11.4. The production of pleated fans. *Monture des Eventeils*. Plate 56, Part 3, Diderot, *L'Encyclopédie* (Diderot 1751–65). *Courtesy of the University of Florida Library, Special Collections Department.*

brisé fan and the pleated fan. The brisé fan is constructed exclusively of rigid slats or sticks (*varillas*) connected to one another by a pin at the base and a ribbon or guide at the top so it could open and close (Fig. 11.1). The sticks of brisé fans are painted, carved, or otherwise decorated (often with elaborate pierced work) from the base to the top, and probably because of this, brisé fans are usually smaller than pleated fans.

Pleated fans are constructed of narrower sticks connected by a pin at the base and are covered over the upper three-quarters of their length by a piece of pliable material (the leaf) that was pleated in order to permit folding (Figs. 11.1, 11.4). In most cases, the leaf was a double sheet of material with the sticks inserted between them, but on the thicker leather or skin fans, the sticks would be visible on the back of the fan (Alexander 1984:33). The sticks of the pleated fans were decorated in the same ways as those of the brisé fans but usually only on their lower quarter or third, since the upper portion was covered by the leaf (except when the leaf was a transparent or lacy material). The outer sticks (*padrones*) of both kinds of fans were wider, studier, and often more elaborately decorated, since these were visible and protected the fan when it was closed. The leaf of a pleated fan could be of skin or fine leather, vellum, paper, lace, or cloth. Often elaborately painted, sometimes by the leading artists of the day, the leaf in itself is a small work of art (see, for example, Du Mortier 1993).

Fan sticks vary considerably in width and in length (ca. 7–12 cm). Some sticks for pleated fans were made in two parts, a lower part decorated or carved and a separate but attached upper part comprised of narrower and plainer sticks. The narrower upper sticks were covered by the leaf. The width of a fan, when open, was typically between 12 and 30 cm.

Pleated fans were made in three separate production stages, which included the preparation of the leaf, the preparation of the sticks, and the joining of these to construct the fan. Brisé fans required only the latter two operations. The painting of the leaf was yet another process, done by an artist who might also paint in other media. These stages are shown in detail by Diderot in his *Encyclopédie* (1751–65) (Fig. 11.4).

Fans in Spain

Hand-held fixed fans were used in Spain by upper-status women at the end of the fifteenth century and continued in use through the nineteenth century. Madame D'Aulnoy reported in 1679 that the women of Madrid "always wear a fan, and be it summer or winter, they never cease fanning themselves at the time of the Mass" (1930:218). The first folding fans to be depicted in Spanish paintings appear at the middle of the sixteenth century in such paintings as Antonio Mor's *María de Portugal* (1550) and Cristóbal de Morales's painting of *Doña Juana of Portugal* (1552) (Fig. 11.5). Many of these fans were apparently made of leather. Permeated with scent, they were prized by Spanish nobility for their odor-masking qualities (Ruiz Alcón 1982; Von Boehn 1929:54). French and English men used fans in the seventeenth and eighteenth centuries (much to the contempt of such social critics as Samuel Pepys), but there is little iconographic or literary evidence to indicate that they were used by Spanish men.

Although fans were produced in Spain and

Figure 11.5. Sixteenth-century Spanish pleated leather fan. Detail from Anthonis Mor van Dashort's (Antonio Mor) *Portrait de Jeanne d'Autriche* (1552). *Courtesy of the Royal Museum of Fine Arts, Brussels, Belgium.* #1296.

Italy during the sixteenth century, the first master fan makers and fan-makers guilds are not documented until the early seventeenth century, when both fan makers (*abaniqueros*) and painters of fans (*pintores de abanicos*) are recorded in Madrid (Ruiz Alcón 1982:623). By the end of the sixteenth century, the folding fan had been introduced to the noble classes of Europe, possibly through exchange of gifts to courts allied with the Spanish Hapsburgs, and fans came into widespread use by both men and women of economic means during the seventeenth century (Von Boehn 1929:51–53). Seventeenth-century Spanish fans were frequently made of lace, another famous craft of Spain (Ruiz Alcón 1982:624).

It was during the eighteenth century, however, that fans reached their peak of popularity and accessibility for all social classes throughout Spain, despite the fact that the Spanish fan-making industry was in decline for much of the century. By the second half of the seventeenth century, competition from French fan-making guilds began to diminish the activity and production of the Spanish industry. Spain did not recapture its primacy in fan production until the late eighteenth century, when a royal fan-making factory was established in Valencia (Ruiz-Alcón 1982:624–625).

Fans in the Spanish Americas

Folding fans appear to have been less common in the Spanish American colonies before 1700 than they were in Spain. No fans, for example, are recorded in pre-1630 shipping records as having been imported to the Americas (Torre Revello 1943). Carolus Allard, in his 1695 compendium of costumes of the civilized world (1966), however, shows an elite woman of Havana using a fixed feather fan (and wearing a remarkable parasol hat) (Fig. 11.3).

The relatively few examples of fan sticks recovered and reported archaeologically all date to the eighteenth century. They have been recovered from eighteenth-century shipwreck sites and from well-documented upper-status terrestrial sites in St. Augustine, where they are often associated with needlework items. Additional evidence for the association of fans with upper-status women in the Spanish colonies comes from the Mexican *casta* paintings, which were painted in the hundreds throughout the eighteenth century to depict the physical, occupational, and social characteristics of the nearly 30 categories of race mixture in America (García Saíz 1989). Fans are shown only with Spanish women or Spanish families in these paintings, a typical example of which is titled *"Español. Gente blanca. Casí limpio de origen"* (Spaniards. White people. From practically pure blood) (García Saíz 1989:120; Fig. 11.6).

The only intact sets of fan sticks recovered archaeologically are those from shipwrecks. The *Tolosá*, which sank in 1742 off the coast of the Dominican Republic, carried many items for personal use and adornment, including the articulated base of a pleated folding fan (Fig. 11.7). The fan consists of 13 short, undecorated, flat ivory sticks, which

Figure 11.6. Eighteenth-century pleated fan in Mexico. Detail from *casta* painting, *Spaniards. White people. From practically pure blood*. Andean School, second half of the eighteenth century. *Courtesy of the Museo Nacional de Antropología, Madrid.*

measure only 6 cm in length. The leaf of this fan is missing and probably included supporting sticks of another material.

The 1733 Florida plate fleet wrecks yielded several fragments of fan sticks in ivory and one in tortoiseshell (see Skowronek 1982:136). The ivory fan sticks are carved and painted, and the single intact example measures 15 cm in length. The decoration extends along the entire length of the stick, suggesting that the stick may have been part of a small brisé fan. Another painted ivory brisé fan stick from the 1733 plate fleet wrecks has designs painted in red, black, and gold along the full length of the stick and two small

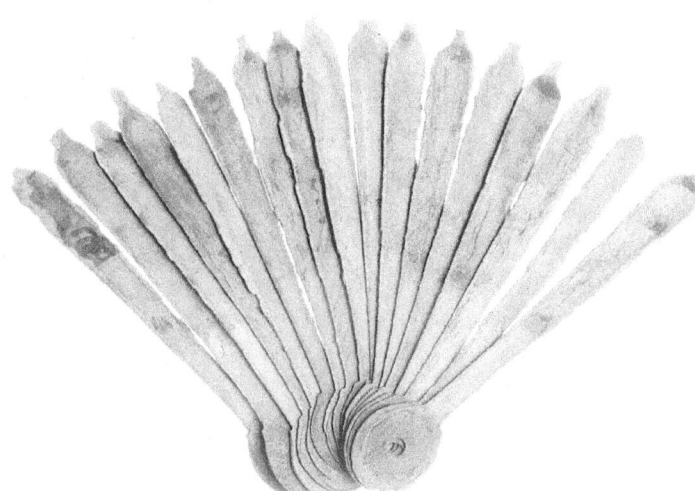

Figure 11.7. Articulated ivory fan sticks, 1724. Length of sticks, 5.2 cm. *El Conde de Tolosá* shipwreck. *Courtesy of the Museo de la Atarazana, Santo Domingo. Photo: James Quine.*

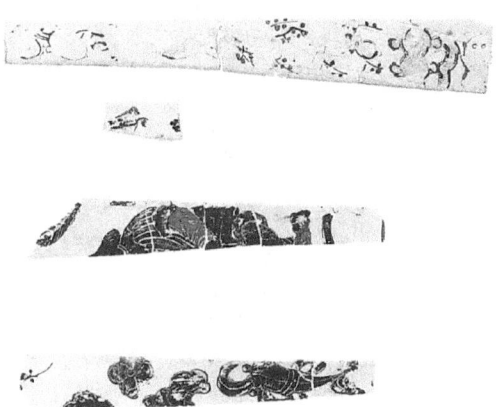

Figure 11.8. Painted ivory fan sticks, 1733. Red, black, and gold paint on ivory. The longest stick measures 10 cm (8MO101) FBAR Lab #S-14. *Photo: James Quine.*

holes at the top edge for connecting the brisé sticks together (Fig. 11.8).

Fan sticks found in the terrestrial sites of St. Augustine are most often made of bone. Many of these are intricately carved (Fig. 11.9), although none has been recovered intact. What may be a *padrón* (guard) stick is particularly ornate.

Umbrellas and Parasols

Like fans, umbrellas and parasols were Asian and Middle Eastern items that were first adopted in Spain and Italy and from there introduced to the rest of Europe (see, for example, Von Boehn 1929:120–150; Lester and Oerke 1954:402–414). "Parasol" generally refers to a sunshade and is usually smaller and lighter than an umbrella. The latter item, as its Spanish name (*paragua*) indicates, is used for protection against rain and is made of a waterproof material.

Parasols were in use by elite people in Spain and Italy by the middle of the sixteenth century. A French traveler, Henry Estienne, described these in 1578 as "a device which certain persons of rank in Spain and Italy carry, or have carried, less to protect themselves against flies than against the sun. . . . it is supported upon a stick, and so constructed that it takes up little room when it is folded, but when it is needed it can be opened forthwith and spread out in a round that can well cover three or four persons" (Lester and Oerke 1954:406). In 1679, the cardinal of Toledo provided parasols "of gold and silver brocade" to protect distinguished visitors from the sun (D'Aulnoy 1930:351).

The social status associated with the parasol extended through the seventeenth century. In 1697, for example, an angry parish priest in St. Augustine charged that "lately the governors have started to use a parasol during religious processions, next to the pall of the sacrament" (Bushnell 1994:186). This showed disrespect for the sacrament, for when the Body of Christ went forth, it alone was entitled to the dignity of a canopy. The crown subsequently ordered the governor of Florida to "desist forthwith from the arrogant custom of carrying a parasol beside the pall of the Holy sacrament . . . being . . . irreverent, and there especially it sets a bad example to the Indians" (Bushnell 1994:186).

The frames for parasols and umbrellas were initially made of wood and later, in an effort to lighten them, of whalebone. The frames of the earliest parasols and umbrellas were essentially the same as those on modern umbrellas, consisting of a rod to which were attached two or more sets of ribs and a fabric or leather shade. Long, slender ribs were attached to the inside of the shade, extending from the outer edge to about halfway in toward the rod, at which point the rib bent inward away from the shade. A second set of shorter and sturdier straight ribs with forked ends connected the shade ribs to the center rod by means of a sliding tube that enclosed the rod several centimeters below its cap. The tube terminated in an everted, grooved collar, which received the forked end of the ribs. Often other sets of smaller ribs served as additional braces and were attached on one end to the cap at the top of the rod. As the sliding tube was pushed up or down along the rod, the ribs folded out or inward, respectively, allowing the umbrella to open and close.

By the eighteenth century, metal frames were in general use, and the ribs from those with copper-alloy frames are sometimes found in archaeological sites (Fig. 11.10). The straight, sturdy, second set of ribs described previously are found most commonly, and an articulated set of these ribs and the grooved tube to which they were attached were re-

Figure 11.9. Eighteenth-century bone fan sticks from St. Augustine. *Left to right:* Carved *padrón* guard stick, length 5.0 cm (SA-24-393); bone fan sticks, lengths: 10.5 cm (SA-7-4-166), 5.3 cm (SA-24-341), 7.5 cm (SA-24-393), 6.5 cm (SA-24-393/340). FLMNH/CSA Collections. *Photo: James Quine.*

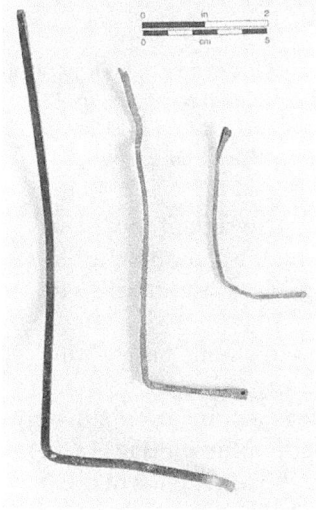

Figure 11.10. Brass umbrella or parasol ribs, ca. 1750. *Left to right:* SA-7-5-5, SA-7-5-4, SA-26-1-228. Vertical portion of leftmost rib, 20 cm. FLMNH/CSA Collections. *Photo: University of Florida Office of Instructional Resources.*

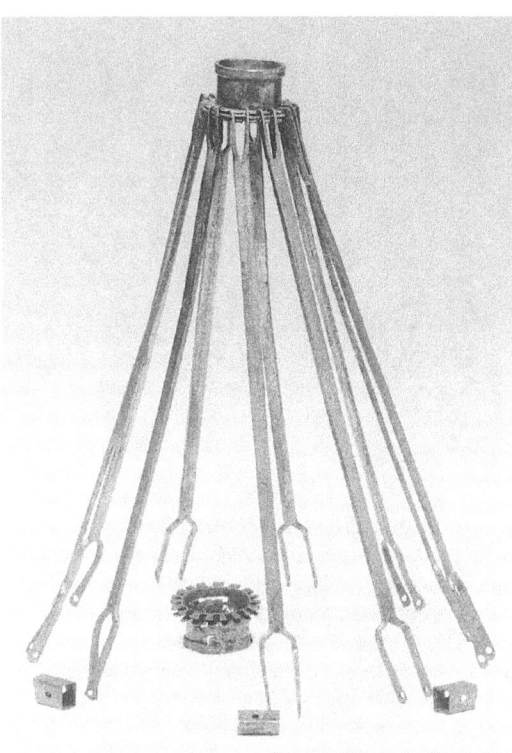

Figure 11.11. Articulated brass umbrella or parasol ribs, 1724. Length of individual rod 12.5 cm. *El Conde de Tolosá* shipwreck. *Courtesy of the Museo de la Atarazana, Santo Domingo. Photo: James Quine.*

covered from the 1742 wreck of the *Tolosá* (Fig. 11.11). The length of the straight ribs recovered archaeologically varies from 13 to 23 cm.

Several of the broken metal parasol ribs recovered from St. Augustine are bent at nearly a right angle at a point approximately two-thirds the length of the rib (Fig. 11.10). These are probably the inner ends of the shade-supporting ribs where they bent inward and were attached to the secondary supporting ribs. These smaller inner ribs often terminate in a small hole rather than in the two-tined fork of the large ribs. Fragments of the lipped tube that connected the ribs to the rod have also been recovered, all dating to the eighteenth or nineteenth century (Fig. 11.12).

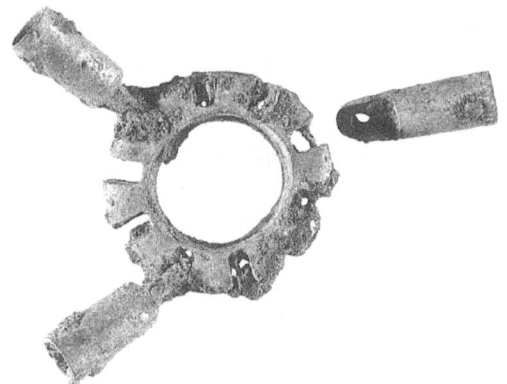

Figure 11.12. Umbrella rod center ring, ca. 1820. The small, movable cylinders attach the ribs to the center ring and permit the umbrella to fold and open. Gilded copper alloy. Outer ring diameter 3.1 cm. St. Augustine (SA-34-2B-1175). FLMNH/CSA Collections. *Photo: University of Florida Office of Instructional Resources.*

Eyeglasses

Eyeglasses (*anteojos*) had been in use in Europe as both an aid to vision and as fashion accessories for centuries when Columbus arrived in the Americas. They were described in an Italian document of 1289 as "glasses known as spectacles . . . these have been recently invented for the benefit of poor old people whose sight has become weak" (Corson 1967:19). The oldest known visual representation is in a portrait of the Italian Cardinal Ugoine, painted in 1352 (Corson 1967:24). Throughout medieval and Renaissance times, eyeglasses appeared with (and probably symbolized) learned and often holy people in paintings.

The demand for eyeglasses increased dramatically after the invention of the printing press and the general availability of printed books, and by the time of Columbus, they were being mass produced and sold by peddlers along with needles, scissors, thimbles, and other notions (Fig. 11.13). Until about 1510, spectacle lenses were round, but after

Items of Comfort and Grooming

Figure 11.13. The spectacles maker (*Der Brillenmacher*), 1568. Plate 65 in the 1568 *Standebuch* of Jost Amman and Hans Sachs. "The spectacles maker makes eyeglasses of different strengths for people from forty to eighty; the frames are of leather or horn" (Amman and Sachs 1967).

that time oval lenses were introduced in response to the development of concave presbyopic lenses for the nearsighted. People wearing these lenses also needed to look over the top of their glasses for clear distance vision, a task that was difficult with the typically large, round lenses (Corson 1967:28–31).

Eyeglasses from the sixteenth through the eighteenth centuries had round or oval double lenses enclosed in frames but lacked the sidepieces characteristic of modern eyeglasses. Frames were most typically of bone, horn, wood, or leather (Fig. 11.14), and metal frames were introduced in the seventeenth century (Corson 1967:43). Frames were often riveted at the nosepiece, permitting some degree of adjustment, but seem in general to have been held in place by hand when they were needed.

Spaniards of the late sixteenth and seventeenth centuries developed a unique solution to the problem of keeping their eyeglasses on, and that was to attach loops of fabric, cord, or leather to the frames and to tie the other end of the loops around their ears (see Corson 1967:46–49). A famous example of this fashion can be seen in El Greco's 1596 *Portrait of the Cardinal Niño de Guevara* (Fig. 11.15). Eyeglasses seem to have enjoyed higher prestige as a fashion accessory in Spain than they did in other European countries (Corson 1967:44). In 1679, Madame D'Aulnoy wrote—probably somewhat exaggeratedly but nevertheless reflecting prevailing notions of Spanish fashion—that there were in Madrid:

> many young ladies with large spectacles on their noses and fastened to their ears. But what seemed strangest to me was that they made no use of them where they were really necessary—they only talked while they had them on. I asked the Marchioness de la Rosa the reason for this. . . . She fell to laughing at my question and told me that it was done to make them look serious. They did not wear them for necessity, but to draw respect. . . . I understand that there are different spectacles according to rank. As a man increases the size of his fortune, he increases the size of his lenses. The grandees of Spain wear them as broad as one's hand. They fasten them behind their ears and leave them off as seldom as they do their collars. (1930:209)

It was not until the first quarter of the eighteenth century that eyeglasses held in place by rigid sidepieces ("temple spectacles") were invented by Edward Scarlett, a London optician (Corson 1967:69). These quickly spread to the rest of Europe and presumably the Americas. The earliest examples were of metal and had sidepieces terminating at the ears in large loops. These are shown in a Spanish broadsheet of 1763 that depicts the variety of spectacles and frames in use in Spain at midcentury (Fig. 11.16).

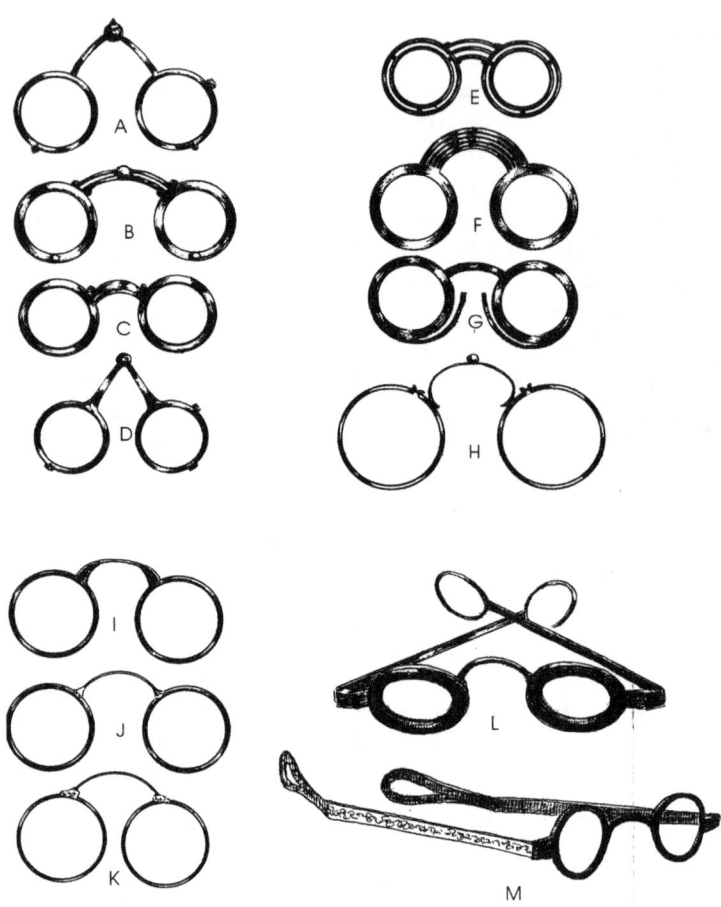

Figure 11.14. Sixteenth- and seventeenth-century eyeglasses. A. Italian, ca. 1510; B. English, 1500–50, horn; C. German, ca. 1500, horn; D. Flemish, ca. 1510–25; E. German, ca. 1550–1600, horn; F. English, ca. 1675; G. German, ca. 1600; H. German, ca. 1630, gilded silver; I. English, mid-eighteenth century, leather and steel; J. English, mid-eighteenth century; K. English folding glasses, tortoiseshell and silver; L. Swedish, 1790–1825, steel; M. American, last quarter of the eighteenth century. Compiled by Pauline Kulstad after Richard Corson (1967:38–58).

No horn or bone spectacles frames have been reported from Spanish colonial archaeological sites, and only a few metal frame spectacles have been reported, all from eighteenth-century contexts. Two examples of round glasses without temple pieces are from the 1741 *Matanceros* shipwreck (Craig 1960:261), and a similar pair was recovered at Santa Rosa Pensacola (1722–52) (Smith 1965:118; Fig. 11.17).

A pair of what are probably copper-alloy temple sidepieces with looped ends were recovered from the 1742 Quicksilver wrecks in the Dominican Republic. A quantity of round lenses with no frames were also recovered from that site, suggesting that parts of eyeglasses were shipped from Europe to be assembled in the Americas (Museo de la Atarazana, Santo Domingo).

Combs

Combs are among the items of personal grooming recovered most frequently from archaeological sites. People have used combs for millennia to groom hair and beards (Lester and Oerke 1954:132–134; Egan and Pritchard 1991:366) and to remove lice and other parasite pests from hair (see, for example, Jan Baart's [1995:179–180] discussion of parasite remains identified in combs found archaeologically in Europe and America;

Figure 11.15. Spanish eyeglasses with ear attachments, 1596. Detail from El Greco's *Portrait of the Cardinal Niño de Guevara* (1596). Metropolitan Museum of Art, H. O. Havermeyer Collection, 29.100.5. *Courtesy of the Metropolitan Museum of Art Photograph and Slide Library, New York.*

Fig. 11.18). Combs as ornaments for women's coiffures or to hold mantillas in place, however, seem to be primarily a nineteenth-century phenomenon (Lester and Oerke 1954:134).

Archaeological evidence from northern Europe suggests that comb making may have been a specialized craft during the early medieval period (Baart 1995:177); however, comb makers do not appear in the various depictions of trades and crafts until the second half of the sixteenth century (Amman and Sachs 1973:67) and are not shown, for example, in the fifteenth-century books of trades such as the Nuremberg *Hausbuch* of about 1425 (Treue and Goldman 1965). In medieval Spain, combs were made from ivory by the members of the *torneros* guild (machinists or lathe operators), who also worked in wood, bone, and horn (Córdoba de la Llave 1990:294).

The form of combs varied little from early medieval times to the eighteenth century, and the most common form recovered archaeologically throughout the American

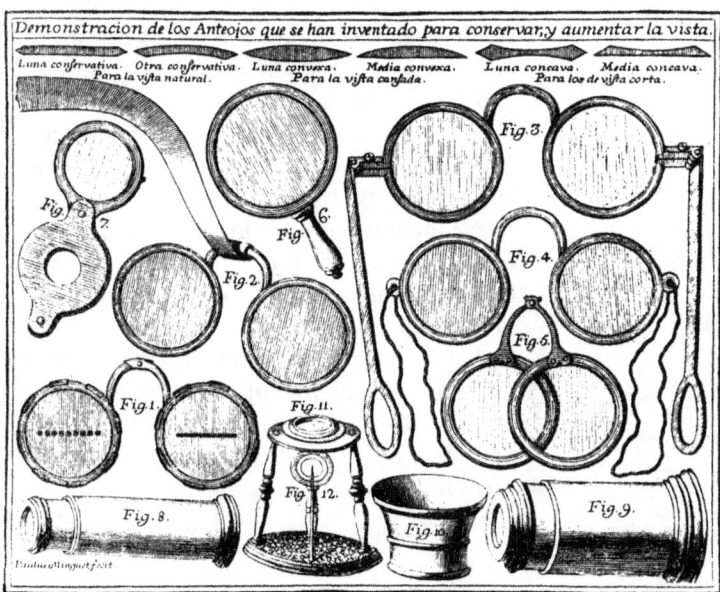

Figure 11.16. Spanish eyeglasses broadsheet, 1763. Pedro Minguet, *"Demonstración de los anteojos que se han inventado para conservar, y aumentar la vista"* (Demonstration of the eyeglasses which have been invented to conserve and augment vision) (Corson 1967:72).

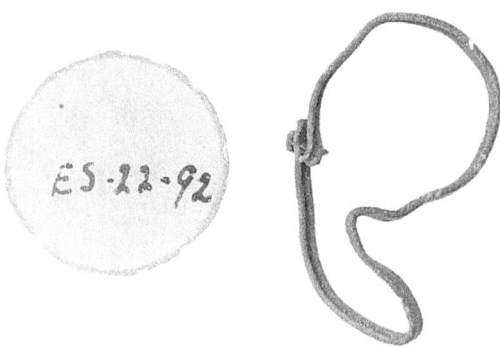

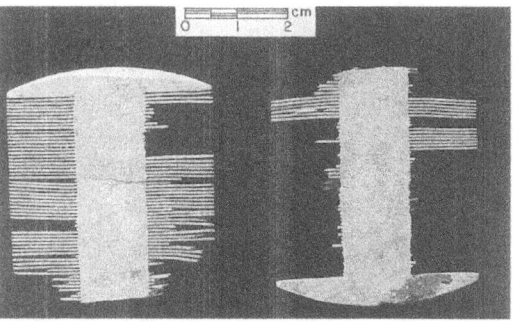

Figure 11.17. Eyeglass lens and metal frames, pre-1750. Diameter of glass 3.1 cm. Santa Rosa Pensacola, Florida (8ES22-92). Florida State University Anthropology Department Collections. *Photo: James Quine.*

Figure 11.19. Double-sided bone combs. Ca. 1750–90. St. Augustine (SA-26-1). FLMNH/CSA Collections. *Photo: James Quine.*

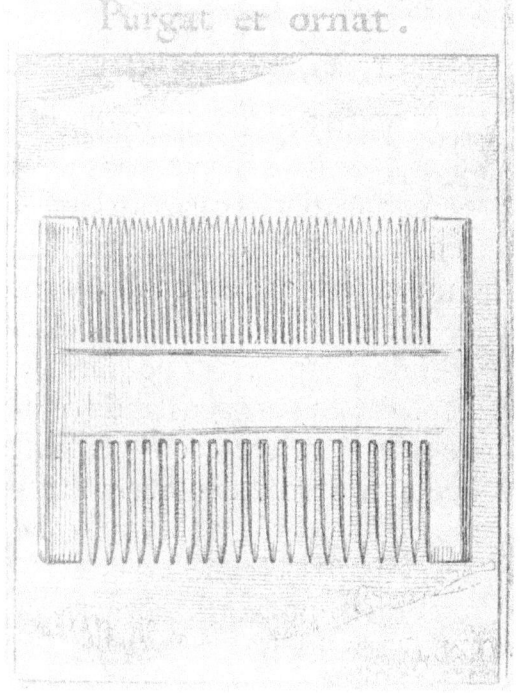

Figure 11.18. *"Purgat et Ornat,"* 1669. Double-sided bone comb for hair grooming and lice removal. In *Sinnenpoppen/Symbols* (Amsterdam 1669). *Courtesy of the Museum Boijmans-van Beuningen, Rotterdam.*

colonial period is the simple, double-sided comb (Fig. 11.19). These generally had teeth of different widths on either side of the comb, one wider for hair and beard combing and one thinner, potentially for parasite removal. Single-sided combs for hairdressing were also used but are less commonly recovered. Those with very large and wide teeth were used primarily for grooming wigs.

Combs were made of ivory, bone, wood, tortoiseshell, horn, and occasionally metal. Amman and Sachs note in their 1568 *Standebuch* that "the combmaker manufactures combs of boxwood, or of horn for commoners, of ivory for barbers and wealthy families, and many other kinds" (1973:67). Torre Revello (1943) records four kinds of combs in the shipping records of cargo bound to the Americas from Spain between 1534 and 1586. These include combs from Paris, combs from Italy, combs of ivory, and *"peines bastardos,"* or common, base combs, probably made of bone or wood.

Randle Holme, in his remarkable compendium of mid-seventeenth-century technology and trivia, gives considerably more information about the kinds of combs in use in England at that time:

> The HORSE or mane comb, a strong wooden comb with a thick back.
> The WISKE comb, have teeth on one side and are wide and slender.

The BACK TOOTH comb, having teeth but on one side.

The BEARD comb, a small sort of comb, almost 4 square.

The DOUBLE comb, two combs, one clasped into the other.

The MERKIN comb.

The PERUWICK comb, having teeth on both sides, one side wider than the other. (Holme 1972:127)

Combs could also be luxury items and ornamental status symbols and were often highly decorated and, in some cases, bejeweled. A beautiful, single-sided, gold comb of this kind, dated 1618 and inscribed with the name of its owner, was recovered from the wreck of the Manila galleon *Nuestra Señora de la Concepción* (Mathers and Shaw 1993:146).

Few combs have been recovered from sixteenth-century archaeological sites, probably for reasons of preservation. During the sixteenth century, boxwood was a particularly favored material for combs (Baart 1995:177). A single wooden comb fragment was reported from a Portuguese context at the early-sixteenth-century site of Qsar es-Seghir (Redman 1986:208), but although it is documented that 54 combs were sent from Spain to St. Augustine in 1569 (Lyon 1992:39), none have been found on American sites of the sixteenth century.

As noted earlier, the great majority of archaeologically recovered combs are double-sided bone combs (Fig. 11.19), and most of these have been reported from eighteenth-century contexts (see, for example, Shephard 1983; Skowronek 1982:137; for a seventeenth-century example from the *Concepción* shipwreck off the Dominican Republic, see Peterson 1979b:15). They are for the most part indistinguishable from the undecorated bone combs used in medieval times (see Egan and Pritchard 1991:371–372).

By the middle of the eighteenth century, single-sided combs were made of bone, wood, horn, and tortoiseshell and had as-

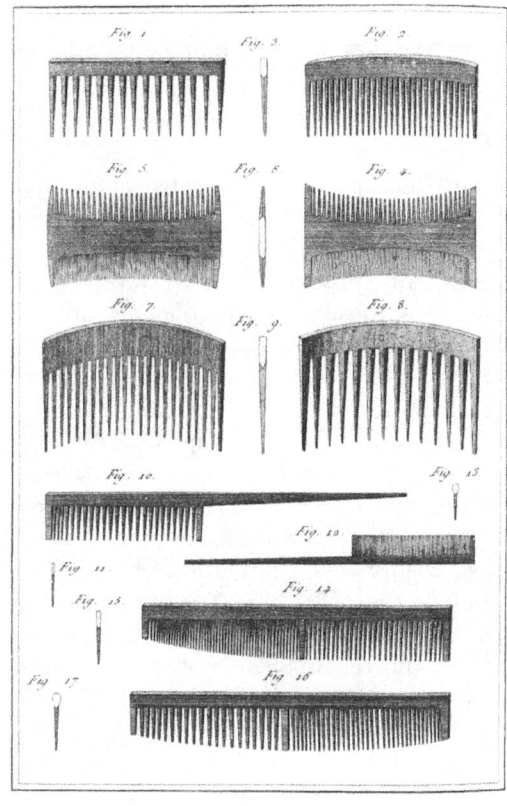

Figure 11.20. Varieties of bone combs and their production. *Tabletier Cornetier.* Plates 121–122, Part 7, Diderot, *L'Encyclopédie* (Diderot 1751–65). Courtesy of the University of Florida Library, Special Collections Department.

sumed the same form as modern pocket combs (Fig. 11.20). A cache of these combs was recovered from the wreck of the French ship *Machault,* which sank in 1760 (Peterson 1977:764; Sullivan 1986:86). The ship also carried double-sided combs made of boxwood (Sullivan 1986), and two-sided combs of wood or bone remained in use throughout most of the nineteenth century, particularly among the poor (Noel Hume 1980:175). With industrialization and the invention of plastic celluloid in 1870, inexpensive mass-produced combs of synthetic materials were readily available by the early twentieth century.

Wigs and Wig Curlers

Wigs were used throughout much of Europe by the middle of the seventeenth century (see Corson 1965:215–225); however, neither Spanish men nor women wore them frequently during that time. The use of the wig did not become de rigueur for public dress in Spain until the Bourbon years of the eighteenth century. Before then, wigs were "mostly for those who had little hair" and could cost as much as 200 ducats (Deleito y Piñuela 1946:225). Most elite people had their hair dressed very extravagantly, however, using their own hair supplemented by a variety of hairpieces known as *pericos, trenzas,* and *arondelas,* and it was reported that in the seventeenth century there were more than 40,000 hairdressers in Madrid alone (Deleito y Piñuela 1946:186, 215). The seventeenth-century tradition of long, dressed hair on men was decried in Spain as it was throughout much of Europe, leading to some of the sumptuary laws passed during that century (Deleito y Piñuela 1946:215).

Wigs may have been used even less frequently in the colonies than in Spain. The only people wearing wigs or powdered hair in any of the eighteenth-century *casta* paintings are identified specifically as Spaniards (García Saíz 1989) (although not all of those identified as Spaniards are wearing wigs or powder). No examples of clay wig curlers like those found on eighteenth-century Anglo-American sites (see Noel Hume 1980:321–323) have been reported from marine or terrestrial Spanish colonial sites in Florida or the Caribbean.

Hairbrushes

Hairbrushes did not come into common use until the late eighteenth century, at least partly because of the nature of hairstyles before that time. As noted, either wigs or elaborate hairstyles involving curls, plaits, and rolls were used in public by many middle- and upper-class Europeans during the seventeenth and eighteenth centuries. These styles were maintained with the various combs discussed previously and would have been put in disarray by a brush (Corson 1965:Chapters 7–10).

Even upper-class Spanish women did not commonly use hairbrushes, as the fanciful Madame D'Aulnoy commented in 1679: "Their hair is as black as jet and very shining, notwithstanding there is cause to think that they comb long with one and the same comb, for t'other day I saw at the Marchioness of Alcañizes her toilet spread, and although she is one of the neatest and richest ladies, the toilet was only furnished with a little bit of calico, a looking glass no bigger than one's hand, two combs, and a little box" (1930:208).

Brushes for hair and other purposes before the late eighteenth century were usually of the form known today as whisk or shaving brushes, that is, with a tuft of bristles or hair at the end of a handle and used primarily to apply powder to the hair. Although such brushes are depicted in illustrations of the fifteenth and sixteenth centuries (see, for example, Amman and Sachs 1973:66; Fig. 11.21), no archaeological evidence for these has been reported from Spanish or Spanish American sites. It is probably this form of brush that was listed in the cargo registers of ships bound from Spain to the Americas, which included *cepillejos de hilo* (odd brushes of thread), *cepillejos de seda con franja de oro* (odd brushes of silk with fringe or trimming of gold), and *cepillos de seda* (brushes of silk) (Torre Revello 1943:780). Brushes of this kind would also have been used to apply cosmetics or hair powder.

Hairbrushes with handles and drilled stocks for bristles appear to be a late-eighteenth-century innovation. They have only been reported from archaeological sites dating to after about 1780, and they are not depicted or described among barbering or hairdressing equipment in such detailed en-

Items of Comfort and Grooming 229

Figure 11.21. The brush maker (*Der Burstenbinder*), 1568. Plate 66 in the 1568 *Standebuch* of Jost Amman and Hans Sachs. "The brush maker manufactures brushes of all qualities for all purposes, from gold-mounded hairbrushes to brushes for scouring glasses" (Amman and Sachs 1967).

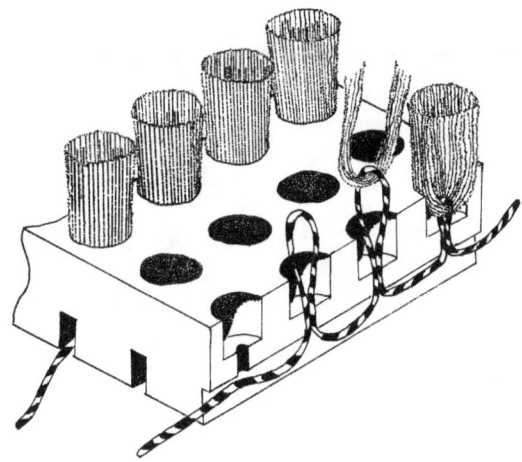

Figure 11.22. Wire method for attaching bristles to a brush stock. After Shackel (1987:47). *Drawing by Pauline Kulstad based on original drawing by Alan Ernstein.*

cyclopedic compilations as Holme's (1688) or Diderot's (1751–65). Brushes shown as part of an eighteenth-century barber's repertoire by Diderot are of the tufted-handle variety.

One of the earliest hairbrushes of modern form recovered archaeologically came from Fort Michilimackinack, occupied by French forces from 1715 to 1761 and by English forces from 1761 to 1781 (Stone 1974:139). The brush was carved of ivory and was 14.5 cm long (8.5 cm of stock and 6.0 cm of handle) and more than 2.0 cm wide. The surviving section had 12 holes drilled in each row, and the reverse had narrow grooves carved parallel to the rows for the insertion of wires. A bit of the wire would be pushed up into each hole and the bristle tufts looped under the wire to secure them. The grooves were then filled with wax, a bone backing, or other filler (Fig. 11.22).

This manufacturing method is characteristic of the bone and ivory brushes reported archaeologically from late-eighteenth-century Spanish colonial contexts. A nearly intact hairbrush stock made in this manner was found in a St. Augustine context dating to between 1790 and 1810 (Fig. 11.23), and a fragment of another was also recovered during the excavation of the Casa Rosa scarp wall in San Juan, Puerto Rico, from a context dating to between 1784 and 1800 (Solís Magaña 1988:117).

A number of nearly intact brushes of this type were also present on the wreck site of the French ship *Scipión*, which sank off the Dominican Republic in 1782 (Borrell 1983a:65–68). These are carved of bone and ivory, with the stocks drilled to hold bristles (Museo de la Atarazana, Santo Domingo) (Fig. 11.24). The holes for the bristles were drilled by hand in either a series of unevenly spaced parallel lines or in a diamond pattern. The brush stocks range from 9 to 12 cm in length and are only slightly different in width from the handles, the whole brush forming a

230 Personal Items and Accessories

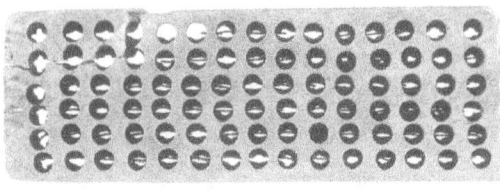

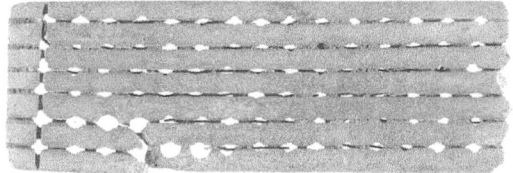

Figure 11.23. Bone hairbrush with wire grooves, ca. 1790. *Top:* Front. *Bottom:* Back. Length, 8 cm. St. Augustine (SA-26-1). FLMNH/CSA Collections. *Photo: University of Florida Office of Instructional Resources.*

rectangle. The narrow, rectangular shape and the irregularity in spacing and size of the drilled holes are characteristic of the earliest bone and ivory hairbrushes dating to the second half of the eighteenth century and occurring most commonly in the final two decades of that century. Brush making became even more standardized after about 1830, with mechanized drills permitting the even spacing and drilling of several bristle holes at a time.

Toothpicks and Toothbrushes

Specialized implements for dental hygiene have been used in Europe and Asia since ancient times (see Egan and Pritchard 1991:377; Motley 1983:101). Toothpicks (*mondadientes*) are the most commonly found dental items before the eighteenth century and were often made as part of cosmetic sets that might also contain other small implements including earspoons, tweezers, whistles, or knives (see, for example, those illustrated in Egan and Pritchard 1991:378–380; Wagner and Taylor 1972:81). One such set, consisting of toothpick, earspoon, and tweezers, was recovered archaeologically at the Ningal Temple at Ur and dated to 3500 B.C. (Motely 1983:101). Toothpicks of fragrant or astringent wood, such as cypress, pine, rosemary, or juniper, have also been used since antiquity as a dentifrice (Motely 1983:101).

Elaborately made toothpicks of gold or silver constituted a subclass of Spanish jewelry for both men and women from the sixteenth through the mid-eighteenth centuries and were often quite valuable (see Muller 1972:103; Frischauer 1934). A toothpick, for example, was listed as part of the estate of a Spanish ship's guardian, Antón de Picardia, who died in St. Augustine in 1566 (Lyon 1992:37).

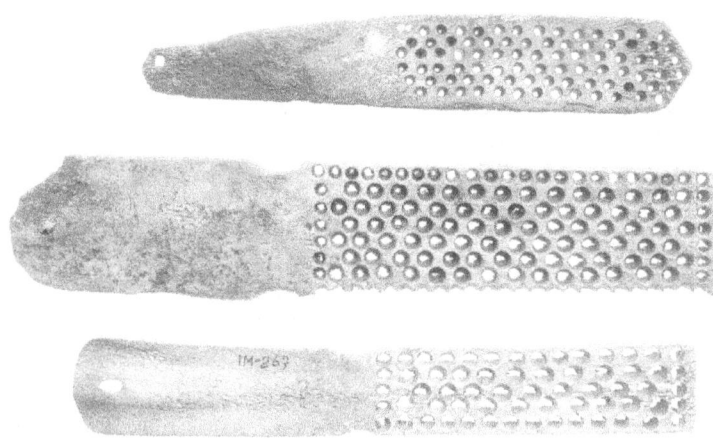

Figure 11.24. French bone and ivory hairbrush stocks, 1782. *Scipión* shipwreck (1782). Length of center brush 18 cm. *Courtesy of the Museo de la Atarazana, Santo Domingo. Photo: James Quine.*

Most of the toothpicks reported from Spanish colonial sites are from shipwrecks and are often made of precious metals. The intact forms and precious composition of these examples undoubtedly influenced their recovery and reporting, and it is likely that toothpicks of wood, bone, or other perishable substances were also used widely in colonial times. Among the earliest Spanish examples recovered archaeologically are two gold toothpicks from the wrecks of the 1588 Spanish Armada. One is a small, straight, tapering pick with a gold animal head at its apex, and the other is a scimitar-shaped pick (Stenuit 1969:760; see also Marx and Marx 1993:103).

The popularity of the scimitar shape continued through the seventeenth century and into the early years of the eighteenth century. A remarkable scimitar-shaped silver toothpick/earspoon in the shape of a narwhal was recovered from excavations at the pre-1650 Jamestown fort (Luccetti and Straube 1999:17–18), and a scimitar-shaped pick cut from a coin was recovered from the 1715 Spanish fleet wrecks in Florida (Wagner and Taylor 1972:129). Several other ornate toothpicks and toothpick-earspoon combinations were also recovered from the ships of the 1715 treasure fleet wrecked off the Florida coast (Fig. 11.25).

Although toothpicks have remained in use through the twenty-first century, they ceded their role as the principal dental hygiene items to toothbrushes (*cepillos de dientes*) during the nineteenth century. Toothbrushes were known in China during the fifteenth century (Mattick 1993, 1998:9; Motely 1983:103); however, they do not appear on American sites until the mid-eighteenth century. The French pioneered the use of the toothbrush in the West during the eighteenth century, and the first dental professional considered the "father of modern dentistry" was the Frenchman Pierre Fauchard (Fauchard 1969). It is thought, however, that the first toothbrushes of the long-handled form famil-

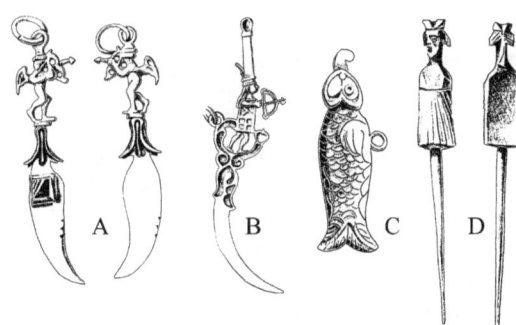

Figure 11.25. Spanish toothpicks, 1715. A. Gold cupid with an emerald (front and back), length 6.2 cm (8SL17) FBAR Lab #L6450; B. Gold cupid toothpick with earspoon, approximate length 6.3 cm (8SL17) FBAR Lab #L-6275; C. Gold fish, length 6.3 cm (8SL17) FBAR Lab #6274; D. Bone anthropomorphic pick, length 9.9 cm (8SL17) FBAR Lab #6458. *Courtesy of the Florida of Bureau Archaeological Research. Drawings: Frank Gilson.*

iar today were produced in England in the 1780s by a William Addis, who invented a method of manufacturing bone brushes from cattle femurs, which were sufficiently strong and dense to withstand manufacture and constant use under moist conditions (Mattick 1993:162).

The earliest Spanish colonial archaeological example of what may have been a toothbrush was recovered from the wreck of the *San José de las Animas*, one of the 1733 Spanish plate fleet ships sunk off the coast of Florida (Skowronek 1982:137; Fig. 11.26). Nearly identical brushes were recovered from the wreck of the *Scipión* (Museo de la Atarazana, Santo Domingo) and from San Juan, Puerto Rico, in a context dating to about 1780 to 1800 (Solís Magaña 1988:117).

The toothbrushes from the *Scipión* and the *San José* are 7 cm long, with 13 small holes drilled in their stocks. The handles are carved with a curve for the finger but are otherwise undecorated. The toothbrush from San Juan is 9 cm long with 10 bristle holes and a straight, tapering handle incised with spiral lines. It is possible that the brushes from the

Figure 11.26. Ivory toothbrush, 1733. Length 7 cm (8MO101) FBAR Lab #L0148. Florida Bureau of Archaeological Research Underwater. For a very similar toothbrush of the same era from San Juan, see Solis (1987:117). *Photo: James Quine.*

San José and the *Scipión* were of French origin, given the abundance of French items imported to the Spanish colonies during the Bourbon years (see Chapter 3), the association of the toothbrush on the 1733 wreck with a number of French items (see, for example, Skowronek 1982:138), and the leadership of the French in dental hygiene.

These very small ivory brushes have only been reported from eighteenth-century sites, and the modern long-handled toothbrush form largely replaced these after about 1780. Long-handled toothbrushes were handmade, usually of bone, in England and France and imported into the Spanish American colonies.

The holes for the bristles in the toothbrush head were drilled by hand until after 1870, when machinery for drilling holes and inserting bristles was patented. Hand-drilled stocks have holes in varying sizes, often irregularly spaced. They frequently have shallow grooves running the length of the each line of holes to be used as a guide. Bristles were attached either by trepanning, which involved boring a hole like a tunnel inside the toothbrush head, or by wire drawing, which was done by cutting a groove on the back of the toothbrush head (see Fig. 11.22). The reverse side of a drawn toothbrush head has linear grooves in it, while the back of a trepanned toothbrush stock is smooth or at least ungrooved. Trepanned brush stock also has small, plugged holes along the top end of the stock where the drilled tunnel holes were made, and this more time-consuming manufacturing method is more characteristic of

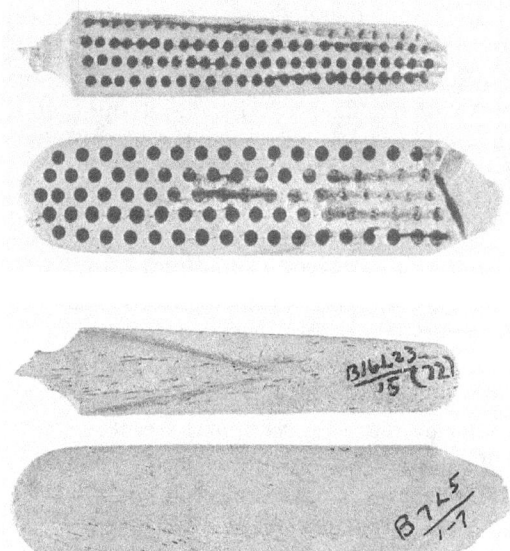

Figure 11.27. Bone toothbrush heads. Top and bottom views. Both toothbrushes had bristles attached by trepanning. *Upper:* ca. 1780–1800; length 6.2 cm; St. Augustine (SA-16-23-15/72). *Lower:* ca. 1800–25; length 7 cm; St. Augustine (SA-7-5-1/7). FLMNH/CSA Collections. *Photo: University of Florida Office of Instructional Resources.*

finely made brushes (for a comprehensive and detailed discussion of toothbrush manufacture, see Mattick 1993, 1998:9–39; Shackel 1987:42–49).

Figure 11.27 shows two Spanish-period bone toothbrush stocks from St. Augustine, both of which were trepanned rather than wire drawn. The earlier of the two is tapered and smaller (4.85 cm long) and bears a raised, elongated triangle carved in relief on the re-

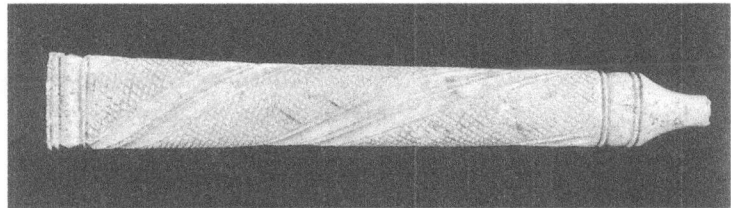

Figure 11.28. Bone handle for toothbrush or other personal maintenance item. Ca. 1800–20. Carved and machine engraved handle, length 10.4 cm, thickness 8.8 mm; rounded oval cross section. St. Augustine (SA-7-4-458). FLMNH/CSA Collections. *Photo: James Quine.*

verse. This was recovered from a context in St. Augustine dating to the third quarter of the eighteenth century. The later (ca. 1800–20) toothbrush stock is larger (5.7 cm long) and has a rounded rectangle form.

Both trepanned and wire-drawn brushes could have ornately carved handles, often decorated with machine turning. This may have been particularly characteristic of French toothbrushes, since many French brush factories grew out of turneries (Mattick 1998:122). An ornately machine-carved handle, slightly cranked (that is, bowed), was recovered from St. Augustine in a context dating to about 1800 to 1820 and undoubtedly once had a handmade head (Fig. 11.28).

By about 1820, toothbrushes had assumed the approximate configuration of modern toothbrushes, although they were often somewhat larger. During the early decades of the nineteenth century, the production of toothbrushes increased both in volume and standardization. In 1835, for example, there were 353 toothbrush makers in London alone, up from nine a century earlier (Shackel 1987:43). After about 1840, toothbrush manufacturers began to engrave their names and logos on the brush handles. In 1830, a method of inserting the toothbrush bristles in grooves rather than holes was patented. Knotted bristles were cemented into the grooves, which were wider at the surface of the toothbrush stock, and this eliminated the need to hand-drill holes. This method, however, did not replace wire drawing and trepanning as methods for attaching bristles.

By 1870, all of these hand-drilling methods were replaced by machine-made stocks when the Woodbury machine for trepanning and attaching bristles was patented (Mattick 1998:25). After this time, most toothbrushes were machine drilled and very regular in form, and mass production made them widely accessible (Mattick 1993:165). For a comprehensive treatment and illustration of nineteenth- and early-twentieth-century toothbrushes, see Mattick (1998).

In general, toothbrushes are very rarely reported from Spanish colonial archaeological contexts dating to before about 1780. The earliest examples are very small, ivory brushes such as that shown in Figure 11.26. By about 1780, bone toothbrushes with bristles attached by trepanning are reported, and there is a suggestion that these were somewhat smaller in the 1780 to 1800 period than they were in the 1800 to 1820 period (Fig. 11.27). These were undoubtedly imported from France or England, and the French examples in particular are thought to have sometimes had ornately carved and turned handles (Fig. 11.28).

The stocks and handles of toothbrushes from this period had the same shapes as stocks and handles of nailbrushes. The two categories of personal hygiene implements

Razors

Razors (*navajas de afeitar*) have existed in one form or another as long as men have shaved, and European metal razors changed very little between Roman times and the nineteenth century. These usually consist of a long, slender, and often tapering blade attached to a handle of the same length, which also served as a sheath into which the blade could be folded. Some razors shown in seventeenth-century engravings include both a handle onto which the blade is fixed and a separate sheath that folds onto and away from the blade.

Razors were made by the *cuchilleros* (cutlers) guild in medieval Córdoba, a city that was particularly renowned for its steel blades. Small items such as penknives, scissors, and razors were made by *cuchilleros* specializing in *arte de menudo* (Córdoba de la Llave 1990:266–267). French and English cutlers also made folding razors, along with scissors and small knife and tool blades (Fig. 11.29; L'Armessin and Valk 1969:Plate 11; see also Noel Hume 1980:179).

The blades of folding razors are most easily distinguished from fixed knife blades by the tips, which in folding razors are squared and blunt rather than pointed. Folding razor blades also lack a tang, having instead a hole in one end of the blade to receive the pivot that attaches the blade to the handle. One side of the blade is straight, and the other usually tapers from a wide tip to a narrow pivot end (see Fig. 11.30). Folding razor blades vary in size, but most range from 10 to 14 cm in length.

Because of the thinness and perishability of

Figure 11.29. Blade merchant. *"Habit de Coustellier."* Late-seventeenth/early-eighteenth-century straight razors and blades shown on coat skirt and head of a *coustellier* (blade merchant) (L'Armessin and Valk 1969:Plate 11).

were distinguished by the proportions of stock to handle: on a toothbrush, the handle is usually about twice the length of the stock and neck, whereas the stock and handle on a nailbrush are approximately equal (see Mattick 1998:124). A certain caution should therefore be taken in interpretation if only the handle or the stock of a brush is recovered.

Figure 11.30. Sixteenth-century straight razor blade. Length 10.5 cm. Puerto Real (1503–78). Hodges Collection, Musée de Guahabá, Limbé, Haiti.

Figure 11.31. Bone straight razor, ca. 1618. Length 14.5 cm, width 1.4 cm, thickness 1.1 cm (8IR22) FBAR Lab #0126. *Courtesy of the Florida Bureau Historic Resources. Drawing: Pauline Kulstad after Frank Gilson.*

the slender iron or steel blades, they are infrequently recovered archaeologically in a recognizable form. One of the earliest archaeological blades from a Spanish colonial site is from Puerto Real, Haiti, and dates to approximately the middle of the sixteenth century (Fig. 11.30). Stone (1974:139) shows eighteenth-century examples from Fort Michilimackinack.

The handles or sheaths were usually made of bone, horn, wood, or ivory before the nineteenth century. These are sometimes preserved, particularly on marine sites; however, in the absence of blades, it can be difficult to distinguish these from handles or sheaths of clasp knives or pocketknives. Handles for razors or folding knives have been reported from the 1724 *Tolosá* wreck (Museo de la Atarazana, Santo Domingo), the 1733 *San José* wreck (Fig. 11.31), the 1741 *Matanceros* wreck (Craig 1960:237), and the 1760 *Machault* wreck (Sullivan 1986:91). Straight razors remained in use through the nineteenth century but gradually were replaced by the safety razor after its invention by K. C. Gillette in 1895 (Corson 1965:583).

Chapter 12
Coins and Weights

Given the prominent role of precious metals in the Spanish American colonization process, it is not surprising that minting of coinage should have been one of the earliest Spanish industries to be introduced in the Americas. Coins have been recovered at nearly every Spanish colonial site and can be an important dating tool, despite the fact that dates are rarely visible on the coins themselves. Coins have been generally underused by terrestrial archaeologists owing to the complexity of the subject and the poor condition of most coins that are reported. Shipwreck sites, in contrast, contain large numbers of coins in good condition, and much useful information about specific coins can be found in reports from these sites (see, for example, Arnold and Weddle 1978; Craig 1988, 2000; Harris 1986; Olds 1976).

The accurate identification and dating of Spanish and Spanish colonial coins of the American colonial period are very complex undertakings, best done by a specialist in the field. It is necessary, for example, for anyone interested in identifying Spanish colonial coins to acquire a basic familiarity with the kinds and denominations of coins produced, the reign dates and insignia of the Spanish monarchs who ruled the colonies, and the identifying characteristics of the colonial mints producing coins in the Americas. For more specific study, it is also important to recognize the various assayers' marks for each mint and the dates during which each assayer was employed.

There are, however, general categories of coins and specific coins that are found more commonly than others in the Spanish colonial sites of Florida and the Caribbean. These coins provide the focus for this chapter, which is intended primarily as a tool for the general identification of archaeological Spanish coin categories and origins and as a guide to more specialized and detailed sources. For this reason, the discussion of coins is organized by those attributes most immediately apparent to the nonspecialist; that is, the metallic composition, size, and denominations of coins. Dating and identification of origin are discussed within each compositional and denomination category.

Denominations, Sizes, and Values of Spanish Colonial Coins

The monetary system used in the Spanish colonies was based on the medieval weight system of the mark (*marco*). The mark was introduced as a standard weight by Alfonso XI of Castile in 1349 and was the equivalent of 230 g (Carerra Stampa 1949:17–18; Lorenzo Sanz 1979:55–59; Nesmith 1955:43). The mark of gold was divided into weights of *onzas, castellanos, tomines, granos,* and *gramos,* and the mark of silver was similarly divided into *onzas, ochavas, adarmes, tomines, granos,* and *gramos* (Table 12.1).

The value of a coin was determined in relation to a mark of silver (Tables 12.1, 12.2). For example, until 1728 there were 67 reales in a mark of silver, and a real was therefore equivalent to 1/67 of a mark (after that date, a mark was equivalent to 68 reales) (Craig 2000:15–16; Lorenzo Sanz 1979:57).

Certain monetary units were used primarily as accounting devices and were not minted as coins. The *ducado* (ducat), for example, was used for commercial accounting in the Spanish Americas as a unit of value equivalent to 375 maravedís (11.03 reales), but it was not minted there as a coin (Lorenzo Sanz 1979:53–54).

Spanish colonial mints produced copper-alloy (*billón* or *vellón*) maravedís, silver reales, and gold escudos or excelentes. Silver and copper coins are the most commonly found types in terrestrial archaeological sites, and marine sites contain the widest variety of silver and gold coins. Spanish coin denominations were based on a system divisible by eight (half, one, two, four, eight), persisting in modern American terminology as the "pieces of eight" associated in popular imagery with pirate treasure.

Spanish American coinage was accepted almost universally worldwide during the eighteenth century, particularly after the appearance of milled "pillar dollars" in 1732. They were legal tender in the United States until 1858, and it has been suggested that the U.S. dollar sign was derived from insignia on these coins (Sedwick 1987:2). The first U.S. silver dollar minted in 1794 was created to be of silver and of weight and fineness equivalent to the Spanish American piece of eight (eight reales) (Sedwick 1987:2). Triangular wedges cut from the milled pillar dollars are recovered from archaeological sites and were used in the place of small denomination coins in the eighteenth-century American colonies. These were referred to as "bits," two bits being one-quarter of a milled dollar coin, and four bits referring to half a milled dollar. The origin of the widely used sports cheer "two bits, four bits, six bits, a dollar" lies in this colonial monetary system.

Silver coins (reales) were produced at all American mints throughout the colonial period. They included denominations of half, one, two, four, and eight reales, and after 1792, a quarter real (the *cuartillo*) was briefly produced. The value and purity of the metal content in silver coins were determined by law, with value and weight based on the mark weight of silver. The decrees establishing the first American mints specified that 67 reales would be struck from each mark of sil-

Table 12.1. Divisions and Weights of the Spanish Mark

Marco	Onza	Ochavas	Adarmes	Tomines	Granos	Grams
Silver						
1	8	50	128	384	4608	230.0465
	1	8	16	48	576	28.7558
		1	2	6	72	3.59447
			1	3	36	1.79723
				1	12	0.59907
					1	0.04992
Gold						
1	8	50		400	4800	230.0465
	1	6.25		50	600	28.7558
		1		8	96	4.6009
				1	12	0.59907
					1	0.04992

Source: After Lorenzo y Sánz 1980:56

Table 12.2. Average Weight, Size, and Value of Common Spanish Coin Denominations

Denomination	x̄ Size (mm)	Weight (g)	Value
Billón Coins			
One maravedí	18.5	0.75	.023 real
Two maravedís	22.5	1.70	.045 real
Four maravedí	26–27.5	2.8–4.0	.091 real
Silver Coins			
Quarter real	10	0.858	0.004 mark/11 maravedís
Half real	15–17	1.716	0.007 mark/22 maravedís
One real	20–22	3.432	0.05 mark/44 maravedís
Two real	27–28	6.856	0.03 mark/88 maravedís
Four real	31–32	13.731	0.06 mark/176 maravedís
Eight real	36–41	27.5	0.12 mark/352 maravedís
Gold Coins			
One escudo	15–17	3.383	16 reales
Two escudo	20–22	6.766	32 reales
Four escudo	24–26	13.532	64 reales
Eight escudo	29–32	27.064	128 reales/ 1,408 maravedís/(1 *onza*)

ver, thereby establishing an average weight of 3.43 g of silver for 1 real.

Until 1732, however, the weight of individual coins could vary because the Spanish mints assessed coinage on the basis of lots rather than on individual coins: as long as each mark of silver produced 67 reales weighing a total of 230 g, the individual coin weights of the lot were not necessarily equal. Each mint had an assayer, who was responsible for testing and guaranteeing the purity of the metal and the correct weight of each coin lot. An initial from the assayer's name was stamped on each coin, testifying that the coins were of the designated value. Assayers' marks varied as assayers changed at the mints, and such marks offer an additional—although often confusing—tool for dating coins (see sections on individual coinages).

Billón coinage, generally known as the maravedí, was produced in the Americas only during the sixteenth century and only at the mints of Mexico City and Santo Domingo. Maravedís minted in Spain have also been reported from sixteenth-century Spanish American sites, although copper coins were produced in most peninsular Spanish mints throughout the colonial period (see Calicó, Xavier, and Trigo 1985).

Maravedís minted in Santo Domingo were valued at 44 to the silver real, although in Spain a real was worth only 34 maravedís (see Estrella Gómez 1979:47, 55; Lorenzo Sanz 1979[2]:54–55). They were the equivalent of "small change" during the sixteenth century, and although they are relatively rare in numismatic collections, they are extremely abundant at many sixteenth-century Caribbean sites, including Concepción de la Vega, Puerto Real, and Santo Domingo. Maravedís were apparently used in quantity and lost frequently.

Copper coins were produced in denominations of one, two, and four maravedís. Table 12.2 shows the average size and weight of Spanish coin denominations; size and weight are generally a more reliable method of determining denomination than is the denomination mark itself (which is often obscured).

Coin Production and Technology

From about 1570 until 1732, all of the *billón* coins and most of the silver coins were the crude, irregularly shaped "cob" type. Before 1570, round silver coins were produced in Mexico and Santo Domingo during the time of Charles II and Joanna coin issue (1536 to ca. 1573, although they reigned 1516–56).

The cob coins of the Americas were not produced primarily for circulation as a medium of exchange but rather as an easily controllable and divisible system for sending huge amounts of silver back to Spain. The tremendous volume of the American mines and mints was not fully realized until about the middle of the sixteenth century, and thus the cob solution to handling these quantities of silver was not developed until then. The vast majority of extant cob coins have come from shipwrecks that had been carrying silver to Spain rather than from terrestrial sites. Cob coins were made in half-, one-, two-, four-, and eight-real pieces (discussed later).

Cob coins are often difficult to identify and date with confidence, since there was little standardization of die designs on cob coins. Wide variations can be found in a single denomination even within a single mint. Cobs were produced by first preparing blanks. Silver refined to at least 90 percent fineness was rolled into rough cylinders of the prescribed size and weight. Slices of variable thickness were made from the cylinders and then snipped with shears to refine size or weight, accounting for the irregularity in both size and shape among cob coins of the same denomination.

The silver blanks were annealed to permit them to take a die (design) impression. One side of the coin die was placed on an anvil, and a blank was place over the die. The die for the other side was engraved or carved on

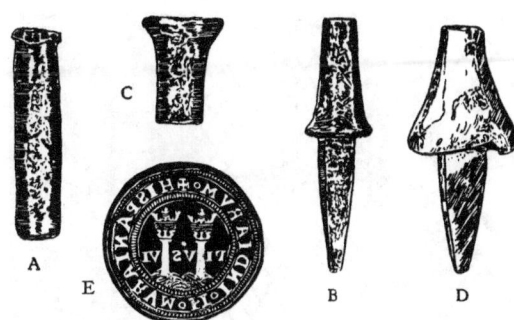

Figure 12.1. Hand hammering coin dies. A, C. Upper dies (*troquel*); B, D. Lower dies (*pila*). The obverse design was stamped into the top of the lower die and the reverse design into the top of the upper die. The lower die was sunk into an anvil by the tongue at its base and the blank coin placed on its top. The top of the upper die was placed over the blank, and the designs were transferred simultaneously by a forceful blow to the end of the upper die. E. Reverse die pattern of a Mexico City one real (late series). *Reproduced with permission from Nesmith (1955:34). Courtesy of the American Numismatic Society.*

a rod of steel, which was positioned over the upper surface of the blank. A strong blow with a hammer to the upper die rod resulted in die impressions on both sides of the blank, often offset or blurred (Figs. 12.1, 12.2). A detailed accounting of cob production can be found in Craig (2000).

In 1732, round, milled coins (that is, produced with a screw press rather than hand hammered) were first made in the colonies. Known as pillar dollars, they were replaced in 1772 by the *busto* coins, which were also milled and showed the monarch's portrait on one side of the coin. Milled coins are round and generally have small ridges encircling their edges.

The Spanish American Mints

A number of different mints, each with its own variable conventions and identifying symbols, were in operation at different times during the Spanish colonial period (Table

Figure 12.2. The coin stamper (*Der Munkmeister*), 1568. From the 1568 *Standebuch* of Jost Amman and Hans Sach. "The coin stamper makes coins of all denominations of proper metal content and weight, artistically stamped" (Amman and Sachs 1973:39).

12.3). Coins from nearly all of them circulated widely throughout Spanish America during specific periods, and it is therefore important to recognize the distinguishing characteristic of each. Although the mint marks for these mints sometimes overlapped, it is usually possible to identify a coin's mint origin by reference to a combination of the dates of mint operation, the insignia and dates for the Spanish monarch represented on the coin, and the unique insignia characteristic of the mints themselves (Tables 12.3, 12.4).

These colonial mints and their products have been studied with widely varying degrees of intensity and scholarship; however, there are useful sources on nearly every one of them. Important overviews of Spanish American coins in general include Adams (1929), Burzio (1958), Craig (2000), Sedwick (1987), and Toribio Medina (1919). The catalog by Calicó, Calicó, and Trigo (1985) also provides excellent illustrations of the range of coins from both Spanish and Spanish American mints between 1504 and 1868. Sources specific to individual mints are provided later.

The Mexico City Mint

The first mint to be established in the colonies was at Mexico City in 1536. One of two American mints authorized by the Spanish crown in 1535 (Nesmith 1955:7–11), it produced silver coins from 1536 until Mexico's independence in 1821 and gold coins from 1679 until the end of Spanish dominion in 1821.

The mint mark for the Mexico mint varies with the date and denomination of the coinage. The earliest coins (during the Charles II and Joanna period) bear a simple "M" mark. Silver coins after this period, as well as gold coins produced between 1679 and 1713, bear a mint mark consisting of a large "M" surmounted by a small "O." Gold coins after 1713 have a large "M" surmounted by a large "X," which is in turn surmounted by a small "O" (Sedwick 1987:6). Assayers' marks for the Mexico mint are shown by Craig (2000:80). Cobs of the Mexico mint tend to have a rectangular shape, but wide variations in form have also been documented (see Craig 2000:89–99).

The Santo Domingo Mint

Although it was authorized in 1535, the Santo Domingo mint did not begin the production of coins until 1542 (Estrella Gómez 1979). The Santo Domingo mint mark was "SD" (sometimes appearing as "SP"), with the two letters often flanking the pillars on the reverse side of the coins. The mint produced copper (*vellón* or *billón*) coins and, after 1545, silver reales. Santo Domingo was notable for the idiosyncrasies, poor quality, and wide variety of designs in its coinage (Estrella Gómez

Table 12.3. Dates and Coin Inscriptions of Reigning Spanish Monarchs of the Colonial Period

Monarch(s)	Reign	Obverse Inscription	Reverse Inscription	Obverse Device	Reverse Device
Ferdinand and Isabella	1475–1504	FERNANDUS ET ELISABET,F	REX ET: REGINA CAST: LEGIO:ARA	Shield of the Catholic kings	Arrows/yoke
Ferdinand	1504–16	FERNANDUS ET ELISABET,F		Shield of the Catholic kings	
Charles I and Joanna*	1516–56	CAROLUS ET IOANNA REGIS	ISPANIARUM ET INDIARUM	Hapsburg shield	Pillars of Hercules
Philip II	1556–98**	PHILLIPUS II	DEI GRATIA HISPANIARUM ET INDIARUM REX	Hapsburg shield or pillars of Hercules	Jerusalem cross in tressure
Philip III	1598–1621	PHILLIPUS III	DEI GRATIA HISPANIARUM ET INDIARUM REX	Hapsburg shield	Jerusalem cross in tressure
Philip IV	1621–65	PHILLIPUS IV	DEI GRATIA HISPANIARUM ET INDIARUM REX	Hapsburg shield/ or pillar and waves***	Jerusalem cross in tressure
Charles II	1665–1700	CAROLUS II	DEI GRATIA HISPANIARUM ET INDIARUM REX	Hapsburg shield or pillar and waves***	Jerusalem cross in tressure
Philip V	1700–1724	PHILLIPUS V	DEI GRATIA HISPANIARUM ET INDIARUM REX	Bourbon shield or pillar and waves***	Jerusalem cross in tressure
Luis I	1724	LUDOVICUS I	DEI GRATIA HISPANIARUM ET INDIARUM REX	Bourbon shield	Jerusalem cross in tressure
Philip V	1725–46	PHILLIPUS V	DEI GRATIA HISPANIARUM ET INDIARUM REX	Crowned Bourbon shield	Pillars of Hercules, PLUS ULTRA
Ferdinand VI	1746–59	FERDINAND VI	DEI GRATIA HISPANIARUM ET INDIARUM REX	Crowned Bourbon shield	Pillars of Hercules, PLUS ULTRA
Charles III	1760–88	CAROLUS III	HISPANIARUM ET INDIARUM REX	Bust of Charles III	Bourbon shield flanked by pillars
Charles IV	1788–1808	CAROLUS IV	HISPANIARUM ET INDIARUM REX	Bust of Charles IV	Bourbon shield flanked by pillars

*Charles and Joanna coins minted only in Americas, 1536–66.
**Philip II did not begin issuing coins in his own name until 1566.
***Shield device on Mexico coins; pillar and waves on South American coins.

1979:83–96; Beltrán 1983:150; Olds 1976:114–115).

Because of its poor quality, the Santo Domingo coinage was referred to at the time as *mala moneda*. Partly because of this, and largely because the population of Hispaniola dropped drastically after 1550 as settlers turned to Tierra Firma in search of riches, the Santo Domingo mint ceased production in about 1558. It briefly resumed the minting of

Table 12.4. Spanish Colonial Mints and Their Marks during the Colonial Period

Mint	Dates of Operation	Mint Mark
Mexico City	1536–ca. 1573	M
	1573–1822	M, M surmounted by "o"
Santo Domingo	ca. 1542–ca. 1587	S/D
Lima	1568–89	P, ☆, P/☆
	1659–60	L
	after 1684	L
Potosí	1575–1810	P
Bogotá	1621–1836	NR, RN, N R, R N, FS, SF (all either with or without a small "o" surmounting the mark)
Cartagena	ca. 1621–ca. 1655	C, N R, R N
Cuzco	1698— Gold coins only	C
Guatemala	1733–ca. 1774	G
	post-1774–ca. 1822	NG
Santiago, Chile	1743–ca. 1817	S
Popayán, Colombia	1758–1820	P

coins in 1578, but Francis Drake destroyed the mint when he sacked Santo Domingo in 1587. It did not again resume serious production during the colonial period (see Burzio 1958:363–364; Estrella Gómez 1979:49–57; Olds 1976:106).

The Lima Mint
The third colonial mint was established in Lima, Peru, in 1565 and began production of coins in 1568. Its first period of operation was from 1568 until 1572, when production ceased until 1575. Coins were minted during a second period from 1575 until 1589, when production was interrupted again. The mint remained closed (except for a few months in 1659–60) until 1683. It reopened that year and continued colonial production until 1824 (Grunthal and Selschopp 1978; Burzio 1958:25–27).

The earliest mint mark for the Lima mint (from 1568 until the 1659 reopening) was a "P" standing for Peru or a star standing for the Star of the Magi, a symbol of the day of Epiphany (January 6) when Lima was founded. The "P" is sometimes also accompanied by a star. Lima coins of the two later periods (1659–10, 1683–1824) bear a mint mark of "L."

The Potosí Mint
Potosí, today in Bolivia, was part of the viceroyalty of Peru in colonial times and a major center for silver mining. The mint was authorized in 1574, and coin production began in 1575, producing only silver cob coins (Murray 1986; Grunthal and Selschopp 1978; Burzio 1945). Assayers' marks for the Potosí mint are shown by Craig (2000:136–137), who also suggests that cobs from the Potosí mint tend to be deeply cracked and irregular around their edges, owing to the use of poorly annealed metal (2000:51).

The first period of production lasted until 1652, when debasement of value and fraud in the mints caused all previous Potosí coinage to be recalled and a new motif to be implemented. Pre-1652 coins bear a crowned shield, and those after that date bear a "pillar and waves" motif (described later). Its mint mark was a "P," shared during the same period by the Lima mint. Motifs, however, distinguish coins from the two centers (discussed later). The Potosí mint closed in 1810.

The Bogotá Mint
A mint was authorized in Bogotá in 1620, and coin production began in 1622. It was the first American mint authorized to pro-

duce gold cob coins (Barriga Villalba 1969; Craig 1988; Sedwick 1987:6). The colonial name for Bogotá was Santa Fe de Bogotá, located in the Nuevo Reino de Granada (the area encompassing what is today Colombia and Venezuela).

A variety of marks were used for the long-lived Bogotá mint, based on these colonial place names. "NR," "RN," "SF," "FS," both with and without a small "o" surmounting the letters, are recorded. The letters might also be arranged vertically, one above the other, and these may or may not be surmounted by a small "o."

The Nuevo Reino de Granada also had a mint at Cartagena, which opened at the same time as the mint of Bogotá but ceased production in about 1655. Its mint mark was either a "C" or "NR" or "RN," shared with Bogotá (Barriga 1969; Sedwick 1987:7).

The Guatemala City Mint

A mint established in Guatemala City in 1731 first issued coins in 1733 (Prober 1957). Until 1753, this mint produced only silver cob-type coins. The Guatemala City mint mark was a "G," and there was a single assayer's mark, "J," used during this period (Sedwick 1987:7). After the mint was destroyed in 1774 by a volcanic eruption, it was reestablished and produced coins with a new mint mark of "NG" (Nueva Guatemala). After that date, the mint produced milled round coins in both gold and silver.

Archaeologically Recovered Coins from Old World Mints

Before the establishment of American mints in the 1530s and 1540s, coins minted in Europe were used in the colonies. Both Portuguese and Spanish coins of the fifteenth and early sixteenth centuries have been recovered from sites dating to before 1550.

The earliest known coins in the Caribbean region are those from the site of La Isabela in the Dominican Republic (1493–98). More than 136 coins have been recorded from the site and have been studied by Alan Stahl (1992, 1995). They provide the most comprehensive depiction of European coin use in the American colonies prior to 1500. Stahl notes that only four of the coins studied were of silver, and the rest were of *billón*. Of the silver coins, only one, a one-real piece, is of Ferdinand and Isabella issue. The other three silver coins were issued during the reign of Henry IV of Castile (1454–74) and include two half reales and a single one real.

Eighty-four percent of the *billón* coins were small-denomination coins known as *blancas*, issued by Henry IV of Castile. These coins bear castles on one side and a lion rampant on the other, symbolizing the joined kingdoms of Castile and Leon. Stahl notes:

> In the early years of Henry's reign, a wide range of *billón* coins had been minted of widely varying weights and produced at poorly-regulated mints. Finally, in 1471, he introduced this relatively well-controlled issue, which appears to have driven all of the earlier *billón* coins out of circulation. This issue was so successful that Ferdinand and Isabella issued no *billón* coins in their own names for the first two decades of their reign; the only low-denomination coins circulating in Spain at the time of Columbus's departures in 1492 and 1493 would have been these old issues of Henry IV. (1992:4–5)

The second most frequently occurring *billón* coin at La Isabela was the Portuguese ceitil, which bears the shield of the reigning monarch of Portugal on one side and a three-turreted castle on the other (Fig. 12.3). Ceitils have also been recovered from sites of the De Soto era in Florida dating to the reign of Alfonso V (1481–1521) (Ewen and Hann 1989:116). In addition to Castilian money, coins from Portugal, Navarre, Aragon, Genoa, Sicily, and Alquilea were recovered from La Isabela, and the full coin assemblage is cataloged and illustrated in Stahl (1995) and Deagan and Cruxent (2002a).

After 1497, Spanish mints produced a series of low-denomination *billón* coins bearing on

Figure 12.3. Blancas and ceitils from La Isabela, 1493–98. *Top: Billón* blanca, Henry IV of Castile, minted in Avila (FS 2105), diameter 2.2 cm. *Bottom: Billón* ceitil, Alfonso V of Portugal (FS 530), diameter 2.4 cm. Parque Nacional de La Isabela, Dominican Republic. *Drawing: Patricia D. Farrior.*

one side the initials of Ferdinand and Isabella along with their yoke and arrows symbol, with the arms of Spain on the other side (Fig. 12.4). These were produced in Spain until after 1566 (Nesmith 1955:38–39) but are relatively uncommon on Spanish colonial sites dating to after 1505 for reasons discussed later. When dominating an assemblage, these coins are a useful index for the period between about 1500 and 1510.

Neither copper nor silver coins produced in Spain bore the name of Charles I or Charles II and Joanna. The names of Ferdinand or Ferdinand and Isabella continued to be used on Spain-minted coins until 1566, when Philip II finally issued coins in his own name. A Spanish-minted coin with the names of Ferdinand and Isabella in an archaeological site, therefore, could date to as late as 1565.

Somewhat more common than these Spanish Ferdinand and Isabella maravedís are Spanish copper maravedís minted in Spain specifically for the colonies. In 1505, Ferdinand mandated that a special series of both copper and silver coins be minted in

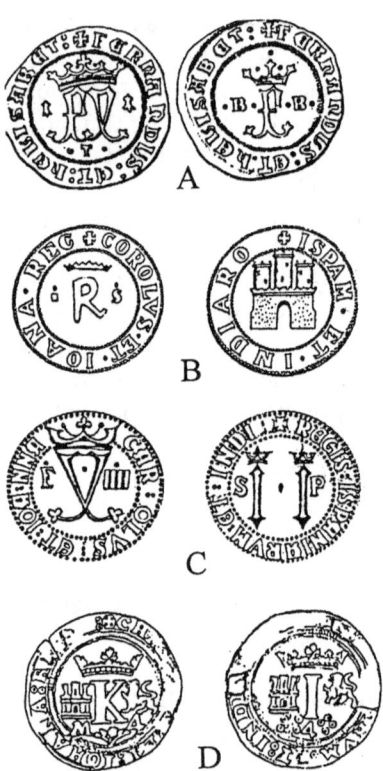

Figure 12.4. Sixteenth-century maravedís. A. *Billón dinero,* probably a maravedí. Ferdinand and Isabella, minted in Burgos for use in Spain, ca. 1505–31; B. Four maravedís, Charles II and Joanna, minted in Santo Domingo, ca. 1541–43; C. Four maravedís, Charles II and Joanna, minted in Santo Domingo, ca. 1544–63; D. Four maravedís, Charles II and Joanna, minted in Mexico City, ca. 1536–60, diameter 2.2 cm. *Drawing: Merald Clark.*

Seville and Burgos exclusively for distribution in Hispaniola (see Estrella Gómez 1979:19–35). The copper coins of the series are distinctive in having the crowned initials of the Catholic kings ("Y" and "F") in gothic script on one side and the crowned gothic "F" on the other.

The silver reales made for the colonies bore the royal arms of Ferdinand and Isabella on the obverse and Ferdinand's initial F, along with his yoke and arrows device, on the reverse (Fig. 12.5). These coins were made in

Figure 12.5. Ferdinand and Isabella reales minted in Seville for America. *Top row:* Obverse. *Bottom row:* Reverse. *Left to right:* One real (diameter 2.5 cm); two reales (diameter 3.2 cm); four reales (diameter 3.7 cm). Found in the foundation of the Church at Puerto Real (ca. 1520–78). Hodges Collection, Musée de Guahabá, Limbé, Haiti. *Photo: Paul Hodges.*

Seville and in Burgos from about 1505 to about 1545. Those made in Seville have an "S" mint mark on either side of the "F," while those minted in Burgos have a "B" mint mark in the same position. Examples of these coins have been reported from sites in the Dominican Republic (Ortega and Fondeur 1978a:141–143; Poladura 1980:10), Cuba (Dominguez 1984:66), Puerto Real (Hodges Collection), Florida (Ewen 1989:117), and Jamaica (Cotter 1970:21). They were gradually replaced after 1536 by the coins of American mints.

Coins from American Mints

Copper Coins from the Mexico City Mint
The Mexico City mint produced copper coins of Charles II and Joanna issue between 1542 and about 1560 (Nesmith 1955:40–43). These were made in one-, two-, and four-maravedí denominations. Their production in Mexico was suspended in the 1560s because the American Indians refused to accept them as currency and tried to destroy and eliminate the coins (Nesmith 1955:40–43).

The distinguishing characteristics of the Mexico City mint copper coinage are, on the obverse, a crowned "K" flanked by a lion and a three-towered castle. This side also bears the mint mark "M" and some version of the inscription "CAROLUS ET IOHANNA REGIS." The reverse depicts a single crowned pillar, also flanked by a lion and castle (Fig. 12.4D). The denomination of the maravedí (most commonly "4") is also on the reverse, with the inscription "HISPANIARUM ET INDIARUM."

Copper Coins from the Santo Domingo Mint
Copper-alloy maravedís of Charles II and Joanna issue were produced in the Santo Domingo mint between 1536 and 1558 and again between 1578 and 1586 (Beltrán 1983:150–151; Burzio 1958:362–363; Nesmith 1955:127, 150). One-, 2-, and 4-maravedí coins were issued during the first period, and 1-, 2-, 4-, and 11-maravedí coins (the latter a "quarter real") were produced during the short second period.

The Santo Domingo Charles II and Joanna maravedís bear a distinctive basic design, on which a wide range of minor variations existed (Figs. 12.6, 12.7). The obverse shows a crowned gothic "Y" with the letter "F" or "E" to the left and the denomination mark to the right. The denomination mark can appear either as Roman or Arabic numerals for the four-maravedí coins ("IIII," "II" with a dot over it, or "4") and as a Roman numeral "II" on the two-maravedí coins. The one maravedís bear a denomination mark of four dots forming a

Figure 12.6. Maravedís. *Top left:* Reverse, Santo Domingo two maravedís. *Center:* Obverse, four maravedís minted in Seville for Santo Domingo (1505–31) (diameter 2.5 cm). *Top right:* Obverse, Santo Domingo two maravedís. *Lower left:* Reverse, Santo Domingo two maravedís. *Lower right:* Obverse, two maravedís minted in Burgos for Santo Domingo (diameter 2.1 cm). All Puerto Real. Hodges Collection, Musée de Guahabá, Limbé, Haiti. *Photo: James Quine.*

Figure 12.7. Four maravedís minted in Santo Domingo. *Left:* Obverse. *Right:* Reverse. Puerto Real. Diameter of bottom coin 2.7 cm. FS 619. FLMNH Collections. *Photo: University of Florida Office of Instructional Resources.*

diamond shape. In some examples, the denomination mark is replaced by a letter "E."

The legend encircling the obverse design is some version of "KAROLUS:ET:IOHANNA:REGIS," which is part of the standard inscription on Charles II and Joanna coins of American issue, that is: "KAROLUS:ET:IOHANNA:REGIS: HISPANIARUM:ET:INDIARUM." On some maravedís, the entire legend is inscribed using both sides of the coin—"KAROLUS ET IOANNA REG" on the obverse and "HISPANIARUM ET INDIARUM" on the reverse. On others, the "KAROLUS ET IOHANNA" portion is repeated on both the obverse and reverse.

The reverse side of these coins bears two crown-topped pillars of Hercules (having pointed ends), usually with a raised dot between them. These pillars are flanked by the letters "S" to the left and "D" or "P" to the right (Figs. 12.4, 12.7).

The one-maravedí Charles II and Joanna Santo Domingo coins have a different obverse design from that of the two and four maravedís. Rather than the crowned pillars, the one maravedís bear a crowned, gothic "K" that appears more like a modern "R."

Although Philip II ascended the throne of Spain in 1556, it was not until 1573 that the Santo Domingo mint was authorized to produce a new coin issue bearing his insignia, and such production did not begin until about 1578, when the second, seven-year phase of the mint's operation was beginning (Estrella Gómez 1979:107–111). Some copper Philip II coins were produced in Santo Domingo, although none have been reported in the archaeological literature.

Table 12.5. Size and Denomination Marks on Reales

Denomination	Approximate Diameter	Denomination Mark
Half real	20 mm	None
One real	26 mm	3 vertical dots (or sometimes none)
Two reales	28–30 mm	"II"
Four reales	37 mm	"IIII" (often surmounted by a dot)
Ten reales	45 mm	"X"

The Philip II maravedís were produced in two- and four-maravedí denominations and are very distinct from those of the Charles II and Joanna period. The obverse bears a three-turreted castle enclosed in a series of connected arcs (quatrefoil). The castle is flanked by the mint mark ("D") to the left and the denomination mark to the right. The reverse bears a crowned lion rampant enclosed in a quatrefoil. The legend "PHILLIPUS II DEI GRATIA HISPANIARUM ET INDIARUM REX" is divided and inscribed around both sides (see Estrella Gómez 1979:110).

Silver Coinage

Silver coins were minted in the Americas in denominations of half, one, two, four, and (rarely) ten reales. The sizes and denomination marks of these are detailed Table 12.5. Die patterns on silver coins from the Spanish American mints varied across space depending on the specific mint and through time with the reigning Spanish monarchs (see Tables 12.3, 12.4). In general, those dating to after the period of Charles II and Joanna issue (that is, after about 1570) were cob coins and nearly always had a Jerusalem cross, usually contained within a series of arcs known as a tressure or quatrefoil, depicted on the coin's reverse. Details of the cross itself and its surrounding tressure vary with individual mints.

The obverse of silver and gold cob coins from American mints can have one of three basic types of designs (each associated with specific mints during specific periods) (Figs. 12.8, 12.9). The earliest of these was the pillars of Hercules motif of two crowned pillars with a scroll across their fronts bearing some version of "PLUS." The pillars might or might not be surmounting waves. This design is restricted to Santo Domingo silver coins, Mexico silver coins from 1536 to 1552, and Lima silver cob coins from 1568 to 1572. The most common obverse design is the shield and arms of the reigning monarch—Castile and Leon, Hapsburg, or Bourbon (Fig. 12.10; Table 12.3).

The third type of obverse design is the pillar and waves design and is based on the earlier pillars of Hercules design. The pillar and waves design consists of two vertical lines and two horizontal lines dividing the obverse side of the coin into nine compartments (in the manner of a ticktacktoe game) (Figs. 12.8, 12.9). The top row of three cells contain information depicting the mint mark, denomination, and assayer; the center three cells contain letters depicting some portion of "PLUS ULTRA"; and the bottom row gives date information.

In summary it can be said that, in general, the pillars of Hercules motif appears on the obverse of silver coins of the following origins: Santo Domingo mint, Mexico City mint before 1552, and Lima mint from 1568 to 1572. In general, the shield motif appears on the obverse of coins of the following origins: all gold cobs except for Peru escudos; all Mexican silver cob coins (1536–1731); Lima silver cobs (1572–88); Bogotá and Cartagena silver cobs before 1652; and Potosí silver cobs before 1652. The pillar and waves motif appears on the obverse of coins of the following origins: Lima and Cuzco gold cobs; Lima silver cobs after 1684 (no production, 1589–1683); Potosí silver cobs after 1652; and Bogotá silver cobs after 1652. Additional details distinguishing the mints from one another are discussed later.

Figure 12.8. Design motifs on Spanish and Spanish American silver coinage. A. One real, Ferdinand and Isabella, Burgos mint for American distribution, ca. 1505–31, diameter 2.8 cm (note presence of Gothic "F" on reverse); B. Eight reales, Ferdinand and Isabella, Seville mint for Spanish distribution, diameter 4.0 cm (note absence of Gothic "F" on reverse); C. One real pillars of Hercules, Charles II and Joanna, Santo Domingo mint, ca. 1545–60, diameter 2.8 cm; D. Four reales pillars of Hercules with waves, Charles II and Joanna, Mexico City mint, ca. 1536–55, diameter 3.2 cm; E. Half real, Charles II and Joanna, Santo Domingo mint, ca. 1545–60, diameter 2.0 cm; F. Eight reales with shield obverse design, Charles II, Mexico City mint, 1689, diameter 4.0 cm; G. Four reales, pillar and waves obverse design, Charles II, Lima mint, 1696, diameter 3.4 cm; H. Pillar dollar, Phillip V, Mexico City mint, 1754, diameter 3.3 cm; I. *Busto*, Charles III, Santiago mint, 1797, diameter 4.0 cm.

Heart- and Pomegranate-shaped Cobs

During the late seventeenth and early eighteenth centuries (particularly during the reign of Philip V), some cobs—primarily at the Potosí mint—were shaped into hearts or, less commonly, pomegranates. These often had a hole drilled through them. The purpose of these coins is unknown, but it has been suggested (Burzio 1945) that these were occasionally issued to demonstrate the love that the monarch held for the people of the region and, alternatively, that they were accidental

Coins and Weights

Figure 12.9. Spanish American cob coins. *Top:* Obverse. *Bottom:* Reverse. *Top left:* One real, Philip II (1556–93), Lima or Potosi, diameter 1.8 cm (SA-24-272). *Top right:* Half real, Phillip V (1700–1746), Mexico City, diameter 1.4 cm (SA-30-3-40). *Center:* Quarter real, possibly Phillip V, Mexico City, diameter 1.2 cm (SA-24-388). *Bottom left:* One real, Phillip IV (1621–65), Potosí, 1660, diameter 1.6 cm (SA-7-7-210). *Bottom right:* Possible counterfeit half real, diameter 1.6 cm (SA-30-3-85). All St. Augustine. FLMNH/CSA Collections. *Photo: James Quine.*

forms enhanced by users and serving as religious symbols (Craig 2000:200).

Half-Real Coins

Motifs and inscriptions on the half-real coins do not correspond to those discussed previously for other silver reales, and it is difficult to determine either the date or the mint for half reales. The reverse of most half-real coins bears the cross (straight or barred for the South American mints; curved or with balls for the Mexico mint) with lions and castles in its quadrant. The obverse side carries a monograph of the reigning king—CAROLVS, FERDANVS, PHILLLIPVS—that is often quite difficult to decipher (Fig. 12.9). Because of the very small size of these coins (ca. 15–17 mm in diameter), the date, mint mark, denomination mark, and assayer's mark rarely appear legible if they are included at all. Half reales are, in general, the least useful silver coins for dating purposes.

Silver Coins from the Santo Domingo Mint

Silver coinage of Charles II and Joanna issue were minted in Santo Domingo between about 1545 and about 1552 (Burzio 1956–58[I]:115; Estrella Gómez 1979:50–51). These were round coins made in the manner of Iberian Spanish reales, and silver cob coins were not produced at all in Santo Domingo (probably because the mint was largely in disuse by the time the volume of American silver provoked the production of cob coins and the volume of the Santo Domingo mint was always very small).

The Santo Domingo mint was authorized to produce Charles II and Joanna issue silver coins in the denominations of half, one, two, three, four, and five, eight, and ten reales. Only half, one, four, and ten reales are documented in collections. The obverse of all but the half-real piece bears a shield containing the arms of Castile and Leon. The shield is surmounted by a crown and is flanked on the left by the letter "F" or "P" (presumably assayers' marks) and on the right by the denomination mark.

The reverse of these coins bears two crowned pillars of Hercules, with a scroll across their fronts. The scroll bears some version of PLUS, from "PLUS ULTRA" ("PLVS," "PV," "PLV," and so forth). The pillars are flanked by the Santo Domingo mint mark—an "S" to the left and a "D" or "P" to the right. Sometimes

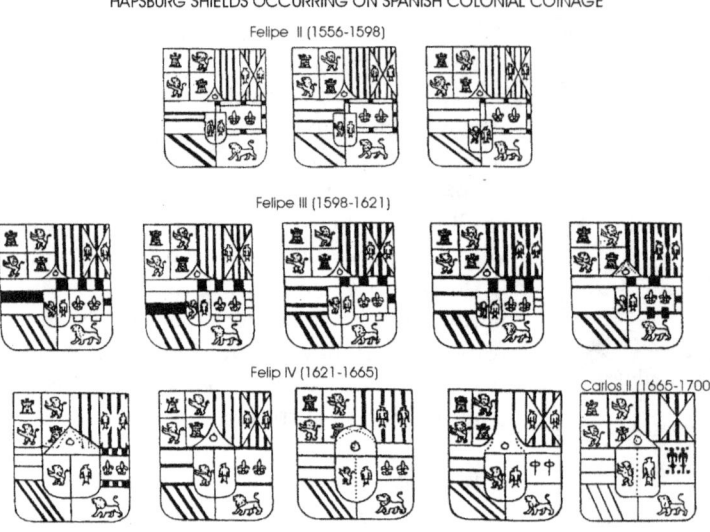

Figure 12.10. Obverse (shield) motifs on Mexico City silver coins.

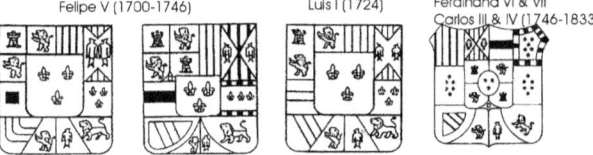

this placement is reversed, with the "S" to the right and the "D" or "P" to the left of the columns. The base of the pillars can vary considerably in shape and decoration, but only the pillars on the ten-real coins are resting on waves. Inscribed around both the obverse and reverse edges is "CAROLUS + ET + IHOANA + REGIS + HISPANIARUM + ET + INDIARUM," most often with half of the inscription on each side but sometimes with the first half repeated on both sides.

The ten-real piece is unique in Spanish American colonial coinage, and these were made only in Santo Domingo. None have been reported from terrestrial archeological sites. As noted, the pillar bases on the reverse rest on stylized waves. The denomination mark is the Roman numeral X.

The half-real pieces do not bear specific assayers' marks or denomination marks, but they are distinct in their obverse design. Instead of bearing a shield with the arms of Castile and Leon (as do all the other silver reales from Santo Domingo), the half-real pieces show a Greek-style "K" and "Y," representing the initials of the monarchs. The letters are connected at the base, and each is surmounted by a crown. There is usually a raised dot between the letters and sometimes two small crosses at the base.

Production of Charles II and Joanna reales ceased in Santo Domingo by about 1552. There was, however, a second very brief period of silver coin production that took place in the Santo Domingo mint during the first half of 1578. These were primarily round, four-real coins of Philip II issue and are very rare (see Estrella Gómez 1979:107–109, 151). They are easily distinguishable from the earlier Charles II and Joanna coins by the presence of the Hapsburg shield on the obverse, with the Santo Domingo mint mark ("s") to the left and the denomination mark to the right of the shield. The reverse bears a Jerusalem cross enclosed in a quatrefoil with castles and lions in the four quadrants of the cross. The legend around the coins reads "PHILIPPUS * II * DEI * GRATIA * HISPANIARUM * ET * INDIARUM +."

Silver Coins from the Mexico City Mint
CHARLES II AND JOANNA PERIOD. Coins of the Charles II and Joanna period of issue (1536–72) bear the shield of Spain with lions and castles on the obverse and two crowned pillars crossed by a banner with some version of "PLUS" inscribed on it on the reverse (Fig. 12.8D). They are also distinctive in being round in shape (as contrasted with the later irregular silver cob coins). "Early" Mexican silver Charles II and Joanna reales (ca. 1536–42) are distinguished from the "late" series (1543–72) by several details (Nesmith 1955:95):

1. Waves are absent beneath the pillars on the reverse side of the early series coins and are present beneath the pillars on late series coins;
2. The motto "PLVS VLTRA" is inscribed on a ribbon or panel in the early series but simply on the background in the late series;
3. Charles's name is spelled "CHAROLVS" on the early series coins and spelled "CAROLVS" on late series coins; and
4. The shape of the crown over the pillars is different (see Fig. 12.4C, D).

HAPSBURG ERA (1556–1700). Mexican silver coins from about 1550 to about 1700 were of the irregularly shaped cob variety. They all bore a version of the Hapsburg shield on the obverse, along with a legend inscribing the monarch's name (Table 12.3; Fig. 12.10). After 1609, a four-digit date was often (but not always) impressed in Arabic numerals above the shield, at the top of the coin, although these are only rarely legible (Craig 2000:80; Sedwick 1987:26). To the right of the shield, the denomination is indicated by Roman numerals, and to the left is often a mint mark and assayer's mark.

The reverse of the coins has a Jerusalem cross with curvilinear-ornamented terminals, either floriated or ball-shaped ends. These curvilinear ends on the Mexican coin crosses are a distinctive Mexican characteristic, helping to distinguish them from the South American mints, whose Jerusalem crosses ended simply and abruptly or with a T-bar. The cross is enclosed in a tressure. Within the four quadrants of the cross are two lions and two castles. This side bears some version of the legend "HISPANIARUM ET INDIARUM REX."

BOURBON ERA (1700–32). After 1700, the coin insignia changed in response to the ascension of the first monarch of the House of Bourbon, Philip V. The obverse of these coins bears the Spanish Bourbon shield, most readily distinguished from the preceding Hapsburg arms by the use of three fleurs-de-lis in the center device of the shield, replacing the lion and bird in the center of the Hapsburg shield. The Bourbon shield changed somewhat in detail between 1700 and 1715, and these changes have been summarized in Figure 12.10. The reverse of the Bourbon reales continues the use of the Jerusalem cross in its tressure, with lions and castles in the corners. The most comprehensive treatment to date of variation in Mexican cob coins is provided by Craig (2000).

PILLAR DOLLARS (1732–72). A major change in the coinage of the Mexico mint took place after 1732, when the first milled coins were produced. These coins were perfectly round with milled edges and were also known as pillar dollars. The obverse of these coins bears the two pillars of Hercules, with two globes, representing the Old and New Worlds, placed between them (Fig. 12.11). A scroll on one column reads "PLUS," and a scroll on the

Figure 12.11. Mexico City Phillip V pillar dollar, 1733. Diameter 4 cm. *Courtesy of the Florida Bureau of Archaeological Research.*

other reads "ULTRA" (indicating "more beyond"). Around the edge of the pillar side of the coins is the legend "UTRAQUE UNUM" (both are one), and the date of the coin is below the pillars. This design replaced the Jerusalem cross of the earlier cob coins. The reverse side of the pillar dollars bears the crowned Bourbon shield, with the legend "HISPANIARUM ET INDIARUM REX" around the edge and the name of the reigning monarch (for example, "PHILLIP V").

BUSTOS (1772–1821). The milled pillar dollars continued in production in Mexico until 1772, during the reign of Charles III. At that time, Charles decreed that his portrait, often in Roman garb, be imprinted on the obverse of Spanish coins. The date was inscribed below the portrait, and around the monarch's bust was the legend "DEI GRATIA" and "CAROLUS III" (Fig. 12.12).

The reverse of these Mexican *bustos* bears a crowned Bourbon shield in the center, flanked on either side by a pillar with a scroll. One scroll reads "PLUS" and the other "ULTRA." The legend around the edge of the coin is some version of "HISPANIARUM ET INDIARUM REX." These coins were produced until Mexican independence in 1821.

Silver Coins from the Lima Mint
There were three periods of silver coin production at Lima during the colonial era. The first, from 1568 until 1571, produced distinctive quarter-, half-, one-, two-, four-, and

Figure 12.12. Mexico City Charles IV *bustos*. *Top:* Obverse. *Bottom:* Reverse. *Left:* 1796 (SA-7-7-410). *Center:* (SA-23-92). *Right:* 1799 (SA-7-7-18). All St. Augustine. Diameter of top center coin, 2.5 cm. FLMNH/CSA Collections. *Photo: James Quine.*

eight-real coins. The motif on these coins is unique in that they are copies of the Mexico Charles II and Joanna silver cobs showing the shield of Castile and Leon but with the inscription of the Hapsburg Philip II (since Philip ascended the throne in 1556 and the Lima mint did not open until 1568).

The obverse on these first-period Lima coins bears the shield associated with Charles II and Joanna, with two lions and two castles in four quadrants. This is surrounded by a version of the legend "PHILIPPVS II DEI GRATIA HISPANIARUM ET INDIARUM" extending around both sides of the coin. The mint mark "P" was placed to the left of the shield.

The reverse of these first-period coins shows the crowned pillars of Hercules, always over waves, with the banner and legend of "PLVS VLTRA" across the front. An assayer's mark is to the left and a denomination mark to the right of the pillars.

Although similar to the earlier Mexican silver, Lima coins are readily distinguishable from them in that Mexican coins with the Charles II and Joanna shield are round and bear the CAROLUS ET IOANNA legend, while those of Lima are cobs and bear the PHILLIPVS legend. In addition, Lima coins of the early period bear a mint mark of "P," while those of Mexico bear an "M."

The Lima mint was closed from 1572 until 1575, when it began production of the second series of Lima silver coins. This second period of production lasted until 1581, and the mint remained closed for more than a century after this date, until 1683 (with the exception of a few months in 1659–60). Silver cob coins of the 1575 to 1581 period differ from the earlier coins in that the later coins bear the Hapsburg shield with the PHILLIPVS inscription on one side and a cross enclosed in a tressure or quatrefoil on the other (Fig. 12.9). This design is also shared by Mexican coins of the same period; however, the Lima coins can be distinguished from Mexican counterparts by their mint marks ("P" or "P" with a star) as well as by the form of the cross. The arms of crosses on Mexican silver coins always end in a curvilinear or ball-shaped terminal, while those of the South American mints end in a T-bar or plain straight terminal.

When the Lima mint reopened in 1683, it used a different mint mark, "L" or "LM" for Lima, and it adopted yet another set of designs. Silver coins made between 1683 and 1752 in Lima bear the cross enclosed in a tressure on one side and the pillar and waves design on the other.

This pillar and waves design (evolved from the earlier pillars of Hercules motif) divided the coin face into nine sections like a ticktacktoe board described earlier (Figs. 12.8G, 12.9). On the Lima coins, the top three cells contain, from left to right, an "L" (mint mark), the coin denomination (usually an Arabic numeral), and a letter representing the assayer. The center row of three cells contain, from left to right, "PLV," "SVL," and "TRA." spelling out "PLVS ULTRA." The bottom row of three cells contain, from left to right, a repeat of the letter in the top right cell representing the assayer, a two-digit number representing the last two digits of the mining date (for example, 1672 would be represented as "72"), and a repeat of the mint mark "L." The date of the coin was also sometimes reproduced on the other side of the coin at the base of the cross, and after 1700 the last three rather than the last two digits often appear in the date.

These coins were produced until 1752, when production of cob coins ceased and round, milled pillar dollars were introduced. The Lima pillar dollars used the same design and motif as the Mexican pillar dollars, which were first produced in 1732. The reverse of these coins bears the pillars of Hercules, with two globes, representing the Old and New Worlds, placed between them (see Fig. 12.12). A scroll on one column reads "PLUS," a scroll on the other reads "ULTRA," and the legend "UTRAQUE UNUM" (both are one) appears around the edge of the pillar side of the coin. The date of the coin is below the pillars, and the mint mark, "L." is inscribed on each side of the date. This design replaced the Jerusalem cross of the earlier pre-1572 cob coins. The obverse side of the Lima pillar dollars bear the crowned Bourbon shield, with the legend "HISPANIARUM ET INDIARUM REX" around the edge and the name of the reigning monarch (for example, "PHILLIP V").

The pillar dollars were produced in Lima until 1772, when coinage shifted to the Charles III *bustos* bearing that monarch's portrait on the obverse. The date was inscribed below the portrait, and around the monarch's bust was the legend "DEI GRATIA" and "CAROLUS III."

The reverse of the Lima *bustos* bore a crowned Bourbon shield in the center, flanked on either side by a pillar with a scroll. One scroll reads "PLUS" and the other "ULTRA." The legend around the edge of the coin is some version of "HISPANIARUM ET INDIARUM REX." If the mint mark "LM" appears (and it often does not), it is placed after the "REX" in the reverse inscription. These coins were produced until Peruvian independence in 1824.

Silver Coins from the Potosí Mint
The "silver mountain" of Potosí (in the colonial viceroyalty of Peru) was discovered in 1545 in what is today Bolivia. Mining operations began in 1562, and by 1575 a mint producing silver cob coins was established there (Burzio 1945:2–3).

The Potosí mint produced exclusively silver cob-type coins until 1773, in denominations of half, one, two, four, and eight reales. All used the "P" mint mark. The mint was plagued by mismanagement and corruption during the first half of the seventeenth century, and many of the Potosí coins of this period do not conform to the standards or weights prescribed by law (Burzio 1945:6–7; Craig 2000:22–38).

During the first seventy-five years of operation (1575–1651), the Potosí silver cobs bore the shield and inscription of the reigning monarch on the obverse, with the "P" mint mark and the assayer's mark to the left of the shield and the coin denomination to the right of the shield. Dates occasionally appear on Potosí cobs of this type after 1617; if they are present, they are found included in the inscription around the obverse edge (Sedwick 1987:27). The reverse of these coins had the standard South American Jerusalem cross ending in straight or T-bar terminals enclosed in a tressure.

During the first six years of production, coins from the Potosí mint shared both their mint mark ("P") and their obverse and reverse designs (shield/cross) with those from the Lima mint of the same time period. In many cases, however, it is possible to distinguish products of the two mints. If there is a star accompanying or in place of the "P" mint mark, for example, the coin is from the Lima mint. Assayers' marks do not all overlap during this period (see Burzio 1945). Between 1575 and 1581, for example, Lima assayers' marks include "R," "X," "M," "B," "L," and "D," while Potosí assayers' marks include "R," "B," "A," and "Q" (Sedwick 1987:8–11). Only "R" and "B" overlap.

In 1651, corruption in the mint was so pronounced that the crown ordered the recall of all existing Potosí cobs and the re-issue of a new design, although large numbers of the early design were undoubtedly taken out of circulation and hoarded. From 1561 to 1772, Potosí silver cob coins bore the cross enclosed in a tressure on the obverse and the pillar and waves design described previously for Lima on the reverse. However, during this period, the Lima mint was in operation only after 1683 and used the mint mark "L." Some students of Spanish American coinage (for example, Sedwick 1987:29) furthermore point out that Lima and Potosí pillar and waves coins can be distinguished by the form of the waves. When the points of the waves beneath the bottom center (date) cell of the motif point down, the coin is from Lima. When they point up, it is from Potosí.

In 1773, Potosí produced its first round, milled coins. These were the *busto* coins of the Bourbon kings Charles III and Charles IV described earlier but bearing the Potosí mint mark.

Silver Coins from the Colombia Mints
Silver coins of the Colombian mints (particularly that of Cartagena) are rarely encountered on terrestrial archaeological sites. The mint at Bogotá was established in 1620, with a branch mint at Cartagena. Silver cobs of quarter, half, one, two, four, and eight reales were struck, and the first gold coins in the Americas were struck here as well (see Barriga Villalba 1969; Craig 1988:57).

The mint mark for the Bogotá mint can be

quite variable, including "NR" and "RN" (for Reino Nuevo) and "SF" and "FS" for (Santa Fé). These can appear either vertically or horizontally arranged. The Cartagena mint might include any of these or a "C." Silver cobs from these mints have a reputation for being cruder in execution than other cob coins (see, for example, Craig 2000:167; Sedwick 1987:26, 31).

From 1620 until about 1650, the silver reales had on the reverse the cross enclosed in a tressure motif. The obverse showed the Hapsburg shield, and the inscription of the reigning monarch (PHILLIPVS; see Table 12.3) was arranged around the edges of both sides.

After 1650, the coins were changed to include the pillar and waves motif on the obverse, replacing the shield design (Barriga Villalba 1969:72–75). Colombian silver cob coins of the pillar and waves type are quite distinct from those of other mints. Sedwick describes them as

> the crudest cobs of all. . . . The pillars are usually either "fat," and bent like two parentheses, or very thin, like an "I". The mintmark, date, assayer, and denomination may be located anywhere on that side, in any order, in either horizontal or vertical position. The waves may go up or down, but are mostly level. There is never a tic-tac-toe diagram. The strangest of features . . . is the PLVS VLTRA, carelessly engraved and often haphazardly spaced without regard to symmetry, its unconcatenated letters wandering above or within the pillars. In short, no two varieties of design ever seem to be similar. (1987:31)

This pillar and waves motif persisted on the cob coins of Colombia until 1655 in Cartagena (when production at that mint ceased) and until 1756 in Bogotá, when round, milled pillar dollars began production (Burzio 1945:51). Although generally round in shape, the Nuevo Reino pillar dollars were sometimes irregular and not truly circular in form (see, for example, Cayón y Castán 1977:107).

After 1772, during the reign of Charles III, pillar dollars were replaced by the milled *busto* coins, showing the bust of the emperor on one side and the Bourbon shield flanked by pillars on the other side. *Busto* reales were produced to the end of the colonial period.

Silver Coins from the Guatemala Mint

The mint in Guatemala City was established in 1733 and produced only silver cob coins until 1753, when production ceased. There was a single assayer, marked by "J," during the life of the mint (Sedwick 1987:14).

Guatemala reales are distinctive both in their shape and legends. The cobs generally have a roughly square or rectangular shape, comprised of straight edges. The reverse of these coins shows the two globes topped by a crown and flanked by the pillars of Hercules. The obverse side of the coin shows a crowned shield containing the arms of the reigning monarch, with the date below the shield and the mint mark on either side of the date. In some cases the quadrants within the shield, which are symmetrical on other coins, are irregular in size on the Guatemala cobs.

The Guatemala half reales are distinct from the half reales of other American mints in that they show the same motifs as the higher denominations. Unlike other half-real coins, they do not bear the rulers' monograms.

Round, milled pillar dollars were first produced at Guatemala in 1754 and were produced until 1772, when the change was made to the *busto* dollar. After being destroyed and rebuilt after 1774, the mint continued production until 1822.

Gold Coinage

Gold coins recovered archaeologically have been reported almost exclusively from shipwreck sites. They were issued in Spanish American mints as escudos in denominations of half, one, two, four, and eight escudos.

Gold coins were first produced in the Americas at the mint of Santa Fe de Bogotá, which was authorized to strike gold coins in

1622. Bogotá was the only place minting gold coins until 1679, when the Mexico City mint began production, and in 1696 Lima began to produce escudos. The mint at Cuzco produced one- and two-escudo pieces during only one year, 1698 (see Craig 1988).

In general, the designs and motifs on gold cobs followed those of their silver counterparts, with some minor variations. All gold cobs have the Jerusalem cross on the reverse, but the curvilinear form characteristic of the terminal ends of the cross on Mexican silver coins (discussed earlier) is not always found on gold coins (Sedwick 1987:20).

Most of the crosses on gold coins are surrounded by a tressure; however, the Lima and Cuzco coins of denominations greater than one escudo are not enclosed in a tressure. The Peruvian coins are also distinct from Mexican and Bogotá gold cobs in that they have lions and castles portrayed in the quadrants of the cross. The Mexican and Colombian gold coins all have fleurs-de-lis in the cross quadrants.

The obverse of gold cobs can bear one of two designs: either the shield or the pillar and waves described previously for silver cob coins. All gold cobs from Mexico bear the shield motif on the obverse. A date is sometimes present at the 11 o'clock position in the encircling legend. Gold cobs from Bogotá also bear the shield obverse design. Unlike other Spanish American coins, if a date is present on a Bogotá gold coin, it appears on the reverse (Sedwick 1987:26).

Lima and Cuzco gold cobs of denominations greater than one escudo bear the pillar and waves design on the obverse. As with silver coins, the last three digits of the date are sometimes shown in the design. Lima gold cob coins were produced until 1750 (Calicó, Calicó, and Trigo 1985:325–326).

One-escudo coins from Lima and Cuzco are quite distinct in their design. The obverse of these coins has a single castle portrayed, with a mint mark to the left and the assayer's mark to the right of the castle. A three-digit date appears under the castle. The reverse has a Jerusalem cross with fleurs-de-lis in the quadrants.

Several round, cob-type, eight-escudo pieces from the Guatemala mint dating from 1733 to 1745 are listed in the Calicó catalog (Calicó, Calicó, and Trigo 1985:260). These coins, although not milled, bear the bust of the king (Philip V) on the obverse and the crowned Bourbon shield typical of the silver *bustos* on the reverse.

During the reign of Philip IV (1700–46), gold cob coin production (like silver) ended in Mexico, and cobs were replaced by round, milled "dollars." Gold milled coins appeared in Mexico in 1733 but were unlike the milled silver pillar dollars that appeared at the same time. Rather than the pillars and scrolls seen on the silver milled coins, the gold coins bore the bust of the reigning monarch encircled by his or her inscription, with the date shown below the bust. The reverse bore the shield of the monarch surmounted by a crown and encircled by a legend such as "MAGNA.SEQOUR.NOMINA," "INITIUM.SAPIENTIAE.TIMOR.DOMINI," or "AUSPICE.DEO.IN.UTROQ.FELIX." The mint mark is in the legend at the base of the shield, the assayer's mark is to the left of the shield, and the denomination mark is to the right (Fig. 12.11H). This bust-type gold coin continued to the end of the colonial era, changing portraits as the rulers changed.

The production of bust-type milled gold coins began in Lima and in Santiago de Chile in about 1750, in Bogotá in 1756, in Popayán (southern Colombia, with a mint mark "P") in 1758 (Calicó, Calicó, and Trigo 1985:328, 327), in Guatemala (with a new mint mark of "NG" after 1774), and in Potosí by 1778 (Murray 1986:2482).

Summary

As noted initially, the precise dating of Spanish American coins can be a very complex undertaking, and if site interpretation depends on this, a numismatist should be consulted. There are, however, general guidelines that can be applied to distinguish major categories of such coins.

General coin types in the Spanish American regions can include copper-alloy coins; round, milled silver coins (before 1550 and after 1732); cob-type silver coins (ca. 1550–1732); and gold coins. Copper-alloy Spanish American coins are restricted to the maravedís minted in Santo Domingo and Mexico City during the middle third of the sixteenth century. The motifs associated with these two mints are quite distinct and cannot easily be confused.

Round, milled silver coins were briefly produced at the Mexico City and Santo Domingo mints during the reign of Charles II and Joanna (1515–56). They were not made in the Americas again until after 1732, when production of the easily identifiable pillar dollars and later the *busto* coins began.

The majority of coins from archaeological sites are the irregular silver cob coins, minted throughout the Americas between about 1560 and 1730. The obvious first step in identification is to identify the denomination of the coin and its mint region. The former can be identified by the size and weight of the coin (Table 12.2) and the latter either by the mint mark (if present) (Table 12.4) or by the design motifs of the coin.

The reverse of nearly all Spanish American cobs bear the Jerusalem cross, usually within a tressure. The shape of this cross provides a useful distinction between the Mexico and South American mints, in that the ends of the crosses on Mexican coins are curved, ball shaped, or floriated, while the ends of the crosses on South American coins are either straight and plain or T-barred.

The obverse design on these coins provides more specific distinguishing information. Three general obverse designs were used: the pillars of Hercules motif, the shield motif, and the pillar and waves motif. These motifs occur on the obverse of coins from specific mints at certain times. The pillars of Hercules motif was used during the sixteenth century and appears on the obverse of silver coins from the Santo Domingo mint (all periods), the Mexico mint before 1552, and the Lima mint from 1568 to 1572.

The shield motif depicts the coat of arms of the reigning family (Hapsburgs or Bourbons) and dates to before 1650 for silver cob coins. It appears on the obverse of all gold cobs except for Peru escudos, all silver cobs from Mexico minted after 1552, Lima silver cobs minted between 1572 and 1588, and all silver cobs from Potosí, Bogotá, and Cartagena minted before 1652.

The pillar and waves motif appears on the obverse of gold cob coins from Peru (Lima and Cuzco) and on all silver cob coins from South American mints after 1652.

The identification of these motifs should permit identification of a coin's origin and its general date based on periods of operation for the mint and its obverse designs (Table 12.4). Dating of such coins can be refined in a number of ways, the most obvious of which are: identification of the reigning monarch's insignia (Table 12.3); written dates appearing on the pillar and waves design; assayers' marks (consult sources discussed earlier for each mint); and minor variations in crosses, shields, and inscriptions (consult a numismatic specialist).

Jetons

Metal tokens, or jetons, were used throughout the Middle Ages as a calculating aid and are like coins in size and appearance. They are round, made of nonprecious metal, and struck with a wide variety of designs that might represent the jeton's maker, its intended user, religious motifs, city coats or arms, rulers, or other themes (Bernard 1981; Van Beek 1986). The system of calculating with numismatic jetons was developed in Europe by the end of the twelfth century and was used until the early sixteenth century, by which date it had been largely superceded by

Figure 12.13. Counting tokens used in calculation. Woodcut, signature LV recto of "Arithmeticae" from *Margarita Philosophica,* by Gregor Reisch, contrasting calculation with Arabic numerals and counting tokens. Published in Freiburg, Germany, in 1503. *Courtesy of the Bodleien Library, University of Oxford.* Shelfmark Douce R534.

Figure 12.14. Nuremberg counting jeton. Copper alloy, late fifteenth century. Diameter 2.95 cm. La Isabela (FS 1503.1). Parque Nacional de La Isabela, Dominican Republic. *Drawing: Merald Clark.*

arithmetic systems of numeric calculation (Bernard 1981; Van Beek 1986).

Figure 12.13 shows the manner of use for counting jetons in the early sixteenth century. Calculations took place on a board or cloth with a series of horizontal lines. Each line was assigned a value in Roman numerals, from the bottom up, depending on the quantity and complexity of the calculations to be done. The value "157" would have one counter placed on the C line, five counters on the X line, one counter on the V line, and two on the I line. Vertical lines separated numbers that could be added or subtracted horizontally across the board.

Most examples of counting jetons found in American sites were produced in Nuremberg, Germany, which was the center for jeton (*Rechenpfennig*) production from the fifteenth through the seventeenth centuries (Van Beek 1986:204). Figures 12.14 and 12.15 show examples of jetons from Spanish colonial sites, and examples of archaeologically recovered seventeenth-century counting jetons are shown by Cotter and Hudson (1957:90).

Jetons continued to be produced in significant quantities in Nuremberg after the mid-sixteenth century, but they functioned primarily as devices for advertisement, commemoration, or propaganda rather than as calculating aids (see, for example, Noel Hume 1980:158–159). The size of jetons gradually diminished through the seventeenth century (Van Beek 1986), and they were used widely

Coins and Weights

Figure 12.15. Eighteenth-century commemorative peace jeton. Copper alloy, showing Louis XV on the obverse and Peace and Liberty on the reverse, ca. 1725–50, diameter 2.4 cm St. Augustine (SA-7-4). FLMNH/CSA Collections. *Reproduced from Shephard (1983:95) with permission. Drawing: Stephen Shephard.*

in the trade between English colonists and American Indians during the seventeenth and eighteenth centuries (Noel Hume 1980:171–173). Medals and jetons were also made specifically as presentation pieces to commemorate alliances and peace agreements with American Indians (Stahl 1990) and are sometimes found on Spanish colonial sites (see Fig. 12.15).

Weights

The establishment and verification of a standard measure for weights in the American colonies were matters of considerable concern to the Spanish crown. Legislation was enacted in the 1520s to ensure that each town used standard weights and measures and to establish the office of the *fiel marcador*, who was responsible for verifying and sealing (marking) all weights used for commerce (Carrera Stampa 1949:3–4). After 1559, merchants in New Spain were obliged to have their weights verified and marked with the municipal seal specific to the town. In Mexico City, this seal consisted of a circle contain-

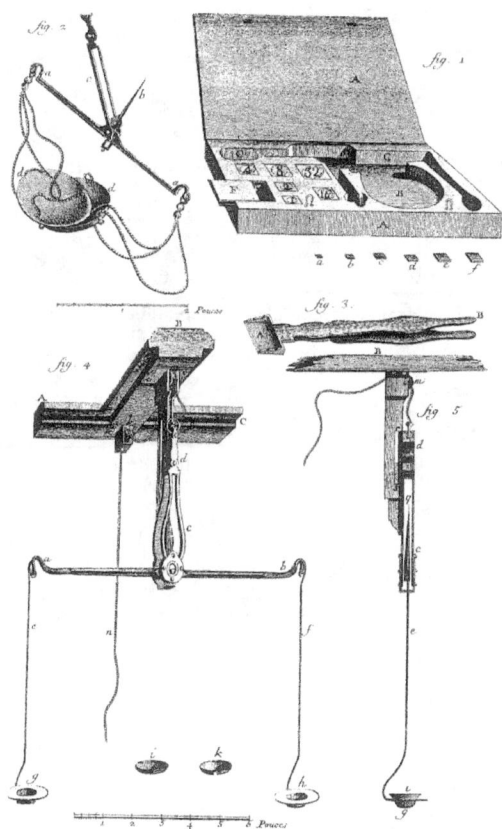

Figure 12.16. Coin scale and weight set. *Balancier.* Plate 5, Part 5, Diderot, *L'Encyclopédie* (Diderot 1751–65). *Courtesy of the University of Florida Library, Special Collections Department.*

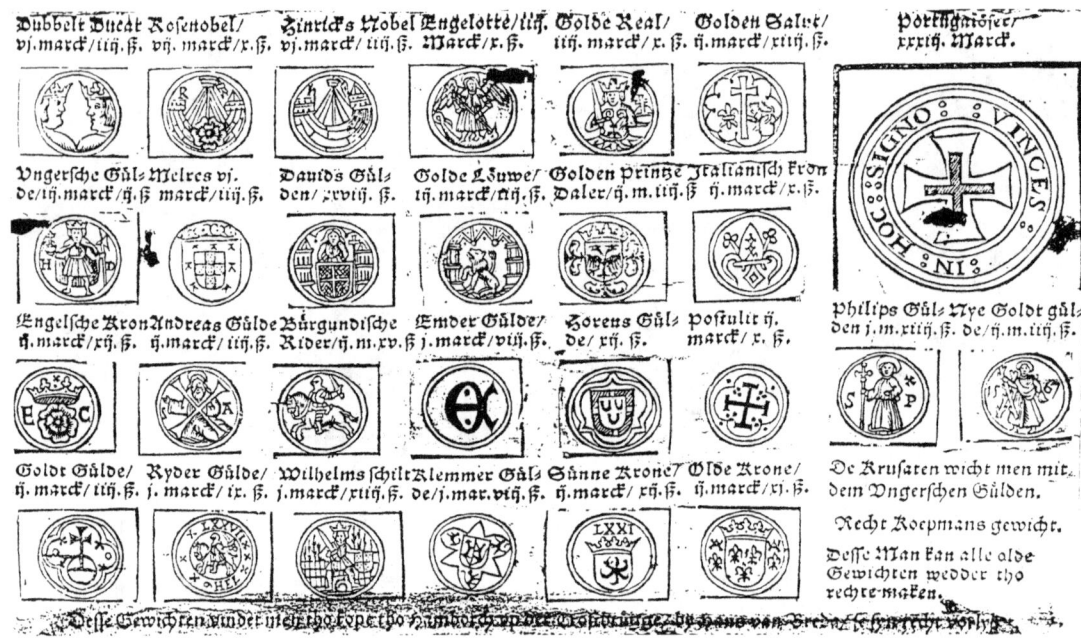

Figure 12.17. Sixteenth-century coin weight box. Label on the inner lid of a Hamburg coin weight box (1587) shows and identifies the designs on a variety of weights for European gold coins. *Courtesy of the Germanisches Nationalmuseum, Nuremberg.*

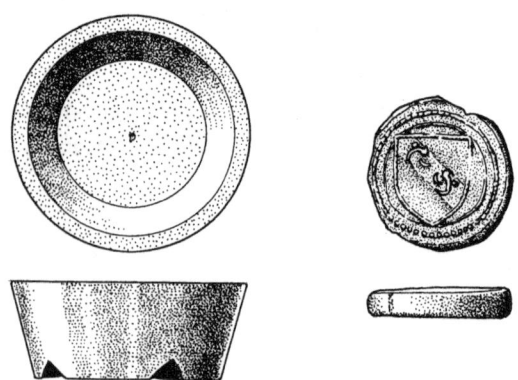

Figure 12.18. Fifteenth-century Spanish weights. Copper alloy, La Isabela (1493–98). *Left:* One cup of a nested weight set (top diameter 2.0 cm, height 1.0 cm, weight 14.2 g). *Right:* Coin weight (diameter 1.5 cm, weight 4.5 g). Parque Nacional de La Isabela, Dominican Republic. *Drawing: Merald Clark.*

ing "MO." In Puebla de los Angeles, the mark was a Greek alpha, and other towns had other marks (Carrera Stampa 1949:5, 9). Table 12.1 shows the standard weight units for Spanish silver and gold, and these were also applied to other commercial products.

Coin Weights

Because the intrinsic value of a colonial-era coin was based on its weight, a means to verify that weight was essential. Coin weights served in this capacity and have been used for as long as coins have been minted (Kisch 1965:129–134). Each coin weight was made to correspond to the exact weight of a specific coin and was impressed with a design that was easily recognizable as representing that coin (often including part of the coin's motif or inscription). This was particularly important during times of widespread illiteracy and equally widespread use of coin weights by merchants (Kisch 1965:132). Kept in a

Figure 12.19. Sixteenth-century copper-alloy weights from Concepción de la Vega (1496–1502). *Clockwise from top:* Diameter 2.3 cm, weight 20.3 g; diameter 1.5 cm, weight 4.4 g; diameter 1.3 cm, weight 3.4 g; diameter 1.3 cm, weight 3.4 g; diameter 1.6 cm, weight 4.3 g; diameter 1.3 cm, weight 4.3 g; diameter 1.2 cm, weight 2.0 g; 1.5 cm square, weight 8.5 g. *Center:* Diameter 3.3 cm, weight 49.9 g. Parque Nacional de Concepción de la Vega, Dominican Republic. *Photo: James Quine.*

Figure 12.20. Spanish coin or pharmaceutical weights. *Left:* Early-eighteenth-century copper-alloy weight with chemical symbol for antimony inscribed, 1.7 cm by 1.6 cm., weight 7.43 g (SA-34-2-365). FLMNH/CSA Collections. *Right:* Late seventeenth or early eighteenth century, copper alloy, 1.7 cm by 1.4 cm, weight 6.7 g (8DU53). FLMNH Collections #HTC-DU-53-S. *Photo: University of Florida Office of Instructional Resources.*

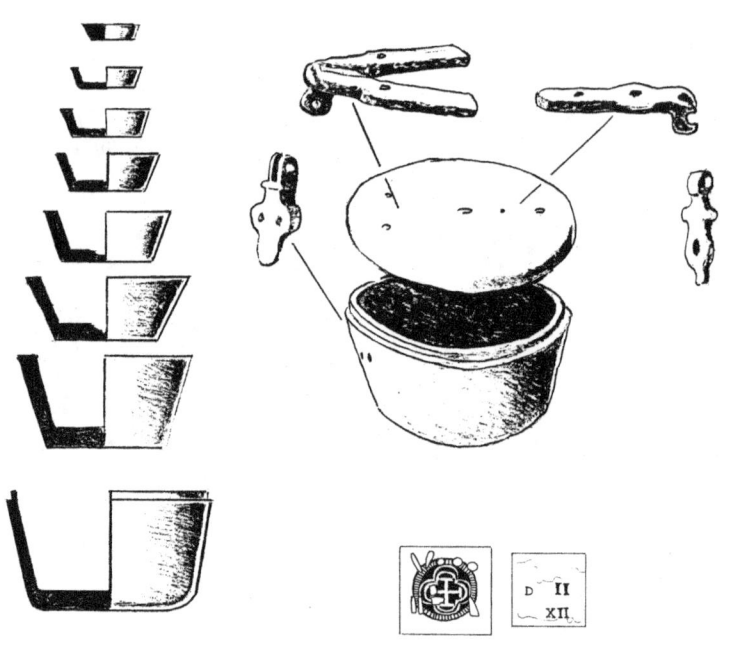

Figure 12.21. Weights from 1715 Florida shipwrecks. *Left and upper right:* Complete set of eight nested cup weights. Weights of smallest to largest cups: 1.95 g, 2.1 g, 4.0 g, 7.6 g, 14.8 g, 27.3 g, 56.1 g; outer cup: 92.45 g including lid. Diameter of top 4.0 cm, (8IR23) FBAR Lab #L030. *Lower right:* Coin weight. Top is 1.7 cm square, with Jerusalem cross inscription. Back is 1.4 cm square, with numerical inscriptions. Weight 12.06 g (8IR19) FBAR Lab #L3993. *Courtesy of the Florida Bureau of Archaeological Research. Drawing: Frank Gilson.*

compact box along with a scale, coin weights were used by merchants and bankers in sets representing a variety of coins and denominations (Figs. 12.16, 12.17). Although coin weight sets were produced in most countries, they were most often manufactured in Germany or Holland and exported throughout Europe. Those found in the Spanish American colonies are most likely to have been made in Germany or Spain.

In Spain and in the Spanish colonies, the weights themselves were nearly always made of brass (Kisch 1965:134) and during the sixteenth and seventeenth centuries were most frequently round in shape (Figs. 12.18, 12.19). Those found in late-seventeenth- and eighteenth-century Spanish American contexts are most often square (Figs. 12.20, 12.21) and may have been produced in the Low Countries rather than in Spain itself.

Coin weights of France, Holland, Germany, Italy, and Belgium were usually square, while English coin weights were round, quadrangular, or hexagonal (Kisch 1965:134). Weights were sometimes fitted with a small knob at the top to permit easy withdrawal from the boxes (Mannis 1992:41).

Nested Weights

From the sixteenth century to the present, brass nested weights (also known as cup weights) were used widely in the Spanish colonies and throughout Europe for a variety of weighing tasks. Nested weight sets were made up by a series of graduated, cup-shaped weights that fit into one another, and the largest (outer) cup usually had a hinged lid that enclosed the nested set into a compact unit (Figs. 12.21, 12.22). They were made in a wide range of sizes depending on their intended purpose, with sets ranging in weight from 21.5 kg or more to a few grams (Kisch:1965:126). Regardless of their size, however, the weight of the outer lidded cup was equal to the sum of the weights of all the smaller cups. The second largest cup weighed the sum of all the subsequently smaller cups

Figure 12.22. Eighteenth-century nested cup weights. *Balancier*. Plate 4, Part 3, Diderot, *L'Encyclopédie* (Diderot 1751–65). *Courtesy of the University of Florida Library, Special Collections Department.*

and was also half of the outer cup's weight. This relative weight ratio continued down to the smallest cup, which contained a disk that weighed the same as the smallest cup and fit neatly inside of it (Kisch:1965:126). These small disks and the hinged lids of nested weight sets are the parts recovered most frequently from archaeological contexts.

Nuremberg had a virtual monopoly on the production and distribution of nested brass weights from the sixteenth through the eighteenth centuries, and the weights were adjusted to the local weight standards of the country to which they were to be sent (Kisch 1965:126–127, 168). It has been suggested that the sets were relatively unadorned during the sixteenth century, with plain, round, flat tops and simple latches, while in the sev-

Figure 12.23. Sixteenth-century cup weights. *Top:* Outer cup and cap with handle. Height 3.0 cm, top diameter 5.0 cm. *Bottom:* Lids with handles. *Left:* Diameter 5.4 cm, weight 75.6 g. *Right:* Diameter 4.0 cm, weight 41.2 g. Concepción de la Vega (1502–62). Parque Nacional de Concepción de la Vega, Dominican Republic.

enteenth century the outer cups became considerably more elaborate, with bands of decoration molded around the outside of the outer cup and a carrying handle attached to two molded or carved vertical posts (Kisch 1965:129). The archaeological evidence suggests, however, that decorated lids and carrying handles were features of the sixteenth century as well, since several examples have been recovered from the ruins of Concepción de la Vega, which was destroyed in 1562 (Fig. 12.23). By the eighteenth century, the ornate decoration diminished, and most examples after 1700 are simple.

Nested weights produced in Nuremberg during this entire period were required by law to be marked with the sign of the master from whose workshop they came. The most comprehensive study of Nuremberg nested weight master signs is that of Stengel (1915), and the most accessible English-language source is Kisch (1965). Some of these master signs, synthesized by Kisch, are shown in Figure 12.24.

Other Weights

Weights intended for weighing all manner of things—from a few grams of drugs to a few tons of commercial produce—were produced in an almost infinite range of sizes and shapes (see Kisch 1965:79–147). Pharmaceutical weights therefore differed from coin weights in their designs, which include symbols of pharmaceutical units (Kisch 1965:140–142). Table 12.6 shows apothecary measures and symbols used in New Spain. Larger scale weights were used for a variety of commercial tasks, and a marked scale weight from London, recovered from an eighteenth-century context in St. Augustine, is shown in Figure 12.25.

Scales

Weights were used with scales to weigh money or other items. Two basic kinds of scales were used for this purpose: the balance

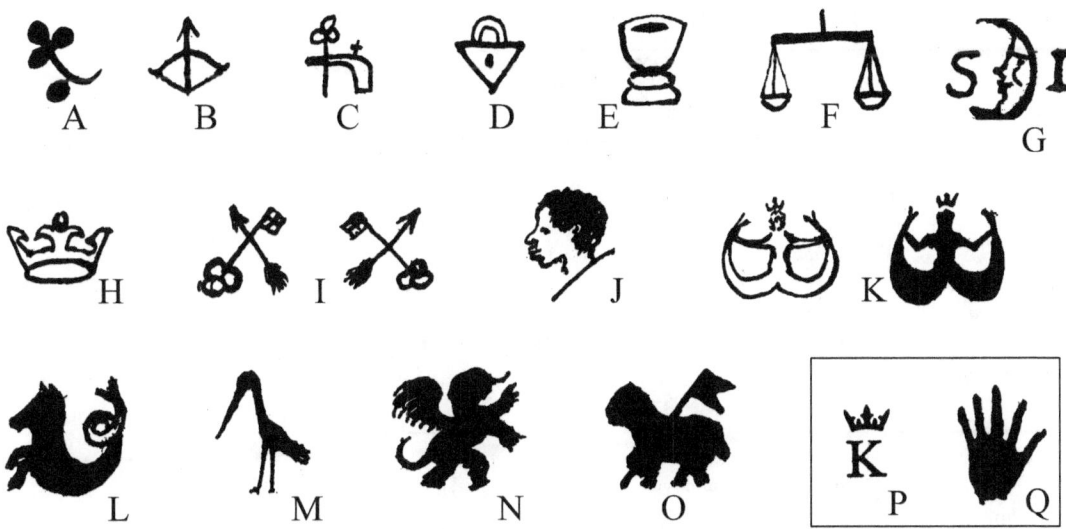

Figure 12.24. Examples of mastersigns on Nuremberg and other weights. A. Clover, sixteenth century; B. Bow and arrow, ca. 1650–1725; C. Spigot and clover, late seventeenth century; D. Lock, ca. 1650–1750; E. Goblet, eighteenth century; F. Scales, eighteenth century; G. Crescent moon with initials, ca. 1560–1800; H. Crown, sixteenth century, also post-1791; I. Crossed key and arrow, ca. 1650–1700s; J. African head, ca. 1600–1800; K. Mermaids, ca. 1650–late eighteenth century (depending on accompanying initials); L. Seahorse, ca. 1750–early nineteenth century; M. Stork, 1670–1800 (depending on accompanying initials); N. Griffin, 1650–1700; O. *Agnus dei* lamb, sixteenth and seventeenth centuries; P. French weight mark (an initial surmounted by a crown), most commonly eighteenth century; Q. Antwerp weight mark (a hand with initials and other symbols), late sixteenth to mid-eighteenth centuries; most common in seventeenth century. All dates are approximate and based on documented examples of dated weights. For greater detail on variations of these and other mastersigns, see Kisch (1965:175–185), from which this information is drawn.

scale (*balanza*) and the steelyard or scale beam (*romana*) (Fig. 12.26). The balance scale had two equal arms (beams) fitted through a vertical suspension rod at the center of the beam. Pans of equal weight were suspended by equal-length strings from each arm. The coin or other object to be weighed was placed in one pan and weights in the other. When the beam was horizontal and perpendicular to the suspension rod, the coin and the weights were equal.

An improvement in balance scales for coins was made in the eighteenth century with the development of the Nuremberg ducat scale. In addition to the vertical shear through which the beams fit, this scale also had a vertical pointer attached to the beam's center

Table 12.6. Pharmaceutical Weight Measures Used in New Spain

Unit	Equivalent	Grams	Troy Ounces	Symbol*
Libra	12 *onzas*	345.180	11.097	
Onza	8 *dracmas*	28.765	.925	℥,ʒ
Half *onza*				℥S or ℥
Dracma	3 *escrúpulos*	3.595	.116	ʒj or ʒi
Half *dracma*				ʒS or ʒ
Two *dracmas*				ʒij or ʒii
Escrúpulo	20 *granos*	1.198	.039	℈j or ℈i
Half *escrúpulo*				℈S or ℈
Grano		.059	.0016	

Source: After Carrera Stampa 1949:17

*After Kisch 1965:141–42. One half of any unit symbolized by S or β

Onza (Ounce) = ℥

Escrúpulo (Scruple) = ℈

Dracma (Dram) = ʒ

Figure 12.25. English scale weight used in Spanish Florida. Brass, late eighteenth century. Diameter 6.6 cm. The dagger is the symbol of the London Guildhall before 1826; the pitcher or ewer symbol represents the Founders Company (guild) before 1826. The "A" indicates that it is the avoirdupois (rather than troy) weight system. FLMNH/CSA Collections. *Photo: James Quine.*

point. An arched and notched arm was attached to one of the arms and passed through the shear to connect with the vertical pointer (Fig. 12.26). When the two weight pans were in equilibrium, the pointer and the shear were both vertical. When a coin was less than its expected weight, the indicator would be skewed away from the shear at an angle, and the notches on the arched arm could show at a glance the degree to which the weight was off. Many ducat scales had one pan that weighed exactly one ducat more than the other. When a ducat of correct weight was placed in the lighter pan, the arms would be horizontal and perpendicular to the pointer. Balance scales have been used since ancient

Coins and Weights

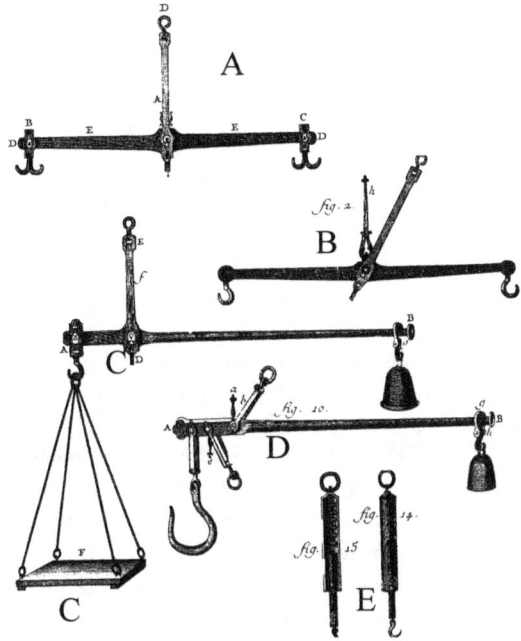

Figure 12.26. Colonial-era scale types. A. *Balanza*, or simple balance scale; B. Balance scale with indicator to measure degree of weight discrepancy; C. *Romana*, or steelyard scale with unequal arms on either side of fulcrum, counterweight, and increments marked along the beam; D. *Romana* scale with indicators; E. Spring scales. From Plate 2, Part 2, Diderot, *L'Encyclopédie* (Diderot 1751–65). *Courtesy of the University of Florida Library, Special Collections Department.*

times for a variety of purposes, but the terminals of the arms on those used to weigh gold and coins can sometimes provide an indication of date and origin (Kisch 1965:39–41; Fig. 12.27).

Unlike the balance scale, the *romana* scale had its suspension hook or shear offset from the center of the beam to create arms of unequal length (Fig. 12.26). The short arm had a pan or a clip suspended from it to hold the item being weighed, while a moveable counterweight was suspended from the longer arm. The beam itself typically had an engraved or inlaid scale, and when the counterweight was moved along the long arm of the beam, the point at which it caused the beam to be exactly horizontal indicated the weight of the object in the pan. Although they have not been reported specifically as such, fragments of these scales—pans, weights, beam sections, or hooks—are undoubtedly present in archaeological assemblages of the Spanish colonies.

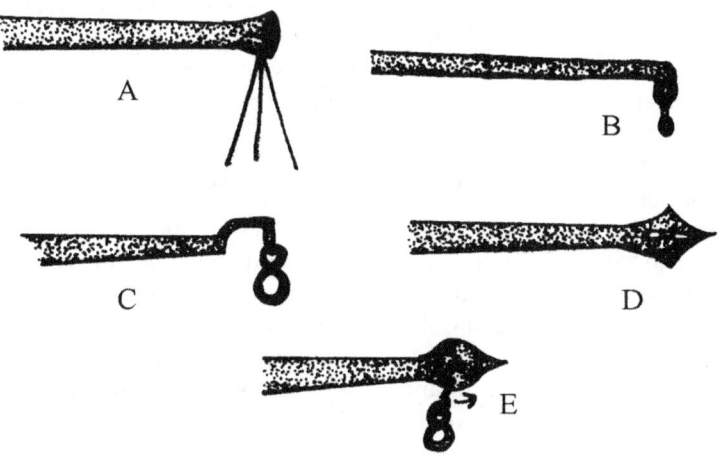

Figure 12.27. Arm terminals on small scale beams. A. Trumpet form, Cologne, sixteenth–seventeenth centuries; B. Spatula form, Germany, seventeenth century; C. Gallow or swan neck form, used throughout Europe, eighteenth century; D. Rhomboid form with holes for hook suspension, French, eighteenth century; E. Round box form; England, Germany, Austria; late eighteenth and early nineteenth centuries. *Drawing: Pauline Kulstad, after Kisch (1965:38).*

Chapter 13
Personal Firearms

Firearms were an important accouterment for Spanish colonial men, both as weapons and as social symbols. As one social historian of the Spanish colonies points out, "Weapons were part of the hidalgo's wearing apparel" (Bushnell 1978:34). As such, they are considered here as portable personal possessions. This chapter will attempt to outline the general categories and chronologies for handheld personal weapons used commonly in the circum-Caribbean Spanish colonies and to identify those basic elements that date and distinguish them. Other categories of guns, such as larger military-issue weapons and artillery, will be considered in a future volume. The discussion of guns here necessarily emphasizes those elements of firearms that are recovered archaeologically; that is, the nonperishable parts of commonly used weapons that were lost, broken, or discarded on sites.

This discussion is intended to serve only as a general guide for organizing and categorizing archaeologically recovered firearms. Anyone attempting to do specific identification and analyses of individual guns should consult a specialist, as well as the sources cited throughout this chapter. As most serious students of Spanish guns are quick to caution, identifying and dating Spanish firearms are quite complex and often confusing tasks. A number of circumstances contribute to this difficulty, not the least of which is inconsistent and often overlapping use of gun terminology in documentary accounts. Another is the fact that ignition systems (which provide the most basic functional and chronological clues) overlapped with one another by as much as a century. Behavioral factors in the colonies also pose problems for firearm dating and identification. These factors include the Spaniards' extreme conservatism in their adoption of new weapons technology in the colonies, a practice that led to widespread use of outdated arms, which was further exacerbated by the tradition of frequent repair and makeshift parts replacements on Spanish weapons (Brinkerhoff and Chamberlain 1972:20; Brown 1980:36–38; Lavin 1965:168; Neal 1956:2, 20; Peterson 1956:17–18).

Although the pistol is the quintessential personal firearm, both long arms and pistols are considered together here. After the first pistols (wheel locks) were produced in Germany during the early decades of the sixteenth century, pistol and long-arm ignition systems evolved in the same ways, and the differences between them is primarily one of size. The locks and hardware on pistols is formally similar to but smaller in size than those of muskets or rifles.

Firearms during the Age of Exploration

The earliest firearms in the Americas arrived with Christopher Columbus in the late fifteenth century. Documentary sources indicate that Columbus brought at least 100 *espingardas* and 100 *hacabuches* to La Isabela for use by his infantry (Brown 1980:35–36; Deagan and Cruxent 2002a, 2002b; Karcheski 1990). These are thought to have been simple,

Table 13.1. Bore Diameters of Spanish Military Long Arms

	Inches	Centimeters
Sixteenth-century military matchlock *mosquete*	.80–.90	2.0–2.3
Sixteenth-century matchlock *arquebuce*	.65–.75	1.6–1.9
Miquelet patilla *escopeta*	.60	1.5
Eighteenth-century French-style Flintlock *fusile* and *carabina*	.69	1.75

smooth-bore, muzzle-loading guns, either small, hand cannons or heavy, handheld guns. Solid lead ball shot recovered from the site of La Isabela ranges from 17.5 to 23.0 mm in diameter (.69–.90 caliber) and 27 to 33 g in weight and was probably used in these guns. Caliber as used today and throughout this chapter refers to bore or ball diameter measured in hundredths of an inch (Table 13.1).

A fragment of the breech end of a small, bronze, octagonal *hacabuche* was collected at La Isabela by John Goggin (Fig. 13.1) and identified by Walter Karcheski of the Higgins Armory Museum. Karcheski notes that it is "the breech end of the hand firearm, probably a *hacabuche*. The overall form, the positioning of the touch hole with the pan on the side of the barrel, and the presence of barrel lugs all support a date in the late 15th/early 16th century" (Karcheski, personal communication, April 28, 1992). Karcheski also notes the similarity of the strapwork design on the gun fragment to that found on Hispano-Flemish armor of the late fifteenth century. The barrel of this fragment has been badly distorted by fire and explosion but appears to have been approximately 14 mm (.55 caliber) in inner diameter.

The caliber of the lead ball shot from La Isabela is slightly larger than that from other early Spanish colonial sites, such as the Molasses Reef wreck site in the Bahamas, which is thought to date to the very early sixteenth century (Kieth 1987). The Molasses Reef firearms, identified as *arcabus*-type weapons, had bore diameters of about 14 mm or

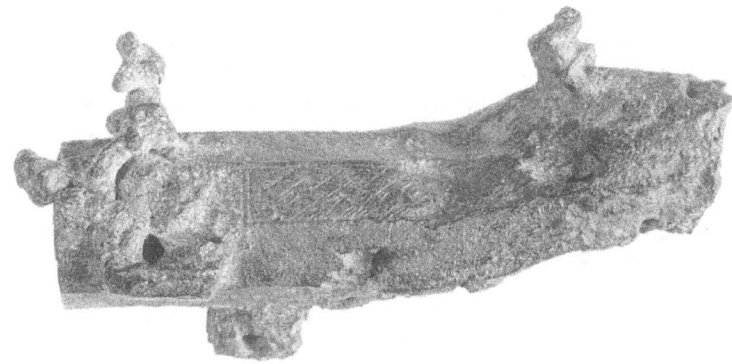

Figure 13.1. Fifteenth-century *hacabuche* barrel fragment. La Isabela (1493–98). Breech end of a bronze *hacabuche*, collected by Emile Boyrie and John Goggin in 1951. Late-fifteenth-century attributes include the touch hole and the pan on the side of the barrel, the barrel lugs, and the strapwork design. FLMNH Collections #93-34-1HTC. Identified by Walter Karcheski, Higgins Armory Museum, and James Lavin, College of William and Mary.

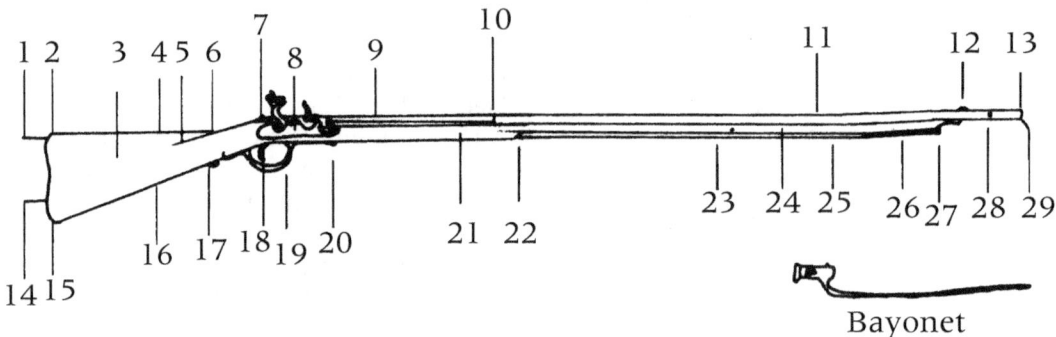

Figure 13.2. Firearm nomenclature. Based on Brown (1980:395).
1. Heel of buttstock
2. Buttplate tang or finial
3. Butt
4. Buttstock comb
5. Buttstock flange
6. Nose of comb
7. Breech plug
8. Gun lock
9. Breech
10. Barrel moulding
11. Barrel
12. Front sight
13. Muzzle
14. Buttplate
15. Toe of buttstock
16. Belly of stock
17. Rear trigger guard tang
18. Trigger
19. Trigger bow
20. Front trigger guard tang
21. Forestock
22. Ramrod guide
23. Rear ramrod thimble
24. Stock (barrel lug) pin
25. Middle ramrod thimble
26. Front ramrod thimble
27. Ramrod
28. Bayonet lug
29. Bore

.55 caliber (Simmons 1987). The terms *hacabuz* and *arcabuce* appear in Spanish records after about 1513 (Karcheski 1990:5) and refer to a handheld, muzzle-loading weapon that probably had a snaphaunce- or matchlock.

Firearms were never as useful as the crossbow in the earliest years of exploration and colonization. Not only were the firearms of the early sixteenth century awkward and difficult to maintain, but they were also subject to malfunction and deteriorated quickly in the tropical climate (during one of Juan Ponce de Leon's early slaving expeditions, for example, all of the firearms were ruined by the humidity) (Karcheski 1990).

Guns were also very expensive. Before 1530, no major gunsmithing industry existed in Spain, and imported German and Italian weapons or obsolete Spanish weapons were used (Lavin 1965:40, 51). It was during the reign of Charles V (1519–56) that a modern gunsmithing industry was developed by Simon and Pedro Marquarte, brought to Spain from Augsberg in 1530 (Neal 1955:1; Lavin 1965:70–71).

The earliest products of the Spanish gun foundries were matchlock, wheel lock, and snaphaunce guns, all of which were gradually replaced by flintlocks after 1600. Not all of the products of the Spanish armories appear to have been commonly used in the Americas, however, where the matchlock and miquelet flintlock muskets were dominant. Figure 13.2 shows the component parts of muskets and their nomenclature.

Matchlocks

The matchlock, the earliest form of firearm ignition, was already in use in Europe at the time of Columbus's first voyage to the Americas. By 1550, matchlocks had outstripped the crossbow as the primary military weapon in the New World. The basic principle of the matchlock mechanism was to bring a lighted "match" into contact with priming powder in the weapon's pan in order to fire the charge inside the gun barrel. Figure 13.3 shows the basic components of the matchlock, which included a lock plate attached to the stock of the gun; a serpentine, which held the lighted match and moved it over the pan; a trigger; and a sear and spring that were attached to both the trigger and the serpentine. The sear and spring operated the serpentine in the early-sixteenth-century matchlocks, and the trigger on these locks was often screwed directly into the sear. These early matchlock triggers were quite similar in appearance to those found on sixteenth-century crossbows (Fig. 13.4) and generally did not have a trigger guard (see Peterson 1956:13–18). They also often had the powder pan attached to the gun barrel (as in Fig. 13.1), while later sixteenth- and seventeenth-century versions had the pan attached to the gun's lock plate.

The matchlock is most often referred to in sixteenth-century accounts as the *"arquebuce"* (harquebus or arquebuss) or *"mosquete"* (musket). These were primarily size distinctions. The *mosquete* was a long military weapon some 1.8 m (6 ft) in length and up to 13.5 kg (30 lb) in weight, with a standard bore of 12 gauge. It had a squared or octagonal breech and took an .80 to .90 caliber ball (Lavin 1965:44; Brown 1980:48). The *mosquete* had the earlier type of sear and spring attached directly to the trigger and required a forked rest from which to be fired (Fig. 13.5).

Although the term *"arquebuce"* was used to refer to a variety of weapons during colonial times, it properly describes a lighter version of the matchlock that could be fired without a rest and was more commonly issued than the *mosquete* (Brown 1980:39–42; Peterson 1956:13–14). Sixteenth-century Spanish harquebuses were commonly 1.4 to 1.5 m (about 4.5 to 5.0 ft) in length and weighed 6 to 8 kg (14 to 18 lb). They used a .65 to .75 caliber ball (Brown 1980:39–42). During the

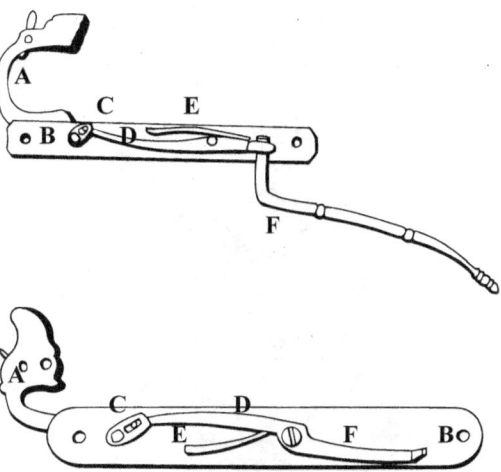

Figure 13.3. Matchlock diagrams. *Top:* Sixteenth-century matchlock with separate lever trigger attached to the sear. *Bottom:* Later matchlock with integral sear trigger. A. Serpentine; B. Lockplate; C. Link; D. Sear; E. Spring; F. Trigger. *Drawing: James Quine after Peterson (1955:13).*

Figure 13.4. Matchlock trigger. Iron. Total length (including curved sections) 16.5 cm. *Nuestra Señora de Atocha.* 1622. FBAR Lab #2019. *Courtesy of the Florida Bureau of Archaeological Research. Drawing: James Quine.*

Figure 13.5. Seventeenth-century musketeer with matchlock. Dutch soldier with matchlock, ca. 1608, showing burning matchcord and gunrest for use while firing. Image first appeared in de Gheyn (1608) and is reproduced from Mora (1804). *Courtesy of the Castillo de San Marcos National Monument, St. Augustine.*

seventeenth century, the term "harquebus" was used by English colonists to describe wheel lock guns (Peterson 1956:14). The term "caliver" was for a short time (ca. 1540–60) synonymous with "harquebus," but gradually by about 1630 "caliver" came to refer to a matchlock weapon between a *mosquete* and *arquebuce* in size (Peterson 1956:13; Brown 1980:86).

The matchlock was the most widely used military weapon in the Spanish Americas until about 1650. During the seventeenth century, it underwent certain alterations, but these occurred at erratic and inconsistent rates; as many students of firearms technology have cautioned, one must use the entire gun to achieve an accurate date (see, for example, Peterson 1956:18). This is obviously not possible for most archaeologists, but some general trends can be identified. Characteristics of matchlocks during the first decades of the seventeenth century include: the attachment of the powder pan to the lock plate rather than to the barrel or stock, as in earlier guns; the use of a modern-appearing trigger rather than the earlier crossbowlike trigger; the addition of a trigger guard; the attachment of the trigger to the sear by means of a catch mechanism rather than by directly screwing it into the sear; the appearance of a more curved, oval lock plate rather than the typically straight-sided rectangle found on earlier matchlocks; and the addition of an iron side plate (Peterson 1956: 14–17, 21–22; Brown 1980:50).

Matchlock firearm parts have only rarely been recovered from Spanish colonial terrestrial sites. One complete example was recovered from a context in St. Augustine dating to the third quarter of the sixteenth century (Fig. 13.6). It has been suggested to be of New World production because of the absence of a thumbscrew on the serpentine (Levy 1977; M. L. Brown, personal communication, 1979). Serpentines, triggers, and a fuse tube from matchlocks have been recovered from Santa Elena, South Carolina (South 1983:24, 1984:58; South, Skowronek, and Johnson 1988:96–100; Fig. 13.7), and in a somewhat later context, 34 matchlock muskets were recovered from the wreck of the *Atocha* (1622) (Matthewson 1986:55).

The matchlock had a number of disadvantages as a military weapon, most obviously the danger of accidental conflagration from the proximity of the burning match and the powder. It was also difficult to protect powder from the elements, and the need to keep the match smoldering at all times had the military handicap of alerting the enemy to the soldiers' positions.

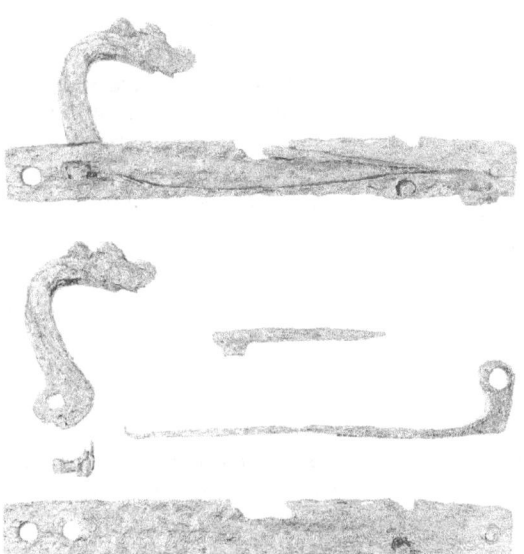

Figure 13.6. St. Augustine matchlock. Iron, ca. 1580. Length of lockplate 16.6 cm. St. Augustine (SA-34-1-21). Top view shows assembled lock; bottom view shows serpentine (top left), sear spring (top right), tumbler and sear linkage (below serpentine), sear lever (center), and lockplate (bottom). The absence of a thumbscrew on the serpentine suggests that this lock may have been made locally. Trinity Episcopal Church Collection, St. Augustine. *Photo: James Quine.*

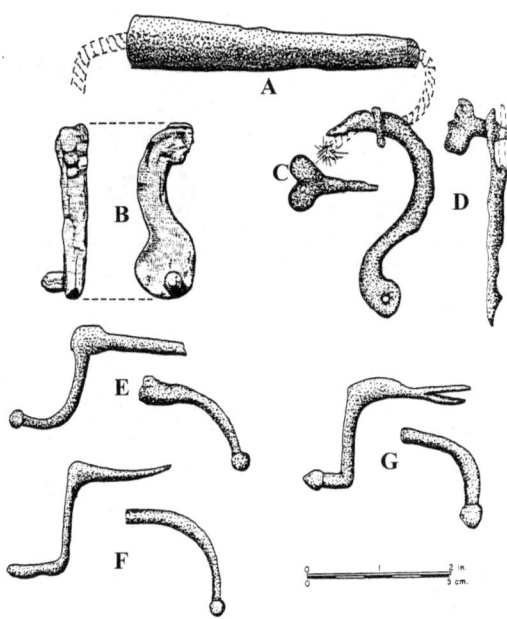

Figure 13.7. Matchlock elements from Santa Elena. All iron, ca. 1566-1587. A. Fuze tube (#38BU162C-171); B. Side and front views of serpentine (#38BU162D-20B); C. Wingnut (#38BU162E-40D); D. Side and edge views of serpentine (#38BU162E-42D); E-G. Side and end views of three matchlock triggers (#s 38BU162D-20B, 38BU162D-6B, 38BU162C-362). From South, Skowronek, and Johnson (1988:Fig. 52). *Courtesy of the South Carolina Institute of Archaeology and Anthropology and Stanley South.*

Other types of more effective locks had been developed in Germany during the first decades of the sixteenth century and were shortly afterward introduced to Spain by the Marquartes (see Neal 1955:1–3; Lavin 1965:51–52; Peterson 1956:21). These new locks forms included the wheel lock (Fig. 13.8) and the snaphaunce lock, which was the predecessor of the flintlock. The complexity of these locks and their greater expense apparently prevented their large-scale adoption by troops in the colonies until after about 1625 (Peterson 1956:21), although it is known both documentarily and archaeologically that wheel locks were in use in the Indies during the sixteenth century (Lavin 1965:47). Several wheel elements from wheel lock guns were found at Puerto Real (1503–78) (see Fig. 13.9). In Spanish Florida, however, matchlocks remained the predominant firearm type in the garrison, and in 1706 they still constituted 38 percent of the weapons listed in the royal armory (Brown 1980:115, 168).

Wheel Locks

The wheel lock was the first major improvement on the matchlock and eliminated the burning match. Figures 13.8–13.10 show the elements of a wheel lock mechanism. The

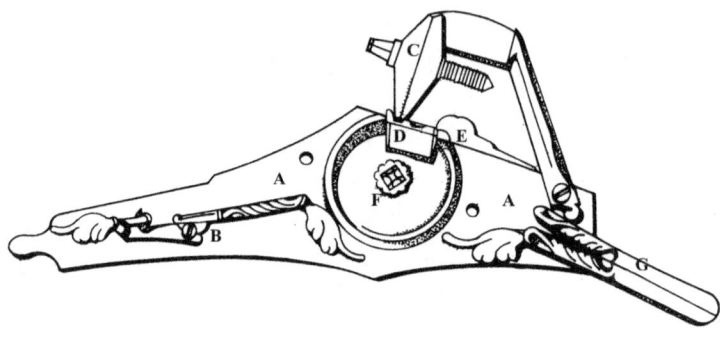

Figure 13.8. Wheel lock diagram. A. Lockplate; B. Safety; C. Doghead; D. Pan; E. Pan cover; F. Wheel housing with shank in center; G. Dog head spring. *Drawing: James Quine after Peterson (1955:17).*

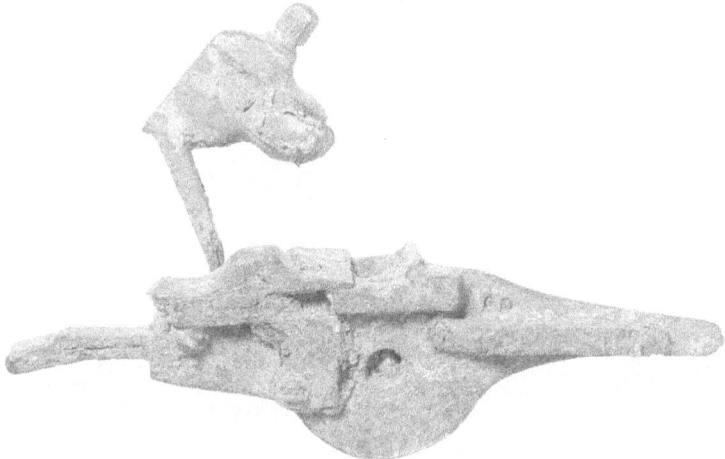

Figure 13.9. Wheel lock. Iron, sixteenth century. Length 17.2 cm. F. E. Williams Collection. *Courtesy of Jack Williams. Photo: James Quine.*

spark to ignite the powder was produced by a revolving metal wheel that struck against a piece of pyrite gripped in a small vise known as a dog head. The dog head intruded into the powder pan from above, while the wheel revolved below. A hole in the bottom of the pan allowed the wheel to intrude into it and come into contact with the pyrite in the dog head, thus producing a spark and igniting the powder in the pan.

On the inside of the lock (the side against the gunstock and opposite the cock), the serrated wheel was attached to a strong, v-shaped mainspring by means of a short chain. Before firing, the wheel was wound with the chain around it and held in place by the sear, which was lodged in the wheel. The trigger was also attached to the sear, and when pressed, it released the sear. This in turn released the mainspring, allowing the wheel to turn and contact the pyrite, showering the powder with sparks. During the process, the pan cover was automatically opened by a special pan-cover release.

The wheel was wound with the chain by means of a small instrument known as a spanner (see Fig. 13.11). These functioned something like a socket wrench, with the spanner's head fitting into the center of the wheel. Complete spanners have been recovered archaeologically from seventeenth-century English colonial sites (see, for example, Peterson 1956:60–61), but very few spanner fragments have come from Spanish colonial sites in the circum-Caribbean area.

Wheel locks are additionally distinguished by the pan set into the lock itself above the wheel housing and by the distinctively

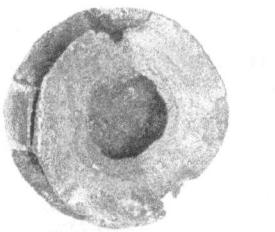 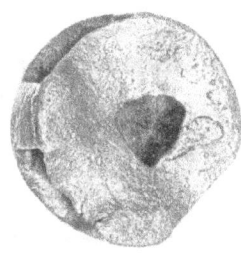

Figure 13.10. Wheel lock pans. Bronze, 2.1 cm. Top diameter 0.6 cm thick. Puerto Real (1503–78). Hodges Collection, Musée de Guahabá, Limbé, Haiti. *Photograph: James Quine.*

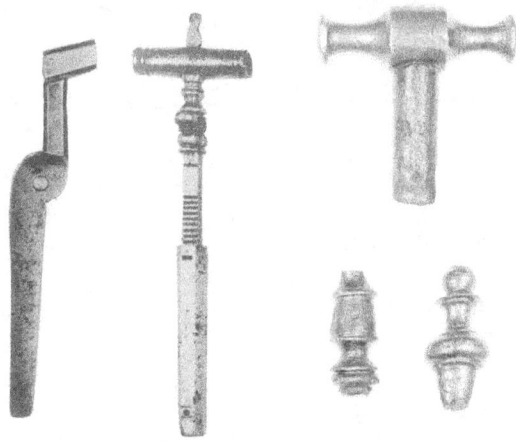

Figure 13.11. Wheel lock spanners. *Left:* Two complete German spanners, sixteenth–seventeenth centuries. *Courtesy of the Tojhosmuseet, Cophenhagen. Reproduced from Brown (1980:55) with permission of Smithsonian Institution Press. Right:* Possible brass spanner fragments found in association with wheel lock pans. Length of hammerlike fragment 5.3 cm, head width 5.2 cm. Puerto Real (1503–78). Hodges Collection, Musée de Guahabá, Limbé, Haiti. *Photograph: James Quine.*

shaped dog head, which was quite unlike the cocks on later flintlocks. Wheel locks also lack a frizzen or battery (a plate against which the flint in the later flintlocks struck to produce a spark).

Wheel locks recovered archaeologically can also be identified by the circular boss on the lock plate that housed the wheel itself (Figs. 13.8–13.10). Circular lock housings have been recovered apart from the locks themselves and appear similar to large bobbin thread holders (Fig. 13.10).

The use of the wheel locks by Spaniards in the New World seems to be restricted to the period of about 1570 to 1625 (see Lavin 1965:47,69; Peterson 1956:24–25, 60; Brown 1980:57). They do not appear to have ever been a dominant form in the Spanish colonies and, when used, were most commonly on pistols. The wheel lock's relative scarcity had to do not only with the competing miquelet locks and matchlocks but also with the fact that wheel locks were more expensive than matchlock guns. In 1593, a matchlock harquebus cost 4 ducats, while a comparable wheel lock cost 15 ducats (Brown 1980:58). Wheel lock guns may have been used more frequently as personal firearms of the elite rather than as military weapons.

The invention of the wheel lock made possible the widespread production and use of pistols. The first wheel lock pistols were produced in Germany during the first decades of the sixteenth century (Brown 1980:56) and in fact gave rise to the first gun control legislation when Maximilian decreed a ban on wheel lock pistols in 1517 in response to increased pistol-related deaths (Brown 1980:56). Charles V armed German cavalry soldiers with wheel lock pistols known as dags in 1544 (see Brown 1980:57), although these were apparently not common in the Spanish colonies.

Snaphaunce Locks, Doglocks, and Flintlocks

The snaphaunce lock, as it is referred to today, was the precursor of the later flintlock and does not appear to have been widely used in the Spanish colonies. It is thought to have been developed in Germany or the Low Countries some time around the middle of the sixteenth century (Brown 1980:68–69) and was the first of the locks to operate on the principle of striking a piece of flint against a steel face to produce a spark. In the snaphaunce lock, this was accomplished by a flint held in a vise at the end of a roughly s-shaped arm, known as the cock (Fig. 13.12). Opposite the cock on the top of the lock plate was a trough-shaped pan with rounded ends for powder. A heavy, v-shaped mainspring, sear, and tumbler on the inside of the lock (that is, the reverse side of the lock from the side with the cock attached) supplied the power to activate the firing process. When the cock was drawn back, the spring was compressed. It was released by pulling the trigger, which was attached by the sear to the cock, and propelled the cock forward to strike the battery to produce sparks that fell into the pan below.

Distinctive features of the snaphaunce lock include its uniquely shaped, armlike battery, which was separate from the pan cover. The trough-shaped pan perpendicular to the lock and with rounded ends is also unique (Fig. 13.12). Examples of snaphaunce locks have been excavated at Williamsburg (Noel Hume 1980:213), Jamestown (Cotter and Hudson 1957), and New York (Peterson 1956:27). None have been reported from Spanish colonial sites.

Improvements on the snaphaunce lock by 1620 led to the seventeenth-century flintlock variation known as a doglock and, later, the English flintlock. The doglock (Fig. 13.12) is distinguished by the combination of the pan cover and battery into a single piece, coupled with a safety latch anchored behind the bottom of the cock. This safety latch was known as a dog and gave its name to the lock itself. Doglocks were primarily used by the English between about 1625 and 1670 (see Peterson 1956:28–32; Noel Hume 1980:213).

Without the dog safety latch, such locks combining the pan cover and battery were known as half-cockable flintlocks or English flintlocks. They were developed during the first decades of the seventeenth century but were not commonly used by English soldiers until after about 1675 (Noel Hume

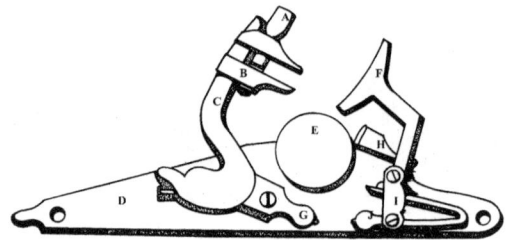

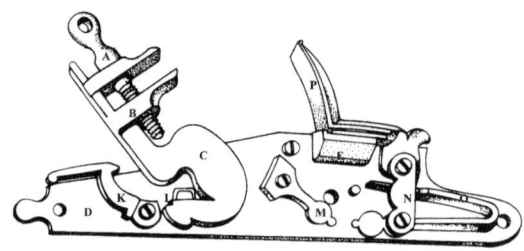

Figure 13.12. Snaphaunce and doglock exteriors. A. Cock jaw screw; B. Cock jaws; C. Cock; D. Lockplate; E. Priming pan; F. Battery; G. Buffer; H. Pan cover; I. Bridle; J. Spring; K. Dog; L. Sear lug; M. Buffer; N. Bridle; O. Frizzen spring; P. Frizzen. *Drawing by James Quine after Peterson (1955: 23).*

1980:213). They are distinguished from the doglock by the absence of the extended dog safety latch and the presence of a notched tumbler that held the cock in a "half-cocked" position. The tumbler was attached to the inside base of the cock and was operated by a sear. Locks of this kind—which included many variations—were used by the English army until the nineteenth century and are frequently found on Spanish sites of the eighteenth century.

Miquelet Locks

The relative rarity of snaphaunce, doglock, and wheel lock firearms on Spanish sites of the seventeenth century is probably related to the late-sixteenth-century development of the miquelet lock in Spain. Attributed to Simon Marquarte II, this sturdy, flint-using lock remained essentially the same until it was replaced by percussion weapons in the nineteenth century (Neal 1955:6). It was the official military firearm in the colonies until 1728, when the French lock (discussed later) was adopted (Brinkerhoff and Chamberlain 1972:29). It replaced both the wheel lock and matchlock in Spain and was in use during the same periods as the snaphaunce, doglock, and flintlock guns in the English colonies.

Certain distinctive characteristics set the miquelet apart from the other flint-using locks. The primary difference is the location of the heavy, v-shaped mainspring on the exterior of the lock plate (that is, the same side on which the cock is mounted) rather than on the interior as in other flintlocks (Figs. 13.13–3.15). This allowed a more massive spring and powerful action than provided by an interior spring mechanism. One end of the mainspring bore directly upon a projection at the base of the cock. Pulling the trigger would cause a horizontal movement of the spring to achieve an upward pressure against the rear of the cock, throwing it (and the flint held in its jaws) forward onto the battery to produce sparks.

Miquelet locks also had an L-shaped frizzen, combining a deeply ridged battery face and pan cover in one piece (Fig. 13.15). While this feature is also found on most post-snaphaunce flintlocks, its occurrence in combination with the exterior, upwardly moving mainspring identifies the miquelet.

The face of the miquelet battery was ridged. Before 1650, a separate raised and ridged face was attached to the battery, coming within 3 mm of either side of the battery itself. After 1650, the ridges extended to the outer edges of the battery. Furthermore, securing pins known as *fieles* were used prior to 1660 on Spanish miquelets (Lavin 1965:164). These were small, metal pins inserted vertically through the top of the lock plate into the screws that secured the frizzen to the lock plate (Fig. 13.13).

A ring-type cockscrew was the most com-

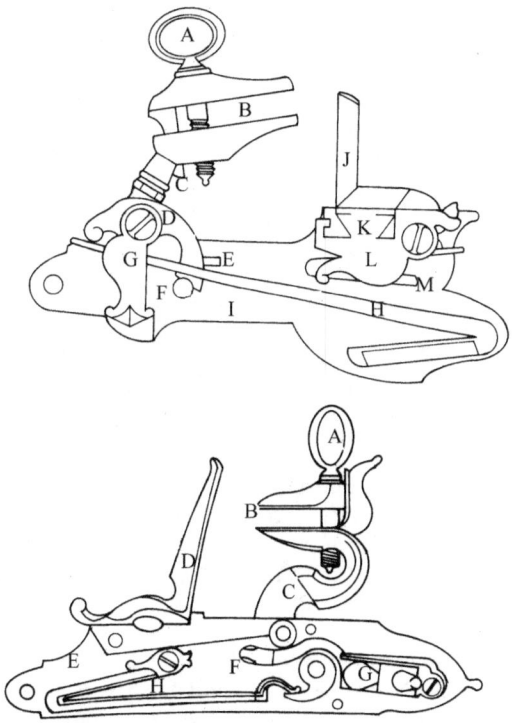

Figure 13.13. Miquelet *a la patilla* and *a la moda* locks. *Top: A la patilla* lock. A. Cock jaw ring screw; B. Jaws; C. Cock; D. Cock foot (*patilla*); E. Full cock sear; F. Bolt for half cock sear; G. Cockscrew bridle; H. Mainspring; I. Lockplate; J. Battery or frizzen with ridged face; K. Pan; L. Battery screw bridle; M. Battery spring. *Bottom: A la moda* lock. A. Cock jaw ring screw; B. Jaws; C. Cock; D. Battery; E. Lockplate; F. Half cock sear (expanded); G. Full cock sear (expanded); H. Mainspring. *Drawing by James Quine after Lavin (1965:171, 183).*

mon form on miquelets and helps to distinguish them from other kinds of flintlocks. The ring allowed quick adjustment of the flint as well as a thumb brace for cocking the gun, which was a useful feature with the heavy miquelet mainspring. The jaws of miquelet cocks were typically squared off at the ends, and the lock plate itself was typically "wasp-waisted," that is, thinner in the center. During the seventeenth century, the jaws of the Spanish flintlock cock were at an obtuse angle to the base of the lock, but after about 1750

Figure 13.14. Miquelet gunlock exterior. Miquelet lock from a wall gun recovered from the St. Marks River, Florida. Length 15 cm. F. E. Williams Collection. *Courtesy of Jack Williams. Photo: James Quine.*

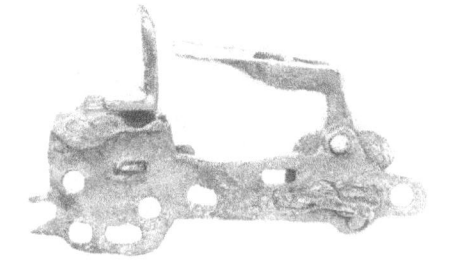

Figure 13.15. Miquelet locks. *Top:* Pre-1704. Length 12.3 cm. 8JE1 (Aspalaga Landing Spanish mission site). Florida Bureau of Archaeological Research. *Center and bottom:* Front and back of a small miquelet lock. Maximum lockplate length 10.6 cm. St. Augustine, ca. 1740 (SA-36-4-F13). FLMNH/CSA Collections. *Photos: James Quine.*

the jaws assumed a position of a right angle to the lock (Neal 1955:27; Lavin 1965:166).

The miquelet lock provided a very powerful and reliable ignition system owing to its general sturdiness, the massive external mainspring, the serrated battery face, and the relatively stronger stock permitted by the external nature of the mainspring (thus eliminating the necessity of removing wood from the stock to house an internal mainspring). Some have suggested that the evolution of this system was at least partly in response to the poor quality of flint found in Spain (Lavin 1965:168; Neal 1955:10).

The miquelet characteristics discussed earlier describe the *patilla* type miquelet lock, which was the most widespread and popular miquelet lock between about 1600 and 1825 (Lavin 1965:169; Neal 1955:3–6). This lock was typically 12.0 to 16.5 cm long and 3.0 to 3.5 cm wide (Fig. 13.13; Brown 1980:173). The *patilla* lock was used on the popular *escopeta,* or light musket, issued to foot and mounted troops between about 1630 and 1728. The *escopeta* used a .60 caliber ball (Brown 1980:172; Brinkerhoff and Chamberlain 1972:20).

Other varieties of the miquelet lock were also present in Europe during this time, including the *agujeta* lock (with two sears, a downward motion on the cock by the mainspring, and a dog safety latch); the *invención,* or *la Romana,* lock (with a separate v-shaped battery spring mounted above the main-

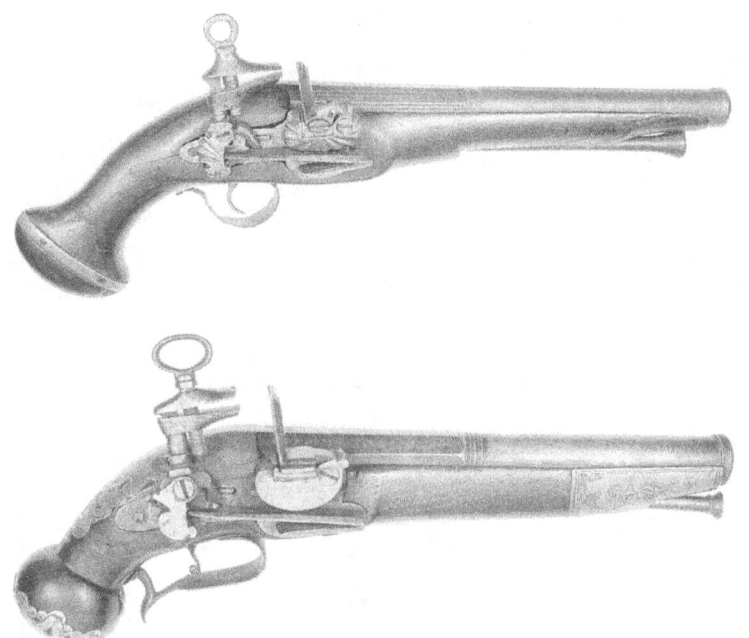

Figure 13.16. Ripoll miquelet pistols. *Top:* Dated 1661. Shell-shaped battery; ovoid pommel; wood butt. Barrel length 25.5 cm. Marked: "AR MAN GUER." *Bottom:* First half of the eighteenth century. Brass ball-shaped pommel, metal ramrod, curved trigger guard. Length of barrel 26 m. Marked: "MA." F. E. Williams Collection. *Courtesy of Jack Williams. Photos: James Quine.*

spring in front of the battery); and the *a la moda* miquelet lock, which was modeled on the French flintlock and adopted for Spanish military use in 1728 (Fig. 13.13; Lavin 1965:170–182; Neal 1955:52–54). The *patilla* lock, however, is of primary interest to students of the Spanish colonial era and dominated the New World firearm assemblage until the adoption of the French lock after 1728.

Ripoll Miquelet Pistols

The town of Ripoll, located north of Barcelona, was a renowned center of gun making during the seventeenth and eighteenth centuries (see Neal 1955:33–40). It was particularly well known for its miquelet lock pistols, which had a distinctive style unique among Spanish pistols of the period (Fig. 13.16). They featured a very short stock ending in a ball-shaped pommel butt and were usually from 25.0 to 35.5 cm in overall length (Neal 1955:36). During the seventeenth century, the pommel butt tended to be ovoid rather than ball shaped, but by the eighteenth century nearly all known examples had a ball-shaped pommel. The wood of the stock is usually inlaid with brass, iron, or silver designs of scrolls and arabesques. The trigger guard on Ripoll pistols was also distinctive in its pronounced spur, which supported a second finger to allow a firmer grip on the weapon when firing (Fig. 13.16, bottom). The barrels of these pistols were fluted or faceted at the breech end and plain toward the muzzle, and the locks (which varied considerably in form to fit particular guns) were generally signed by the maker.

One of the most distinctive traits of the Ripoll locks is the pattern engraved or cut on the inside of the jaws of the cock (which held the leather-covered flint). Unlike the cock jaws of other Spanish locks, which were simply roughened or filed to give better purchase on the flint, those of Ripoll were cut with symmetrical, geometric linear designs.

A very popular weapon in the Spanish colonies during the eighteenth century was the *trabuco,* or carbine-blunderbuss. This gun had a flared, usually brass barrel that fired

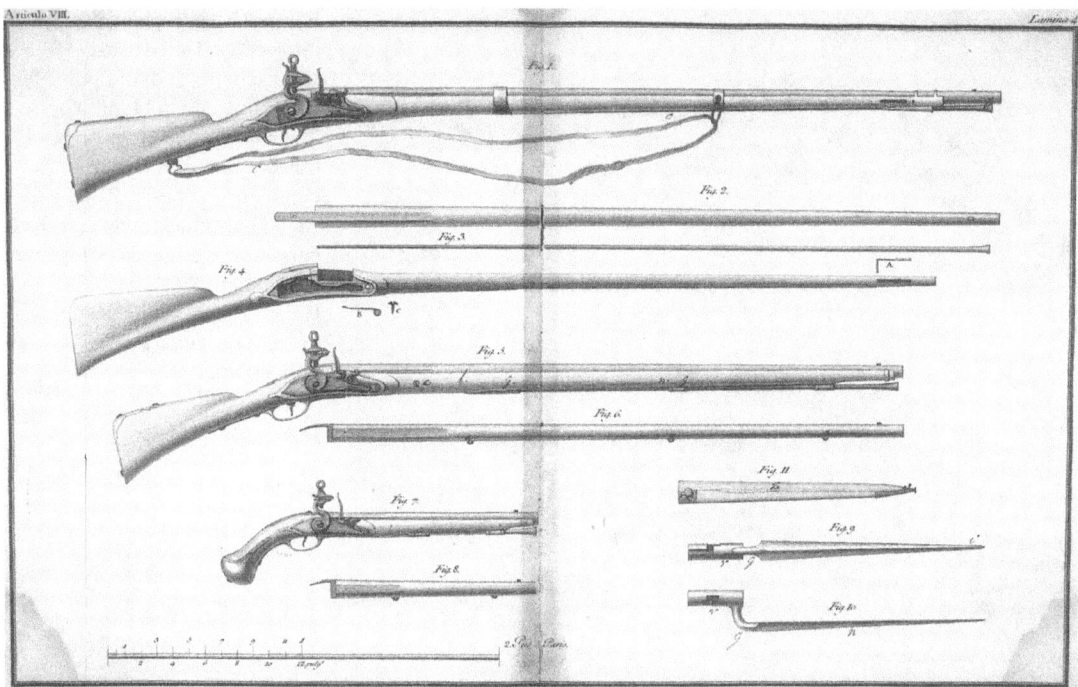

Figure 13.17. Spanish military-issue firearms, 1752. Figure 1: 1752 fusil musket; Figure 2: Musket barrel (top); Figure 3: Iron ramrod; Figure 4: Musket stock with barrel band retaining spring; Figure 5: 1752 *carabina* musket; Figure 6: *Carabina* barrel; Figure 7: Cavalry *pistola;* Figure 8: Pistol barrel; Figure 9: Socket bayonet, top view; Figure 10: Socket bayonet, side view; Figure 11: Bayonet scabbard. From Mora (1804), Articulo 8, Lamina 4. *Courtesy of the Castillo de San Marcos National Monument.*

scattering shot in the manner of a blunderbuss. It weighed about 2.8 kg (6 lb) and was about 1.2 m (38 in) long, with a barrel of about 58.0 cm (23 in), flaring at the muzzle to a diameter of from 3.0 to 3.8 cm (1.25 to 1.50 in). The *trabuco* was mounted with a *patilla* miquelet lock, typically measuring 14 by 3 cm (5.75 by 1.25 in). The best known were made in Ripoll and featured elaborate brass inlay on the stock in the form of animals and plants (Brinkerhoff and Chamberlain 1972:44; Brown 1980:171).

Flintlocks

The fusil, a light flintlock musket, was first adopted by the Spanish military in 1703, although it did not become standard issue to Spanish troops until after 1728 (Brown 1980:166). The fusil weighed about 4 kg (9 lb), used a .69 caliber ball, and was carried by officers or noncommissioned officers (Brown 1980:40, 168; Fig. 13.17). It originally used a modified miquelet lock but after 1728 adopted the French lock. It has been suggested that very early fusils may have marked the transition between matchlocks and flintlocks and that the *fusiles de mecha* noted in the Florida colony in 1706 may have, in fact, had dual match and flint ignition systems (Brown 1980:168). A flintlock carbine (*carabina*) was also introduced in 1730 that was lighter than the fusil, weighing about 3 kg (6.5 lb), but used the same .69 caliber ball (Brown 1980:131; Fig. 13.17).

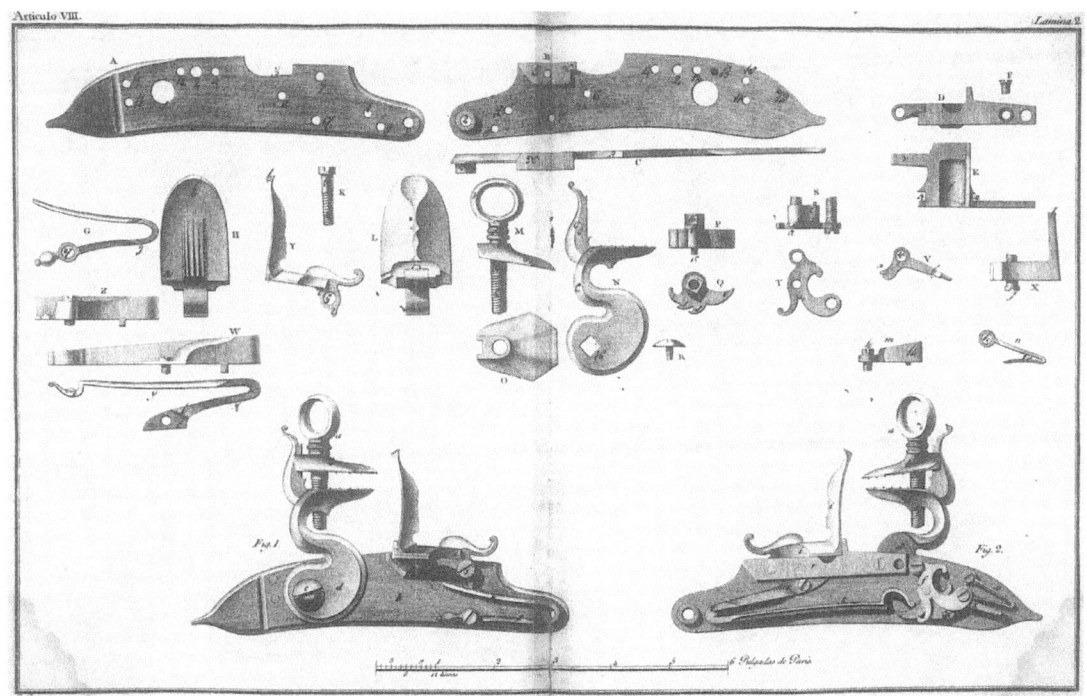

Figure 13.18. Lock components of the 1752 *a la francesa* lock. Figure 1: Assembled lock, exterior; Figure 2: assembled lock, interior. A. Lockplate (*plantilla*) exterior; B. Lockplate interior; C. Lockplate (*canto*), top view; D. Priming pan (*cazoleta*) interior; E. Priming pan, top view; F. Priming pan screw; G. Steel spring (*muelle de rastrillo*); H. Steel (*rastrillo*); K. Steel screw; L. Steel, rear view; M. Cock jaw screw (*tornillo pedrero*); N. Cock (*gatillo*); O. Lower cock jaw; P. Tumbler (*nuez*), top view; Q. Tumbler, side view; R. Cock screw; S. Sear bridle (*brida*), top view; T. Sear bridle, side view; V. Sear (*calzo*); W. Mainspring (*muelle grande*); X. Sear, top view; Y. Steel, side view; (m) Sear spring (*muelle de fiador*), top view; (n) Sear spring, side view. From Mora (1804), Articulo 8, Lamina 2. *Courtesy of the Castillo de San Marcos National Monument.*

The French, or "a la Francesa," Lock

The ascension of Philip V (1700–46), the first Bourbon king of Spain, brought French influence to many aspects of Spanish life, including weaponry technology. In 1728, a standard .69 caliber, French-type flintlock was introduced and adopted by the military, and in 1752 it was made regulation for Spanish soldiers (Brinkerhoff and Chamberlain 1972:28; Brown 1980:170–171; Lavin 1965:183). Unlike the miquelet lock, the *a la francesa* lock had an inner mainspring and a smooth battery face. They were used in fusil muskets. After 1730, the smaller carbine musket (*carabina*) and carbine pistol (*pistola*) were introduced and were carried by mounted troops (Brown 1980:170–171; Fig. 13.17). Details of these guns are shown in Figures 13.17–13.19. After 1755, Spanish military guns carried an iron ramrod, fitted to the gun barrel by a metal guide tube (thimble) and band (Fig. 13.19). Before that time, they had wooden ramrods, fitted with a ramrod tip.

The hardware for these weapons was also distinctive, including side plates for muskets and pistols, trigger plates and guards, ramrod carriers, and other fastenings (Fig. 13.19). A number of these elements have been recovered archaeologically from eighteenth-century domestic sites in St. Augustine (Fig. 13.20).

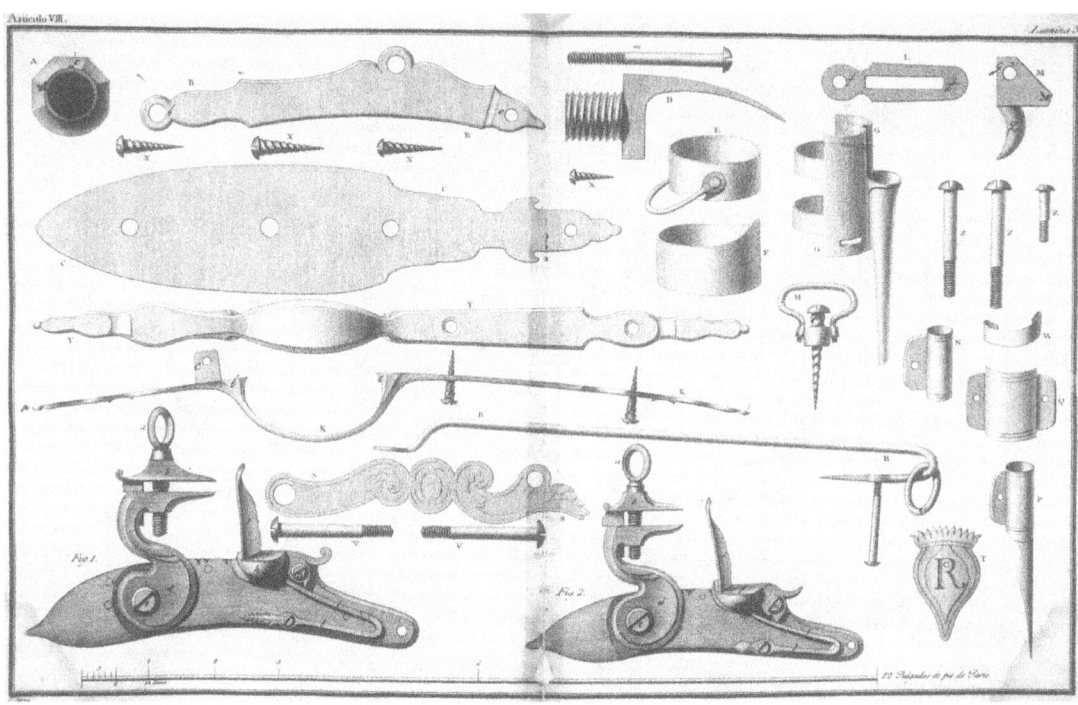

Figure 13.19. Hardware on 1752 issue Spanish firearms. Figure 1: 1752 musket lock, exterior; Figure 2: 1752 pistol lock, exterior. A. Barrel, front view with sighting stud; B. Musket sideplate (*escudo*); C. Musket buttplate (*cantonero*) with heel finial; D. Breech plug with tang (*tornillo de recámara*); E. Midbarrel band (*abrazadera del medio*) with ring sling swivel; F. Lower barrel band (*abrazadera del inferior*); G. Ramrod guide with upper barrel band (*abrazadero superior*), front view; H. Rear sling swivel (*sortija del parta fusil*); K. Trigger guard with screws (*guardamonte*); L. Trigger plate (*planchuela del disparador*); M. Trigger (*disparador o gatillo*); N. Ramrod thimble (*casquillos por donde pasa la banqueta*); P. Rear ramrod guide; Q. Pistol fore-end cap; R. Carbine slide bar with ring (*gancho de la carabina*); S. Pistol sideplate (*escudo de la carabina*); T. Thumbplate (*Escudo superior de pistoles y carabina*); V. Lockplate screws; W. Pistol barrel fore-end band (*chapa*); X. Buttplate screws; Y. Trigger guard, bottom view; Z. Lockplate screws for musket (*tornillos pasadores*) (m) Breech plug tang screw. From Mora (1804), Articulo 8, Lamina 3. *Courtesy of the Castillo de San Marcos National Monument.*

According to the 1728 ordinance that introduced the French lock, all weapons produced for the crown were to be marked (although this mandate was not always observed). These marks were frequently on the lock plate behind the cock, consisting of a letter designating the armory in which it was made and a crown or fleur-de-lis over it denoting royal ownership (Brown 1980:173; Brinkerhoff and Chamberlain 1972:30). After 1750, a proof mark, usually the letters "EX," appeared on the gun's barrel or lock. Guns with these marks were probably not personal firearms.

Although the French lock was standard military issue, sporting and personal guns did not necessarily conform to military standards. Spanish miquelet locks continued in use through the eighteenth century (Neal 1955:16), along with English, French, and German firearms. English, French, and northern European flintlocks had their mainsprings on the inside of the lock plate (that is, the side opposite that on which the cock is mounted) and usually had a grooved, solid-head cock jaw screw (Fig. 13.21). Figures 13.21–13.23 show the component elements of some northern European and French flintlocks.

The international character of Spanish gun use in the eighteenth century is reflected in the pieces recovered from shipwrecks. Figure 13.24, for example, shows English, French, and German pistol components recovered from the 1733 wreck of the Spanish *San José de las Animas*, and similar examples also occur on contemporary terrestrial sites in St. Augustine. A pair of 1710 English "Queen Anne" pistols of this sort, with faces cast on the butt plates, are shown in Figure 13.25. Sources useful for the study, identification, and dating of colonial era non-Spanish European firearms include, among many others, Blackmore (1962), Brown (1980), Hamilton (1968), Noel Hume (1970), Peterson (1956), and Russell (1959).

In 1791, the miquelet lock was reintroduced to replace the French lock of the 1728–91 period, which had proven too fragile for military use (Brinkerhoff and Chamberlain 1972:31). The 1791 miquelet had the characteristic external mainspring, a heavier and less wasp-waisted lock plate, and a distinctive cock design. It retained all of the brass furniture, ramrod, sling swivels, barrel, and stock of the 1752 French flintlock model (Brinkerhoff and Chamberlain 1972:31).

Spanish New World firearms of the nine-

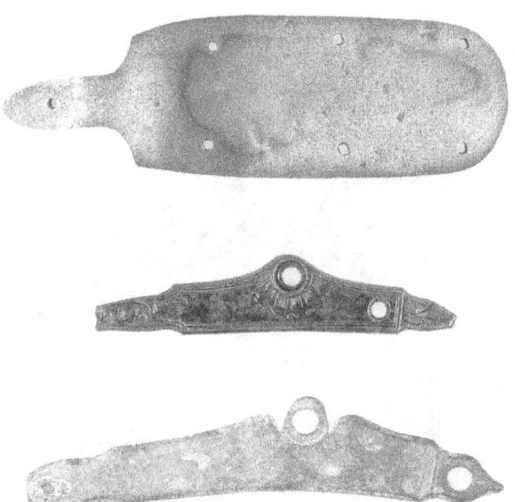

Figure 13.20. Spanish gun hardware, eighteenth century. *Top:* Musket buttplate, brass, ca. 1740. Length of buttplate 13.8 cm. Length of tang 3.6 cm. St. Augustine (SA-36-4-F8). *Center:* Musket sideplate, brass, ca. 1728–52. Length 12.2 cm. St. Augustine (SA-7-5-19). FLMNH/CSA Collections. *Bottom:* Musket sideplate, brass, ca. 1690–1740 (Peterson 1956:58). Length, 15.2 cm. Castillo de San Marcos Collections, #1675.

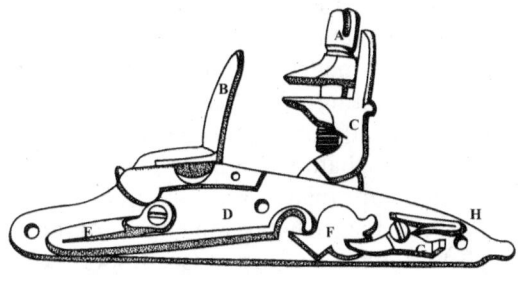

Figure 13.21. Northern European flintlock. Dutch or English type, late seventeenth century. Interior view. A. Cockjaw screw; B. Frizzen; C. Cock; D. Lockplate; E. Mainspring; F. Tumbler; G. Sear; H. Sear spring. *Drawing by James Quine after Peterson (1956:32).*

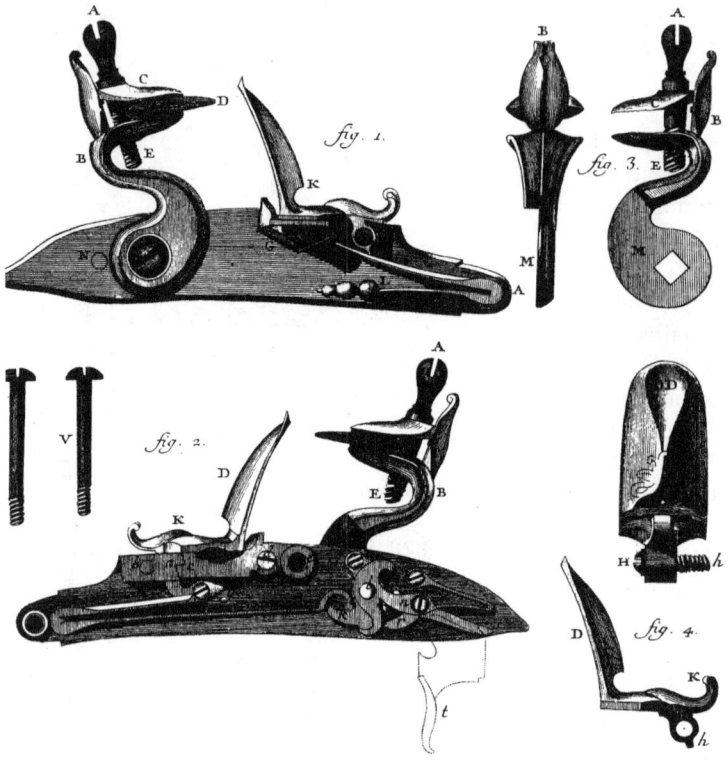

Figure 13.22. French flintlock, ca. 1750. *"Arquebusier."* Figure 1: Assembled lock, exterior; Figure 2: Assembled lock, exterior; Figure 3: Cock; Figure 4: Battery or frizzen. Plate 5, Part 1, Diderot, *L'Encyclopédie* (Diderot 1751–65). *Courtesy of the University of Florida Smathers Library, Special Collections Department.*

teenth century are characterized by wide variety and frequent change. After 1803, a new *a la moda* lock model was introduced to the military, featuring a flat, heavy cock with an exposed sear (Brinkerhoff and Chamberlain 1972:36). The hardware on the post-1803 regulation guns (plates, ramrods, inlay, and so forth) increasingly resembled that of the English Brown Bess musket (see Noel Hume 1980:216; Peterson 1956:165; Neumann and Kravic 1975:208–211).

Between 1802 and 1815, the Spanish military also used a variety of experimental miquelet and *a la moda* lock forms in addition to those described previously (Brinkerhoff and Chamberlain 1972:36). In 1815, they returned to a variation of the French lock of 1752. This new French-style lock had a reinforced cock and new hardware design, and it continued in use until the introduction of percussion firearms in the 1830s.

Firearm Accessories

Effective use of guns required the use of a number of accessories related to ammunition, firing, and maintenance, and many of these are represented archaeologically. Ammunition was obviously of primary importance and throughout the colonial period was in the form of lead balls or shot. Most colonial military firearms used single balls loaded into the muzzle along with powder and wadding.

Spain was one of the first countries to standardize the caliber (bore diameter) of its military musket, which was established at between .80 and .90 by 1535. This was not the case for guns produced outside of Spain or for hunting and personal weapons in Spain (Brown 1980:49, 51). Units of measurement varied from country to county and from region to region, and a gun's caliber was ex-

Personal Firearms

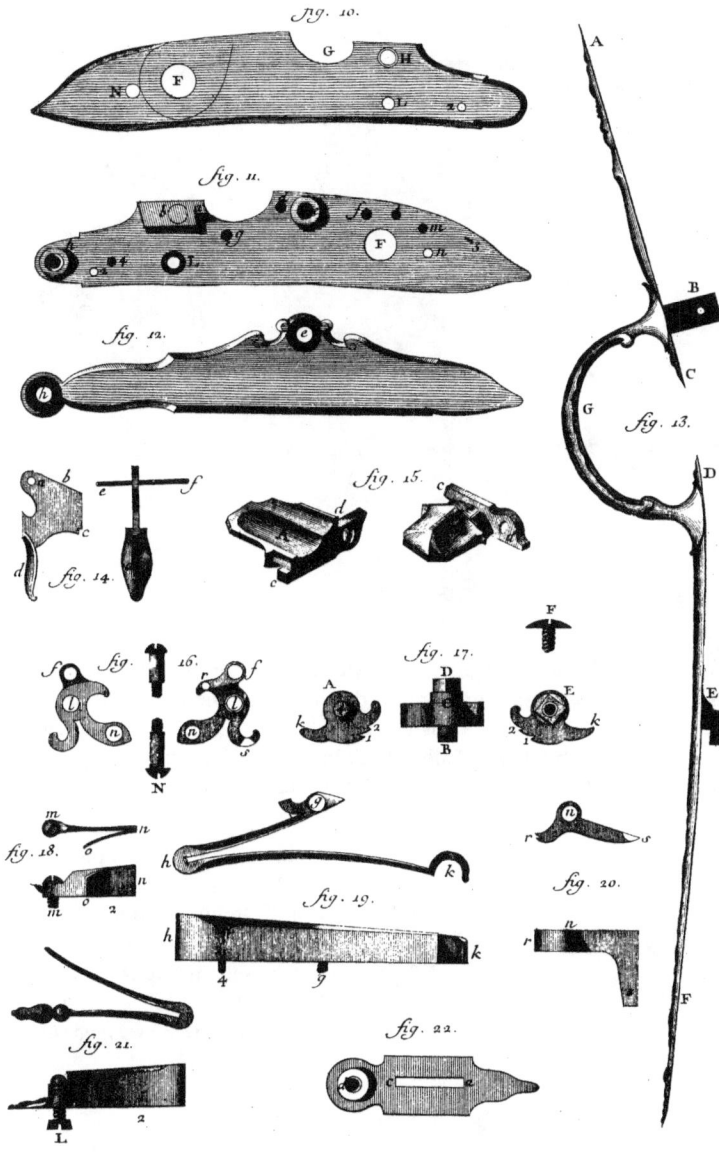

Figure 13.23. French flintlock components, ca. 1750. *"Arquebusier."* Figure 10: Exterior lockplate; Figure 11: Interior lockplate; Figure 12: Sideplate or counterplate; Figure 13: Trigger guard with finials (A, F) and lugs (B, D); Figure 14: Trigger; Figure 15: Priming pan; Figure 16: Tumbler bridle and bridle screws; Figure 17: Tumbler; Figure 18: Sear spring; Figure 19: Mainspring, top and side views; Figure 20: Sear; Figure 21: Battery spring, top and side views; Figure 22: Trigger guard. Plate 224, Volume 6, Diderot, *L'Encyclopédie* (Diderot 1751–65). *Courtesy of the University of Florida Smathers Library, Special Collections Department.*

pressed in the units of measurement used in the place of manufacture.

Although military guns were made to reasonably consistent specifications, the size of the shot they used varied considerably (Fig. 13.26). The shot had to be of a slightly smaller caliber than the barrel bore to allow it to move through the barrel and to take black powder residue on the inside of the barrel into account. The powder, ball, and a wad of paper were shoved into the barrel with a ramrod (see Peterson 1956:16).

The reason for a shot also influenced the size of the ball that was used. For accuracy and deadly force, a ball just slightly smaller than the barrel bore would be ideal, to allow for free movement and a tight fit. For hunting, however, the type of prey might determine the shot size. Greater numbers of small scatter shot would be more effective to hunt

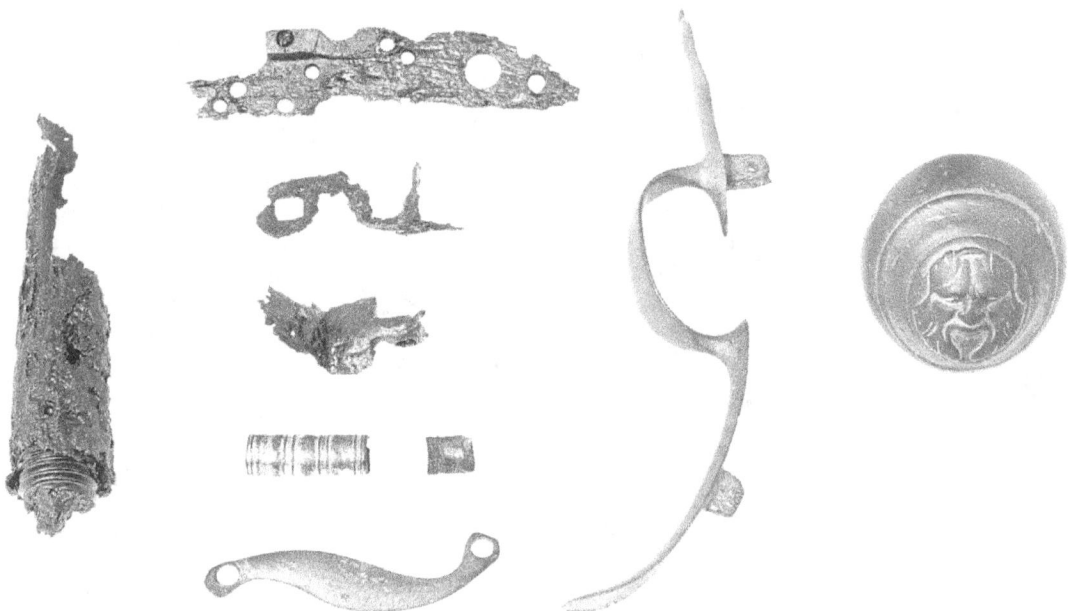

Figure 13.24. Flintlock pistol elements, 1733. Left Barrel fragment, length 11.0 cm. *Top to bottom, center left:* Lockplate, probably English, length 8.4 cm; cock fragment; brass ramrod thimble fragments, length of longer fragment 2.7 cm (FBAR Lab #2045); brass sideplate, English or French, length 7.3 cm (FBAR Lab #2959). *Center right:* Trigger guard (part of FBAR Lab #0540). *Right:* Silver buttplate, German (part of FBAR Lab #0540), 5.5 cm by 2.2 cm. 8MO101. Florida Bureau of Archaeological Research. *Photo: James Quine.*

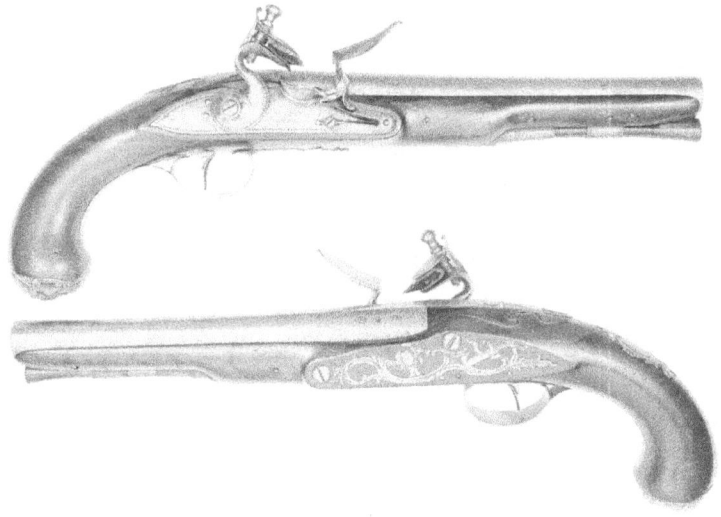

Figure 13.25. English pistols, 1710. Pair of Queen Anne pistols, English, dated 1710. Buttplate has face motif similar to that seen in Figure 13.24. F. E. Williams Collection. *Courtesy of Jack Williams. Photo: James Quine.*

Personal Firearms

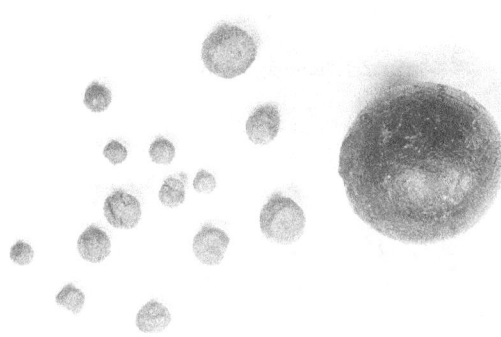

Figure 13.26. Lead shot and ball. Shot diameters range from .25 cm to 2.0 cm. Second half of the sixteenth century, 8SJ31 (Fountain of Youth Park site), St. Augustine. FLMNH Collections. *Photo: University of Florida Office of Instructional Resources.*

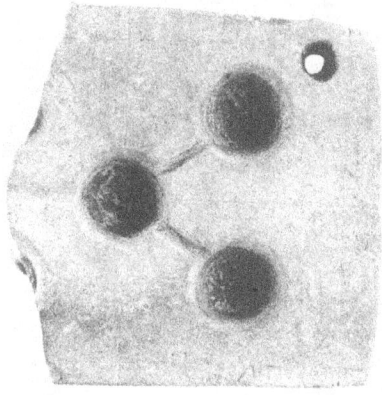

Figure 13.27. Stone shot mold, La Isabela, 1493–98, 5.5 cm by 5.6 cm. For multiple shot of 16 mm diameter each. Parque Nacional de La Isabela, Dominican Republic.

birds than the larger shot used to hunt deer, for example.

Single-shot balls were usually cast in molds, which have been recovered from both military and domestic contexts in Spanish colonial sites. The earliest molds are from La Isabela in the Dominican Republic (1493–98) and are two-piece stone molds that produced balls ranging from 13 to 45 mm in diameter (Fig. 13.27). Three iron molds for making a single shot of approximately 75 mm in diameter were recovered at sixteenth-century Santa Elena, South Carolina, by Stanley South (South, Skowronek, and Johnson 1988:94–95; Fig. 13.28). Although the molds were for single balls, the lead sprue (strips of surplus lead used in casting) indicates that multiple shot molds were also present at the site (South, Skowronek, and Johnson 1988:88; Fig. 13.29). A late-sixteenth-century brass shot mold used to produce four balls each of shot of 6 mm and 8 mm balls was recovered in St. Augustine and is shown in Figure 13.30.

Shot at Santa Elena ranged from 3.15 mm (.14 caliber) to 20 mm. Two modes of frequency in size occurred of 6 to 8 mm and 12 to 14 mm (Carl Steen in South, Skowronek, and Johnson 1988:87). Shot found in sixteenth-century contexts at the contemporary

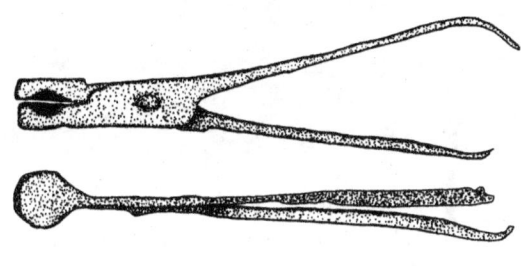

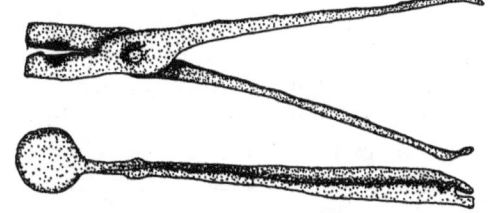

Figure 13.28. Sixteenth-century shot molds for single lead balls. Iron, Santa Elena, South Carolina (1566–87). Length of upper mold 13.3 cm. #s 38BU162-74 and 38BU162C-144B. South, Skowronek, and Johnson (1988:Fig. 49). *Courtesy of the South Carolina Institute of Archaeology and Anthropology and Stanley South.*

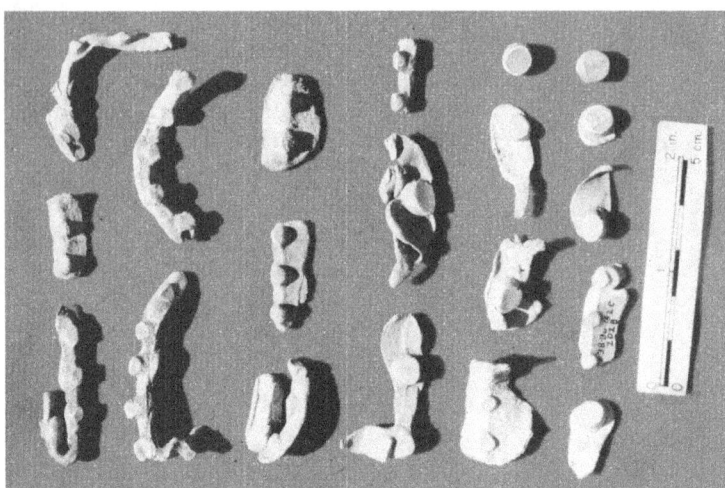

Figure 13.29. Lead sprue from multiple shot molds. Sprue sow and sprue from gang mold. Santa Elena, South Carolina (1566–87). #38BU162, various proveniences. South, Skowronek, and Johnson (1988:Fig. 43). *Courtesy of the South Carolina Institute of Archaeology and Anthropology and Stanley South.*

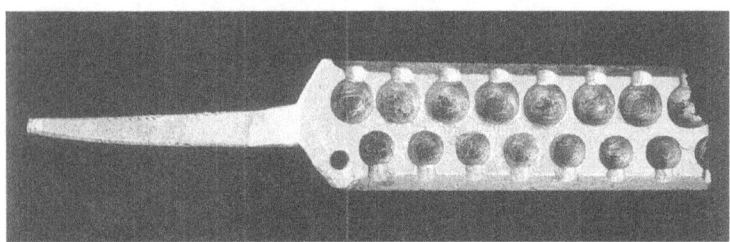

Figure 13.30. Multiple shot mold. Brass, late sixteenth century. For multiple shot of 6 mm diameter and 8 mm diameter. Maximum length 12.3 cm. St. Augustine (SA-23-137). FLMNH/CSA Collections. *Photo: James Quine.*

Spanish site of the Fountain of Youth Park, thought to be the first Spanish campsite in St. Augustine (ca. 1565), ranged from 2 to 39 mm. Eighty-five percent of the shot measured between 10 and 15 mm, which is close to the second size mode noted at Santa Elena. Nearly all of those in the 2 to 5 mm size category were recovered from 15 mm (1/16 in) screen samples and soil flotation samples. These small shots were used in multiples to produce scatter shot in the manner of a shotgun.

Before about 1550, most shot was cast. After that time, shot was either rolled from rough lead wire in a shot roller or, more typically, mass produced using a trencher or shot colander (Fig. 13.31; Brown 1980:63–64). This latter technique involved pouring molten led through a sieve with holes of the desired shot size and allowing the lead drops to fall into cold water, where they hardened into roughly spherical shot (see Brown 1980:64–65 for a seventeenth-century description of this method of shot production).

This process for making shot was used until the mid-eighteenth century, when the shot tower was invented in England (Brown 1980:193). These were tall towers with the melting furnace for lead and the perforated trenchers at the top and vats of water at the base. After the molten lead was poured through the perforated trencher, the long fall produced a nearly perfect spherical shape before the shot fell into the water and hardened. Huge quantities of very round shot could be produced with a shot tower, which is still in use today.

Gunpowder was, of course, an essential element in the effective use of guns, although it is generally not recovered archaeologically. Gunpowder consisted of various proportions of saltpeter, charcoal, and sulfur, depending upon its intended use; the higher the proportion of saltpeter, the finer the powder

Figure 13.31. Colander method for making lead shot. From Vita Bonfadini, *La caccia dellárcobugio*, Venice 1691. In Brown (1985:64). *Courtesy of Smithsonian Institution Press. Drawing by M. L. Brown.*

Figure 13.32. Sixteenth-century powder flasks. Late sixteenth century, probably German or Austrian. *Left:* Linen over wood with iron fittings; dimensions: 3.49 cm by 17.9 cm by 5.25 cm. *Right:* Leather over wood with iron fittings; dimensions: 20.2 cm by 20.3 cm by 5.4 cm. See also Karcheski (1990:14) and Wickman (1985:10). F. E. Williams Collection. *Courtesy of Jack Williams. Photo: James Quine.*

(Biringuccio 1990:412–415). Nevertheless, as the early-sixteenth-century metallurgist Vannoccio Biringuccio noted, "If you wish it to be good, each powder should have three points: the first is that it be composed of materials that are free from gross earthiness; the second, that it be finely powdered and its parts well mixed together; the third, that it be well-dried of every moisture. If it is like this, whatever it may be, you will always have its effects very strong and powerful" (Biringuccio 1990:412).

The third condition was particularly difficult for the Spaniards in the tropical, humid, circum-Caribbean region. Powder was carried in powder flasks, which were designed to keep powder dry and conveniently at hand. At least two varieties recovered archaeologically were used in the Spanish colonies, one wooden and trapezoidal in form and another made from the horns of cattle (see Nickel 1985; Karcheski 1990:14; Brown 1980:43–44). Both of these were relatively uncommon until 1550, when firearms superseded crossbows as the most common projectile weapon in the Americas.

The trapezoidal or rectangular wooden powder flask (Fig. 13.32) was in use between about 1550 and 1650 and the powder horn varieties from at least 1560 through the end of the eighteenth century (Brown 1980:43–44; Karcheski 1990:14; Nickel 1985). The more elaborate wooden flasks were probably manufactured in Europe (Karcheski 1990:14; Nickel 1985). Lids for both kinds have been recovered archaeologically; those for the wooden flasks are rectangular in shape, and those for the horns are circular (Fig. 13.33). Both types of lids had a center spout, and most had a spring lever on the base of the cap that served to open the flask itself and to

Figure 13.33. Powder container lids. *Left:* Iron powder flask lid, ca. 1580, 5.0 cm by 3.2 cm. St. Augustine (SA-34-1-16). *Right:* Brass powder horn lid, ca. 1740, maximum length 7.25 cm. St. Augustine (SA-7-5-15). FLMNH/CSA Collections. *Photos: James Quine*

measure a standard charge of powder into the spout for easy loading. Nonintact archaeological examples can have a central hole for the spout and a hole in the cap for the charging spring (Fig. 13.33).

Powder horns were much more commonly used by non-Iberian European settlers in America (Nickel 1985:4), although they were adopted by the Spaniards by at least 1560, when the viceroy of Mexico sent Don Tristan de Luna in Pensacola "one hundred and ten or one hundred and twenty horn flasks which will preserve the powder better in a damp, cold country better than wooden ones; they will last longer, and be useful for loading and priming. If they work well, let me know, and I will send some more" (quoted in Brown 1980:44). The preferred horns for powder containers among all European groups in the Americas were those of the Spanish longhorn cattle, prized for their stoutness. Horns were purchased in large quantities from Spanish centers in the West Indies, Mexico, and South America by contractors buying leather for the British army (Nickel 1985:2).

Although paper cartridges containing a ball and individual charge of powder were developed by the mid-seventeenth century (requiring a cartridge box), the powder horn retained its utility and popularity for sporting and personal weapons until after about 1820, when the metal breech-loading cartridge was developed and adopted (Peterson 1956:64–65).

Many other firearm accessories and accessories associated with military activities (rather than with personal possessions) have been recovered archaeologically, including mounted guns and artillery, cleaning equipment, cartridge cases, bandolier bags, and armor. These have, for the most part, come from military contexts and are therefore not included here but rather will be discussed in a future volume.

Chapter 14
Pastimes

In 1497, as Columbus was preparing to return to Hispaniola on his third voyage, Ferdinand and Isabella commanded him to include in his contingent *"some musicians and instruments for the entertainment of the people there,"* recognizing that the colonists needed familiar forms of diversion (in Parry and Keith 1984:220). The residents of Spanish America continued through the entire colonial period to seek avenues of amusement and relaxation in both public and private settings.

Many of the traditional Spanish and American Indian entertainments of the colonial period are not reflected in the archaeological record. Religious festivals, dancing, song, and theater, for example, were as ubiquitous in the colonies as they were in Spain but left few artifact remains (for comprehensive discussions of these activities in Spanish and Spanish colonial life, see Deforneaux 1966:128–144; Deleito y Piñuela 1946; Díaz-Plaja 1995; García Guinea 1999; López Cantos 1992; Oliveira Marquez 1971:242–268).

Many other leisure activities, however, did have archaeologically recoverable objects associated with them, and this chapter addresses the portable material correlates of some of the more commonly pursued of these pastimes in the Spanish colonies. The discussion does not deal with such landscape-level manifestations of entertainment as ballgame courts, bowling (*boliche*) courts, bullrings, cockfighting rings, theaters, or pleasure gardens, all of which were present in the Spanish colonies, but rather with portable items that were used or owned by individuals. It is furthermore restricted to the material objects associated with those activities that have been reported with some regularity from archaeological sites. These activities and objects include games and gambling, toys, musical instruments, writing and reading equipment, and the rituals of tobacco use.

Many of the objects discussed in Chapter 10 relating to needlework (particularly lace making) might be considered as artifacts related to pastimes, particularly for elite Spanish women. They also, however, relate to the production of clothing elements and for that reason were included in the earlier chapter. The same might be argued for some of the weaponry-related items treated in Chapter 13, since hunting was a favored pastime among the elite.

Games and Gambling

Games, claims at least one scholar, were at the heart of the Spanish soul (López Cantos 1992:269). Spaniards of all classes were passionately committed to games of chance, and gambling houses were common both in Spain and in the colonies (see Deforneaux 1966:214; López Cantos 1992:269–271). Dice and board games had been popular in Iberia since at least the early Middle Ages and probably before that time. Dice are among the most ancient of gaming items, and dice of the same size and shape as modern examples have been recovered from Egyptian tombs and in Roman sites (Bell 1960; Austin 1934, 1940). Dice excavated from Roman sites are not notably distinct in shape, size, or markings from those found on Spanish colonial sites.

Dice and dice games are closely related to the ancient game of *astragalus,* or "knucklebones," which in the classical world was nearly always depicted as a game played by girls and women (Tylor 1971:70–71). This game involved the use of sheep or goat astragali (knucklebones), which, when tossed, would fall on one of four sides, each given a specific value (Fig. 14.1). The game remained popular in Europe through the seventeenth century and beyond. Peter Breugel, for example, depicts girls playing knucklebones in *Children's Games,* painted in 1560. Zooarchaeologists analyzing materials from colonial sites should carefully scrutinize any excavated sheep or goat astragali to detect wear that might have resulted from gaming rather than butchering.

The *Tratado de ajedrez, dados y tablas* (Treatise on chess, dice and board games) (ca. 1283), written by the Christian King Alfonso X of Castile, illustrates and explains many of the gambling and board games involving dice that were prevalent in both Christian and Moslem Spain at that time (Fig. 14.2). These included dice rolling, backgammon, chess, and checkers. All of these games remained popular through the American colonial era.

Gambling games, particularly those using dice, were regularly prohibited by Spanish authorities from the thirteenth century onward because of the apparently general obsession with the game and the great harm it did to the often pauperized losers (recounted in D'Aulnoy 1930:317–318; Deforneaux 1966:219; Hinojosa Montalvo 1999:71–72; Oliveira Marquez 1971:252–253). Both the practice and the prohibitions came to the Americas with the Spaniards. During the sixteenth century, women and priests were expressly forbidden to play dice, but to no apparent avail (López Cantos 1992:303–314). To have a gaming house in America was a profitable venture, and because of this they

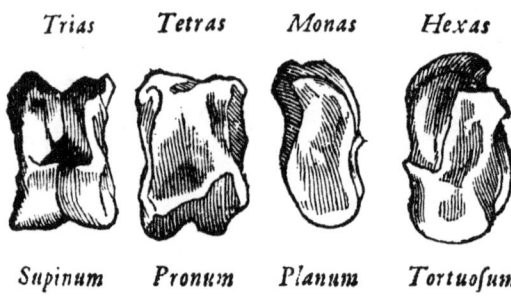

Figure 14.1. *Astragalas* (Knucklebones). Showing the sides as used in gaming. After Hyde (1694).

were frequently monopolized by government officials (as in sixteenth-century Puerto Rico and Honduras) (López Cantos 1992:304).

Dice games were also apparently a domestic entertainment, as suggested by the eighteenth-century Mexican *casta* paintings (Fig. 14.3). It is no surprise, therefore, that dice are found frequently on colonial sites. All of those reported from Spanish colonial sites are made of bone, although ivory was used quite commonly for dice before the seventeenth century (Egan 1997).

A die is a small cube with each of its six sides bearing from one to six indented circles. The circles or dots can be simple holes, holes within incised circles, or sets of incised circles, and there does not seem to be evidence that the design of the circles has chronological significance. Both simple holes and holes surrounded by incised circles, for example, have been reported from Santa Elena, South Carolina (1566–87) (South, Skowronek, and Johnson 1988:169), as well as from late-eighteenth-century contexts in St. Augustine (for example, FLMNH Lab #SA-7-4-291).

The placement of the numerical designators on the faces of the die cube is invariably done so that the numbers on opposite faces of the cube add up to seven (one opposite six, two opposite five, and so forth). This has been the arrangement since Roman times for "regular" dice; however, it has been noted that late medieval dice (thirteenth through fifteenth centuries) were often "nonregular,"

Pastimes

Figure 14.2. Gambling with dice in thirteenth-century Spain. Detail from the *Tratado de ajedrez, dados y tablas* (ca. 1283). Illustrated manuscript in the Biblioteca El Escorial, Madrid. #T.1.6. *Copyright © Patrimonio Nacional.*

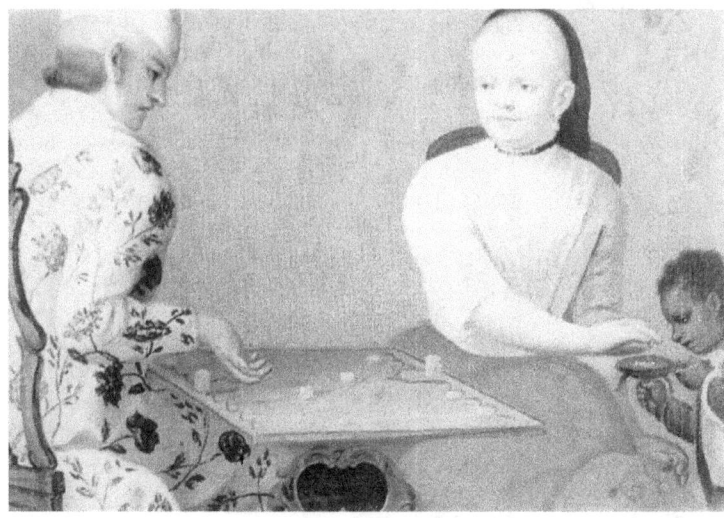

Figure 14.3. Dice games in eighteenth-century Mexico. Anonymous *casta* painting, ca. 1780. Detail from *Spaniard and Albino woman, Torna Atrás. Courtesy of the Museo Nacional de Arte y História, Mexico City.*

having the dots placed in random positions, not necessarily with values on opposite faces adding up to seven (Egan 1997:2).

On regular dice the six, three, and two are on three adjacent sides of the die (Fig. 14.4). Modern dice are generally "right-hand dice," that is, when the face with one dot is on top and the die is oriented with the three and two facing the viewer, the face with three dots will be on the viewer's right. Conversely, when the face with six dots is on top, the two will be on the viewer's right.

This modern right-handed alignment was the one most frequently used on colonial dice but was by no means the only one (Fig. 14.5). Of seven die recorded from sixteenth- through late-eighteenth-century Spanish colonial contexts, five were left-handed and only two were right-handed (both of those were from the period of ca. 1780–1800). The direction of the diagonal on which the dots are aligned can also differ, resulting in 16 possible combinations of dot patterns (Potter 1992, reproduced in Egan 1997). On sixteenth- through eighteenth-century English sites, by far the most fre-

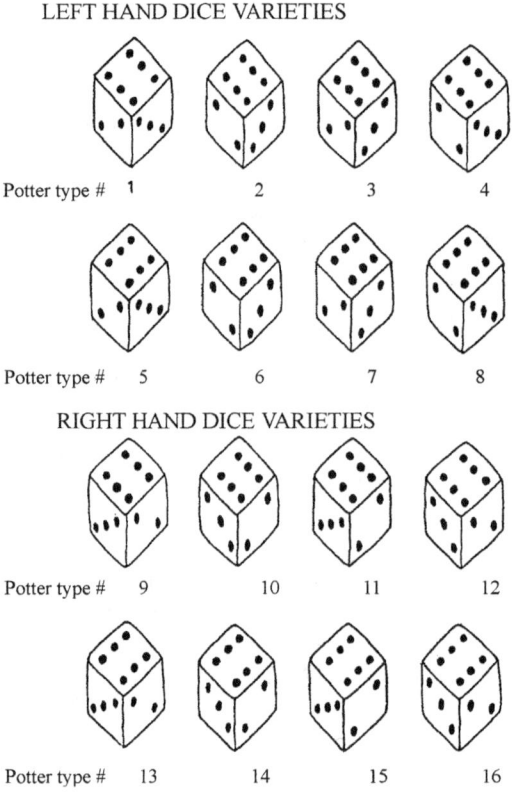

Figure 14.4. Variants of dice layout arrangements. After Potter (1962), as reproduced in Egan (1997:3).

Figure 14.5. Spanish colonial dice. *Top:* Bone, late seventeenth century. San Luis de Talimali, FS 5074. *Courtesy of the Florida Bureau of Archaeological Research, the San Luis Archaeological and Historical Site, and Bonnie McEwan. Center:* Bone, "parabolic" shape. Both St. Augustine, late eighteenth century. SA-26-1-73, SA-342B-1150. *Bottom:* Bone, mid-eighteenth century. St. Augustine (SA-7-4-291). Bottom, left die is a 1.1 cm cube. *Photos: James Quine.*

quently occurring pattern is that defined by Potter as Type 16 (Fig. 14.4). Unfortunately, most dice reported from Spanish colonial sites are shown from only a single angle, and it is not currently possible to determine accurately the relative frequency of these types. Based on the small sample available for study at this level of analysis, however (N = 5, all eighteenth century), Type 16 does not predominate on Spanish sites as it seems to on English sites. One of the dice observed was Type 5, one Type 8, one Type 14, one Type 16, and one either a Type 6 or Type 8. It would be most useful for archaeological reports to contain this information.

False, or "fixed," dice have also been reported from English sites (Egan 1997), and ordinances against weighting of dice were in force in sixteenth-century Spain (Hinajosa Montalvo 1999:72). Such dice may have only high numbers on every side or may have had weights inserted to "load" them and make them fall with high numbers showing. False dice can also be made with different-sized faces (an imperfect cube) so that the die tends to fall on the longer side.

Dice of a curious shape, best described as cubes with curved faces, or "parabolic cubes," have been reported from several eighteenth-century Spanish contexts (Fig. 14.5). Although the faces of the dice are flat, their corners rise above the face in points. The five examples from St. Augustine are all from contexts dating to about 1750 to 1800; however, a cache of similar dice was recovered from the 1724 *Tolosá* shipwreck (Apesteguí, León, and Borrell 1996:115). Those from the

Tolosá are reported to be approximately 1.0 cm on a side, while those from St. Augustine range from 0.6 to 0.7 cm on a side. The dot patterns on these dice are quite variable, including both left- and right-handed varieties, and Potter's Types 14, 16, and 8. The dots on several of these appear to have been crudely handmade.

Dice in general do not provide particularly useful chronological information, except perhaps for the "parabolic cube" dice that have been reported only from contexts dating between 1725 and 1800. Size varies considerably through time, as does the manner of inscribing dots (simple holes or holes in incised circles). The pattern of placing the dots on the die faces (left- or right-handed) and the 16 types proposed by Potter (1992) may have potential for distinguishing Spanish from English dice.

Dice were often used in conjunction with board games such as backgammon (*tablas*), which has existed in some form for several thousand years (backgammon boards and counters have been excavated in Babylonian and pharoaic Egyptian tombs). Backgammon was played in the early Middle Ages in Spain using dice and counters and was outlined in some detail in Alfonso X's *Tratado*. It has been played throughout Europe since that time and was brought to America with the Spaniards.

Backgammon, like a number of other board games such as checkers (*damas*) and parchisi (a form of East Indian backgammon that allows four to play), was played using counters (Fig. 14.6). Board-game counters were apparently made in an endless variety of shapes, sizes, and materials (see Bell 1969:137–143). Those reported from Spanish colonial archaeological sites, however, have been simple disks of bone or more commonly of pottery (Figs. 14.7, 14.8). Crudely shaped disks of glazed or unglazed European and American Indian pottery are found on virtually all Spanish colonial sites in St. Augustine and have also been reported from Caribbean sites and shipwrecks of the sixteenth through

Figure 14.6. Board game players, ca. 1560. Two men play what appears to be backgammon. Detail of Jost Amman engraving (Amman 1968:Plate 124).

eighteenth centuries (Ewen 1991:132; Skowronek 1982; Solís Magaña 1988:114). These have ranged in size from 1.5 to 4.0 cm in diameter and are generally interpreted as gaming pieces (Fig. 14.7). It is also possible that they may have served other functions, such as for stopping bottles and jars; however, the frequency with which they occur on Spanish colonial sites, coupled with the well-documented passion for gaming, suggests that at least some of these were used as game counters. They were easy to make, durable, cost free, and easily distinguishable from one another. Gaming disks chipped from broken pottery have also been excavated in eighteenth-century Amsterdam (Tokyo Metropolitan Edo-Tokyo Museum 1997:123).

Figure 14.7. Ceramic gaming pieces. All from a single deposit in St. Augustine, ca. 1740. *Top row:* All green-glazed olive jar. Diameter of top left 4.2 cm. *Center row:* Left, San Luis polychrome majolica, diameter 3.5 cm; center and right, unglazed olive jar. *Bottom row:* All unglazed olive jar. Diameter of bottom left piece 4.6 cm. (SA-36-4-286, 382). FLMNH/CSA Collections.

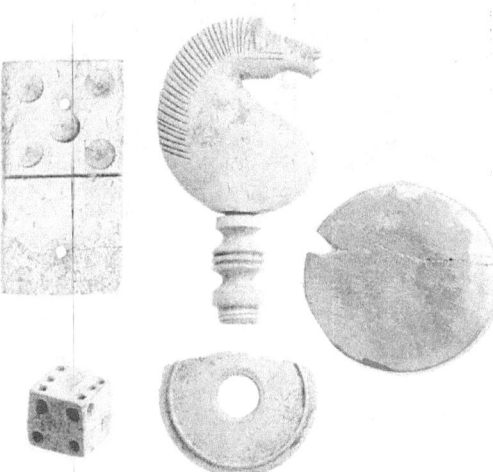

Figure 14.8. Bone gaming pieces. Domino: Top of two-piece bone domino, ca. 1750, 3.5 cm by 1.8 cm, St. Augustine (SA-7-4-184). Die: Bone, ca. 1750, 0.7 cm square sides, St. Augustine (SA-26-1-172). Chessman (knight), ca. 1760. The base is threaded to receive the knight. St. Augustine (SA-7-4-495). Notched circular game piece: Bone, ca. 1730–50, 3.0 cm in diameter, St. Augustine (SA-7-4-59). *Photos: James Quine.*

Other board and table games that enjoyed popularity in the Spanish colonies could not rely on generic, homemade counters. Dominoes (*dominó*) and chess (*ajedrez*) each require standard pieces that meet specific requirements, and both of these games were played widely throughout Spanish colonial America. Chess was a game of the educated, although priests were forbidden to play in the sixteenth-century Caribbean colonies because of the distraction created by their frequent obsessions with the game (López Cantos 1992:263). The chess pieces themselves offered a rich opportunity for artistic expression, and many medieval sets were made from crystal, gold, rose quartz, or ivory and survive primarily in museums. General conventions to designate the various pieces of king (*rey*), queen (*reina*), bishop (*alfil*), knight (*caballo*), rook (*torre* or *roque*), and pawn (*peón*) are observed (Fig. 14.9), but there has always been a tremendous amount of variation in the execution of the pieces through both time and space (for a very comprehensive survey of chess pieces from antiquity to the present, see Liddell 1937).

One of the few chess pieces reported archaeologically from a colonial-period site is a bone knight in the form of a horse, shown in

Figure 14.9. Gaming pieces. *Top row:* Bone chess pawns and two-piece domino from Caracas, ca. 1780–1830. Length of left pawn, 3.4 cm. Domino on top is 4 cm by 2 cm (after Sanoja et al. 1998:241, 254.) *Bottom row:* Shapes of chess pieces, ca. 1616 (after Liddell 1937:37). *Drawings: Pauline Kulstad.*

Figure 14.10. Possible gaming piece elements. Bone disk has a threaded hole in center and may have served as a base for a game piece. The bone finial is threaded both inside the hole at the bottom and outside at the top and may have served as a joining element in a gaming piece. Both Puerto Real, ca. 1550–70. Disk diameter 3.2 cm, FS 3344. Finial length 1.3 cm, FS 3125. See also Ewen (1991:81). *Photo: James Quine.*

Figure 14.8. Two bone pawns from a nineteenth-century context in Caracas retain the general form of the pawns shown in Alfonso X's *Tratado* (Sanoja Obediente et al. 1998:241; Fig. 14.9). Recognizable chess pieces in general are rarely reported, probably because most of those in common use were made of perishable wood. Chess pieces were probably lost less frequently than other kinds of items, and others in fragmentary form may not have been recognized as chess pieces. It is likely that at least some of the "unidentified bone objects" in site reports were once parts of chess sets (for example, Fig. 14.10). Examples of French gaming pieces from the first half of the eighteenth century can be found in Stone (1974:120).

The game of dominoes also requires specially formed and marked pieces. These consist of flat rectangles divided in half and marked on each half with dots representing values from one to six. The marking dots are similar to those of dice in that they can be a single hole (usually filled with a color that contrasted with the tile body) or a hole surrounded by a concentric circle.

Most accounts of domino history suggest that the game was introduced to Italy from China in the mid-eighteenth century and spread from there to Europe. Although the English encyclopedist Randle Holme's discussion of games in 1680 outlines chess, checkers, and billiards in some detail, he makes no mention of dominoes (Holme 1972:262–265). The earliest dominoes recovered archaeologically from Spanish colonial sites date from the middle of the eighteenth century (Shephard 1983:94), and others have been reported from early-nineteenth-century contexts in Caracas (Sanoja Obediente et al. 1998:254). These eighteenth- and early-nineteenth-century dominoes were constructed of two superimposed flat tiles joined by a pin. The top tile bears the numerical dots, and the lower tile serves as a base (Figs. 14.8, 14.9). The eighteenth-century example from St. Augustine measures 3.4 by 1.3 cm, somewhat smaller than the nineteenth-century domino from Caracas, which measures 4.2 by 2.2 cm. Several modern examples measured for comparison were consistently 5.0 by 2.5 cm, possibly suggesting a tendency for dominoes to increase in size through time.

This suggestion is supported by the dominoes recovered from the excavation of the Place Royale in Quebec. The earliest domino at that site dated to the second half of the eighteenth century and measured 3.5 by 1.5 cm. Several dominoes dated to the nineteenth century measured 4.3 by 2.3 cm, and a twentieth-century example from the site was 7.0 by 2.4 cm. All were made of polished bone (Tremblay and Renaud 1999:46–51).

Spaniards were also fervent devotees of *boliche*, or bowling, which was brought to America with the earliest settlers. It is said that Pizarro's men played at *boliche* in the streets of Cuzco (López Cantos 1992:249–260). *Boliche* was well established throughout Mexico and the Caribbean during the sixteenth century and provided yet another opportunity for gambling. During the seventeenth century, a number of regulations were established in various places to restrict *boliche* to weekdays and to forbid playing by priests, people who owned no property, slaves, children, and people who lived solely on what they earned from working (López Cantos 1992:255).

Boliche, like most other European games, had origins in Greek and Roman sports, which included versions of bowling (see, for example, Balsdon 1969). The game was very popular during medieval times and was known variously as *bocci, bowles, quills,* and *kugel*. The game was played with a small, wooden bowling ball that, as in the modern game of bowling, was aimed at a set of pins or other objects. Breugel's *Children's Games* shows two types of bowling games being played, one aiming a ball at a target and the other aiming the ball at a stack of additional balls. There were undoubtedly an infinite number of variations.

By the sixteenth century, the "bowling

Figure 14.11. Wooden pin fragment and ball, possibly used in eighteenth-century *boliche*. St. Augustine, ca. 1720–40, found together in an eighteenth-century well. The top of the presumed pin is 11.0 cm in length, and the worn wooden ball is approximately 10.5 cm in diameter. SA-7-6-F14. FLMNH/CSA Collections.

pin" shape of the modern game was being used as a target and was typically about 40 cm in length and 1.5 kg in weight (Tremblay and Renaud 1999:128). The balls themselves were also of wood and, with diameters in the vicinity of 10 to 15 cm, were much smaller than those used in the modern game of bowling. Since most of the implements used in *boliche* were of wood, very few have survived archaeologically. A worn wooden ball possibly used in *boliche* was recovered from a mid-eighteenth-century well in St. Augustine, along with the head of what might be a pin (Fig. 14.11).

Children's Games and Toys

Board games and ball games were played both by children and adults in the colonies. There were also, however, categories of toys and games that were strongly associated with the presence of children. Serious archaeological attention to children as active participants in the past has been a fairly recent phenomenon (see, for example, Lillenhammer 1989), and toys provide one of the few archaeological reflections of children's activities. Children's thimbles were discussed in Chapter 10, and they might be considered as a reflection of girls' pastimes (although they more likely reflected girls' education and chores). Certain amulets and *chupetas,* discussed in Chapter 5, also indicate the presence of children.

Iconographic sources are particularly useful for material expressions of children's toys and games. Breugel's *Children's Games* depicts 24 games being played (one of the best sources to review these in detail is the Canadian Museum of Games and Archives Web site: www.ahs.uwaterloo.ca). Games that are played with objects include knucklebones, hoop rolling, bowling, and tops.

The eighteenth-century *casta* paintings (synthesized in García Saíz 1989) are also a rich source of imagery for toys used by all classes of children in eighteenth-century Mexico. The most common toys associated with young boys were toy horses and hobbyhorses (Fig. 14.12; see also Fig. 7.1). Elaborate hobbyhorses were also featured in the sixteenth-century paintings of royal Spanish boys by such artists as Alonso Sánchez Coello. One of the earliest records of a hobbyhorse is on a Chinese painted ceramic pillow of the Sung Dynasty (A.D. 900–1279) in the Metropolitan Museum of Art (Ketchum 1981:13). Other toys in the *casta* paintings included peashooters, kites, miniature animals, miniature ceramic dishes, and dolls. The latter two categories were the only ones associated with girls.

A number of toys or toy-related artifacts have been recovered from Spanish sites, and others undoubtedly have gone unrecognized. People have created small items for the amusement of children in nearly all times and places, and these are often idiosyncratic and unique, such as the object in Figure 14.13, thought to have been a toy bug.

Among the most common toys from eighteenth-century contexts are miniature ceramic figurines, depicting animals, birds, and people (Fig. 14.14; see also Peterson 1977:743 for a group of exotic South American ceramic animal figures from the 1733

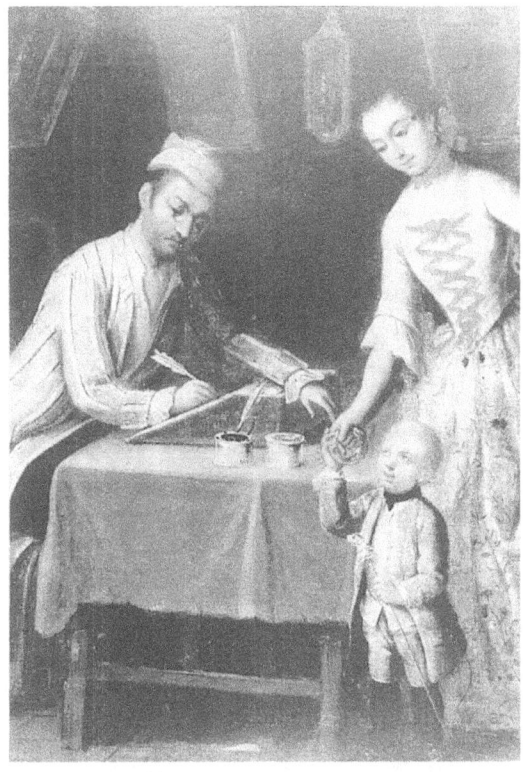

Figure 14.12. Child with hobbyhorse. *Casta* painting by Andrés de Islas, late eighteenth century. From *Spaniard and Morisco Woman, Albino. Courtesy of the Museo de América, Madrid.*

Florida plate fleet wrecks). A group of ceramic miniatures, including animals, shoes, ceramic vessels, and musical instruments, was recovered from the 1766 wreck of *El Nuevo Constante* (Pearson and Hoffman 1995:189–192). Most of these were made from the Mexican ceramic type known as Guadalajara Polychrome, which was apparently exported in significant quantities from Mexico to Spain during the eighteenth century (Deagan 1987:44–46). These may have been doll accessories, children's playthings, or novelties for adults. Care should be taken in interpreting all ceramic human figure parts as components of toys or dolls, since many small saints' images (*santos*) were also made of unglazed ceramics during the colonial era.

Figure 14.13. Wire bug. Possibly created as a toy or diversion. Twisted copper wire body and wings, gold thread head, ca. 1730–40. Maximum length 4.2 cm. St. Augustine (SA-36-4-257). FLMNH/CSA Collections. *Photo: James Quine.*

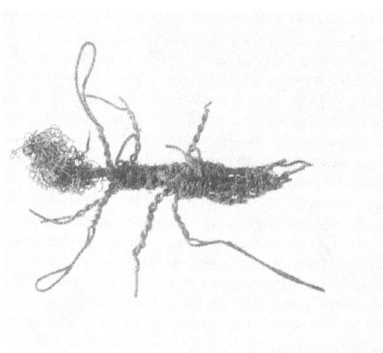

Figure 14.14. Ceramic figurines. St. Augustine, ca. 1720–40. *Left:* Fragment of a human figurine, length 4.5 cm (SA-342-36). *Center:* Dog head, length 2.3 cm (SA-7-4-216). *Right:* Dog head, length 3.0 cm (SA-36-4-340). FLMNH/CSA Collections. *Photo: James Quine.*

Dolls sewn in cloth and carved of wood have been made and used since ancient times and were probably the most common toys in use during the colonial period (they are also, however, among the least enduring objects in the archaeological record). It has been suggested that in Spain, at least, the association of dolls as toys for young girls in paintings emerged at the beginning of the sixteenth century, when very elaborate dolls appear in portraits of noble or wealthy children (Alcaide 1982:631–632).

There was a demand for dolls and puppets among the Spanish elite of the sixteenth century, and most were imported from France, which was a center of doll and toy making at that time. These included marionettes and automated dolls that moved when wound up, although the latter were usually showpieces rather than playthings (Alcaide 1982:632–633). Less-privileged children undoubtedly had humbler wooden or cloth counterparts; however, few recognizable examples of wooden doll parts have been reported from sites dating to before the nineteenth century.

Glazed and bisque porcelain doll faces, legs, and arms were being produced by the early nineteenth century, and by midcentury, Germany and France were the major producers and exporters of china dolls throughout the world (Ketchum 1981:36; Noel Hume 1980:317–319; Tremblay and Renaud 1999:102–103).

Children in the Spanish colonies (as in most times and places) played games requiring skill and dexterity, including several varieties of marble games and spinning tops. Marbles are small, spherical objects used in games that require aiming one marble at others and hitting them. Early marblelike games were played with fruit pits and round pebbles, and glass marbles excavated from Roman and Egyptian sites are very little different from those used in the eighteenth and nineteenth centuries (see, for example, Bauman 1970:7; Ketchum 1981:4). Little is known of the game in medieval times, and few marbles are reported from medieval sites.

Marbles seem to have gained a resurgence in popularity during the seventeenth century, and stoneware examples have been found in late-seventeenth-century Dutch contexts (Tokyo Metropolitan Edo-Tokyo Museum 1997:151). The most common type of marble from the seventeenth to mid-nineteenth centuries was made of stone, although marbles

Figure 14.16. Wooden spinning top with iron pin. St. Augustine, ca. 1720–40. Length 5.6 cm. SA-7-6-F14. FLMNH/CSA Collections.

Figure 14.15. Marbles. St. Augustine, ca. 1750–70. *Top and bottom left:* Pale gray stone, diameter 1.5 cm. *Center right:* Glazed, marbleized cream and dark brown clay, diameter (slightly irregular) 1.5 cm. All SA-7-7-315. FLMNH/CSA Collections.

of molded glass were also in use during the eighteenth century. Germany became a center for the manufacturing of glass marbles. Their peak period of production and export occurred in the 1740s and declined thereafter throughout the nineteenth century (Bauman 1970:17–19; Tremblay and Renaud 1999:57; Randall 1971:102). Stone remained the most common marble material until the 1870s, when glazed porcelain, baked clay, and translucent or transparent glass were first widely used (Randall 1971:102).

Marbles have been reported only from eighteenth- and nineteenth-century contexts in Spanish colonial sites. The majority are of stone, although examples of opaque, swirled glass similar to those from Roman sites have been noted (Fig. 14.15).

Spinning tops are another widespread child's toy found in many parts of the world and have been known since at least Roman times. These are seldom recovered archaeologically because they were usually made of wood. Both pin (or peg) tops and whipping tops have been reported from seventeenth- and eighteenth-century sites, and both are depicted by Breugel in *Children's Games* and the *Fight between Carnival and Lent* (1559). Pin tops were usually pear shaped and mounted on a metal pin or peg (Fig. 14.16). A string was wound around the peg, and the top was set into motion by casting it on to a surface and quickly unwinding the string. Whipping tops have long, narrow necks and bulbous bodies and are kept in motion by striking the top as it turns with a whip (examples of both pin tops and whipping tops have been recovered by Jan Baart from seventeenth century contexts in Amsterdam; see Tokyo Metropolitan Edo-Tokyo Museum 1997:150). Both kinds of tops are still being made and used today.

Noisemakers and Music

Noise-making toys have sometimes also survived in the archaeological record. Ceramic whistles in the shapes of birds or animals have been recovered from eighteenth-century St. Augustine sites as well as from shipwrecks of the same period. Buzzers, whizzers, or whirligigs are also present on Spanish sites spanning the colonial period were used in medieval and earlier times throughout Europe. These simple toys, made of ceramic, metal, or wood, are flat disks,

Figure 14.17. Whizzers. *Left:* Pewter, diameter 4.1 cm. St. Augustine, late eighteenth century. *Right:* Ceramic (olive jar), diameter 3.4 cm. Puerto Real, ca. 1550–78. FLMNH Collections.

usually having serrated edges, with two holes drilled in the center through which a string is passed (Fig. 14.17). When the string ends are twisted and rapidly pulled apart, the whizzer spins and vibrates, creating a buzzing noise. Whizzers have been found on sites dating from the sixteenth century through the end of the eighteenth centuries (for a discussion of whizzers on English colonial sites, see Noel Hume 1980:320–321).

The Jew's harp (which has nothing to do with either Jews or harps) is a noise-making instrument of great antiquity that was probably used both by children and adults. It is known in Spain as the *birimbao* or *guimbarda* and was also known in medieval Europe as a *trump*. In its most common European form, the Jew's harp is a lyre-shaped iron or brass frame with a circular or oval head and two extending arms. A piece of very thin and flexible metal (the tongue) is attached to the inner center of the head, extending beyond the edge of the arms and bent at a right angle to the arms. The tongues rarely survive on archaeological examples. The instrument is brought to the player's mouth, and the two extended arms are placed against the front teeth (Fig. 14.18). The tongue of the instrument is then vibrated by plucking with the player's fingers or tongue. Sounds are varied

Figure 14.18. A Jew's harp being played. Detail from Plate 30 of the *Triumph of Maximilian*, by Hans Burkmair (ca. 1520; reprint, New York: Dover, 1968).

by changes in breathing and changing the size of the oral cavity.

Forms of the Jew's harp have been used throughout Asia and Europe since before the Christian era. It has generally been considered as a folk instrument, although a depar-

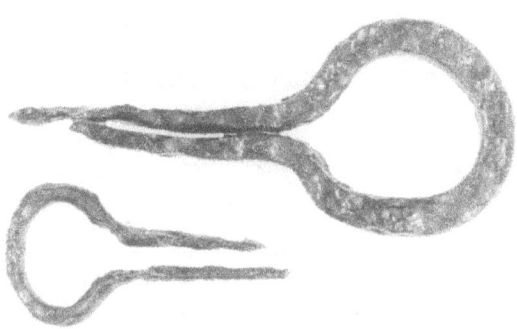

Figure 14.19. Steel Jew's harps. Large harp, length 8.5 cm. Small harp, length 5.0 cm. Puerto Real, ca. 1503–78. Hodges Collection, Musée de Guahabá, Limbé, Haiti. *Photo: James Quine.*

ture from this occurred between about 1750 and 1850, when formal European music for the Jew's harp was often composed and performed (see Fox 1988). Jew's harps were popular items in English trade with the American Indians and were also used in English communities such as Jamestown and Williamsburg (see Corson 1989:40; Cotter and Hudson 1957:84).

Jew's harps vary considerably in size, with archaeological example ranging from about 3.5 to 6.6 cm in length (Fig. 14.19). Most are made of iron, although during the eighteenth century brass frames became more frequent. Of the 122 Jew's harps excavated at Fort Michilimackinack, 65 percent had brass frames. The majority of examples reported from sixteenth- and seventeenth-century contexts, however, have iron frames. Comprehensive consideration of all aspects of the Jew's harp can be found in Fox (1988).

Performing or listening to music was an entertainment and a pastime activity for Spanish colonists from the first days of colonization. Stringed instruments such as lutes, guitars, violins, and their relatives and woodwinds and drums were present in most parts of the Spanish Americas throughout the colonial era, coexisting with American Indian and African musical traditions. There is a very extensive literature dedicated to colonial-era music in Spain and the Spanish Americas, as well as to the syncretic blending of non-European and European musical expression in America, and an adequate consideration of these topics is beyond the scope of this chapter. Introductory sources that are useful for archaeologists (in that they deal with the details of instruments as well as their music) include Bermudez (1992), Corona Alcalde (1993), Hayes (1928–30), and Saldivar (1987).

Relatively few artifacts related to musical instruments other than Jew's harps have been reported from archaeological sites. As with so many leisure items, the factors of perishable composition, restricted contexts of use, and special care in curating them render musical instruments less likely to enter the archaeological record. Certain parts of stringed instruments, such as tuners and string pegs, were often carved from bone or ivory and sometimes survive archeologically. Bone tuning pegs from guitars or *vihuelas* have been reported from contexts dating to the first half of at least two eighteenth-century Spanish sites and are shown in Figure 14.20. A portion of a small, wooden guitar neck was also recovered from the 1733 Spanish plate fleet wrecks (James Levy, personal communication, 2000).

The tambourine came to America with Columbus, who (probably on the basis of trade with West Africa) noted that the people of the Caribbean were delighted to trade food and gold for *sonajes de latón,* the disks attached to tambourines (Morison 1963:72–73). Although a popular trade item, the tambourine also continued as part of the Spaniards' musical repertoire both in Spain and Spanish America. Brass disks that appear to have been *sonajes de latón* for a tambourine are seen in Figure 14.20, and these are identical to tambourine disks as shown by Ribera in 1637 (Juseppe de Ribera, *Girl with a Tambourine* [1637], reproduced in Pérez-Sánchez 1992:127).

304 Personal Items and Accessories

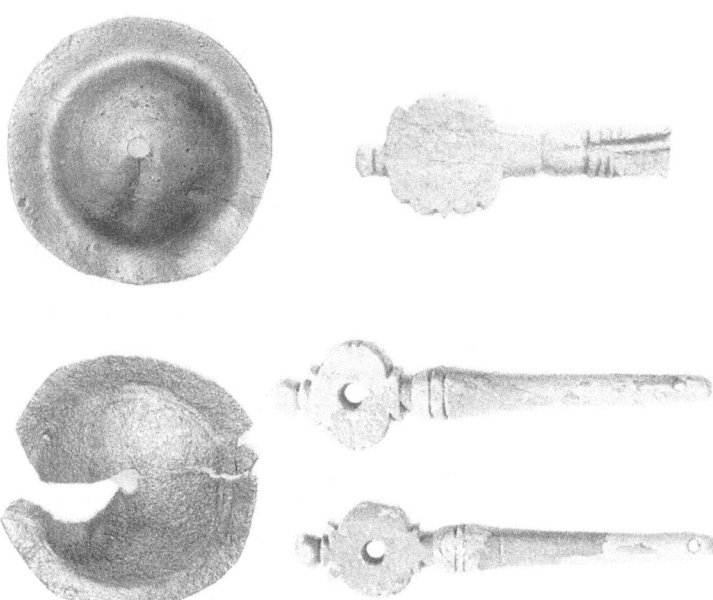

Figure 14.20. Music-related artifacts. *Left:* Brass tambourine jingles, diameter 4.0 cm, Puerto Real, ca. 1503–78. Hodges Collection, Musée de Guahabá, Limbé, Haiti. *Top right:* Single locally-made bone tuner, length 5.5 cm. St. Augustine, eighteenth century, no number. *Bottom right:* Pair of ivory tuners for a stringed instrument, length 7.5 cm, 1733, 8MO101 (*San José* shipwreck). *Courtesy of the Florida Bureau of Archaeological Research. FLMNH/CSA Collections. Photos: James Quine.*

Reading and Writing

Reading and writing were possibly the most common leisure activities among educated colonists, and writing equipment was imported to the colonies from the early sixteenth century onward (Table 14.1). *"Escribanía"* can refer to portable writing desks or writing equipment, and the items shipped to the colonies apparently included both.

Either as sets of writing materials (*aderezos de escribanía, escribanías con sus herramientos*) or as desks (*escribanías ordinarios, de Sevilla,* and *de cinta*), there was considerable variation in cost and probably quality. The most expensive *escribanías* were those noted as *de cinta,* which can mean narrow bands of fluted or pleated decoration, and these may have been more ornate than others.

The equipment used for writing in the sixteenth through eighteenth centuries included quill pens, inkwells, penknives, and sometimes a container of blotting powder or pounce (see, for example, Figs. 14.21, 14.22). Letters were often sealed with wax and the seal of the person writing it. The pens themselves, of course, have not survived archaeologically, but remains of several other categories of writing equipment have been reported from Spanish colonial sites.

Quill pens were used for writing until the middle of the nineteenth century, when metal pen nibs became common. Juan de Yciar, a Spanish calligrapher and scribe writing in 1550, asserted that most scribes agreed that a feather from the right wing of a domestic goose was the preferred source for quill pens, the left-wing feathers being more difficult for right-handed people to hold properly (Yciar 1960:38–39). The knife used to cut and trim the quill pen "should be of good steel, well-tempered and should have a good shape and sharp edges. The handle should be rather stout and square so that it does not slip from the hand when being used . . . the blade should be straight and concave, the point should fall a little forward with its back or angles squared and not rounded, and with a slight edge so that one can scrape the pen. . . . It is best to keep it exclusively for the purpose of trimming pens" (Yciar 1960:36–37). Knives of this type re-

Table 14.1. Writing Equipment Imported to the Spanish Colonies, 1523–1613

Item	1523	1590	1613	Cost
ADEREZOS DE ESCRIBANIA (sets of writing equipment)		288	18	500 maravedís to 8 reales each
ESCRIBANIAS (writing desks)	12	60		12–20 reales/dozen
ESCRIBANIAS CON SUS HERRAMIENTOS (with their tools)			12	5 reales each
ESCRIBANIAS CON TINTEROS (with inkwells)		32		50 maravedís each
ESCRIBANIAS DE SEVILLA (from Seville)			12	4 reales each
ESCRIBANIAS DE CINTA (banded or with scrollwork)		7		6 reales each
ESCRIBANIAS ORDINARIOS (ordinary)			48	4 reales each

mained in use through the eighteenth century (Figs. 14.21, 14.22).

Although metal tips for pens did not come into common use until the middle of the nineteenth century, they were known much earlier. Yciar writes that "black letters" in church manuscripts (that is, large, elaborate lettering) are "usually written with a pen of brass or iron or steel. These are all right for those who are used to them" (Yciar 1960:30).

Inkwells recovered from sixteenth-century Spanish colonial contexts are most often ceramic and usually made of majolica. They were square in shape, containing a circular depression in the center to hold ink. A square flange extended around the edge of the vessel, pierced by holes in which pens could be placed (Fig. 14.23). Paintings of the era sometimes show small, simple glass tubes containing ink attached to the sides of writing desks, and fragments of tubular glass may in fact have originally come from ink containers. Spanish paintings of the sixteenth and seventeenth centuries also depict metal inkwells with square, octagonal, or cylindrical shapes. Few objects identified as inkwells have been reported from seventeenth- or eighteenth-century sites; however, the eighteenth-century Mexican *casta* paintings show round inkwells, similar in construction (apart from the shape) to those of the sixteenth century (see Fig. 14.12). Similar examples in pewter have been recovered from eighteenth-century shipwrecks (FBAR Conservation Lab Collections; Skowronek 1982:151).

Ink used for writing with quill pens needed to be dried before the document could be moved or folded. This process was aided by using pounce, a very fine sand or powder that could absorb excess ink on the surface of the paper. Blotting material was often dispensed by a shaker with a perforated metal top. Examples have been reported archaeologically from sixteenth- and eighteenth-century sites in Florida, including a six-sided

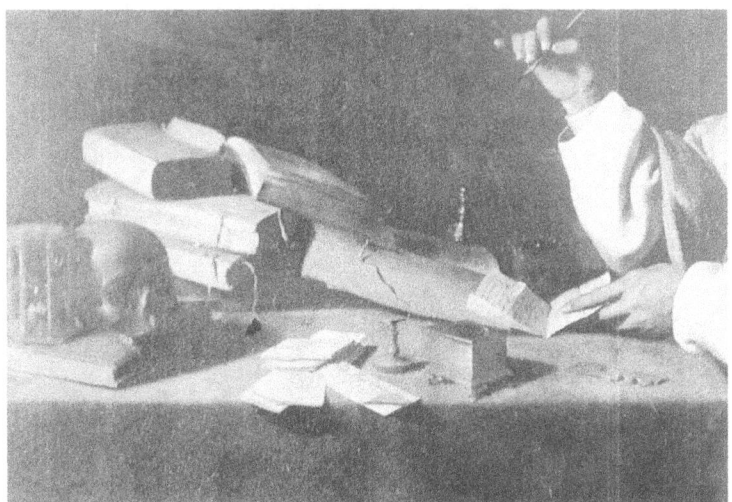

Figure 14.21. Seventeenth-century writing equipment. Detail from Zurburan's *Fray Gonzalo de Ilescas* (ca. 1639). The painting shows the quill pen, inkwell, penknife, and seal used typically for writing during the colonial period. Cat. #148, Real Monasterio de Santa María de Guadalupe, Cáceres. *Courtesy of the Real Monasterio de Santa María de Guadalupe.*

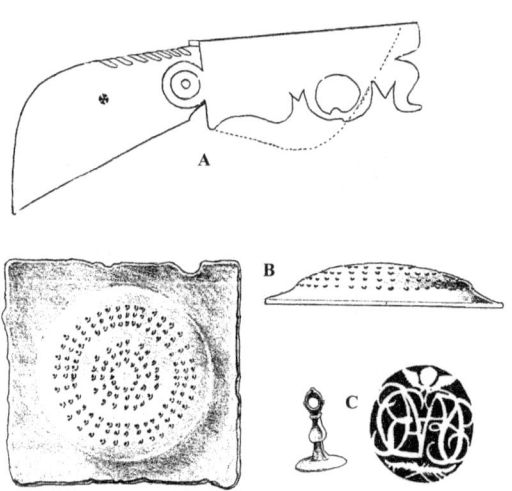

Figure 14.22. Eighteenth-century writing equipment. A. Penknife, copper-alloy handle with steel blade, 1733. Maximum open length 13.9 cm (8SL17) FBAR Lab #0466. B. Pewter lid to a pounce shaker, 1715. Top and side views. 8.0 cm square (8IR19) FBAR Lab #L6459. C. Silver seal with enlarged detail of seal engraving, 1715. Length 2.6 cm, maximum seal diameter 3.6 cm (8IR23) FBAR Lab #L6473. *Courtesy of the Florida Bureau of Archaeological Research. Drawing: Frank Gilson.*

Figure 14.23. Majolica inkwell. Caparra blue majolica inkwell, ca. 1500–50. Concepción de la Vega (FS 222). Top: 7 cm square. Parque Nacional de Concepción de la Vega, Dominican Republic. *Photo: James Quine.*

shaker made of mother-of-pearl and brass recovered from one of the 1733 Florida plate fleet wrecks (Fig. 14.24). Copper-alloy lids from pounce shakers have been found at both sixteenth- and eighteenth-century Spanish sites (see Fig. 14.22).

Books provided an opportunity for reading and relaxation for literate (and usually elite) colonists. Although the pages and covers of

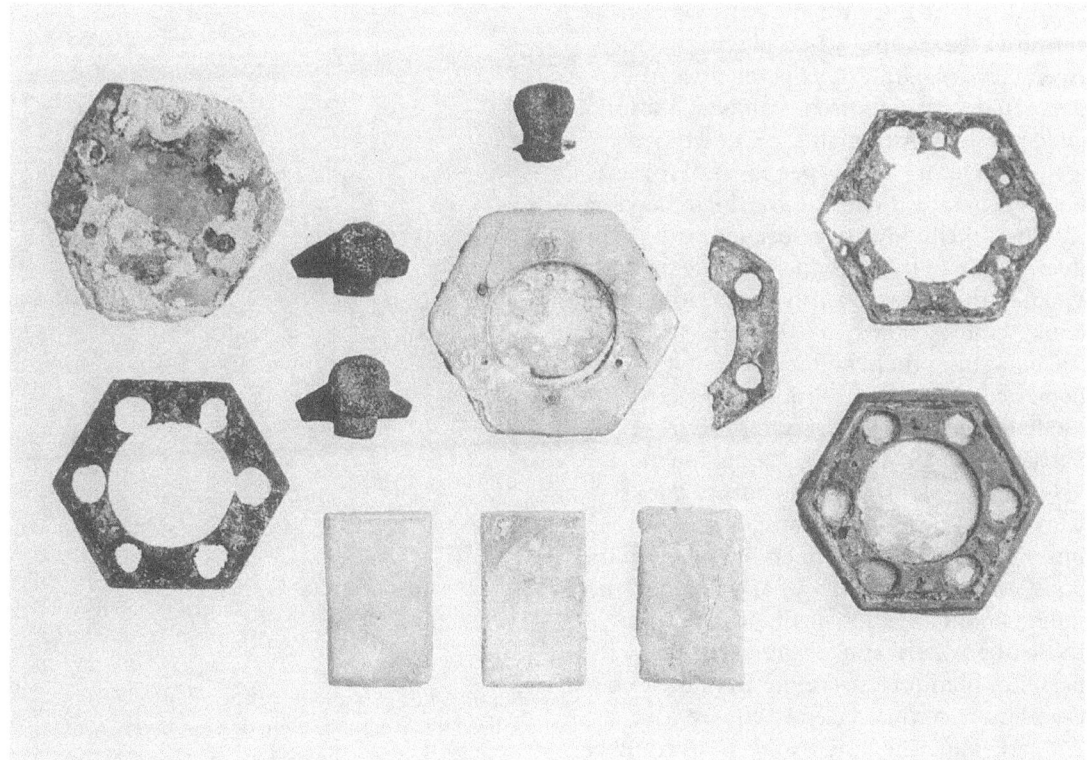

Figure 14.24. Eighteenth-century desk accessory pieces. Pen holder and pounce shaker. Brass and mother-of-pearl six-sided container with ball feet, 1733. Diameter of six-sided plate elements, 6.0 cm by 6.4 cm. Dimensions of side plates, 2.6 cm by 4.0 cm. 8MO101. *Courtesy of the Florida Bureau of Archaeological Research. Photo: James Quine.*

the books themselves rarely survive in the archaeological record, metal elements of book bindings and book fasteners are found quite frequently. Spaniards brought books to the Americas from the first days of exploration (for a discussion of Columbus's interest in books, see Deagan and Cruxent 2002b; Taviani 1985:445–452).

Printing and binding of books began in the Americas in Mexico in 1535 (Torre Revello 1940:93–95). The printing of religious books, catechisms, dictionaries, and grammars of Mexican Indian languages was soon a thriving industry, and 251 known books were published in the Americas in the sixteenth century, rising to 1,818 in the seventeenth century and 6,890 in the eighteenth century (Torre Revello 1940:103). Bookbinders were also actively binding these volumes.

The extent to which the books were exported to the other Spanish colonies is unclear, but the only other places with active presses prior to the eighteenth century were Lima (1584); Puebla de los Angeles, Mexico (1640); and Guatemala (1660). During the eighteenth century, presses were established at Havana (1707), Oaxaca (1720), Bogotá (1738), Nueva Valencia (Venezuela) (1764), Quito (1760), New Orleans (1769), Cartagena (1769), Santiago de Chile (1776), Buenos Aires (1780), Santo Domingo (1782), Trinidad (1786), Santiago de Cuba (1792), and Guadalajara (1793) (Torre Revello 1940:93).

Books of the fifteenth and early sixteenth centuries were sturdily bound with wooden covers (boards), thickly covered by leather decorated with embossed, stamped, and/or gilded designs. Although the wood boards, leather covering, and paper pages of these books generally do not survive in archaeological sites, the hardware associated with them does. Books of this early period bore ornate metal hardware used variously to close the book, to protect the book's corners, to secure the book from theft, and to decorate the book's cover (Carrión Gútiez 1994; Needham 1979; Roberts and Etherington 1982:1–2; Sarriá Rueda 1994; Weale 1962:xiii–xv).

Fifteenth- and sixteenth-century books were closed by hinges, straps, or clasps mounted on the outer (opening) edges of the book's covers (Fig. 14.25). Early Spanish and Italian books are often distinguished from those of northern and western Europe by the presence of four clasps rather than the two clasps more common elsewhere (Weale 1962:xii–xiii). The hinges and clasps could be quite elaborately decorated with gilding and enamel work and were often accompanied by decorative metal bosses or plaquettes embedded in the leather cover to provide additional decoration (Figs. 14.26, 14.27).

By the middle of the sixteenth century, the wood boards (covers) of books were largely replaced by pasteboard covers, the books themselves were smaller in size, and books were printed in larger quantities. For all of these reasons, metal clasps and corner brackets were no longer either functionally necessary or economically viable (Roberts and Etherington 1982:1–2; Sarriá Rueda 1994; Weale 1962:xiii–xv). From about 1550 until about 1640, books were often closed with fabric ties attached to the closing edges of the covers (Fig. 14.25), but after the mid-seventeenth century even these became uncommon except on Bibles.

Spanish book hardware from early sites in the Caribbean tended to be strongly Mudejar in style, reflecting the major impact and en-

Figure 14.25. Sixteenth-century books. From Albrecht Dürer, engraving of *Erasmus of Rotterdam*, 1526. The image shows books with metal hardware and closures as well as tie closures. National Gallery of Art, Lessing J. Rosenwald Collection, #1943.3.3554. *Photograph © Board of Trustees, National Gallery of Art, Washington, D.C.*

during influence of Moorish art and science not only on the Spanish material world but also on Spanish scholarship and learning. Examples of book hardware from the early-sixteenth-century sites of Concepción de la Vega and Puerto Real in Hispaniola are often intricately cast with gilded and enameled raised designs (Figs. 14.26, 14.27). Those from Concepción de la Vega are the most ornate, and many of them were recovered from the site of the town's Franciscan monastery (ca. 1512–62). Book hardware from Puerto Real tends to be somewhat less ornate, except for the examples recovered from the church excavations (Willis 1984).

It is difficult to distinguish metal ornamentation used on very large books from that used to decorate saddles and furniture; how-

Figure 14.26. Book hardware, Concepción de la Vega. Ca. 1500–50. Copper alloy with gilding and enamel. Length of top left clasp, 6.5 cm. Parque Nacional de Concepción de la Vega, Dominican Republic. *Photo: James Quine.*

Figure 14.27. Book clasps and hardware, Puerto Real. Copper alloy, some with gilding and enamel, ca. 1520–78. Length of leftmost clasp, 9.0 cm. Hodges Collection, Musée de Guahabá, Limbé, Haiti. *Photo: James Quine.*

ever, furniture and saddlery decoration in general probably required a more robust manner of attachment than did book ornaments, and book ornamentation is more likely to occur in a religious context.

Although metal clasps were not common on books after the mid-sixteenth century, there are archaeological examples known from the seventeenth century that are thought to have been used on missals or Bibles. Figure 14.28 shows a distinctive type of book clasp found on two mid-seventeenth-century mission sites in Florida that may have been part of the missionary friars' equipment. It is possible that metal fasteners continued to be used on religious books through the first half of the seventeenth century.

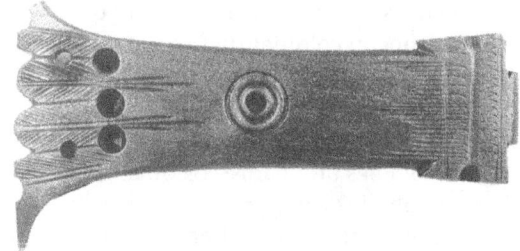

Figure 14.28. Book clasp type associated with Florida missions. Mid-seventeenth century. Copper alloy. Length, 7 cm. Examples have been found at the Franciscan monastery in St. Augustine (SA-42A) and at the Santa Catalina mission on Amelia Island (8NA41). FLMNH Collections (SA-42-A). *Photo: University of Florida Office of Instructional Resources.*

Tobacco Use

Although the Spaniards were the first Europeans to use tobacco as a form of relaxation or leisure, they did not adopt the distinctive, archaeologically recoverable tradition of pipe smoking that was so common in the Anglo colonies. Cigars and cigarillos were the favored forms of tobacco use among both male and female Spanish colonists, even into the nineteenth century (see, for example, Boyd 1958). This tradition may have been owing to the influence of the native peoples encountered by the Spaniards in the Caribbean, Mexico, and Brazil, who smoked tobacco as cigars or ingested it by sniffing. Native Americans in the areas first settled by the English used pipes, probably providing the original impetus for the English clay pipe tradition, which began in the 1570s (Noel Hume 1980:296).

Whatever the origins of the traditions of tobacco use adopted by the Spaniards and the English, the clay tobacco pipe fragments found in such abundance on Anglo-American colonial sites are extremely rare in Spanish contexts dating prior to the eighteenth century. Even on eighteenth-century and later Spanish sites, kaolin pipe fragments are much less frequent than they are on other European colonial sites of the same period (see, for example, Deagan 1983:246–247; Santiago 1980; Shephard 1983; Skowronek 1982; Smith 1965).

Tobacco pipes on Spanish colonial sites of the first half of the eighteenth century are nearly always of Dutch or English origin, and the products of American pipe makers appear occasionally in contexts dating to after about 1770. In Spanish St. Augustine, at least, these are very frequently the molded Moravian bowls designed to take a reed stem.

The identification and dating of European and Euro-American tobacco pipes have been the foci of a great many useful studies, and most pipes on Spanish colonial sites can be identified by reference to these sources. An ambitious series of publications on the archaeology of the clay tobacco pipe has been published intermittently by the BAR International Series, and several of these volumes are useful for researchers working in the Spanish colonies (Davey 1979, 1981a, 1981b, 1983, 1985). Other good beginning sources for English pipes include the studies by Atkinson and Oswald (1961), Oswald (1951, 1961, 1975), and Noel Hume (1980:296–313). Dutch pipes and their markings are discussed by Atkinson and Oswald (1972), Omwake (1965), and Walker (1971a). American pipes of the types found on Spanish sites have been documented by South (1965, 1999) and Walker (1971b, 1975).

A distinctive category of locally made pipes referred to as colonoware pipes has been recognized and documented by archaeologists working in English colonial sites of the Chesapeake and southeastern regions of the United States. Colonoware pipes occur primarily in seventeenth-century and early-eighteenth-century contexts. These pipes are generally made of terra-cotta clay, are handmade or molded, and have European pipe shapes decorated with non-European artistic motifs. Their manufacture and use have been attributed variously to enslaved Africans, American Indians, and creolized multicultural peoples (for a summary discussion and illustrations of these pipes and the various interpretations of them, see Emerson 1988, 1999; Mouer 1993; Mouer et al. 1999).

Similar pipes have been reported from Spanish and African *cimarron* (escaped slave) sites in the Caribbean, from both sixteenth- and seventeenth-century contexts. These are all handmolded of terra-cotta or dark brown local clays, and some appear to be stub-stem, elbow-type pipes intended to receive a separate stem. Most of the extant bowl fragments are poorly smoothed and are decorated with bands of molded, incised, and rouletted geometric designs (although rouletting seems to be less frequent on these pipes than it is on the Chesapeake examples) (Fig. 14.29). A few examples are undecorated.

Elbow pipes from seventeenth-century *cimarron* sites have been reported from Cuba and the Dominican Republic. These are either undecorated or decorated with a series of straight and cross-hatched incised lines (Arrom and García Arévalo 1986:64–65; see also Deagan and MacMahon 1995:14).

A similarly decorated pipe bowl fragment was recovered from a pre-1562 context at Concepción de la Vega. This was thinner and rounder and more burnished than the *cimarron* examples, although it was decorated in a similar fashion (Fig. 14.29). Three examples from what is thought to be a late-sixteenth-century "buccaneer" context at La Isabela are also shown in Figure 14.29. These are thinner than the *cimarron* examples, with a rounder bowl shape, and they include molded as well as incised designs.

The colonoware pipes from the *cimarron* sites are almost certainly African in origin and/or inspiration, since documentary sources are quite explicit about the identification of the sites' inhabitants as *cimarrones* (Arrom and García Arévalo 1986). The earlier pipes are from sites with European and African and American Indian inhabitants; however, after about 1530 the dramatic loss of American Indian populations in the region makes this a less likely source or origin for the locally made pipes (Deagan and Cruxent 2002b).

Spanish American colonists most commonly smoked cigars, but snuff (a finely ground form of tobacco inhaled through the nose) was also a favored method of ingesting tobacco (probably introduced by the Taíno). Although the ingestion of tobacco by sniffing had been practiced in Spain and Portugal for some time, snuff did not become widespread in western Europe until the mid-seventeenth century, when it was made fashionable by

Figure 14.29. Red clay pipe bowl fragments from the Dominican Republic. *Top left:* Molded design (top width 1.8 cm); *Top right:* Incised and molded design; *Bottom left:* Incised design. All La Isabela, post-1500. Parque Nacional de La Isabela, Dominican Republic. *Bottom right:* Incised design on dark red clay (maximum width 1.7 cm). Concepción de la Vega, ca. 1503–62. Parque Nacional de Concepción de la Vega, Dominican Republic.

Louis XIII and the French court. It remained the stylish way to use tobacco until the first decades of the nineteenth century, when the thousands of English and French troops who fought in Iberia during the Napoleonic peninsular war were introduced to cigar smoking. They in turn introduced cigars to their respective countries after returning from the war (1815), and cigars quickly replaced snuff as the fashionable form of social smoking (Scott and Scott 1981:3–4).

The use of snuff required a small container that could be carried on the person, and snuff containers provided an opportunity for display and extravagance among the well-to-do. Numerous fine snuffboxes of the seventeenth and eighteenth centuries survive in European museums. These are often miniature works of art, made of precious metals, jewels, ivory, enamelwork, gold, and tortoiseshell (see, for example, Le Corbeiller 1966). Less-affluent users of snuff had boxes of wood, tin, pewter, or papier-mâché. An example of a gold snuffbox recovered from a 1715 Florida shipwreck is shown in Figure 14.30, and others are illustrated by Skowronek (1982) and Borrell (1983a, 1983c). Most of these are thought to be of French origin, and some in fact bear such inscriptions in French as *Mon plaisir* (FBAR Lab #8MO101-L2654).

Snuffboxes were made in a vast array of shapes and sizes, ranging from about 5 to 8 cm in diameter or on a side. It is not always possible to distinguish snuff containers from the small, ornate boxes used for sweets, pomander, or trinkets, since these were also popular with both men and women during the seventeenth and eighteenth centuries. Snuffboxes did, however, always have a hinged lid that fit securely to the bottom of the box, since the purpose of the box was to avoid spilling snuff in one's pocket. A box without evidence of a hinged lid was probably not used to carry snuff.

Snuff did not replace cigars in the Spanish colonies, and men and women of the Spanish Americas continued smoking hand-rolled cigars as a form of relaxation well beyond the colonial era (see, for example, Vega 1981).

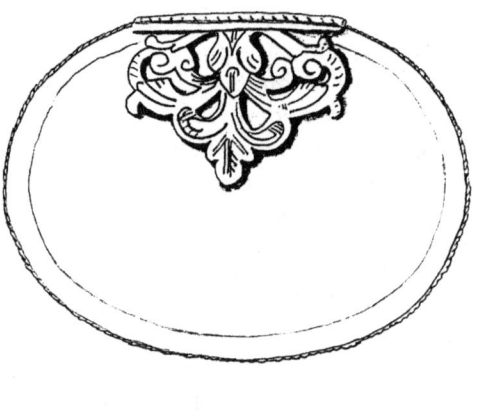

Figure 14.30. Gold snuffbox. 1715. Top view and rear hinge view. Top: 6.2 cm by 4.7 cm; thickness 2.2 cm (8SL17) FBAR Lab #L6276. *Courtesy of the Florida Bureau of Archaeological Research. Drawing: Frank Gilson.*

Glossary

Alcalde:	Justice of the peace in a Spanish colonial town, serving functions similar to those of a mayor. *Alcaldes* were elected each year from the members of the town council (see *Cabildo*) and had jurisdiction over criminal proceedings and enforcement of ordinances.
Alhóndiga:	A large structure used in the earliest colonies as a combined storehouse, stockroom, customs house, and administrative center.
Almojarifazgo:	Customs duties levied on imported and exported goods.
Arondela:	A hairpiece, usually to add length and volume.
Arroba:	A measure of weight comprising approximately 14.3 kg (about 25 lb).
Asiento:	An exclusive permit and contract to import slaves to the Spanish Americas.
Audiencia:	A council or tribune governing administrative and judicial affairs in a colony. It was presided over by the governor or viceroy of the colony.
Baldric:	A broad belt extending diagonally across the body from shoulder to waist, intended for the suspension of sword or other military equipment.
Bezel:	The part of a ring or ornament that surrounds and holds fast the stone.
Bezoar stones:	Renal calcifications found in deer, often mounted in settings and used as amulets.
Billón:	An alloy of copper with small amounts of silver, used for low-denomination coins in medieval and early modern Europe and America.
Caballero:	A knight or the highest category of untitled nobility.
Cacique (m), *Caciqua* (f):	A term used by Europeans to refer to chiefs among the American Indians, and particularly those inhabiting the circum-Caribbean region. (alternate form: *cassique*).

Cartouche:	An oval or oblong shape or design enclosing an emblem.
Casa Real:	Literally the Royal House, or a public building in which affairs of the crown were conducted (treasury, customhouse, and so forth).
Casta:	In the Spanish colonies, a person of mixed-race heritage. The many varieties of *castas* were depicted in a series of paintings done in eighteenth-century Mexico.
Cédula:	An official decree, most often set forth by the crown.
Cofradía:	A confraternity or religious fraternity of laypeople devoted to a saint or other religious devotion. Members of a *cofradía* were involved in works to benefit the Church and the membership.
Convento:	A monastery for friars.
Converso:	A Jewish convert to Catholicism in the Spanish world.
Corsair:	A ship (or one of its crew members) not licensed by a legitimate government, which preys on and tries to capture other vessels (usually of a different nationality).
Criollo:	A person of Spanish ancestry born and living in the Americas. This term also can refer to the forms of items or practices generated in the Americas by criollos.
Doctrina:	An American Indian Catholic parish.
Doublet:	Tight-fitting, buttoned vest worn by Spanish men.
Emic:	An anthropological term that refers to the meaning of something from the internal perspective of the person experiencing it (see also etic).
Entrada:	The entry of a Spanish (or other foreign) force into an area that was previously unexplored and unsettled by Europeans.
Etic:	An anthropological term referring to the meaning of something from the perspective of the external observer (see also emic).
Fanega:	A unit of weight or volume comprising about 4 *arrobas,* 44.8 kg (100 lb), or 1.6 bushels.
Feature:	A term used by archaeologists to designate a disturbance to the earth left by a recognizable cultural (or natural) activity, event, or process in the past.
Flota:	The annual Spanish trading fleet that gathered goods from Mexico, usually sailing to and from Veracruz and Seville. It met and joined with the *galeón* fleet in Havana for the transatlantic trip to Spain.

FS#:	Abbreviation for "Field Specimen Number," a number assigned in the field to each lot of associated excavated material assumed to represent a group of materials deposited as part of the same event or process.
Galeón:	The annual Spanish trading fleet that gathered goods from South and Central America, usually sailing to and from Cartagena and Seville. It met and joined with the *flota* in Havana for the transatlantic trip to Spain.
Hidalgo:	An untitled member of the minor Spanish nobility (derived from *hijo de algo,* or "son of somebody").
Hidalguía:	The Spanish Castilian ideal of nobility.
Idiotechnic:	In archaeology, objects that function to express ideology or belief systems.
Latón:	Tin. It is also sometimes used to refer to brass.
Maravedí:	The lowest denomination *billón* (copper-alloy) coin in the Spanish Americas, worth about 1/44 of a real. They were produced in the Mexico and Santo Domingo Spanish American mints between about 1536 and 1550.
Marian devotion:	Devotion to the Virgin Mary.
Mestizo (m), Mestiza (f):	A person of mixed European and American Indian parentage.
Moravian:	Settlers from Moravia (Germany) who immigrated to the southeastern United States in the eighteenth century and are well known for their pottery-making traditions (including pipes).
Morisco(m), *Morisca* (f):	A Muslim converted to Christianity.
Mudejar:	A Muslim living under Christian rule. The term also refers to a Muslim-influenced artistic style in late medieval and early Renaissance Christian Spain.
Obverse:	Numismatic term used to refer to the side of a coin bearing the symbol of the monarch who issued it. The other side is known as the "reverse." Also used to designate the top or visible side of a button.
Operculum:	A hard covering over the opening of some gastropod shells when the animal is completely retracted.
Otolith:	A small, calcareous body found in the inner-ear cavities of vertebrates.
Palo de Brasil:	Brazil wood, or dyewood, usually of the genus *Caesalpinia.* Red in color, it was used as a source of dye and for ornamental objects.
Patronato Real:	Royal patronage of the Catholic Church, which

	included privileges of participation in Church administrative affairs.
Peninsular:	A Spaniard born in Iberia.
Pietá:	Representation of the Virgin Mary holding and mourning the dead body of Christ.
Pragmatica:	An imperial or papal decree with the force of law.
Presidio:	A fortified town on a frontier, existing principally for the defense of the empire.
Quintal:	A Spanish weight measure equivalent to four arrobas (about 46 kg).
Real:	Silver coins used in Spain and its colonies during the colonial era. One real was equivalent to approximately 44 or 34 maravedís (in Spain and the Americas, respectively).
Relación:	A report or account.
Reliquary:	A container for safeguarding or displaying the relics of saints or other holy objects.
Repartimiento:	In the Spanish colonies, an allocation of Indians assigned to one of their conquerors for purposes of forced labor.
Rescate:	Illegal trade, particularly between Spanish citizens of the American colonies and non-Spanish foreign nationals; smuggling.
Rouletting:	Designs comprised of lines of small, incised, vertical tics.
Seriation:	Placing things into a series by some logical principle of ordering. In archaeology, this is usually done as a method of dating.
Situado:	A government subsidy of goods and specie provided to military presidio colonies.
Sociotechnic:	In archaeology, objects that function to reflect or communicate social identity.
Sonajero:	A rattle or small object intended to make sounds. These were commonly given to Spanish babies to protect them against evil.
Syncretism:	The blending of two distinct cultural traditions to produce a new, recombinant mode of expression.
Taíno:	The indigenous people of the Caribbean at the time of European arrival (1492).
Technomic:	In archaeology, this refers to objects that function primarily in the technological spheres of human activity.

Glossary

Terminus post quem (TPQ):	A relative dating method used by archaeologists. It means "date after which," or the latest date after which a deposit must have entered the ground. Usually the TPQ is provided by the latest dated object in a deposit.
Timucua:	The indigenous inhabitants of northeast Florida and southeastern Georgia at the time of European arrival (1513).
Tonelada:	A unit of measure for the carrying capacity of ships. During most of the sixteenth century, this was equivalent to 1.4 cubic meters.
Trenza:	A hair braid.
Vellón:	See *Billón*.
Venera:	Symbol of a cult, saint, religious order, knighthood, confraternity, and other religious organizations.
Vihuela:	A small Spanish guitar-type instrument played during the colonial era.
White metal:	A general term used to describe any alloy of metal containing predominantly tin or lead, which gives it a whitish color.
Zoomorphic:	Having a shape or form derived from an animal.

References

Abbitt, Merry
    1973   The eighteenth-century shoe buckle. In Five Artifact Studies. *Colonial Williamsburg Occasional Papers in Archaeology* 1:25–53.

Adams, Edgar H.
    1929   *Catalogue of the Guttag collection. Coins of the Americas.* New York: privately printed.

Ahlborn, Richard
    1991   Religious devices from Santa Catalina de Guale, Georgia, 1566–1686. Unpublished manuscript submitted to the American Museum of Natural History, New York.

Alarcón Román, Concepción
    1987   *Catálago de amuletos del Museo del Pueblo Español.* Madrid: Ministerio de Cultura.

Alcaide, Soledad Nieto
    1982   Juguetes. In *Historia de las artes aplicadas e industriales en España,* edited by Antonio Bonet Correa, 631–638. Madrid: Ediciones Cátedra.

Alexander, Helene
    1984   *Fans.* London: B. T. Batsford.

Allard, Carolus
    1966   *Orbis habitabilis oppida et vestitus.* (1695). (The towns and costumes of the inhabited world). Amsterdam: Teatrum Orbis Teattarum, Ltd.

Allender, Mark T.
    1995   Sixteenth-century European contact sites along the Florida Gulf coast. Master's thesis, University of Florida.

Allerton, David, George Luer, and Robert Carr
    1984   Ceremonial tablets and related objects from Florida. *Florida Anthropologist* 37(1):5–54.

Amades, Joan
    1951   Piedras de virtud. *Revista de dialectología y tradiciones populares* (Madrid) 7:84–131.

Amman, Jost
1968 *A pictorial archive of decorative renaissance woodcuts*. New York: Dover.

Amman, Jost, and Hans Sachs
1973 *The book of trades (*Standebüch*)*. (1568). New York: Dover.

Anders, Andrén
1997 *Between artifacts and text: Historical archaeology in global perspective*. New York: Plenum Press.

Anderson, Lawrence
1956 *El arte de la platería en México*. Mexico City: Editorial Porrua.

Anderson, Ruth M.
1979 *Hispanic costume 1480–1530*. New York: Hispanic Society of America.

Andrews, Kenneth
1978 *The Spanish Caribbean: Trade and plunder, 1530–1630*. New Haven, Conn.: Yale University Press.

Angulo Íñiguez, Diego
1954 *Ars hispaniae, Historia universal del arte hispánico*. Vol. 12 (*Pintura del siglo* 16). Madrid: Editorial Plus Ultra.

Anonymous
1926 *Catálago de medallas religiosas con inscripciones españoles y latinas*. Sales catalog on file. London: Victoria and Albert Museum Library.
1950 *Catálogo de la colección de cuernos talladas y grabadas*. Madrid: Museo del Pueblo Español.
1951 *Catálogo de la colección de collares*. Madrid: Museo del Pueblo Español.
1952 *Catálogo de la colección de sonajeros*. Madrid: Museo del Pueblo Español.

Apestegui, Cruz, Carlos León, and Pedro Borrell
1996 *Navegantes y náufragios: Galeones en la ruta del mercurio*. Madrid: Editores Lundwerg.

Arana, Luis
1971 A private library in 1680: Will of Pedro Bénedit de Horruytiner. *El Escribano* (St. Augustine Historical Society) 8(3):165–167.
1972 A bitter pill for the widow Cendoya. *El Escribano* (St. Augustine Historical Society) 9(2):73–77.

Arfe, Juan de
1698 *Quiltador de oro, plata y piedras*. Madrid.

Armstrong, Nancy
1986 Los abanicos del Museo Lázaro Galdiano. *Goya* (193–195):131–142.

Arnold, Barto, and Robert Weddle
　1978　*The nautical archaeology of Padre Island, Texas.* New York: Academic Press.

Arranz Márquez, Luis
　1991　*Repartimientos y encomiendas en la isla Española.* Santo Domingo: Fundación García-Arévalo.

Arrom, Juan J., and Manuel García-Arévalo
　1986　*Cimarrón.* Santo Domingo: Fundacion García-Arévalo.

Artes de México
　1968　Virgenes de México. *Artes de México* 15(113).

Atkinson, David, and Adrian Oswald
　1969　London clay pipes. *Journal of the Archaeological Society of London* 32.
　1972　A brief guide for the identification of Dutch clay tobacco pipes found in England. *Post-Medieval Archaeology* (London) 6:175–182.

Austin, R. G.
　1934　Roman board games. *Greece and Rome* (London) 4.
　1940　Greek board games. *Antiquity* 14(1):257–271.

Avery, George
　1996　The 1996 annual report for the Los Adaes Station Archaeology Program. Department of Social Sciences, Northwestern State University of Louisiana, Natchitoches.
　1997　Pots as packaging: The Spanish olive jar and Andalucian transatlantic commercial activity, 16th–18th centuries. Ph.D. diss., University of Florida.

Axtell, James
　1995　Columbian encounters: 1992–1995. *William and Mary Quarterly* 52(4):649–696.

Baart, Jan
　1995　Kammen/Combs. In *One man's trash is another man's treasure: The metamorphosis of the European utensil in the New World,* edited by Alexandra van Dongen, 175–188. Rotterdam: Museum Boymans-von Beuningen.

Baker, Henry
　1968　Archaeological investigations at Panama la Vieja. Master's thesis, University of Florida.

Balsdon, J. P.
　1969　*Life and leisure in ancient Rome.* New York: McGraw-Hill.

Baroja de Caro, Carmen
　1945　*Catálago de la colección de amuletos.* Madrid: Museo del Pueblo Español.
　1947　*Catálago de la colección de pendientes.* Madrid: Museo del Pueblo Español.

1952 *Suplemento de catálago de la colección de pendientes.* Madrid: Museo del Pueblo Español.

Barriga Villalba, Antonio María
1969 *Historia de la casa de moneda.* 2 vols. Bogotá: Banco de la República.

Barrio Lorenzot, Francisco del
1920 *Ordenanzas de gremios de la Nueva España.* Mexico City: Dirección de Talleres Gráficos, Secretario de Gobernación.

Bauman, Paul
1970 Collecting antique marbles. Albany, N.Y.: Wallace Homestead Books.

Beaudry, Mary, ed.
1988 *Documentary archaeology in the New World.* Cambridge: Cambridge University Press.

Beaudry, Mary, Lauren Cook, and Stephen Mrozowski
1991 Artifacts and active voices: Material culture as social discourse. In *The archaeology of inequality,* edited by R. McGuire and R. Paynter, 150–191. Oxford: Basil Blackwell.

Bell, R. C.
1960 *Board and table games from many civilizations.* London: Oxford University Press.
1969 *The boardgame book.* London: Cavendish House.

Beltrán Martínez, Antonio
1983 *Historia de la moneda Española.* Madrid: Editorial Vico y Sega.

Benson, Carl A.
1967 The Phillips mound: A historic site. *Florida Anthropologist* 20(3–4):146–163.

Benson, George
1976 *The cross: Its history and symbolism.* New York: Hacker Art Books.

Berges, M.
1984 *Joyas populares.* Catálogo de la exposición en el Museo Arqueológico Nacional. Madrid: Museo del Pueblo Español.

Bermudez, Egberto
1992 Instrumentos musicales latínoamericanos del período colonial. *Revista musicál de Venezuela* 12(30–31):155–162.

Bernard, F. P.
1981 *The casting counter and the counting board.* (1917). Oxford: Oxford University Press.

Berners, Dame Juliana
1962 *Indumentaria Española en tiempos de Carlos V.* Madrid: Editorial A.
1966 *The book of St. Albans.* New York: Abercrombie and Fitch.

Binford, Lewis
1962 Archaeology as anthropology. *American Antiquity* 28:217–225.

Biringuccio, Vannoccio
  1990 *The Pirotechnica.* (1540). Translated and edited by Cyril S. Smith and Martha Teach Gnudi. New York: Dover.

Blackmore, Howard L.
  1962 *British military firearms (1650–1850).* New York: Arco Publishing.

Blair, Craig
  1960 *Diving for pleasure and treasure.* Cleveland and New York: World Publishing.

Bock, Freidrich
  1935 *Deutsches handwerk im mittelalter.* Leipzig: Inselverlag.

Bond, Stanley, Valerie Bell, and Susan Parker
  1994 Archaeological excavations at the Puente site (SA24) and Potters parking lot (SA23), St. Augustine, Florida. Unpublished project report on file, Historic St. Augustine Preservation Board, St. Augustine, Fla.

Boone, James
  1980 *Artifact deposition and demographic change: An archaeological case study of medieval colonialism in the age of expansion.* Ann Arbor, Mich.: University Microfilms.

Borrell, Pedro
  1983a *Arqueología submarina en la República Dominicana.* Santo Domingo: Museo Casas Reales.
  1983b *Historia y rescate del galeón* Nuestra Señora de la Concepción. Santo Domingo: Museo Casas Reales.
  1983c *The Quicksilver wrecks.* Santo Domingo: Museo Casas Reales.

Bouchardon, Chaumont
  1737–1744 *Etudes prises dans le bas peuple ou Cris de Paris* (60 plates). Paris.

Boulton, Alfredo
  1952 *La Margarita.* Barcelona: I. C. Seix y Barral Hnos.

Bourne, Edward
  1907 Columbus, Ramon Pané and the beginnings of American anthropology. *Proceedings of the American Antiquarian Society* 17:310–348.

Bouza Brey, F.
  1949 El lagarto en la tradición popular gallega. *Revista de dialectología y tradiciones populares* (Madrid) 5:531–550.

Boyd, E.
  1958 The use of tobacco in Spanish New Mexico. *El Palacio* 65(June):103–106.
  1961 A bronze medal of sixteenth-century style. *El Palacio* 68(2):124–128.

Boyd, Mark F., Hale G. Smith, and John W. Griffin
   1951 *Here they once stood: The tragic end of the Apalachee missions.* Gainesville: University of Florida Press.

Boyrie Moya, Emile de
   1964 *La casa de piedra de Ponce de León en Higuey.* Santo Domingo: Editora del Caribe.

Brain, Jeffrey
   1975 Artifacts of the Adelantado. *Conference on Historic Sites Archaeology Papers* 8:129–138.
   1979 *Tunica treasure.* Boston and Salem: Peabody Museums.

Brill, Robert
   1986 Laboratory studies of some European artifacts excavated on San Salvador Island. In *Proceedings of the first San Salvador conference: Columbus and his world,* edited by D. Gerace, 247–292. San Salvador, Bahamas: College Center of the Finger Lakes.
   1992 Preliminary remarks on the analysis of glasses from La Isabela, Dominican Republic. Paper read at the American Association for the Advancement of Science, Chicago.

Brinckerhoff, Sidney, and Pierce Chamberlain
   1972 *Spanish military weapons in colonial America, 1700–1821.* Harrison, Pa.: Stackpole Books.

British Museum
   1976 *Jewelry through 7000 years.* London: British Museum.

Brown, Ian
   1975 Historic trade bells. *Conference on Historic Sites Archaeology Papers* 10:69–82.
   1979 Bells. In *Tunica treasure,* edited by J. Brain, 197–205. Boston and Salem: Peabody Museums.

Brown, M. L.
   1980 *Firearms in colonial America.* Washington, D.C.: Smithsonian Institution Press.

Burgess, George, and Carl Clausen
   1976 *Gold, galleons and archaeology.* New York: Bobbs-Merrill Company.
   1982 *Florida's golden galleons.* Stuart, Fla.: Florida Classics Library.

Bury, Shirley
   1982 *Jewelry summary catalogue.* London: Victoria and Albert Museum.
   1984 *An introduction to rings.* London: Victoria and Albert Museum.

Burzio, Humberto F.
   1945 La ceca de la villa imperial de Potosí y la moneda colonial. *Publicaciones del Instituto de Investigaciones Históricas* 88. Buenos Aires: Peuser.
   1956–58 *Diccionário de la moneda Hispánoamericana.* 3 vols. Santiago de Chile: Fondo histórico y bibliográfico José Toribio Medina.

1958   La ceca de Lima. *Publicación 5*. Madrid: Fábrica nacional de moneda y timbre numismática.

Bushnell, Amy Turner
1982   *The king's coffer*. Gainesville: University of Florida Press.
1994   Situado *and* Sabana: *Spain's support system for the presidio and mission provinces of Florida*. American Museum of Natural History Anthropological Papers 7. New York: American Museum of Natural History.

Butzer, Karl, and Elisabeth Butzer
1989   Historical archaeology of medieval Muslim communities in the Sierra of eastern Spain. In *Medieval Archeology*, edited by C. Redman, 217–236. Medieval and Renaissance Texts and Studies. Binghamton, N.Y.: SUNY.

Calicó, Ferrán, Xavier Calicó, and Joaquín Trigo
1985   *Monedas españolas desde Juana y Carlos a Isabel II. (1504–1868)*. Barcelona: Gabinete Numismático Calicó.

Calicó, Xavier
1953   *Aportación a la historia monetaria de Santa Fé de Bogotá:* Barcelona: X y F Calicó.

Calvert, Abert F.
1907   *Spanish arms and armour.* New York and London: John Lane.

Caple, Chris
1995   Factors in the production of medieval and post-medieval brass pins. In *Trade and discovery: The scientific study of artefacts from post-medieval Europe and beyond*, edited by D. Hook and D. Gaimster, 221–234. British Museum Occasional Papers 109. London: British Museum.

Carillo y Gariel, Abelardo
1959   *El traje en la Nueva España*. Mexico City: Instituto Nacional de Antropología e Historia.
1989   *Campañas de México*. Mexico City: Universidad Nacional Autónoma de México, Instituto de Investigaciones Estéticas.

Caro Álvarez, J. A.
1973   La Isabela, Santo Domingo, R.D. *Boletín del Museo del Hombre Dominicano* (Santo Domingo) 3:48–52.

Caro Baroja, Julio
1950   *Catálogo de la colección de cuernos tallados y grabados*. Madrid: Museo del Pueblo Español.
1952a *Catálogo de la colección de medallas*. Madrid: Museo del Pueblo Español.
1952b *Catálogo de la colección de sonajeros*. Madrid: Museo del Pueblo Español.
1973   *Las brujas y su mundo*. Madrid: Alianza Editorial.
1974   La mágia en Castilla durante los siglos XVI y XVII. In *Algunos*

mitos españoles, edited by J. Caro Baroja, 185–303. Madrid: Ediciones del Centro.

Carrera Stampa, Manuel
   1949   The evolution of weights and measures in New Spain. *Hispanic American Historical Review* (February 1949) (pt. 1):2–22.

Carrión Gútiez, Manuel
   1994   La encuadernación Española. In *Historia ilustrada del libro Español de los incunables al siglo XVII,* edited by Hipólito Escolar, 395–446. Madrid: Fundación German Sánchez Ruipérez.

Casanowicz, Immanuel
   1909   The collection of rosaries in the United States National Museum. *Proceedings of the United States National Museum* 36:333–359.
   1929   Collections of objects of religious ceremonial in the United States Museum. *United States National Museum Bulletin* 148:24–61.

Castañega, Fray Martín de
   1946   *Tratado de las supersticiones y hechicerías* (1529). Madrid: Sociedad de Bibliófilos Españoles.

Catholic Church
   1883   Medals of the Roman pontiffs from Martin V (1417) to Leo XIII (1883) coined at the Roman mint. Translated from the Italian catalog. (Microfilm, filmed by Microfilming Corporation of America). Original in Ryan Memorial Library, St. Charles Seminary, Overbrook, Philadelphia.

Chaney, Ed
   1993   Survey and evaluation of archaeological resources in the Abbott Tract and North City, St. Augustine (with special reference the Fountain of Youth Park site, 8-SJ-31). Master's paper on file, Florida Museum of Natural History, University of Florida, Gainesville.

Chaney, Ed, and Kathleen Deagan
   1989   St. Augustine and the La Florida colony: New lifestyles in a new land. In *First Encounters,* edited by J. Milanich and S. Milbrath, 166–182. Gainesville: University Press of Florida.

Chatelaine, Verne
   1941   *The defenses of Spanish Florida, 1565–1763.* Carnegie Institute of Washington Publication 511. Washington, D.C.

Chaunu, Huguette, and Pierre Chaunu
   1957   *Seville et L'Atlantique (1504–1650).* Vol. 7, *Constructión Graphique.* Ecole Practique des Hautes Etudes. Paris: SEVPEN.

Chiovaro, F.
   1967   Relics. In *The New Catholic Encyclopedia* 11:234–240. San Francisco: Robert Appleton Company.

Christian, William
   1981   *Local religion in sixteenth-century Spain.* Princeton, N.J.: Princeton University Press.

Cipriano de Utrera, Fray
   1947   *La immaculada concepción.* Santo Domingo: Imprenta Franciscana.

Clausen, Carl
   1965   *A 1715 Spanish treasure ship.* Florida State Museum Occasional Contributions in Anthropology 12. Gainesville: University of Florida.

Cleland, Charles
   1971   *The Lasenen site.* Publications of the Museum, Anthropological Series 1(1). East Lansing: Michigan State University.

Cockrell, Wilburn S.
   1980   The trouble with treasure. *American Antiquity* 45:333–349.

Cockrell, Wilburn S., ed.
   1981   *In the realms of gold.* Proceedings of the Tenth Conference on Underwater Archaeology. Society for Historical Archaeology.

Cohen, Jeremy
   1997   Preliminary report on the 1996 field season at Concepción de la Vega, Dominican Republic. Master's paper on file, Florida Museum of Natural History, University of Florida, Gainesville.

Coleman, Satis N.
   1928   *Bells: Their history, legends, making and uses.* Chicago: Rand McNally.

Contreras y López de Ayala, Juan
   1951   *Catálago de la colección de rosarios.* Madrid: Museo del Pueblo Español.
   1952   *Catálago de la colección de collares.* Madrid: Museo del Pueblo Español.

Córdoba de la Llave, Ricardo
   1990   *La indústria medieval en Córdoba.* Córdoba: Caja Provincial de Ahorros de Córdoba.

Corona Alcalde, Antonio
   1993   La vihuela, el laud y la guitarra en el Nuevo Mundo. *Revista de musicología* 16(3):1360–1372. Proceedings of the XV Congreso de la Sociedad Internacional de Musicología: Culturas Musicales del Mediteráneo y sus Ramificaciónes.

Corson, Richard
   1965   *Fashions in hair: The first five thousand years.* New York: Hastings House.
   1967   *Fashions in eyeglasses.* Chester Springs, Pa.: Dufour Editions.
   1972   *Fashions in makeup from ancient to modern times.* London: Peter Owen.

Cotter, C. S.
　1948　The discovery of the Spanish carvings at Seville. *Jamaican Historical Review* 1(3):227–233.
　1970　Sevilla Nueva: The story of an excavation. *Jamaica Journal* 4(2):15–22.

Cotter, John, and Paul Hudson
　1957　*New discoveries at Jamestown.* Washington, D.C.: Government Printing Office.

Council, R. Bruce
　1975　Archeology of the Convento de San Francisco. Master's thesis, University of Florida.

Cowgill, J. M. de Neergaard, and N. Griffiths
　1987　*Knives and scabbards.* Medieval Finds from Excavations in London 1. London: Museum of London.

Craig, Alan K.
　1988　*Gold coins of the 1715 Spanish plate fleet: A numismatic study of the state of Florida collection.* Tallahassee: Florida Bureau of Archaeological Research.
　2000　*Spanish colonial silver coins in the Florida collection.* Gainesville: University Press of Florida.

Cruxent, José M.
　1990　The origin of La Isabela. In *Columbian Consequences,* vol. 2, edited by D. H. Thomas, 251–260. Washington, D.C.: Smithsonian Institution Press.

Cruxent, José M., and Irving Rouse
　1958　*An archeological chronology of Venezuela.* 2 vols. Pan American Union Social Science Monographs 6. Washington, D.C.

Cruz Valdevinos, José M., and Andrés Escalera Ureña
　1993　*La platería de la Catedrál de Santo Domingo: Primada de América.* Santo Domingo and Madrid: Patronato de la Ciudad Colonial de Santo Domingo.

Cusick, James
　1993　*Ethnic groups and class in an emerging market economy: Spaniards and Minorcans in late colonial St. Augustine.* Ann Arbor, Mich.: University Microfilms.

Cusick, James, ed.
　1997　*Culture contact: Interaction, culture change and archaeology.* Carbondale: Southern Illinois University Press.

D'Aulnoy, Madame Marie-Catherine
　1930　*Travels into Spain.* (1691). Broadway Travelers Series. London: George Routledge.

Davenport, Millia
　1948　*The book of costume.* New York: Crown Books.

Davey, Peter. ed.
- 1979 *The archaeology of the clay tobacco pipe.* Vol. 2, *The United States of America.* Oxford: BAR International Series 60.
- 1981a *The archaeology of the clay tobacco pipe.* Vol. 5, *Europe 2.* Oxford: BAR International Series 177.
- 1981b *The archaeology of the clay tobacco pipe.* Vol. 6, *Pipes and kilns in the London region.* Oxford: BAR International Series 178.
- 1983 *The archaeology of the clay tobacco pipe.* Vol. 8, *America.* Oxford: BAR International Series 175.
- 1985 *The archaeology of the clay tobacco pipe.* Vol. 9, *More pipes from the midlands and southern England.* Oxford: BAR 146 (i–iii).

Davies, P. N., J. Illsley, D. C. Jones, O. Roberts, and S. Wignall
- 1981 Nautical archaeology in Wales: A progress report. *Underwater archaeology: The challenge before us,* edited by Gordon Watts, 33–57. San Marino, Calif.: Fathom Eight.

Dávila Rodríguez, Arturo
- 1989 *María en la religiosidad popular de Puerto Rico.* Bogotá: Consejo Episcopal Latinoamericano.

Davis, Mary L., and Greta Pack
- 1963 *Mexican jewelry.* Austin: University of Texas Press.

Deagan, Kathleen
- 1972 Fig Springs: The mid seventeenth century in north-central Florida. *Historical Archaeology* 6:23–46.
- 1976 *Archaeology at the Greek Orthodox Shrine.* Florida State University Notes in Anthropology 16. Tallahassee.
- 1981 Downtown survey: The discovery of 16th century St. Augustine in an urban area. *American Antiquity* 46:626–633.
- 1983 *Spanish St. Augustine: The archaeology of a colonial creole community.* New York: Academic Press.
- 1985 The archeology of 16th century St. Augustine. *Florida Anthropologist* 38(1–2):6–33.
- 1987 *Artifacts of the Spanish colonies of Florida and the Caribbean, 1500–1800.* Vol. 1, *Ceramics, glassware, and beads.* Washington, D.C.: Smithsonian Institution Press.
- 1988 Neither history nor prehistory: The questions that count in historical archaeology. *Historical Archaeology* 22(1):7–12.
- 1992a La Isabela, foothold in the New World. *National Geographic* 181(1):40–53.
- 1992b Preliminary report on laboratory analyses of materials recovered from La Isabela, Dominican Republic (1493–1498). Project report on file, Florida Museum of Natural History Historical Archaeology Lab, University of Florida, Gainesville.
- 1996 Colonial transformations: Euro-American cultural genesis in the earliest Spanish colonies. *Journal of Anthropological Research* 52(2):135–160.

1999 Final report on the *Proyecto para la conservacion y desarollo de los recursos fisicos-rurales y humanos en los Parques Nacionales de la República Dominicana: La Isabela y Concepción de la Veg*a. Project report submitted to the Dirección Nacional de Parques, Santo Domingo, and U.S.A.I.D., Santo Domingo. On file, Florida Museum of Natural History, University of Florida, Gainesville.

Deagan, Kathleen, ed.
1995 *Puerto Real: The archaeology of a sixteenth-century Spanish town in Hispaniola.* Gainesville: University Press of Florida.

Deagan, Kathleen, and José Cruxent
1993 From contact to criollos: The archaeology of Spanish colonization in Hispaniola. In *The meeting of two worlds: Europe and the Americas 1492–1650,* edited by Warwick Bray, 67–104. Proceedings of the British Academy 81. Oxford: Oxford University Press.
1997 Medieval foothold in the Americas. *Archaeology* 50(4):54–61.
2002a *Archaeology at La Isabela: America's first European town, 1493–1498.* New Haven, Conn.: Yale University Press.
2002b *Columbus's outpost among the Taínos: Spain and America at La Isabela, 1493–1498.* New Haven, Conn.: Yale University Press.

Deagan, Kathleen, and Darcie MacMahon
1995 *Fort Mose: Colonial America's fortress of freedom.* Gainesville: University Press of Florida.

DeBles, Arthur
1925 *How to distinguish the saints in art.* New York: Art Culture Publications.

Deetz, James
1977 *In small things forgotten.* Garden City, N.J.: Anchor-Doubleday.
1993 *Flowerdew Hundred: The archaeology of a Virginia plantation 1617–1864.* Charlottesville: University Press of Virginia.

Defourneaux, Marcel
1966 *Daily life in Spain in the golden age.* Palo Alto, Calif.: Stanford University Press.

Deleito y Piñuela, José
1946 *La mujer, la casa y la moda en la España del rey poeta.* Madrid: Editorial Esposa-Calpe.

Dennis, Faith
1943 *Renaissance jewelry.* New York: Metropolitan Museum of Art.

Denson, Robyn
1991 Interim report on the Oklawaha River survey. Project report on file, Florida Museum of Natural History, University of Florida, Gainesville.

Díaz-Plaja, Fernando
1995 *La vida cotidiana en la España medieval.* Crónicas de la historia 11. Serie la vida cotidiana. Madrid: Editorial EDAF.

Diderot, Denis
   1751– *Encyclopédie; ou Dictionnaire raisonne des sciences, des arts et de*
   65   *metiers, par un societé de gens de lettres.* 17 vols. Paris: Briasson.
   1959 *A Diderot pictorial encyclopedia of trades and industry.* (1752). 2 vols. New York: Dover.

Di Peso, Charles
   1976 That other revolution. *Archaeology* 29(3):190–195.

Domínguez, Lourdes
   1978 La transculturación en Cuba (s. XVI–XVII). *Cuba Arqueológica* 1:33–50. Santiago de Cuba: Editorial Oriente.
   1981 Arqueología del sitio colonial Casa de la Obrapia o de Calvo de la Puerta, Habana Vieja. *Santiago* (Havana) (41):63–82.
   1984 *Arqueología colonial cubana: Dos estudios.* Havana: Editorial de ciencias sociales.

Duarte, Carlos
   1984 *Historia del traje durante la época colonial Venezolana.* Caracas: Fundación Pampero.

Duby, Georges, and Phillippe Braunstein
   1988 The emergence of the individual. In *A history of private life II: Revelations of the medieval world,* edited by Georges Duby, 507–632. Cambridge: Belknap Press of Harvard University Press.

Duchet-Suchaux, Gaston, and Michel Pastoureau
   1996 *Guía iconográfica de la Biblia y los Santos.* Madrid: Alianza Editorial.

Du Mortier, Blanca
   1992 *Fans and fan leaves 1650–1800.* Amsterdam: Zutphen.
   1993 Print sources for eighteenth-century fans. *Magazine Antiques* (January):144–153.

Dusenbury, Elsbeth
   1960 Crosses in the collection of the museum. *The Museum* (Newark [N.J.] Art Museum) 12(2):1–27.

Egan, Geoff
   1997 Dice. *Datasheet 23.* In *Finds Research Group 700–1700, Datasheets 1–24.* Oxford: University of Oxford Reprographic Unit.

Egan, Geoff, and Frances Pritchard
   1991 *Dress accessories c. 1150–1450.* Medieval Finds from Excavations 3. London: Museum of London.

Elliot, John H.
   1961 The decline of Spain. *Past and Present* 20:52–75.
   1963 *Imperial Spain 1492–1716.* New York: St. Martin's Press.

Elliot, John H., ed.
   1991 *The Spanish world, civilization and empire, Europe and the Americas, past and present.* New York: Harry Abrams.

Ellis, Florence
    1987   The long lost "city" of San Gabriel del Yunque, second oldest European settlement in the United States. In *When cultures meet: Remembering San Gabriel del Yunque Oweenge,* 10–38. Santa Fe, N.M.: Sunstone Press.

Elworthy, F. T.
    1895   *The evil eye.* London: J. Murray.

Emerson, Matt
    1988   Decorated clay tobacco pipes from the Chesapeake. Ph.D. diss., University of California, Berkeley.
    1999   African inspirations in a New World art and artifact: Decorated pipes from the Chesapeake. In *"I, too, am America": Archaeological studies of African-American life,* edited by Theresa A. Singleton, 47–82. Charlottesville: University Press of Virginia.

Emilio, Luis Fenollasa
    1911   *Catalogue: The Emilio collection of military buttons: American, French, British and Spanish, with some other countries; and non-military, in the Museum of the Essex Institute.* Salem, Mass.

Espinosa, P.
    1911   Flagellants. *The Catholic Encyclopedia* 6:635–637. New York: Encyclopedia Press.

Estrella Gómez, Miguel
    1979   *Monedas Dominicanas.* Santo Domingo: Sociedád Dominicana de Bibliófilos.

Evans, Joan
    1970   *A history of jewelry 1100–1870.* 2nd ed. Boston: Boston Book and Art Publishers.
    1976   *Magical jewels of the Middle Ages and of the Renaissance.* New York: Dover.

Ewen, Charles
    1985   The Ximenex-Fatio house: A view from the backyard. In *Indians, slaves and colonists: Essays in honor of Charles H. Fairbanks,* edited by K. Johnson et al., 57–69. Gainesville: Department of Anthropology, University of Florida.
    1987   From Spaniard to creole: The archaeology of Hispanic-American cultural formation at Puerto Real, Haiti. Ph.D. diss., University of Florida.
    1991   *From Spaniard to creole.* Tuscaloosa: University of Alabama Press.

Ewen, Charles, and John Hann
    1998   *Hernando de Soto among the Apalachee: The archaeology of the first winter encampment.* Gainesville: University Press of Florida.

Fairbanks, Charles
    1968   Early Spanish colonial beads. *Conference on Historic Sites Archaeology Papers* 2(1):3–21.

1972 The cultural significance of Spanish ceramics. In *Ceramics in America*, edited by I. Quimby, 141–174. Charlottesville: University Press of Virginia.

Farmer, David H.
  1982 *The Oxford dictionary of saints*. Oxford: Oxford University Press Paperbacks.

Farnik, J. M.
  1967 Reliquaries. In *The New Catholic Encyclopedia* 12:335–336. San Francisco: Robert Appleton Company.

Fauchard, Pierre
  1969 *Chirurgien dentiste. (The surgeon dentist, or Treatise on the teeth.)* Translated from the 2nd ed. (1746) by Lilian Lindsay. Pound Ridge, N.Y.: Milford House.

Faulkner, Alric, and Gretchen Faulkner
  1987 *The French at Pentagoet, 1635–1674*. Special Publications of the New Brunswick Museum and Occasional Publications in Maine Archaeology 5. New Brunswick: Maine Historic Preservation Commission.

Ferguson, George
  1961 *Signs and symbols in Christian art*. Oxford: Oxford University Press.

Fernández, Alejandro, Rafael Munoa, and Jorge Rabasco
  1984 *Enciclopédia de la plata Española y virreinal Americana*. Madrid: Editorial de Arte.

Ffoulkes, Charles
  1988 *The armorer and his craft*. New York: Dover.

Fiosconi, Cesár, and Guserio Jordam
  1974 *Espingarda Perfeyta* or *The perfect gun*. (1718). Translated and edited by Rainer Daenhardt and W. Keith Neal. London: Sotheby Parke Benet Publications.

Foster, George
  1960 *Culture and conquest*. Viking Fund Publications in Anthropology 27. New York: Wenner-Gren Foundation.

Fox, Leonard, comp. and ed.
  1988 *The Jews harp: A comprehensive anthology*. London: Associated University Presses.

Frothingham, Alice
  1941 *Hispanic glass*. New York: Hispanic Society of America.

Gallo, Miguel Mujica
  1967 *The gold of Peru*. Recklinghausen, Germany: Verlag Aurel Bongers.

Gannon, Michael V.
  1965 *The cross in the sand*. Gainesville: University Press of Florida.

1992 The new alliance of archaeology and history in the eastern Spanish Borderlands. *William and Mary Quarterly* 49:321–334.

García Arévalo, Manuel
1978 La arqueologia Indo-Hispano en Santo Domingo. In *Unidades y variedades, ensayos en homenaje a José M. Cruxent,* edited by Erika Wagner, 77–127. Caracas: Centro de Estudios Avanzados.

García Guinea, Miguel Ángel, ed.
1999 *Fiestas, juegos y espectáculos en la España medieval.* Actas del VII curso de cultura medieval. Madrid: Ediciones Polifemo.

García Saíz, Maria C.
1989 *Las castas Mexicanas.* Mexico City: Olivetti.

Garibay, A. M.
1967 Guadalupe, Our Lady of. In *The New Catholic Encyclopedia* 6:821–822. San Francisco: Robert Appleton Company.

Gavin, Peter
1999 *Patterns of pillage: A geography of Caribbean-based piracy in Spanish America 1536–1718.* American University Studies Series 25. Vol. 5. New York: Peter Lang.

Gheyn, Jacob de
1608 *The exercise of armies: A seventeenth century military manual.* Amsterdam. Manuscript copy, Castillo de San Marcos National Monument Library.

Gibson, Charles
1966 *Spain in America.* New York: Harper and Row.

Gillaspie, William
1961 Juan de Ayala y Escobar: Procurador and entrepreneur: A case study of the provisioning of Florida 1683–1716. Ph.D. diss., University of Florida.

Goggin, John
1951 Ft. Pupo: A Spanish frontier outpost. *Florida Historical Quarterly* 30(2):139–192.
1952 *Space and time perspective in northern St. Johns archaeology, Florida.* Yale University Publications in Anthropology 47. New Haven, Conn.
1960 Spanish trade beads and pendants. Manuscript on file, Florida Museum of Natural History, University of Florida, Gainesville.
1968 *Spanish majolica in the New World.* Yale University Publications in Anthropology 72. New Haven, Conn.

Gómez Tabanero, José
1977 Azabeche, amuleto de la vieja Europa y ambar negro de Asturias. *Boletín del Instituto de Estudios Asturianos* (Oviedo) 31(90–91):383–413.

González, José
1980 Conferéncia del Arq. José Gonzáles. In *Objetos y ambientes de la*

Concepción de la Vega, coordinated by Atala de Poladura, 34–50. Catálogo de la exposición. Santo Domingo: Museo Casas Reales.

González, Justo
 1969 *The development of Christianity in the Caribbean.* Grand Rapids, Mich.: William B. Eerdmans.

González Mena, María Angeles
 1982 Bordados, pasamanerías y encajes. In *Historia de las artes aplicadas y industriales en España,* edited by Antonio Bonet Correa, 389–406. Madrid: Ediciones Cátedra.

Goodwin, William
 1946 *Spanish and English ruins in Jamaica.* Boston: Meador.

Gordon, Gardner, and Kathleen Deagan
 1992 Report on the 1992 excavations at the Fountain of Youth Park site (8-SJ-31) in St. Augustine, Florida, with an interpretive summary of 50 years of archaeology. Manuscript on file, Florida Museum of Natural History, University of Florida, Gainesville.

Graham, J. T., and Maurice Stevenson
 1987 *Weights and measures.* 3rd ed. Shire Album 14. Ayelsbury, England: Shire Publications.

Graham, Winston
 1972 *The Spanish Armadas.* Garden City, N.J.: Doubleday.

Gregory, Hiram, and Clarence Webb
 1965 European trade beads from six sites in Natchitoches Parish, Louisiana. *Florida Anthropologist* 28(3)(pt. 2):15–44.

Greif, Helmut
 1984 *Talks about thimbles: A cultural historical study.* Klagenfurt, Austria: Fungerhutmuseum Creglingen.

Griffin, John W.
 1960 Preliminary papers on the site of the mission of San Juan del Puerto, Fort George Island, Florida. *Papers of the Jacksonville Historical Society* 4:63–66.

Griffin, John W., and Hale G. Smith
 1948 *The Goodnow mound, Highlands County, Florida.* Contributions to the Archaeology of Florida, No. 1. Florida Park Service, Tallahassee.

Grove, Sylvia
 1966 *The history of needlework tools and accessories.* Feltham, England: Country Life Books.

Grunthal, Henry, and Ernesto Selschopp
 1978 *The coinage of Peru.* Frankfurt and Main: Numismatischer Verlag P.N. Schulten.

Guazzo, Francesco Mariá
 1988 *Compendium Maleficarum.* (1608). The Montague Summers edition, translated by E. A. Ashwin. New York: Dover.

Halbirt, Carl
    1996   The Plaza de la Constitución. Paper prepared for the Plaza rededication ceremony, August 15, 1996. City of St. Augustine (Fla.) Division of Planning and Building.

Hamilton, Earl
    1938   The decline of Spain. *Economic History Review* (first series) 8:168–179.

Hamilton, Jennifer, and William Hodges
    1982   Bayahá: A preliminary report. Typescript. Musée de Guahabá, Limbé, Haiti.
    1995   The aftermath of Puerto Real: Archaeology at Bayahá. In *Puerto Real: The archaeology of a sixteenth-century Spanish town in Hispaniola,* edited by K. Deagan, 375–419. Gainesville: University Press of Florida.

Hamilton, T. M.
    1968   *Early Indian trade guns, 1625–1775.* Contributions of the Museum of the Great Plains 3. Lawton, Okla.: Museum of the Great Plains.

Hamilton, T. M., and K. O. Emery
    1988   *Eighteenth-century gunflints from Ft. Michilimackinac and other colonial sites.* Mackinac Island, Mich.: Mackinac Island State Park Commission.

Hanke, Lewis
    1949   *The Spanish struggle for justice in the conquest of America.* Washington, D.C.: American Historical Association.

Hann, John
    1986   Church furnishings, sacred vessels and vestments held by the missions of Florida: Translation of two inventories. *Florida Archaeology* 2:147–164.
    1988   *The Apalachee.* Gainesville: University Press of Florida.
    1991   Inventory and auction of the estate of Captain Don Fransisco de la Rua, deceased in 1649 in St. Augustine Florida. In *America's Ancient City: Spanish St. Augustine 1565–1763,* edited by K. Deagan, 492–541. New York: Garland Press.
    1996   *A history of the Timucua Indians and missions.* Gainesville: University Press of Florida.

Hann, John, and Bonnie G. McEwan
    1998   *The Apalachee Indians and Mission San Luis.* Gainesville: University Press of Florida.

Hardin, Kenneth
    1986   The Santa Maria Mission Project. *Florida Anthropologist* 39(1–2):75–83.

Haring, Clarence H.
  1947 *The Spanish empire in America.* New York: Harcourt, Brace and Jovanovich.
  1964 *Trade and navigation between Spain and the Indies in the time of the Hapsburgs.* (1918). Gloucester, Mass.: Peter Smith.

Harman, Joyce
  1969 *Trade and privateering in Spanish Florida 1721–1763.* St. Augustine, Fla.: St. Augustine Historical Society.

Harris, Neil
  1986 Coins of the *Nuestra Señora de Atocha. Numismatist* 99(10):2017–2042.

Hawkins, Nancy, ed.
  1986 Uncovered French Quarter burials analyzed. *Archaeology News* (Louisiana Division of Archaeology) 3(1):1–2.

Hayes, Gerald R.
  1928–30 *Musical instruments and their music, 1500–1750.* 2 vols. London: Oxford University Press.

Heim, Bruno Bernard
  1978 *Heraldry in the Catholic Church.* Atlantic Highlands, N.J.: Humanities Press.

Hernández Tápia, Concepción
  1970 Despoblaciónes de la isla de Santo Domingo en el Siglo XVII. *Anuário de Estudios Americanos* (Madrid) 27:281–320.

Hildburgh, W. L.
  1906 Notes on Spanish amulets. *Folklore* (London) 17:454–472.
  1914 Notes on Spanish amulets (third series). *Folklore* (London) 25:204–212.
  1915 Notes on Spanish amulets (fourth series). *Folklore* (London) 26:404–416.
  1940 Caravaca crosses and their uses as amulets in Spain. *Folklore* (London) 51:241–58.
  1942 Lunar crescents as amulets in Spain. *Man* (London) 42:73–84.
  1950–51 Psychology underlying the employment of amulets in Europe. *Folklore* (London) 61–62:231–251.
  1951 Some Spanish amulets connected with lactation. *Folklore* (London) 62:430–448.

Hill, Erica
  1995 Thimbles and thimble rings from the circum-Caribbean region, 1500–1800: Chronology and identification. *Historical Archaeology* 29(1):84–92.

Hinajosa Montalvo, José
  1999 Juegos, fiestras y espectáculos en el reino de Valencia: Del caballero andante al moro juglar. In *Fiestas, juegos y espectáculos en*

la España medieval, edited by M. A. García Guinea, 67–91. Actas del VII curso de cultura medieval. Madrid: Ediciones Polifemo.

Hinnebusch, W. H.
- 1967 The Rosary. In *The New Catholic Encyclopedia* 12:667–670. San Francisco: Robert Appleton Company.

Hinton, David
- 1982 *Medieval jewelry*. Shire Archaeology Series. Aylesbury, England: Shire Publications.

Hodges, William
- 1979 How we found Puerto Real. Typescript. Musée de Guahabá, Limbé, Haiti.
- 1991 Silver medal-locket found at Montholón, Haiti. *Occasional Newsletter of the Musée de Guahabá* 2. Limbé, Haiti.

Hodges, William, and Eugene Lyon
- 1995 A general history of Puerto Real. In *Puerto Real: The archaeology of a sixteenth-century Spanish town in Hispaniola*, edited by K. Deagan, 83–112. Gainesville: University Press of Florida.

Hoffman, Charles
- 1986 Archaeological investigations at the Long Bay site, San Salvador, Bahamas. In *Proceedings of the first San Salvador conference: Columbus and his world*, edited by D. Gerace, 237–245. San Salvador, Bahamas: College Center of the Finger Lakes.

Hoffman, Kathleen
- 1994 The development of a cultural identity in colonial America: The Spanish-American experience on La Florida. Ph.D. diss., University of Florida.

Hoffman, Paul
- 1980 *The Spanish crown and the defense of the Caribbean 1535–1585*. Baton Rouge: Louisiana State University Press.

Holme, Randle
- 1972 *A store house of armory and blazon*. (1688). Menston, England: Scholar Press.

Holmes, Edwin
- 1985 *A history of thimbles*. London: Cornwall Books.
- 1987 Sewing thimbles. *Datasheet* 9. In *Finds Research Group 700–1700, Datasheets 1–24*. Oxford: University of Oxford Reprographic Unit.

Holweck, Frederick
- 1910 The Immaculate Conception. In *The Catholic Encyclopedia* 6:678–681. New York: Encyclopedia Press.

Hoover, Herbert C., and Lou H. Hoover, ed.
- 1950 *De Re Metallica* (Georgius Agricola, 1556). New York: Dover.

Hoover, Robert, and Julia Costello, eds.
- 1985 *Excavations at Mission San Antonio 1976–1978*. Monograph 26. Institute of Archaeology, University of California at Los Angeles.

Hostos, Adolfo de
    1938   *Investigaciones históricas.* On file, Castillo de San Marcos National Monument Research Library, St. Augustine, Fla.

Howe, Jane
    1956   Spanish bells in New Mexico. *New Mexico Historical Review* 31(2):148–153.

Hyde, Thomas
    1976   Mandagorias, seu, Historia shahiludii . . . Oxonii: E Theatro Sheldoniano. (1694). In *Early English books, 1641–1700,* 568:5. Ann Arbor, Mich.: University Microfilms International.

Jelks, Edward
    1967   The Gilbert site: A Norteño focus site in northeastern Texas. *Bulletin of the Texas Archaeological Society* 37.

Jones, Grant
    1978   The ethnohistory of the Guale coast through 1684. In *The anthropology of St. Catherine's Island.* Vol. 1, *Natural and cultural history,* edited by D. Thomas. American Museum of Natural History Anthropological Papers 52(22).

Jones, Mark
    1979   *The art of the medal.* London: British Museum Publications.

Jones, William
    1967   A report on the site of San Juan del Puerto, a Spanish mission site, Fort George Island, Florida. Manuscript on file, St. Augustine Historical Society, St. Augustine, Fla.

Judge, Joseph
    1986   Where Columbus found the New World. *National Geographic* 170(5):566–572, 578–599.
    1988   Exploring our lost century. *National Geographic* 173(3):330–363.

Kamen, Henry
    1978   The decline of Spain—an historical myth? *Past and Present* 81:24–50.
    1991   *Spain 1469–1714: A society of conflict.* New York: Longham.

Kapitzke, Robert
    1999   *Religion, power and politics in colonial St. Augustine.* Gainesville: University Press of Florida.

Karcheski, Walter, Jr.
    1990   *Arms and armor of the conquistador, 1492–1600.* Gainesville: Florida Museum of Natural History.

Ketchum, William C.
    1981   *Toys and games.* Smithsonian Illustrated Library of Antiques. Washington D.C.: Cooper-Hewitt Museum.

Kieth, Donald
    1987   The Molasses Reef wreck. Project report, Institute for Nautical Archaeology, Texas A&M University, College Station.

King, Julia
    1981   An archaeological investigation of seventeenth-century St. Augustine, Florida. Master's thesis, Florida State University.

Kirkman, James
    1974   *Fort Jesus: A Portuguese fortress on the east African coast.* Oxford: Claredon Press.

Kisch, Bruno
    1965   *Scales and weights; a historical outline.* New Haven, Conn.: Yale University Press.

Knight, Franklin
    1978   *The Caribbean.* New York: Oxford University Press.

Koch, Joan K.
    1980   Nuestra Señora de la Soledád: A study of a church and hospital site in colonial St. Augustine. Master's thesis, Florida State University.

Kohler, Charles
    1963   *A history of costume.* New York: Dover.

Kubler, George
    1940   *Mexican architecture of the sixteenth-century.* New Haven, Conn.: Yale University Press.

Kuncze, Leo F.
    1885   *Systematik der weihmünzen.* Raab. (British Public Library 7737.b.7).

Langedijk, Catherine, and Herman Boon
    1999   *Vingerhoeden en naairingen uit de Amsterdamse bodem.* Amsterdam: De Archeologische Werkgemeenschap voor Nederland (AWN).

Lanllier, Jean, and Anne-Marie Pini
    1983   *Five centuries of jewelry in the West.* New York: Arch Cape Press.

L'Armessin, Nicolas de, and Gerard Valk
    1969   *Fantastick costumes of trades and professions.* (ca. 1650–90). London: Holland Press.

Las Casas, Bartolomé de
    1965   *Historia de las Indias.* 2 vols. Mexico City: Fondo de Cultura Económica.
    1985   *Historia de las Indias.* 3 vols. Santo Domingo: Ediciones del Continente.

Lavin, James
    1965   *A history of Spanish firearms.* New York: Arco.

Lea, Henry C.
    1968   *A history of auricular confessions and indulgences in the Latin Church.* (1896). Vol. 3. 3rd ed. New York: Greenwood Press.

LeCompte, Elise
    1988   Thimbles from the archaeological collections of the Florida

Museum of Natural History. Manuscript on file, Florida Museum of Natural History, University of Florida, Gainesville.

Le Corbeiller, Clare
  1966 *European and American snuff boxes, 1730–1830*. New York: Viking Press.

Leone, Mark, and Parker Potter
  1988 Introduction: Issues in historical archaeology. In *The recovery of meaning in historical archaeology in the eastern United States*, edited by M. Leone and P. Potter, 1–22. Washington, D.C.: Smithsonian Institution Press.

Lesage, Robert
  1960 *Vestments and church furniture*. New Haven, Conn.: Hawthorne Books.

Lesley, Parker
  1968 *Renaissance jewels and jeweled objects*. Baltimore: Baltimore Museum of Art.

Lester, Katherine M., and Bess V. Oerke
  1940 *Accessories of dress*. Peoria, Ill.: Manual Arts Press.
  1954 *Accessories of dress*. Peoria, Ill.: Charles A. Bennett Publications.

Leutenneger, Benedict, trans. and ed.
  1977 *Inventory of the Mission San Antonio de Valero, 1772*. Office of the State Archaeologist Special Report 23. Austin: Texas Historical Commission.

Levy, James
  1977 Report on conservation and reconstruction of a circa 1580 matchlock from St. Augustine. Lab report submitted to the Historic St. Augustine Preservation Board, July 11, 1977. On file, Florida Museum of Natural History, University of Florida, Gainesville.

Lewis, M. D. S.
  1970 *Antique paste jewelry*. Boston: Boston Book and Art.

Liddell, Donald M.
  1937 *Chessmen*. New York: Harcourt, Brace.

Lietch-Wright, John
  1978 *Anglo-Spanish rivalry in North America*. Athens: University of Georgia Press.

Lillenhammer, Grete
  1989 A child is born: The child's world in archaeological perspective. *Norwegian Archaeological Review* 22(2):89–105.

Limón Delgado, Antonio
  1981 *Costumbres populares andaluzas de nacimiento, matrimonio y muerte*. Seville: Artes Gráficas Paduras.

Linate, Claudio
   1956 *Trajes civiles, militares y religiosos de México.* (1828). Mexico City: Imprenta Universitaria, Universidad Nacional Autónoma de México.

Lister, Florence, and Robert Lister
   1987 *Andalucian ceramics in Spain and New Spain.* Albuquerque: University of New Mexico Press.

Little, Barbara
   1994 People with history: An update on historical archaeology in the United States. *Journal of Archaeological Method and Theory* 1(1):5–40.

Little, Barbara, ed.
   1992 *Text-aided archaeology.* Boca Raton, Fla.: CRC Press.

Logan, Patricia
   1977 The *San José de las Animas:* An analysis of the ceramic collection. Master's thesis, Florida State University.

Long, George
   1964 Excavations at Panamá Vieja. *Florida Anthropologist* 18(2):2–11.
   1967 Archaeological investigations at Panamá la Vieja. Master's thesis, University of Florida.

Lope de Vega
   1989 *Espistolaria (Obra completa).* Madrid: Real Academia Española.

López Cantos, Angel
   1992 *Juegos, fiestas y diversiones en la América Española.* Colecciones MAPFRE, Relaciones entre España y América, 10. Madrid: Editorial MAPFRE.

López-Penha, José Ramón Báez
   1992 *Por qué Santo Domingo es así?* Santo Domingo: Banco Nacional de la Vivienda.

López y Sebastian, Lorenzo
   1986 Sevilla la Nueva, Arqueología. Manuscript on file, Jamaica National Historic Trust, Kingston.

Lorenzo Sanz, Eufémio
   1979 *Comercio de España con América en la época de Felipe.* Vol. 2, *Tomo I: Los mercaderes y el tráfico Indiano.* Simancas: Institución Culturál Simancas.

Lorenzot, Francisco del Barrio
   1920 *Ordenanzas de grémios de la Nueva España.* Mexico City: Secretaria de Gobernación, Dirección de Talleres Gráficos.

Loucks, J. Lana
   1979 Political and economic interaction between Spaniards and Indians: Archaeological and ethnohistorical perspectives on the Spanish mission system in Florida. Ph.D. diss., University of Florida.

1993 Spanish-Indian interaction in the Florida missions: The archaeology of Baptizing Springs. In *The Spanish missions of La Florida,* edited by B. McEwan, 193–216. Gainesville: University Press of Florida.

Luccetti, Nicholas, and Beverly Straube
  1999 1998 interim report on the APVA excavations at Jamestown, Virginia. Jamestown: Association for the Preservation of Virginia Antiquities.

Luján Muñoz, Luís
  1975 *Historia de la mayólica en Guatemala.* Guatemala City: privately printed.

Lyon, Eugene
  1976 *The enterprise of Florida.* Gainesville: University Press of Florida.
  1979 *The search for the* Atocha. New York: Harper and Row.
  1985 List of material culture items brought to Florida, 1565–1580. Manuscript on file, St. Augustine Foundation, Inc., Flagler College, St. Augustine, Fla.
  1988 Toward a typology of Spanish colonial nails. In *The artifacts of Santa Elena,* edited by S. South, R. Skowronek, and R. Johnson, 325–330. Anthropological Papers 7. South Carolina Institute of Archaeology and Anthropology, Columbia.
  1992 Richer than we thought: The material culture of sixteenth-century St. Augustine. *El Escribano* (St. Augustine Historical Society) 29.
  1997 The first three wooden forts of Spanish St. Augustine, 1565–1571. Project historical report for *Archaeology at Florida's first Spanish fort.* On file, St. Augustine Foundation, Inc., Flagler College, St. Augustine and the Florida Museum of Natural History, University of Florida, Gainesville.

MacAlister, Lyle
  1984 *Spain and Portugal in the New World.* Minneapolis: University of Minnesota Press.

MacMurray, Judith Angley
  1973 The definition of the ceramic complex at San Juan del Puerto. Master's thesis, University of Florida.

Maintfort, Robert
  1979 *Indian social dynamics in the period of European contact.* Publications of the Museum. East Lansing: Michigan State University.

Malé, Emile
  1931 *L' art religieux de la fin du moyen age en France: Étude sur l'iconographie du moyen age et sur ses sources d'inspiration.* Paris: Armand Colin.
  1932 *L'art religieux aprés le Concile de Trent.* Paris: Libraire Armand Colin.

Maloney, Clarence, ed.
　1976　*The evil eye.* New York: Columbia University Press.

Mandel, Massimiliano
　1990　*Scissors.* Wigston, England: Magna Books.

Manucy, Albert
　1997　*Sixteenth-century St. Augustine.* Gainesville: University Press of Florida.

Manucy, Albert, and Ricardo Torres-Reyes
　1973　*The forts of Old San Juan.* Old Greenwich, England: Chatham Press.

Marrinan, Rochelle
　1993　Archaeological investigations at Mission Patale 1984–1992. In *The Spanish missions of La Florida,* edited by B. McEwan, 44–294. Gainesville: University Press of Florida.

Martí, Samuel
　1971　*La Virgen de Guadalupe y Juan Diego.* Mexico City: Ediciones Euroamericanas.

Martin, Colin
　1975　*Full fathom five.* New York: Viking Press.
　1978　*La Trinidad Valencera:* A Spanish Armada wreck. *Archaeology* 31(1):38–47.

Martin, Colin, and Geoffrey Parker
　1988　*The Spanish Armada.* New York: W. W. Norton.

Martín, Luis
　1983　*Daughters of the conquistadores.* Tucson: University of Arizona Press.

Marx, Robert
　1973　*Port Royal rediscovered.* Garden City, N.J.: Doubleday.
　1983　*Shipwrecks of the western hemisphere.* New York: Bonanza Books.

Marx, Robert, and Jennifer Marx
　1993　*The search for sunken treasure.* Toronto: Key Porter Books.

Mason, Anita
　1974　*An illustrated dictionary of jewelry.* Illustrated by Diane Packer. New York: Harper and Row.

Mateu y Llópes, F.
　1934　*Catálago de los ponderales monetarios del museo arqueológico nacional.* Madrid: Museo Arqueológico Nacional.
　1946　*La moneda Española.* Barcelona: Editorial Alberto Martín.

Mathers, William M.
　1990　Nuestra Señora de la Concepción. *National Geographic* 178(3):39–56.

Mathers, William, and Nancy Shaw
　1993　*Treasure of the* Concepción. Manila: Pacific Sea Resources.

Matthewson, Duncan
  1986 *Treasure of the* Atocha. New York: Pisces Books.
Mattick, Barbara
  1993 The history of toothbrushes and their nature as archaeological artifacts. *Florida Anthropologist* 46(3):162–184.
  1998 Bone toothbrushes of the 19th & 20th centuries: A history and a typology based on brushes from the Roberts collection. Master's thesis, Florida State University.
May, Florence Lewis
  1938 Laces and embroideries. In *The Hispanic Society of America Handbook,* edited by Archer Huntington, 299–314. New York: Hispanic Society of America.
McCauley, H. Berton
  1946 Toothbrushes, toothbrush materials and designs. *Journal of the American Dentistry Association* 33:283–292.
McConnell, Bridget
  1990 *A collector's guide to thimbles.* London: Wellfleet Books.
McConnell, Sophie
  1991 *Metropolitan jewelry.* New York: Metropolitan Museum of Art, and Boston: Little, Brown.
McEwan, Bonnie
  1983 Spanish colonial adaptation on Hispaniola: The archeology of Area 35, Puerto Real, Haiti. Master's thesis, University of Florida.
  1988 An archaeological perspective on sixteenth-century Spanish life in the Old World and the Americas. Ph.D. diss., University of Florida.
  1991a The archaeology of women in the Spanish New World. *Historical Archaeology* 25(4):33–41.
  1991b San Luis de Talimali: The archaeology of Spanish-Indian relations at a Florida mission. *Historical Archaeology* 25(3):36–60.
  1992 *Archaeology of the Apalachee village at San Luis de Talimali.* Florida Archaeological Reports 28. Tallahassee: Florida Bureau of Archaeological Research.
  1993 Hispanic life on the seventeenth-century Florida frontier. In *The Spanish missions of La Florida,* edited by B. McEwan, 295–321. Gainesville: University Press of Florida.
  1995 Domestic adaptation at Puerto Real. In *Puerto Real: The archaeology of a sixteenth-century Spanish town in Hispaniola,* edited by K. Deagan, 195–284. Gainesville: University Press of Florida.
McEwan, Bonnie, ed.
  1993 *The Spanish missions of La Florida.* Gainesville: University Press of Florida.

McEwan, Bonnie, Michael W. Davidson, and Jeffrey Mitchem
   1997   A quartz crystal cross from the cemetery at Mission San Luis, Florida. *Journal of Archaeological Science* 24(6):529–536.

McNickle, Andrew J.
   1962   *Spanish colonial coins of North America: Mexico mint.* Mexico City: Sociedad Numinsmática de México.

Mead, J.
   1967   The Passion. In *The New Catholic Encyclopedia* 10:1059–1061. San Francisco: Robert Appleton Company.

Meaney, Audrey L
   1981   *Anglo-Saxon amulets and curing stones.* Oxford: BAR British Series 96.

Medina, J. T.
   1924   *Medallas Europeas relativas a América.* Publicaciones del Instituto de Investigaciones Históricas 24. Buenos Aires: Casa Jacobo Peuser.

Meinberg, C.
   1967   The cross. In *The New Catholic Encyclopedia* 4:473–479. San Francisco: Robert Appleton Company.

Meyers, Albert, and Elizabeth Hopkins, eds.
   1988   *Manipulating the saints: Religious brotherhoods and social integration in post-contact Latin America.* Hamburg: Wayasbah.

Milanich, Jerald T.
   1995   *Florida Indians and the invasion from Europe.* Gainesville: University Press of Florida.

Miller, Dwight
   1970   *Street criers and itinerant tradesmen in European prints.* Stanford Art Books 11. Palo Alto, Calif.: Stanford University Press.

Miller, George
   1980   Classification and economic scaling of 19th century ceramics. *Historical Archaeology* 14(1):1–41.

Mitchem, Jeffrey
   1992   Analysis of beads and pendants from San Luis de Talimali (8LE4): The *convento* and church. In *Archaeology at San Luis: The church complex,* edited by Gary Shapiro and Richard Vernon. *Florida Archaeology* No. 6, pt. 2, 241–249. Tallahassee: Florida Bureau of Archaeological Research.
   1993   Beads and pendants from San Luis de Talimali: Inferences from varying contexts. In *The Spanish missions of La Florida,* edited by B. McEwan, 399–417. Gainesville: University Press of Florida.

Mitchem, Jeffrey M., and Dale L. Hutchinson
   1987   Interim report on archaeological research at the Tatham Mound, Citrus County, Florida: Season III. Miscellaneous Project Report

Series No. 30. Florida State Museum, University of Florida, Gainesville.

Mitchem, Jeffrey M., and Bonnie McEwan
1988 New data on early bells from Florida. *Southeastern Archaeology* 7(1):39–48.

Moell, C. J.
1967 Devotion to the Sacred Heart. In *The New Catholic Encyclopedia* 12:818–820. San Francisco: Robert Appleton Company.

Mora, Don Tomás de
1804 *Tradato de artillería para el uso de la Académia de Caballeros Cadetes del Real Cuerpo de Artillería.* Madrid: La Impreta Real. Translation by Luis Arana, 1976, Castillo de San Marcos National Monument.

Morales, Gaspar de
1977 *Libro de las virtudes y propiedades de las piedras preciosas* (1598). Prologue and introduction by Juan Carlos Ruiz Sierra. Madrid: Editora Nacional.

Morales Padrón, Francisco
1952 *Jamaica Española.* Escuela de Estudios Hispano-Americanos, Publication 67, Seville.
1992 *Andalucia y América.* Madrid: Editorial MAPFRE.

Morison, Samuel E.
1963 *Journals and other documents on the life and voyages of Christopher Columbus.* Translated and edited by S. E. Morison. New York: Heritage Press.

Morris, J. J.
1967 Sacred Heart, iconography of. In *The New Catholic Encyclopedia* 11:820. San Francisco: Robert Appleton Company.

Morris, John W.
1995 Report on excavations at 8-SJ-34, St. Augustine (1994). Project report on file, Florida Museum of Natural History, University of Florida, Gainesville.

Motley, Wilma E.
1983 *Ethics, jurisprudence and history for the dental hygienist.* Philadelphia: Lea and Febiger.

Mouer, Daniel
1993 Chesapeake creoles: The creation of a folk culture in colonial Virginia. In *The Archaeology of 17th century Virginia,* edited by T. Reinhart and D. Pogue, 105–166. Virginia Archaeological Society Special Publication 30. Richmond.

Mouer, Daniel, Mary Ellen Hodges, Stephen Potter, Susan Henry Reynaud, Ivor Noel Hume, Dennis Pogue, Martha McCartney, and Thomas Davidson
1999 Colonoware pottery, Chesapeake pipes, and "uncritical assump-

tions." In *"I, too, am America": Archaeological studies of African-American life*, edited by Theresa A. Singleton, 83–115. Charlottesville: University Press of Virginia.

Mulhern, P. F.
    1967   Medals, religious. In *The New Catholic Encyclopedia* 9:547–549. San Francisco: Robert Appleton Company.

Muller, Patricia
    1972   *Jewels in Spain 1500–1800*. New York: Hispanic Society of America.

Mummenhof, Ernst
    1901   *Der handwerker in der deutschen vergangen heit*. Leipzig: E Diederichs.

Murray, Glenn S.
    1986   Potosí and its historic mint. *Numismatist* 99(12):2472–2488.

Neal, W. Kieth
    1956   *Spanish guns and pistols*. London: G. Bell and Sons.

Needham, Peter
    1979   *Twelve centuries of bookbindings: 400–1600*. New York: Pierpont Morgan Library and Oxford University Press.

Nesmith, Robert
    1955   *The coinage of the first mint of the Americas at Mexico City 1536–1572*. Numismatic Notes and Monographs 131. New York: American Numismatic Society.

Neumann, George C., and Frank J. Kravic
    1975   *Collector's illustrated encyclopedia of the American Revolution*. Harrisburg, Pa.: Stackpole Books.

Nevinson, J. L.
    1977   Buttons and buttonholes in the fourteenth-century. *Costume* 11:38–44.

New Catholic Encyclopedia
    1967   Religious orders of men in Latin America. In *The New Catholic Encyclopedia* 12:302–303. San Francisco: Robert Appleton Company.

Nickel, Helmut
    1985   Introduction to *Powder horns in the southern tradition*, edited by Patricia Wickman. Exhibition catalog. Tallahassee: Museum of Florida History.

Noel Hume, Ivor
    1961   Sleeve buttons: Diminutive relics of the seventeenth and eighteenth centuries. *Antiques* 79(4):380–383.
    1980   *A guide to the artifacts of colonial America*. 5th ed. New York: Knopf.
    1983   *Martin's Hundred*. New York: Alfred Knopf.

Norris, Andrea, and Ingid Weber
   1976 *Medals and plaquettes from the Molinari collection at Bowdoin College.* Brunswick, Maine: College Press.

O'Callaghan, J. F.
   1967a Knights of Alcantara. In *The New Catholic Encyclopedia* 8:215. San Francisco: Robert Appleton Company.
   1967b Knights of St. James. In *The New Catholic Encyclopedia* 8:220. San Francisco: Robert Appleton Company.

O'Connor, E. D.
   1967 Immaculate conception. In *The New Catholic Encyclopedia* 6:378–382. San Francisco: Robert Appleton Company.

Olds, Dorris
   1976 *Texas legacy from the Gulf: A report on sixteenth-century shipwreck material from the Texas tidelands.* Texas Memorial Museum Miscellaneous Papers 5. Austin.

Oliveira Marquez, A. H.
   1971 *Daily life in Portugal in the Middle Ages.* Madison: University of Wisconsin Press.

Olsen, Stanley J.
   1963 Dating early plain buttons by their form. *American Antiquity* 28:551–554.

Olsen, Stanley J., and J. Duncan Campbell
   1962 Uniform buttons as an aid in the interpretation of military sites. *Curator* 4(4):346–352.

Oman, Charles
   1967 The jewels of Our Lady of the Pillar at Saragossa. *Apollo* 80:400–406.
   1968 *The golden age of hispanic silver.* London: Victoria and Albert Museum.

Omwake, H. G.
   1965 White kaolin pipe bowls and pipe stems. In *Archaeological excavations at Santa Rosa, Pensacola,* by Hale Smith, 41–49. Florida State University Notes in Anthropology 10. Tallahassee.

Orser, Charles
   1996 *A historical archaeology of the modern world.* New York: Plenum Press.

Ortega, Elpidio
   1971 Informe de las excavaciones arqueológicas realizadas en la plazoleta y en la Calle Juan Barón. *Revista Dominicana de Arqueología y Antropología* 1(1):25–37.
   1980 *Introducción a la loza común o alfarería en el período colonial de Santo Domingo.* Santo Domingo: Fundación Ortega Álvarez.
   1982 *Arqueología colonial de Santo Domingo.* Santo Domingo: Fundación Ortega Álvarez.

Ortega, Elpidio, and J. M. Cruxent
 1976 Informe preliminar sobre las excavaciones en las ruinas del Convento de San Francisco. *Actas del XLI Congreso Internacional de Americanistas* 3:674–689.

Ortega, Elpidio, and Carmen Fondeur
 1978a *Arqueología de los monumentos históricos de Santo Domingo.* San Pedro de Macorís: Universidad Central del Este.
 1978b *Estudio de la cerámica del periodo Indo-Hispano de la antigua Concepción de la Vega.* Serie Científica 1. Santo Domingo: Fundación Ortega Álvarez.
 1979 *Arqueología de la Casa del Cordón.* Serie Científica 2. Santo Domingo: Fundación Ortega Álvarez.

Osma y Scull, G. J.
 1916 *Catálogo de azabaches compostelanos.* Madrid: Instituto de Valencia de Don Juan.

Oswald, Adrian
 1951 The English clay tobacco pipe. *Archaeological Newsletter* (London) 3(10):154–159.
 1961 The evolution and chronology of English clay tobacco pipes. *Archaeological Newsletter* (London) 7(3):55–62.
 1975 *Clay pipes for the archaeologist.* British Archaeological Reports 14. London.

Owsley, Douglas, Charles Orser, Robert Montgomery, and Claudia Holland
 1985 An archaeological and physical anthropological study of the first cemetery in New Orleans. Project report submitted to the Division of Archaeology, State of Louisiana, Baton Rouge.

Oxea, Fernández, and José Ramón
 1965 Amuletos luñares toledanos. *Revista de dialectología y tradiciones populares* 21:147–155.

Paar, Karen L.
 1999 "To settle is to conquer": Spaniards, Native Americans and the colonization of Santa Elena in sixteenth-century Florida. Ph.D. diss., University of North Carolina, Chapel Hill.

Pabellón de España
 1992 *Treasures of Spanish art.* Exhibition catalog, Pabellón de España, Expo 92, Sevilla. Seville: Electa España.

Palm, Erwin
 1952 La Fortaleza de la Concepción de la Vega. *Memória del V congreso histórico municipal interamericano* (Santo Domingo) 2:115–118.

Pantel, A. G., J. Sued Badillo, Aníbal S. Rivera, and Beatriz Pantel
 1988 Archaeological, architectural and historical investigations of the first Spanish settlement in Puerto Rico, Caparra. Project report

submitted to the Foundation of Archaeology, Anthropology and History of Puerto Rico, San Juan.

Parker, Susan R.
1999 The second century of settlement in Spanish St. Augustine: 1670–1763. Ph.D. diss., University of Florida.

Parry, J. H.
1969 *The Spanish seaborne empire.* New York: Knopf.
1990 *The Spanish seaborne empire.* (1966). Berkeley: University of California Press.

Parry, J. H., and Robert Keith
1984 *New Iberian world: A documentary history of the discovery and settlement of Latin America to the early 17th century.* New York: Times Books; Hector and Rose.

Payne, Blanche
1965 *History of costume.* New York: Harper and Row.

Pearson, Charles
1981 *El Nuevo Constante.* LASAC Anthropological Study 4. Louisiana Department of Parks and Recreation, Baton Rouge.

Pearson, Charles, and Paul Hoffman
1995 *The last voyage of* El Nuevo Constante. Baton Rouge: Louisiana State University Press.

Pérez-Bueno, Luis
1952 *Catálago de la colección de cruces del Museo del Pueblo Español.* Madrid: Museo del Pueblo Español.

Pérez Montás, Eugenio
1984 *República Dominicana: Monumentos históricos y arqueológicos.* Publication 380. Mexico City: Instituto Panamericano de Geografía e Historia.

Pérez-Sánchez, Alfonso Emilio
1992 The baroque. In *Treasures of Spanish Art.* Exhibition catalog, Pabellón de España, Expo 92, Sevilla. Seville: Electa España.

Perry, Mary Elizabeth
1990 *Gender and disorder in early modern Seville.* Princeton, N.J.: Princeton University Press.

Peterson, Harold
1956 *Arms and armor in colonial America, 1586–1723.* New York: Bramhall House.

Peterson, Mendel
1975 *Funnel of gold.* New York: Little, Brown.
1977 Reach for the New World. *National Geographic* 152(6):724–767.
1979a Graveyard of the Quicksilver galleons. *National Geographic* 154(12):850–863.
1979b *Treasure of the* Concepción. Chicago: John G. Shedd Aquarium.

Phillips, Carla Rahn
 1986 *Six galleons for the king of Spain: Imperial defense in the early seventeenth-century.* Baltimore: Johns Hopkins University Press.
 1987 Time and duration: A model for the economy of early modern Spain. *American Historical Review* 92:531–562.
 1990 The growth and composition of trade in the Iberian empires, 1450–1750. In *The rise of merchant empires: Long distance trade in the early modern world, 1350–1750,* edited by James Tracey, 34–101. Cambridge: University of Cambridge Press.

Pike, Ruth
 1961 Seville in the sixteenth-century. *Hispanic American Historical Review* 41:1–30.
 1966 *The Genoese in Seville and the opening of the New World.* Ithaca, N.Y.: Cornell University Press.
 1972 *Aristocrats and traders: Sevillian society in the sixteenth-century.* Ithaca, N.Y.: Cornell University Press.

Poladura, Atala de, coord.
 1980 *Objetos y ambientes de la Concepción de la Vega.* Catálogo de la exposición. Santo Domingo: Museo Casas Reales.

Polhemus, Richard
 1988 Spanish buttons from Santa Elena. In *Spanish artifacts from Santa Elena,* edited by S. South, R. Skowronek, and R. Johnson, 411–416. Anthropological Studies 7. South Carolina Institute of Archaeology and Anthropology, Columbia.

Pollard, Hugh B. C.
 1973 *A history of firearms.* New York: B. Franklin.

Pope, J. Keith
 1979 *Decade of adventure.* Singer Island, Fla.: Singer Island Press.

Potter, E. C.
 1992 On being interested in the extreme. *International Journal of the Royal Society of New South Wales* 125:451–453.

Potter, Parker
 1982 The translation of archaeological evidence into economic understanding: A study of naming, context and nineteenth-century ceramics in Rockbridge country, Virginia. Master's thesis, Brown University.

Powell, John
 1994a Spanish colonial artifacts of the Gulf Coast region, part 1. *Military Collector and Historian* 46(1):2–11.
 1994b Spanish naval insignia from *El Cazador. Military Collector and Historian* 45(2):90.

Price, Percival
 1984 Bells. In *The New Grove dictionary of music,* 2:203–216. London: MacMillan.

Proske, Beatrice G.
  1938 Sculpture. In *The Hispanic Society of America handbook,* 57–102. New York: Hispanic Society of America.

Provoyeur, Pierre
  1996 Tableware, jewelry and devotional objects. In *Treasures of the San Diego,* edited by Jean-Paul Desroches, Gabriel Casal, and Franck Goddio, 258–259. Manila: National Museum of the Philippines.

Quimby, George
  1966 *Indian cultures and European trade goods.* Madison: University of Wisconsin Press.

Radisch, William
  1988 Classification and interpretation of stars from Santa Elena: Some problems and potential solutions. In *The artifacts of Santa Elena,* edited by S. South, R. Skowronek, and R. Johnson, 145–151. Anthropological Papers 7. South Carolina Institute of Archaeology and Anthropology, Columbia.

Randall, Mark E.
  1971 Early marbles. *Historical Archaeology* 5:102–105.

Reade, Bryan
  1951 *The dominance of Spain.* Vol. 3, No. 4, in *Costume of the western world,* edited by James Laver. London: George C. Harrap.

Real Academia Española
  1939 *Diccionário de la lengua Española.* Madrid: Real Academia Española.

Redman, Charles
  1986 *Qsar es-Seghir: An archaeological view of medieval life.* New York: Academic Press.

Redman, Charles, and James Boone
  1979 *Qsar es-Seghir (Alcácer Ceguer): A 15th and 16th century Portuguese colony in North Africa.* Lisbon: Centro de Estudios Históricos Ultramarinos da Junta de Investigacoes Cientificas do Ultramar.

Reid, William
  1976 *Weapons through the ages.* New York: Crescent Books.

Reitzer, Ladislas
  1960 Some observations on Castilian commerce and finance in the sixteenth-century. *Journal of Modern History* 32(3):213–223.

Riaño, Juan F.
  1890 *The industrial arts in Spain.* London: Chapman and Hall.

Roberts, Matt, and Don Etherington
  1982 *Bookbinding and the conservation of books: A dictionary of descriptive terminology.* Washington, D.C.: Library of Congress.

Robinson, William
  1976 Mission Guevavi: Excavations in the *convento. Kiva* 42(2):135–175.

Roig, Juan Fernández
  1950 *Iconografía de los santos.* Barcelona: Ediciones Omega.
Romero, Leandro Estébanez
  1981 Sobre las evidéncias arqueológicas de contacto y transculturación en el ámbito Cubano. *Santiago* (Havana) 44:77–108.
Rouse, Irving, and José Cruxent
  1963 *Venezuelan archaeology.* New Haven, Conn.: Yale University Press.
Rowe, Donald F.
  1975 *The art of jewelry 1450–1650.* Chicago: Chicago Art Institute.
Ruiz Alcón, María Teresa
  1982 Abanicos. In *Historia de las artes aplicadas e industriales en España,* edited by Antonio Bonet Correa, 621–629. Madrid: Ediciones Cátedra.
Russell, Carl P.
  1959 *Guns on the early frontier: A history of firearms from colonial times through the years of the western fur trade.* Berkeley: University of California Press.
Saldivar, Gabriel
  1987 *Historia de la música en México (épocas precortésiana y colonial).* Toluca: Ediciones del Gobierno del Estado de México.
Salgado Jerrera, Antonio
  1977 *La brujería en Hispanoamerica.* Mexico City: Costa-Amic.
Salillas, Rafael
  1905 *La fascinación en España.* Madrid: Eduardo Arias.
Salmeron, África León, and Natividad de Diego y Gonzáles
  1915 *Compendio de indumentaria Española.* Madrid: Imprenta de San Francisco de Sales.
Salton, Mark M.
  1969 *The Salton collection: Renaissance and baroque medals and plaquettes.* Brunswick, Maine: Bowdoin College Museum of Art.
Sánchez-Barba, Mario Hernández
  1992 *Castilla y América.* Madrid: Ediciones MAPFRE.
Sankalia, H. D., and M. G. Dikshit
  1952 *Excavations at Brahmapuri (1945–46).* Deccan College Monograph Series 5. Poonan.
Sanoja Obediente, Mario, Iraida A. Vargas, Gabriela Alvarado, and Milene Montilla
  1998 *Arqueología de Caracas. Tomo 1. Escuela de Música José Angele Lamas.* Biblioteca de la Acadèmia Nacional de la Historia 177. Caracas.
Santiago, Pedro J.
  1980 *Estudios sobre comercio marítimo, naufragios y rescate submarino en la República Dominicana.* Santo Domingo: Museo Casas Reales.

Santiago Cruz, Francisco
　1960　*Las artes y los gremios en la Nueva España*. Figuras y Episodios de la Historia de México 77. Mexico City: Editorial Jus.

Sarría Rueda, Amalia
　1994　Los inícios de la imprenta. In *Historia ilustrada del libro Español de los incunables al siglo XVII*, edited by Hipólito Escolar, 35–94. Madrid: Fundación Germán Sánchez Ruipérez.

Saunders, Rebecca
　1988　*Excavations at 8NA41: Two mission-period sites on Amelia Island, Florida*. Miscellaneous Project Reports 35. Florida Museum of Natural History, University of Florida, Gainesville.

Schnieder, Janet
　1981　*Shipwrecked 1622*. Exhibition catalog. Flushing, N.Y.: Queen's Museum.

Schurz, William L.
　1939　*The Manila galleon*. New York: E. P. Dutton.

Schuyler, Robert L.
　1977　The spoken word, the written word, observed behavior and preserved behavior; the contexts available to the archeologist. *Conference on Historic Sites Archeology Papers*, vol. 10, pt. 2, 99–120.
　1988　Archaeological remains, documents and anthropology: A call for a new culture history. *Historical Archaeology* 22(1):36–42.

Scott, Amoret, and Christopher Scott
　1981　*Smoking antiques*. Shire Album 66. Aylesbury, England: Shire Publications.

Sedwick, Frank
　1987　*The practical book of cobs*. Maitland, Fla.: privately printed.

Shackel, Paul
　1987　*Personal discipline and material culture: An archaeology of Annapolis, Maryland, 1695–1870*. Knoxville: University of Tennessee Press.

Shapiro, Gary, and Bonnie McEwan
　1992　Archaeology at San Luis: The Apalachee council house. *Florida Archaeology* No. 6, pt. 2, 1–170. Tallahassee: Florida Bureau of Archaeological Research.

Shapiro, Gary, and Richard Vernon
　1992　Archaeology at San Luis: The church complex. *Florida Archaeology* No.6, pt. 2, 177–271. Tallahassee: Florida Bureau of Archaeological Research.

Shephard, Stephen
　1983　The Spanish *criollo* majority in colonial St. Augustine. In *Spanish St. Augustine: The archaeology of a colonial creole community*, edited by K. Deagan, 65–97. New York: Academic Press.

Sheppard, T., and J. F. Musham
　1924　*Money scales and weights*. London: Spink and Sons.

Sherbowitz-Wetzor, O. P., and C. Toumanoff
  1967   The knights of Malta. In *The New Catholic Encyclopedia* 8:217–220. San Francisco: Robert Appleton Company.

Simmons, Joe J.
  1988   Wrought iron ordnance: Revealing discoveries from the New World. *International Journal of Nautical Archaeology and Underwater Exploration* 17(1):25–34.

Simmons, Marc
  1987   The Spaniards of San Gabriel. In *When cultures meet: Remembering San Gabriel del Yunque Oweenge*, 39–61. Santa Fe, N.M.: Sunstone Press.

Simmons, Marc, and Frank Turley
  1980   *Southwestern colonial ironwork*. Santa Fe: Museum of New Mexico Press.

Simonis, J.
  1904   *Art du medailleur en Belgique*. Brussels: Jemeppe.

Singleton, Teresa
  1977   The archaeology of a pre-eighteenth-century house site in St. Augustine. Master's thesis, University of Florida.

Skeabek, A. H.
  1967   Bulla. In *The New Catholic Encyclopedia* 2:88–89. San Francisco: Robert Appleton Company.

Skowronek, Russell K.
  1982   Trade patterns of 18th century frontier New Spain: The 1733 *Flota* and St. Augustine. Master's thesis, Florida State University.

Sluiter, Engel
  1985   *The Florida situado: Quantifying the first eighty years, 1571–1651*. Gainesville: University of Florida Libraries.

Smith, Bradley
  1968   *Mexico: A history in art*. New York: Doubleday.

Smith, Hale G.
  1956   *The European and the Indian: European-Indian contacts in Georgia and Florida*. Florida Anthropological Society Publication 4 and Notes in Anthropology 2. Florida State University, Tallahassee.
  1962   *El Morro*. Notes in Anthropology 6. Florida State University, Tallahassee.
  1965   *Archaeological Excavations at Santa Rosa, Pensacola*. Notes in Anthropology 10. Florida State University, Tallahassee.

Smith, Jody Brant
  1983   *The image of Guadalupe*. New York: Doubleday.

Smith, Marvin
  1981   European and aboriginal glass pendants in North America. *Ornament* 5(2):21–23.
  1983   Chronology from glass beads: The Spanish period in the South-

east, 1513–1670. In *Proceedings of the 1982 glass trade bead conference*, edited by C. Hayes, 147–158. Research Records 16. Rochester, N.Y.: Rochester Museum and Science Center.

1987 *Archaeology of aboriginal culture change in the interior Southeast.* Gainesville: University Presses of Florida.

Smith, Marvin, and M. E. Good
1982 *Early sixteenth-century glass beads in the Spanish colonial trade.* Greenwood, Miss.: Cottonlandia Museum Publications.

Smith, Roger
1993 *Vanguard of empire: Ships of exploration in the age of Columbus.* New York: Oxford University Press.

Smith, Roger, Denise Lakey, Thomas Oertling, Bruce Thompson, and Robyn Woodward
1982 Sevilla La Nueva: A site survey and historical assessment of Jamaica's first European town. Project report on file, Institute of Nautical Archaeology, College Station, Texas.

Smith, Roger, James Spirek, John Bratten, and Della Scott-Ireton
1995 *The Emanuel Point ship archaeological investigations 1992–1995.* Tallahassee: Bureau of Archaeological Research, Division of Historical Resources, Florida Department of State.

Solís Magaña, Carlos
1988 *Colonial archaeology of San Juan de Puerto Rico: Excavations at the Casa Rosa scarp wall, San Juan National Historic site, Puerto Rico.* Project report, Office of Archaeological Research Report 52. Tuscaloosa: Alabama State Museum of Natural History.

South, Stanley
1964 An analysis of buttons from Brunswick Town and Fort Fisher. *Florida Anthropologist* 17(2):113–133.
1965 Anthropomorphic Pipes from the Kiln Waster Dump of Gottfried Aust—1755 to 1771. *Florida Anthropologist* 18(3)(pt. 2):49–60.
1977 *Method and theory in historical archaeology.* New York: Academic Press.
1979 *The search for Santa Elena.* Research Manuscript Series 150. South Carolina Institute of Archaeology and Anthropology, Columbia.
1980 *The discovery of Santa Elena.* Research Manuscript Series 165. South Carolina Institute of Archaeology and Anthropology, Columbia.
1982 *Exploring Santa Elena.* Research Manuscript Series 184. South Carolina Institute of Archeology and Anthropology, Columbia.
1983 *Revealing Santa Elena.* Research Manuscript Series 188. South Carolina Institute of Archeology and Anthropology, Columbia.
1985 *Excavation of the Casa Fuerte and wells at Ft. San Felipe 1984.* Research Manuscript Series 196. South Carolina Institute of Archaeology and Anthropology, Columbia.
1988 Santa Elena: Threshold of conquest. In *The recovery of meaning,*

edited by M. Leone and P. Potter, 27–72. Washington, D.C.: Smithsonian Institution Press.

1999 *Historical archaeology in Wachovia: Excavating eighteenth-century Bethabara and Moravian pottery.* New York: Klewer Academic/Plenum Publishers.

South, Stanley, and Chester B. DePratter
1996 *Discovery at Santa Elena: Block excavation 1993.* Research Manuscript Series 222. South Carolina Institute of Archaeology and Anthropology, Columbia.

South, Stanley, Russell Skowronek, and Richard Johnson, eds.
1988 *The artifacts of Santa Elena.* Anthropological Papers 7. South Carolina Institute of Archaeology and Anthropology, Columbia.

Spaer, Maude
1994 The Islamic glass bracelets of Palestine: Preliminary findings. *Journal of Glass Studies* (Corning, N.Y.) (34):44–62.

Spencer, Brian
1990 *Pilgrim souvenirs and secular badges.* Salisbury Museum Medieval Catalog, pt. 2. Salisbury, England: Salisbury and South Wiltshire Museum.

Stahl, Alan
1990 Indian peace medals, official and unofficial. *Médailles* (1990):38–48.
1992 The coinage of La Isabela, 1493–1498. *Numismatist* 105:1399–1402.
1995 Coins from the excavations at La Isabela, D.R., the first European colony in the New World. *American Journal of Numismatics* (second series) 5–6:189–207.

Stengel, Walter
1918 Die merkzeichen der Nürenberger goldschmiede. In *Mitteihagen aus dem Germanischen Nationalmuseum Nürnberg,* 107–155. Nuremberg: German National Museum.

Stenuit, Robert
1972 *Treasures of the Armada.* London: David and Charles.

Stenuit, Robert, and Bates Littlehales
1969 Priceless relics of the Spanish Armada. *National Geographic* 135(6):745–777.

Stone, Lyle
1974 *Fort Michilimackinack 1715–1781.* Publications of the Museum. East Lansing: Michigan State University.

Strauss, Walter, ed.
1973 *The complete etchings, engravings and drypoints of Albrecht Dürer.* New York: Dover.

Stuhlman, Robin
   1995   Cultural formation in sixteenth century Spanish Florida. Master's thesis, University of Florida.

Sullivan, Catherine
   1986   *Legacy of the Machault.* Ottawa: National Historic Sites and Parks Branch, Parks Canada.

Symes, Martha, and M. E. Stephens
   1965   The Fox Pond site, A 272. *Florida Anthropologist* 18(2):65–76.

Taillard, A.
   1941   *Platería sudamericana.* Buenos Aires: Editores Peuser.

Tait, Hugh, and Charlotte Gere
   1978   *The jewelers art: An introduction to the Hull gift to the British Museum.* London: British Museum.

Tamburini, G. M.
   1640   *Virtu et arti essercitate en Bologna.* 11 plates. Bologna.

Taviani, Paolo Emilio
   1983   *I viaggio di Colombo.* 2 vols. Rome: Instituto Geografico de Agostini Novaro.
   1985   *Christopher Columbus. The grand design.* Translated by William Weaver. London: Orbis.

Thomas, David Hurst
   1988   Saints and soldiers at Santa Catalina: Hispanic designs for colonial America. In *The recovery of meaning,* edited by M. Leone and P. Potter, 73–140. Washington, D.C.: Smithsonian Institution Press.
   1993   The archaeology of mission Santa Catalina: Our first fifteen years. In *The Spanish missions of La Florida,* edited by B. McEwan, 1–34. Gainesville: University Press of Florida.

Thomas, David H., ed.
   1989   *Columbian Consequences.* Vol. 1, *The Spanish borderlands west.* Washington, D.C.: Smithsonian Institution Press.
   1990   *Columbian Consequences.* Vol. 2, *The Spanish borderlands east.* Washington, D.C.: Smithsonian Institution Press.
   1991   *Columbian Consequences.* Vol. 3, *The Spanish borderlands in Pan-American perspective.* Washington, D.C.: Smithsonian Institution Press.

Thurston, Herbert
   1907   Bells. *The Catholic Encyclopedia* 2:18–25. Appleton, N.Y.: Encyclopedia Press.
   1913   Medals, devotional. *The Catholic Encyclopedia* 10:111–115. Appleton, N.Y.: Encyclopedia Press.

Toke, Leslie St. L.
   1910   Flagellants. *The Catholic Encyclopedia.* Vol. 6. (reprinted by New Advent www.newadvent.org/cathen/06089c.htm).

Tokyo Metropolitan Edo-Tokyo Museum
    1997   *Unearthed cities: Edo, Nagasaki, Amsterdam, London, New York.* Exhibition catalog. Tokyo: Tokyo Museum.

Toribio Medina, José
    1919   *Las monedas coloniales Hispano-Americanas.* Santiago de Chile: Imprenta Elzeviriana.

Torre Revello, José
    1932   *El gremio de plateros en las Indias occidentales.* Publicaciónes del Instituto de investigaciones históricas 61. Buenos Aires.
    1940   *Orígenes de la imprenta en España y su desarrollo en América Española.* Buenos Aires: Institución Cultural Española.
    1943   Merchandise brought to America by the Spaniards (1534–1586). *Hispanic American Historical Review* 23(4):773–780.
    1945   *La orfebrería colonial en Hispanoamérica y particularmente en Buenos Aires.* Buenos Aires: Institución Cultural Española.

Torres Petitón, Francisco
    1988   *Colección Vega Vieja.* Vol. 1, *Brevísima cronología de la Concepción.* La Vega, Dominican Republic: Imprenta Enriquillo.

Toussaint, Manuel
    1967   *Colonial art in Mexico.* Austin: University of Texas Press.

Tremblay, Katherine, and Louise Renaud
    1999   *Le jeux et les jouets de Place Royale.* 2nd ed. Quebec: Groupe Harcarte.

Trens, Manuel
    1946   *María: Iconografía de la Virgen en el arte Español.* Madrid: Editorial Plus Ultra.

Treue, Wilhelm, and Katherine Goldman
    1965   *Das hausbuch der Medelschen Zwolfbruderstiftung zu Nurnberg. Deutsch handwerkbilder des 15 und 16 jahrhunderts.* Munchen: Bruckmann.

Tylecote, R. F.
    1972   A contribution to the metallurgy of 18th and 19th century brass pins. *Post-Medieval Archaeology* 6:183–190.

Tylor, E. B.
    1971   The history of games. (1879). In *The study of games,* edited by E. A. Avedon and B. Sutton-Smith, 63–76. New York: John Wiley and Sons.

Van Beek, Bert
    1986   Jetons—their use and history. In *Perspectives in numismatics,* edited by Saul Needleman, 195–220. Translated by Robert Shulman. Chicago: Ares.

Varela, Consuelo
    1987   La Isabela, vida y ocaso de una ciudad efémera. *Revista de Indias* (Seville) 47 (181):733–744.

Vargas, Iraida A., Mario Sanoja Obediente, Gabriela Alvarado, and Milene Montilla
    1998   *Arqueología de Caracas: Tomo 2. San Pablo Teatro Municipal.* Biblioteca de la Académia Nacional de la Historia 178. Caracas.

Vargas Ugarte, Ruben
    1947   *Historia del culto de María en Iberoamérica y de sus imágenes y santuarios más celebrados.* Buenos Aires: Editorial Huarpes.

Vega, Bernardo
    1979   *Los metales y los aborígenes de la Hispaniola.* Santo Domingo: Museo del Hombre Dominicano.
    1981   La heréncia indígena en la cultura Dominicana de hoy. In *Ensayos sobre la cultura Dominicana,* 9–53. Museo del Hombre Dominicano, Serie Conferencia 10. Santo Domingo.

Veloz Maggiolo, Marcio, and Elpidio Ortega
    1992   *La fundación de la villa de Santo Domingo.* Colección Quinto Centenario, Serie Historia de la Ciudad 1. Santo Domingo.

Vernon, Richard, and Bonnie G. McEwan
    1990   *Investigations in the church complex and Spanish village at San Luis.* Florida Archaeological Reports 18. Tallahassee: Florida Bureau of Archaeological Research.

Vicens Vives, Jaime
    1969   *An economic history of Spain.* Princeton, N.J.: Princeton University Press.
    1970   The decline of Spain in the seventeenth-century. In *The economic decline of empires,* edited by Carlo Cipolla, 121–167. London: Methuen.

Von Boehn, Max
    1929   *Ornaments.* New York: Benjamin Blom.

Von Hoelle, John
    1988   Thimbles, archeology and the New World. *Thimbletter* (1988):3–7.

Wagner, Kip, and Lonn Taylor
    1972   *Pieces of eight.* New York: E. P. Dutton.

Walker, Iain
    1971a   The manufacture of Dutch clay tobacco pipes. *Northeast Historical Archaeology* 1(1):2–7.
    1971b   Note on the Bethabara, North Carolina, tobacco pipes. *Conference on Historic Site Archaeology Papers* 1969(4):26–36.
    1975   The American stub-stemmed clay tobacco-pipe: A survey of its origins, manufacture, and distribution. *Conference on Historic Sites Archaeology Papers* 1974(9):97–128.

Wallerstein, Immanuel
    1974   *The modern world system I: Capitalist agriculture and the origins of the European world economy in the sixteenth century.* New York: Academic Press.

Walsh, Marie
  1934 *Mission bells of California.* San Francisco: Hart Wagner.
Walters Art Gallery
  1979 *Jewelry, ancient to modern.* New York: Viking Press, in cooperation with Walters Art Gallery, Baltimore.
Walton, Timothy
  1994 *The Spanish treasure fleets.* Sarasota, Fla.: Pineapple Press.
Ward, Christopher
  1993 *Imperial Panamá. Commerce and conflict in isthmian America.* Albuquerque: University of New Mexico Press.
Waters, Gifford
  1998 Excavations at the Nombre de Dios site, 8-SJ-34. Master's paper, University of Florida.
Weale, James
  1962 *Bookbindings and rubbings of bindings in the Victoria and Albert Museum.* Vol. 1, *Introduction.* (1898). London: Holland Press.
Weiditz, Christoph
  1994 *Authentic everyday dress of the Renaissance* (the "Trachtenbuch," 1529). New York: Dover.
Weisman, Brent
  1992 *Excavation on the Franciscan frontier: Archaeology of the Fig Springs mission.* Gainesville: University Press of Florida.
White, D. P.
  1977 The Birmingham button industry. *Post-Medieval Archaeology* 11:67–79.
Williams, Eric
  1970 *From Columbus to Castro: The history of the Caribbean.* New York: Vintage Books.
Williams, Maurice
  1982 The Castillo de San Marcos: A cross cultural test of the determinants of artifact patterning. Master's thesis, Florida State University.
Willis, Raymond
  1976 The archeology of 16th century Nueva Cádiz. Master's thesis, University of Florida.
  1982 Nueva Cádiz. In *Spanish colonial frontier research,* edited by H. Dobyns, 27–40. Albuquerque: Center for Anthropological Studies.
  1984 Empire and architecture at 16th century Puerto Real, Hispaniola. Ph.D. diss., University of Florida.
Witthoft, John
  1967 A history of gunflints. *Pennsylvania Archaeologist* 36(1–2).

Wood, Casey, and F. Marjorie Fyfe
 1961 *The art of falconry, being the* De Arte Venandi cum Avibus *of Frederick II of Hohenstaufen.* (1248). 3rd ed. Stanford, Calif.: Stanford University Press.

Woods, Alfred
 1999 Field report on the 1997–1998 field survey at Concepción de la Vega. Project report submitted to the Dirección Nacional de Parques, Santo Domingo, and U.S.A.I.D. On file, Florida Museum of Natural History, University of Florida, Gainesville.

Woodward, Robyn P.
 1988 The Charles Cotter collection: A study of the ceramic and faunal remains. Master's thesis, Texas A&M University.

Worth, John
 1992 *The Timucua missions of Spanish Florida and the rebellion of 1656.* Ann Arbor, Mich.: University Microfilms.

Wright, Irene
 1939 *Rescates:* With special reference to Cuba, 1599–1610. *Hispanic American Historical Review* 5(3):33–61.

Yciar, Juan de
 1960 *Arte Subtilissima.* (1550). London: Oxford University Press.

Yoh, Alison
 1993 Buttons from Spanish contexts in St. Augustine, Florida. Database and comments, on file, Florida Museum of Natural History, University of Florida, Gainesville.

Zapata Gollán, Agustín
 1988 *Supersticiones y amuletos.* Santa Fe, Argentina: Editorial Colmegna.

Zierden, Martha
 1981 The archaeology of a nineteenth-century second Spanish period homesite in St. Augustine, Florida. Master's thesis, Florida State University.

Index

A

Académia de las Ciéncias de Cuba, 19
Addis, William, 231
Aderezo, 109, 134, 135, 136
Agate, 91, 99, 95, 130
Aglets, 159, 160, 174–176
Agnus Dei (Lamb of God), 81–82
Ahlborn, Richard, 51
Alfonso X of Castile, 292
Alfonso XI of Castile, 236
Allard, Carolus, 219
Amber, 89, 95, 96, 99, 100
Ambergris, 68
American Museum of Natural History, 15
Ammunition, 269, 284–285
Amulets, 73, 87, 131; animal products as, 95, 102; beads as, 99–100; bells as, 141–142; childrens', 91, 103–104; fish as, 105; forms of, 95–102; glass, 102–103; Roman and Phoenician, 89; material properties of, 90, 93–95
Andalucía, 48, 61, 201
Apalachee Indians, 16
Armor, 188
Asiento, 27, 30
Atocha shipwreck, 29, 79, 84
Augustinian Order, 47

B

Backgammon, 292, 295
Bahamas, 7
Ball shot, lead, 269, 284–285, 287
Baptizing Springs, Florida, 14
Barcelona, Spain, 31, 108, 279
Bayahá, Haiti, 11, 14
Beads: as amulets, 99; on bobbins, 210, 211; Chevron, 131; as clothing adornment, 159; in jewelry, 126, 131–132; Nueva Cádiz, 131; in rosaries, 66–72
Beetles, 95
Bell founding, 139, 151
Bells: on animals, 138, 139, 150; as amulets, 141–142; bayou, 147; cast rumbler, 147–149; chime and open bells, 149–154; Clarksdale, 145–146; as dress accessories, 139; flanged-edged, 145–146; flush-edged, 146; Flushloop 146–147; handbells, 150, 151, 152; harness bells, 146, 148; mission bells, 150, 153; Roman, 139; Sabana Yegua, 145; Saturn 145, 146; for ships, 152, 153–154; taxonomy, 138–139; as trade goods, 138
Belt hooks, 192
Bermuda, 7
Billón, 237, 238, 243
Binford, Lewis, 5
Biringuccio, Vannoccio, 288
Blades, 234
Blair, Clay, 22
Blancas, 243, 244
Blotting pounce, 305
Blunderbuss, 280
Bobbins, lace, 210–211
Bogotá, Colombia, 255–256; mint, 242–243, 255
Boliche, 298
Books, 306–309; bookbinding, 308–309; hardware and fasteners, 308–309; printing in Spanish colonies, 307
Borrell, Pedro 22
Boulton, Alfredo, 12
Bourbon monarchy, 30, 251, 254, 281
Bourbon shield, 252, 255
Bowling. *See Boliche*
Boys, 299. *See also* Children

Bracelets, 134–136
Breugel, Peter, 299
Buckles: armor, 185–187, 188; baldric, 184, 189–191; clothing and shoe, 181, 182, 184, 185, 186, 187; figure-eight, 183, 186; harness, 184, 194, 189–191, 194; manufacturing, 184; spur, 187–189; sword, 182; taxonomy, 180–181
Bullae, 82
Bullfighting, 291
Burgos mint, 245
Bustos, 239, 252, 255, 256
Buttons, 157–174; bone, 165–167; crystal, 158–160; glass, 158, 163–164, 172–173; horsehair, 160; jeweled, 171–172, 173; metal, 159, 162–163, 164–165, 166, 167–171; military, 159–160, 162, 168–170; production and commerce, 157–158, 160–161; shell, 172, 173; sleeve, 172, 173; thread, 164, 165; two-piece manufacture, 170–171; taxonomy, 161

C

Cádiz, Spain, 26, 30
Caliber, 284
Caliver, 272
Cap Haitien, Haiti, 11
Caparra, Puerto Rico, 11
Caracas, Venezuela, 297
Carmelite Order, 45
Carrera de Indias, 24, 26, 27, 28
Cartagena, Colombia, 21, 254; mint of, 242
Cartridges, 290
Casa de Contratación, 26, 30, 31
Casa Rosa, San Juan, 18
Casas Grandes, Mexico, 71
Cassolet, 131
Casta paintings, 91, 120, 127, 134, 136, 157, 219, 228, 293, 299, 305
Castillo de San Marcos, Florida, 17
Catalonia Company, 30
Catholic Church, 5, 151; iconography, 47–49, 55, 74, 83, 101; influence in material culture 37–38, 41, 107
Cats, 89
CEDAM, 22
Ceitil, 243, 244
Celluloid, 227

Cemeteries, 37, 58, 70, 83, 88, 134
Chains, ornamental, 108, 133–134
Charles II, King of Spain, 239, 240, 244, 245, 246, 250, 251, 252–254, 256
Charles III, King of Spain, 33, 253, 255
Charles V, Holy Roman Emperor, 26, 27, 270, 275
Checkers, 292
Cherubs, 154
Chess, 292, 295, 296
Chessmen, 296
Chestnuts, 89, 95
Childbirth, 89, 95, 105
Children, 88, 89, 95, 91, 102, 103–104, 105, 141, 205, 298
Christ, 42, 44–47, 51, 55, 56, 63–64, 69, 73–74, 97, 101, 154; Child, 38, 44, 46, 73, 80, 89, 123; Passion of, 58, 80, 84
Chupadores, 92, 102–103
Cigars, 310–311
Cimarrón sites, 310–311
Cladagh design, 126
Claws, as amulets, 102
Clothing, 181, 183; French-influenced, 158, 165; Moorish, 157; ornaments on, 176–178; Spanish, 157–158, 160, 175, 184
Cockfighting, 291
Cofradías, 49, 63–65, 72–73
Coins: *bustos*, 239, 252, 255, 256; Byzantine, 104; cob-type, 239, 247, 251, 254, 256; copper-alloy in, 256; denominations of, 237–239; gold, 255–256, 247; inscriptions on, 241; milled, 239, 256; production of, 239
Colombia, mints in, 254–255
Colonialism, 4
Colonoware. *See* Pipes
Columbian quincentenary, 3, 5
Columbus, Christopher, 7, 10, 11, 74, 84, 138, 140, 216, 224–228, 268, 291, 303
Combs, 228–229
Comisión para la Puesta en Valor del Sitio Histórico de La Vega Vieja, 10
Compendium maleficarum, 87, 141
Compostela, Spain, 73, 94, 132
Concepción shipwreck, Dominican Republic, 22
Concepción de la Vega, Dominican Republic, 9–10, 49, 57, 82

Contraband trade, 14, 28–29, 158, 170
Convento de San Francisco, Santo Domingo, 125
Coral, 68, 69, 89, 91, 92, 94, 96, 120, 131
Córdoba, Spain, 157, 195, 201, 206, 234
Corsairs, 29
Cortés, Hernán de, 216
Cotter, C.S., 11
Council of Trent, 47–48
Covarrubias, Alvaro, 89
Craft guilds, 31–32, 157–158, 176, 180, 201, 202, 218, 225, 234
Crosses: Alcántara, 64; Avellan, 63; Caravaca, 60–62, 80, 89, 105; Dominic, 65, 73, 94; ecclesiastical, 56; forms of, 55–56, 65; Jerusalem, 247, 251, 252, 254, 256; Maltese, 64; reliquary, 61; Santiago, 64, 94
Crossbows, 271
Crucifixes, 54–65; skeleton, 57
Cruxent, José, 8, 12
Crystal, 58–59, 79, 89, 92, 95, 96, 100, 120, 131
Cuenta de leche, 91, 99, 100
Cufflinks. *See* Buttons, sleeve
Cup weights. *See* Weights, nested
Cuzco mint, 242, 256

D

D'Aulnoy, Madame Catherine, 66, 81; on amulets, 87, 89; on bells, 127; on eyeglasses, 223; on fans, 218; on hairdressing, 136, 228; self-flagellation and, 85; on Spanish jewelry, 109, 127, 134
Dados. *See* dice
Dags, 275
Dancing, 291
Death, 89
De León site, St. Augustine, 19
Deer, 95, 102, 287
Dental hygiene, 230
Depositional processes, archaeological, 106
Dice, 291–295
Dirección Nacional de Parques of the Dominican Republic, 10, 22
Doglock, 276
Dolls, 299, 300
Dominican Order, 45, 47, 48, 50, 65, 88
Dominican Republic, 7–10, 22, 31, 123

Dominoes, 296, 297–298
Drums, 303
Ducat, 237
Durer, Albrecht, 75
Dutch West India Company, 29

E

Earrings, 108, 120, 126–130
Earspoon, 230
Earthquake, 9
El Morro, Puerto Rico, 20
El Nuevo Constante shipwreck, 23
Emeralds, 109
Emmanuel Point shipwreck, Florida, 21
Enamels, 108, 132, 133
Eros, 73
Escopeta, 269, 278
Escribanías, 304
Escudos, 255
Espingardas, 268
Ethnicity, 3, 4
Evangélios, 95
Evil eye, 89, 94–95, 102, 104, 105
Eyeglasses, 222–226

F

Fairbanks, Charles, 15
Fairs, trade, 26
Fans, 215–220; brisé, 217, 219; feathers, 216, 219; pleated, 217; as status markers, 219
Fauchard, Pierre, 231
Female activities. *See* Women
Ferdinand, King of Spain, 37, 243, 244, 291
Festivals, 291
Fiel marcador, 259
Fig Springs, Florida, 15, 125
Figa. *See* Higa
Figurines, 299–300
Filigree, metal, 130, 160
Firearms, identification of, 268; nomenclature, 270. *See also* individual firearm types
Fish, as amulets, 105
Flagellation, 72, 84–86
Flintlocks and flintlock muskets, 276, 280, 283, 285; *carabina*, 269, 280; *fusile*, 269; English flintlock, 276; *mosquete*, 269, 271

Florida Bureau of Archaeological Research, 15, 21, 22
Florida Museum of Natural History, 12, 13, 14, 15, 19
Florida State University, 12, 17, 18
Flota, 26, 33
Foodways, 3
Fort Jesus, Mombasa, 7
Fort Liberté, Haiti, 11
Fort Michilimackinack, Michigan, 125, 215, 229, 235
Fort Pentagoet, Maine, 215
Fountain of Youth Park site, St. Augustine, 12
Fox Pond site, Florida, 15
Franciscan Order, 15, 16, 44, 47, 48, 49–51, 54, 69, 82, 88, 123, 309
French Guinea Company, 28, 30
French influence on Spanish material culture, 109, 125, 181, 231; in clothing, 158, 165, 183; in tobacco use, 311; in weaponry, 281
French colonial sites, 129
Friars Minor. *See* Franciscans

G

Galeónes, 26, 33
Games: counters, 295–296; courts, 291; and gambling, 291–298
Gardens, 291
Gargantillas, 131–132
Gender, 4, 107, 123
Genoa, Italy, 27
Germany, 27
Gillette, K.C., 235
Girls, 135, 205, 292, 299. *See also* Children.
Girona shipwreck, 21
Glassmaking, 31
Goggin, John, 11–12, 15, 16
Gold mining, 9
Goldsmiths, 31, 185
Griffin, John W., 16, 19
Grommets, 84
Guadalajara Polychrome pottery, 299
Guadalupe shipwreck, Dominican Republic, 22
Guarnición, 176–177
Guatemala mint, 242, 243, 255–256
Guazzo, Francesco, 87, 88
Gueux, Revolt of, 42
Guitars, 303

Gun hardware, 281–283, 286
Gunlocks: agujeta, 278; a la moda, 279, 284; a la Romana; 279; French, 277, 281; flintlocks, 276, 280, 283, 285; matchlock, 270–273, 280; miquelet, 276–279, 283; snaphaunce, 275–276; wheel lock, 273–275
Gunpowder, 288
Guns. *See* firearms
Gunsmithing industry, 270

H

Hacabuche, 268, 269
Hairbrushes, 228–230
Hair ornaments, 136–137
Hairpieces, 228
Hairpins, 108
Haiti, 30
Halbirt, Carl, 17
Half-real, 249, 250
Hamilton, Jennifer, 14
Handbells, 150, 151, 152
Hapsburg shield, 251, 255
Havana Company, 30
Havana, Cuba, 19, 26, 33
Hearts, as amulets, 101
Henry IV of Castille, 243
Heyn, Piet, 29
Hieronymite Order, 45, 47
Higas, 88, 89, 91, 92, 93, 95–99
Higgs site, Florida, 17
Hildbergh, W.L., 88
Hispanic Society of America, 73
Hispaniola, 9, 27
Historical Archaeology, 4
Hobbyhorses, 299
Hodges, William, 11, 14
Holme, Randle, 216, 226, 297
Holy Family, 47
Holy Trinity, 54
Hook-and-eye fasteners, 176
Horns, as amulets, 102; cattle, 289–290; deer, 102; powder, 289–290
Hospital le Bon Samaritain, Haiti, 11
Hostos, Adolfo de, 11
Hunting, 287, 291
Hurricanes, 18, 28

I

IHS symbol, 51, 74
Iconography, Catholic, 47–49, 55, 74, 83, 101
Ideology, 3, 5, 37
Immaculate Conception, 47, 48–50, 54, 55, 64, 73, 74; *veneras,* 77
India, 135
Indulgences, 42–43, 65, 81
Inkwells, 305, 306
Inquisition, 65, 105
Instituto de Don Juan de Valencia, 97
Instituto Nacional de la Cultura Puertorriqueña, San Juan, 11, 18
Intercolonial trade, 33–34
Intermarriage, 34
Isabella, Queen of Spain, 37, 135, 216, 243, 244, 291
Italy, 27

J

Jacksonville, Florida, 12, 14
Jamaica, 30
Jamaica National Trust, 11
Jamestown, Virginia, 231
Japan, 216
Jesuit Order, 47, 50, 83, 74, 101, 123
Jet, 65, 73, 89, 93–94, 96, 120, 131, 132
Jetons, 42, 256
Jewelry: gender specific, 107, 123; Native American, 107–108; popular, 106; in Spain, 108; Spanish-American, 107, 109. *See also* individual pieces
Jewels, paste, 120, 122, 129, 130
Jew's harp, 302–303
Joanna, Queen of Spain, 239, 240, 244, 245, 246, 250, 251, 252–254, 256
Jones, William, 14

K

Karcheski, Walter, 269
Kites, 299
Knights of Alcántara, 64
Knights of Malta, 64
Knights of Santiago, 64, 73
Knucklebones, 292
Knurling, 199–200, 204

L

Lace, 210–211, 218; lace-making, 193, 209–211; metallic lace, 176–177
Lace tips. *See* Aglets
Lactation, 91, 95, 99
Lagrimario, 101
La Isabela, Dominican Republic, 7–8, 10, 24, 31, 56, 83, 122, 243, 268
Lasanen site, Michican, 50
Lazo ornament, 108, 134
Lead sprue, 288
Lesser Antilles, 29
Lice, 226
Lightning, 95
Lima mint, 252–254
Limbé, Haiti, 11, 12
Llibres de Passanties, 108
Lope de Vega, Félix, 27
López, Lorenzo, 11
Los Adaes site, Louisiana, 69
Louis XIII of France, 311
Louisiana Department of Culture, Recreation and Tourism, 23
Lourdes, France, 46
Loyola, Ignatius, 84
Luna, Tristán de, 21
Lunar crescents, 103
Lutes, 303
Luther, Martin, 49
Lyon, Eugene, 159

M

Machault shipwreck, 215
MacMurray, Judith, 14
Madrid, Spain, 11, 31, 85, 228
Mala moneda, 241
Manila galleons, 7, 56, 102, 109, 227
Mantillas, 225
Maravedís, 244, 245–247, 256
Marbles, 300–301
Marquarte, Simon and Pedro, 270, 273, 276
Marx, Robert, 22
Matanceros shipwreck, 22, 52, 56, 120
Matchlock, 270–273, 280; *arquebuce,* 269, 271
McEwan, Bonnie, 16
Medalla de Santa Elena, 92

Medallion, 66
Medals: devotional, 41–54; miraculous, 54; peace, 259
Men, 218
Menéndez de Aviles, Pedro, 13, 15, 64, 97, 124
Mercantilism, 24–25
Mercederian Order, 47
Merchants, 26–28
Mercury, 22, 89
Mermaids, 92, 103, 132
Mexico City Cathedral, 152
Mexico City mint, 238, 240, 245, 251, 256
Mica, 81
Militia, Cuban, 170
Mints, 31: Bogotá, 242–243; Burgos, 245; Cartagena, 242; Cuzco, 242, 256; Guatemala, 242, 243, 255, 256; Lima, 242; Mexico City, 238, 240, 245, 251, 256; Peru, 256; Popayán, 242; Potosí, 242; Santiago, 242; Santo Domingo, 238, 240–242, 256; Seville, 245
Miquelet locks, 276–279, 283–284
Missionary orders and missionaries, 46–47, 82, 83, 123, 151
Mission sites and missions, 14, 15, 16, 50, 58, 69, 70, 80, 151
Mobile, Alabama, 18, 125
Moctezuma, 216
Molasses Reef shipwreck, 269
Monetary system, Spanish, 236
Monte Cristi, Dominican Republic, 14
Moorish influence in Spanish material culture, 5, 105, 130, 139, 157, 160, 178, 216
Moorish design elements, 108, 130, 160
Morales, Gaspar de, 93
Mor, Antonio (Anthonis Mor van Dashort), 163, 218
Morgan, Henry, 12
Morocco, 7
Moscow, 151
Mosé, Florida, 103
Mount Tabor, 62
Mudejar style, 308
Muller, Patricia, 106
Murillo, Bartolomé, 48–50
Musée de Guahabá, Haiti, 12, 14
Museo de la Atarazana, Santo Domingo, 22

Museo de la Ciudad de la Havana, 19
Museo de las Casas Reales, Santo Domingo, 10, 19, 20, 22
Museo del Pueblo Español, Madrid, 67, 76, 88, 92, 107
Museum of Games and Archives, 299
Museum of Florida History, 22
Music, 303
Musket, 280

N
National Museum of American History, 67
National Park Service, 18
Necklaces, 108, 118, 120, 134
Needle cases, 196–197
Needles, 222, 195–196
Needlework, 207, 209, 291
Netherlands, The, 27, 29, 203
New Orleans, 81
Noel-Hume, Ivor, 207
Noisemakers, 301–302
Nombre de Dios site, St. Augustine, 13, 27
Nuestra Señora de Guadalupe, 43, 75
Nuestra Señora de la Leche, 72
Nuestra Señora de los Milagros shipwreck. *See* Matanceros
Nuestra Señora del Pilar (Zaragoza), 55, 78
Nuestra Señora del Rosario, 65
Nuestra Señora de Santa Maria de Nieva, 75, 76
Nueva Cádiz, Venezuela, 12, 57
Nuremberg, Germany, 108, 198, 201, 225, 258, 263, 264

O
Oñate, Juan de, 47
Order of the Golden Fleece, 73
Order of the Holy Sepulchre, 83
Ortega, Elpidio, 19
Our Lady of Hal, 42
Ovando, Nicolas de, 11, 86

P
Pablo Bush Romero Museum, 22
Padre Island shipwrecks, 7, 21
Panama City, Panamá, 12
Panamá Viejo, Panamá, 12, 13

Parasols, 220–222
Parchisi, 295
Paris, 226
Parris Island, South Carolina, 13
Paste stones, 120, 122, 129, 130
Patilla lock, 278
Patronato Real, 37
Pearls, 108, 109
Peashooters, 299
Pendants and necklaces, 108, 128, 130–134; Punta Rassa Teardrop, 128
Penknives, 304, 306
Pens, 304
Pensacola, Florida, 18, 21
Petaloid bells, 148–149
Phillip II of Spain, 6, 24, 244, 247, 250
Pieta, 76
Pilgrim's tokens, 42
Pillar and waves design, 247, 253, 254, 255, 256
Pillar dollars, 237, 239, 251, 253, 255, 256
Pillars of Hercules, 246, 249, 251, 252, 255, 256
Pinchbeck, 120
Pins, 193–195, 205, 210
Pipes: colonoware, 310–311; tobacco, 310
Pirates, 26, 28, 30
Pirotechnia, 139
Pistols, 275, 279–280, 286
Pizarro, Francisco, 298
Place Royale, Quebec, 298
Plaquettes, 42
Plate fleet shipwrecks, Florida, 22, 53, 64, 125, 126
Pocket knives, 235
Pomegranates, 248
Ponce de León, Juan, 11, 270
Popayán mint, 242
Popes, Catholic, 37, 42, 49, 56, 81–82, 151; Gregory V, 49; Innocent III, 82; Paul V, 49; Pius V, 42
Portobello, Panama, 21, 27, 28
Port Royal, Jamaica, 11
Portugal, 27, 28–9, 243–244
Potosí mint, 242, 254
Powder flasks, 289–290
Powderhorns, 289–290

Pragmaticas, 97, 107, 108, 177
Presidios, 33
Price inflation, 28
Processual archaeology, 3–4
Puebla de los Angeles, Mexico, 31, 260
Puerto Real, Haiti, 11–12, 14, 57

Q

Qsar-es-Seghir, Morocco, 7, 134
Quartz, 95
Quicksilver shipwrecks, Dominican Republic, 22, 52, 77, 80

R

Race, 4
Radisch, William, 84
Ramrods, 281
Ranching, 9
Razors, 234–235
Reading, 304
Relics and reliquaries, 78–81, 130
Rings, finger, 83–84, 120, 122–126; thimble, 197
Ripoll, Spain, 279
Roman sites, 186, 291, 300
Rome, 43, 46, 51
Rosary, 40–41, 43, 65–72; beads, 66–72; Dominican, 65; Feast of, 65; Franciscan, 66

S

Sabana Yegua, Dominican Republic, 123, 142
Sacred Heart of Jesus, 73, 83
Salamanca, Spain, 48
San Antonio de Valera mission, 153
San Esteban shipwreck, 57
Sánchez Coello, Alonso, 163
San Francisco de Potano mission, 15
San Gabriel del Yunque, New Mexico, 47
San Juan de Guacara mission, 14
San Juan del Puerto mission, 14
San Juan, Puerto Rico, 11, 18, 20
San Luis de Talimali, Florida, 16, 58, 70–71
San Luis pendants, 128
San Martín de Ayacuto mission, 15
San Pedro Quiationi, 131
Santa Catalina de Guale, Georgia, 15, 47, 58, 71
Santa Elena, South Carolina, 13, 126, 162

Santa Fe de Bogotá, Colombia. *See* Bogotá
Santa Fe la Vieja, Argentina, 88, 96
Santa María mission, Florida, 75
Santa Rosa Pensacola, 18, 125
Santiago de Chile, 242, 256
Santo Domingo, Dominican Republic, 19, 22, 33, 49; mint of, 238, 240–242, 249–251, 256
Santos, 299
Savaneta, Trinidad, 74
Scales, weighing, 264–267
Scarlett, Edward, 223
Scissors, 206, 222, 234, 255–256; embroidery, 207, 209; industrial, 207; ornamental, 206, 208; taxonomy, 206
Seahorse, 91
Seals and stamps, 81, 306
Segovia, Spain, 76
Sequins, 179
Serpentines, 271, 272, 274
Sevilla Nueva, Jamaica, 11
Seville, Spain, 26, 48, 50, 157, 245
Shakers, blotting powder, 305–306
Shapiro, Gary, 16
Shears, 206
Shells: as amulets, 101–102; Trochus, 100, 102; scallop, 73, 94
Shield motif, 247, 250, 251, 252, 255
Shipwrecks, 17, 20–23, 28, 37, 51, 106, 136, 197, 219, 236, 283
Shoe buckles, 122
Shot molds, 287–288
Silversmiths, 31, 109
Sisters of St. Joseph, 17
Situado, 33–34
Slaves, African, 27, 310
Smith, Hale, 12, 17, 18, 19, 20
Smith, Roger, 21
Smuggling. *See* Contraband trade
Snaphaunce locks, 275–276
Snuff and Snuffboxes, 311–312
Social identity, 4
Social status, 3, 219, 221
Soledad cemetery, Florida, 71
Solís, Victor, 108
Sonajeros, 92, 103, 104
South Carolina Institute of Archaeology and Anthropology, 14

South Seas Company, 28, 30
South, Stanley, 14
Southeast Archaeological Center of the National Park Service, 17, 18, 20
Spanish Armada shipwrecks, 7, 21, 47, 64, 79, 124
Spanish longhorn cattle, 290
Spanners, 274, 275
St. Agatha, 91
St. Anthony of Padua, 51
St. Augustine, 72
St. Augustine, Florida, 12, 16–17, 18, 19, 68
St. Benedict, 43
St. Bernadette, 46
St. Bernard of Siena, 43, 54
St. Catherine of Alexandria, 73, 82
St. Catherine's Island, Georgia, 15
St. Christopher, 44, 103
St. Francis of Assisi, 51, 54, 82
St. Helena, 55, 78, 82
St. James, 51, 64, 69
St. John of Capistrano, 54
St. John the Evangelist, 51
St. Lucy's bean, 102
St. Paul, 51, 81, 82
St. Peter, 51, 81, 82
St. Rose of Lima, 43
St. Teresa, 89
Stahl, Alan, 243
Stars, copper-alloy, 84–86, 89, 178–179
Straight pins. *See* Pins
Strap tips, 191
Suárez de Deza, Pedro, 82
Sueltos, 26, 28, 30
Sumptuary laws, 133, 176–177, 228. *See also Pragmaticas*
Syncretism, 5–6; Moorish-Spanish, 5–6; in music, 303; Spanish-American-African, 6, 34, 75; in religion, 75; Spanish-Indian, 10, 75

T

Taíno Indians, 123, 138, 140, 145
Talismans, 87
Tallahassee, Florida, 16, 18
Tambourines, 303, 304
Taxes and duties, 26, 28
Taxonomy, artifact, 3

Teeth, as amulets, 102
Texas Antiquities Commission, 21
Theaters, 291
Thimbles, 159, 197–206, 222; children's, 205; Dutch, 203–205; English, 204–205; Hispano-Moresque, 201; Nuremberg, 201–202; production, 198–200, 201, 205
Thirty Years War, 29
Thomas, David H., 15
Thomas Mound site, Florida, 76
Thread, 160
Timucua Indians, 14–15, 72
Tinkler cones, 128, 129
Tinning, 194
Tobacco, 310
Tokens. *See* Jetons
Tolosá shipwreck. *See* Quicksilver shipwrecks
Tonsure, 199, 203
Toothbrushes, 231–234
Toothpicks, 103, 230–231
Tops, spinning, 301
Toys, 298–301
Trabuco, 280
Trade, intercolonial, 33–34
Treasure Salvors, Inc., 21
Treaty of Tordesillas, 28
Trepanning, 232
Triggers, 271, 272
Trinidad Valencera shipwreck, 21
Tuners, instrument, 303, 304
Tweezers, 230
Typology, artifact, 4

U
Umbrellas, 220–222
Unicorns, 108, 132
Universidad Complutense, Madrid, 11
University of Alabama, 18
University of Florida, 8, 10, 11, 12, 14, 17
U.S. National Park Service, 20

V
Valencia, Spain, 48
Veloz Maggiolo, Marcio, 19
Veneras, 72–78, 93
Victoria and Albert Museum, 100
Vihuelas, 303
Violins, 303
Virgin Mary, 46, 47, 63, 73, 77, 86, 97, 123, 154; veneras to, 74–78. *See also* Immaculate Conception and Nuestra Señora

W
War of Jenkin's Ear, 30
War of the Spanish Succession, 28, 30
Weights, 237, 259–264; coin, 260–262; nested, 262–264; pharmaceutical, 261, 264, 266; scale, 266
Wheel locks, 273–275
Whistles, 230
Whizzers. *See* Noisemakers
Wig curlers, 228
Williamsburg, Virginia, 215
Willis, Raymond, 12
Witchcraft and magic, 87
Witches, 141
Women, 34, 63, 66, 89, 100, 105, 193, 218, 292; amulets for, 91, 99; Spanish, 216, 219, 228
Woodbury machine, 233
Writing and writing equipment, 304–307

X
Ximenez-Fatio site, St. Augustine, 19

Y
Yciar, Juan de, 304

Z
Zaragoza, Spain, 77
Zurbarán, Francisco de, 48
Zarcillos, 127

www.ingramcontent.com/pod-product-compliance
Lightning Source LLC
Chambersburg PA
CBHW080533300426
44111CB00017B/2708